ColdFusion® 5 Developer's Guide

About the Author

Michael Buffington has been a strong advocate for ColdFusion for more than five years. In 1998, Michael started PricePulse, Inc., which later changed its name to Price.com, Inc. Price.com is a leading price-comparison search engine using ColdFusion as part of a solid web application platform.

Michael is always busy doing something. In addition to being a complete geek, he enjoys skateboarding, illustration, web design, photography, surfing, playing the guitar, and travelling. Visit michaelbuffington.com to learn more about the author, or to see what project he is currently working on.

ColdFusion® 5 Developer's Guide

Michael Buffington

Osborne/**McGraw-Hill**

New York Chicago San Francisco
Lisbon London Madrid Mexico City
Milan New Delhi San Juan
Seoul Singapore Sydney Toronto

Osborne/McGraw-Hill
2600 Tenth Street
Berkeley, California 94710
U.S.A.

To arrange bulk purchase discounts for sales promotions, premiums, or fund-raisers, please contact Osborne/**McGraw-Hill** at the above address. For information on translations or book distributors outside the U.S.A., please see the International Contact Information page immediately following the index of this book.

ColdFusion® 5 Developer's Guide

1234567890 CUS CUS 01987654321

ISBN 0-07-213225-6

Publisher Brandon A. Nordin
Vice President & Associate Publisher Scott Rogers
Acquisitions Editor Jim Schachterle
Project Editor Jody McKenzie
Acquisitions Coordinator Tim Madrid
Technical Editor Erik Goodlad
Copy Editor Susan Cohen
Proofreader Nancy McLaughlin
Indexer Irv Hershman
Computer Designers Tara A. Davis, Elizabeth Jang & Kelly Stanton-Scott
Illustrators Michael Mueller & Lyssa Wald
Series Designer Roberta Steele
Cover Series Designer Greg Scott
Cover Illustrator Eliot Bergman

This book was composed with Corel VENTURA™ Publisher.

Contents at a Glance

Contents

Acknowledgments

First I need to thank everyone who put up with my constant moanings of "I have a chapter to write." I think it was probably harder for them to hear my complaints than it was for me to write the chapters. I both thank and apologize to anyone who had to hear any of that.

I'll make this simple: thanks to Howard Shen and Hadi Setiadi, for forcing ColdFusion 1.5 down my throat, Scott Fleming, Jared Scott, Jamie Alhstrom, Stacey Jensen (and the entire Jensen family), Lee Schultz, "Wojo" Joe Wojiehowski, Bob Remieka, Joseph "Flash" Seymour, Tony Meadows, Richard Wrightsman, Steven Ng, and the entire Price.com team. And to my Mom, who set the example that writing a book is a humanly possible event (even while raising four rowdy kids).

A special thanks goes out to Erik Goodlad, who not only did the technical editing of this book but who is also a good friend. Erik truly went the extra mile, making sure every line of code in this book worked, and often put as much time into a chapter as I did. I may have complained when he made fun of me for every mistake, but I'm very grateful for his efforts.

My wife made it very clear that she didn't want to be thanked in the book, but I simply had to do it—my conscious wouldn't allow me to do otherwise. Writing a book is not an easy event, and it's especially difficult when your life is surrounded by difficult circumstances. During the writing of the book there were some very difficult times: I spent 45 days 3,000 miles away from home and family, got laid off twice, and faced some big life-changing decisions. There were times when it would have been easy to quit, but she encouraged me and supported me with love, kindness, and patience. She deserves a lot of credit for this book. I'm eternally grateful that she is my wife and that she and I were able to share this experience.

Introduction

In the past six years, ColdFusion has gained an impressive following, and with the merger between Allaire and Macromedia, the popularity of ColdFusion is sure to increase. ColdFusion has proven to be a simple yet incredibly powerful web application, with both excellent support and a huge community support system.

I started using ColdFusion in 1995, when the program was truly in its infancy. A coworker of mine was really excited about the product, almost to the point that I was skeptical of his claims of what the product could do. Within a year, I was developing web sites that could do incredible things—or at least things that were incredible at the time. I was creating dynamic sites driven entirely off databases, with full content management systems. ColdFusion was an incredible step forward, and presented opportunities like no other program had done to date. The simplicity of ColdFusion's tag-based language couldn't be beat, and I knew from that point forward that ColdFusion would have an impact on developers just as it did on me.

Now, six years later with the release of ColdFusion 5.0, the program is better than the original by leaps and bounds, yet the concept of a simple tag-based language remains. While competing products like ASP and PHP have started to gain a following, ColdFusion will always have the advantage of pure simplicity, and that's why I feel so strongly about the language.

For me, writing a book on ColdFusion is truly a dream come true, and it's a good way to share what I've learned about the platform.

Who Should Read This Book

This book has been designed to offer the most to ColdFusion developers who have some ColdFusion experience under their belts and want to extend themselves further. Technically speaking, the book is written for intermediate to advanced developers, but we all know that terms like "intermediate" and "advanced" don't always accurately describe a developer's ability. It often happens that a ColdFusion developer who has been writing code for a few years hasn't used a particular set of tags but excels in other areas. With this kind of developer in mind, the book has been designed to cover more advanced ColdFusion topics.

None of the basics of developing ColdFusion applications is covered in this book. We assume that you at least know how to successfully write simple applications that do things like retrieve data from a database using the <CFQUERY> tag, and output data from a query using the <CFOUTPUT> tag. We don't go over the basics of pound-sign usage, or how to set and output variables simply because covering everything, including the basics, wouldn't allow for an effective text on how to get the most out of ColdFusion.

Despite the more advanced tilt of this book, adventurous beginners are not left in the dark. I would imagine that with some effort and experimentation, beginning developers could gain a lot from this book. Beginning developers who want to get an idea of ColdFusion's capabilities might also benefit from the material as well, and developers who use this text along with the other books in this series will benefit most of all.

What's in This Book

This book is divided into three distinct parts, each of which has its own theme, if you will. It's possible to jump from Part I to Part III, but to get the most out of the book, it's best to follow along in a linear fashion. The following sections describe what can be found in each part.

Part I

Part I primarily focuses on installing the software needed to successfully run a ColdFusion application. From my years of writing ColdFusion applications, and managing both ColdFusion developers and large-scale ColdFusion projects, I've discovered that one of the most overlooked yet crucial pieces of a good ColdFusion application starts with focusing on installing the software correctly.

This part of the book will talk about how to install ColdFusion on both Windows platforms and Linux platforms. It will also discuss the Apache and IIS web server installations, and SQL Server 2000 and MySQL installations.

One of the goals of Part I is to show you how easy it is to set up a ColdFusion application on Linux. Linux continues to gain steady followers, and as time goes on it will likely become even more popular. Having a chapter devoted to Linux is crucial for advanced developers who will need to know how to gracefully handle the situation when the time comes.

Installation instructions and tips will be extensive for both platforms. My general indifference toward Microsoft and gaining enthusiasm for Linux might be easy to read between the lines, but both platforms will be given equal coverage.

Part II

Part II introduces a sample application. The application itself is an online skateboard supply store. I have a serious love of skateboarding, and I took full advantage of using it to make the sample application a little more interesting.

Part II covers a lot more than just talking about lines of ColdFusion code. We'll cover everything from project development cycles to project management to writing optimal code. The project itself can be used as a real-world application, but the more important goal of the project is to give a real-world example of a ColdFusion application from start to finish.

Part III

Part III covers advanced topics that either were given little coverage in Part II or no coverage at all. It will fill the gaps for intermediate or advanced developers who have gone several years without ever using the <CFHTTP> tag, for instance.

PART

I

Installation & Overview

OBJECTIVES

- How to install and optimize IIS 5.0
- Quick overview of the SQL Server 2000 installation
- How to install and optimize ColdFusion 5.0

CHAPTER

1

Windows 2000 Installation and Optimization

IN THIS CHAPTER:

Internet Information Server 5.0

SQL Server 2000

Installing ColdFusion 5.0

To make full use of ColdFusion as an application server, it is important to have all of the supportive pieces of software in place and working well. ColdFusion by itself can do nothing—it must sit behind a Web server. Knowing how to properly set up a web server like Internet Information Server (IIS) 5.0 can add to the performance of your application and reduce the amount of administration required. Even though, technically, ColdFusion doesn't require a database to work with, we know that database connectivity is one of ColdFusion's strong points, and is usually the reason for using ColdFusion. Having a strong database solution will also aid in the success of your application.

In this chapter, we'll cover how to install IIS 5.0 on a Windows 2000 Advanced Server, as well as installing ColdFusion 5.0. Simply describing how to install these programs would not only not be very useful, but it would help insomniacs of the world better than any sleeping pill known to man. Within the installation overviews, we'll squeeze in plenty of real-world examples of what works well with ColdFusion, and what doesn't. I think after we're through, you'll be surprised how much each component of the web server depends on the other components to work well.

Internet Information Server 5.0

Internet Information Server (IIS) hands users' requests to ColdFusion, and also hands ColdFusion output to users. If IIS isn't working correctly, your entire application's performance will suffer. Because of the role IIS plays in your application, paying attention to its setup and performance can make the difference between a good application and a problematic one.

Because of the essential function IIS performs with ColdFusion, I'll be giving it a good amount of focus. Configuring IIS properly is probably one of the most overlooked tasks of a ColdFusion developer. It's an easy mistake to make, as a default IIS installation works pretty well. However, you have to consider IIS 5.0's roots. Microsoft made it primarily to serve ASP applications. Out of the box, it works great for running ASP applications, but with ColdFusion, certain setup techniques should be considered. After all, we want our ColdFusion application to be well received by the users we're serving it to, and tuning IIS will help us achieve that goal.

IIS 5.0 is a useful piece of software that efficiently serves ColdFusion applications. But IIS 5.0 is not the only solution. As a ColdFusion advocate, I preach the good points of ColdFusion, and gain much satisfaction by talking about the bad points of its opponents. But, when it comes to the servers for ColdFusion applications, I am not married to one server over another. In Chapter 2, I'll talk about how to set up

Apache and ColdFusion on a Linux server. Relatively few ColdFusion developers have experience with ColdFusion and Linux, yet more and more companies are adopting Linux as a viable and cost effective platform.

IIS 5.0 comes with every version of Windows 2000, but this book will cover every version of Windows 2000 except Windows 2000 Professional. Windows 2000 Professional disables a lot of the features that will be discussed.

Windows 2000 Professional Edition is basically a workstation, not a server. For now I'll spare you my opinions on Microsoft licensing; now is not the time or place. It's important, however, to know how the limitations of a workstation license can affect you. IIS 5.0 on Windows 2000 Professional Edition will allow no more than ten connections at a time to IIS. An example scenario would be if three people were logged into your FTP site, only seven people would be able to connect to your web site, making a total of ten connections. So it's a total of ten connections to any one of the IIS components, period. Additionally, you can only have one web site. You don't have the ability to create a new web site as you would in any other Windows 2000 installation. Every other Windows 2000 edition gives you the ability to have "unlimited" connections. (Of course hardware and bandwidth bottlenecks will always prohibit unlimited connections, but you get the idea.)

The limitations of Windows 2000 Professional may not be a problem for some people; in fact, for a single developer it's great. Using Windows 2000 Professional works great for me when I've developing something on my own that doesn't require a ton of hardware or all the other features of the more expensive licenses of Windows 2000. It's a cost effective way for me to get a prototype application off the ground. When I'm ready for the project to go live, I move it to a staging machine, then a production machine, then make an official launch.

I've known teams of developers who use Windows 2000 Professional on a development server, and then stage it on another Windows 2000 Pro server for testing, with the final, production server being a Windows 2000 Advanced or similar server. This has its disadvantages, as you've probably already pictured a 10-20 employee company testing a web site that only allows ten connections at a time. It might work for some, but not all. Every situation is different, and every situation needs a different solution.

IIS 5.0 only runs on Windows 2000. Out of curiosity once I actually isolated the IIS 5.0 install files and tried to install IIS 5.0 on a Windows NT 4.0 server. It's probably no surprise that it didn't work, but at least I tried. I don't learn very quickly sometimes, and I wasn't ready to take defeat that easily, so I tried installing IIS 5.0 from my Windows 2000 Advanced CD on my Windows 2000 Professional server. Guess what? Didn't work. Microsoft is more clever than I, and in fact, later on I did some reading up in my licensing agreement, and apparently I'm not supposed to be poking around like that, if I translate the legal jargon correctly. My suggestion: do what you need to do. Get the correct license for the job; there's no way around it, technically, or legally.

Microsoft has put together a very powerful piece of software with IIS 5.0, and there is a lot you can do with it. Yet, it would take an entirely separate 700-page book to go into every possible feature of IIS 5.0. Out of the box IIS is pretty good, but as I said, it needs some tweaks to work even better with ColdFusion.

You may not be willing or able to make the jump from Windows NT to 2000, and may feel that this section is entirely useless to you. If you're still using NT 4.0 and IIS 4.0, you can still use a lot of this information. Not much has changed on the surface from IIS 4.0 to IIS 5.0, but IIS 5.0 runs much faster than IIS 4.0. It takes advantage of performance gains in Windows 2000, and has been optimized itself. I'd recommend upgrading from NT to 2000, if just for the performance gains.

Some of the screenshots for IIS 4.0 and 5.0 may differ, but if you've used either of them at all, you should be able to crossover without too much difficulty. I won't be pointing out the differences between the two. I want to quickly cover the performance gains of IIS so that I can get into the core of this book. Translating between 4.0 and 5.0 might get confusing, and might unduly remove focus from the main topic, ColdFusion.

IIS 5.0 is built from the ground up to serve web applications. It also does a good job at serving static HTML pages, but its main strength is in serving applications. While Microsoft puts a huge focus on serving ASP applications, they're smart, and built what they call the ISAPI.

The ISAPI is basically an API for either Internet Services (hence, the IS in ISAPI), or IIS. API's are nothing new to most developers. If you need to talk to a certain piece of software, you keep your fingers crossed and hope there is an API already built for it, because the API lets you quickly and easily talk to that piece of software without having to learn about the details of how that software works. The ISAPI is no different. The ISAPI let's you interact with IIS similarly to an API, without having to know the details about how IIS serves its data to users.

IIS likes to cache things. If a user requests a certain HTML file, it will serve that HTML file, and then hold onto it in its memory, waiting for someone else to request that HTML file. If someone requests the same HTML file, IIS hands it off to the user much more quickly than if IIS had to go and read the file off the disk. Caching is where IIS gets a lot of its performance gains.

IIS is good at handling system resources. It's also sensitive to system load, gathering more resources depending on the amount of people who are requesting data. We'll talk about how to make sure your application is getting the attention it needs from IIS a little later on.

Installing IIS 5.0

Installing IIS is relatively simple; you may have already installed it while installing Windows 2000. To see if you have it installed, do the following:

1. Open up your Control Panel.
2. Double-click the Add/Remove Programs icon.
3. Click Add/Remove Windows Components.
4. Check to see if the second option, Internet Information Services, has a check next to it.

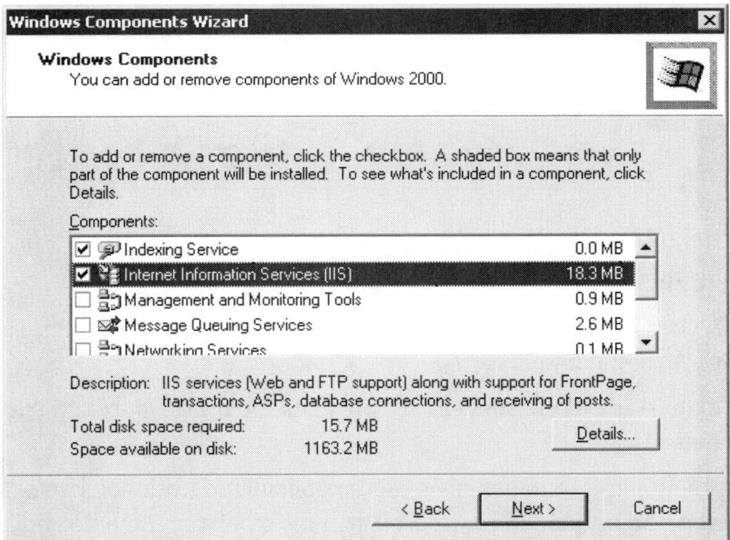

Your list of options may differ slightly from my machine, but the concept is the same. If the Internet Information Services (IIS) option doesn't have a check next to it, you need to install it.

Follow these steps to install IIS:

1. Select the desired IIS subcomponents. There are several possible subcomponents available, but if we want a truly slim ColdFusion server, we only need three subcomponents to run ColdFusion.

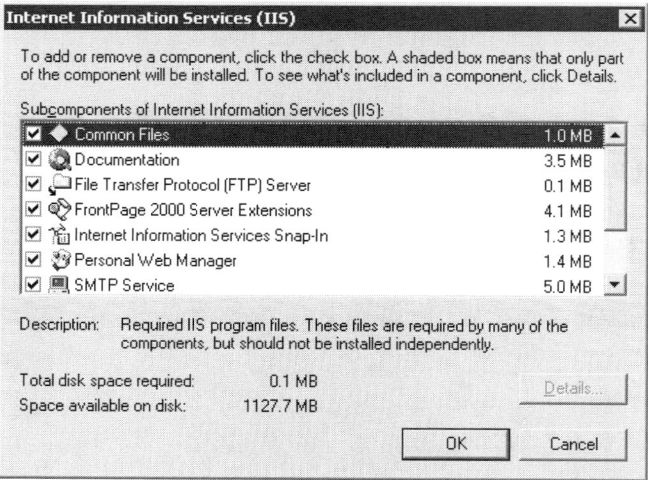

2. Select the following three subcomponents:
   - **Common Files** Includes all the core IIS program files
   - **Internet Information Services Snap-in** Includes the management console components for IIS
   - **World Wide Web Server** Represents the most important part of the IIS installation

   Any of the other components should be considered optional, or should be installed on an as needed basis. You will always have the option of adding subcomponents to your IIS installation later on.

3. The install program will determine what files it needs to complete the installation, and will ask for your Windows 2000 Installation CD-ROM if you haven't installed IIS on this machine before. If you have installed IIS, it may or may not ask for the CD-ROM, depending on the subcomponents you've selected

to install. After IIS is finished copying and installing the subcomponents, click Finish.

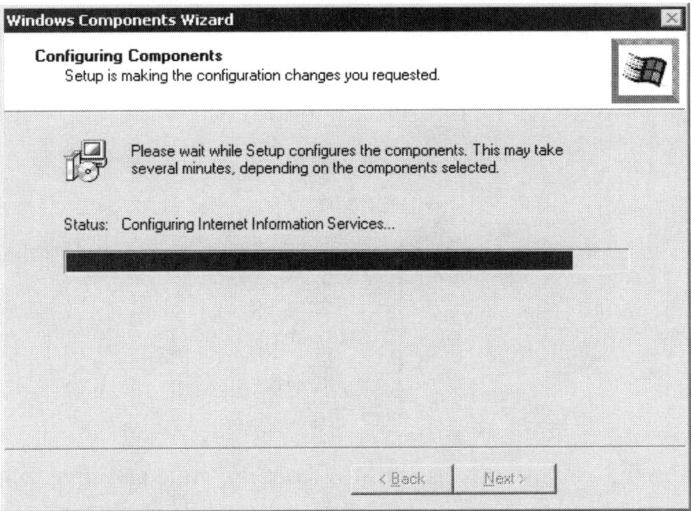

The IIS 5.0 Hierarchy

With the release of IIS 4.0, Microsoft introduced a new interface that they call the management console (MMC). It offers a common interface that manages and manipulates different services within the Windows platforms. You see a lot of it on Windows 2000, and SQL 2000's Enterprise Manager uses it as well.

IIS 5.0 uses the management console as a GUI interface to IIS's metabase. The metabase is like a mini-registry, set aside just for IIS. It stores settings in a hierarchical manner, and can be manipulated through the GUI, although there are other ways to manipulate the metabase.

IIS uses a hierarchy to display and maintain its data. Each point on the hierarchy is officially called a *configurable unit* according to Microsoft. While the term means exactly that, a configurable unit, it's a mouthful, and is difficult to use all the time. I prefer calling this an *object*, or a *node*. Most of us are familiar with both of the terms; I'll refer to it as a node from now on.

There are several different kinds of nodes. We'll mostly be focusing on web sites, as that's where most of the settings we're concerned about will be set. There are Web servers, web sites, home directories, virtual directories, and files, like HTML files or images. The hierarchy looks like this:

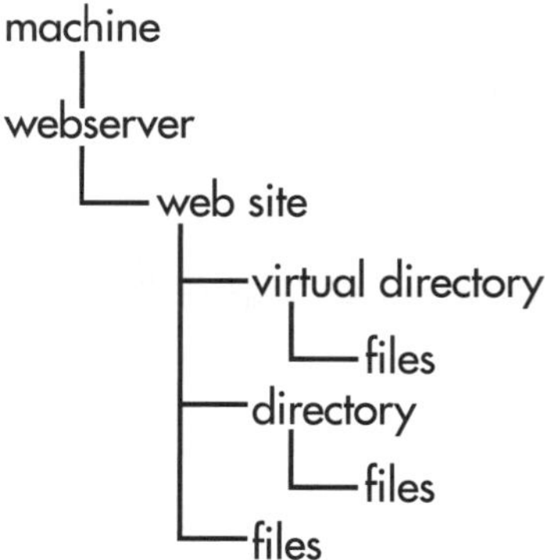

Each node on the tree inherits its settings from the node above it, which is also referred to as a parent node. Each node should, whenever possible, inherit its settings from its parent node. You could apply settings to each node individually, one at a time, but you shouldn't, and I'll tell you why in a second. You've seen in the management console that nodes sit at different levels within the hierarchy. A web site might have virtual directories beneath it, with files beneath that. Every node has a parent, and most nodes have children. That's not really an earthshaking tidbit of information, but it is important to know for performance reasons.

IIS stores settings for a node in the metabase. If the children of that node are to inherit the same settings, it doesn't duplicate the data in the metabase, it simply flags the child node, indicating that the child node should inherit its settings from its parent. Again, not earthshaking.

You can see where it's important for the metabase not to duplicate its data when you start thinking about traffic levels. If your site has high traffic levels, accessing data from the Web server as quickly as possible is a requirement. Not only do you not have the hardware resources to waste, you don't have the time. You need to answer that user's request as quickly as possible, or they might start using a faster competitor.

If you were to set each node by hand, bypassing the ability to have child nodes inherit settings, you would indeed be creating duplicate data that would ultimately slow down the server.

Now, let's be crazy and say that performance doesn't matter. Either you have the most powerful server on the block, or you *want* your site to be slow. All performance issues aside, you still benefit from taking advantage of the inheritance features. If you ever need to add a new web site, or any other child node, you simply have to do less work, because the node you create will inherit its settings from its parent. Taking advantage of IIS's hierarchy inheritance speeds up your server and makes administrating the server easier.

How IIS 5.0 and ColdFusion Work as a Team

IIS is built to be an application server. While it's mostly optimized to work with Microsoft's ASP, it still does an excellent job when teamed with ColdFusion. It's important to understand how IIS handles the user's request for a ColdFusion template, and what happens in the process.

While IIS is a powerful server, it can really only perform three types of tasks when a user requests something from it:

- Return a static file
- Launch a CGI program
- Launch an ISAPI extension

Static Files

Static files are files in your Web directory that are expected to do nothing. They're simply HTML files with no server-side coding in them, or any other special features that the server should be concerned with. Images files, such as GIF files or JPG files are also considered static files.

CGI Programs

CGI programs are executable files. Specifically, IIS will execute files that end with .exe when a user makes the request. The CGI program performs its task, and hands off the output to IIS. IIS displays the output, and everyone is happy, except the server. CGI is slow. Each user that makes a request to a CGI program opens up a new thread, which can really bring a busy server to its knees.

ISAPI Extensions

An Internet Server Application Programming Interface (ISAPI) extension is what we're most interested in. ISAPI allows a developer to create a DLL that is loaded once when IIS starts, and is ready to take requests at any time. Rather than opening a new thread for each request, the request is performed in the already open ISAPI thread. This is faster and less resource demanding than the only alternative, CGI.

When you install ColdFusion, the installation program automatically sets up a *Script Map*, which maps the ColdFusion ISAPI-enabled .dll to .cfm files. These DLL's are also sometimes referred to as ISAPI *filters*.

ColdFusion has been using ISAPI for the past few versions, but it used to use CGI. I did some performance testing a few years back comparing the two, and the performance increase from CGI to ISAPI was fantastic. My ColdFusion templates more than tripled in speed, while my server's resources were nowhere near the levels they were with CGI.

Ways to Tweak IIS 5.0 for Performance

A default IIS 5.0 installation runs quickly, but there are some things you can do to make it faster when running ColdFusion templates.

Good hardware always makes a difference. If you have plenty of memory, a fast CPU and fast hard drives, IIS is going to run faster. Also, Reducing the number of programs running on your IIS box is important. You should be running nothing more than the bare minimum Windows 2000 installation, turning off any OS feature that's not being used. In a live production environment, only IIS and ColdFusion should be running on the box. I highly recommend not running IIS, ColdFusion, and SQL 2000 on one box. If you want to be reminded of the good old days of computers when the 286 was the fastest kid on the block, running everything on one box will certainly remind you of those days.

There's a sort of obscure tweak for IIS 5.0 that may go away with final release of ColdFusion 5.0. With ColdFusion 4.5.1 SP2 running on Windows 2000, it's actually been reported that there can be performance degradations. Adjusting the Application Protection level can overcome this degradation. Even if this tweak has no effect on the final release of ColdFusion 5.0, it at least shows a good example of how to get into the IIS 5.0 settings.

There are steps you can take if you're being affected by this bug. Navigate to your Internet Services Manager either through Control Panel | Administrative Tools | Internet Services Manager, or Start | Programs | Administrative Tools | Internet Services Manager, and follow these steps:

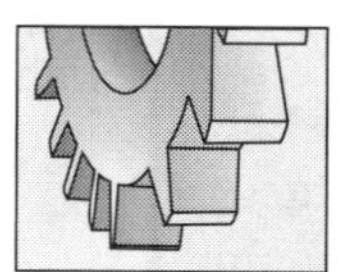

TIP

I usually create a shortcut on my desktop for the Internet Services Manager. I find that I end up using it a lot, and having the shortcut saves me a lot of time (or at least it feels faster, which is good enough for me).

1. Right-click on the web site, and select properties.
2. Click the Home Directory tab.

3. Towards the bottom is a drop-down list called Application Protection – Select Low (IIS Process). Click apply, then close all windows (including IIS).
4. From Administrative Tools | Services, stop and start IIS Admin Service and World Wide Web Publishing Service.

ColdFusion-Specific Settings

Script mappings within IIS are what allow IIS and ColdFusion to work together. While we haven't installed ColdFusion yet, there are already several script mappings that we can take a look at.

Open up the management console for IIS, and then follow these steps:

1. Right-click on a web site, and select Properties.
2. Click the Home Directory tab.
3. Click Configuration.

Your screen should look something like Figure 1-1. This is a list of all the script mappings for this particular web site. Select an extension, and click Edit. The first box contains the path to the ISAPI executable. The second box contains the extension for the type of file that the executable will process. The third box is only available if All Verbs is not selected. The verbs box allows you to selectively limit the script to do certain HTTP tasks, such as GET, HEAD, and POST. I usually set my templates to enable All Verbs, as I don't necessarily want to limit my scripts to certain operations. You'll probably find that you rarely need to limit the verbs.

Later, when we install ColdFusion, I will return to Script Mappings. The ColdFusion installation will automatically insert its script mapping into the list upon installation. In Part III, I'll talk about some tricks that can be used by using the Script Mappings section of IIS.

The IIS Metabase

Since the first release of Windows NT, and then with Windows 95, we've been using the Windows registry to maintain settings for our computers. The registry is a database of sorts, which allows us to store settings or program information with different data types (like binary, hex, or decimal). The registry also offers a major advantage over the old text file methods, organizing information in a hierarchal system. But with

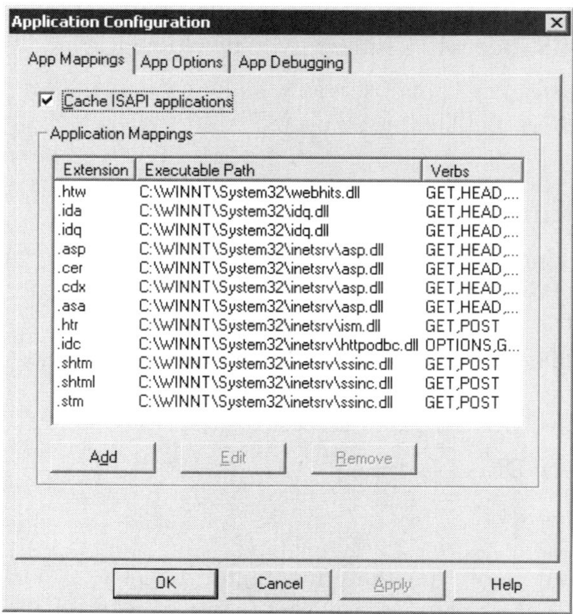

Figure 1-1 *A list of script mappings in IIS*

the size of the registry and the amount of information stored in it, it makes sense to have a separate registry just for IIS, which is what we call the *metabase*.

With the ability to edit multiple levels of nodes within the IIS hierarchy, the metabase is an obviously more efficient way to store web site information. Additionally, with the requirement of serving HTTP requests as fast as possible, the metabase is a quick alternative to the much slower Windows registry.

There are a few differences between the metabase and Windows registry. The metabase is stored in a binary file call METABASE.BIN, which is stored in the systemroot/system32 directory of your Windows 2000 installation. Just like the Windows registry, the metabase can store binary data, as well as textual data. The metabase adds something that the Windows registry doesn't have, and that's inheritance.

The following illustration is a visual example of how IIS child and parent relationships work. The top of the tree shows the Web service itself. The lefthand branch shows a web site with several settings. The nodes below the web site inherit their properties from the web site. The righthand branch shows a web site with several settings as well.

The difference is that the nodes below the righthand web site have their own explicit settings:

Node: Web Server
Set Properties:
Default Document: *index.htm, inheritance on*
Max connections: *10, inheritance on*

Node: Web Site
Inherited Properties:
Default Document: *index.htm, inheritance on*
Max connections: *10, inheritance on*

Node: Virtual Directory
Inherited Properties:
Default Document: *index.htm, inheritance on*
Max connections: *10, inheritance on*

Node: Web Site
Set Properties:
Default Document: *bunny.htm, inheritance off*
Max connections: *9000, inheritance off*

Node: Virtual Directory
Set Properties:
Default Document: *main.htm, inheritance off*
Max connections: *175, inheritance off*

It should be noted that the above example is merely an illustration of the concept of inheritance, and not a perfect real-world example of how inheritance works.

In the Windows registry, properties are stored by their names. In the IIS metabase, each property is assigned a unique numeric identifier. This identifier aids in performance as it's quicker to make numerical comparisons than it is to make string comparisons. The properties are accessed much quicker than the standard Windows registry because of this.

Another nice feature of the metabase is that there is an API just for the metabase. Developers can add settings to the metabase through installation scripts or other mechanisms right from their programs. An example of a program that takes advantage of this is the ColdFusion installation. During the install it adds entries into the metabase that make it possible for IIS to serve ColdFusion templates.

IIS Security Features

IIS provides security features that are fully integrated with Windows 2000. Five methods of authentication are supported so that you can confirm the identity of anyone requesting access to your web sites.

Anonymous Authentication

Anonymous authentication allows anyone access without asking for a user name or password. While it doesn't actively ask for a user name and password, it's still a method of authentication, in that it allows access to certain resources, just like any other form of authentications. Anonymous Authentication provides *no* security whatsoever, and is only included in this section because IIS allows you to pick it as a security method.

Basic Authentication

Basic authentication prompts the user for a user name and password, which are sent unencrypted over the network. This is probably the most commonly seen form of authentication on the Web. It provides a quick an easy way to allow only certain logins to access the directories you've set aside to be password protected. This provides a low amount of security, as the unencrypted password could potentially be intercepted.

Digest Authentication

Digest authentication is a new feature that operates much like Basic authentication except that each password is sent as a *hash* value. A hash value is a number derived from the password, from which it is not easy to decipher the original text. This provides a relatively high degree of security. Even if someone managed to get the hash value, they'd have to know how the hash value was derived in order to know the password. Digest authentication is available only on domains with a Windows 2000 domain controller.

Integrated Windows Authentication

Integrated Windows authentication uses hashing technology to identify your user without actually sending the password over the network. Integrated Windows authentication used to be called *NTLM*, or Windows NT Challenge/Response authentication. This provides a relatively high degree of security, although is usually best used for things like company intranets, where a resource is located on a Windows 2000 domain.

Certificates

Certificates are digital credentials that can be used for establishing a Secure Sockets Layer (SSL) connection. They can also be used for authentication. During the login process, the server checks the clients' digital identification. Client certificates can be obtained from a mutually trusted source. The certificates usually contain identifying information about the user and the source that issued the certificate. This is probably the most secure method of authentication, although you'll probably rarely use it.

Logging

Another often overlooked part of IIS is how to set up the logging properly. Every time an HTTP request is made to IIS, by default, a log entry is made. The way IIS sets up its default logs is usually inadequate for most organizations. Figures 1-2 and 1-3 show the default IIS settings.

To edit log settings, right-click on the web site, select Properties, then the Web Site tab. Click the Properties button in the lower right hand part of the dialog box.

In Figure 1-3 we see that under New Log Time Period, Daily is selected. This is probably adequate for most sites, but if your application gets a high degree of traffic, it might be a better idea to set the log files to hourly. I've found that it's easier to deal with hundreds of 5MB log files than it is to deal with a dozen 10–20GB log files.

Log file sizes add up quickly. Every request a user makes is logged, as well as the response from the server. When a user requests an HTML page, every item on the page that has to load, whether it be a style sheet, an image, or an audio file, will make an entry in the log file. One page view from a single user could easily put 10–20 lines into your logs. The location where you store your log files is very important as well. You should never have your log files building up on a slow drive,

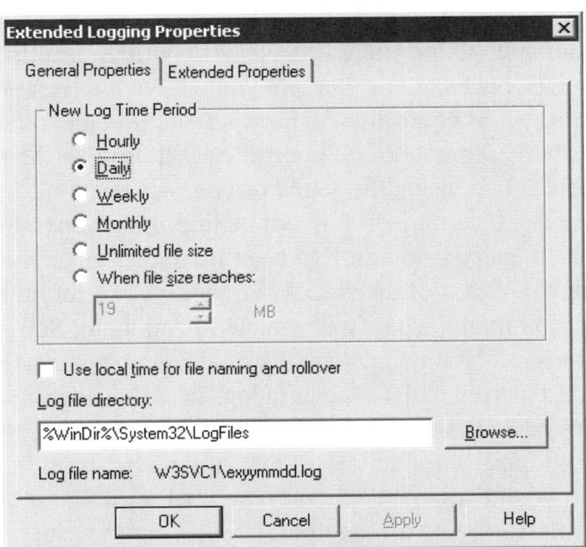

Figure 1-2 *The general logging properties*

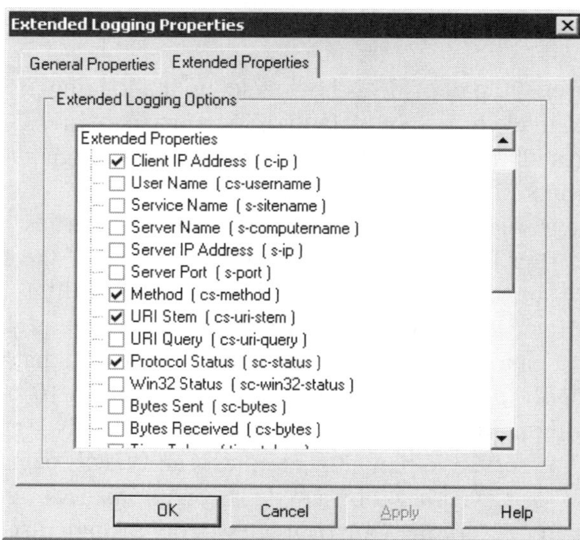

Figure 1-3 *The default extended settings just don't capture enough*

especially a Raid 5 system. A Raid 5 system is built for redundancy, not speed. Each time a user hits your site the log file will have to be written multiple times according to the Raid 5 spec. It's much better if you put your active log files on a very fast drive with its own separate SCSI controller. IDE drives should be avoided as well, as they use the CPU to write. A separate SCSI controller will provide the fastest read/write times to your log files, increasing the speed of your server.

Backing up your log files may or may not be important depending on your application. In almost every situation I've been in, log files were vital in measuring the success or lack of success of the site. After about 5 or 6 months however, the log files are less important than the data extrapolated from them. Some would probably argue that 5–6 months is a bit too much, but I consider it a bit of a safety net. Of course, if resources and space permit and you require log files, I'd suggest keeping all of them on whatever type of backup mechanism you prefer. I've known organizations that will routinely offload old log files on to CD-ROMs or tape backups.

I've also known organizations that don't care for log files at all. If you don't care about log files, turn off logging all together. Not having to write to a disk for every hit will make things noticeably quicker, as well as save you a lot of time and effort maintaining the files.

You have the option of using ODBC to store your logging information. I think the limitations and other disadvantages make it a much less desirable option than the ASCII log files.

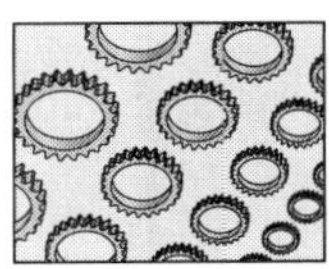

NOTE

ODBC stands for Open Database Connectivity. *ODBC is a data access application interface (API) which allows data access to any database with ODBC compliant drivers. You might already be very accustomed to ODBC because it's primarily what allows ColdFusion to connect to several different types of databases.*

The most important limitation is that ODBC logging limits you to how many columns you're able to track. ODBC doesn't let you add any extended tracking properties to the logging, which, depending on your situation could be a serious limitation. Also, you might be setting yourself up for a bottleneck. The speed at which you can write to the database should be quicker than it is to write to the recommended fast SCSI hard drive, writing to a small file. You'll also have to rely on your database server to do any optimizing of the logs, which might add too much administration to the logging process. And finally, it might be difficult to analyze the data once it's stored. You'll either have to find a web-based log-processing package that supports an ODBC source, or you'll need to write the queries to do the processing yourself—another administrative cost.

If you're going to be using your log files to extrapolate marketing information, the default settings in IIS are just not enough. Table 1-1 shows the default column selections. You can set the log files to give you information like where they came from or even what kind of browser they have. This kind of information is very important in knowing where your traffic is coming from or how you should design your site. Table 1-1 provides a list of the possible properties to track.

SQL Server 2000

Microsoft SQL Server 2000 is an excellent database solution to use with ColdFusion. While ColdFusion is designed to work with quite a few RDBMS products, it is probably best designed to work with SQL Server. SQL Server 2000 is the Microsoft Corporation's latest version of their extremely popular and well-supported SQL Server line.

New SQL Server 2000 Features

SQL Server 2000 Enterprise includes over 50 new features and enhancements that make an already powerful database server even more powerful. I'd like to highlight some of the features that I think are most relevant and important to ColdFusion developers.

Field	Appears As	Description
Date	date	The date the activity was logged
Time	time	The time the activity was logged
Client IP Address	c-ip	The IP address of the client that accessed your server
User Name	cs-username	The name of the Windows user who accessed your server
Service Name	s-sitename	The Internet service that was running on the client computer
Server Name	s-computername	The name of the server on which the log was generated
Server IP	s-ip	The IP address of the server on which the log entry was generated
Server Port	s-port	The port number to which the client connected
Method	cs-method	The action the client was trying to perform (such as, GET, POST)
URI Stem	cs-uri-stem	The resource accessed (HTML page, CGI, or script)
URI Query	cs-uri-query	The query the client submitted with the request (The bold text is an example: index.htm**?cat=1**)
HTTP Status	sc-status	The HTTP status code of the action (such as, 404, 405)
Win32 Status	sc-win32-status	The status of the action, in Win32 terms
Bytes Sent	cs-bytes	The number of bytes sent by the server
Bytes Received	sc-bytes	The number of bytes sent from the client to the server
Time Taken	time-taken	The length of time the action took
Protocol Version	cs-version	The protocol (such as, HTTP 1.1, FTP)
User Agent	cs(User-Agent)	The browser agent code (such as, Mozilla 4.5)
Cookie	cs(Cookie)	The content of the cookie sent or received, if it exists
Referrer	cs(Refer)	The URL the user came from, just before this action.

Table 1-1 *A List of the Possible Columns to Select for Your Log Files*

XML Views

XML Views allow you to view and access relational data using XML techniques by mapping XML elements and attributes to relational schema. XML is used as a standard formatting of data that can be passed to different applications or database servers without losing information about how the data is formatted. For instance, a comma-delimited list of values doesn't tell the reader what the data type of each value is. XML documents can include that kind of information, and can even pass complex structures like related tables to XML-capable applications.

SQL Server 7.0 didn't just let you play with XML out of the box. You had to download an update that allowed you to read and manipulate XML structures. All versions of SQL Server 2000 are now XML friendly, although the XML support still leaves a lot to be desired. XML data can be generated with relative ease, but importing XML data isn't even supported on a standard SQL Server 2000 installation. An XML Tools Update that makes the task of importing possible must be downloaded from Microsoft. Even with the update, importing XML data is a bit tedious. I'll go over some importing examples in Chapter 18, which covers XML in more depth.

If you wanted to quickly and easily allow other organizations to access your site's data, either through syndication channels or however you might want to structure it, you could use SQL Server 2000 to create an XML view that you could then allow other organizations to access that data.

URL and HTTP Access

You can now access data on your SQL Server 2000 server via a web browser, using a URL. You can also append SQL statements to the URL, as well as define XML templates.

This is a pretty heavy-duty feature. There are a lot of things to consider when you realize that your precious SQL server may be open to the public via a web browser. Because of the security risk this feature exposes, I won't recommend using it on your application server.

Another thought might come to mind when absorbing the weight of this new feature: what about ColdFusion? Does this negate the need for ColdFusion if I can use SQL alone to output data to a Web browser, formatting it with an XML template? Well, if all ColdFusion could do was output data and format it, then perhaps that might be a valid concern, but we know that ColdFusion is far more than a tool to pull data from a database. While SQL Server 2000 can output data to the Web, it is not an application server like ColdFusion. You cannot easily implement program logic into SQL's Web output, or maintain sessions, or do all of the many powerful things that ColdFusion can. The best thing to do is embrace the feature, and use it where it makes the most sense.

SSL Security

Now that SQL has the ability to make it live to the world, this feature is a no-brainer. SQL Server 2000 now allows you to protect your server using SSL (Secure Sockets Layer) connections and Kerberos. C2-level certification is expected sometime after the release.

32 CPU SMP System Support

If you're using Windows 2000 DataCenter Server, you can put SQL Server 2000 on SMP systems with as many as 32 processors. I've seen very few applications that would require even more than 4–6 active SQL processors, but it is possible to require this kind of power. If you ever need it, SQL Server 2000 could in theory do it.

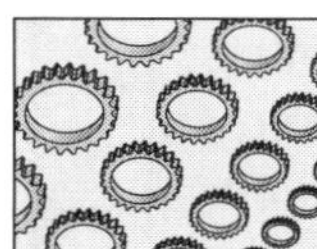

NOTE

SMP stands for symmetric multiprocessing, *which is a general term for systems that have several processors that run in parallel under a single operating system. Each processor has equal access to the input/output systems of the system. In more basic terms, SMP systems are systems with more than one CPU.*

64GB RAM support

If you're using Windows 2000 DataCenter, SQL 2000 can use up to 64GB of memory. This is a lot of RAM. Again, I doubt that most ColdFusion applications would ever need a SQL Server 2000 server with 64GB of RAM, but it is possible, and SQL Server 2000 can do it.

User-Defined Functions

This is a nice one. I use a lot of functions in SQL-stored procedures, and this feature allows me to make my own functions in SQL to reuse when needed.

Installing SQL Server 2000

This section consists of a brief overview of how to install SQL Server 2000, discussing parts of the installation that might be either useful or harmful to your ColdFusion application. While you can choose many ways to install SQL Server 2000 depending on the situation, this is just one of them.

Installing the Prerequisites

If you're installing SQL Server 2000 on a Windows 95 box (which I wouldn't suggest doing), then you'll need to install the Common Controls Library Update, located on the Install Prerequisites tab from the main installation menu.

If you're running Windows 2000, you already have all the prerequisites, and we can move on to installing the SQL 2000 components.

Install the SQL Server 2000 Components

If you're installing SQL Server 2000 Enterprise Edition, you have three installation choices available:

- **Install Database Server** Installs the core database server, along with all of its associated components.
- **Install Analysis Services** Installs the SQL Server 2000 Analysis server, a tool used to perform OLAP (Online Analytical Processing), and data-mining functions.
- **Install English Query** Allows users to ask plain English questions to retrieve data.

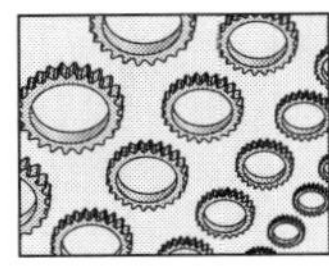

NOTE

SQL Server 2000 Enterprise Edition requires Windows 2000 Advanced server or greater. You can install the client components of SQL Server 2000 Enterprise on a Windows 2000 Professional operating system, but that's about it.

We're going to install the database server. While useful, the other components don't directly interact with ColdFusion, so we'll ignore them for now.

1. Click SQL Server 2000 Components to begin the installation.

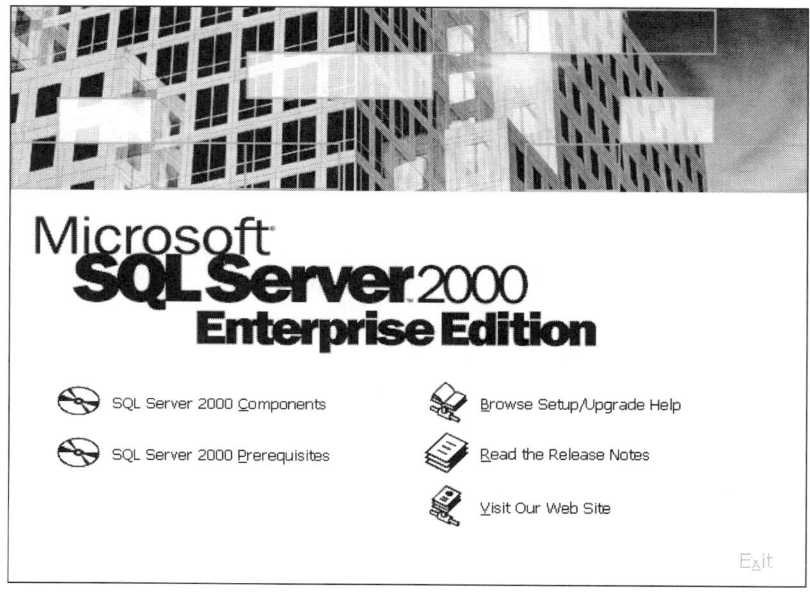

2. Click Install Database server.

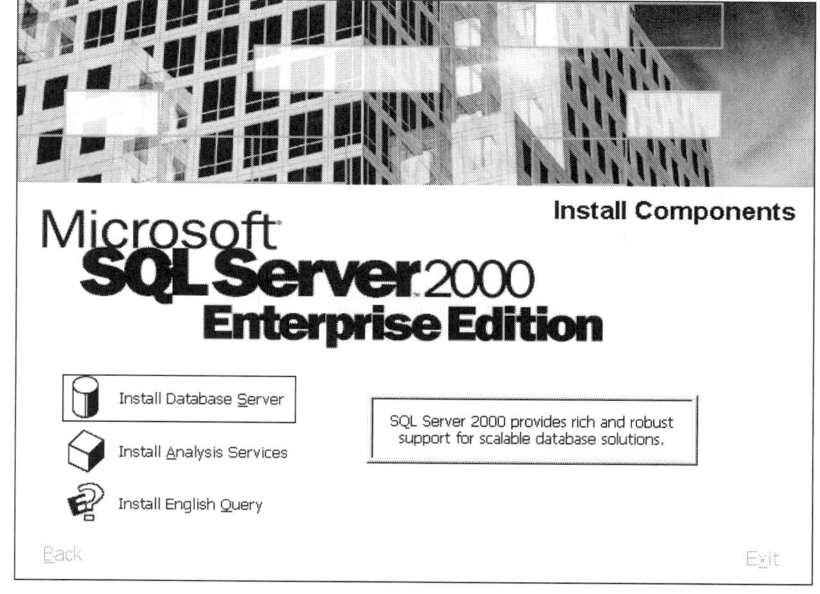

3. Click Next.
4. While you have the option to install SQL Server 2000 to a remote machine, for the sake of simplicity, install on the local machine. Select the Local Computer radio button and click Next.

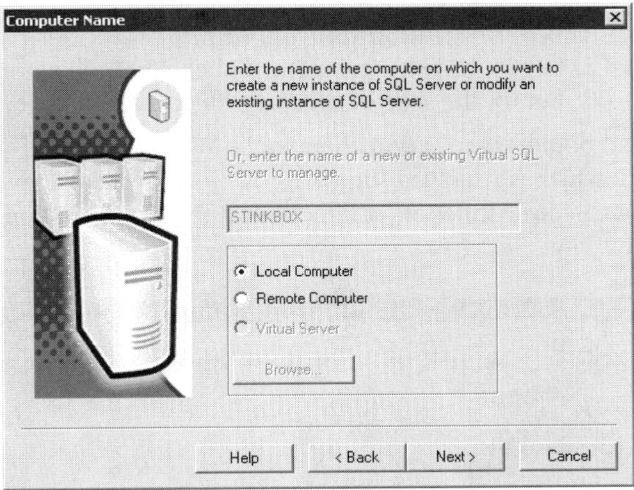

We want to install a new instance of SQL Server 2000, although it is possible to upgrade an older SQL Server installation (SQL Server 6.5 or SQL Server 7.0). Even if I already have SQL installed, I usually like to create a new instance, and migrate my old server to the new server gradually, just to play it safe.

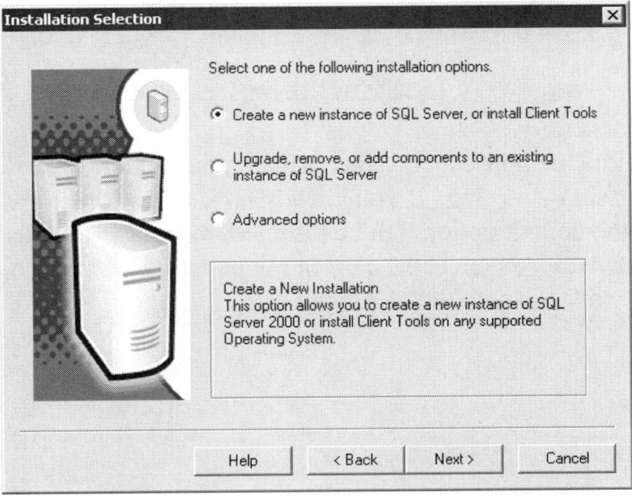

5. Enter a name and company name and click Next.

6. To legally use SQL Server 2000, you must accept the license agreement. Read it diligently, I don't think it could happen, but you certainly wouldn't want Microsoft showing up at your door asking for your firstborn. Of course I'm trying to be funny. I wouldn't think for a second that Microsoft would ever do anything like that, but it is a good idea to read the license agreement if you haven't already. When you're finished, click Next.
7. Enter your CD key in the next screen, then click Next. This is all relatively brainless stuff, but for the sake of accuracy I want to include every step.
8. Next, install both the server and client tools. We have the option to only install client tools, which is what you should probably do on a development workstation so that you can access the server later. Select the second option, Server and Client Tools, and click Next.

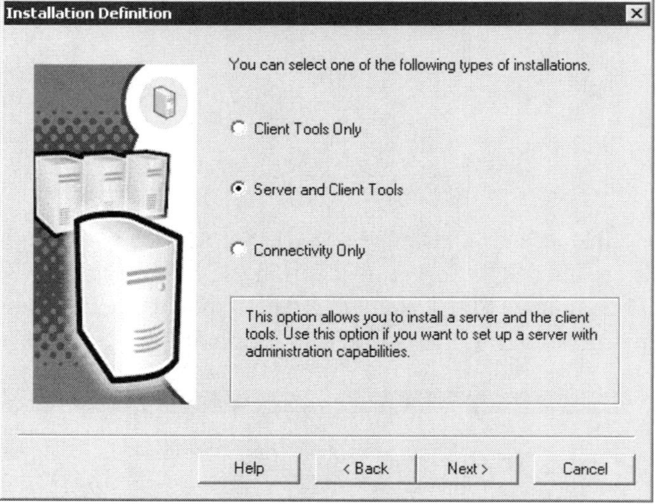

9. Now it's time to choose an instance name. You can leave the default instance name, or assign your own. If you already have SQL Server installed on your machine, the default option will be disabled, meaning you must come up with an instance name, which is the case in my particular installation. Assign a name and click Next.

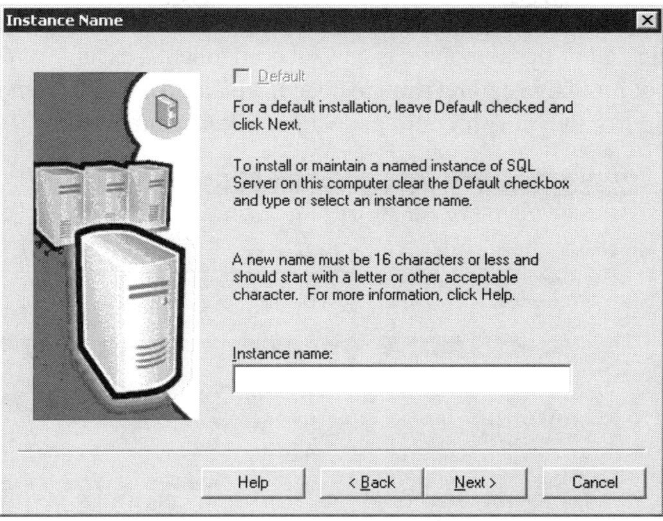

This is where you get to decide what drives to install the server on, and what kind of installation you'd like. Choose a Custom installation, and decide where you'd like to install the program and data files.

10. It is recommended that you install the data files on a fairly quick drive, separate from the Program Files drive. We'll go into more detail about drive related performance issues later on. For now, select the options that best suit your situation, and click Next.

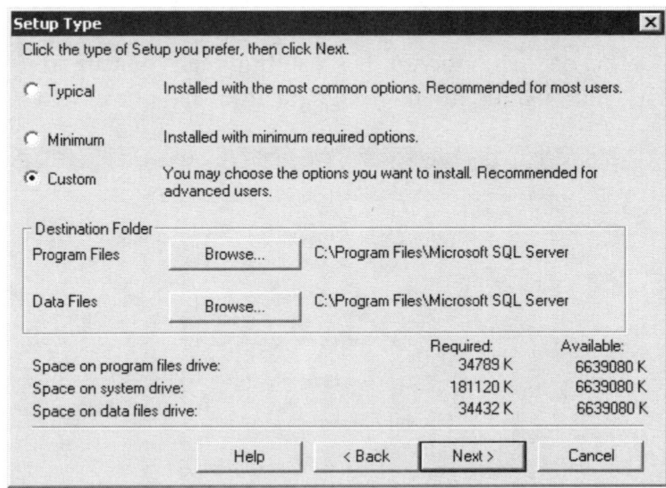

11. Select everything but the Code Samples subcomponent, and click Next. We want pretty much all of the components and subcomponents, except for the sample code. I usually don't like installing sample code if I plan on using the server in a staging or live environment, as it could pose a potential security risk.

12. Assign a user account to the SQL Server 2000 services. I like to have each service use the same Domain User account. Prior to setting up SQL Server 2000, I usually make an account just for the SQL Server 2000 services called something identifiable like "sql_agent." I do this partly for security reasons, and also to help track down issues if they ever arise. Knowing there's only one place this domain account is used is helpful at times, and helps make my job easier. How you handle this one is up to you. It's a setting that you can pretty much set and forget. Use your best judgment, assign a name, and click Next.

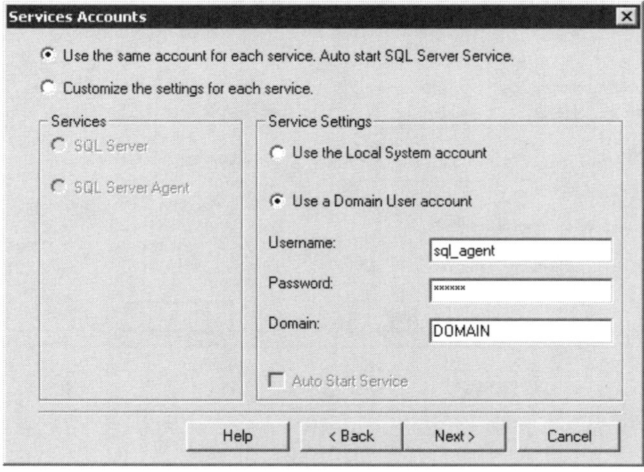

13. Set the authentication mode for the server. We want to select Mixed Mode, because it will allow backwards compatibility with SQL Server 7, but more importantly, with ColdFusion as well. The *sa login* is the SQL System Administrator login. Choose your password carefully, and whatever you do, don't leave it blank. An outside user can gain complete control over your SQL Server if they know the *sa* password, and leaving the password blank is a sure-fire way to getting hacked. Choose Mixed Mode, enter a *good* password for your *sa* account, and click Next.

Authentication Mode

Choose the authentication mode.

Windows Authentication Mode

Mixed Mode (Windows Authentication and SQL Server Authentication)

Add password for the sa login:

Enter password:

Confirm password:

Blank Password (not recommended)

Help | < Back | Next > | Cancel

TIP

Passwords should be a mix of numbers and letters, and should be hard to reverse engineer. While it might seem clever for me to choose a password like buffington1234, it's obvious that even though the password is a mix of letters and numbers, it's still easy to guess. A password like dH2odq39da would be much more difficult to guess. But a password like that is nearly impossible to remember. I find it helpful to develop a password system. For instance, I can generate a pretty difficult to crack password by picking a phrase that makes sense to me like "Sometimes Steve Ballmer Frightens Me," and combing it with another sequence of numbers that makes sense to me, like 9876. The end result, s9s8b7f6m, creates a password that's very hard to guess.

14. Collations aren't new to SQL Server, but how SQL Server 2000 let's you use them is new. A collation specifies the bit patterns that represent each character and the rules by which characters are sorted and compared. During the SQL Server 2000 installation, you're able to modify the default collation settings. The subject of using collations properly is a complicated one. Most database solutions will use the default collation settings. Click Next to continue.

15. Choosing which network libraries to use is up to you and your network setup. Usually I leave named pipes alone, and make a slight modification the TCP/IP. I usually set the port for TCP/IP to 1434, as it's reserved by the Internet Assigned Number Authority as a SQL Server port. Sometimes for security reasons you may choose to use another port. Assign your port and click Next.
16. Set your licensing modes, which depends on what kind of license you have purchased. You've probably seen this before, so do what you think suits your needs best (within your legal rights). I usually purchase a "per-processor" license. Select the option that suits you best, and click Next.

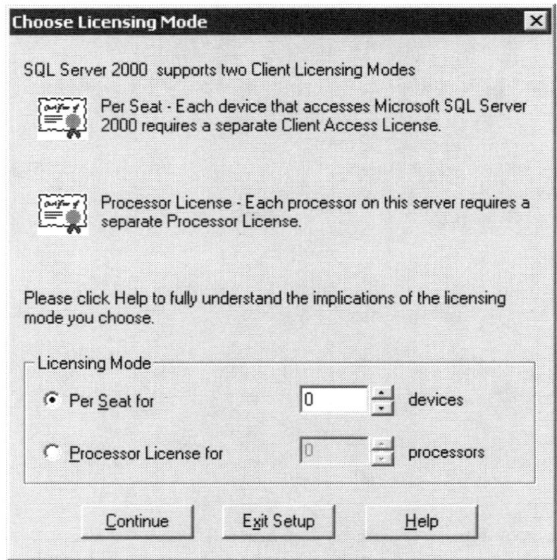

Now that we've got all the options and settings out of the way, the SQL Server 2000 installation will start. It displays a prompt that recommends shutting down certain tasks before continuing in order to avoid a reboot. I've gone through the install at least a dozen times on different machines, and regardless of which services I shut down, it always has to restart at the end of the installation. Expect to do a restart at the end, despite what it tells you, and shut down what you think you should shut down.

Once you've completed that step, the installation program copies the files, configures the subcomponents, and restarts the server. Almost every administrative task can be done from another machine with the SQL Server 2000 client tools installed, which makes it very easy to run your SQL Server 2000 box remotely.

Overview of the Enterprise Manager

The Enterprise Manager is a powerful tool used to perform administration tasks in SQL Server 2000. It uses the Microsoft Management Console, or MMC, so some of its features may be familiar to you. Earlier we installed IIS 5.0, which also uses the MMC. The MMC is a tool used to administer things like IIS, SQL Server, and other network and system administrative tasks.

The Enterprise Manager organizes SQL Server in a hierarchal system similar to IIS 5.0. This makes it easy to quickly perform administrative tasks. Figure 1-4 shows an example of the Enterprise Manager.

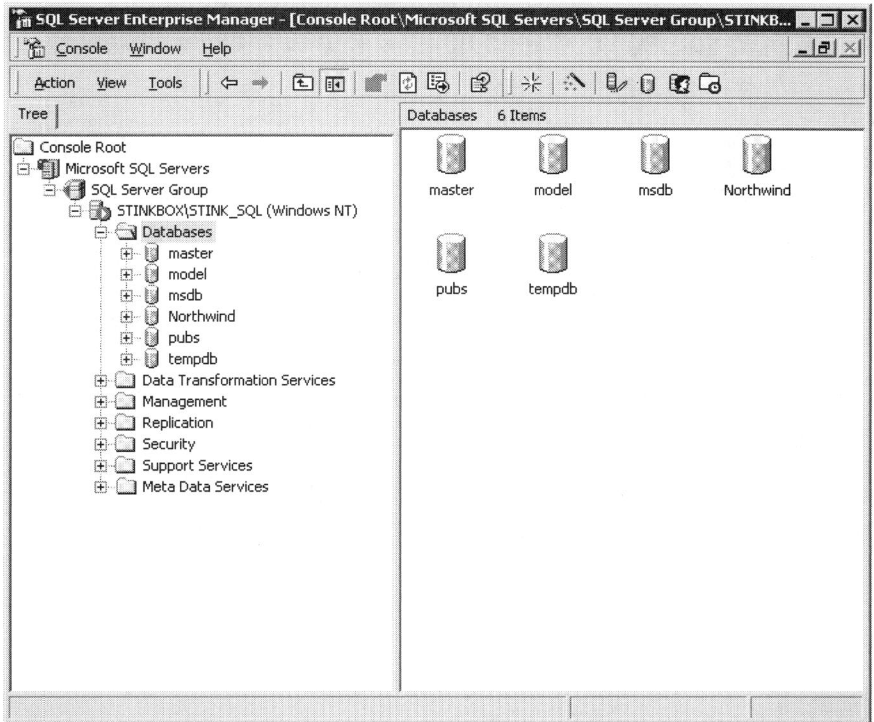

Figure 1-4 *An example of how the Enterprise Manager organizes its parts.*

I won't go into all the details of the Enterprise Manager just yet. We'll be going into more detail as we perform certain tasks later with the Enterprise Manager.

TIP

You can open multiple Enterprise Manager windows at one time. This makes it easy to perform administrative tasks in one window while the other window is busy.

Registering a Server

To use the Enterprise Manager on a separate machine, you'll need to add your recently install SQL Server to your Enterprise Manager. Before you can, you'll need to set up an alias for the server you just set up. To do this, take the following steps:

1. Click the Start menu. Select Programs, and then Microsoft SQL Server.
2. Click Client Network Utility. You'll see the screen shown in Figure 1-5.

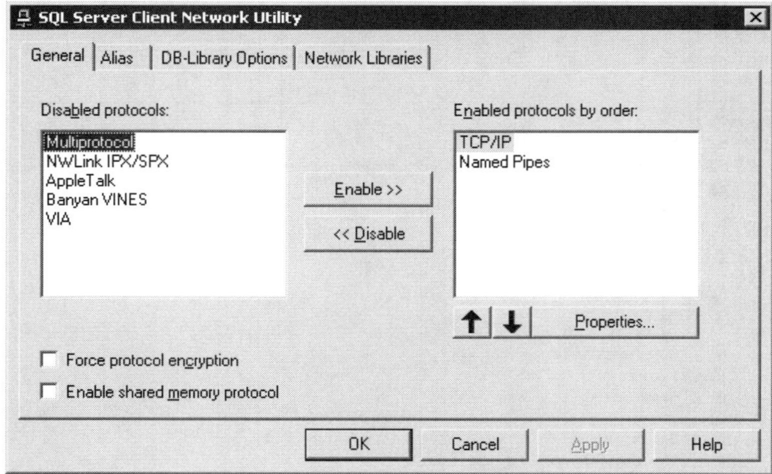

Figure 1-5 *The SQL Server Client Network utility*

We'll use TCP/IP to connect to the server. This isn't the fastest or most secure way to connect to the server, but it works well and is quick and easy to set up.

1. Click the Alias Tab.
2. Click Add.
3. Select the TCP/IP option and assign whatever kind of name you want in the Server name field; the IP address and port are what really matter. You (the client) will refer to the alias when communicating with the server, and the Client Network Utility will translate that into an IP address and port. Give the server a sensible name, and you can choose to dynamically figure out the port, or you can assign it manually. The Server Alias field should be your name for the server, and the Server Name field should be the IP address of the server. Yes, it's a bit confusing, especially when the Server Name field is automatically filled in the same as the Server Alias.

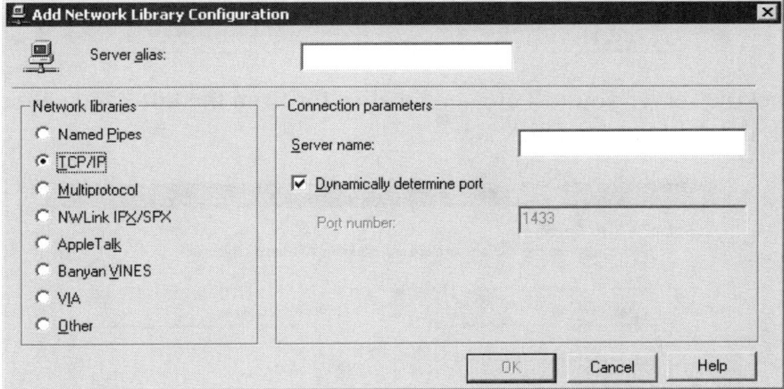

4. Now, back in the Enterprise Manager, expand the Microsoft SQL Servers node, and then expand the SQL Server Group node. The SQL Server Group node is probably empty. It's time to add your server.
5. Right-click on the SQL Server Group node, and then select New SQL Server Registration. The wizard starts.

6. For now, let's continue to use the wizard and click Next.

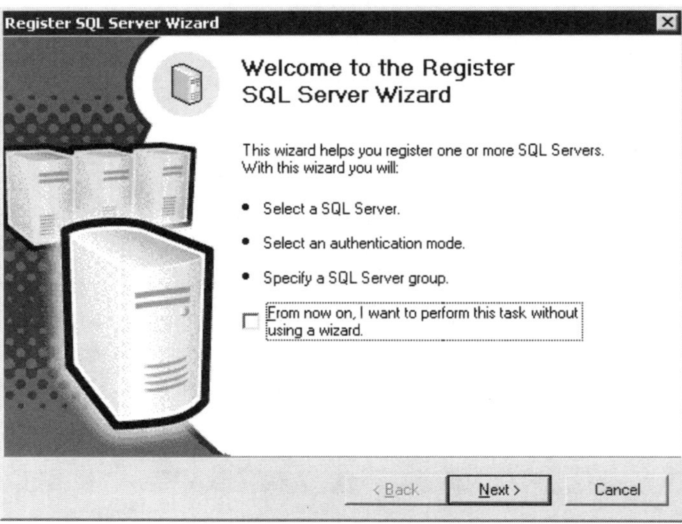

7. Select the server you just created an alias for from the left-hand column, and click the Add button. Click Next.

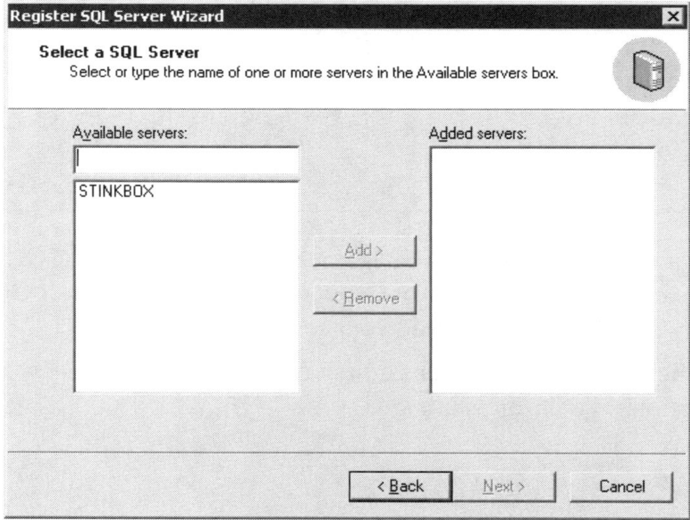

8. If your client is not on the same network as your SQL Server, you need to use SQL authentication to gain access to the box. Select the SQL Server Authentication option and click Next.

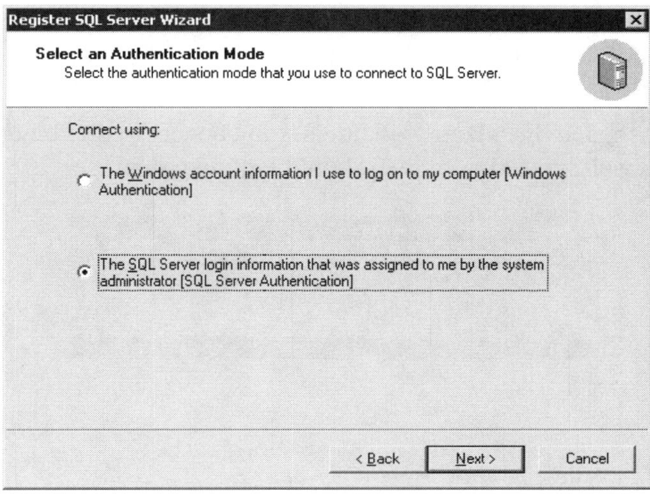

9. Enter the user name and password you'll be using. Normally, I would have set up an account on my SQL Server specifically for me, but because this is the first I've connected to the SQL Server to any type of administration, I'll use the *sa* account I created during the installation of SQL Server 2000.

10. It's important to know who's connecting to your SQL Server for several reasons. Giving each client a separate login will help you track down potential application performance issues more quickly. It will also help you keep an eye on your box. Each login can have separate auditing, making it easy for you to know who's doing what on your box. Before we install ColdFusion, we'll set up a SQL security account for our first ColdFusion datasource. For now, enter your account information, and click Next.

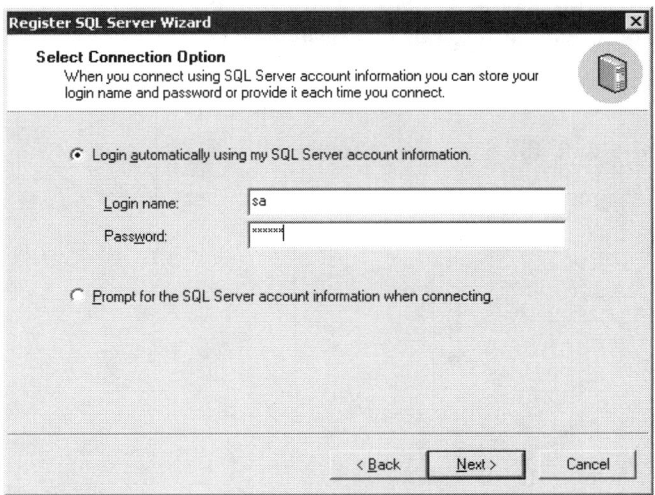

11. The next step will ask you if you want to add your newly registered server to the Microsoft SQL Servers group, or create a new top-level group. Choose the option that works best for you, and click Next.
12. Click Finish, and the wizard will attempt to connect to the remote SQL Server. If all goes well, your final screen should look like this:

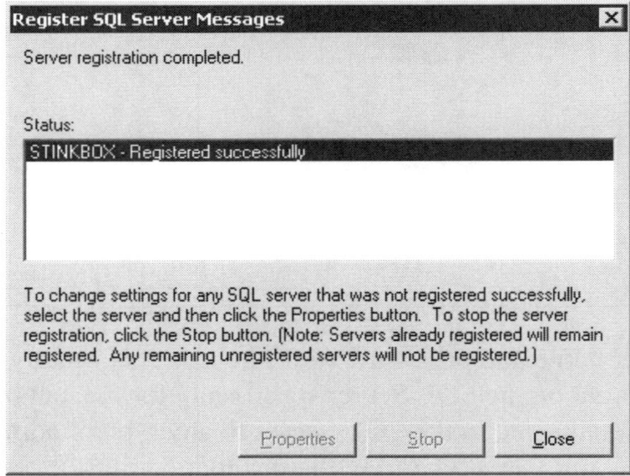

Now you'll be able to perform administrative tasks as if you were sitting in front of the actual server.

Creating a Test Database

Now that we've registered a server, it's time to create the database we'll be using for our sample ColdFusion application.

Before starting, you need to consider a few things. Here's a quick list of questions to ask yourself before creating your database:

- What physical drive will this database reside on?
- How rapidly will this database grow?
- Will I be diligent in monitoring the database size regularly?

The questions are important, because they're some of the first decisions you'll have to make about your database.

1. To create a new database, expand your database server within the Enterprise Manager, then right-click on the databases folder. Select New Database. You'll see the screen shown in Figure 1-6.
2. The first question you're asked is what you want to name the database. Name it something that makes sense. Believe it or not some people try to go crazy here and name their databases with all sorts of scientific names like "db30xlrev" (no joke). I'm going to name my database "skateshop." Because we're going to be building an online store and I love skateboarding, I've chosen to sell skateboards. Name the database whatever you like, and leave the Collation settings alone for now.

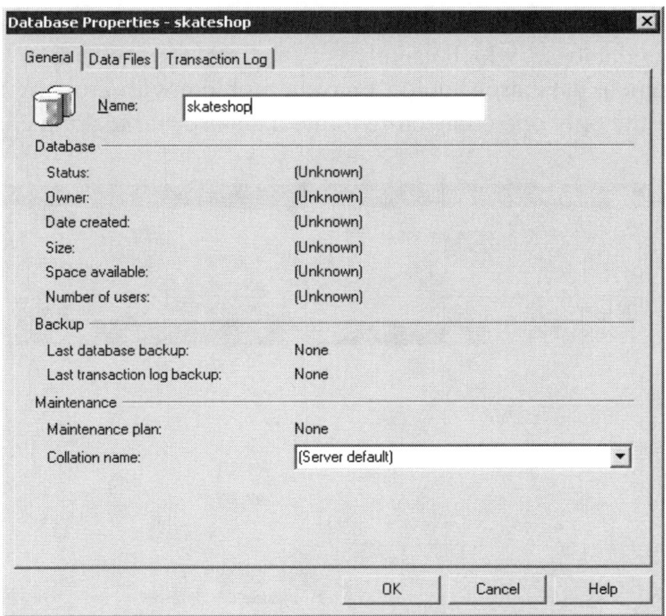

Figure 1-6 *Giving your database a name*

3. Click the Data Files tab.
4. Automatically, the Enterprise Manager suggests a name for a data file, the location, and how to grow the database file. Figure 1-7 shows what it suggested for my skate shop database.

But, since this is simply a development server, I'm not going to change anything here.

However, if I were setting this up for a production server, I'd want to make sure my data files were on a very fast, separate drive. I also wouldn't allow SQL Server to automatically grow the database. Space is always limited, and I don't want SQL to hit a dead end when trying to grow the database. What I would do instead, in a production environment, is create a SQL job that would monitor the amount of data in the data file, and if the data was approaching a certain size, expand the database file. I'd also have a step in there that would alert me via e-mail if the file were running out of space. If I set it to automatically grow, it'll grow and grow, and eventually, hit a snag, without any fair warning. Figure 1-7 shows what SQL Server automatically suggests for my database, which usually isn't optimal for production servers.

My development database shouldn't have a problem with growing too rapidly because I'll be the only one connecting to the database and making changes. I know

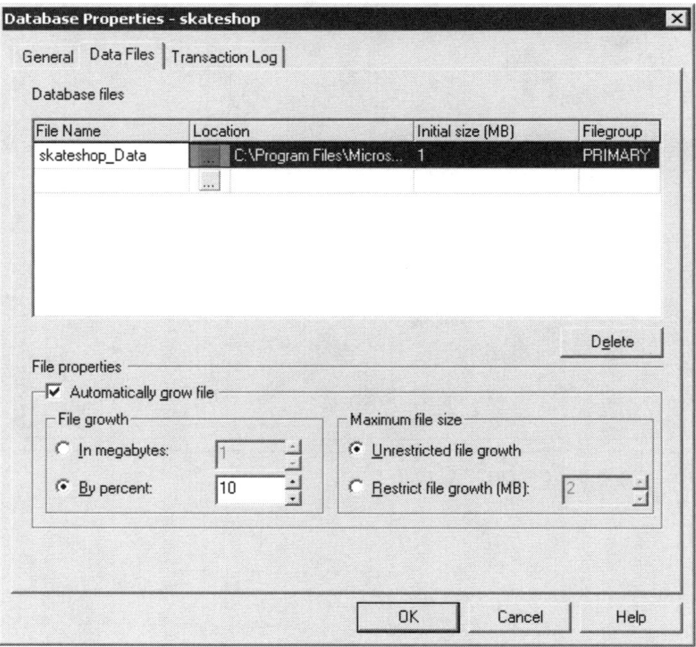

Figure 1-7 *Enterprise Manager automatically suggests file names and locations for your database.*

I'm capable of many things, but in this case, I cannot single-handedly fill a 20GB drive just by doing "normal" things to my database.

The same goes for the transaction logs. The transaction log stores information about database activity. This makes it possible to restore data back to a previous state. In a development environment, the default settings work just fine. In a production environment, speed is vital. Storing a transaction log on a separate, fast, disk is highly recommended. Transaction logs are written in a *serial fashion*, which means that when written to, the drive head remains in the same place so that the next write can be performed very quickly.

Also, in a production environment, it's a good idea to make sure your transaction logs have enough room to grow. If the transaction log has to automatically grow, it slows the logs down considerably. Each time it grows, a virtual log file is created, and transaction logging has to wait for the log to expand. I'd set up a job that would monitor the size, just like my production database size-monitoring job, and expand it ahead of time so that it wouldn't have to expand on the fly.

Once you decide how you'll setup the data files and transaction logs, click OK and your database is created.

If you select your database and look at its tables, you might see a bunch of oddly named tables, stored procedures, and views. Figure 1-8 shows an example.

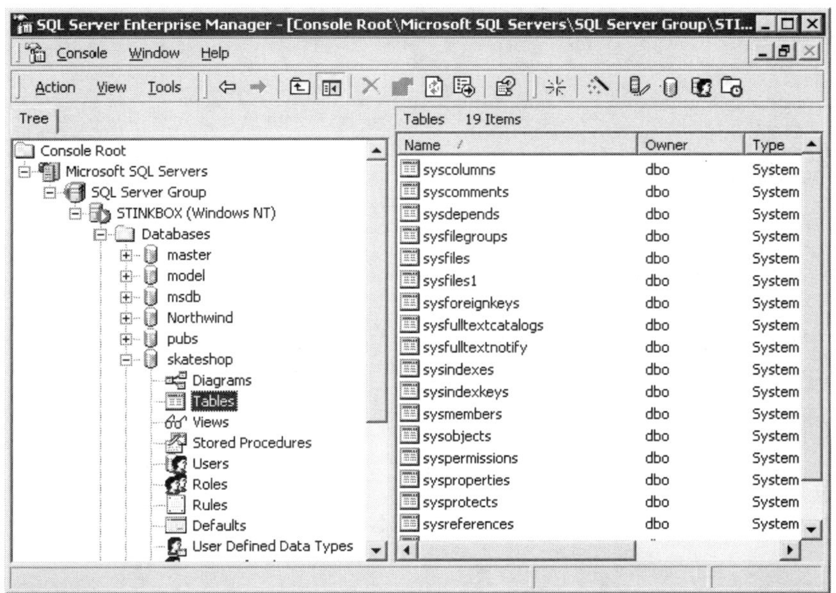

Figure 1-8 *System tables all over the place*

These odd tables are system tables, or better yet, system objects. Put simply, system objects are used by SQL to store information about your database, and perform tasks on your database. You will probably never need immediate access to these objects. You certainly don't need to see them every time you open your Enterprise Manager.

We can hide the system objects in Enterprise Manage. Right-click your SQL Server in Enterprise Manager and select Edit SQL Server Registration Properties. Your screen should look like this:

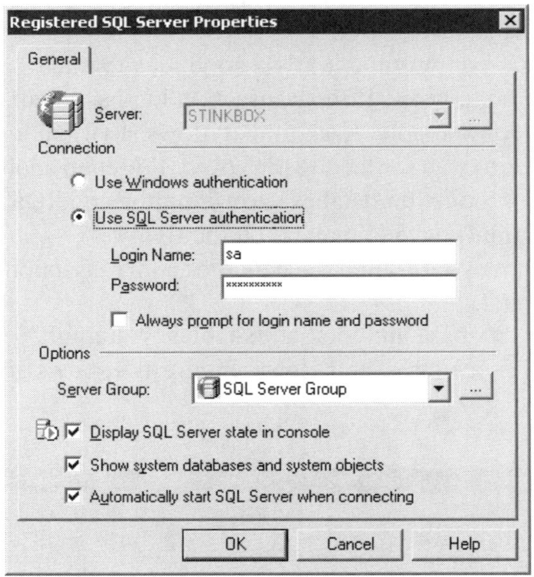

1. Uncheck the "Show system databases and system objects" option.

2. Click OK, and you should know have a fresh, uncluttered database, ready for tables and store procedures.

The system objects still exist in the database, they're just not cluttering your view in the Enterprise Manager. If you ever need access to them, you can have them show the same way we hid them. They're also available to SQL commands in SQL Query Analyzer.

Setting Up Security Roles

Before doing anything with the database, we want to set up some security roles. We could easily ignore this step, but inevitably something would happen a few months from now that would make us regret the day we ever skipped this step. And, because we're professionals, we know that security is very important. Of course, what we say and do don't always align, and I'll be the first to admit that I shine on this step far too often. It's difficult, and requires some foresight. I know though, that if you just get it out of the way and move on, your job will be easier in the long run.

Every situation calls for different security measures. If you're dead serious about security, I'd suggest that in addition to this section that you study how SQL Security works. Because it's a complicated subject, I'm not able to give a complete and comprehensive guide on it. I'm limited to giving a somewhat detailed how to on setting up accounts.

In our application, I want three main accounts. I want an administrative account for my client computer, a general account for my Skate Shop application, and an limited security account for my Skate Shop application.

1. First, I'll create an administrative account other than the default *sa* account. This one will be fairly easy because it's basically a duplicate of the *sa* account.

2. To add the account, expand the Security folder underneath SQL Server.

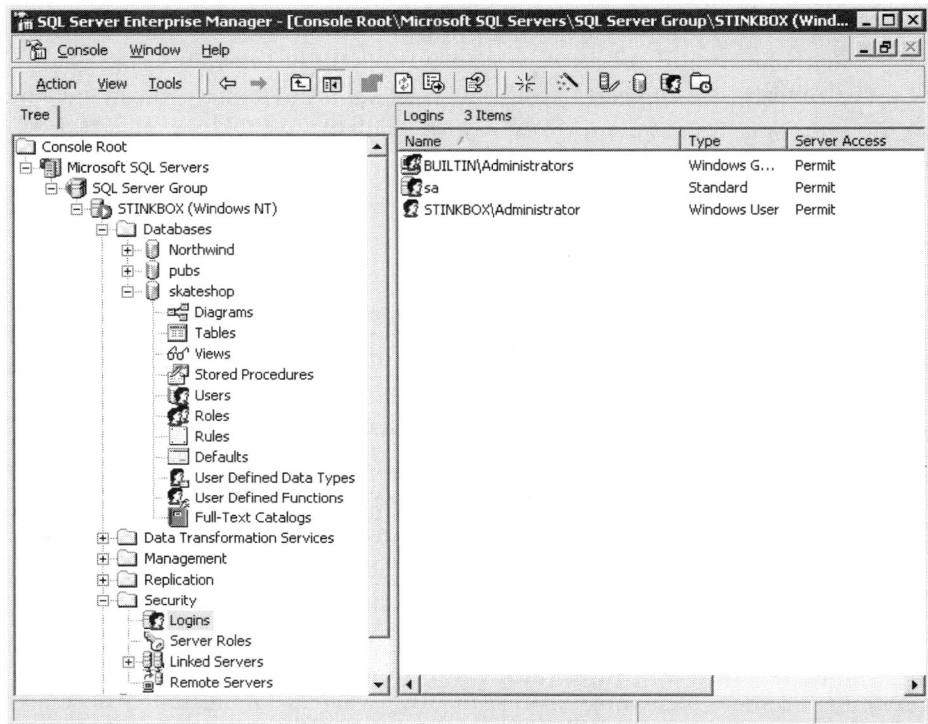

3. Right-click anywhere in a blank area in the right pane, and select New Login.
4. Because I'll be logging in remotely with this account, I want to use SQL Server authentication. I'll add my name as "mike," and I'll enter a secure password.

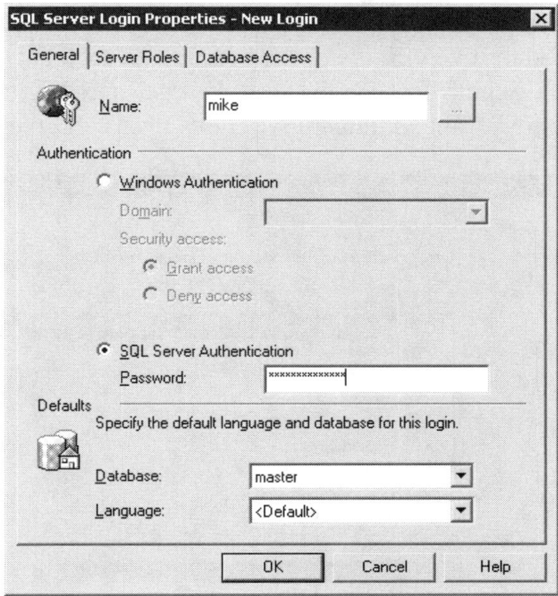

5. I want the default database to be "master," although I could just as easily choose "skateshop." I want the default language also, which on our server is English.
6. Click on the Server Roles tab. This is where I assign administrative privileges to my account. Check System Administrators.

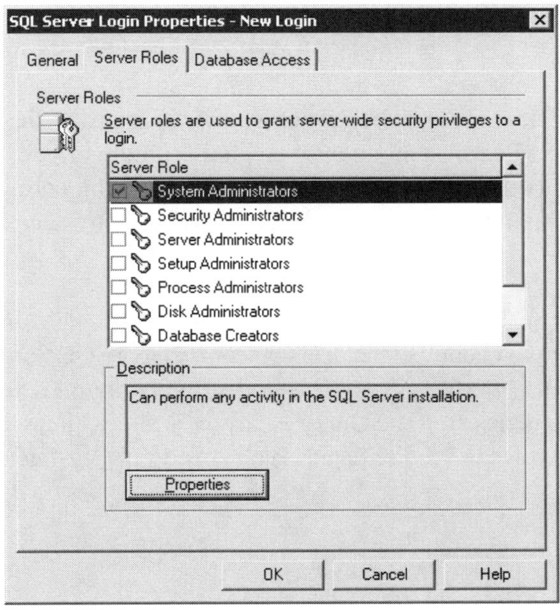

7. Click on the Database Access tab. Since I want administrative access over each database, I need to select fill the check box next to each database, and in the Database Roles window, I need to select "public" and "db_owner." Doing this for each database I want administrative rights over will give me full control.

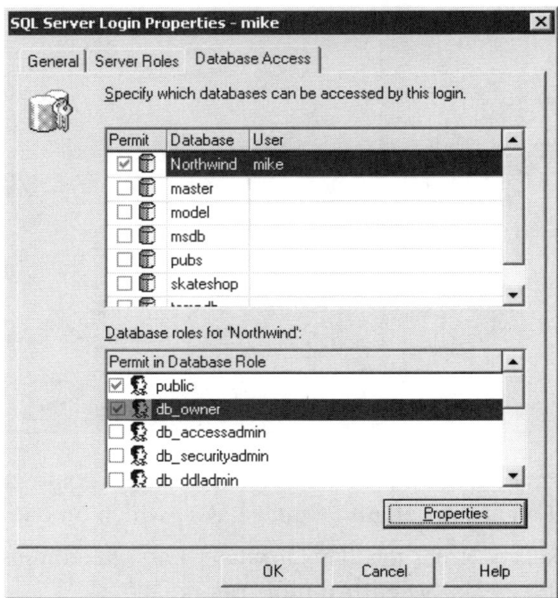

8. When you click OK, you'll be asked to confirm your password, and the account will be created.

Now I can go back into my SQL Server Registration properties, and instead of using the *sa* account, I can use my newly created account.

My other accounts follow the same process. By selecting certain settings in the Server Roles and Database Access tabs, I can allow or deny access to certain users.

Query Analyzer Overview

The Query Analyzer is a client tool that lets you connect to a SQL Server and execute SQL from a command line interface. It also has tools that help you determine where the bottlenecks in your queries are. The Query Analyzer is an excellent tool for ColdFusion developers. With it, you can browse database objects, run SQL statements, retrieve results, and query analysis tools that help you pinpoint bottlenecks in your code. Figure 1-9 shows my Query Analyzer.

Using the Query Analyzer is pretty straightforward. The toolbar on the upper right-hand side is where you can select different tools with the program.

Typically when developing a ColdFusion application I have this program open at all times. I can quickly create and debug stored procedures, and gather information on tables and databases. It's a simple yet invaluable tool. I'll be going into more details about one of the most important parts of the Query Analyzer in Part II, when we start building our application.

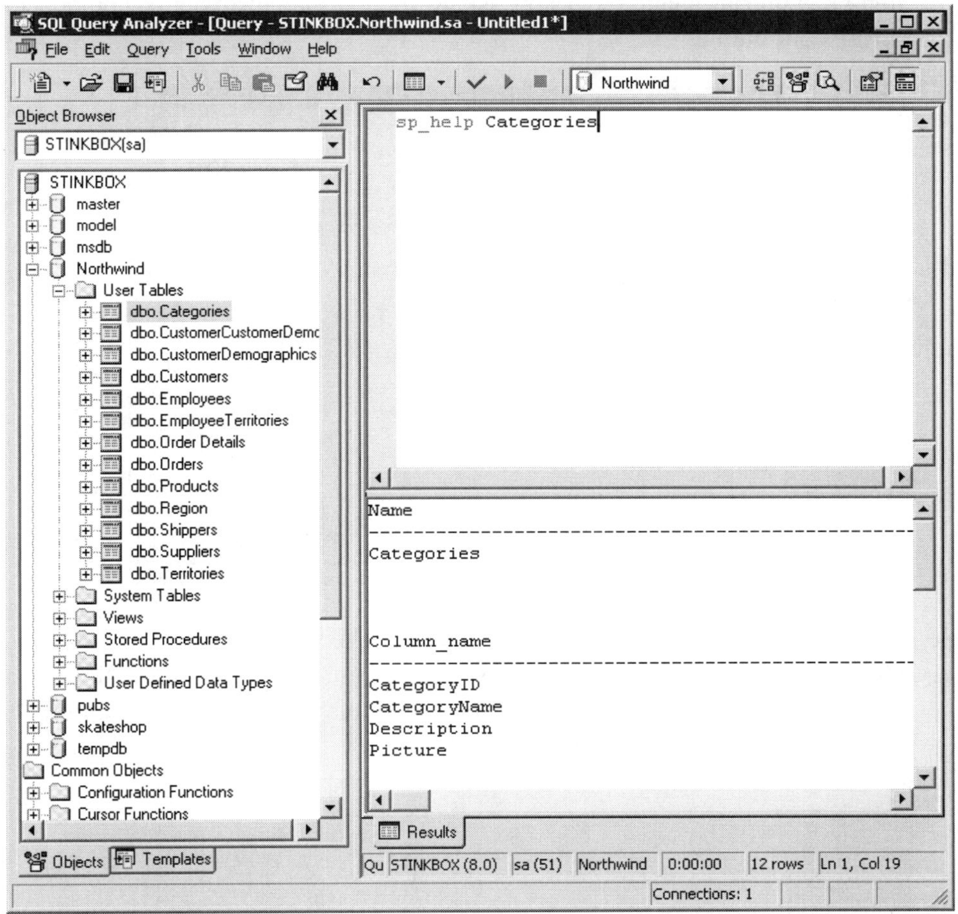

Figure 1-9 *The Query Analyzer is a simple yet powerful tool, invaluable to any ColdFusion developer.*

Installing ColdFusion 5.0

This section gives a quick rundown of the installation process, and stops at certain intervals to point out a few things. ColdFusion is very easy to install, although there are some points about the installation that I'd like to talk about.

1. Start the setup by either clicking Install ColdFusion 5.0 on the menu that comes up when you insert the CD-ROM, or running the setup.exe program.
2. The first dialog shown checks the system requirements. If certain requirements aren't met, the installation will stop, asking you to install the required components before continuing.

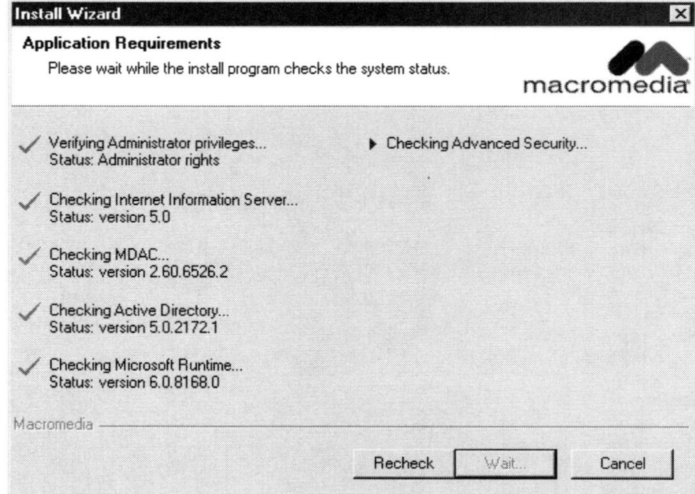

3. Click Next on the next dialog box to begin the installation.
4. The next screen is the general License Agreement dialog box that tells you to kill any other programs, and that if you pirate this program you'll promptly be

put in jail, etc. Click Next once you've let that sink in. Agree to the license by clicking on Yes to proceed. Clicking on No will abort the installation.

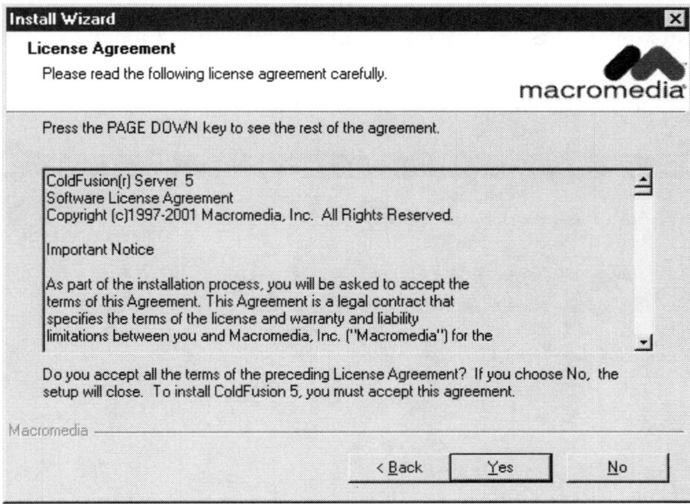

5. Enter your Name, Company name, and serial number. Click Next.

Install Wizard
Customer Information
Please enter your information.
macromedia
Please enter your name, the name of the company for whom you work and the product serial number.
User Name:
Michael Buffington
Company Name:
Serial Number:
Previous Serial Number:
Status
A blank serial number entitles you to a 30-day ColdFusion 5 Enterprise Evaluation. After 30-days, ColdFusion will revert to Single IP mode.
Macromedia
< Back
Next >
Cancel

6. Select the IIS server, and click Next. The ColdFusion server automatically detects the presence of a web server. It should see our IIS 5.0 server.
7. By default, the installation wants to place the program files for ColdFusion in C:\CFusion. There's really no need to change this. I have changed it, however, and didn't have any problems. Click Next when you're satisfied with the choices you've made for the ColdFusion installation location and the root Web directory.

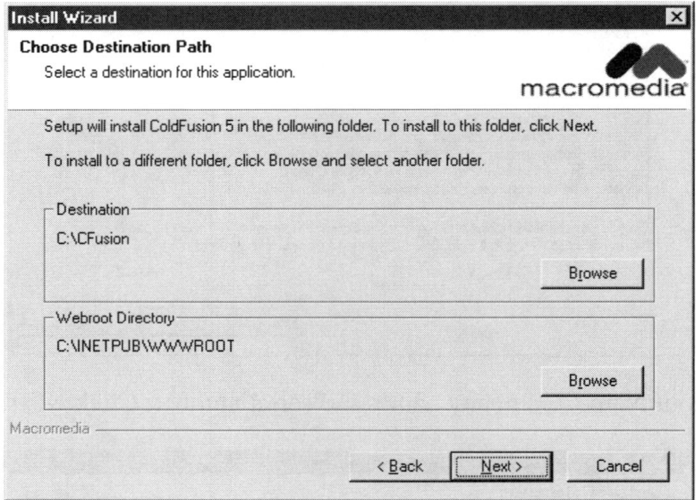

The next dialog box is where we get to choose some detailed installation options. Here's a description of the options:

Option	Description
ColdFusion Program Files	Contains all the required components of ColdFusion.
Documentation	Contains HTML documentation on ColdFusion, and ColdFusion-related topics, like server administration, and CFML language references.
Advanced Security	Installs the advanced security files and added functionality.
CFXAPI Tag Development Kit	Installs libraries and header files to aid in the construction of CFX tags.
ClusterCats Load Balancing and Failover	Installs a program that works in tandem with ColdFusion to provide high availability.

For this installation I'm selecting the program files, CFXAPI, and documentation only. Because I'm installing this on a development box, I don't need failover support.

If I were installing ColdFusion on a production server, I'd only install the program files and the failover support (if I planned to use that at all). There's no reason to install the documentation or the CFXAPI libraries on a production server.

8. Select the options you'd like to install, and click Next.

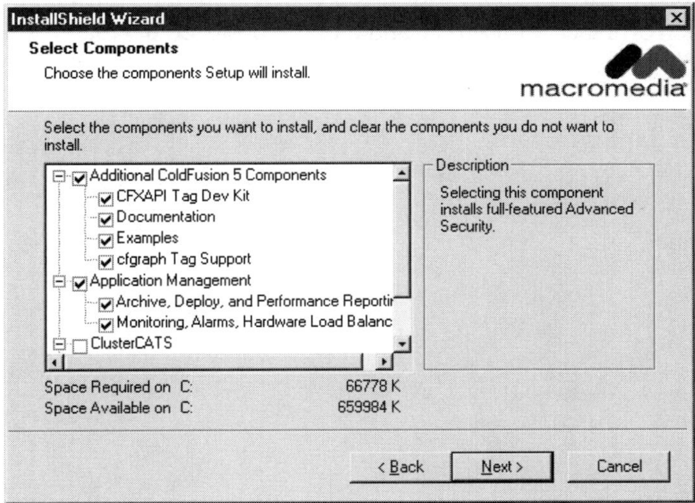

9. On the next two screens, you'll be choosing passwords. Select a secure password for your ColdFusion administrator and a *different* password for ColdFusion Studio access. I've known far too many ColdFusion installations that used identical passwords for both, or no passwords at all. You *must* pick good passwords. If someone gained control over your ColdFusion administrator, they could potentially cause a lot of damage.

10. The next few screens don't ask for input, and once you get through them, ColdFusion will start installing. You will need to restart your computer once the installation is complete.

To verify the installation, enter the following URL into your browser: http://127.0.0.1/cfide/administrator/docs/testinstall.cfm

Wrapping Up

We've seen how to setup ColdFusion 5.0 with IIS 5.0 and SQL Server 2000. Using ColdFusion with IIS and SQL Server is by far the most widely used configuration for serving ColdFusion applications. There is a ton of support available, and plenty of people who share similar experiences, and similar difficulties. In the next chapter, we'll show you how to set up a ColdFusion configuration on a Linux box, complete with a high-performance web server and a built-for-speed database.

CHAPTER

2

Linux Installation and Optimization

IN THIS CHAPTER:

Setting Up Apache as Your Web Server

Setting Up MySQL

Installing ColdFusion 5.0

Linux has proven itself as a stable web application platform. Combined with a number of freely available software packages, you can set up a ColdFusion application that runs entirely on Linux. I should give fair warning though: if you're in any way unfamiliar with Linux, I don't suggest setting up a Linux server as your production server. There are a lot of intricacies of the Linux operating system that, if unknown, can cause potential security holes, as well as serious performance issues. This chapter should help those with Linux experience set up a 100 percent Linux ColdFusion server. Of course, if you're brave and want the experience, dive in—just don't expect to run before you've learned how to walk.

The instructions and examples I give in this chapter use the Redhat Linux 6.2 operating system. I chose Redhat Linux 6.2 because it is one of the most widely used Linux distributions, and probably has the most support available. Redhat Linux 7.0 is available but not yet in wide use. The commands and instructions I use may or may not work on other versions of Redhat due to possible version differences.

If you haven't yet set up your Redhat box, I'd suggest setting it up as a server. This installs the essential packages needed to run a server, and avoids installing unnecessary programs like games and office applications. It also installs the libraries that Apache, ColdFusion, and MySQL might use.

Apache is probably one of the most popular pieces of web server software for the Linux environment; some might argue that it's the most popular web server, period. For users accustomed only to Windows environments, Apache in most ways is equivalent to IIS. And although Apache is used widely on Linux machines, it's also available for Windows platforms. We'll be using Apache as our Linux-based web server because there is no such thing as IIS on a Linux platform.

MySQL is a free database server, and is a worthy equivalent of Microsoft's SQL Server. Because there is no SQL Server available for Linux platforms, we'll be using MySQL as our Linux-based database server.

Setting Up Apache as Your Web Server

The Apache web server is the collective effort of about 11 core developers who wanted to improve the NCSA (National Center for Supercomputing Applications) 1.3 web server. Over the years, Apache has become a powerful and professional standalone package, and according to http://www.netcraft.com, it is the most widely used web server on the Internet. Apache is free and can be downloaded from http://www.apache.org.

The installation of Apache is relatively simple. If you've installed Redhat Linux as a server type, Apache may already be installed. To see if Apache is installed, log in as root, and type the following into the terminal:

```
httpd status
```

If Apache is installed, you should get some type of status, either indicating that the server is running, or that there is a problem with the server. If the httpd command is not found, then the server probably is not installed, or was not installed correctly.

You can also use the Redhat Package Manager (RPM) to see if Redhat Linux installed Apache when you set up your server. To find out if RPM knows about any Apache installations, use the following:

```
rpm -q apache
```

If Redhat Linux installed Apache, you should see something like "apache-1.3.12-2". If Redhat Linux didn't install Apache, you should see something like "package apache is not installed."

We'll be using the 1.3.12 Apache server that comes with Redhat Linux 6.2. As I write this, Apache 2.0 is available, but is not yet in wide use, making it more difficult to find support. The 1.3 versions have been stable for some time now, and it's best, in my opinion, to stick with something you know is stable, especially in a production environment.

If you know Redhat Linux has already installed Apache as part of the Redhat Linux installation process, you can quickly see what version it is. Log in as root, and in the terminal, type:

```
httpd -v
```

This will report what version the software is. If Redhat Linux installed Apache 1.3.12 or greater, you're in good shape and don't need to install Apache. If it's older than 1.3.12, then you should remove the old version before installing a new version.

To remove Apache, type the following:

```
rpm -e apache
```

Some installed RPM packages may require Apache to work properly, so take care when removing the old version. Keep in mind that this will only remove a Redhat-installed version of Apache. The developers of Apache don't normally use RPM to package Apache, so this command would not work with a normal, non-RPM installation of Apache.

Installing Apache

For best results, you should remove old versions of Apache before you begin installing the new version. It is possible to run multiple instances of Apache, but it can get complicated if you're trying to troubleshoot one instance while another instance is running.

We're going to download and install an RPM distribution of Apache, found on http://www.redhat.com. The following URL should directly bring you to the distribution:

http://www.redhat.com/swr/i386/apache-1.3.14-3.i386.html

If you're unable to find that URL, the Downloads section on the Redhat site lets you search for RPMs. Search for Apache, and find the Apache 1.3.14 web server. The 1.3.14 distribution will work just fine for what we need. The installation process is simple. Just download the RPM file, and type the following into a terminal as root:

```
rpm -i apache-1.3.14-3.i386.rpm
```

This command should install all the necessary binaries and configuration files in the default Apache directories. To double-check the installation, you can use:

```
rpm -q apache
```

This command returns a version number of Apache.You can also see if the configuration files were installed, which should indicate that the installation went well:

```
ls -l /etc/httpd/conf/httpd.conf
```

If a file is there, chances are everything went smoothly. If problems occur, check the Apache documentation at http://httpd.apache.org/docs.

Before we test to see if Apache is serving HTTP requests, take a look at the configuration files. Rarely have I seen an Apache installation work right after an install. There are certain parts of the configuration files that cannot be set by the RPM installation and must be set by hand.

Configuring the Apache Web Server

Apache typically stores its configuration files in /etc/httpd/conf. I say *typically* because depending on how Apache was installed, these files could end up in a different place.For our Redhat Linux 6.2 installation, however, this is where they are found.

The configuration files are where all values are set for Apache, much like the Internet Information Server (IIS) metabase. Apache uses three different configuration files. Actually, that's not entirely true. Apache *can* use three configuration files, and has in the past relied on three configuration files. The only reason it is still able to use three files today is for historical reasons. Let me give a little background on these files:

- **httpd.conf** This file contained directives, or instructions, on the actual operation of the server. It included settings for the log files, how to manage resources, and so on.
- **srm.conf** This file contained directives for the file system. It controlled what directories were available to the web server, and whether or not to show a default document or a directory listing.
- **access.conf** This file controlled security for certain directories.

In the past, it made sense to have each file contain organized directives for the server, but as time went on, certain directives started to cross over into different categories. For instance, when setting up a Virtual Host using the <VirtualHost> directive, certain parts of this directive contained subdirectives that would logically go in httpd.conf, and certain parts would logically go in access.conf. It was more difficult, inefficient, and sometimes impossible to always separate directives into three different files. So, with more current releases of Apache, only one file is truly required, httpd.conf. Apache, upon startup, still looks at the old files, and still executes directives contained in these files, but it won't go crazy and have problems if the files are empty.

If you don't want Apache to bother with the old files, you can put the following directives in the httpd.conf file:

```
AccessConfig /dev/null
ResourceConfig /dev/null
```

This stops Apache from even checking the files upon startup. If you were to simply delete the files without these directives in your httpd.conf file, Apache would report an error upon startup.

If you open /etc/httpd/conf/httpd.conf in an editor (for simple, quick editing I use gnotepad+, although any ASCII editor will do), you will see what Apache calls *directives*. These directives are commands issued to the Apache server upon startup. They determine how your server will behave. Because we're using a newer version of Apache, all of our directives are contained in the http.conf file (even though you'll find three of the configuration files we talked about earlier).

When I start messing around with my httpd.conf file, I make a backup of it first. I mess the file up often, and if I'm in a hurry, it's much easier to revert back to my old version rather than spend some time trying to figure out what I did wrong that is making my Apache server go nuts. All you have to do is copy the file you know works, and call it httpd.conf.backup or whatever makes sense to you. When doing a new install, I copy the original configuration files into a backup folder, so I have the original installation files handy if I ever need them (in case I *really* screw things up)

The original installation files do a good job of organizing the directives, as well as including some of the most common directives. We really don't have to do too much editing to the file to make our server work.

Lines that start with # are not processed by Apache, and are used for comments. In the original configuration files there are *tons* of comments, which are very valuable. I'd suggest reading over them. You'll gain a better understanding of how Apache works if you do. But the configuration files also suggest, in the comments, that you read the Apache documentation before messing with things. And I would agree. Apache is very powerful. If it's not configured correctly, it may not perform well, or even at all.

Let's take a look at the first group of directives—the directives that control the operation of the Apache server itself. Historically, these directives would have been the only directives to appear in the httpd.conf file, and the original configuration files maintain that theme. Keeping the directives as organized as possible will help keep you sane, and will make your job of tracking down issues much less difficult. Notice that I didn't say "easy." I might be a baby about this, but I find that it's usually a pain trying to figure how an Apache problem. It's certainly never fun. You may have a knack for this kind of thing; personally I find managing configuration files difficult, which makes it all the more important for me to keep things organized.

I'll list the directives and their values out in the order they appear in my original configuration files. It's not required that they appear in this order, but again, it doesn't hurt to be organized. Also, keep in mind that these are not all of the possible directives—they're only the ones in my configuration file. The Apache documentation has a full list of all possible directives, but I think you'll find that you won't use anything other than what's in the original configuration files.

ServerType standalone Indicates that the server is a standalone server. The other possible server type is *inetd*, which will spawn a new Apache process each time someone hits it. Spawning off a new Apache process for each hit sounds like it's not very resource friendly, and you're right, it's not. It is helpful sometimes during testing, when you've made some changes to the server, and you don't want to start and stop the server. Personally, I never use it. If I make changes, I start and stop the server to test the changes.

ServerRoot "/etc/httpd" Tells Apache where the program files and directories exist for the server. This must be a full path, and should not contain a slash (/) on the end. This directive is used later if you ever refer to an absolute path like "logs/kerbapple." The ServerRoot value would be placed in front of the "logs/kerbapple," making a full and complete path. I would not mess with this, unless the path is incorrect. If you install Apache somewhere else, then change it; otherwise, it is smart to leave it.

LockFile /var/lock/httpd.lock It's best to leave this setting alone. If you change the directory to a directory that is not secure, you could set your server up for denial of service attacks. When Apache creates a lock file it appends its main server process ID on the end. If a user creates a lock file with a process ID on the end, it could potentially make it impossible to start the Apache server. It's probably safe to say though that if you're machine is insecure enough for a user to write a file to a directory, that you have bigger problems than not having your server start. Still, every bit of security counts.

PidFile /var/run/httpd.pid Apache records its process ID here. Don't change this if you don't need to. Again, this shouldn't be in an insecure directory.

ScoreBoardFile /var/run/httpd.scoreboard Do not change this unless you're running multiple instances of Apache. You don't want multiple instances of Apache using the same scoreboard file. The scoreboard file is used to store internal process information. Depending on your Linux installation, you may or may not have a scoreboard file.

Timeout 300 Controls how long it should take for a send or receive to timeout. The value is in seconds, so the default value would be five minutes in this case. This is far too long in my book, but is an appropriate setting for Apache. It is not set any lower than 300 seconds because, according to the Apache documentation, "there may still be odd places in the code where the time is not reset when a packet is sent."

KeepAlive On Determines whether or not you'd like to keep connections alive. When you keep connections alive, you can get more than one request per connection, which can help speed things up. This is good to have on, so I'd leave it.

MaxKeepAliveRequests 100 Lets you control how many requests are allowed per connection. Setting it to 0 allows an unlimited number, but Apache recommends setting the number high for maximum performance. 100 is good for right now.

KeepAliveTimeout 15 Number of seconds Apache should wait for before closing the connection. If a request is made within 15 seconds, the connection is kept alive; otherwise the connection is kept closed. 15 seconds is good for now.

MinSpareServer 5 Sets how many idle server processes should be sitting around. Apache dynamically adjusts how many processes it should run to handle requests based on traffic load. If load is high, Apache uses more processes. If load is low, it uses fewer processes. This setting is the minimum amount of processes you'd like to use. If your server gets a consistent load, it might be a good idea to set the process amount higher. For now, let's leave this the way it is. The best way to set this is to watch your load, and see how many processes are typically used. If on average it's using, say, 20 processes, it might be good to always allocate at least 20 processes to Apache.

MaxSpareServer 15 Controls what the maximum level of processes allowed to run should be. This is similar to the MinSpareServer directive. If you get a lot of traffic spikes, it might be good to set this number high. Apache won't actually use the processes until it needs them, but it will only use 15 in this case at the most during spike levels. A good way to determine what the best setting would be to watch normal traffic load. If you're consistently spiking at 14 processes, you might want to increase the MaxSpareServer amount to be safe. It's not a good idea to set this process too high. Apache suggests that 15 is the highest you should set it. I'd suggest that it depends on your system resources. If at 15 processes you're not even pushing 50 percent CPU utilization, it's probably safe to increase it.

StartServers 8 Controls how many servers to start with. A good rule of thumb is to set it roughly halfway between the MinSpareServer value and the MaxSpareServer value.

MaxClients 150 Limits how many people can connect at a time. If the number of connections made to the server is more than 150 in this case, they will be locked out. This sounds crazy! Although the number in this case might be a little low, the directive itself is important. You don't want a server to allow so many active connections that it crashes the server. I usually suggest that with a load balancing solution, this setting isn't really important (unless it's too low). Your load balancing solution should take action before the server is ever maxed out. I'd set MaxClients a little higher than 150 for a production server—300 should cover you. For a development server it's fine.

MaxRequestsPerChild 100 This is the amount of allowable requests to a child process. On Linux, this setting isn't really an issue, and is mainly here for operating systems like Solaris that are prone to memory leaks. After 100 requests the child will exit, clearing out any memory leaks. 100 is a good number.

Now we get to check out the modules. I won't talk about each module that Apache loads by default, and I'd even suggest leaving the default setup intact until you really know what you're doing. The modules that Apache loads provide the functionality of the Apache server. There's a module, for instance, that allows Apache to execute CGI scripts. Without these modules, Apache would not have very many extra functions.

When we install ColdFusion, we'll see that ColdFusion adds its entries into the modules portion of the httpd.conf file. This loads the libraries needed to invoke the ColdFusion engine when processing CFM files. It's similar in a way to IIS script mappings, although the two are quite different otherwise.

For each LoadModule directive, there's a matching AddModule directive. The LoadModule directive looks like this:

```
LoadModule module_name module_directory/modulefile.so
```

The AddModule directive looks like this:

```
AddModule mod_file.c
```

It's important to make sure that if you change, add, or remove a LoadModule directive, that you also change, add, or remove the matching AddModule directive.

We get to look at the "Main" server directives now, or the directives that control how documents get served by Apache. The directives in this section handle any user request that isn't handled by the <VirtualHost> containers to follow. Every setting in this part of the file can also show up in a <VirtualHost> container, overriding any of the "main" settings. After this configuration file section, we then look at the <VirtualHost> container.

Port 80 No rocket science here. The default port for HTTP is 80. If you change this to anything other than 80, users will have to add a port into the URL to get to your site. Don't change this unless you know what you're doing.

User nobody If you wanted to run the Apache server as a different user other than "nobody" you could change this. Apache will run with whatever rights the user you assign to it has, so keep that in mind. Using "nobody" limits the rights, which is good for security reasons. You may run CGI applications or ColdFusion scripts that need more rights, either to write to the disk, or read certain things. You'd be able to adjust that here.

Group nobody Similar to user nobody, described previously.

ServerAdmin root@localhost The e-mail address of the web site administrator (you!). Users will see this e-mail address if Apache errors. I usually setup a dedicated e-mail account for this purpose alone. Make sure you check that e-mail account also, don't let it collect dust. Use it to help keep your server in tiptop shape.

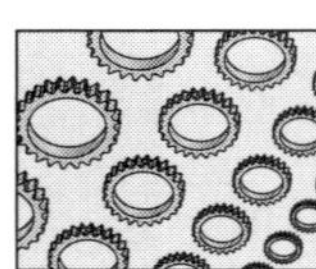

NOTE

It is a bit unclear where the web site administrator e-mail shows up on your site. The standard Apache error pages typically don't show the e-mail address. The Apache documentation simply recommends putting it in—where it shows up is a good question.

DocumentRoot /home/httpd/html This is the full path to your root HTML directory. This is where you keep you're the index.html file for your site.

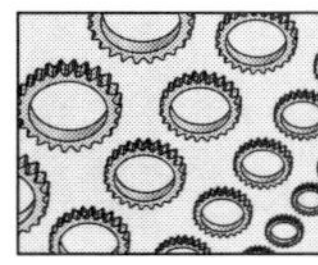

NOTE

Some RedHat installations place your default HTML directory someplace else, like "/var/www/html". Wherever it is, this directory is where Apache serves HTML documents from. Later, ColdFusion might also ask for this directory, so keep it handy.

The next portion of the file allows us to add directory-specific access instructions. The first <Directory> container we see in the configuration file looks like this:

```
<Directory />
     Options FollowSymLinks
     AllowOverride None
</Directory>
```

The first tag indicates what directory we want to set options for. In this case, it's the root directory (/). The first directive, Options FollowSymLinks, tells Apache that the server will follow symbolic links in this directory. For instance, if you set up a symbolic link /wwwroot to /home/httpd/html, it would follow that link. The second directive tells the server to ignore any .htaccess files, which override settings in the httpd.conf file. You can place a file called .htaccess in web directories that contain directives similar to the httpd.conf file. In this case, we don't want anyone to be able to override the settings for our root directory, so we disallow it here.

From this point on, if we want a directory to have any type of settings enabled, we have to enable those settings. To setup our "main" web server directory, let's examine the sample:

```
<Directory /home/httpd/html>
     Options Indexes Includes FollowSymLinks
     AllowOverride None
     Order allow, deny
     Allow from all
     DirectoryIndex index.html index.cfm
</Directory>
```

The Options directive indicates that we want to allow Indexes, which means that if there is no default index.html, and that we want a directory listing instead. If this option were not enabled, a directory listing would not show if the index.html file wasn't there—it would simply show a 404 error. We want to allow server-side includes by specifying Includes, and we want to follow symbolic links. Also, note that the actual path on your machine may differ.

Again, by using AllowOverride, we disallow an .htaccess file to override our settings.

Order allow, deny Determines the order in which access is given. By default, we want to allow access to the site, unless the client meets certain criteria that would deny he or she access. It's not entirely as simple as I put it, but for now, this will work well for us.

Allow from all Allows all clients to have access to the site. I could also change the "all" part of this directive to "10.1.2.3," which would be a specific IP. Only that IP would have access.

DirectoryIndex index.html Where we define the default document. We could also set it outside of the <Directory> container, which would apply it to all directories.

Everything else in httpd.conf is pretty easy to figure out, so we won't go into much more detail about the remainder of the file. With what I've covered, and the Apache documentation, you should be able to quickly write your own httpd.conf file.

There are GUI interfaces to the httpd.conf file. If you run linuxconf as root, you can drill down to the Apache section, and edit just about everything we've covered. I have noticed however that linuxconf adds some extra quotation marks here and there that can mess up your file, but they're easy to catch and fix. Also, if you go to http://gui.apache.org you can find several GUI interfaces in production for Apache. Personally, I find it easiest to edit the file by hand.

Verifying the Installation

A quick way to check to see if your configuration files are working correctly is to check the status of the server. Type the following in a terminal as root:

```
httpd status
```

If you get no reply, your server should be configured correctly, or at least there are no errors.

In a web browser, try accessing your server by using http://127.0.0.1, which is the loop back IP. You should see a default Apache screen. If you get an error, it's likely that you need to remove the following directive from your httpd.conf file:

```
<Files ~>
     AllowOverride AuthConfig FileInfo Indexes Limit Options
     Order allow,deny
     Deny from all
</Files>
```

The default configuration file added the container above, and it unfortunately is malformed. It may work on some systems, but it doesn't on my Redhat 6.2 installation (which means it might not work for yours either). Delete it or replace it with the following, then stop and start the server:

```
<Files ~ "^\.ht">
     AllowOverride AuthConfig FileInfo Indexes Limit Options
     Order allow,deny
     Deny from all
</Files>
```

To start and stop the server, open up a terminal window in root, and type **httpd stop** to start the server, and **httpd start** to start it again.

Setting Up MySQL

MySQL is an open source relational database management system. Basically, it's free, and can do many of the things that Microsoft's SQL Server can do. There are arguments from the pro Microsoft camp that it doesn't come close to SQL Server's performance, as well as counter arguments from the open source camp claiming it outperforms SQL Server. I take each side's opinion with a grain of salt. Both sides have their good points and bad points. One of the best points about MySQL is that it's free.

MySQL (pronounced like "My Ess Que Ell" and not like "My Sequel") was created by a Swedish company named MySQL AB, and currently is run by a team of about 20 developers. The original developers claim that they started MySQL with the intentions of using *mSQL* for their own fast low level routines. mSQL is a small, lightweight database server written by Hughes Technologies. They began to realize that mSQL wasn't fast enough or flexible enough for their needs, so they built a new database system. They made their API to MySQL almost identical to mSQL to help aid in porting mSQL applications to MySQL.

It's unclear exactly how the name MySQL came about. One of the founders has been naming a number of his libraries and tools with the "My" prefix for over ten years, while the other founder of MySQL AB has a daughter named My. Either way, it worked out to be a useful name.

MySQL is feature rich. Here are just some of its features:

- Fully multithreaded, using kernel threads. This means that it's capable of using multiple CPUs if available.
- Provides several APIs available in C, C++, Java, and more.
- Works on several different platforms including Linux, Windows, and Mac OS X.
- Allows over 25 different data types.

- Allows full T-SQL support.
- Offers ODBC Support (Connect to MySQL with ColdFusion, or MS Access).
- Claims it can support databases with over 50 million records.
- Allows clients can connect to MySQL using TCP/IP or Named Pipes.

Although MySQL can do a lot, there are some actions it cannot perform. MySQL *doesn't* have the following:

- Does not allow subselects (SELECT … WHERE IN (SELECT ….)).
- Does not support transactions (they claim where speed is of utmost importance, transactions aren't important).
- Does not support stored procedures or triggers.
- Does not support foreign keys.
- Does not allow you to create views like in SQL Server 2000.
- Does not allow you to use '--' to start a comment. (You use # instead.)

In this section, we'll be downloading a source version of MySQL, compiling it, and installing it. As previously discussed, it's assumed that you're using Redhat Linux. If not, some of the commands issued may or may not work for your system. It's also assumed that you have the ability to compile programs on your Linux installation. If you are unable to compile programs, you should either install the packages that will allow you to compile, or find a RPM version of MySQL.

I must stress that this section only shows one possible way of installing MySQL, on one particular version, Redhat 6.2. The MySQL documentation is practically required reading if you plan on doing any work with MySQL. If you run into a problem that we haven't discussed, the MySQL documentation should probably cover it. I'd also suggest taking advantage of the MySQL mailing list. More information about the mailing list can be found at http://www.mysql.com/documentation/lists.html.

Installing MySQL

You can download the source files for MySQL at http://www.mysql.com/downloads. From there, select the newest stable version, then download the Tarball source file. The file name should be something like mysql-3.23.35.tar.gz. If you're downloading a different version, use that version number wherever I refer to the 3.23.35 version.

To untar and unzip the source package, type the following:

```
gunzip < mysql-3.23.35.tar.gz | tar xvf -
```

This will create a directory called mysql-3.23.35.tar.gz, which contains all the source files. Move to that directory, and check out the various README files and INSTALL files. These files contain version specific information about MySQL.

MySQL comes with a handy configuration script. Use the following command to kick off the script:

```
./configure --prefix=/usr/local/mysql
```

The --prefix=/usr/local/mysql indicates that after you're done compiling, you'd like to install the MySQL executables in /usr/local/mysql. You could also specify a lot of other options, but we don't need to worry about that right now. We want to get this compiled so we can start using it.

The configure script inspects your system and makes sure that you have all the tools needed to compile MySQL. If there are problems, it will report errors. The most common error occurs when the configure script is looking for threading libraries. If you have Redhat 5.0 or greater installed, you should already have threading libraries. If the configure script finishes without any errors, you're ready to start compiling.

Compiling is very simple. Make sure you're in the mysql-3.23.35 directory, and type the following:

```
make
```

That will start the compilation. MySQL is a pretty complex program, and it takes a while to compile the software. Depending on the speed of your machine, it could take some time.

When the software compilation is finished, type the following:

```
make install
```

This should happen pretty quickly, certainly much faster then the MySQL compilation. MySQL is now installed on your machine. Before we can use it, we need to run a few MySQL scripts that setup the default tables.

Type the following to setup the default tables:

```
scripts/mysql_install_db
```

Verifying the Installation

To verify the installation, type the following:

```
cd /usr/local/mysql
./bin/safe_mysqld --user=mysql &
```

If you get a message that looks something like the following, you may have a problem:

```
[root@kerbapple mysql]# Starting mysqld daemon with databases from
var/lib/mysql
010117 16:34:45 mysqld ended
```

Look through your systems user list. If there is no mysql user, you need to create one with permissions to read and write to the MySQL installation directories. After you've created the user, try starting the server again:

```
bin/safe_mysqld &
```

If it's working correctly, you should see a message similar to this:

```
Starting mysqld daemon with databases from /usr/local/mysql/var
```

Once again, we want to verify the installation. Type the following:

```
bin/mysqladmin version
```

You should get a detailed list of the version of MySQL you're running. It should look similar to this:

```
Server version      3.23.35
Protocol version    10
Connection          Localhost via UNIX socket
Uptime:             10 min 21 sec
```

If you run into trouble, I highly recommend reading the MySQL installation documents. It is by no means a simple program, and there are several places where the installation can screw up. I'd be doing you a disservice if I didn't also recommend that you pick up a book about MySQL.

Creating a Test Database

Before we can test the functionality of MySQL, we need to create a test database. You can create a database from a terminal by typing the following:

```
mysqladmin -u root create mydb
```

You can issue commands to MySQL by saving your commands into a text file, and then using the **mysql** executable to run the commands.

Here's an example—I've saved a sequence of SQL statements in a text file called sql.dump:

```
USE mydb
CREATE TABLE animals (id tinyint(4) DEFAULT '0' NOT NULL AUTO_INCREMENT,
animal_type varchar(30), PRIMARY KEY (id), UNIQUE id (id));

INSERT INTO animals VALUES (1, 'Cat');
INSERT INTO animals VALUES (2, 'Dog');
INSERT INTO animals VALUES (3, 'South African Monkey Toad');
```

I will then issue the following command in my terminal:

```
bin/mysql -u root < sql.dump
```

You shouldn't get any feedback from this if the commands were completed successfully. To actually pull some of that data back, issue the following:

```
bin/mysql
```

This is the main interface to MySQL. At the mysql> prompt, use the following commands:

```
mysql>use mydb
mysql>select * from animals;
```

The first command tells MySQL what database you want to query. The second command will bring back your results. The semicolon is important—it tells MySQL that you're finished with your SQL command. Without it, MySQL continues to wait for more SQL commands. You can execute any SQL command this way, which means that you can do pretty much anything you need to do in MySQL in this program. To exit MySQL, type **/quit** at the mysql> prompt.

To create a user in SQL (which we'll use later when connecting to a data source through ColdFusion), enter the following command at the mysql> prompt.

```
GRANT ALL PRIVILEGES ON *.* TO coldfusion@"*" IDENTIFIED BY
'monkeywrench' WITH GRANT OPTION
```

This creates a user named coldfusion with the password monkeywrench. The syntax of the command allows the user, coldfusion, remote read and write privileges on all of the MySQL databases. You can easily give certain users access to just a particular database, or to local users only, with different rights and privileges. For more information, check out the MySQL documentation, which you can find at http://www.mysql.com/doc/.

You can also use a graphical interface for MySQL. There are several available written by independent developers. I think that the program MySQL GUI, located at http://www.mysql.com/downloads/gui-clients.html, works best with MySQL.

Installing ColdFusion 5.0

Compared to what we're used to with Linux, the ColdFusion installation is pure joy. I've installed a lot of Linux programs, and none install as smoothly nor are as straightforward, as ColdFusion 5.0 for Linux.

To install ColdFusion, log in as root and copy the coldfusion-50-linux.tag.gz from the installation CD-ROM or network location to a local temporary directory. Run the following command to unzip the file:

```
gunzip coldfusion-50-linux.tar.gz
```

Once that command has finished, run the following command to untar the file:

```
tar -xvf coldfusion-50-linux.tar
```

The tar program will create the coldfusion-50 directory. Change to the directory and type **./cfinstall** to start the installation.

After starting the install process, feel free to choose whatever options you'd like to install. Again, as with ColdFusion 5.0 for Windows, you should pick secure passwords for the ColdFusion Administrator and Remote Development Services (RDS). I wouldn't recommend installing the examples applications or documentation on a production server. ClusterCats can be installed at a later time if you don't need it yet.

One of the best things about ColdFusion for Linux is that its system requirements are far less than for a Windows server. I have a test server that I dual-boot between Windows 2000 Advanced and Redhat Linux 6.2, and both servers have ColdFusion installed. While I haven't done any formal tests yet, there is a noticeable speed difference between the sample applications on each platform. Linux seems much faster. This could be a combination of a lot of things, but it's interesting to point out, just the same.

The ColdFusion installation program automatically adds the LoadModule and AddModule directives to your Apache configuration files. If for some reason the installation doesn't add the directives, you can add them manually to your httpd.conf file. You'll need the following entries:

```
LoadModule coldfusion_module libexec/mod_coldfusion.so
AddModule mod_coldfusion.c
```

ColdFusion installs drivers to connect to MySQL databases, so you should be able to easily setup a data source using the *mydb* test database we created in MySQL earlier.

To test ColdFusion, point a browser to:

http://127.0.0.1/cfide/administrator/index.cfm

This should load the ColdFusion Administrator.

To add a test data source, go into the data sources menu, add a MySQL data source, and make sure to use the correct database name and IP. (For this server, 127.0.0.1 works because ColdFusion and MySQL are on the same server.) Use the coldfusion login we created earlier, enter the password **monkeywrench**, and click Add.

Wrapping Up

I've shown that with a little bit of practice, it's possible to configure a 100 percent Linux ColdFusion server. For companies or individuals on a tight budget, Linux provides a sensible alternative. I think we've also seen that setting up a 100 percent Linux ColdFusion server isn't exactly easy. There are certain trade-offs—we've seen that we can spend some money on Microsoft products that install with relative ease, and we've seen that we can pinch pennies, but spend more time setting up. Whether you choose Linux or Windows is up to you—from this point forward everything I talk about is platform-unspecific. Now let's see what's new in ColdFusion 5.0.

CHAPTER

3

New ColdFusion 5.0 Features

IN THIS CHAPTER:

ColdFusion Administrator

Database Connection Support

New Tags

New Functions

User Defined Functions

Queries of Queries

ColdFusion 5.0 adds a number of new and powerful features that either didn't exist in ColdFusion 4.5, or were lacking somewhat in functionality. In this chapter, I show off each feature in detail, and present some scenarios in which you might use it. This is a great chapter for those who are familiar with ColdFusion 4.5 and need to study the new features.

ColdFusion Administrator

The first notable change in the ColdFusion Administrator is the new look and feel. If you've ever played with Allaire Spectra, 1.5 you'll notice the similarities. Figure 3-1 shows the new Administrator. The Administrator is divided into three major sections, with each section having its own navigation and menu options. We look at each section, and describe each possible menu option. Some of the menu options are nearly the same as previous versions of ColdFusion, but there are subtle changes here and there, so to be thorough, we'll go over each part.

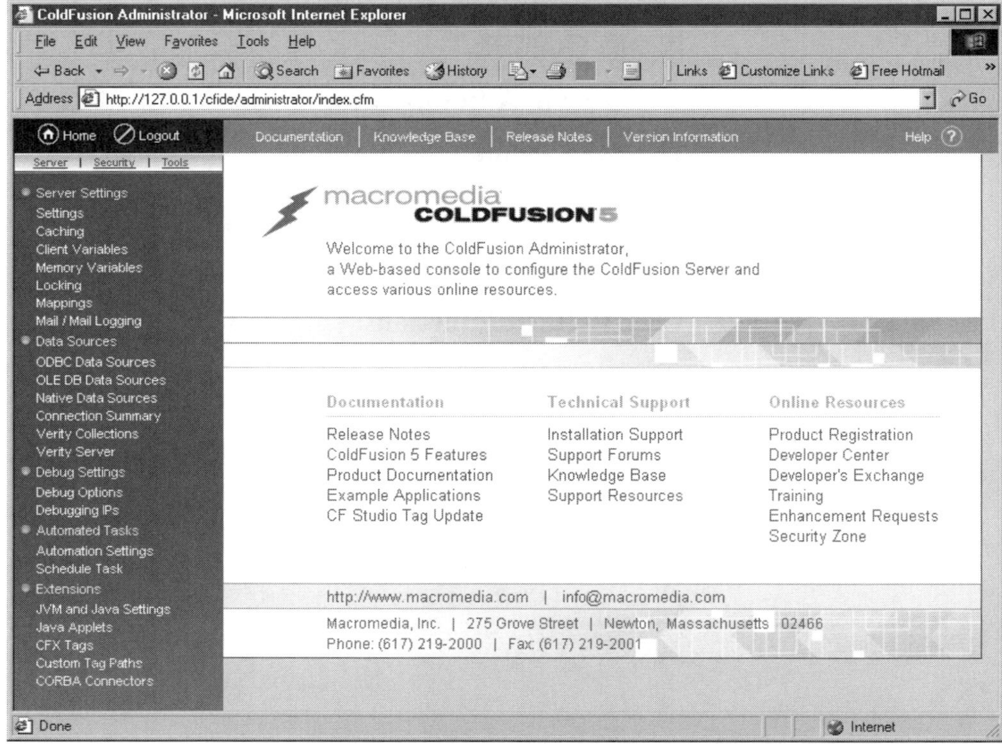

Figure 3-1 *The ColdFusion Administrator for 5.0 has a new and improved look.*

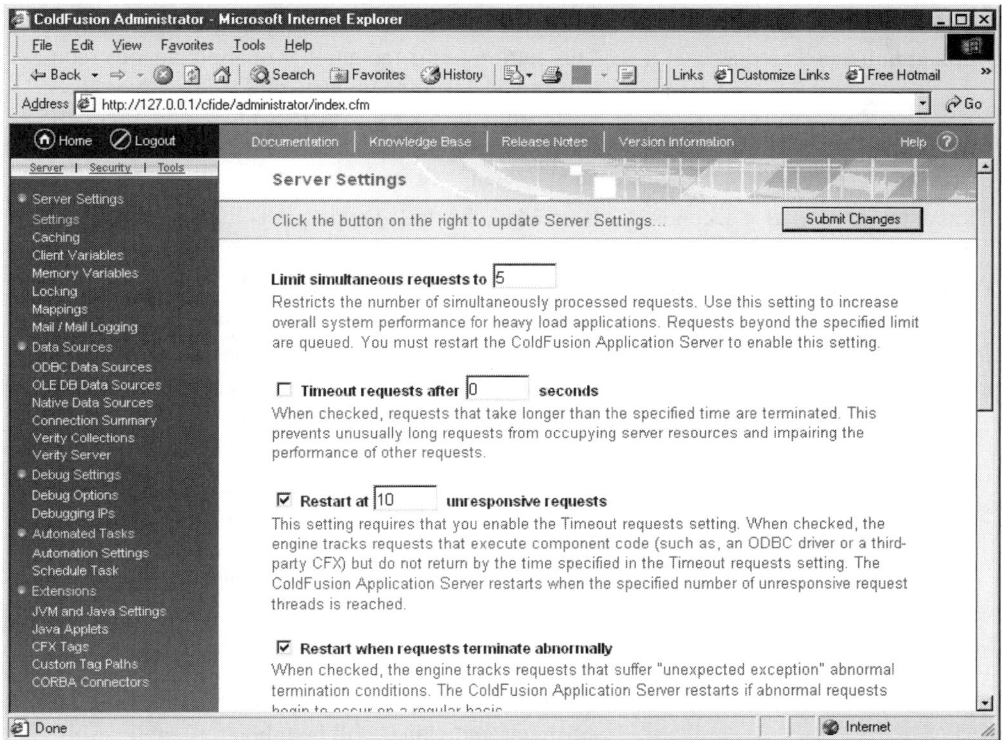

Figure 3-2 *Settings page*

Server Menu

The Server menu is accessed by clicking the Server link towards the upper-left of the ColdFusion Administrator. After logging in, you automatically end up at this menu. A lot of these possible menu options will seem familiar to users of ColdFusion 4.5, but there are, as I said, some subtle changes here and there. Let's break down each option.

Server Settings

On the Server menu, options are grouped according to their purpose. Server settings deal with memory, caching, mail server options, and things of that nature.

Settings This is where the core ColdFusion settings are displayed and updated (see Figure 3-2). There are eight possible settings. The following table gives a brief description of each of these eight settings.

Setting	Description
Limit simultaneous requests to *n*	This setting limits the number of simultaneous requests that can be executed on the ColdFusion server at any given time. If this value were set to 5, and 5 requests were currently being executed, then other requests would need to wait their turn.
Timeout request after *n* seconds	If enabled, this kills any requests that exceed the amount of time entered.
Restart at *n* unresponsive requests	If enabled, this setting instructs ColdFusion server to restart after the set amount of requests.
Restart when requests terminate abnormally	When enabled, the ColdFusion server restarts when abnormal requests occur. Abnormal requests usually indicate that perhaps the server memory has become corrupt, or other unpleasant problems that are easily fixed with a service restart.
Suppress white space by default	When enabled, ColdFusion strips unnecessary white space from the ColdFusion template upon execution. Stripping white space from the returned HTML document reduce the size of the HTML document that the user needs to download.
Enforce strict attribute validation	When enabled, any incorrect attribute passed to CFML tags will cause an error. When disabled, unnecessary attributes and values will be ignored. Enabling this setting can increase template execution speed and expose incorrect coding practices.
Missing template handler	If a file is specified, then the file acts as a default template, which is executed whenever a user requests a ColdFusion page that doesn't exist.
Sitewide error handler	If a file is specified, whenever an error occurs, the file executes. This can be useful for tracking errors, showing more descriptive error messages, and so on.

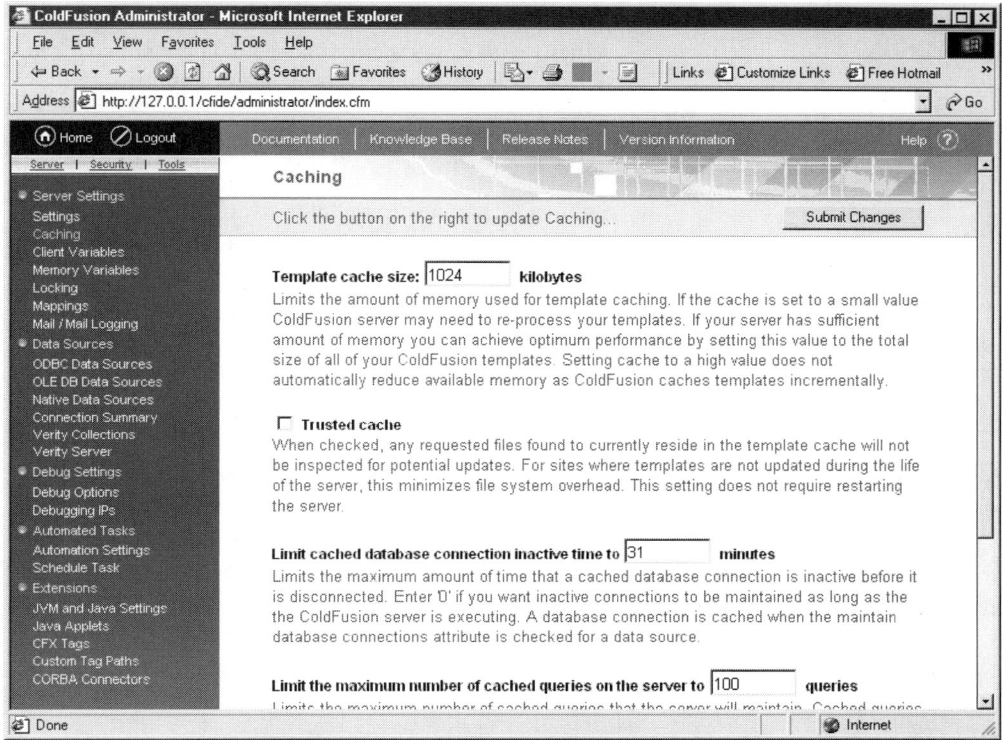

Figure 3-3 *Caching page*

Caching Caching is an important part of any application, and certain settings in the ColdFusion Administrator have an effect on what kind of caching you can do, among other things (see Figure 3-3). Here's the list of possible settings and their descriptions.

Setting	Description
Template cache size: *n* kilobytes	As caching is used in a ColdFusion application, the data that is cached is stored in memory on the server. This setting gives you control over how much memory is used for caching on the server.

Setting	Description
Trusted cache	When enabled, updates of cached data are not checked. This can improve the performance of templates that never change.
Limit cached database connection inactive time to *n* minutes	This setting works in conjunction with the "Maintain database connections" setting on data sources. If the number of minutes is anything over 0, then the server will maintain an inactive connection to the database at a maximum of the value entered.
Limit the maximum number of cached queries on the server to *n* queries	In ColdFusion, the capability exists to cache queries. This setting limits the number of possible queries. New queries replace the oldest queries if the query limit is met.

Client Variables One of the new features in ColdFusion Server 5.0 is the ability to define a default client variable storage mechanism. Client variables are used with the <CFAPPLICATION> tag to track things like user preferences, or variables specific to a certain client. Previous to version 5.0, developers were stuck with using the Registry for the default client variable storage mechanism unless they set up a specific store to use with the <CFAPPLICATION> tag. With ColdFusion 5.0, the default client variable storage mechanism can be chosen (see Figure 3-4). The following options are available.

Storage Name	Description
Cookie	Stores client variables on the user's browser in the form of cookies.
Registry	Stores client variables in the Windows 2000 registry. (This option isn't available on non-Windows operating systems.)
Custom Datasource	Datasources can be assigned for use as client variable storage mechanisms; the datasource must be created first, then added using the drop-down menu.

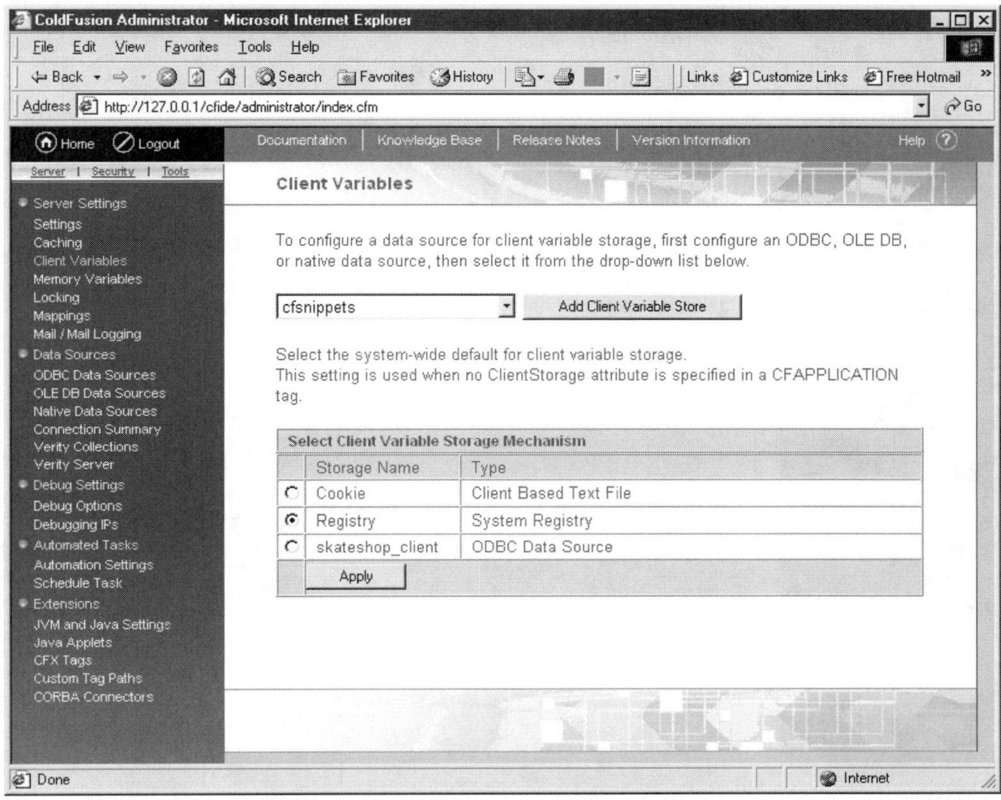

Figure 3-4 *Client Variables page*

Memory Variables Memory variables now have their own page as well, where settings related to memory variables can be applied (see Figure 3-5). On this page of the Administrator, administrators can define the default timeout values for application variables and session variables. Using the <CFAPPLICATION> tag, developers can set their own timeout values, but the ColdFusion Administrator has the final say. If the developer wants a session variable to timeout in an hour, but the Administrator has been told to time out session variables within 20 minutes, the session variable will time out within 20 minutes. If the tables are turned, and the developer sets a time out value less than the timeout value of the Administrator, the developer's timeout value will be used.

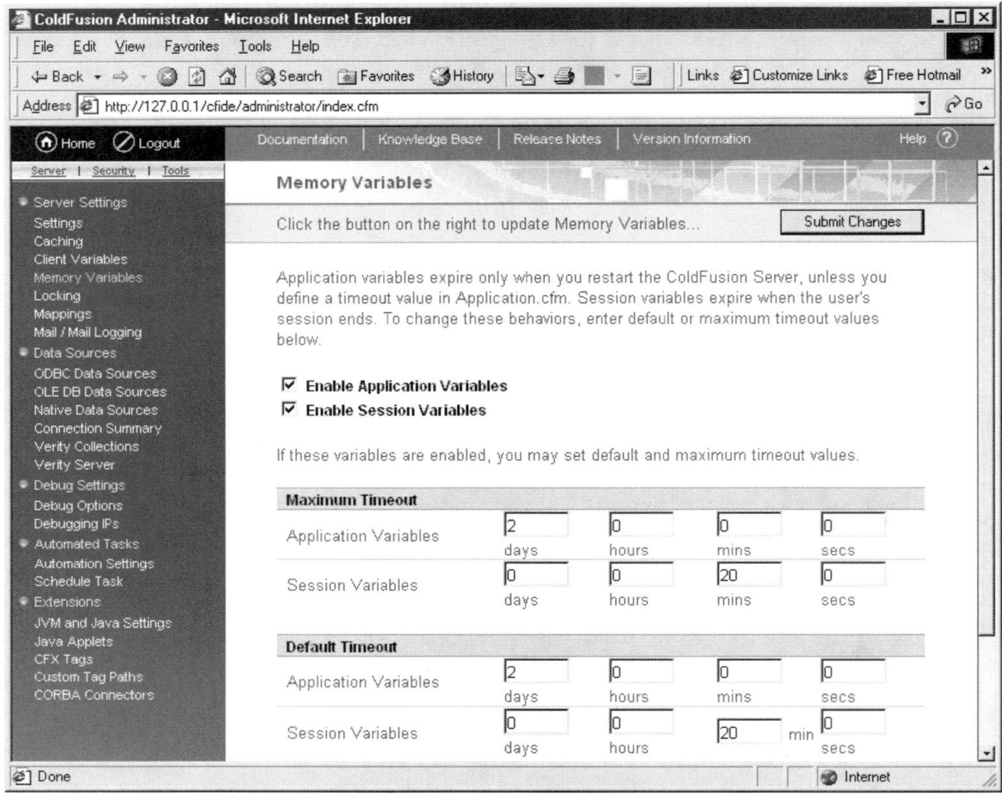

Figure 3-5 *Memory Variables page*

Besides setting the default timeout values, you can also enable or disable the use of session and application variables from this page. I've given it a lot of thought, and personally, I can't give a good reason why you would want to disable session or application variables on the server, except for cases where memory is a scare resource.

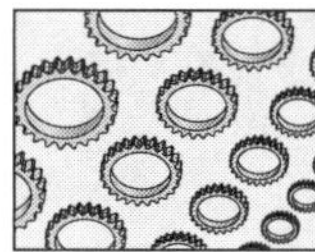

NOTE

You might notice a lot of talk about things like application variables or session variables. These different kinds of variables, and how they're used, will be explained as we progress in the book.

Locking Locking is an important subject in ColdFusion, and we'll spend some more time in Chapter 10 on the finer points of locking. For now, it's sufficient to understand that locking is needed to avoid data corruption on shared variables. Session, application,

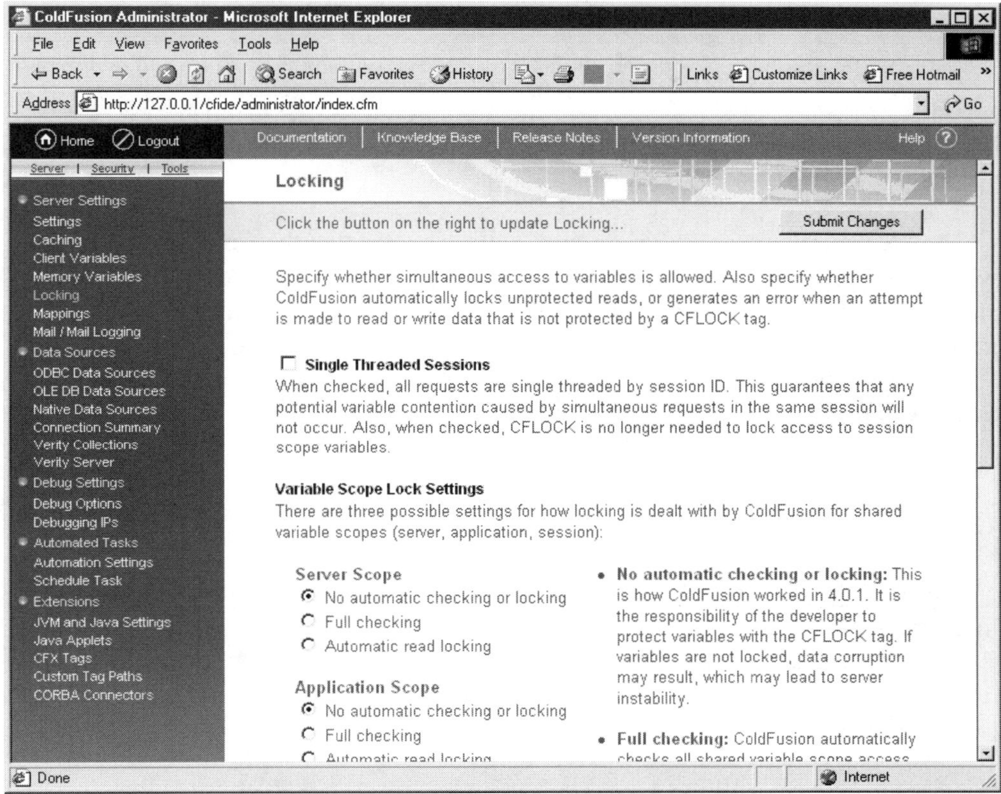

Figure 3-6 *Locking page*

and server variables are shared variables, and therefore need to be locked when being set to prevent data corruption.

The following table describes each setting relating to locking in ColdFusion (see Figure 3-6).

Setting	Description
Single Threaded Sessions	When enabled, the <CFLOCK> tag is no longer needed because ColdFusion will single-thread each process that writes a variable to within the session scope. This prohibits simultaneous requests from possibility writing corrupt data to the variable. This setting only pertains to session variables.

Setting	Description
Variable scope settings	Server, application, and session scope variables can all be set to one of the following options: No automatic checking or locking Full checking Automatic read locking

The "No automatic check or locking" setting means that the ColdFusion server will do nothing to try and save the developer from possible conflicts when reading and writing shared memory variables. With this setting enabled, the only way to implement locking is by using the <CFLOCK> tag.

The "Full checking" setting basically locks variable assignments in the same way as shown here:

```
<cflock scope="session">
   <cfset session.UserID = 1230394>
</cflock>
```

This setting will probably make more sense when we discuss the <CFLOCK> tag in Chapter 10.

The "Automatic read lock" setting automatically locks a variable when it is being read. It will not check variable writes though—<CFLOCK> must be used when writing to a variable when this setting is enabled.

Mappings This page allows you to define logical mappings to physical locations on a drive (see Figure 3-7). Creating mappings can come in handy when using the <CFMODULE> tag to call custom tags from a specific directory within the application. But that is not the only reason to use them, as they can also allow you to access directories from a ColdFusion application that might otherwise be inaccessible (for example, something that lies outside of the shared wwwroot directory).

Notice in Figure 3-7 that C:\INETPUB\WWWROOT\ is mapped to /. Whenever we want to refer to the C:\INETPUB\WWWROOT\ directory within our ColdFusion application, rather than specifying the long form, we'd use the mapping name instead. For example, both of the following lines of code would be referring to the same directory; one uses the actual relative path, the other uses the mapping name:

```
<cfinclude template="../../functions.cfm">
<cfinclude template="/functions.cfm">
```

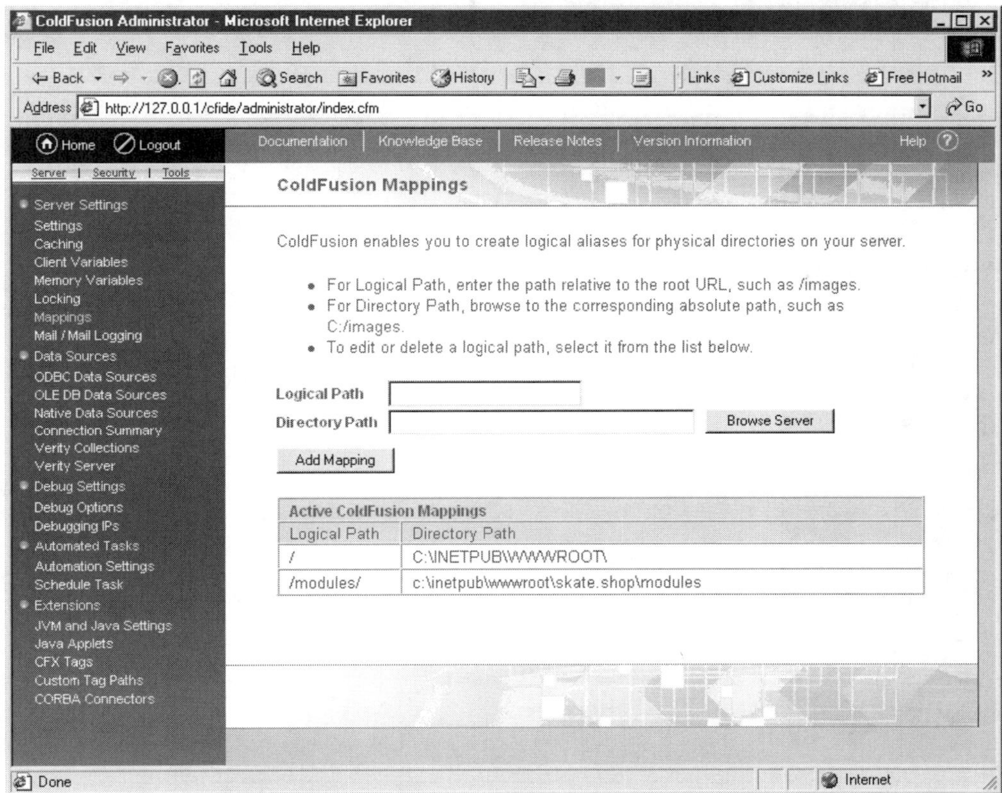

Figure 3-7 *Mappings page*

Mail/Mail Logging Using a tag like <CFMAIL>, developers can perform e-mail related tasks in their code. The Mail/Mail Logging settings page allows the developer to control certain mail-related settings (see Figure 3-8). The following table lists and describes the possible settings.

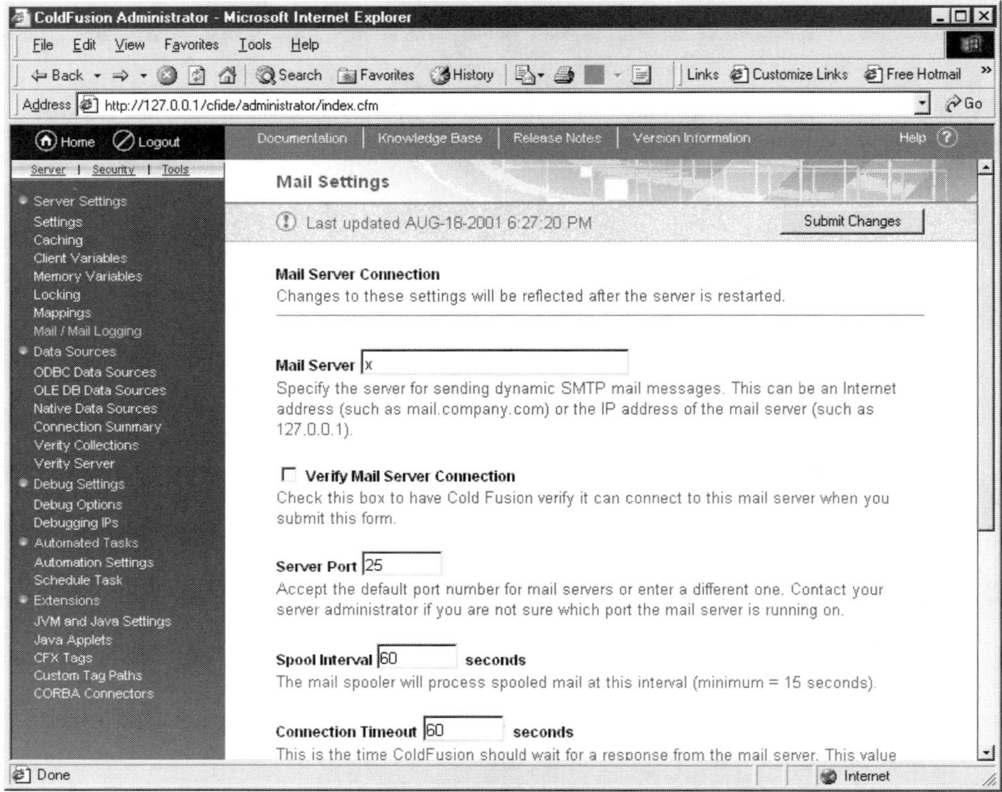

Figure 3-8 *Mail/Mail Logging page*

Setting	Description
Mail Server	This setting allows you to assign a default mail server. If a developer omits the server attribute on a tag like <CFMAIL>, this server will be used instead. If it's left blank, and the developer omits the server attribute, then there will be an error in their code; but if it's blank and they *do* supply the server attribute, there will be no error. Any IP address or domain name will do, as long as the mail server can accept e-mail from the server. Some e-mail administrators disallow the ability for programs like ColdFusion to send out mail, but if you work closely with your e-mail administrator, these problems are very easy to solve. For instance, if the e-mail administrator only allows certain IP address to use the SMTP server, they can simply add the ColdFusion server's IP address to the acceptable IP list. Every situation is different, but most easily remedied.

Setting	Description
Verify Mail Server Connection	This setting triggers the ColdFusion Administrator to check the connection to the SMTP mail server when the changes for this page are applied. It doesn't affect any part of a developer's application—it's simply a handy tool for whoever is setting up the connection between ColdFusion and the e-mail server.
Server Port	This is the server port of the SMTP server. It's almost always port 25, although e-mail administrator can easily change it.
Spool Interval *n* seconds	ColdFusion holds onto outgoing e-mails, or spools them, within this time period. This relieves both the ColdFusion server and the e-mail server from having to make a connection for each e-mail that originates from the ColdFusion server. The smallest spooling interval allowed is 15 seconds. If you enter a number smaller than this, the ColdFusion Administrator will warn you, and discard the value. ColdFusion holds outgoing e-mails in the C:\CFUSION \Mail \Spool directory until they are sent to the SMTP server.
Connection Timeout *n* seconds	This is the amount of time ColdFusion waits before giving up on a response from a server. Some servers under a lot of load, or older servers, might take a while to respond. This value helps reduce issues related to slow servers.
Error Log Severity	Errors related to e-mail will be stored in the C:\CFUSION \Log\mail.log file. There are three possible severity levels: Information, Warning, and Error. If you use the Information severity level, you'll probably get more log entries than you would if you'd used the Error severity level.
Log All E-Mails Sent By ColdFusion	This setting, when enabled, will store every e-mail sent through ColdFusion to the C:\CFUSION\Mail\Log\ directory. This might be helpful in debugging, but could get out of hand if a lot of e-mail originates from your ColdFusion server. Also, it's likely to slow things down when you're doing bulk mailings. Imagine a large web site community with 10 to 20 thousand e-mail addresses, and when looping over that list, sending e-mail to every one, and then writing and storing that same e-mail to file. Things could get clogged up pretty quickly if you weren't careful. While the e-mail would be automatically written to disk in the spool director, another write would occur when writing the e-mail to the log. Use at your own risk.

Datasources

With the new ColdFusion Administrator, anything that stores data is, not surprisingly, called a *datasource*. What we're used to, as ColdFusion developers, when we hear "datasource" is probably something like a database connection to an Access or SQL Server database. But ColdFusion considers Verity collections as datasources as well, including several other less familiar datasources. We talk about these less familiar datasources as we explain the settings pages for each option. We then continue to follow the same format as we have been: looking at a screenshot of the particular settings page, and then talking about what each setting does.

ODBC Datasources Most of us are probably familiar with this menu, as ColdFusion has used this format for the past few versions. From this page, we can see existing ODBC datasources, or add new ones (see Figure 3-9). Clicking the name of an existing datasource will bring up the datasource's properties, and clicking the Verify link will determine if the datasource is set up and working correctly.

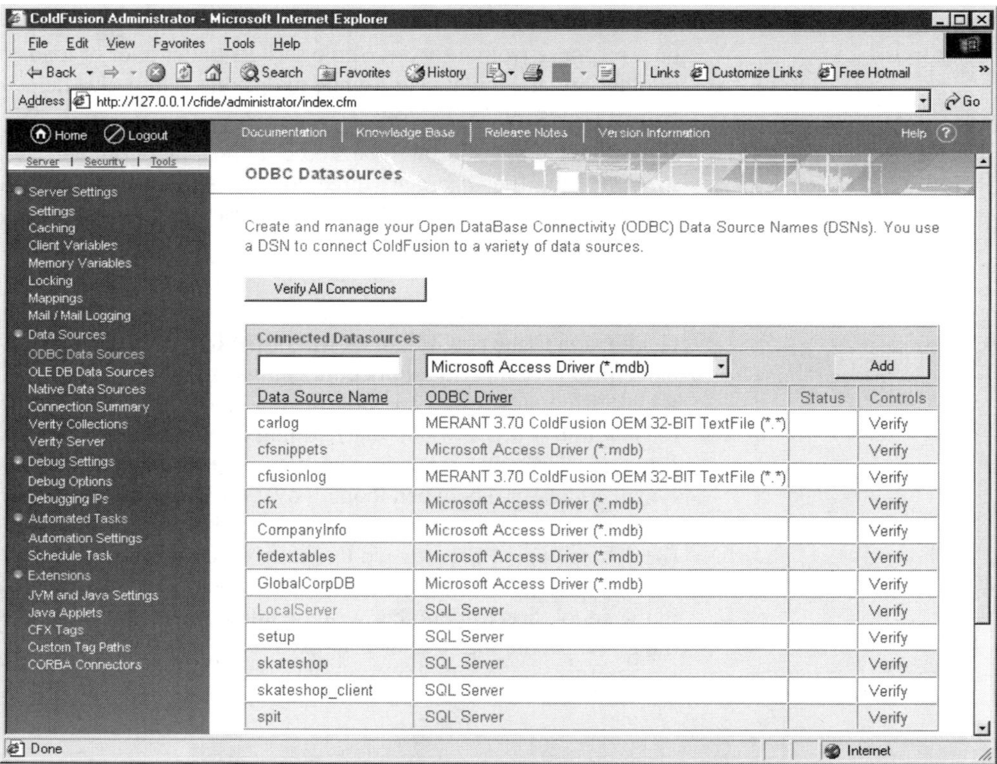

Figure 3-9 *ODBC Data Sources page*

The datasource properties page allows the administrator to enable or disable settings related to that particular datasource. Figure 3-10 shows a datasource properties page, with the advanced settings visible. These settings can be exposed by clicking on the CF Setting button, which appears when you first click on a data source to view its properties.

The datasource properties page can be different depending on the database driver. You'll see towards the top of this properties page that the driver type is SQL Server. For the most part, ColdFusion default settings for database drivers are sufficient for most applications. This wasn't always the case though, as developers began fine-tuning their settings they quickly realized that the default settings were not acceptable. ColdFusion 4.5 and ColdFusion 5.0 have done a good job in setting the default values to be acceptable for most environments.

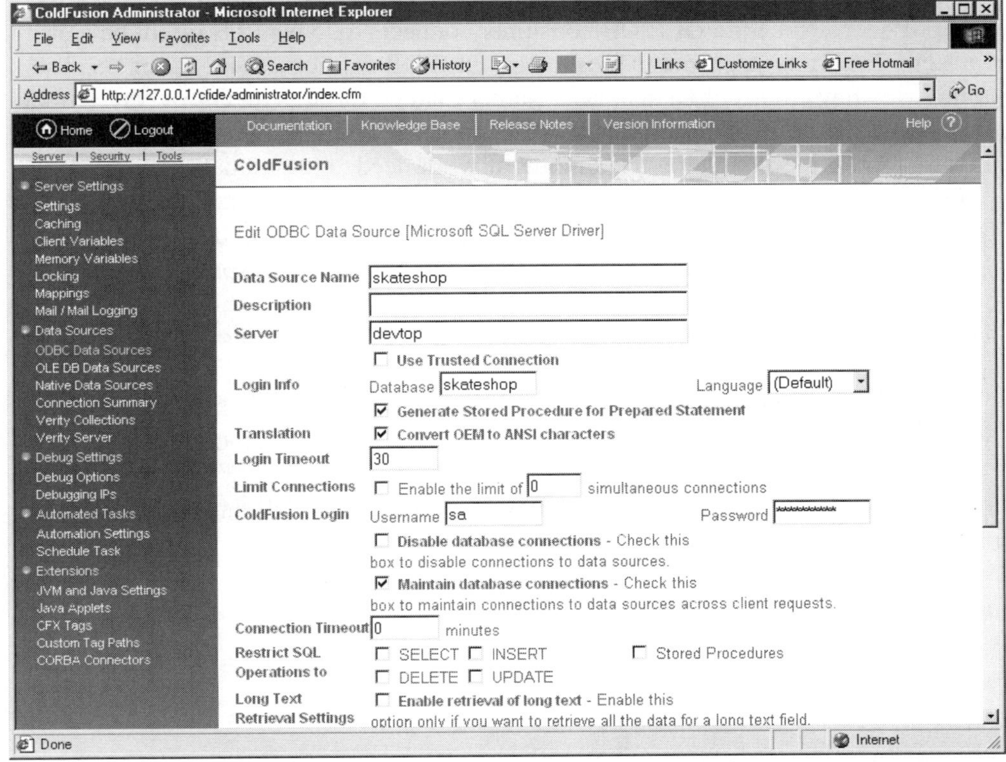

Figure 3-10 *Advanced ODBC datasource settings*

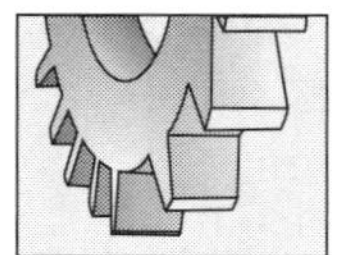

TIP

Don't name your datasource cookie *or* registry*. These are reserved names. Seems like a kind of common sense tip, but I can see myself naming a datasource* cookie*, and then pulling my hair out trying to figure out what was wrong. Rogaine probably doesn't appreciate this tip because of all the hair pulling I'll be preventing.*

OLE DB Datasources The Object Linking and Embedding for Databases (OLE DB) datasources page looks nearly identical to the Open Database Connectivity (ODBC) datasources page, so we'll forgo the screenshot. Setting up a datasource is also nearly the same as setting up an ODBC datasource.

OLE DB is a Microsoft technology that works on nearly the same principle as ODBC in that it acts as the middleman between the application and the database, except that it can connect directly to a database by using what is called an OLE DB consumer and an OLE DB provider. Each OLE DB-capable database will have its own provider, which the OLE DB consumer connects to. Now, this might be a bit too technical at this stage, but in most cases, OLE DB datasources are faster because of the way they connect to a database. Rather than go through an ODBC driver that translates data retrieval algorithms for each database type, they connect directly to the proper provider, reducing the amount of work needed to pull data.

But there is a downside to using OLE DB datasources. Some databases are strictly ODBC databases, and when used with an OLE DB datasource will be slower, because there are now two middlemen. The ColdFusion application will speak to the ODBC OLE DB provider, which will then speak to the ODBC Driver, which is simply too much work. At this point, using OLE DB is counterproductive, and ODBC should simply be used alone.

There is also an issue with complexity: if you're unfamiliar with how OLE DB works, it might be better to play it safe and stick with ODBC, although adding an OLE DB datasource isn't all that difficult.

Let's look at a screen shot of an already configured OLE DB datasource, using the SQLOLEDB provider:

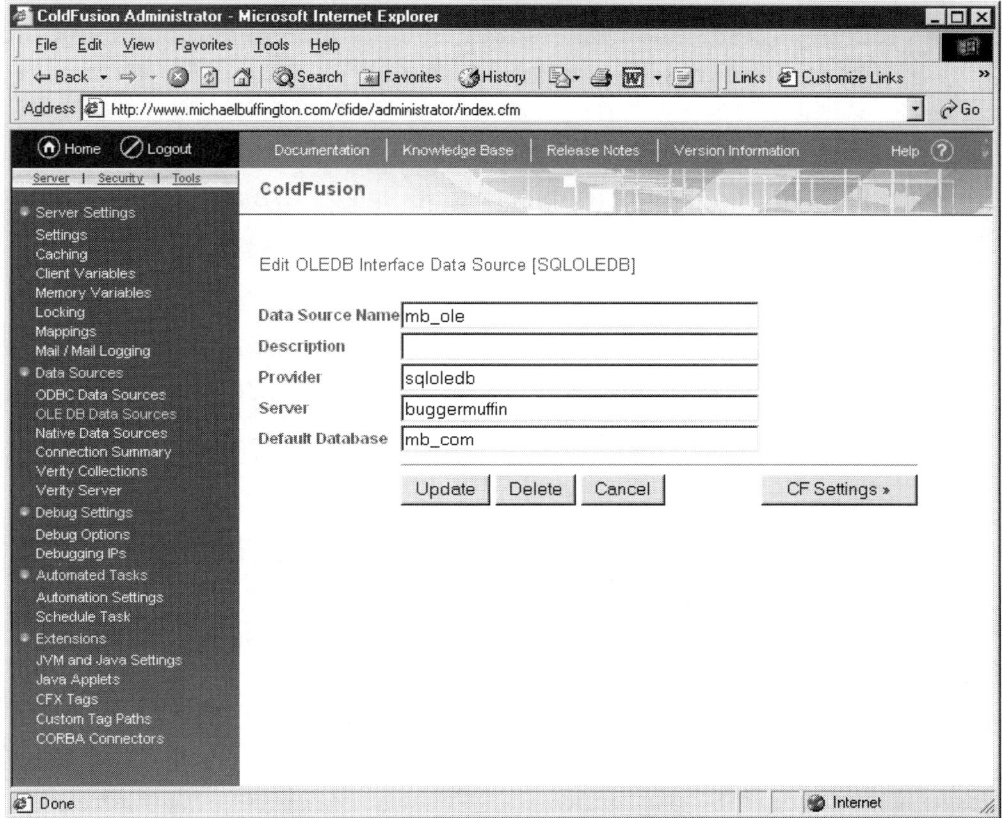

The only big difference between setting up this datasource and setting up an ODBC datasource is the Provider field, which contains *sqloledb* in this example. If you were connecting to an Access database, you would type **Microsoft.Jet.OLEDB.4.0** (or something similar depending on what version of the Jet engine is on your machine).

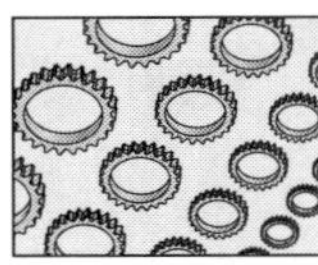

NOTE

Even if you use the drop-down menu to select a datasource provider, you still have to type in the OLE DB provider name in the Provider box of the datasource details page. That's a little bug that's been around for a while; maybe in future versions it will be fixed.

Allaire has written some articles on how to set up OLE DB datasources for a number of different providers, as well as a document describing how to best set up Microsoft Access datasources at the following URLs:

```
"Configuring OLE DB Data Sources in ColdFusion"
http://www.allaire.com/Handlers/index.cfm?ID=14632&Method=Full

"Using Microsoft Access Databases in a Production Environment"
http://www.allaire.com/Handlers/index.cfm?ID=1540&Method=Full
```

Native Datasources For developers using Oracle, Sybase, DB2, or Informix databases, this is the menu used to create those datasources. Just as Microsoft-centric databases use ODBC and OLE DB, native drivers require some type of client component to be installed on the ColdFusion server in order to work properly. Each of the listed databases work differently in how they connect, so it would be hard to give a full description here of how each one works.

The menu for adding native driver datasources is much like the previous datasource examples, so we'll skip that screenshot.

Connection Summary This page allows you to view all of the active datasources, regardless of whether they are ODBC, OLE DB, or native driver datasources. (See Figure 3-11.) By clicking the Release button, all active datasource connections will be reset. The datasources will be connectionless until the first connection is made, and then you're back to where you started—datasources with cached connections. Cached connections are not exactly a bad thing, but it might help to reset all connections if a particular datasource seems to be acting funny. It's too bad you can't release connections on a single datasource. Maybe we'll see a change in the next version.

If you click the datasource name, the Administrator tries to verify the connection. By combining every datasource type to a single page like this, it's much easier to quickly verify each connection without having to dig through menus.

Verity Collections First of all, let me offer a disclaimer. Verity collections aren't for the inexperienced. They can be very frustrating for beginners, and even for advanced programmers who are simply unfamiliar with the territory.

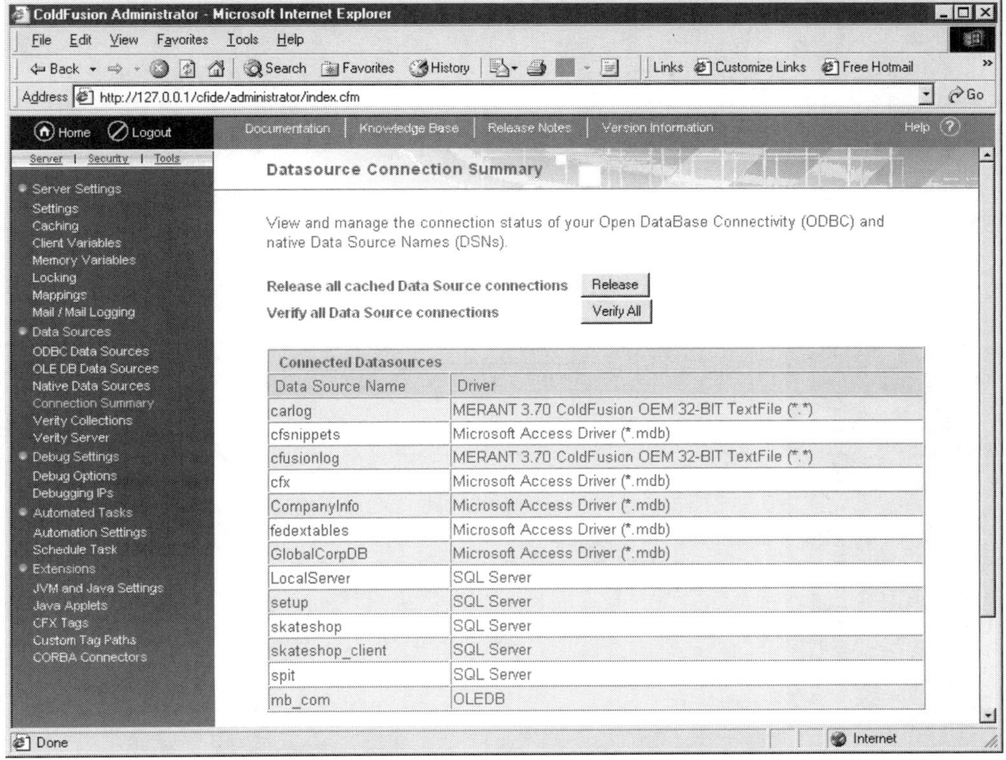

Figure 3-11 *Connection Summary page*

Verity is the ColdFusion built-in full text search engine. It is a sort of subprogram to ColdFusion that is tightly integrated with the ColdFusion Engine. It creates collections, or *indexes*, on a set of documents or data in a format that the Verity engine is comfortable with, and as a developer, you can use CFML tags to allow full text search capabilities within your site.

This page allows new collections to be created, or existing collections to be mapped (see Figure 3-12). When a collection is created, a directory is created with the name of the collection in the path specified. Verity will store its collection files in this directory. Once a new collection has been created, the collection will show up in a list at the bottom of the page.

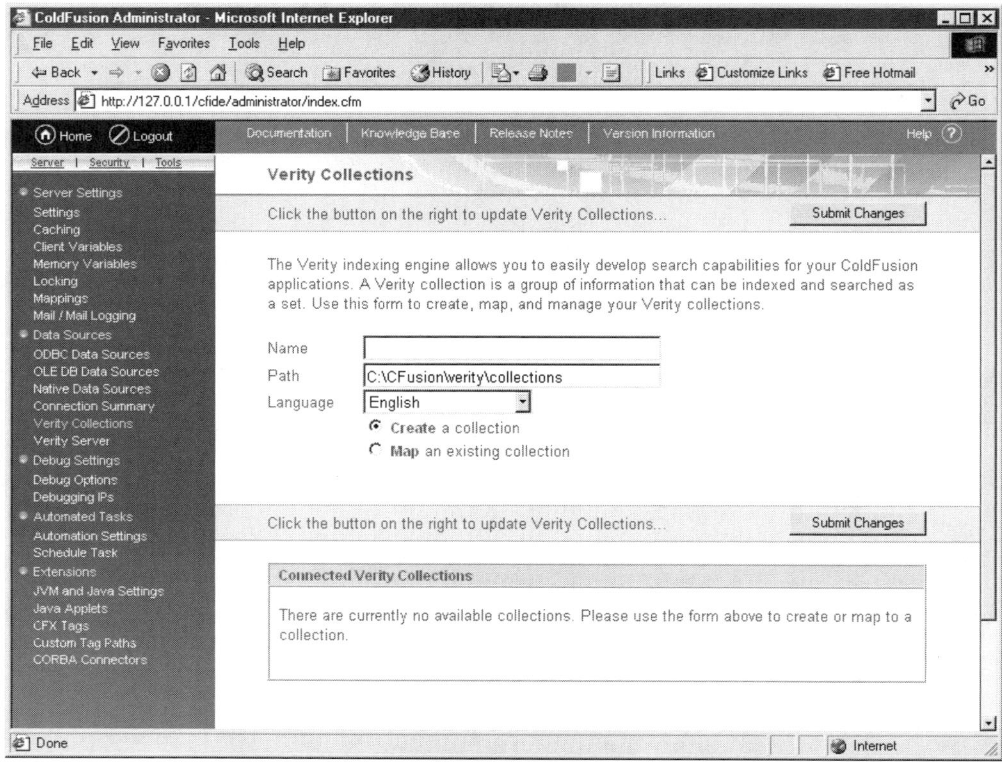

Figure 3-12 *Verity Collections page*

Once the collection is created, new options are available for the collections. These options allow the developer to performance maintenance tasks on the collection.

Verity Server Verity searches can be run from a Verity K2 server. Normally, ColdFusion and its tightly integrated Verity subcomponent perform the full text Verity searches. Sometimes, due to traffic levels, a separate server is a wise idea. This page allows you to set up a connection to a K2 server (see Figure 3-13). The —K2 Server is a separate, standalone piece of software available through the Verity web site at: http://www.verity.com/products/enterprise/index.html.

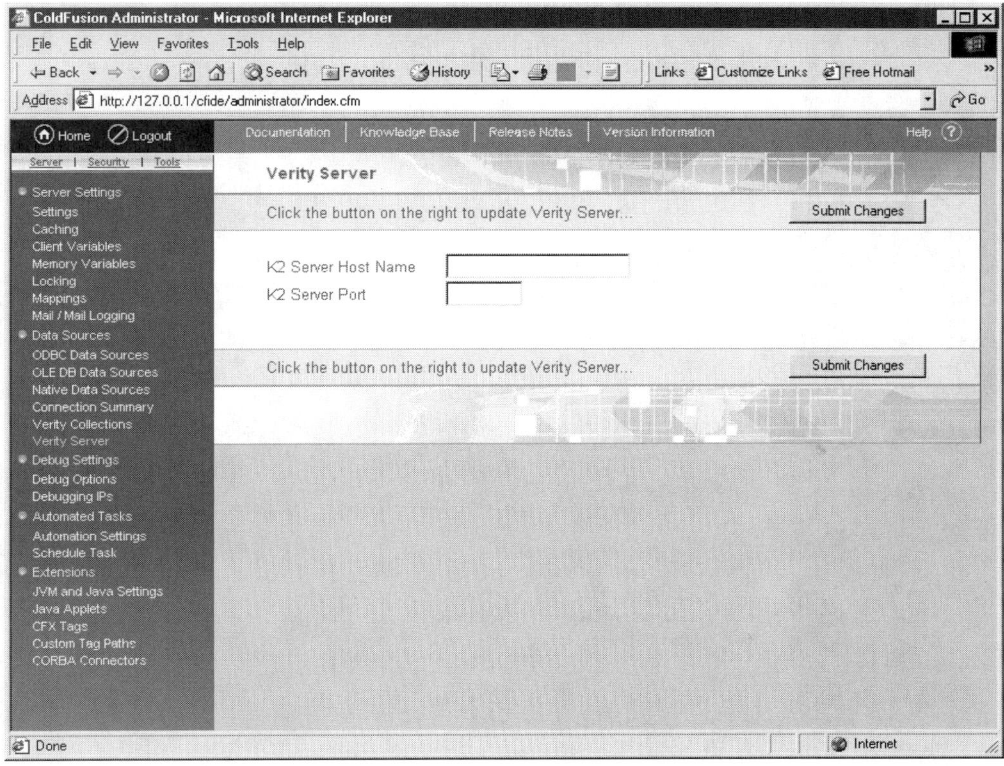

Figure 3-13 *Verity Server page*

Debug Settings

The debug settings section would be a developer's best friend if a section of a web site could be a best friend. The types of setting that can be enabled or disabled in the following pages pertain to everything debugging-related.

Debugging Options This page is where all the fun happens. This is where every possible piece of diagnostic information, aside from log files, can be exposed. Debugging as a topic is covered extensively in Chapter 13, so we'll try to curb the excitement as much as possible in this section, and just get to the point. The following table lists each setting and provides a brief possible description of the setting (as shown in Figure 3-14).

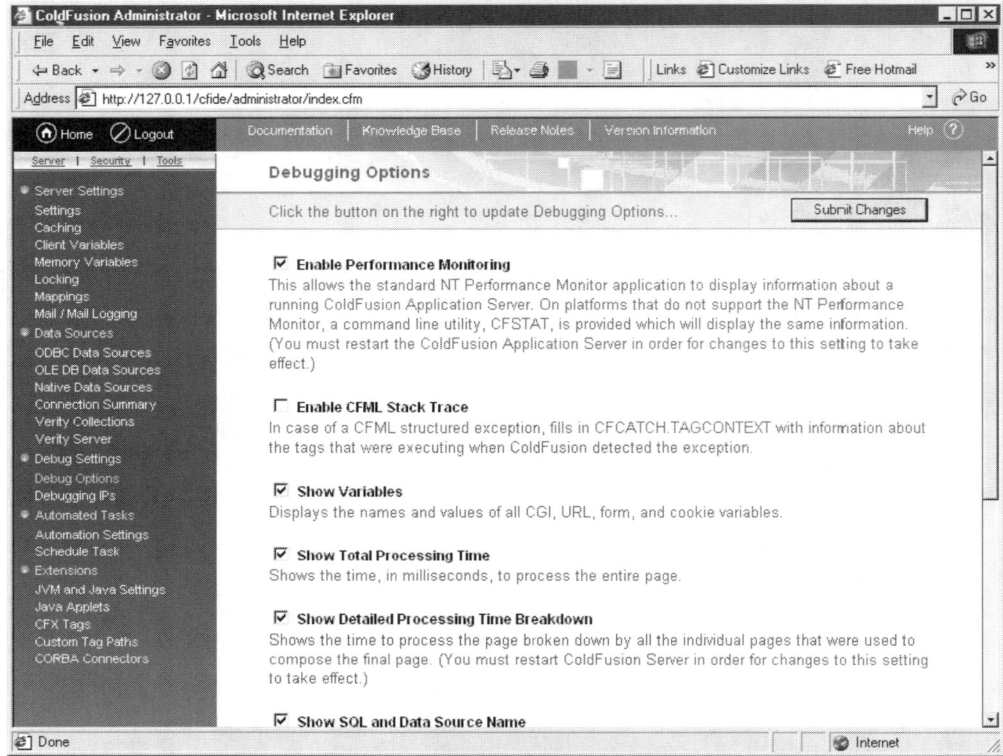

Figure 3-14 *Debugging Options page*

Setting	Description
Enable Performance Monitoring	When enabled, this setting allows you to view real-time ColdFusion performance-related, statistical data in the Windows 2000 Performance Analyzer. For nonWindows machines, this setting enables the use of the command line program CFSTAT.
Enable CFML Stack Trace	When enabled, this setting exposes information about what tags executed in a CFML document when an error occurs. Personally, I'd recommend that you avoid this setting, as there is a performance loss when it's enabled.

Setting	Description
Show Variables	When this setting is enabled, all CGI, URL, FORM, and COOKIE variables present in an executed template will be displayed, with their names and values in the debugging information at the bottom of the content generated by the template.
Show Total Processing Time	Enabling this setting is like seeing the results of a stopwatch after a 100-meter sprint or a 5,000-meter run. This setting displays the amount of time it takes for your template to execute.
Show Detailed Processing Time Breakdown	This setting lets you choose to display a detailed breakdown of how fast your template executed. Each included file or custom tag will be shown, along with its individual time in the debugging info.
Show SQL and Data Source Name	If a database error occurs and this setting is enabled, the SQL statement that was attempting to execute will be exposed in the error message, along with the datasource name.
Show Query Information	With this setting enabled, queries, along with their execution times, are exposed in the debugging information.
Display the Template Path in Error Messages	When an error occurs, the template path of the template with the error is displayed if this setting is enabled. Included templates and custom tags also show their template paths in the event of an error, which helps the developer figure out which file they need to look for.

As I mentioned earlier, Chapter 13 has detailed information about how to use the debugging information to your advantage.

Debugging IPs You probably don't want all of your servers' debugging information available for the entire world to see, so you'll want to use this page to restrict debugging information to certain IPs. If you enable all the debugging settings in the previous page, and do not restrict the display of the debugging information to a particular IP, the debugging information will be visible to everyone. It's a good idea to put the 127.0.0.1 IP in the list (see Figure 3-15) to avoid being shamed by having all your behind-the-scenes stuff show. That's like going to school in just your underwear, or worse.

Automated Tasks

ColdFusion allows developers to schedule ColdFusion scripts to run at certain times and intervals. The following pages allow us to configure the automation system, as well as add and configure automated tasks.

Automation Settings This page only has two settings, so we'll bypass the Setting/ Description table for this section and just talk about each setting in good old- fashioned paragraph form. (See Figure 3-16.)

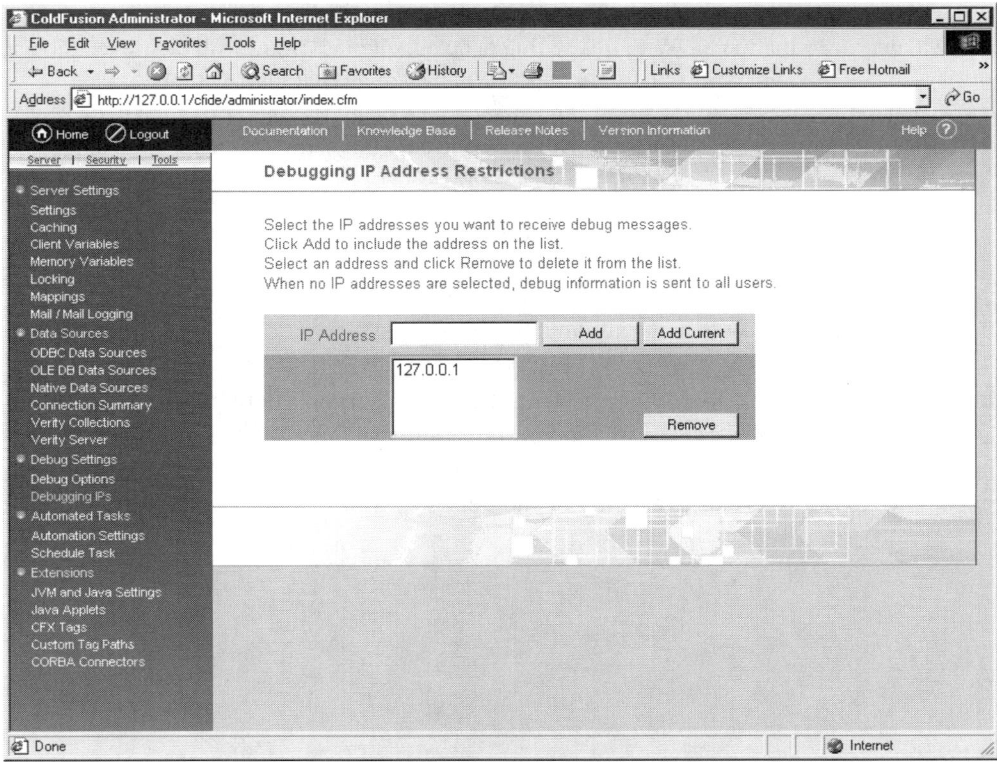

Figure 3-15 *Debugging IP Address Restrictions page*

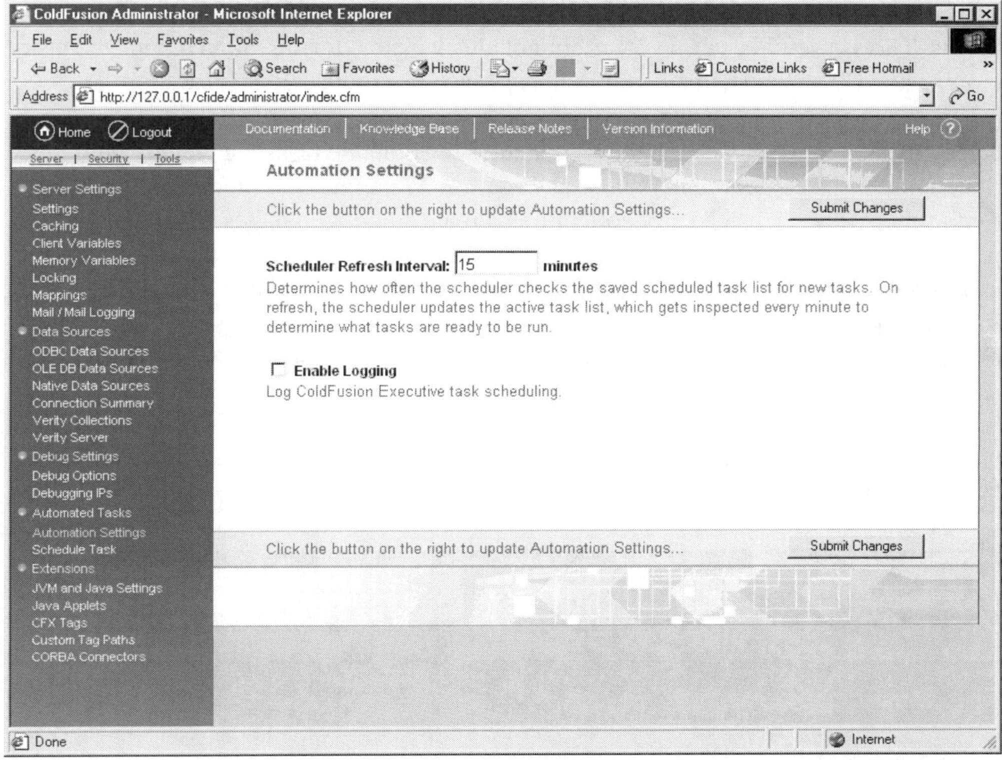

Figure 3-16 *Automation Settings page*

The first setting, Scheduler Refresh Interval: *n* minutes, controls how often the scheduler should look for new scheduled tasks. We see how to add a scheduled task in the next section, but it's safe to share, at this point, that when you add a scheduled task, the ColdFusion scheduling system doesn't immediately recognize it. The task is only recognized once the scheduler has refreshed itself, and this is the number that controls it.

Unless you're adding several scheduled tasks an hour, there's really no need to have this number be very low. In fact, by default, ColdFusion sets this number to 15 minutes, which in my opinion is way too low. I only very occasionally need to add a scheduled task to my servers, and I usually have it perform at a very unreasonable time of night, like 3:00 A.M. or something, to avoid slowing the server during peak times. If I add a task at 3:00 P.M. that doesn't need to execute until 3:00 A.M., I can get away with having my refresh time be three or four hours, or even more. In my case, entering 240 minutes would work just fine. Your situation may differ.

The second setting, Enable Logging, does exactly that. It enables you to log scheduled events. This is useful because you might not always know for sure if an automated task has executed. The logs will tell you if it has, which can reduce your frustration.

Schedule Task This page is where we actually schedule the tasks we want to automate. Scheduled tasks can come in handy, as Figure 3-17 suggests. You can create tasks to do things like refresh Verity collections, create static web pages from dynamic pages, perform site maintenance tasks, pull data from another site, and more. You can do pretty much anything, as long as it doesn't require a human to make it work. It would be impossible for the Scheduler to process a form that required form data before it could finish processing. The Scheduler isn't a human, it doesn't know what to put in the form elements—it just executes things.

To add a scheduled task, click the Schedule New Task button. Fill out the form with the proper information, and click Submit Changes. For more information about how to create scheduled tasks, turn to Chapter 8.

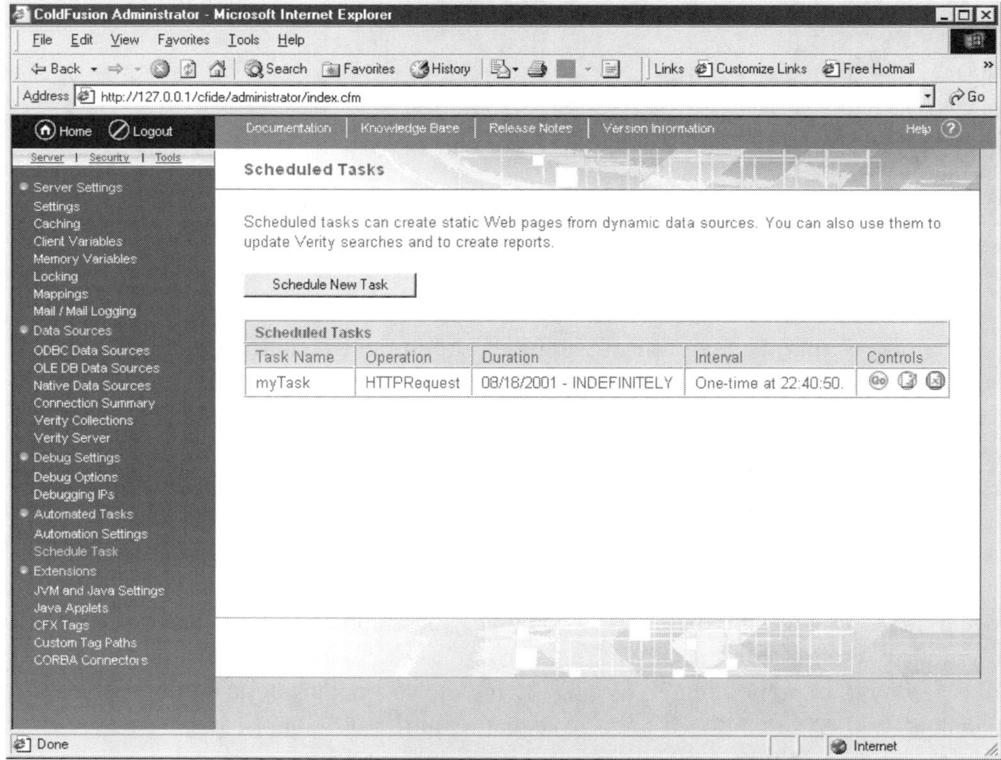

Figure 3-17 *Scheduled Tasks page*

After you submit the changes, the task will show up in the active task list. There are three icons in the Controls column of the table that list the tasks:

- **Go Icon** This immediately executes the selected task.
- **Notepad Icon** Clicking this icon allows you to edit the task. This is the same as clicking the task name.
- **Red X Icon** Clicking this icon deletes the task.

Extensions

The extensions section of the ColdFusion Administrator allows for the registration and settings of external objects like Java Applets, ColdFusion CFX tags, and other extension-related settings. We talk more about extensions to ColdFusion in Chapter 15.

JVM and Java Settings This page allows you to apply Java-related settings (see Figure 3-18). ColdFusion supports Java Objects, Enterprise Java Beans, Java Servlets,

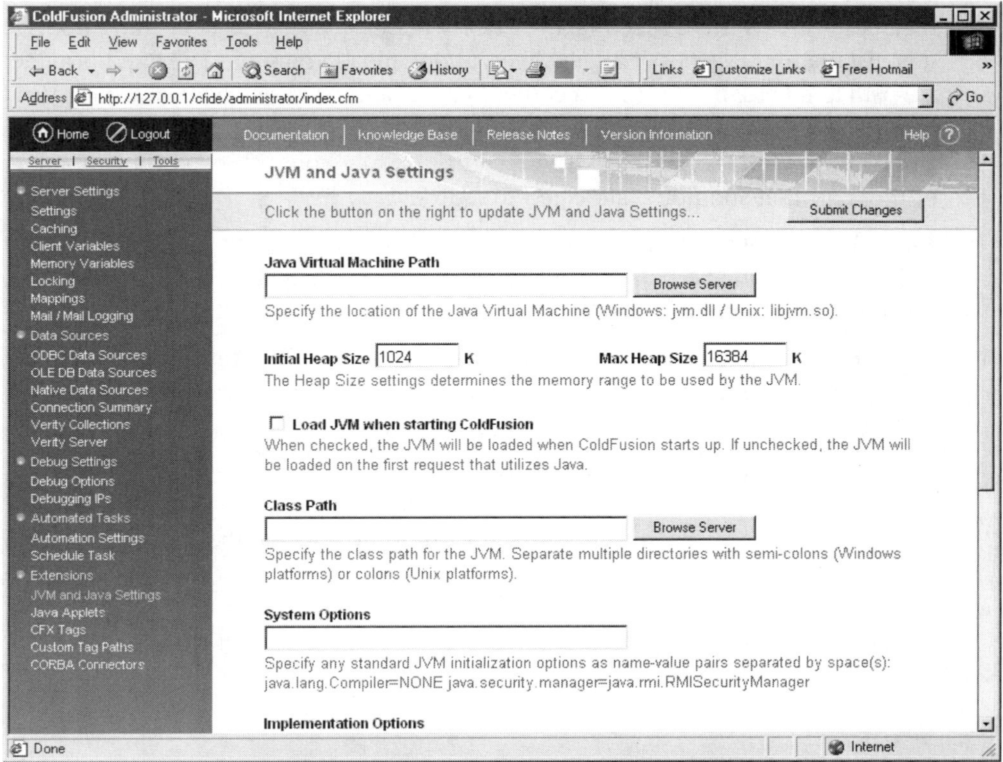

Figure 3-18 *JVM and Java Settings page*

as well as Java-based CFX tags. Java can be used to perform server-side operations that are far too difficult or impossible for ColdFusion to execute. For instance, imagine expecting ColdFusion to do batch image processing. Not only is it not possible for ColdFusion to manipulate images, even if it could, it probably wouldn't be the best language to use.

Let's show each of the possible settings for this page, and discuss each in detail:

- **Java Virtual Machine Path** A virtual machine is required to execute Java code, whether you're using ColdFusion or not. Rather than compiling code specifically for different platforms, Java Virtual Machines are created for each platform, making the code itself completely portable. For example, a program written in the C++ language and compiled on a Linux machine will not execute on a Windows 2000 machine. The same source code could be compiled on a Windows 2000 machine, and it would then work on a Windows 2000 machine. Java code isn't compiled per se, it's built into byte code, which is then interpreted by a Java Virtual Machine.

  ColdFusion installs version 1.2 of the Java Development Kit (JDK 1.2), which includes a Java Virtual Machine (JVM). By default, Java extensions run through this installation. It is possible, however, to download your own JVM and provide the path to it here. If no path is specified, Java extensions use the ColdFusion JVM.

- **Initial and Max Heap Size** These settings allow you to specify the amount of memory that should be allocated to the JVM.
- **Load JVM When Starting ColdFusion** When this setting is enabled, the JVM will be loaded when ColdFusion starts up. If it's disabled, the JVM is loaded the first time a Java extension is requested.
- **Class Path** This setting allows you to specify multiple paths to your Java classes. Separate multiple directories with semicolons on Windows-based platforms, and colons on Unix-based platforms.
- **System and Implementation Options** These settings are optional, and will rarely need changing. They allow you to set JVM startup settings. If you're using the JDK 1.3 on a Linux machine, Allaire recommends that the following option be entered into the Implementation Options box:

  -XX:+AllowUserSignalHandlers

- **CFX Jar Path** This setting allows you to change the path for the cfx.jar file. This file is what enables Java-based CFX tags to execute, and will probably not need to be changed.

Java Applets This page allows you to register new Java Applets to be used with the <CFAPPLET> tag (see Figure 3-19). To add a new applet, click the Register New Applet button. To edit the applet, click the applet name, or click the Notepad icon.

CFX Tags CFX tags are custom-built extensions that work seamlessly within ColdFusion. CFX tags can be written in C++ and Java. CFX tags must be registered before they can be used with ColdFusion.

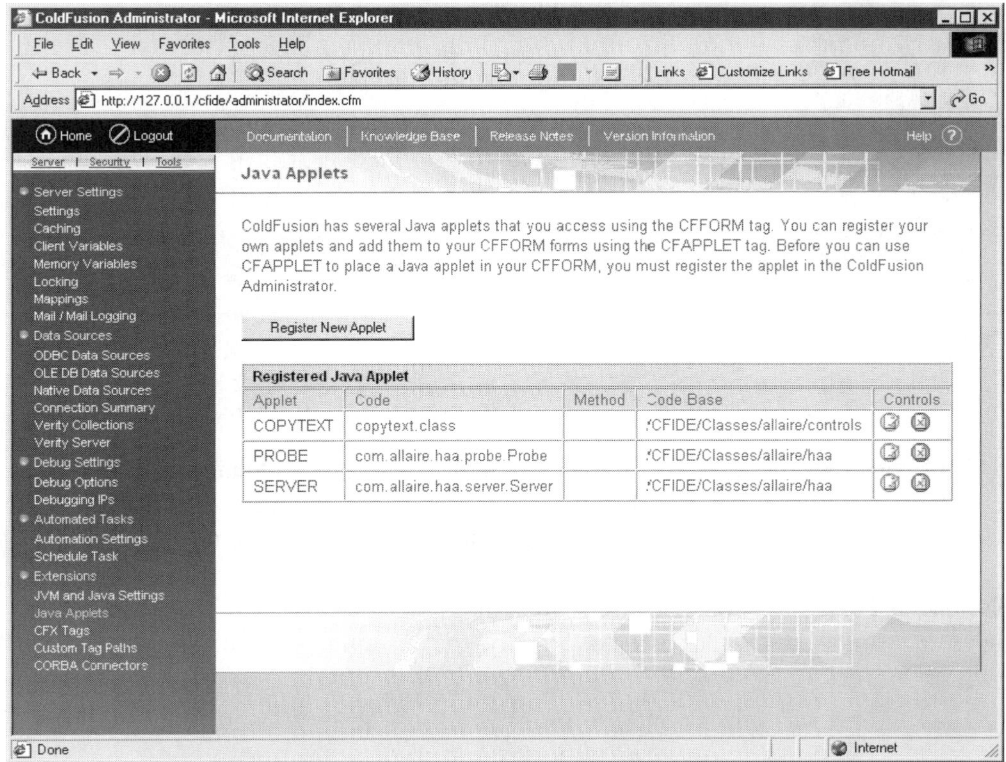

Figure 3-19 *Java Applets page*

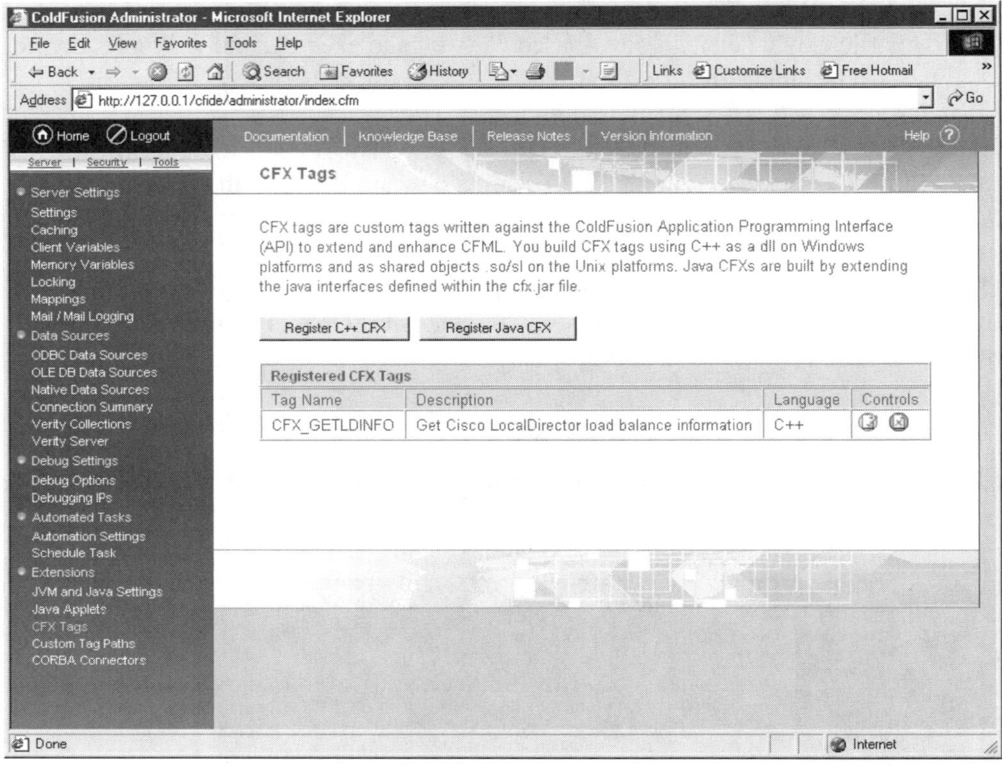

Figure 3-20 *CFX Tags page*

This page lists the registered CFX tags, and allows you to add new CFX tags (see Figure 3-20). To edit a CFX tag, click the tag name. Figure 3-21 shows the CFX properties page, which is also identical to the screen to add a new CFX tag.

Custom Tag Paths Custom tags are written in CFML, and can be used just like other tags are used in ColdFusion. Normally, the custom tags are placed in the

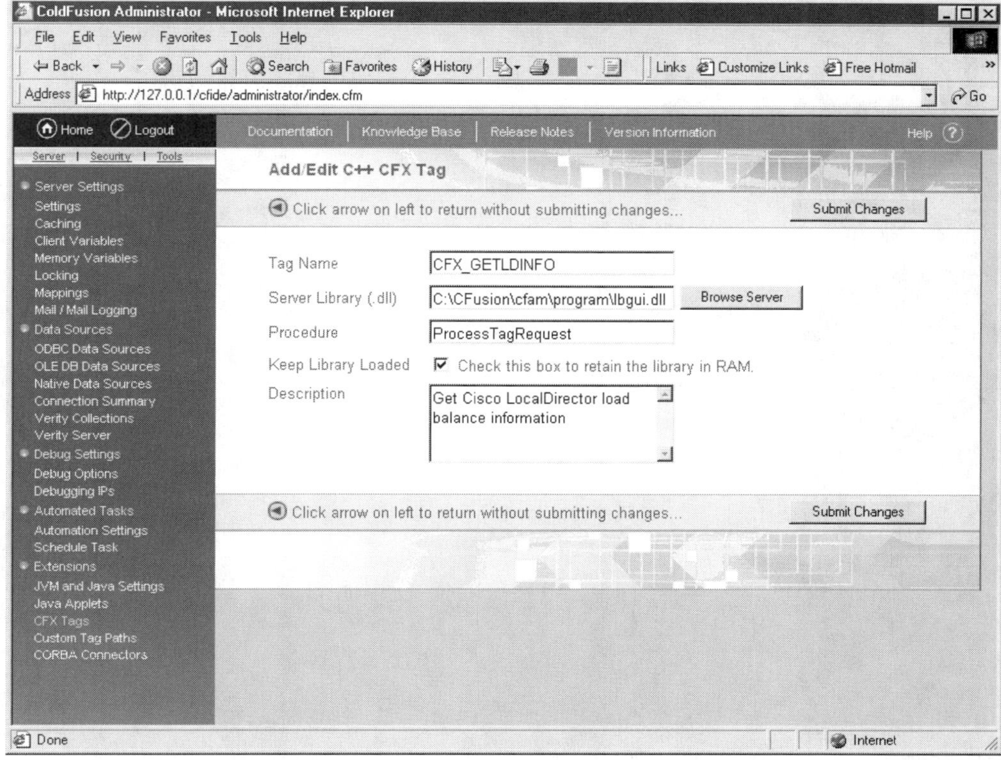

Figure 3-21 *Editing a CFX tag*

C:\CFUSION\CustomTags directory. This page allows you to add new custom tag paths other than the default custom tags (see Figure 3-22). We talk extensively about custom tags in Chapter 15.

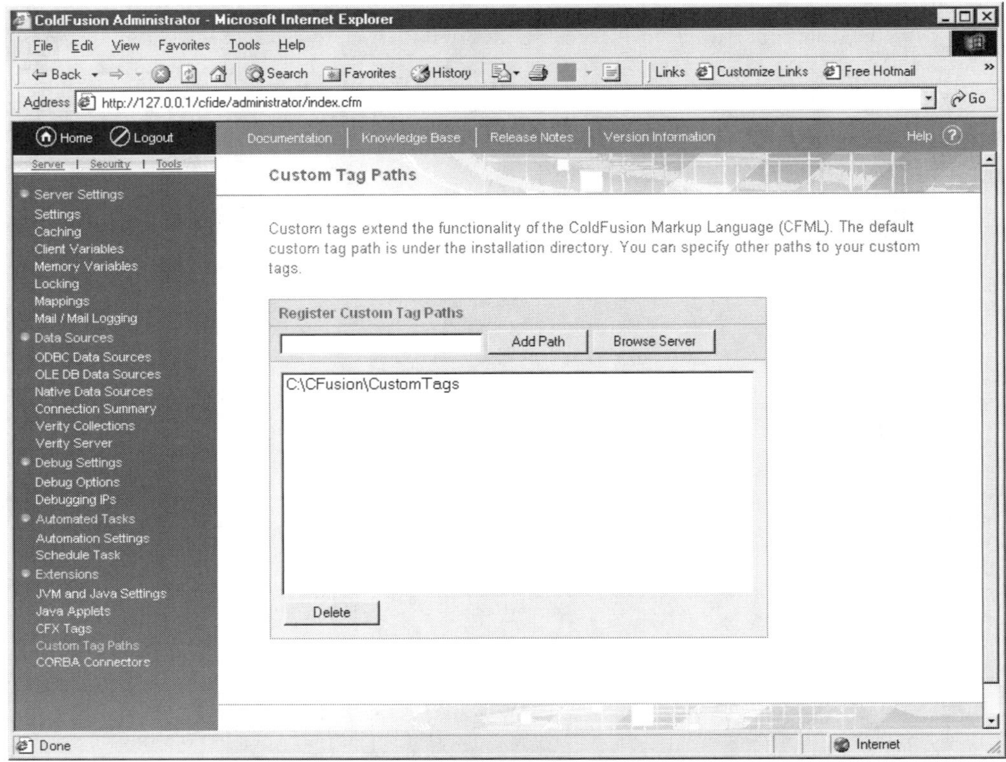

Figure 3-22 *Custom Tag Paths page*

CORBA Connectors First of all, let me mention that ColdFusion developers rarely use CORBA connectors. Because of this, we won't be talking much about CORBA in this book (although it does get a general overview in Chapter 10). CORBA is really only used when things like Java or COM objects cannot be used. If you'd like to learn more about CORBA, visiting the CORBA web site at http://www.corba.org should help.

This page allows you to register new CORBA connectors and view currently installed CORBA extensions (see Figure 3-23). To add a new extension, click on the Register CORBA Connector button. To edit an existing CORBA extension, click the extension name.

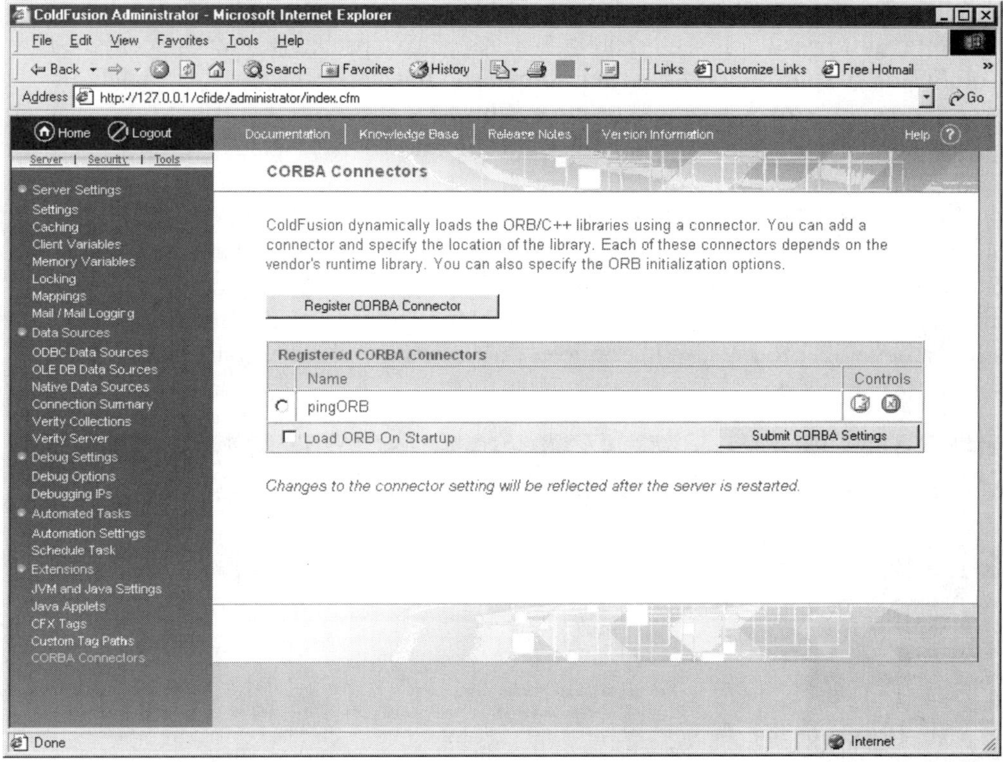

Figure 3-23 *CORBA Connectors page*

Security Menu

The security menu is accessed by clicking on the middle Security link towards the upper-left corner of the ColdFusion Administrator. This portion of the Administrator is broken down into two major parts: Basic Security and Advanced Security. We go over each option within these major sections, just as we've done with previous options.

Basic Security

This is where general security settings are applied. There are three possible settings pages: CF Admin Password, Tag Restrictions, and CF Studio Password. We look at each in detail.

CF Admin Password This page allows you to set or change the ColdFusion Administrator password (see Figure 3-24). As you've probably already seen, the ColdFusion Administrator is a powerful tool, and if access is gained by a malicious user, then a lot of damage could be done. Choose a password that is not easy to guess, and only allow trusted Administrators to know what the password is.

Tag Restrictions This page allows you to allow or disallow the use of certain tags and tag attributes (see Figure 3-25). Some tags, when used in a shared environment, can pose a security risk. For example, the <CFDIRECTORY> tag could expose information about your customers, and combined with the <CFFILE> tag, could allow a developer to read, write, or delete files from a customer's directory—a serious security risk.

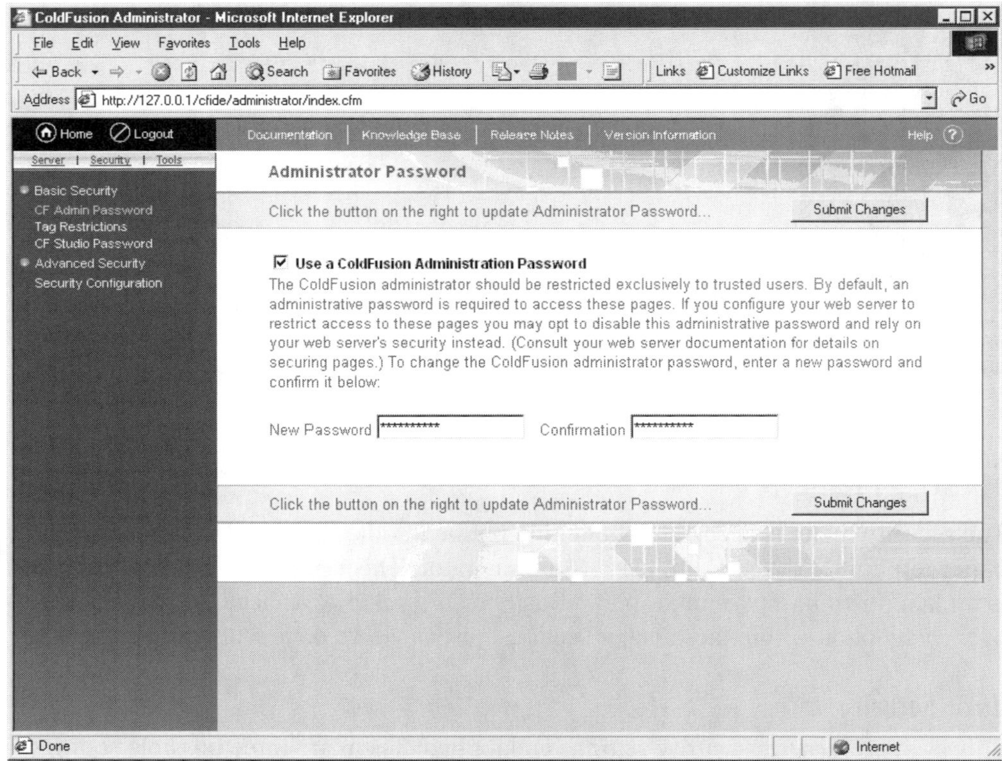

Figure 3-24 *Administrator Password page*

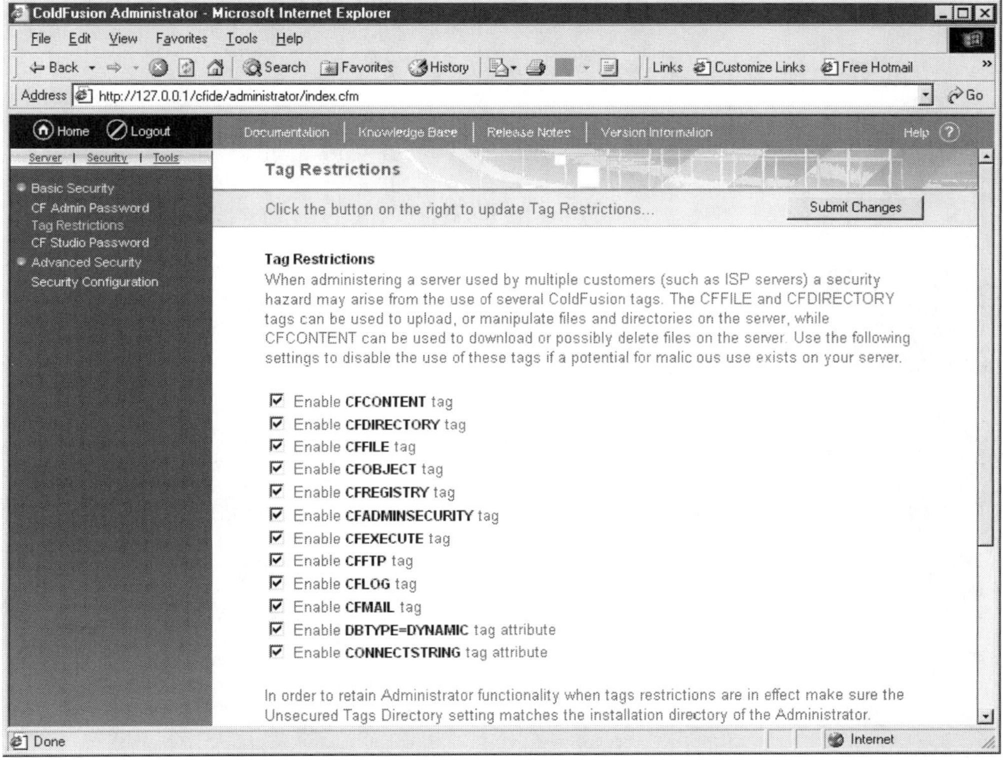

Figure 3-25 *Tag Restrictions page*

Because the ColdFusion Administrator makes extensive use of the some of the tags that can be disabled, the path to the Administrator can be entered. Any CFML listed in this directory will be allowed to use the disabled tags. ColdFusion automatically fills in this value upon installation, and typically it doesn't need to be changed.

To save the changes, click the Submit Changes button.

CF Studio Password ColdFusion Studio integrates with the ColdFusion server, and in order to gain access, a password can be enabled. It's highly recommended that you enable a password, and make the password something that is hard to figure out. Figure 3-26 shows this page.

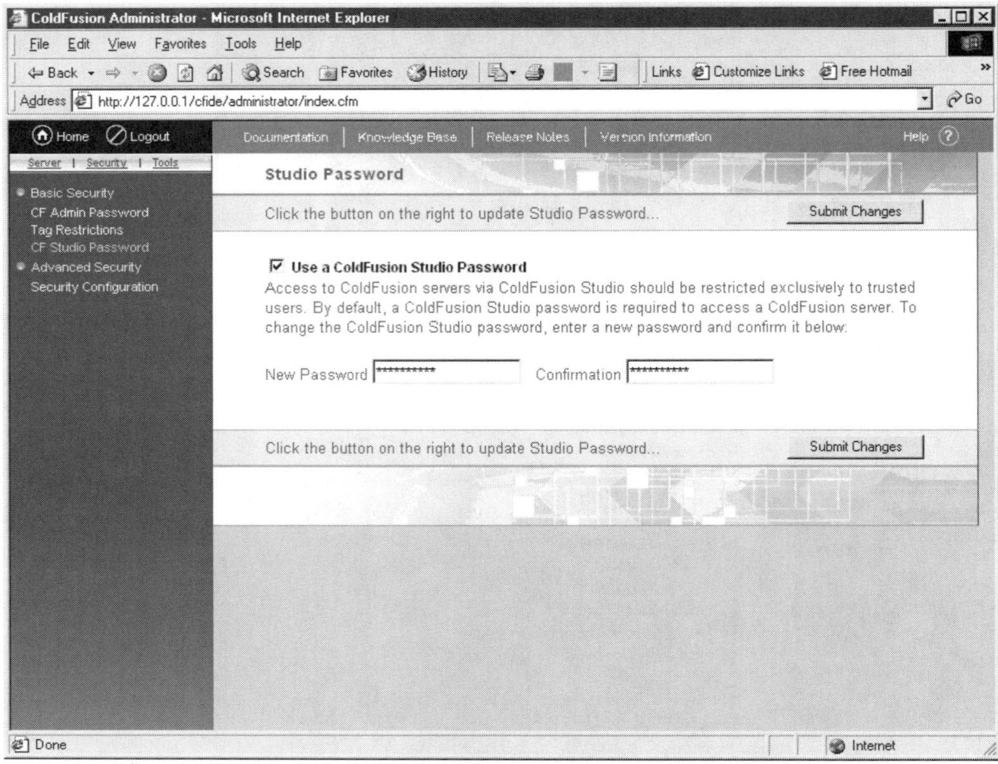

Figure 3-26 *Studio Password page*

Advanced Security

When you click the Security Configuration menu option for the first time, you get a pop-up window basically stating that Microsoft Access does not make an adequate Policy Store location. Because we focus on SQL Server 2000 in this book, we'll walk through the Upsize Wizard to upsize our Advanced Security Policy Stores to SQL Server 2000, but first, a word about some Advanced Security topics.

Advanced security is based on four concepts: User directories, Resources, Policies, and Security contexts. Let's break down each of these concepts to better understand how they related to Advanced security.

- **User Directories** User directories store user names, passwords, and the groups that a user belongs to. User directories can be stored in LDAP directories, Windows NT Domain security stores, and ODBC datasources.

- **Resources** Resources are items that you want to secure. This can include directories, CFML tags, or specific actions on a particular datasource. Whether or not a resource can be accessed is enforced using security-related CFML tags. Resources are not secure unless you specifically secure them.
- **Policies** Policies are the rules that determine which resources are secured. Resources without a security policy are, by default, fully secured. An example of a policy would be if you created a policy that gave the development team access to a certain directory, but not the marketing team.
- **Security Contexts** Security contexts allow you to group policies to help simplify the task of administration. The number of security contexts is unlimited.

Now, back to the Policy Store Upsize Wizard. We'll go through each step, describing what needs to be done at each one.

Click the Start Security Wizard button on the Policy Store Upsize Wizard pop-up window. You will be taken through the following steps:

1. *Introduction: What do I need to run the wizard?* This window gives a description of the steps that the Wizard will perform. The window also gives warnings on what may be required of you during the Wizard. Click the Next button when you're ready to begin.
2. *Choose your ODBC DSN to use as your security policy storage device.* This step asks that you select a datasource to use as the security store. At this point, a datasource probably hasn't been set aside, so it's a good idea to create one. The ColdFusion Administrator should still be open in the background, so leave this window open, create a database that will store your security information, register the datasource, and then refresh Step 2 of the Wizard. Make sure the datasource is an ODBC datasource, not an OLE DB or Native Driver DB. Once the datasource is created, refresh the page, select the datasource, and click Next.
3. *Installing the DSN information.* Step 3 verifies that the DSN is installed. Click Next to continue.
4. *Installing the default schema for the database*. Step 4 creates the required tables and relationships in the database. Click Next to continue.
5. *Setting security password for the selected DSN.* Step 5 applies a password to the data source. Do as the instructions say at this step by running C:\CFUSION\Bin\smconsole.exe. Click the ODBC tag, and enter the correct password into

the available boxes. Click the Test Connection button to verify that the password is correct. Click Next to continue.

6. *Restarting the security services.* Step 6 restarts the Site Minder services. Click Next to continue.
7. *Resetting the security password.* Step 7 resets the security password to a temporary value so that the Wizard can make security related changes. The password can be manually reset in a later step. Click Next to continue.
8. *Importing default data into the new Policy Store.* Step 8 creates a new default Policy Store in the datasource. Click Next when it's completed.
9. *Creating a Policy Store administrator password.* The temporary password set in Step 7 can now be reset by hand. Choose a password that isn't easy to guess. Click Next once the password is entered.
10. *Setting ColdFusion Advanced Security administration password and restarting ColdFusion services.* Step 10 resets all security services as well as the ColdFusion Server. This is the last step of the Upsize Wizard. Click the Close Window button to close the window.

We talk in detail about how to set up and use Advanced Security in Chapter 10.

Tools Menu

Another one of the new useful features introduced in ColdFusion 5.0 is the Tools menu. This menu provides access to several tools, including the new log file-management system, server reports, web site probes, and archival and deployment features.

Logs and Statistics

ColdFusion 5.0 has made a big improvement over previous versions when it comes to logging. Log files take on a more important role, as seen with the redesign of the log file-management system. Let's look at each menu option in detail.

Logging Settings This settings page will look familiar to developers who have used ColdFusion 4.5. It allows you to set logging-related settings (see Figure 3-27). The following table describes each setting.

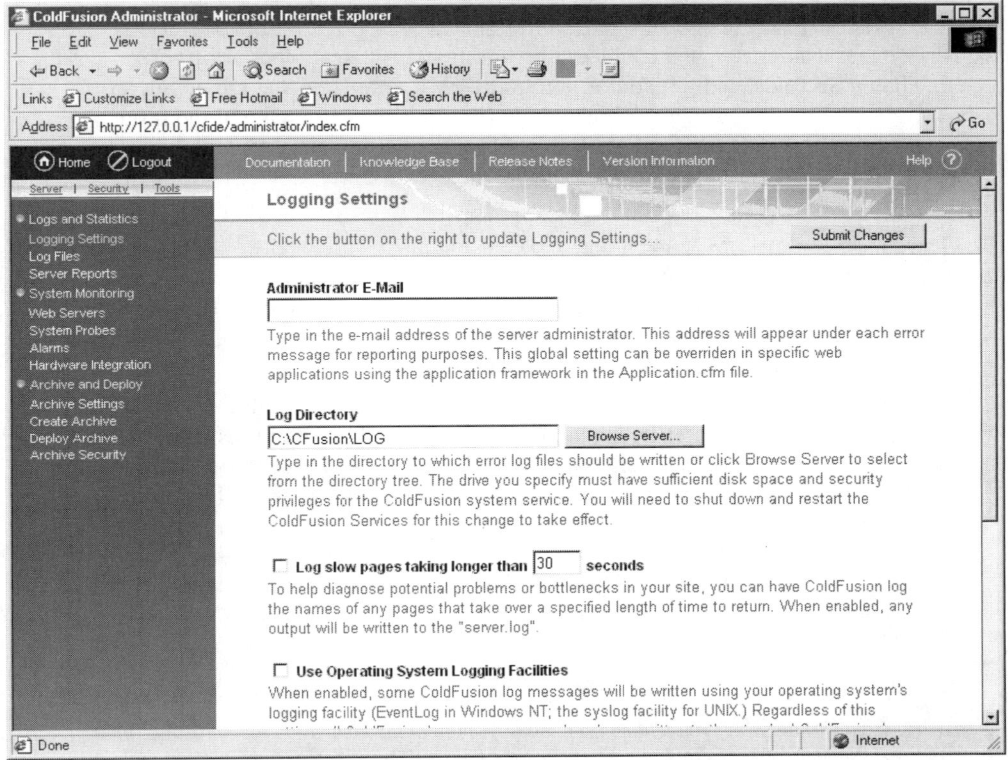

Figure 3-27 *Logging Settings page*

Setting	Description
Administrator E-mail	If an e-mail address is entered here, it will show up on standard ColdFusion error messages.
Log Directory	By default, ColdFusion uses the C:\CFUSION\Log directory. This setting can specify any directory you'd like it to, as long as the ColdFusion service has high enough permissions to read and write to the drive. A new directory will not be recognized until the ColdFusion service is restarted.

Setting	Description
Log Slow Pages Taking Longer Than *n* Seconds.	When enabled, this setting helps a developer or server administrator pinpoint CFML templates that are taking an unreasonable amount of time to execute. One of the fastest ways to speed up a server is to eliminate slow CFML pages. One CFML can make the entire server slow. Enabling this setting is highly recommended.
Use Operating System Logging Facilities	When enabled, ColdFusion makes use of the system's global logging system. On Windows NT and 2000 machines, entries will be made in the Event Log. On UNIX systems, entries will be made in syslog. Even with this setting enabled, ColdFusion logs will still be written to.
User Version 5.0 Logging Format	This setting controls whether or not the ColdFusion server writes its logs in the new, standardized ColdFusion 5.0 format, or in older formats. If this setting is changed, the ColdFusion services must be stopped, and the previous log files need to be moved or renamed before the services can be started again. The ColdFusion 5.0 log format allows for a higher degree of functionality with the new log management system.

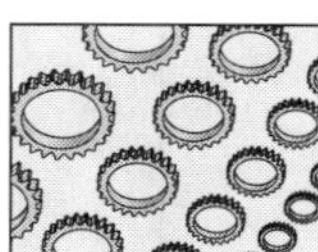

NOTE

Erik Goodlad, the technical editor for this book, noticed an interesting quirk in the ColdFusion Administrator. When you update a setting anywhere in the ColdFusion Administrator, then immediately after the update, an information box at the top of the screen indicates that the setting for that page was last updated a few milliseconds ago. This information is stored to the cfadmin.log file. The quirk is that once you leave the page, the information box is gone. So—what's the point of displaying the last updated date if you're only going to see it immediately after an update? You clicked it so you know it was just updated. Wouldn't it be more beneficial to see the information when going to the page, regardless of anything you might have just done? Fortunately, for those who must see this kind of information, the information is stored in the cfadmin.log file, but it would really make more sense to see the information on the affected page at all times.

Log Files ColdFusion 5.0 introduces a new log file system that is much improved over previous versions of ColdFusion. In previous versions of ColdFusion, it felt as if the log files were just there if you felt like looking at them. Indeed, there were no specialized tools for viewing them. In the older Administrators, you could save the files to a new location, or view them in plain text format. For large log files, neither of these actions was very appropriate; who wants to start 10MB worth of log file entries?

ColdFusion 5.0 has made the new log file-management system much more user-friendly, with tools to filter the content, as well as a cleaner, easier to read format. Now, rather than being displayed in raw text format, the log files are polished up and color-coded.

The first new thing we see with the log file-management system is the main menu, as shown in Figure 3-28. The log files are organized in an easy-to-read HTML table, and you can have actions applied to each log file by clicking one of the icons in the right-hand column.

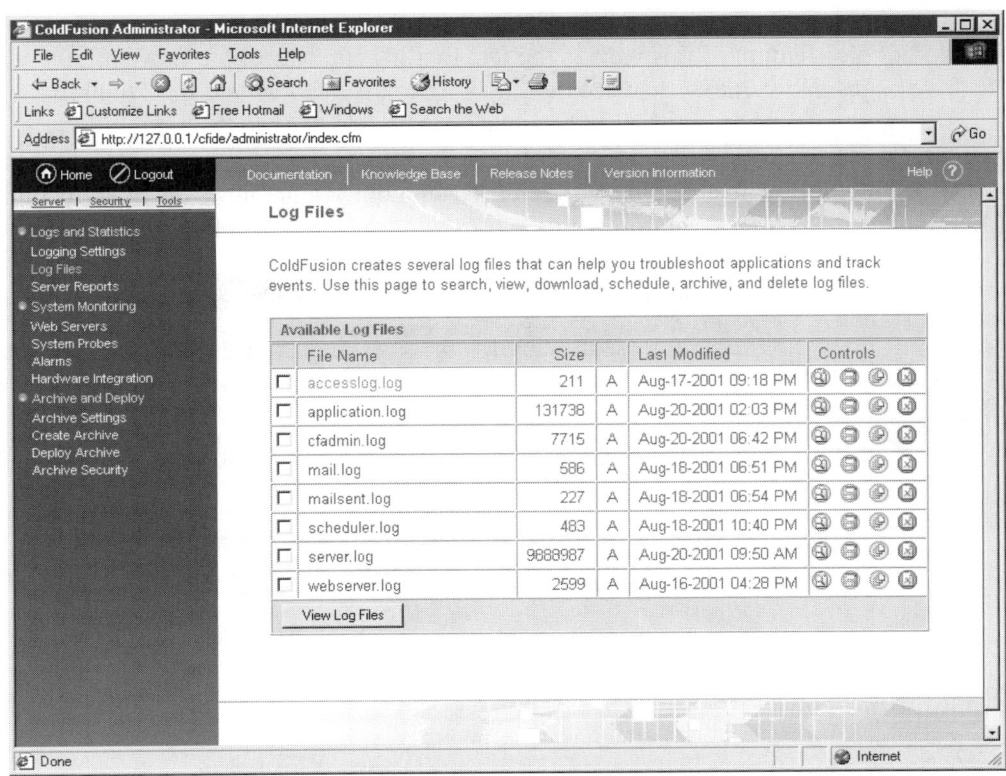

Figure 3-28 *Log Files page*

Each icon, when clicked on, allows you to perform a different task related to the log file. There are four possible tasks, as listed here in order from left to right as shown on the page:

- Search/View Log File
- Download Log File
- Store Log File
- Delete Log File

This Search/View Log File view (shown in Figure 3-29) is drastically different than viewing log files in the previous versions of ColdFusion. Prominently displayed towards the top of the page are check boxes that allow you to change the view to Compact Mode or Raw Data. Clicking the View Raw Data box displays the text file as a plain text file, with no formatting or filtering capabilities. The same log file in compact mode shows less data, requiring you to click the Compact View box to see full information again.

Another nice feature of this view is the fact that log file entries are now split on to separate pages. Now, rather than seeing the entire log file in a single shot, the log file is split into several pages, with links to advance from one page to the next, and back to previous pages.

Despite all the new features in the logging system, one feature takes the blue ribbon. Clicking the Launch Filter button will pop up a window that looks like this:

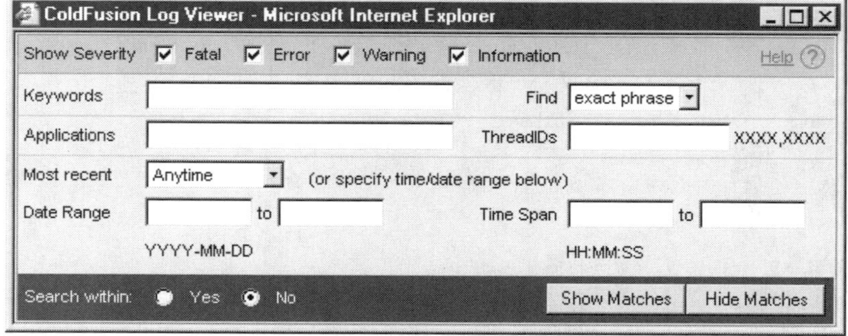

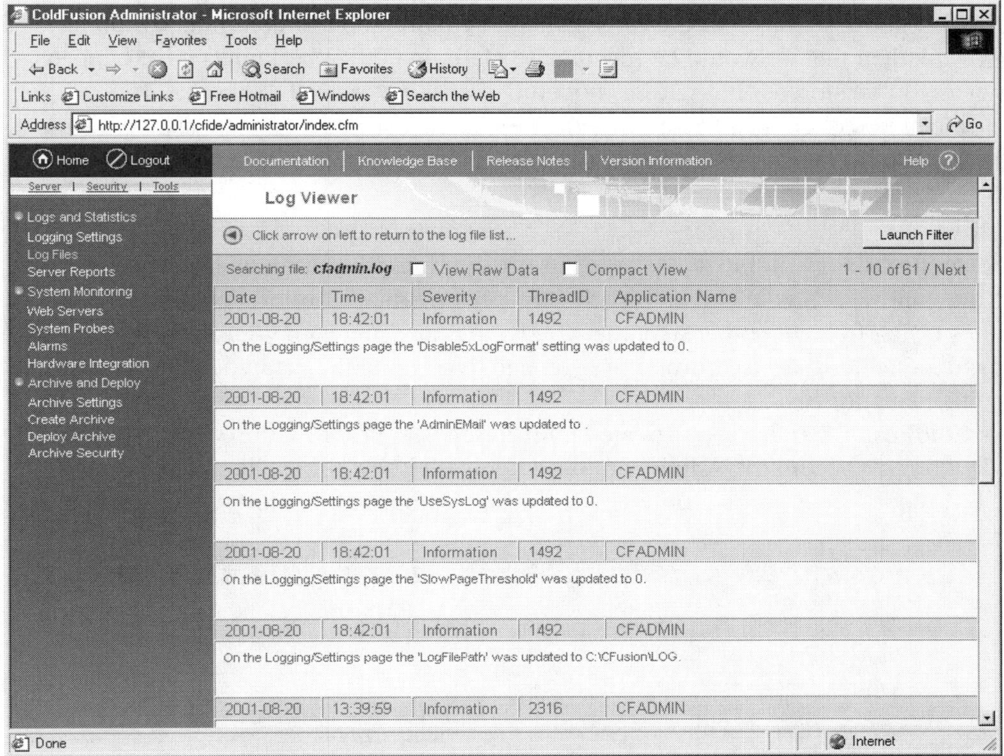

Figure 3-29 *Search/View Log File view*

This pop-up allows you to filter your log file content so you only see what you want to see. This feature alone makes the new log file-management system a powerful tool for administrators who manage servers. Rather than wading through hundreds and thousands of log file entries, administrators can narrow down exactly what they're looking for, and maintain focus on the task at hand, whatever it may be.

Clicking the Download Log File view icon allows you to immediately download the log file. If on a slow connection, it's always a good idea to check the file size before downloading a log file, as they can be very large at time.

When you click the Store Log File view icon, the log file will be removed from the log file list and stored in the default log file directory (usually C:\CFUSION \ Log) with a number file extension. For instance, if you decided to store the cfadmin.log file for the first time, it would be renamed to cfadmin.001. If cfadmin.001 already existed, then the file would be renamed to cfadmin.002. Who knows what happens when you've stored 999 log files; hopefully we'll never need to know.

When you click the Delete Log File view icon, a window appears asking if you really want to delete the log file. Once you click the Delete button, the log file will be gone forever, so choose wisely.

Server Reports ColdFusion 4.5 was, in my opinion, a bit weak on the reporting side. You could watch your server with the NT performance monitor, and read through piles of log files, but other than that you were pretty much on your own. In order to get detailed long-term information, you had to compile the data yourself, which was neither fun nor easy.

ColdFusion 5.0 has sophisticated built-in reporting (see Figure 3-30). You can view reports within the Administrator that let you know things like your average CFM requests per second, or even the average amount of memory ColdFusion uses.

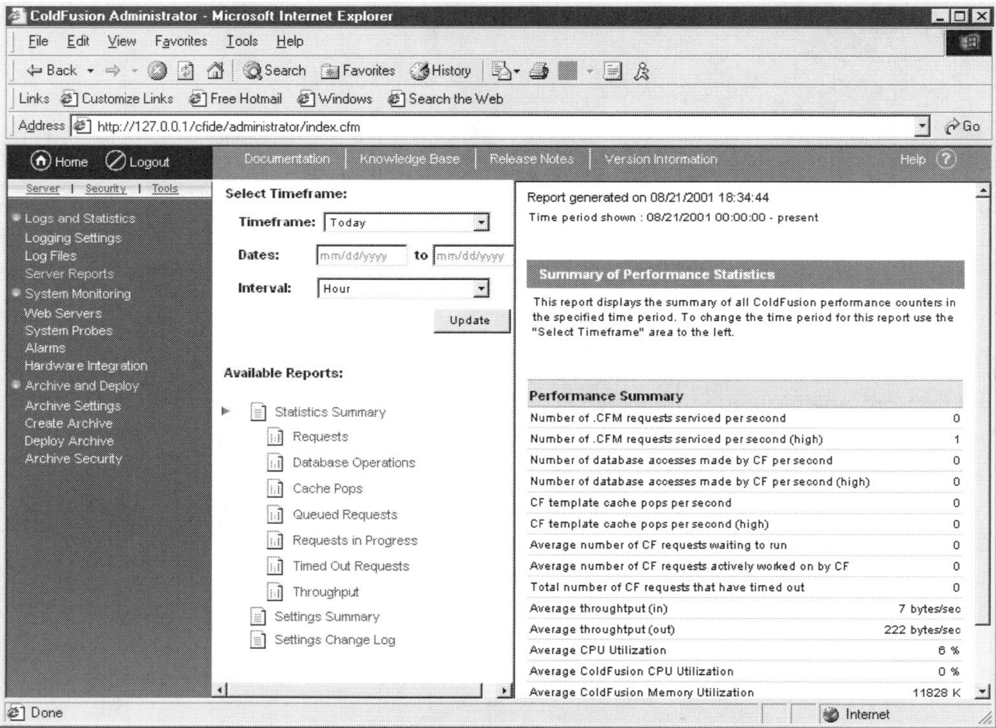

Figure 3-30 *Server Reports page*

The amount of data available is truly amazing when you think about what ColdFusion 4.5 made available.

Let's go over each type of report available in the Server Reports page:

- **Statistics Summary** Gives a general overview of your ColdFusion server's performance. With this report you can quickly, at a glance, determine whether your server is running quickly or falling behind. It's interesting to note in the following screenshots how little traffic my server gets. I'm not ashamed of a low traffic box!
- **Requests** Gives more specific, detailed information about what kind of requests you're getting. One of metrics I really enjoy seeing is the "Average CF memory usage" metric. This is a good indicator for me if I have enough RAM installed on my server.

The rest of the following reports look very similar to the screenshots, so I'll not make you look at nearly identical screenshots for each report.

- **Database Operations** Provides detailed information about the statistics of your database connections, including how many connections are being made, what types of average response time you're getting, and so on.
- **Cache Pops** Not to be confused with Corn Pops, *cache pops* occur when a template in cache has been removed to allow another template to be cached. This happens when the memory allocated for caching templates is too low. It's good to know if it's happening, and this report will give you an idea of how much room you should be giving to your templates. Eating enough Corn Pops to make your head explode is a good "brick-and-mortar" (or real-world) example of a cache pop. Please don't try that at home.
- **Queued Requests** This is an important report. *Queued requests* are requests that are waiting in line for running requests to finish. A queued request is a slow request, and you should try to get these numbers as low as possible. All of the ColdFusion 5.0 server reporting should help you determine how to keep these numbers low, by pinpointing errors or slow-running requests in the log files, or by pointing out things like cache pops, database bottlenecks, etc.
- **Requests in Progress** These are the running requests. Ideally, this number should be as low as possible, although on a busy server they will probably never be zero. If the number of running requests exceeds the allowable simultaneous running requests (set in the Server > Server Settings > Settings section), the request will be queued, which we know is a bad thing. If too many requests

turn into queued requests, a lot of people begin to wait for their page to finish processing, and we know that is a bad thing also. Jakob Nielsen (http://www.useit.com) of usability fame (or infamy depending on how you feel) determined through testing that while a user is looking at your site, he or she also has several of your competitors open in different browsers at the exact same time. I hope that underlines the importance of keeping your running requests low. This report is important in helping determine the speed of your server.

- **Timed-Out Requests** Ouch! A timed-out request is worse than a queued request. It's a completely dead request. Have you ever stood in a long line at Disneyland to ride a 45-second ride? So have I. Now imagine if people started to keel over and die in line, Disney would go absolutely nuts trying to fix that (in a Disney sort of way of course). Pretend your running request are people enjoying the ride, the queued requests are people waiting in line, and timed-out requests are people who either starved to death or died of old age. Yes it's morbid, and little weird by normal people standards, but you get the point I hope. Timed-out requests indicate a pretty sizable deficiency in your application. Either your hardware isn't adequate, or you have a part of your application that is taking entirely too long to process, or perhaps you have a problem connecting to a database. This report should, ideally, have all zeros in the "Requests timed out" column.
- **Throughput** This report provides details on how much data is flowing in and out of ColdFusion. If your service provider charges an adjustable rate depending on bandwidth usage, this is somewhat relevant to how much you'll pay at the end of the month. I wouldn't count on this data, however, as an exact figure on bandwidth usage. It simply pertains to ColdFusion, and nothing else. It doesn't track how much bandwidth the images use, or what kind of bandwidth is being taken up by anything else you can think of. Just ColdFusion.
- **Settings Summary** This report is like a gift from heaven for those of us who try in vain setting up truly identical ColdFusion servers. It provides a detail table of the exactly how your server is set up, from the server version to debugging information. The only thing I can figure out is why Allaire didn't make it easy for me to export these settings, to apply on another machine.
- **Settings Change Log** As if the Setting Summary report weren't good enough, now I can see what settings the server had *before* I changed them. This is a great feature for going back to a setting that you know works, after changing a setting that suddenly brought your server to its knees. If you're interested in actually saving the system settings to a file, read the "Archive and Deploy" section later in this chapter.

System Monitoring

ColdFusion 5.0 provides a number of new tools that perform active system monitoring. The new features include load-balancing hardware integration, system probes that monitor system performance, and e-mail-based notifications. We look at each section within the system monitoring section in detail.

Web Servers The section of the system-monitoring area allows you to set up load threshold levels for multiple servers (see Figure 3-31). On a single-server application, this page isn't exactly something one needs to worry about. In a multiple-server environment with load-balancing hardware, this menu allows you to define which servers are active in the cluster farm, and it displays what the activity level for each machine is currently at. You may also completely restrict access to a particular server—be aware that once the restricted box is checked, the changes are immediate.

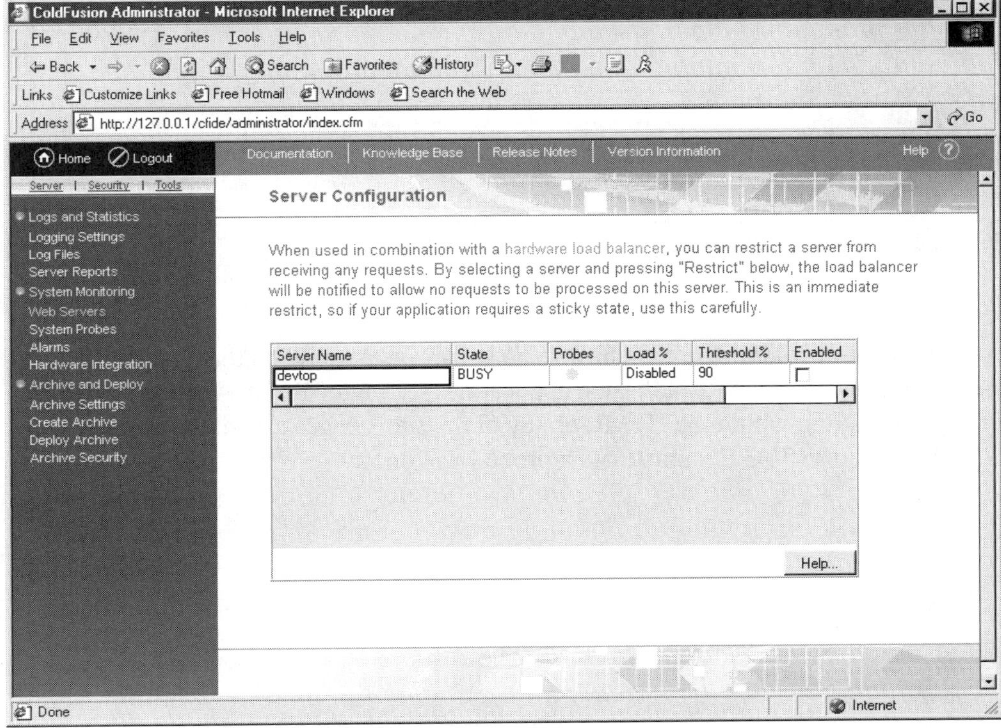

Figure 3-31 *Web Servers page*

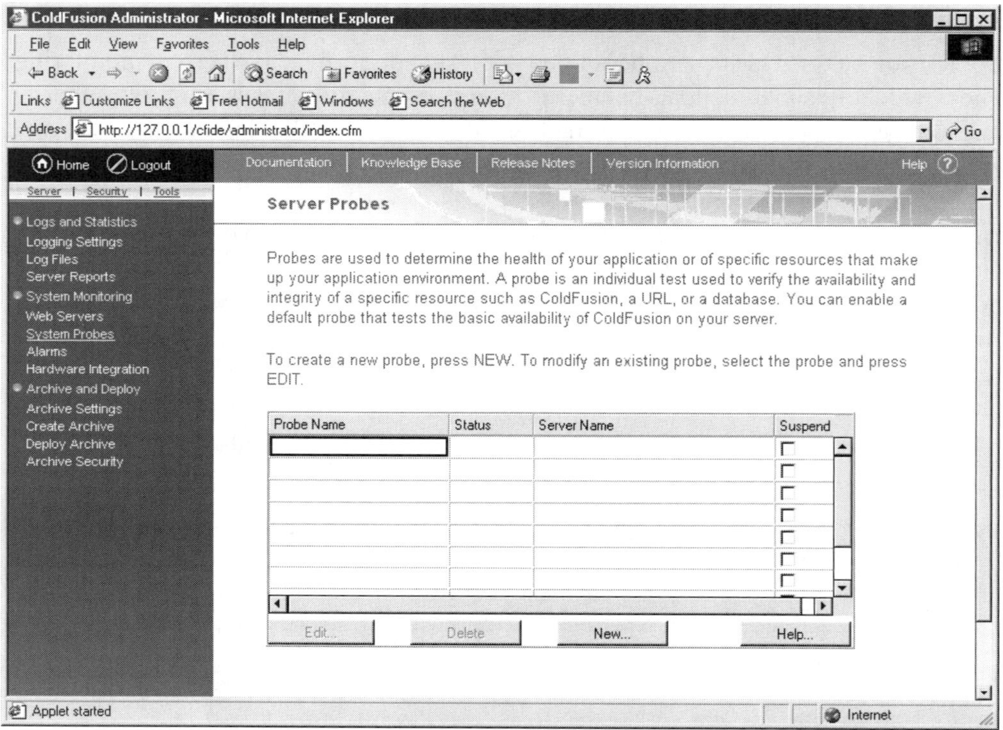

Figure 3-32 *System Probes page*

System Probes ColdFusion 5.0 allows you set up system probes that can be used to monitor the health of your ColdFusion application (see Figure 3-32). A probe can check for a certain string within the HTML of any of the site's pages to indicate that the site is healthy. Figure 3-33 demonstrates a probe I use on my server.

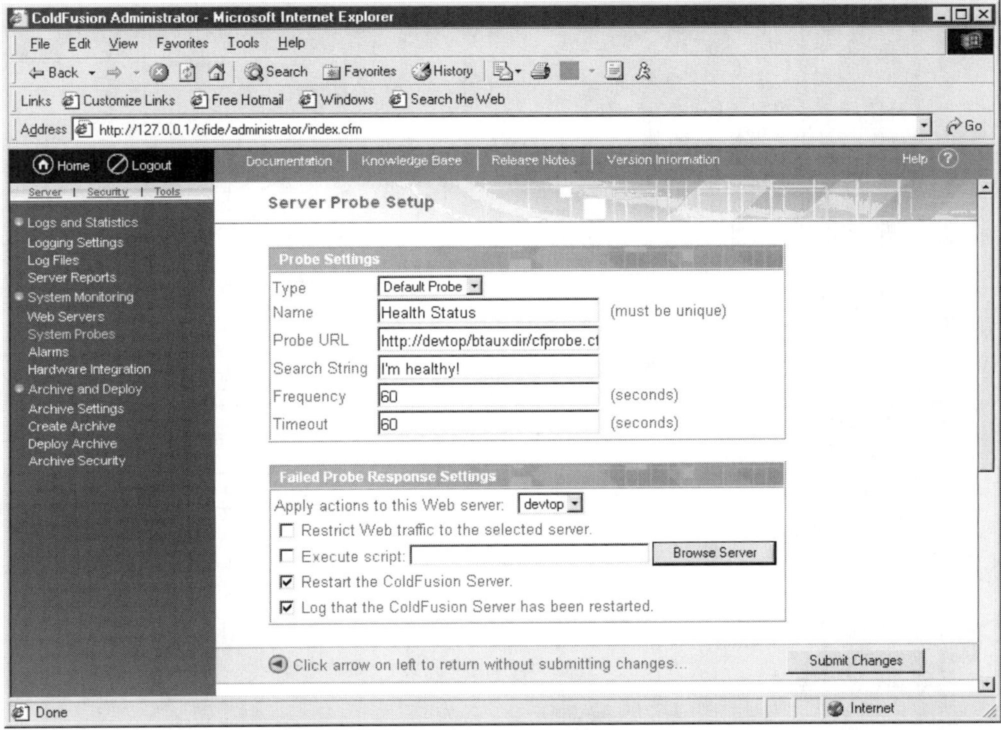

Figure 3-33 *Example of a server probe setup*

Alarms A useful feature of ColdFusion 5.0 is the ability to send e-mail to a list of recipients when the server has problems (see the Alarms page in Figure 3-34). On some of my servers I've set the ColdFusion Administrator to e-mail my e-mail capable phone, and it has come in very handy at times. There are, of course, ways to

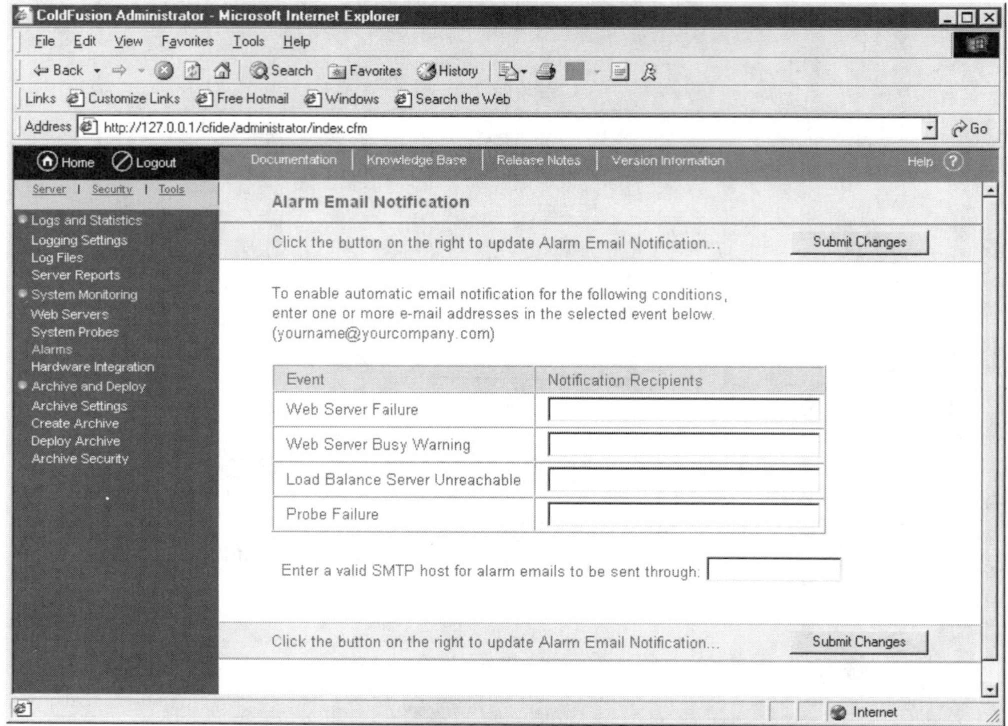

Figure 3-34 *Alarms page*

e-mail your phone when the server is down outside of ColdFusion, but ColdFusion does it so well, why bother with anything else?

Hardware Integration This section allows you to make a connection between a Cisco Local Director load-balancing switch (see Figure 3-35). ColdFusion has the ability to report to the Local Director about its status, and the Local Director in turn uses that information to decide which server to send a user to.

Archive and Deploy

ColdFusion 5.0 introduces a new feature in the ColdFusion Administrator called Archiving and Deployment. Using the ColdFusion Administrator, developers or site administrators can define a set of ColdFusion and other ColdFusion application-

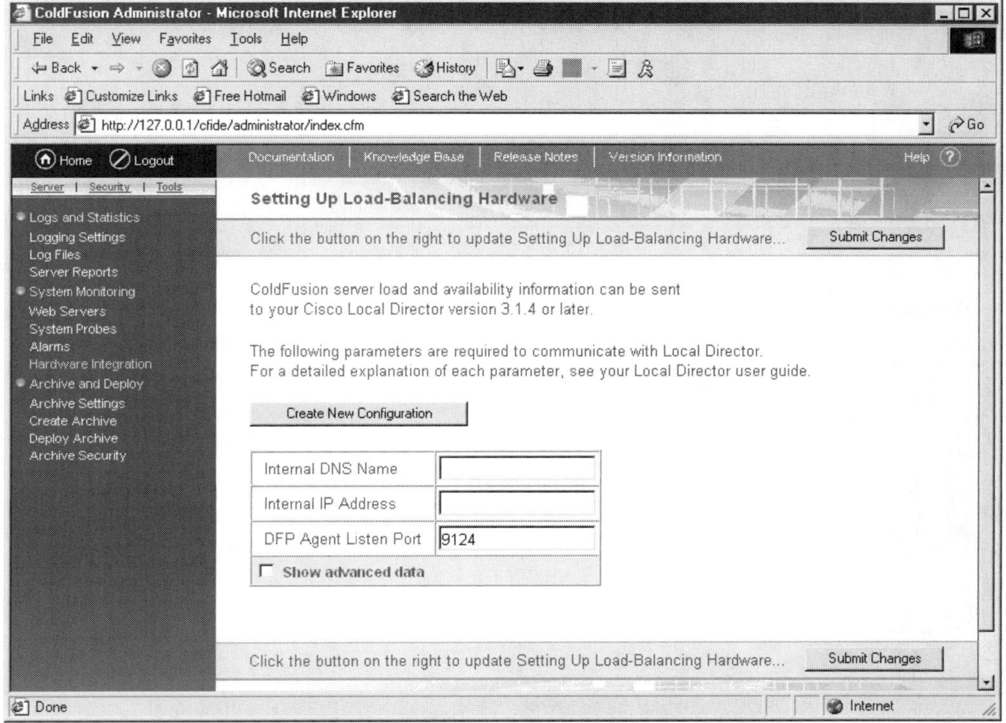

Figure 3-35 *Hardware Integration page*

related files, and make an archive that can be deployed later, or simply used as a means of backup.

The files in an archive are compressed just like a .zip file might be compressed, except that ColdFusion uses Sun Microsystem .jar compression technology. The files archives themselves are actually named .car (for *C*oldFusion *Ar*chive).

Archives can also store ColdFusion Administrator settings, making ColdFusion applications truly portable from one machine to another.

Let's briefly look at the menus within this section.

Archive Settings This page is where general archive-related settings are entered (see Figure 3-36). Let's look at each possible setting.

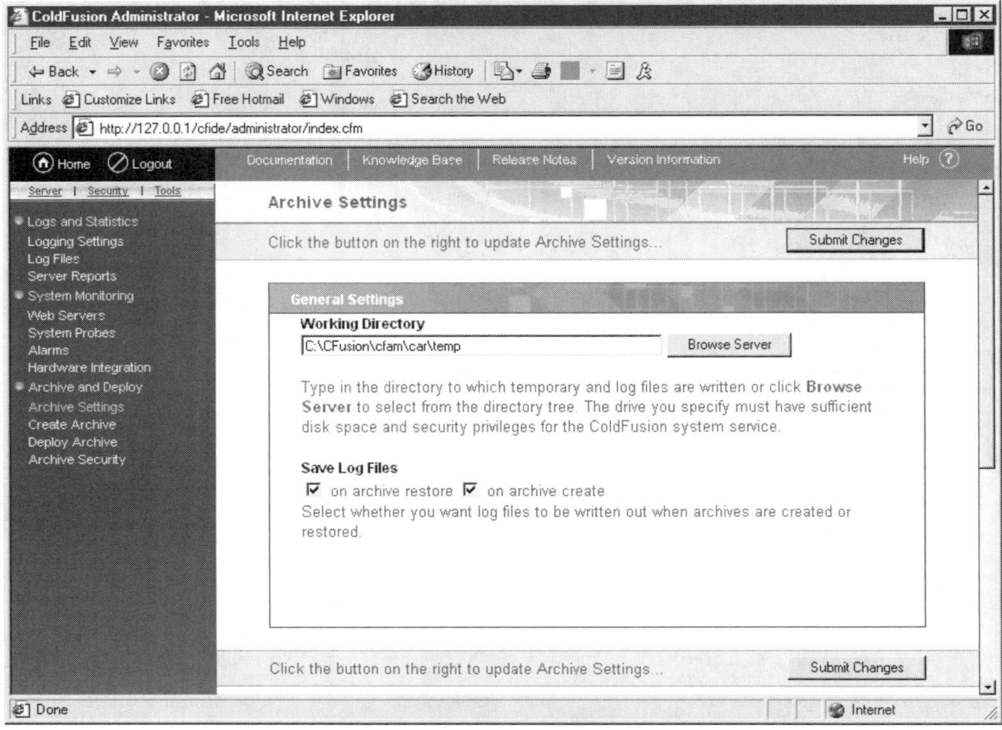

Figure 3-36 *Archive Settings page*

- **Working Directory** This directory is used by ColdFusion as a temporary folder for archival purposes. Care should be taken when you choose the drive and path; for each archive you need about double, if not triple, the space of the final archive available on the drive. The ColdFusion service must also have read and write permissions on that path.
- **Save Log Files** There are two possible settings under the Save Log Files subheading; on archive and archive create. Both are selected by default, and indicate that all archival actions are logged.

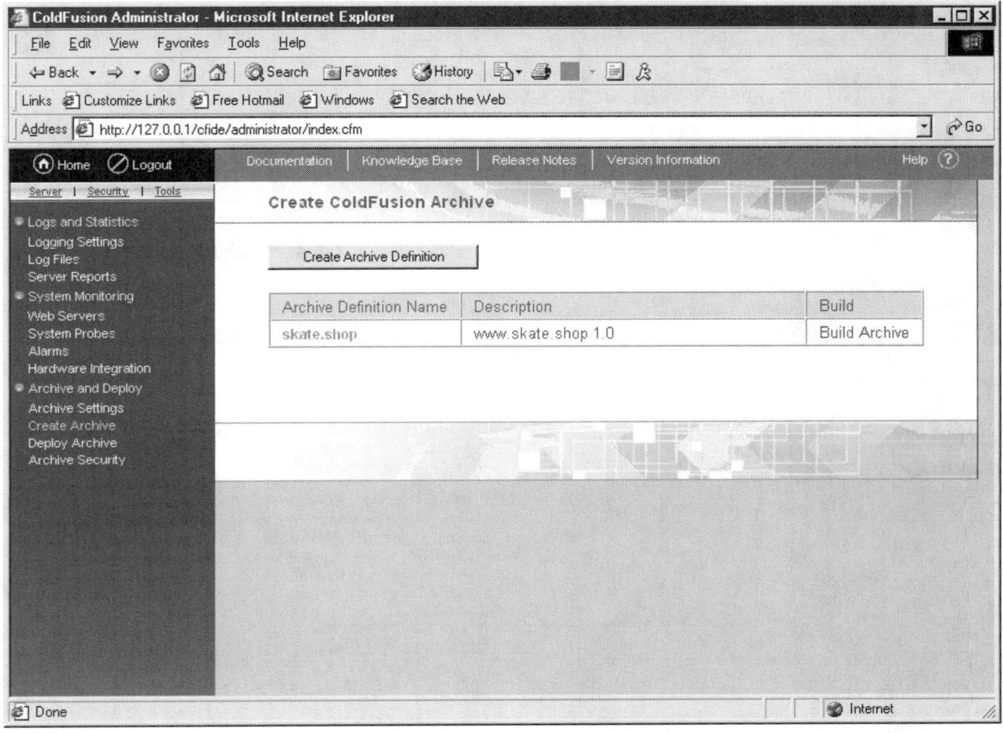

Figure 3-37 *Create Archive page*

Create Archive The Create Archive menu allows you to build a new archive (see Figure 3-37). Archives can contain almost anything you can think of when it comes to your ColdFusion application, including data source settings, CFX tags, mappings, and more. Figure 3-38 shows the first step in creating the www.skate.shop 1.0 archive. Each of the steps listed on the left pane can be configured to create a custom archive for your needs. The archive can then be scheduled to be built on a one-time basis, or even on a recurring basis.

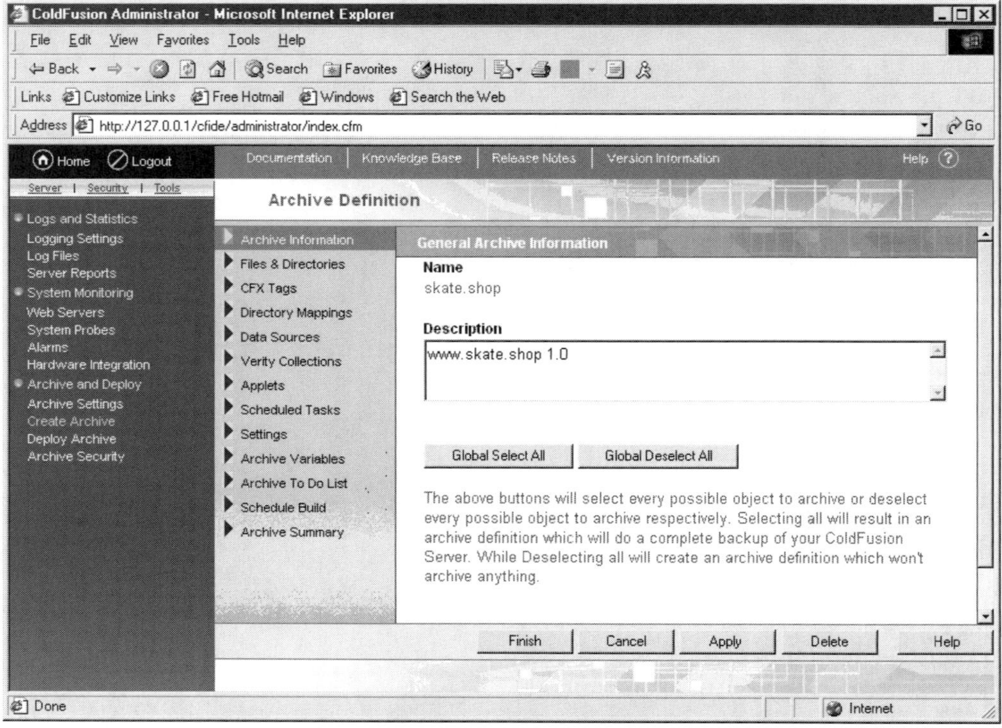

Figure 3-38 *The first step in creating an archive*

Deploy Archive Once an archive has been created, it can be retrieved and deployed on the server using the Deploy Archive page (see Figure 3-39). The archive itself doesn't have to originate from the same server—it can be on a different server, as long as you can get to it using FTP or HTTP. Once you've selected an archive and clicked Next, the archive restoration process will begin.

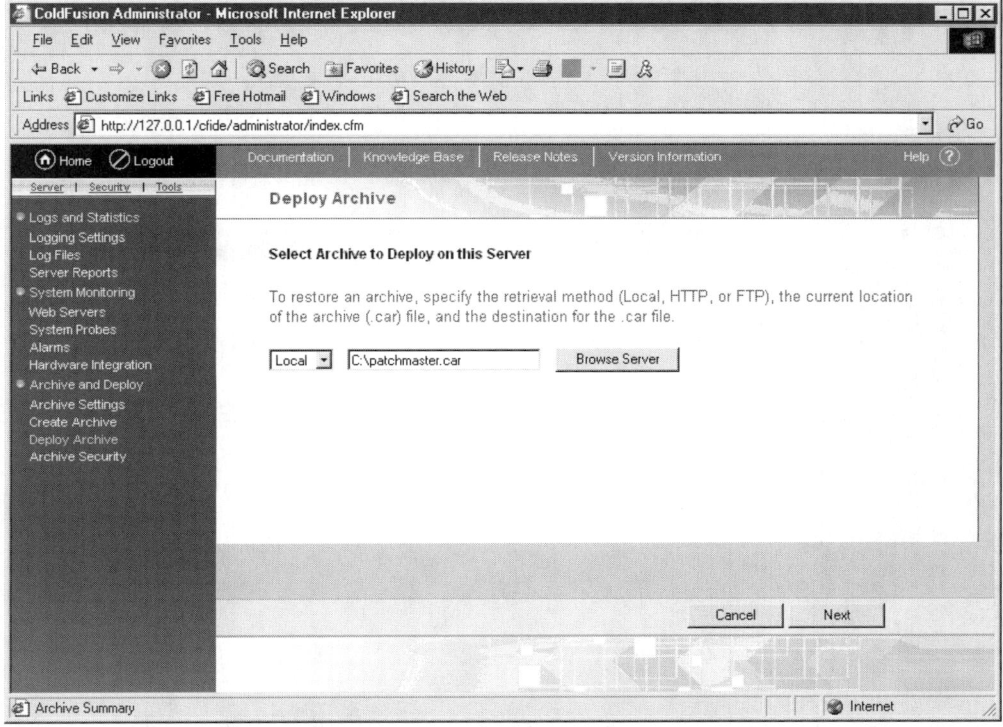

Figure 3-39 *Deploy Archive page*

Archive Security Archives can be signed with a digital key, or a certificate. Digital keys can be obtained from trusted sources like VeriSign. For more information about how to obtain a security certificate, visit http://www.verisign.com.

This menu also allows you to verify the signature of an archive received from another party (see Figure 3-40). The utility actually contacts the digital signature provider to see if the signature is indeed correct, and trusted. The digital signature provider informs you if the key, or signature, is forged or incorrect and shouldn't be trusted.

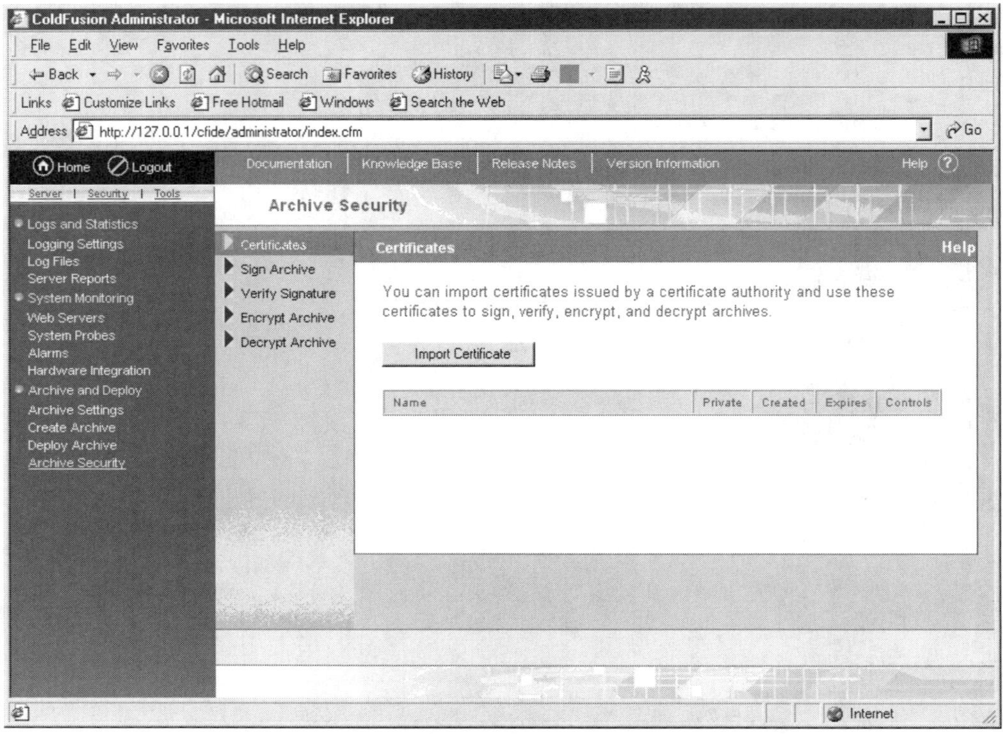

Figure 3-40 *Archive Security page*

Archives can also be encrypted using your own private key. If you intend to pass the archive on to another party, they'd need to know the private key to unlock the archive. Decrypting an archive involves the same process, but in reverse order. You need to know the key that the other party encrypted the archive with in order to decrypt it.

Database Connection Support

ColdFusion 5.0 now allows for a number of different ways to connect to a datasource through tags like <CFQUERY>. The *connectString* attribute has been introduced for tags that connect to a data source, and this new attribute allows you do a lot of interesting things.

The *connectString* attribute allows you to pass parameters to the data source that you otherwise wouldn't able to pass. For example, you could pass an application id value, which the SQL Server DBA would be able to use to determine which ColdFusion applications were using the most resources on the SQL Server.

The *connectString* attribute, combined with the *dbtype* attribute, allow a developer to make a connection to a database without setting up a datasource in the ColdFusion Administrator. We'll see some examples of how to use the *connectString* attribute effectively in Chapter 11.

New Tags

ColdFusion 5.0 introduces five new tags that provide functionality long requested by developers since the release of the last version. In this section, we talk about four of those five new tags. We're leaving out <CFGRAPHDATA> because it's a subtag of <CFGRAPH>, which we'll cover here.

It might take the wind out of some peoples' sails to know that there are only five new tags, but for those people I offer this explanation: Allaire, now Macromedia, has always been committed to compatibility. They have always been sensitive to developers who are upgrading from one server version to another. Maintaining a high amount of focus on compatibility, the developers of ColdFusion have always been careful about adding to or taking away its functionality. If a pile of new tags were introduced with every new server version, compatibility might go straight down the tubes.

<CFLOG>

To help compliment the new ColdFusion logging support, <CFLOG> has been introduced. <CFLOG> allows you to write an entry into the log files programmatically. Prior to ColdFusion 5.0, a developer had no control over log files, except. With <CFLOG>, programmers can include log writing as part of their error handling routines, or even non-error-related events.

To get an idea of what can be done with <CFLOG>, let's look at the following snippet of code. The code will record when a particular IP address accesses a template:

```
<cfif cgi.remote_addr eq IPToTrack>
   <cflog
   file="accesslog"
```

```
    application="no"
    thread="no"
    text="#cgi.remote_addr# has made contact">
</cfif>
```

In this example, we make a log entry for each time a user with a particular IP address executes the code. The file attribute in this case allows us to create our own log file in the C:\CFUSION\Log directory. There's no need to include the extension, and the file is created if it doesn't already exist. You cannot specify where you'd like log files to be created.

The following table shows the available <CFLOG> attributes, and their purposes.

Attribute	Description
text	This is the text message to write to the log. This attribute is required.
log	Optional. If you don't use the file attribute, then this attribute is required. This attribute has two possible values: Application (writes entries to the Application.log file) Scheduler (writes to the Schedule.log file)
file	Optional. When a filename is indicated, the file will be created in the C:\CFUSION\Log directory if the file doesn't already exist. Omit the extension name of the log (e.g., "AccessLog").
type	This attribute is optional, and indicates the severity of the log entry. The following values are valid: Information (default) Warning Error Fatal information
thread	Optional. This attribute accepts either a "yes" or "no" value. If the value is "yes," the current thread ID will be applied to the log entry. The default value is "yes."
date	Another optional "yes/no" attribute, if the date attribute is "no", the date will be excluded from the log entry. The default value is "yes."
time	Optional. If time is "no", the time will be excluded from the log entry. The default value for this attribute is "yes."
application	This optional attribute controls whether or not the name of the current application should be included in the log. This, of course, requires that the <CFAPPLICATION> execute before hand, with an application name assigned.

If you specify a file with the *file* attribute, the file will be available in the ColdFusion Administrator under the Tools | Log Files page. All of the features available to the default ColdFusion log files are also available to your custom log file. Based on what we learned earlier about the Logging System in ColdFusion, this has obvious benefits, such as the ability to filter the log file data.

The <CFLOG> file is a beneficial new tag that helps the developer create more robust applications, complete with the ability to write custom log entries for any number of different reasons. There is, however, the possibility of overdoing it; too many entries in the log file can clog up hard drive space, as well as slow the server down in general due to frequent disk writes. Discretion should be exercised when using the <CFLOG> tag, but don't let that warning stop you from using it entirely.

<CFFLUSH>

One of the biggest complaints made by both ColdFusion developers and users of ColdFusion sites in the past was that when users accessed ColdFusion-driven sites, the pages would take forever to load, until suddenly all the HTML was dumped to the browser at once. Normally, HTML is fed to the browser in a streaming fashion. The browser takes the HTML code as it streams and renders it on the fly.

Normally, the ColdFusion server will process ColdFusion templates entirely before being handed off to the web server. The web server will then pass the processed ColdFusion template to the user's browser just as it would any other HTML file. When ColdFusion is processing the ColdFusion template, it can give the user the illusion that things are moving slowly because of this lag. In reality, the speed isn't as slow as it's perceived, and this is something that <CFFLUSH> helps with in a great way.

<CFFLUSH> allows the developer to release whatever ColdFusion has completely processed to the web server, which in turn hands the completed HTML code to the user's browser. If the user is receiving content while the page is still processing, the lag time is no longer a factor. While the user will probably receive the final HTML document in about the same amount of time as they would without <CFFLUSH>, the perception is that the page is faster.

I suggest that the <CFFLUSH> enabled template might result in equal "final" times because it's hard to quantify the difference in speed. There are a lot of factors to take into account. For instance, in order to measure the exact amount of time it takes for a ColdFusion template to process isn't difficult; ColdFusion automatically provides those kinds of numbers in its debugging information, but once the document is handed off to the web server, more factors come into play. The system load of the web server is a factor at that point, but more importantly, the following factors make it very difficult to measure speed differences:

- The quality of the user's connection.
- The speed of the user's connection.
- The speed of the user's computer.
- The user's operating system.
- The user's browser (i.e. Opera, Internet Explorer, or Netscape to name the big ones).
- The version of the user's browser; some older browsers render HTML slower than newer ones.

Simply put, because of all of the things that can make a user's actual speed different, it's not safe to make an assumption that <CFFLUSH> can affect the "bottom line." It is, however, safe to assume that when <CFFLUSH> is used effectively that the user's perception of speed is improved greatly. If they simply believe that *something* is happening, the perception of speed is improved.

Let's look at an example of how to use <CFFLUSH> in your application. The example is just a snippet of code taken from an imaginary application, although you could easily use the snippet in any CFML template.

```
<cfset i = 1>
<cfloop from="1" to="1000" index="i">
   <cfoutput>#i#</cfoutput>
   <cfflush>
</cfloop>
```

In this example, for every iteration, or cycle of the loop, the <CFFLUSH> tag will send whatever the template has processed to the browser. If you were to execute this code, rather than waiting for the entire template to finish processing before seeing any numbers, with the <CFFLUSH> in place users would see numbers appear one after another on the screen, each getting "flushed" to the browser as the loop cycles.

It's also possible to be less precise with what gets flushed, using <CFFLUSH> to send content to the browser at certain byte-sized intervals. Consider the following code example:

```
<cfflush interval="100">
<cfset i = 1>
```

```
<cfloop from="1" to="250" index="i">
   <cfset n = 1>
   <cfloop from="1" to="250" index="n">
      <cfif n/200 eq int(n/200)>
         <cfoutput>#RandRange(1,i)#</cfoutput>
      </cfif>
   </cfloop>
</cfloop>
```

This script should take a little longer to run than the first example, due to the nested loop. In this example, the <CFFLUSH> tag is only needed once. Adding the *interval* attribute indicates that ColdFusion should flush the contents to the browser every 100 bytes. Just to make it interesting, the RandRange function will pick a number between one and whatever the value of *i* is, so the random numbers will probably start getting larger towards the end of the template processing.

<CFFLUSH> works by sending the HTML document headers to the browser upon the first execution or interval of the <CFFLUSH> tag. On following executions or intervals, it sends the data generated by ColdFusion to the browser. Because of the way <CFFLUSH> works, it shouldn't be used with ColdFusion tags that modify the header mid page, like <CFHEADER>. The following tags modify the HTML header, and therefore are incompatible with the <CFFLUSH> tag:

- <CFCONTENT>
- <CFCOOKIE>
- <CFFORM>
- <CFHEADER>
- <CFHTMLHEAD>
- <CFLOCATION>

Cookie variables set with the <CFSET> tag are incompatible as well. There are also some issues with using <CFERROR> and the <CFFLUSH> tag. <CFERROR>, when executed without <CFFLUSH>, replaces whatever ColdFusion has already processed with an error template. When used with <CFFLUSH>, anything that <CFFLUSH> has already sent to the browser will appear before the error template assigned in <CFERROR>. While this isn't the end of the world, it could confuse the user, or worse yet, expose information that might not be good to show the user.

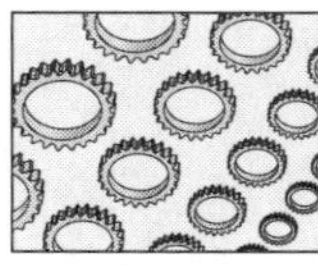

NOTE

We talk extensively about <CFERROR> in Chapter 14.

<CFDUMP>

Often when developing applications that make extensive use of arrays and structures, the meanings of the structures can get confusing. Sometimes it's difficult to figure out what information is getting sent to the structure without writing some code to loop over the structure or array to output the values. It can get even more difficult when the names of the keys in the structure are unknown.

<CFDUMP> provides a quick and easy way to "dump" the contents of a structure, array, or any of the following types of variable to the screen for analysis:

- Simple values. For example, consider the following: <CFSET simplevar = "hello">
- Query values.
- Structures.
- Arrays.
- WDDX values.

To use <CFDUMP>, simple use the following syntax:

```
<cfdump var="#varname#">
```

The *var* attribute is required. <CFDUMP> is a good tool for debugging purposes; in fact, it is designed with no other purpose in mind other than to provide the developer with information about their variables. Beyond debugging, there's not much more one could do with the information produced by <CFDUMP>.

<CFGRAPH>

One of the most interesting new features available to ColdFusion 5.0 is the graphing feature, which is implemented in CFML by using the <CFGRAPH> tag. We show some examples in Chapter 7 when we design an Administrator for a sample application.

To keep things moving along smoothly, we'll refrain from going over any examples here, and stick with talking about what <CFGRAPH> can do. <CFGRAPH> enables developers to create pie, line, and bar graphs using Macromedia Generator. The graphs by default are in the popular Macromedia Flash format, but can just as easily be formatted as GIF or JPG files.

Using <CFGRAPH>, developers can show a user an accurate and updated chart on the fly. <CFGRAPH> allows for a lot of customization, and is easily one of the most powerful new features in ColdFusion 5.0.

<CFSAVECONTENT>

<CFSAVECONTENT> allows the developer to save any information contained between the <CFSAVECONTENT> tags to a variable. Here's an example:

```
<cfsavecontent variable="newcontent">
   <cfoutput>
   #RandRange(1,200)#
   #RandRange(1,200)#
   <cf_customtag>
   </cfoutput>
   This is also included in the newcontent variable.
</cfsavecontent>
```

Everything between the <CFSAVECONTENT> tags is stored to the specified variable. CFML code within the tags is processed as it normally would be, and its generated contents are stored in the specified variable.

New Functions

There is only one new function in ColdFusion 5.0, and while it may only be one, it's a useful one. The function is called GetHTTPRequestData(). The following example uses the <CFDUMP> tag to display the structures created by the GetHTTPRequestData() function:

```
<cfset strHTTPHeader = GetHTTPRequestData()>
<cfdump var="#strHTTPHeader#">
```

User Defined Functions

ColdFusion 5.0 adds a lot of flexibility by introducing user defined functions (UDFs). UDFs allow a developer to create their own functions to perform repetitive tasks. For example, some applications might need to calculate the interest earned on a bank account for a period of a year. ColdFusion doesn't have a function for this, but with UDF, one can be created.

Queries of Queries

One of my favorite new ColdFusion 5.0 features is the ability to query a query. In ColdFusion 5.0, it's now possible to query a query object. For instance, imagine that you've created a query that pulled back a couple thousand records. Now imagine that you'd like to narrow down those thousand records to about ten or fifteen records. Rather than making another database call, you could query the first query, as if it were a table in a database. This obviously increases performance, and it's a quite useful new feature.

Wrapping Up

In this chapter, we've covered every possible new feature of ColdFusion 5.0. While it may seem like the Administrator may have just earned a few new features and face lift, with a few other things tossed in, in reality the new features make ColdFusion 5.0 a much more powerful piece of software. With the introduction of UDF and Query of Queries, the CFML language is greatly strengthened, and that alone might have been reason enough to call it greatly improved. Considering all of the other new features in both the Administrator and with improvements on performance, ColdFusion 5.0 is now more than ever a serious and competitive player in the web application business.

PART II

The Project

OBJECTIVES

- Discover planning methods for the software development process
- Show details of the planning phases for our sample application
- Learn about database forms and normalization
- Design and build the skate.shop database
- Build the skate.shop Administrator tool
- Process orders and create sales reports
- Build a maintenance scheduler
- Test and launch the site
- Monitor site performance and make adjustments as needed

CHAPTER

4

Project Planning

IN THIS CHAPTER:

Planning Methods for Software Development

Planning Our Sample Skate Shop Application

Before we write even a single line of code, we must do some planning. In this chapter, we discuss how to plan the software development process in general, and then we get into the specifics of creating a sample application. While I discuss the details about how to plan the development process, keep in mind that the methods that I suggest are only suggestions. There is no one perfect way. But, if you only take one thing away from this chapter—that you *must* plan your project—I will have accomplished something.

Planning Methods for Software Development

Development cycles apply to ColdFusion applications, just like any other type of software development process. Even if we just sit down with no planning whatsoever and code something, we're still following a development cycle. Consider the development cycle in the life of the application, from birth to maturity.

In ColdFusion development, I've seen three popular planning methods:

- **Back and Forth Method** The choice of the novice, unfortunately, this is probably the most frustrating form of development (especially while learning a new programming language). This method involves a programmer coding something, with requirements determined on the fly, as needed.
- **Waterfall Method** A structured form of development, with at least four phases, which include: requirements, design, development, and launch. Each phase can be broken down into more specific areas of focus. I like to include a testing phase between development and launch.
- **Spiral Method** Also known as the *Iterative method*, it is the Waterfall method, but as an ongoing and infinite process. It consists of the same phases as the Waterfall method, repeating with a new version of software once a launch has occurred.

Let's take a detailed look at the pros and cons of each development method.

Back and Forth Method

I'm sure most of you are familiar with this method. It has no phases; we just sit down with an idea and start coding. Once we've finished the project, we begin to realize that we want to add something here, or take away something there, and we begin to wish we had planned a little more.

The potential for frustration in this method is increased when we're writing the application for a client, or for the company we work for. We start to write an application, and either halfway through or at the end of the project someone who calls the shots adds a new requirement, and we have to go back into our application and squeeze in the new requirement.

The Back and Forth method is by far the most costly method. With little idea of what the final requirements of the project will be, we can spend precious time trying to figure out how to integrate new requirements as they are thought of. The developer begins to go crazy with all the code changes, and the person who calls the shots begins to get frustrated with the process, blaming the developer. The process is slow and cumbersome, deadlines are missed, and bugs are more prevalent.

Don't use this method if you can help it. Even on small, personal projects that beg for you to just speed along, it pays to use any other method but this one. In fact, this method is basically no method at all; development becomes chaotic, and no plan is followed consistently.

Waterfall Method

Unlike the Back and Forth method, this method is structured. Determining our requirements is the first step. Each phase of this method tackles a different development issue. Keep in mind that each phase is not limited to what I'm describing. While some people break the phases down, in this section I focus on only the most important steps. Most key planning issues are covered with the following phases: requirements, design, development, testing, and launch.

Requirements

This is where we brainstorm and lay out all possible requirements for our project. This phase isn't complete until we're absolutely satisfied that no other requirements can be thought of. It's possible that later on more requirements may come up, but we must be as diligent as we can be in finalizing the requirements in this phase. We also must be sure that all requirements are technically possible. If we know that something is impossible, it should not be a requirement. This will save us from having to discover the impossibility in the design phase, where it will result in wasted time and money.

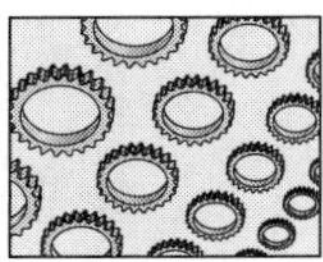

NOTE

In other types of development, like game development, coming up with technically impossible requirements is the norm. Games usually take several years to develop, and by the time the "technically impossible requirement" needs to be developed, it's technically possible, due to the advancements in graphics technology, or whatever it may be.

One of the most successful requirements phase I've seen accomplished was at Price.com. We set aside a room we called the "war room," which was used for nothing but planning. It was an area that didn't need to be cleaned for other meetings, and would remain in the same state from day to day (except for old pizza boxes and flat cans of soda). Its sole purpose was to allow unstructured, unrestricted brainstorming. One of four walls had a whiteboard.

When starting a new project, we would gather a member or two from each department, including management, marketing, development, IT, sales, and content, and we began brainstorming the requirements for the finished product. Someone would write on the whiteboard, and we'd all come up with ideas. While the idea itself might receive constructive criticism, no one was allowed to criticize someone else directly. This helped keep the flow of ideas coming, and helped keep tensions at ease.

Once the whiteboard was full of ideas, we began copying the common ideas onto large sheets of paper that were then taped to the walls. We'd almost always have duplicate ideas on the whiteboard, so the sheet of paper would usually contain a condensed list of the whiteboard contents.

We continued this process until all the ideas were being repeated. These repeated ideas would often end up being the core requirements.

If you're a single person team, you can still do this kind of brainstorming. If you have a project you're executing for a client, brainstorm with the client. You may be the only developer, but there are usually several people involved in the project that can and should be providing valuable insight. If you're a single-person team working on a personal project, brainstorm with friends and family. The more minds you have contributing ideas to the project, the better the final product will be. A final requirements document should come out of this phase, with a checklist of every requirement and descriptions of the project's goals and objectives.

Design

In this phase, we study the requirements, and think about how to execute each. We're not writing code yet; we're just thinking technically about how to actually make our requirements a reality. We develop program flowcharts, devise hardware requirements, prototype interface design, and begin to design our database. This phase is a final screen for impossible requirements, and should also prepare us completely for development. At the end of this phase, we should have no question as to what code to write, what graphics to produce, and how the site structure will be executed.

Development

During this phase, we build the project. It's crucial that this phase consist of development only—no design. If things are changing in this phase, it means we didn't spend enough time on the design phase, and we should stop development immediately.

Testing

If the development phase is complete, it's time to try and break our application. This phase is used to find and fix bugs. Development code goes onto staging servers that are as near as possible to the production servers, or *live servers*. You should have several people with different operating systems and browsers test your application, actively looking for ways to foul up the program.

It's a good idea to keep the bug list in a central location, either in a spreadsheet, a text file, or whatever works best. Developers should be able to look at this document and sign off on a fixed bug, adding comments if needed. Do not cut corners during this phase, because the next phase is the launch, and you don't want bugs in your launch.

Launch

This is the moment we've worked so hard for: the day we unveil our product to our users. If all the phases were executed properly, we should have a successful, bug-free launch. All of the pieces of the puzzle should be in place at this stage. The launch phase is less a phase than it is an event, although valuable information can be gathered to help improve the product. After the launch, we may get complaints or feedback from users. We should be storing this information in a central location (much like the bug reporting), and getting ready to use it to enhance the feature set.

The Waterfall method of development is effective. By defining specific phases of the project, it allows us to keep our minds on what's important when it's important. But, the Waterfall method isn't exactly complete. After watching users use our application, we get an even better idea of how to execute our product. That's where the Spiral method comes in.

Spiral Method

The Spiral method is a looping version of the Waterfall method. After the launch of the product, information is gathered to improve the next version of the site. Once the decision is made to generate a new version, the process is begun again. What makes this different from the Waterfall method is that the process truly starts from the beginning again, and the phases repeat, with a little variation.

Requirements

The project requirements from the first round are re-evaluated. A brainstorming session occurs for any new requirements, and user-requested requirements are discussed as well. A new document outlining the requirements of the next version of the application is written.

Design Just as in the Waterfall method, requirements are planned out. Requirements and features from the previous version are reevaluated, perhaps to speed up the features, or to modify the functionality to better suit the requirements. New program flow is created, as well as flowcharts, graphics, interface design, and so on.

Development

Whether you entirely recode the application or rebuild previous versions of code is up to you. Personally, I like to see the code rebuilt. Newer versions of code are almost always cleaner, faster, and more organized.

Testing

Testing occurs just as it did in the previous version.

Launch

The new version of software is launched just like the previous version.

The Spiral method is also sometimes known as the Iterative method, because it loops infinitely. (Well, eventually you stop making new versions, I'd hope, but you get the idea.)

Other Planning Methods

The three preceding methods are certainly not the only methods available, nor the best, but I believe they're the basis of almost any other method. Some methods may be more efficient than others, and may suit different organizations better. I would stress that you at least follow any organized development cycle. Using the Back and Forth method is an exercise in frustration, and should be avoided. Anything other than that method will most likely be more productive.

Planning Our Sample Skate Shop Application

The first two phases of our development cycle are the *requirements* and the *design* phase. Because I'm developing our sample application from the perspective of a single-person team, I need to cover some development-related issues first, which include preparing the directory structure for our application on the staging server, setting up the web site in Internet Information Server (IIS), and a few other tasks as well.

These tasks allow us to prepare for the coding, which starts in Chapter 6. In a team environment, we'd probably have someone in the design phase whose sole responsibility would be to worry about the *serving* part of our application. During development, they'd worry about setting up IIS, making sure that the developers have development servers, and that the proper directories, based on our design, exist on the server.

Determining Our Project's Requirements

There are several steps within phase one of our development cycle. We'll look at each step in detail, specifically focusing on our sample application.

The Idea—skate.shop

Before we can start a new project, there has to be an idea. I thought it would fun to build an online skateboard shop. I've loved skateboarding since I was a little kid, and still skateboard regularly to this day.

The idea to use a skateboard shop as the sample application isn't a random one. An online store covers a lot of ColdFusion techniques and principles, from beginning to advanced, and can be easily used in a real-world situation. Making the site skateboarding-related keeps it somewhat colorful and casual, and certainly less typical. I could have profiled a computer store, but the idea is to prevent you from falling asleep.

The skateboard shop is not just a sample application—it's also a real-world idea. I've been developing the idea for a while now, and it will likely be opened as a real business sometime soon. Because it's a real idea, the following chapters focus on real-world problems and issues. If you decide to use the code samples in this book to open up a ColdFusion-powered site, then I'll be pleased to know I might have helped or inspired you in some way. If you open up a skateboard shop to compete with me using the code in this book, then I'll simply have to work a bit harder at selling skateboards!

From now on, to be consistent, let us refer to the sample application as skate.shop.

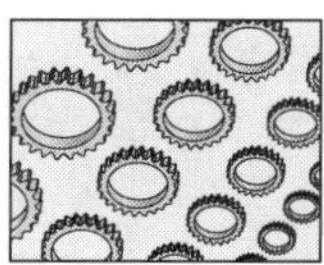

NOTE

I actually own the domain http://www.skate.shop. The domain uses the new top-level domains available at http://www.new.net. If the new domains become widely used, then I'll probably set up shop there. If not, I'll have to use an alternative.

Brainstorming

This is the second-best part of the project (the first being the launch). Every idea is valid, every thought counts, and nothing is yet impossible or unreasonable.

Here's what I do when I brainstorm. For this project, I'm a single-person team, but the same method of brainstorming can be used in a team environment (5–10 people maximum). I get out a piece of paper and begin writing ideas. (See Figure 4-1 for an actual brainstorming session for skate.shop.) The ideas may or may not end up in the final product, but you have the luxury of deciding what's *not* going into the final product. It's much easier to take ideas out of the project than it is to add them.

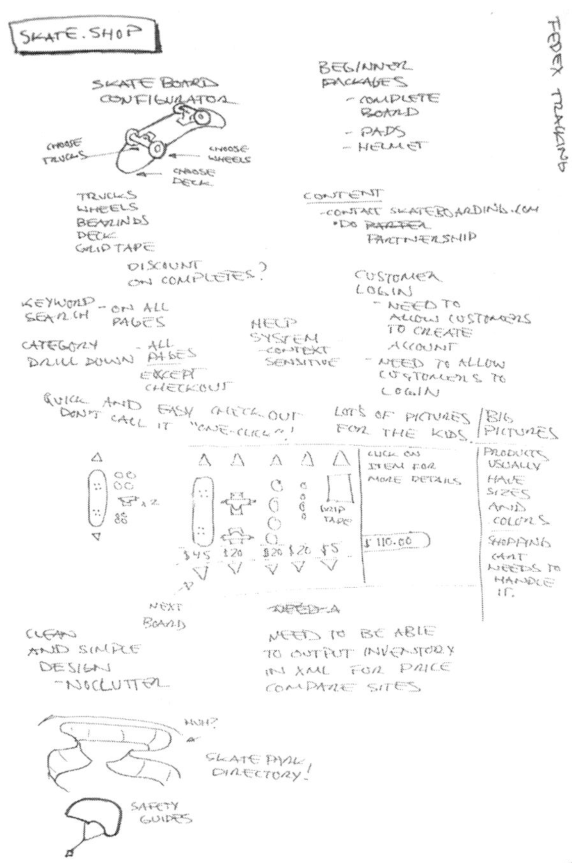

Figure 4-1 *An actual brainstorm session for the skate.shop application.*

I'm a visual person, so I usually doodle. This sketch is actually much cleaner than most of the ones I do. Yes, that is my normal handwriting. Brainstorming isn't always an easy process. Some days the ideas don't flow, and some days they flow like the hot lava out of a volcano (sometimes in the middle of the night when you'd much rather be asleep). I usually have a notepad on me at all times so that I can write down ideas about the site. Then, when I get a chance, I'll update my master list. In a team environment, chances are that with several people in a "war room" type of environment, the ideas will come fairly easily. If no one's cylinders are firing, divert attentions to something else.

I like to refer to Price.com when I talk about brainstorming, because I think we did a good job at it. We were all either young, or young at heart, and if we got stuck with no flow of ideas, we'd do something off the wall.

One of the things we did to divert our attention was invent a new sort of game that we called "Kung Fu Kickball". There were two participants in the game, and they would stand about 20 feet apart. One of the players would try to kick a tennis ball as hard as possible at the other contestant while making an appropriate "Kung Fu" noise. The "receiver" was free to cover certain sensitive or easily damaged areas with their hands, but was not allowed to move. If they were going to get hit in the gut, they'd have to take it. Once the kick was complete, the receiver would then get his/her turn to kick. If the "kicker" failed to make a "Kung Fu" noise they missed a turn kicking. It's sounds completely dangerous and stupid, and it was. We rarely hit each other however, because we just weren't very good at aiming, and inevitably it would be a bystander that got hit. If Erik Goodlad (the technical editor of this book and a co-founder of Price.com) was nearby, it would usually hit him square in the forehead.

The brainstorming session should produce enough ideas to form a list of features, or requirements.

Spotting Requirements

During the brainstorming session, you'll come up with as many ideas as possible. Some of them will be so out of this world that they'll need to be ignored. Some, if analyzed by a doctor, might win you a free vacation to a place where everyone wears white slippers and eats vanilla custard for breakfast. Pull out the best do-able ideas from the brainstorming session, and make a list of them.

You'll probably find that some of the ideas are nearly the same, or can be rolled into the same idea. Try to condense your list as much as possible, combining ideas that are nearly the same. Take your list and prioritize the most important ideas. Here are the ideas I pulled out of my brainstorming session. They're not in any particular order—just the order on the page, and none have been left out:

- Skateboard configurator
- Beginner packages
- Syndicated skateboarding-related content
- FedEx tracking
- Keyword search
- Category drill-down
- Context-sensitive help
- Customer login
- Fast checkout
- Shopping cart
- Web-based order processing

This list of ideas is basically a first round. It is a good idea to have a few more brainstorming sessions and add any new ideas, or get rid of the weaker ones. I think my list of ideas is pretty complete, at least for the purposes of discussion in this book, so we'll make them official.

Making Requirements Official

Once you've decided that your idea list is good, and nothing more can be added, make an official list. I like to make a table with ideas organized by categories, with details of each feature.

This list serves as your final requirements document. Table 4-1 shows how the skate.shop document ended up.

Interface	Description
Keyword search	Customers should be able to search for products using a keyword search engine. Product results should be displayed organized by categories, then manufacturer name, with thumbnail images representing each product.
Category drill-down	Customers are able to click on links, drilling down through categories to a list of product results with thumbnail images representing each product. The fewest number of clicks should be required to find a product. The category drill-down menu is available on every page.
Customer login	Customers can log in to take advantage of user-specific settings, and to speed up the checkout process. New customers are able to create an account, protected by a login and password. New customers can create an account during checkout, or by clicking on a "create account" link.
Fast checkout	Customers are asked as little information as possible, to speed up the checkout process. Order totals should be available as soon as possible in the process. The customer are shown what steps they've completed, what step they're on, and what steps still need to be completed. At the end of the order process, an order number is displayed clearly stating that the order is in the system, and a confirmation of shipping is received by e-mail. An e-mail will is also be sent with the same statements, and other important information.

Table 4-1 *The Final Requirements for skate.shop*

Interface	Description
Shopping cart	Customers are able to preview standard shipping charges by entering their ZIP code into the shopping cart. The shopping cart and its contents is visible on all pages. The shopping cart handles sizes, colors, and quantities.
Content	
Syndicated content	A content provider is used to supply skateboarding-related content.
Help system	Skateboarding-specific terms and jargon are linked to definitions contained in the Help system. Customers are able to click on information links throughout the site that explain how to use the shopping cart, how to check out, and so on. Customers are able to browse the Help system and search the Help system.
Marketing	
Beginner packages	Beginner package promotions appear on the site, allowing customers to purchase a discounted package of products, including skateboards and safety accessories.
Back End	
Order processing	Employees of skate.shop need to be able to see new incoming orders. They need to be able to print orders to hand off to the Fulfillment department. Employees must be able to export e-mail lists and mailing addresses to a text file for later use. Demographic information, such as product popularity and conversion rates, needs to be available.

Table 4-1 *The Final Requirements for skate.shop* (continued)

Designing the Project Feature Set

Sometimes it's easy to confuse the requirements phase with the design phase. When you're in the requirements phase, you're brainstorming. You're defining the scope and abilities of the application. You're defining *what* the program will do.

In the design phase, you're figuring out *how* you're going to execute the project. The design phase lays out the technical specifics of each requirement set forth in the first phase.

Adopting a Code Standard

You'd think having a code standard would be a no-brainer, but you'd be surprised how many projects I've seen that didn't even consider using a code standard. A code standard is way of writing your code that's organized and easy for other developers to work with (without having to read minds), and that follows a certain type of logic that's relatively easy to understand.

ColdFusion as a language works fine with or without a code standard. If you want to make piles of messy spaghetti code, you've got plenty of room to do it with ColdFusion. But spaghetti code is usually crawling with bugs. And fixing those bugs can be an utter nightmare!

Use a code standard! Any code standard will do. Just use one! If you invent your own standard, make sure it's documented. If you don't want to invent your own, people have already done the work for you.

The guys at www.fusebox.org have put together a code standard that has seen widespread popularity, and is getting used more and more all the time. Most organizations that use the Fusebox methodology add their own twists, but for the most part, it follows a well-established standard. People have used the standard on large sites, and haven't seen any performance loss. Those who use it claim it's much easier to work with once you understand the methodology.

I've also been reading more about another ColdFusion code standard called SmartObjects (http://www.smart-objects.com). SmartObjects is different from Fusebox. It requires that some custom tags be installed on the server, and uses a more object-oriented approach.

For skate.shop, we're going to use our own homebrewed code standard. It's simple, so it should be simple to explain, and uses custom tags almost exclusively. Don't be surprised if it looks like Fusebox. It's not exactly intentional, and it's not exactly coincidence either. I've used a lot of different flavors of coding, and Fusebox happens to be one of them. If some Fusebox has rubbed off on me, you may see it in our application.

When I develop a code standard for a project, I make a list of rules on how to handle things. These rules are somewhat driven by the requirements phase, but for the most part originate in this design phase. I put the standard in a document for documentation purposes, and then I make sure my code follows the standard.

The skate.shop Code Standard

I feel that the document can be somewhat informal, or even conversational. It doesn't have to be strictly a technical document. It can simply be paragraphs and examples of how you want the application to be structured. The next few sections set the rules for the skate.shop site.

Top-Level Pages Our site consists of several top-level pages. For example, we'll have an index.cfm for our home page, and a product_details.cfm page for product details. Each of these top-level pages is actually just a shell for a more important document called content.cfm, which controls all the content of the site. I'll describe what it does in a second, but first we need to know the details of our top-level pages. The reason I call the top-level pages "shells" is because, like the shell surrounding the chocolate in M&Ms, our top-level pages surround content.cfm. Here's an example of one:

```
<cfset request.page = "foo">
<cfinclude template = "content.cfm">
```

I do this because the content.cfm file is really where all the action of our application is going to take place. I could get away with not having top-level pages at all, but I think it helps, at least slightly, to clean up and simplify the URL. For example, look at the difference between these two URLs.

```
http://www.skate.shop/content.cfm?page=foo
```

Versus:

```
http://www.skate.shop/foo.cfm
```

You ask, "Who looks at or cares about the URL?" Well, who knows for sure, but I bet some people do, and it's a detail that I like to pay attention to. The URL may end up with a ton of other parameters attached to it, making it seem a bit silly to worry about the URL, but it has other benefits also. If I were trying to hack a site, and I saw that every single action went through a content.cfm file, I might give content.cfm extra focus, and try to break the content.cfm file.

While writing code, it's easier to refer to a top-level page like foo.cfm than it is to refer to content.cfm?page=foo. Why have one file that controls everything in the first place? Well, it's efficient and it helps organize your application. Let's look at some code from a sample content.cfm file:

```
<cfswitch expression="#request.page#">
  <cfcase value="foo1">
  Foo1 related content/logic goes here
  </cfcase>
  <cfcase value="foo2">
  Foo2 related content/logic goes here
  </cfcase>
</cfswitch>
```

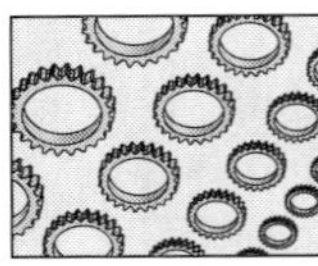

NOTE

*We use the **Request** scope because anything within that scope is available to all custom tags or modules. The variables are scoped just for that particular request, and are purged once the request has been fulfilled. The **Request** scope is a structure, so you can also pass structures to every included custom tag using the **Request** scope. For now, it's not all that important that we know what scoping means; we'll cover it more in Chapter 6.*

In one file, I can quickly look at the top-level logic of nearly every part of my application. Within each cfcase, I'll go further and make sure each block of logic is as efficient and organized as possible, either by using <CFMODULE> or <CFINCLUDE>, or by using custom tags.

Some may not feel that this is efficient, but I've seen this organization work extremely well, even on very large applications, and that's why I continue to use it. You might decide there's a better way, and that is one of the strong points of ColdFusion—it's flexible, and it allows for a lot of creativity.

Content.cfm Content.cfm is like a receptionist. It screens incoming calls, or requests, and routes the caller to the proper channels. Content.cfm should be as organized as possible. There should be minimal amounts of HTML code in the file itself. HTML code should be included using the <CFINCLUDE> tag, or by using <CFMODULE>, or custom tags. It's not required, but it makes the file cleaner. It pays to keep content.cfm clean because you'll be editing it a lot, and if it's not clean, it can become a real headache (but not nearly as big a headache as trying to track down a bug in a half-dozen standalone files with no organization).

Content.cfm keeps your program flow more organized. Because the flow of the application is controlled by content.cfm, and each file within the application is referenced in content.cfm, it's easy to tell what files are involved in the part of the application you're working on. Let's look at a more detailed version of content.cfm:

```
<!--- include any custom functions --->
<cfinclude template="functions/general.cfm">

<!--- include queries --->
<cfinclude template="queries/global.cfm">
<cfinclude template="queries/main_switch.cfm">
<!--- call the general page modules --->
<cfmodule template="modules/general/page_title.cfm">
<cfmodule template="modules/spiderweb/meta_gen.cfm">
<cfmodule template="modules/display/style.cfm">
<cfmodule template="modules/general/html_wrapper.cfm">
```

```
<cfflush interval="10">
  <!--- include the site HTML --->
  <cfmodule template="modules/display/master.cfm">
    <!--- main switch for the pages --->
    <cfswitch expression="#request.page#">
      <cfcase value="home">
        <cfmodule template="modules/pages/home/home.cfm">
      </cfcase>
      <cfcase value="results">
        <cfmodule template="modules/pages/results/results.cfm">
      </cfcase>
      <cfcase value="details">
        <cfmodule template="modules/pages/details/details.cfm">
      </cfcase>
      <cfcase value="checkout">
        <cfmodule template="modules/pages/checkout/checkout.cfm">
      </cfcase>
      <cfcase value="help">
        <cfmodule template="modules/pages/help/help.cfm">
      </cfcase>
    </cfswitch>
  </cfmodule>
</cfmodule>
```

The first four lines of code handle the HTML formatting of our site. They're left out of the main switch because we want them to execute on every page that calls content.cfm. We'll look at each of the modules a little later on.

The <CFSWITCH> tag is where the main logic of our application takes place. If the top-level page is set to "Help," the Help module is loaded. The help.cfm module is a separate application of its own, looking very similar in code structure to content.cfm, except that it sets up a switch that deals with help-specific logic only. Every main page on our site is basically a separate application. Some of the applications pass off information to each other, but for the most part, they worry about themselves.

Separate Application Concept Each main page on our site should be a separate application. The Help module, for example, has its own logic separate from the logic for the rest of the site. For example, here's some sample code from the help.cfm file we call in the content.cfm file:

```
<!--- help switch --->
<cfswitch expression="#request.action#">
  <cfcase value="browse">
```

```
    <cfmodule template="modules/pages/help/browse.cfm">
  </cfcase>
  <cfcase value="search">
    <cfmodule template="modules/pages/help/search.cfm">
  </cfcase>
  <cfcase value="results">
    <cfmodule template="modules/pages/help/results.cfm">
  </cfcase>
  <cfcase value="terms">
    <cfmodule template="modules/pages/help/terms.cfm">
  </cfcase>
</cfswitch>
```

We don't need to include any of the HTML formatting modules in help.cfm, because they're already executed in content.cfm. Some of the included modules in the help.cfm file might also have their own switches.

Designing Program Flow

Our program needs to have a certain flow of logic in order to work at all. We've peeked at a little bit of that logic by looking at the content.cfm file, but we haven't gone into detail about the actual flow of the entire application.

Understanding the Different Parts of Our Application If we look at our project requirements, it's easy to determine that nearly each of the major requirements is a separate application. Most of the applications work closely with the other applications, but in reality, they each deal with their own thing. By separating each of these mini- applications into their own pieces of logic, we'll be much more organized in how we accomplish our task.

The concept of mini-applications also allow different members of the development team to work on different parts. Each mini-application could also follow the Spiral method, with separate planning sessions, design, development, and eventually new versions. For our little skate.shop, we won't be versioning, but we will be planning, designing, and developing. Hopefully most of the planning has already been done, but there are still things to consider, like program logic for each mini-application.

Let's focus on two of the mini-applications, the shopping cart and keyword search and results, so we can get a good idea of how they interact with each other.

Keyword Search Planning

Let's do a little mini planning session for the keyword search. We already know the following about it:

- A user needs to be able to enter a keyword, press Search, and be presented with a list of possible matches to the keyword.
- A list of results with product images for each result, organized by category, then by manufacturer, and then by product name, needs to be shown.

Here are some details we didn't think of in the main planning session. It's OK that we missed them the first time around; the overall requirements for the project are the same, whether we think of new details for each main requirement or not.

If the search doesn't produce any results, launch a little helper application that tries to walk the user through a search, by asking the following questions and making suggestions:

- Spell check the keyword—if it seems misspelled, ask "Did you mean *x*?" You might search for an intentionally misspelled word on Google.com.
- Present the user with a list of categories that might contain the product. (Incidentally, this will be the same category list as in the drill-down box, only larger, and broken down into a hierarchy tree.)
- Inform the user that the shop owners have been notified of the request, and that if they supply their e-mail address, the owner will notify them of the location of the product, or when and if the product will be carried.

With those new features in mind, we're better prepared to begin thinking about how we can accomplish the design task.

Keyword Search Design

When we design our application, or mini-application in this case, it helps to create a document that lists each major requirement, along with a paragraph or two about how to implement it. This document becomes our design document. For each phase of the development cycle, we should have detailed documentation. For the keyword search, we can condense our requirements with proposed implementation of the keyword search feature, as follows.

The keyword search takes input from the user through the text field of a form element, which is used to generate a query using the SQL Server 2000 full text index on the *Products* table. If products exist containing the supplied keyword, a results page lists the results by category, by manufacturer, and then by product name. Each product has an image depicting the product. The thumbnail images are referenced in the *Products* table, and images themselves are stored in a directory on the server.

If no products are found based on the keyword, the following actions are taken, and items displayed:

- The keyword is sent through a custom spell check tag. If the tag determines that the word may be spelled incorrectly, a message is displayed to the user asking if they meant to search on the correctly spelled keyword. The user can click on the message, initiating a search using the correctly spelled keyword. If the spell check tag determines that the keyword is spelled correctly, no message is displayed.
- A full expanded category tree is shown to the user, with the message "Would the product you're looking for be in one of these categories?" The user is free to review these categories just as he/she would normally.
- A message is displayed indicating that the site owners have been notified of the user not being able to find a product. If the user enters an e-mail address, the e-mail address is stored in a separate table solely for product notifications. The site owners send e-mail to the user if the product was found on the site or is added by the site owner, or if it will ever show up at all. Site owners need to be able to let a user know if a product is discontinued, or if the site has no plans to sell the item. The user is also told that the e-mail data entered will be used only for product notification purposes, and that once notified, the e-mail would be purged.

So that's basically *how* the design part of the process is done. We don't need full-blown technical details yet. Major technical details will surface during development, when we write documentation for our modules. It's nearly impossible to pin down every technical detail in the design phase—we may not know yet exactly how we'll program a module—if we did, we'd be developing it, rather than designing it. We will do our best though to make sure that all our bases are covered before hand with flowcharts and pseudocode.

Shopping Cart Planning

Let's do the same thing for the shopping cart. We know our requirements:

- The shopping cart must be able to accept a product ID, and possibly a quantity, size, and color.
- The shopping cart adds up and displays the total price of all the items in the cart.
- The customer is then able to enter their ZIP code into the card for standard shipping and tax information.
- A check button then allows the user to start the checkout process.
- The shopping cart displays on every page.

Here are some new features discovered in a mini-planning session:

- When a user changes the quantity of a product in the cart to zero, the item should be removed from the cart.
- The user should only have to click one button to update multiple products in the cart.

I don't think we need to see the paragraph or two about how to implement this—it's basically an echo of the requirements, with a little more detail than we've seen already. If you feel you need the practice, give the implementation statement a shot.

Making a Draft of the Flow It always helps to use a program like Visio, or to just draw shapes on paper to indicate how the program will flow. Visio costs money, and I'm cheap, so I stick with paper when it comes to relatively simple projects like skate.shop. I sometimes also sketch the flow out on paper first, just so I don't spend a lot of time messing around in Visio with all of its pretty shapes and connector bars. I find that I spend more time in Visio trying to make a fancy flowchart than I do actually making a functional flowchart, so giving myself a rough draft on paper first is helpful. Figure 4-2 showns what my hand-drawn flowchart for the keyword search ended up looking like.

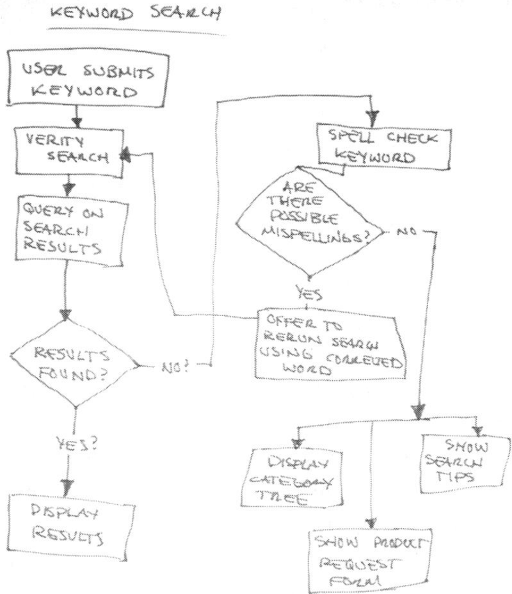

Figure 4-2 *A hand-drawn flow chart for the keyword search portion of the skate.shop application.*

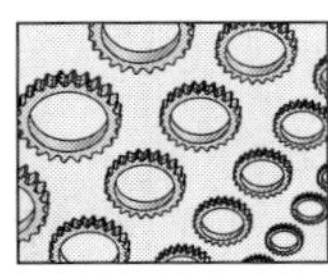

NOTE

People make jokes all the time about how they learned everything they needed to know in Kindergarten, so I won't go there, but I will say that it's pretty ironic that I used to get punished in grade school for drawing little pictures, and now it's an important part of my job.

Each mini-application within our main application should get a flowchart. Eventually, we'll be able to make an overview flowchart with less detail that simply shows how each mini-application deals with the other mini-applications.

Pseudocode I don't know how widespread the use of pseudocode is, but I do know that it helps me a lot in the development process. It's part of the design phase, but you'll probably find yourself doing some pseudocode just to double check the flow of things before you go crazy programming something. Pseudocode is pretend code—you quickly, in nearly plain English, sketch out how the actual code looks for something. Here's an example of some pseudocode for the keyword search:

- User submits form with keyword.
- Keyword is sent to search stored procedure.
- Stored procedure generates results.
- If rows are greater than zero, show results.
- If rows are zero, show help messages.

That's almost so simple it's stupid, and might even seem like an unimportant step. If your mind is crystal clear on how you want to program something, you probably don't need this kind of thing, but if you're like most developers, you probably have a hundred things going on at once, and having a nice little roadmap is a welcome aid.

Another thing writing pseudocode does for you, aside from all the documentation benefits, is that it helps you think abstractly about what the code does. By generating pseudo code, you may discover pitfalls in the logic that may be a lot harder to fix once you've generated a ton of code for a particular application.

Pseudocode, as well as anything else documentation related, helps on a lot of levels. Documentation is used to bring new programmers up to speed. It helps you refresh your memory after a break. It also helps with legal issues, including intellectual property issues, and patent-related things. I'm not a patent lawyer or an intellectual property lawyer, but I've talked with a few in my day, and most are thrilled when a project is fully documented from planning to launch. Nothing makes an IP lawyer more giddy than a pile of documentation.

Finalizing the Flow Once you've gone over your flowchart sketches, more refined Visio charts, and pseudocode, and you're confident the project is planned to the brink of destruction, finalize the process.

Make one master flowchart that shows each mini-application, and how they interact with each other, and make sure everything seems right. This master flowchart serves as your blueprint, and shouldn't change much.

Defining the Hardware Requirements

I bet you thought that with the creation of our final flowchart we were all set, and ready to develop. Not yet, sorry to say. We need to think about what kind of hardware we need. It's usually pretty easy to determine. We know we need a ColdFusion server, and we know we need a database server. Sometimes in your application you may need other pieces of hardware, like a separate Linux box for serving ads, or a CD-ROM jukebox for making large archives of data available to the application.

Skate.shop only needs two boxes initially to run: a ColdFusion box and a SQL Server 2000 box. The standard system requirements should do for both ColdFusion and SQL Server boxes.

In a perfect development world, we'd want to expand the total box count to three ColdFusion boxes and three SQL Server boxes. One ColdFusion/SQL pair would be used for development, and the two remaining pairs would be load-balanced and used to serve the site. No development would ever be done on a live box, and the application wouldn't have a single point of failure. If one of the servers died, then another would still be able to serve requests.

Most organizations take what they can get. Another possible alternative is to have a pair of live boxes, and a pair of development boxes, and if the live boxes die, you switch them out with the development servers. This is risky—you may be running live development code, but it's better sometimes that not being up at all. And keep a current version of the application on the development box; you might be able to transition without much of a glitch.

Never develop on a live box! If you want to give the customer any impression at all that you're flaky, develop on a live box and let them see an error or two. Or, accidentally delete the application, then try to bring it back. It's not worth the risk—get a development box.

Hardware planning is usually pretty easy, and even easier if you have an IT department ready to fulfill your every desire. If you take care of the hardware planning early on, it gives either the IT department or yourself a chance to procure the hardware needed for the job while you develop. Don't wait until the launch to do your hardware planning—you need the right amount of time to test the application on live servers just in case something goes haywire.

Preparing for Development

With our flowcharts, our pseudocode, and our hardware planning completed, we're ready to start preparing for development. While we're not yet developing, we're getting ready for development.

In this phase, we prepare our hardware for development, create the directory structures on the server, set up IIS, and begin setting up our database. Chapter 5 is devoted entirely to the database, so we'll go into full detail there.

Preparing Development Hardware

We do some hardware planning, and determine that the best development environment would be one that closely resembled our production environment. Specifically, for the skate.shop application, I'll be using the following setup. This setup is identical to what I'd use for my production servers. The benefits of having identical servers are obvious—there should be no issues with moving the application from development to production, and I can use the development servers as backups in a crisis. This is just what I decided to use, and it doesn't mean you have to run out and buy the exact same setup, but you probably didn't need that disclaimer.

ColdFusion/IIS Box

- Pentium III 800 MHz
- 384MB RAM
- Two 9GB SCSI drives with separate controllers (one for the operating system, and one for data)
- CD-ROM drive (I'll explain shortly)

SQL Server 2000 Box

- Dual Pentium III 800 MHz
- 1024MB RAM (1GB)
- One 9GB SCSI drive with separate controller for operating system
- One 27GB RAID 5 array (three 9GB drives) for database files
- One 18GB SCSI drive with separate controller for transaction logs
- Tape backup

The ColdFusion box is pretty simple. I feel the amount of RAM is just about right for the application and the operating system, but if you can manage to put in more, it won't hurt. I like putting the operating system drive on a separate SCSI controller card for speed reasons. I don't want any slow downs when a user makes a request. It's more expensive to do it this way, so there are tradeoffs, but I think they're worth it. Fixing bottlenecks are never easy once the application is running on the box. The 9GB drives are more than enough—the entire skate.shop application shouldn't take more than half a GB, but 9GB SCSI drives are about the smallest, most economical drives you can get these days. The CPU speed is also plenty—ColdFusion returns requests faster with a faster CPU, but the difference between a Pentium III 800 and a Pentium 4 1.5GHz isn't going to be noticeable with our application. The cost difference between the two CPUs is very different, so it makes much more sense to go with the 800MHz chip.

The CD-ROM drive is our backup solution for the box. I really only need to back up the data files for our application. Everything else can be reinstalled, or should exist elsewhere. There are log files that might be important, but those should be able to be backed up on a CD-ROM as well. Every morning I can drop a CD into the tray, and a scheduled backup copies everything I need onto the CD. CDs are really inexpensive these days—I can spend $20 or less on 50 CDs, so making a daily backup is very economical. There are obvious disadvantages as well—if the server is in a remote location, you can't load and unload CDs on a daily basis, but the same argument could be made for any physical backup solution.

The SQL box is a lot beefier—it carries the biggest load of our application. I probably went a bit of overkill on this box—our little skate.shop application might not need the 27G RAID, or all of the RAM, but I wanted to set the box up for speed. As I said, 9GB drives are probably the smallest SCSI drives I can find, and I want to have a RAID 5 on the main data drive. RAID 5 stripes the drives, or spreads one piece of data across multiple disks, speeding up the read/write process. It also has a bit of redundancy built in. If one drive dies, the other two take over. It's not the fastest RAID level, but it is a good balance between speed and reliability. I may only need 4GB of space, but a 27GB RAID 5 is probably the cheapest solution I'll be able to find. Actually, it could be even cheaper—Windows 2000 has a software-based RAID 5 solution, but it's slower. I choose to have a separate RAID controller for the drives to keep things as fast as possible.

I have a separate 18GB drive for the transaction logs. Again, I probably don't need that large a drive, but I feel safer knowing I have room. Keeping the transaction logs on their own drive, with their own controller, keeps things very fast. The transaction logs need to be written as quickly as possible—if they're writing to a slow drive, the database is slower than it needs to be. You might be able to get away with using the same controller for the operating system and the transaction log drives, but I think it's best to split them off. It's more expensive, but I want this machine to be as fast as possible.

I decided to use Pentium III 800's, two of them. SQL benefits from having multiple processors, and for the cost, the performance gain is pretty significant. I'd rather have two 800 MHz chips than one 1.5GHz chip. SQL Server benefits from as much memory as possible. For our application, 1,024MB is plenty, and it's about all I'm willing to spend.

Setting up your hardware solution is an important step in the development process, and you should be aware that it can sometimes take the same amount of time to set up your hardware solution, if not more, than to actually develop your application. I see far too many companies look over this very important detail, and companies who aren't willing to buy the proper equipment for the job pay for it in greater amounts later on.

Give yourself plenty of time to make sure you get it done right to begin with. If you don't have the budget, do the best you can, but keep your focus on the most bang for your buck. It doesn't make sense to spend $50,000 on a hardware solution when a $10,000 solution could perform the exact same task. I might be overstating the obvious, but you've probably seen organizations yourself, or even worked for one, that aren't willing to spend the right amount of money and time on the right solution.

Preparing Directory Structures

An organized directory structure aids in keeping our application easy to work with. We planned some of the directory structure when we set up a code standard earlier in this chapter. We should continue with these directories, and duplicate the directories on our server.

Let's look at the skate.shop directory structure. Assume everything starts in the root directory of **skateshop**:

- **images** Contains all the subdirectories for every image on the site.
- **images/general** Contains general site images, like bullets, spacer images, icons, and so on.
- **images/nav** Contains user interface images. Separating these from the general images is especially helpful when you have rollover images for navigation elements—it just keeps it more organized.
- **images/product** Contains subdirectories for product images.
- **images/product/thumbnail** Contains a thumbnail image of each product.
- **images/product/medium** Contains a medium-size image of each product, used in the product details page.
- **images/product/detail** Contains a full-size image of each product.

- **modules** Contains subdirectories for all of our mini-applications, and sitewide code.
- **modules/general** Contains sitewide code.
- **modules/display** Contains general site-formatting code, for the main user interface, etc.
- **modules/pages** Contains the subdirectories for each of our top-level pages, or mini-applications.
- **modules/pages/home** Contains the home page code.
- **modules/pages/search** Contains the keyword search code.
- **modules/pages/details** Contains the product details code.
- **modules/pages/cart** Contains the shopping cart code.
- **modules/pages/help** Contains the Help system code.
- **modules/pages/checkout** Contains the checkout code.
- **modules/pages/login** Contains the customer login code, as well as the new customer creation code.
- **modules/pages/orderstatus** Contains the FedEx tracking code and order status code.
- **modules/pages/admin** The base directory for the Web-enabled Administrator code.
- **modules/pages/admin/orders** Contains the new orders code.
- **modules/pages/admin/demographics** Contains the demographic information.
- **modules/pages/admin/listmanager** Contains the e-mail export list code.
- **modules/pages/admin/general** Contains general administration-related code.
- **modules/tracking** Contains the code used to track user information on the site, such as product popularity.
- **admin** The base directory for our Administrator. It contains top-level pages for the Administrator application.

Create the directories above, and we'll set up IIS to begin serving from our root skateshop directory in a few.

A First Look at Setting Up the Database

For now, we just want to create the database. We'll build the tables and go more into the design issues in Chapter 5. Because the database is such an important part of your application, it deserves an entire chapter. Right, now let's look at just setting it up, without worrying about all of the details yet.

We know that because of our hardware setup, we want to create a new database that places its transaction logs on one drive, and the data files on another. To do that, create a new database in the Enterprise Manager of SQL Server 2000 by right-clicking in the databases pane of Enterprise Manager, and click New Database.

Enter **skateshop** in the Name field, and then click the Data Files tab, shown in Figure 4-3. We can assign a location to the data files for the database. Enter an appropriate location in the Location field, as shown in Figure 4-3. In my hardware setup, this points to my 27GB RAID 5 array, better known as my E: drive. For the sake of simplicity, let's leave the file growth settings where they are. We can always change them later on.

Click the Transaction Log tab, shown in Figure 4-4, and you can do the same thing for your transaction log. The drive I set aside for my transaction log is the D: drive. Again, don't worry about the file growth settings yet.

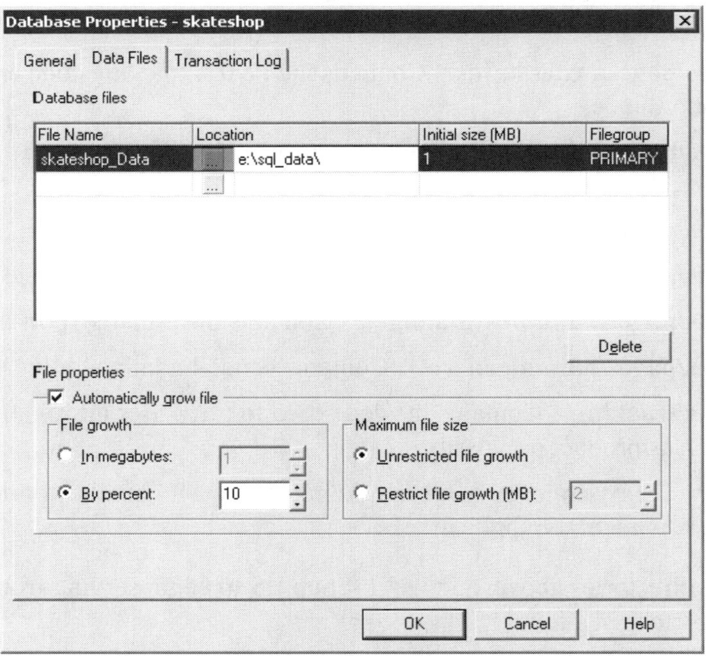

Figure 4-3 *Assigning a location to the data files*

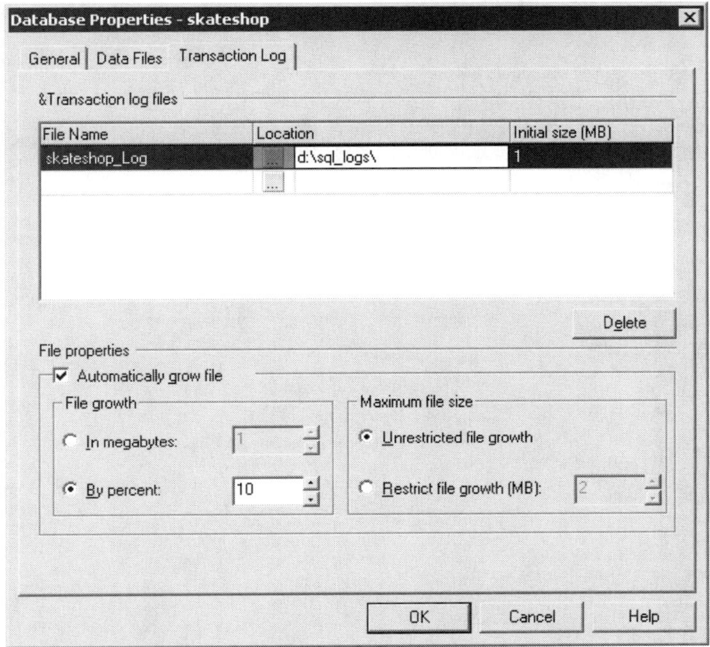

Figure 4-4 *Assigning a location for the transaction log*

Click OK, and our database is created.

We'll come back to creating the database, but for right now we just want it ready for use.

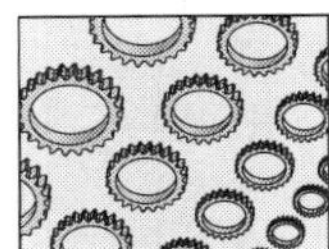

NOTE

I'm describing how I would set up my application on my development servers, but I'm also considering that you probably have one server to play with. Because of that, I'm being a bit unspecific about how and where to create directories, and how to name things. I assume that you should be able to use your own judgment, and do what works best for your situation.

Creating the Datasource

Go into your ColdFusion Administrator, shown in Figure 4-5, and set up the data source for the newly created database.

If you have trouble setting up the data source, make sure you're trying to connect to the right IP and server name, and make sure you're pointing to the right database.

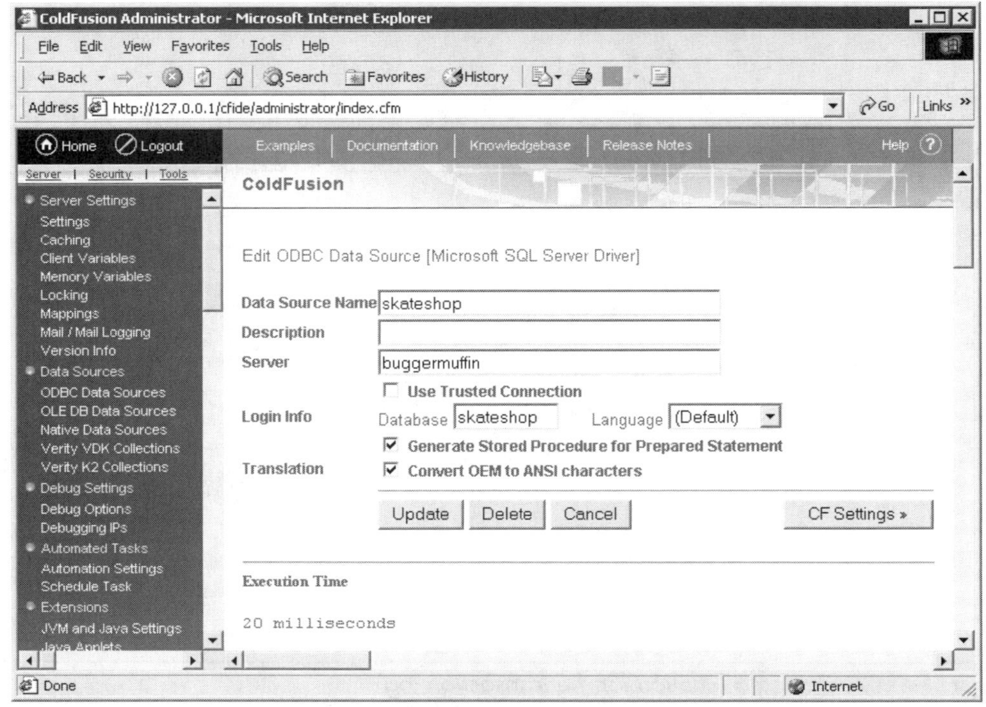

Figure 4-5 *Setting up the data source*

Wrapping Up

This was a pretty heavy chapter. We've discussed software development cycles in detail, and we've started to get our application ready. The next few chapters focus entirely on development: taking the skate.shop application from a list of requirements to a functioning site. If we follow the development cycle, we should have few pitfalls, and our application should be well documented.

CHAPTER 5

The Database

IN THIS CHAPTER:

Background on Database Forms

Referential Integrity

Designing Our Database

Building Our Database

Our application, and most database applications for that matter, will follow the Third Normal Form (3NF for short), which is a set of rules for database structure. When we design our database, we'll adhere to those rules. It's no surprise that there is a first and second form, as well as a fourth and fifth (and a few more variations tossed into the mix). In the next couple of sections, I'll discuss where forms came from, and the differences between the forms. I'll stop at the third level. We're not yet concerned with the fourth and fifth level, or any variations on levels.

Background on Database Forms

Database *normalization* can be simple to explain or it can be incredibly complex, put-you-to-sleep kind of material, so I'll go with the simple route. It's the heart of our application, and it should be exciting. It's not as exciting as winning the lotto, but there is a great deal of satisfaction gained from having a well-designed database.

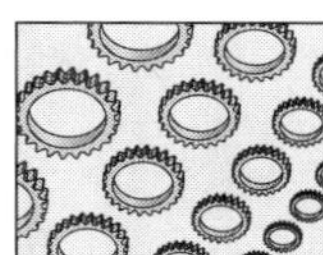

NOTE

Before we get into this, keep in mind that the term normal *in this regard has nothing to do with doing things in a normal, as opposed to abnormal, fashion, nor does it have anything to do with the town where Illinois State University is located. That was a cheap play on words, but I have no shame, so we'll continue.*

The term *normalization* stems from the standardization of database design and storage. The official definition in this regard is conforming to, adhering to, or following a standard, pattern, or type. Basically it means that our database design will follow a set of rules.

Database normalization has been around for a long time in computer terms—since the late 60s. Dr. Edgar F. Codd is considered the inventor of the relational database model, and has also made great contributions towards database normalization. It's no surprise that he became involved in the normalization end of things—relational databases and normalization go hand-in-hand, whether you realize it or not.

Database normalization, put simply, means that you are designing the database structure to be as optimal as possible, with consideration for speed and storage requirements. When we set out to design a database, inevitably it follows a form, and whether we try to or not, it will almost always follow one of the first three forms.

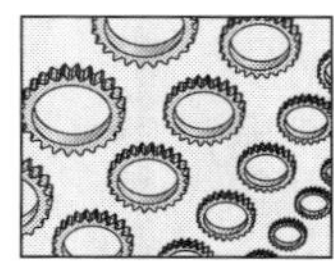

NOTE

The table examples I show in these sections are not our actual skate.shop tables; they're just examples.

First Normal Form

First Normal Form (1NF) suggests that all column values must be atomic. This doesn't mean that the database should be on the brink of explosion, like an atomic missile ready to launch; it should actually be the exact opposite.

Atom stems from the Latin word *atomus*, which literally means "not to cut." My own definition, which is not so literal, translates into "separate each piece of data until it cannot be separated any more." Each column in a row should contain one value, not a list of values. It also means that groups of data should not repeat themselves.

Here's an example of data that doesn't follow 1NF rules:

Order_ID	Customer_ID	Items
1	4	2 small t-shirts, 4 skateboard wheels, 10 stickers
2	35	1 skateboard
3	7	1 hat, 2 pairs of pants

We should see problems with this right off the bat. There's no real order to the Items column; data is placed based on the whims of whoever put the data there in the first place, which might be consistent now, but could easily be changed. Pulling this data out of the table and doing something useful with it would be difficult as well. We'd have to parse the data, and hope that everyone follows the rules. This is probably a database administrator's worst nightmare because it's so hard to manage. The quality of the data is poor because it's probable that someone will add data incorrectly, and it could mess every thing up that is dependent on the rules for the column.

An improvement to the table might look like this:

Order_ID	Customer_ID	Qty 1	Item 1	Qty 2	Item 2	Qty 3	Item 3
1	4	2	Small T-Shirts	4	Skateboard Wheels	10	Stickers
2	35	1	Skateboard				
3	7	1	Hat	2	Pants		

This is an improvement over the first attempt, but it still doesn't follow 1NF rules. We have multiple quantity columns, and multiple item columns, which means multiple groups of data.

The 1NF police wouldn't be happy about this table. We'd have a less difficult time retrieving data from this table, and less potential for the data to get messed up, but it's still not a good structure. If a customer orders more than three items, we'd need another group of columns. It would also be difficult to see how many skateboards were purchased over a period of time. Each column in the three quantity/item groups would need to be scanned for a skateboard.

Let's look at the table in proper 1NF form:

Order_ID	Customer_ID	Quantity	Item
1	4	2	Small T-Shirts
1	4	4	Skateboard Wheels
1	4	10	Stickers
2	35	1	Skateboard
3	7	1	Hat
3	7	2	Pants

This is a much more organized table, and there is no data group repetition. We can more easily see how many skateboards were ordered over a period of time, and customers can order unlimited quantities of items without the database administrator having to add columns to the table.

Keep in mind that our database does not simply follow the 1NF. Each form is applied to the next form, so 3NF will follow the 2NF rules, as well as the 1NF rules.

Second Normal Form

Second Normal Form (2NF) suggests that the tables must be in 1NF form, and that every nonkey column is fully dependent on the primary key. Tables should only store data relating to one table, and that table should be described by its primary key.

That's a lot for your mind to chew on. Go ahead, read it a few times. If it doesn't make sense, don't throw a fit; I literally spent days trying to parse it. I know how to explain 2NF, but the official rules are almost as hard to parse as political figures *almost* admitting guilt. The official rules are confusing. Let's step back, take a look at our 1NF table again, and try and understand the meaning of the 2NF rules.

Order_ID	Customer_ID	Order_Item_ID	Quantity	Item
1	4	1	2	Small T-Shirts
1	4	2	4	Skateboard Wheels
1	4	3	10	Stickers
2	35	1	1	Skateboard
3	7	1	1	Hat
3	7	2	2	Pants

We haven't talked about primary keys yet, so 2NF might be confusing because of that. Primary keys, put simply, are columns that hold unique identifiers to particular rows in a table. For instance, in our proper 1NF table, the Order_ID combined with the Order_Item_ID was a composite, or combined primary key. No two rows share the exact same primary key. Primary keys typically consist of one column.

Based on the rules of 2NF, our 1NF table should be split. Because we're depending on both the Order_ID and Order_Item_ID as our primary key, each of these items should be split off into separate tables. Each nonkey column should be fully dependent, or should have no relation to the primary key. In our 1NF example, a product in the Item field is dependent on the Order_ID column just as much as it's dependent on the Order_Item_ID column.

The best way to explain it is to show our tables split apart, in proper 2NF form. First, the *Orders* tables:

Order_ID	Customer_ID	Order_Date
1	4	5/1/01
2	35	5/9/01
3	7	5/28/01

The primary key in the *Orders* table is the Order_ID column, and each nonkey item is dependent on that key. Customer_ID and Order_Date depend on Order_ID.

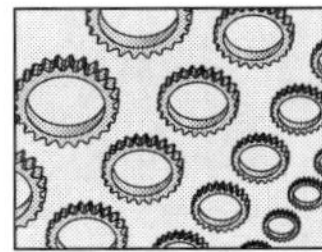

NOTE

SQL Server doesn't disallow naming tables or columns with spaces. However, it is considered a best practice to keep your table or column names to one word. You can make your objects more readable by using underscores (_) or dashes (–).

The *Orders Detail* table:

Order_ID	Order_Item_Num	Quantity	Product_ID	Item
1	1	2	45	Small T-Shirts
1	2	4	27	Skateboard Wheels
1	3	10	221	Stickers
2	1	1	2	Skateboard
3	1	1	346	Hat
3	2	2	54	Pants

In the *Order Details* table, the Order_ID column is a foreign key, and can be used to join the tables in a query later on. Splitting off the tables takes up less space because we're repeating less information, and it is more organized.

The official term used to describe "splitting off tables" is *decomposition.* In this case, our form is using *nonloss decomposition*, because no data is lost in the splitting of tables.

TIP

When creating a primary key in a table, it's very important to give it a unique name. If the table name is Orders, *give the primary key a name like Orders_ID. If you follow the rules of 2NF, and later 3NF, you'll need to be able to use that primary key in another table as a foreign key. If you give it a plain, nondescriptive name like ID, you're going to end up with a confusing foreign key in your tables, and you'll have a very difficult time determining where the foreign key originates. Not to mention the fact that anyone who works on your database later on will want to beat you with a stick for introducing such chaos into their lives.*

Third Normal Form

Third Normal Form (3NF) says a table must be in 2NF, and all nonkey columns must be mutually independent. For example, if we had a price column in the *Order Details* table, and we had another column that calculated the cost of Quantity × Price, that column would be dependent on the Quantity and Price columns, and would break the rules of 3NF. In 3NF, we'd use a query to calculate the cost.

We are all probably most familiar with this form. It's fairly intuitive to come up with a database design that follows the rules of 3NF.

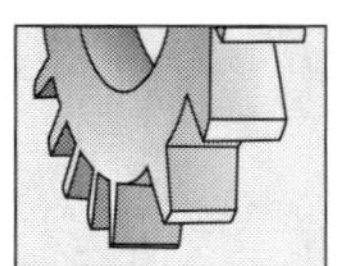

TIP

A rule of thumb I like to use when designing a database is to avoid the repetition of data as much as possible, and to keep in mind that each table must have a descriptive primary key and a matching foreign key in a dependent table. Designing with those thoughts in mind almost always helps me follow 3NF rules.

In order to make our example tables conform to 3NF rules, we'd need to split a *Products* table off, because in the 2NF example, the Product_ID column and the Item column depend on each other.

Imagine trying to change the description of "Skateboard" to "Downhill Skateboard." For every "Skateboard" item in the 2NF example, you'd have to update to the new value. This isn't very efficient, so we should split our tables again.

The *Orders* table should now look like this:

Order_ID	Order_Item_Num	Quantity	Product_ID
1	1	2	45
1	2	4	27
1	3	10	221
2	1	1	2
3	1	1	346
3	2	2	54

Notice that we dropped the Item column, which really only contains product descriptions, and we kept the Product_ID column, which we'll use as a foreign key for the *Products* table.

Product_ID	Description
45	Small T-Shirts
27	Skateboard Wheels
221	Stickers
2	Skateboard
346	Hat
54	Pants

Now, we only have to update product descriptions in one location, the *Products* table. We refer to the primary key, Product_ID, in the *Order Details* table.

Our application follows the 3NF. There are higher levels of normalization, but since 3NF does an excellent job for our purposes, I won't bore you with the other forms.

Here are some tips to remember regarding normal forms discussed here:

- Every form builds on the previous form. You aren't following the rules of 3NF if you're not following the rules of 2NF, and so forth.
- The principles of database design are mostly based on common sense.
- Database design is more an art than a science. The rules may not always apply to your particular situation, and you may want to break the rules if it helps speed up your database.

Keep in mind that the example tables I've shown in this section are just that—examples. Later in this chapter, we design tables based on our own project requirements.

Referential Integrity

Building and maintaining logical relationships between tables are fundamental parts of working with relational databases. It's basically the entire point of having a relational database in the first place. When the proper relationships exist between two tables, we call that *referential integrity*.

When we follow the 3NF rules, we preserve the relationships between our tables. If we didn't maintain these relationships, there would be a potential for data corruption, or at least a possibility that data could be orphaned, lost, or logically corrupt.

One table is the referenced table and the other is the referencing table; primary keys in the referencing table must match foreign keys in the referenced table. Although the relational database model tries to avoid parent/child relationships, sometimes it helps to think of our data this way. Technically, there is no hierarchy to database objects in the database, but logically, we do create parent/child relationships.

Referential integrity enforces consistency across the related tables. We could set up our referential integrity to delete child items in a table if the parent items are also deleted. For example, imagine that we have a *manufacturer* table and we have several tables that have a relationship with the *manufacturer* table. If we delete an item in the *manufacturer* table, we don't want orphaned items in our related tables, so we'd set up referential integrity between each of the related tables. Any item in any of the related tables that referred to the deleted item would also, in turn, be deleted.

Enforcing Referential Integrity

There are several ways to enforce referential integrity. SQL Server 2000 uses a technology it calls Declarative Referential Integrity (DRI), which uses foreign keys constraints defined as part of a table definition that enforce proper relationships between tables. The constraints ensure that proper actions are taken when DELETE, INSERT, and UPDATE statements remove, add, or modify primary or foreign key values. The DRI actions enforced by foreign key constraints can be supplemented with additional referential integrity logic defined in triggers on a table.

Constraints are properties, or rules, applied to a column that prevents certain types of invalid data values from being placed in the column. For example, a *primary key* constraint prevents you from inserting duplicate information into a field that requires unique data (like an INT field with identity turned on). A *check* constraint prevents you from inserting a value that does not match a search condition, and a *not null* constraint prevents you from inserting a null value.

DRI is SQL Server's automatic version of referential integrity, and it does a pretty good job of enforcing referential integrity. But if you're uncomfortable with the automatic version, you can build in your own referential integrity using procedural referential integrity. You can also, as I mentioned earlier, use both at the same time.

You can use procedural referential integrity by creating triggers to enforce relationships. If an item were deleted in a parent table, the delete action could fire off a trigger that also deleted its child items. Procedural referential integrity offers much more flexibility in how the integrity is enforced, but it also requires more of your time and effort to make it work just right.

Using SQL Diagrams to Build Relationships

Before we start using SQL Diagrams to build relationships, let's quickly go over some background on relationships. As we've already read, a relationship works by matching primary key columns with foreign key columns.

There are three different types of relationships used between tables:

- One-to-many relationships
- Many-to-many relationships
- One-to-one relationships

One-to-Many Relationships

A one-to-many relationship is the most common type of relationship. In this type of relationship, a row in table A can have many matching rows in table B, but a row in table B can have only one matching row in table A. For example, the manufacturers and products tables have a one-to-many relationship: each manufacturer produces many products, but each product comes from only one manufacturer.

A one-to-many relationship is created if only one of the related columns is a primary key or has a unique constraint. In SQL Diagrams, the primary key side of a one-to-many relationship is denoted by a key symbol. The foreign key side of a relationship is denoted by an infinity symbol (∞).

Many-to-Many Relationships

In a many-to-many relationship, a row in table A can have many matching rows in table B, and vice versa. You create such a relationship by defining a third table, called a *junction table*, whose primary key consists of the foreign keys from both table A and table B. For example, the *authors* table and the *titles* table have a many-to-many relationship that is defined by a one-to-many relationship from each of these tables to the *titleauthors* table. The primary key of the *titleauthors* table is the combination of the au_id column (the authors table's primary key) and the title_id column (the *titles* table's primary key).

One-to-One Relationships

In a one-to-one relationship, a row in table A can have no more than one matching row in table B, and vice versa. A one-to-one relationship is created if both of the related columns are primary keys or have unique constraints.

This type of relationship is really uncommon. Rather than using a one-to-one relationship, it usually makes sense to just combine the two tables. There are times, however, when you might use a one-to-one relationship though, such as:

- To divide a table that has a large number of columns
- To isolate part of a table for security reasons
- To store temporary data that can easily be deleted by deleting the table
- To store information that applies only to a subset of the main table

The primary key side of a one-to-one relationship is denoted by a key symbol. The foreign key side is also denoted by a key symbol.

Using the SQL Diagram Tool

Let's play with the diagramming tool included with SQL Server 2000. To get to the tool, open up your SQL Enterprise Manager, expand your server tree, expand Databases, and then expand the *Northwind* database. Click Diagrams. Your tree should look something what is shown in Figure 5-1. Follow these steps:

1. Right-click in the Diagrams pane, and click New Database Diagram. The Create Database Diagram Wizard pops up.

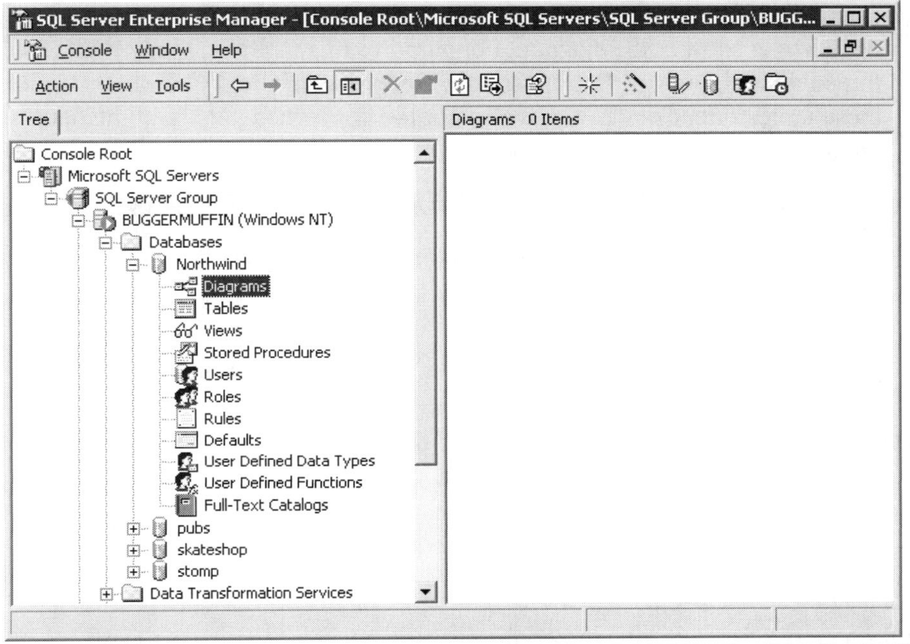

Figure 5-1 *The Enterprise Manager Diagram Tool*

Let's use the Wizard. Click Next:

Create Database Diagram Wizard

Select Tables to be Added

Select one or more tables from available tables box. You may also choose to add related tables.

Available tables

Categories
CustomerCustomerDemo
CustomerDemographics
Customers
Employees
EmployeeTerritories
Order Details
Orders
Products
Region
Shippers

Add >

< Remove

Tables to add to diagram

Add related tables automatically

How many levels of related tables? 1

< Back Next > Cancel

2. This screenshot shows the second step in the Wizard. Here we select the tables we'd like to show in the diagram. For purposes of simplicity, I only want to select three tables right now. Select *Orders*, *Order Details*, and *Customers*. I picked these tables rather randomly; we're not too concerned yet about the details of the tables, we just want to see how SQL Diagrams work.

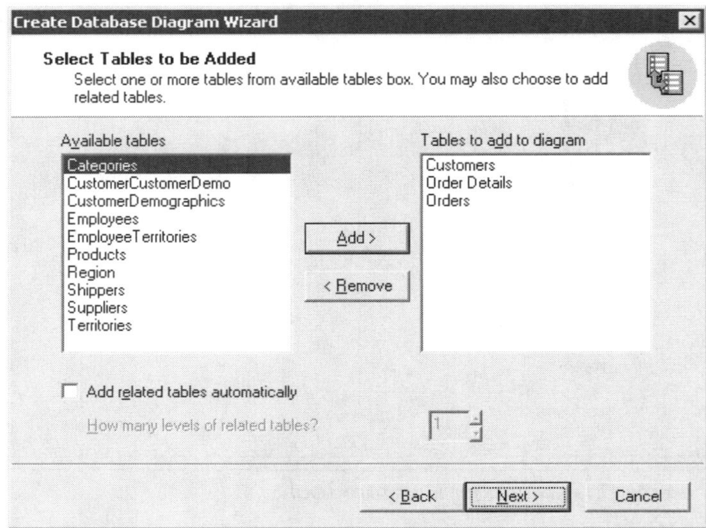

3. Make sure Add Related Tables Automatically is disabled, and click Next. The Wizard confirms the selections:

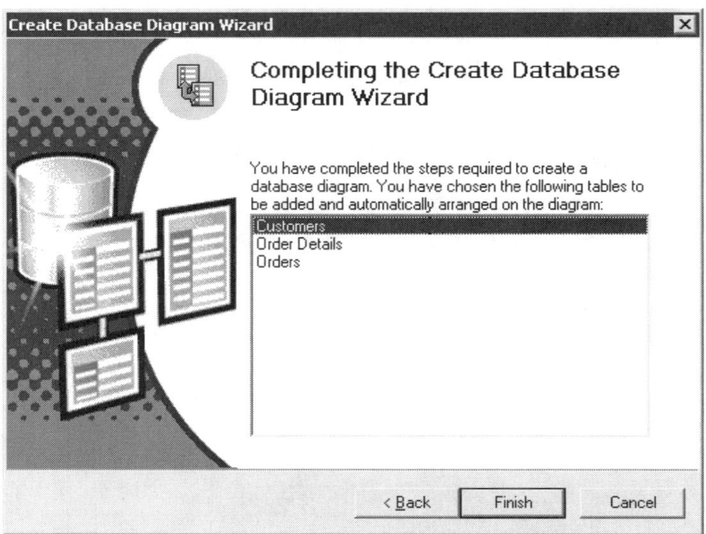

4. Click Finish to generate the diagram. SQL Diagrams automatically lays our tables out in a readable fashion. It doesn't exactly know how to logically place the tables according to your application; based on relationships, it will try and organize the tables as clean as possible. With a very large diagram, you might have to spend some time organizing things. Your diagram should resemble this one:

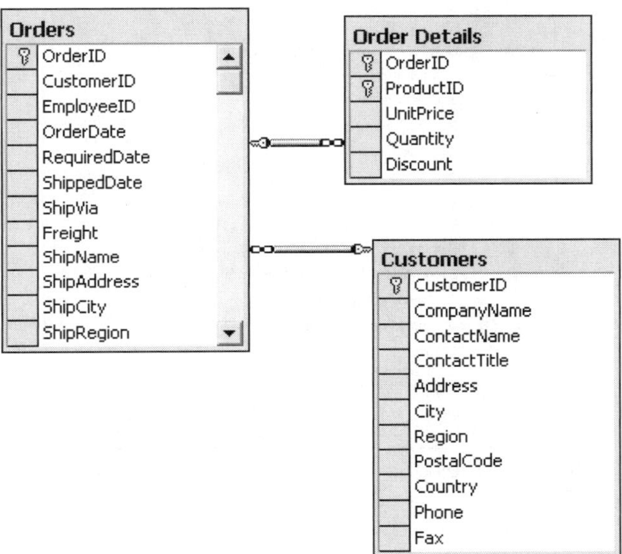

I arranged my tables slightly to fit better, but for the most part, your diagram should look nearly the same.

Now, let's look at the diagram. You'll notice that out of our three visible tables, we have two relationships. There's a one-to-many relationship between *Orders* and *Order Details*, and there's a one-to-many relationship between *Customers* and *Orders*.

Right click on the relationship between *Orders* and *Order Details*, and then click Properties. You'll see the screen shown in Figure 5-2. If you're confused about the details of a relationship, you can use this dialog to help sort out the details.

Let's see what it's like to create a new relationship from an existing one:

1. Close the Properties menu. Right-click a relationship, and select Delete relationship from database.
2. Click Yes to delete the relationship. By the way, I wouldn't do this on a live, active box. Without a relationship, you run the risk of data corruption or other similar problems. This is for development boxes only.

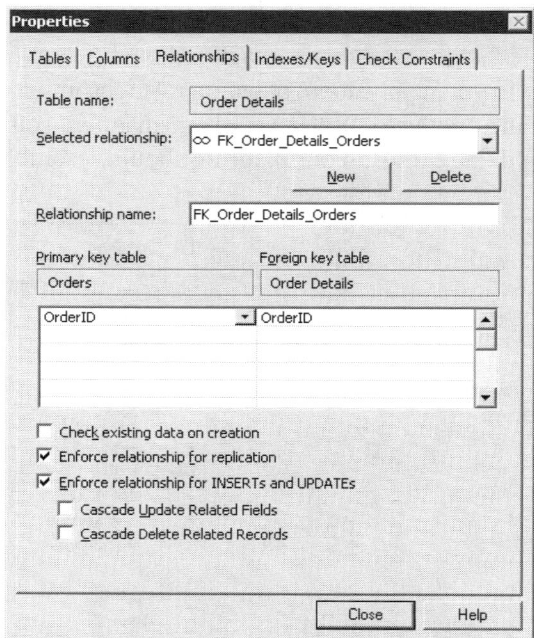

Figure 5-2 *Editing the properties of a relationship between two tables.*

3. To re-create the relationship, click the key symbol on the OrderID column of *Orders*, and drag a relationship over to the OrderID column of *Order Details*.

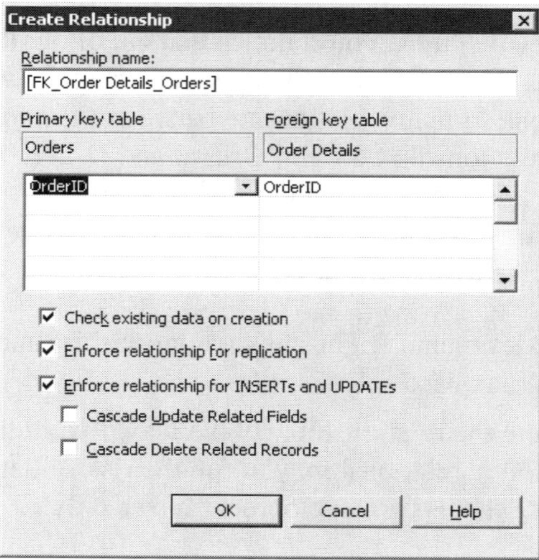

4. A menu pops up confirming the relationship. Click OK to create the relationship. This automatically creates a one-to-many relationship between *Orders* and *Order Details*.

Designing Our Database

Considerable thought should be put into the design of your database. Hopefully, now that we've covered a lot of database theory, we can apply what we've learned to our database. I was really picky about following the rules of 3NF earlier, but I also mentioned that database design is more an art than a science. We don't have to follow everything by the book. Sometimes we'll want to break away from conventional theory, and do something that works well for us, but perhaps not for others. Ultimately, the database designer will know when to deviate from 3NF rules depending on the needs of the application.

In this section, we'll first talk about data types, which help us design for speed and storage, and then we'll talk about the different methods of coming up with table structures.

Data Types

Data types, not surprisingly, specify the kind of data that can be stored in a column, parameter, or variable. It's important to note that data types don't just apply to columns, but parameters in stored procedures, as well as variables, need to have a data type applied when first declared.

There are several reasons why we have data types—the first obvious one is for storage reasons. If every single column in our database were a 400-character string, we'd have some fat database files. With proper data types, that fat database could be drastically reduced in size. I don't need to explain all the reasons why data types are a good thing; anyone with an even dim imagination could come up with reasons why data typing is important.

Understanding the different available data types is important in the design process. It's difficult, and sometimes impossible, to change the columns data type without losing data once the column contains data. Knowing what data types are available also broadens your scope of what can be accomplished. The following is an extensive list of data types available to SQL Server 2000:

Integers:

- ***bigint*** Integer (whole number) data from –2^63 (–9,223,372,036,854,775,808) through 2^63–1(9,223,372,036,854,775,807). A *very* large number that should only be used if needed, storage size for this data type is 8 bytes. There are 18,446,744073,709,551,616 possible integers using BIGINT. In America, we call that over 18 quintillion. In England, and other countries, it would be 18 trillion. (Thanks to Jim Loy at http://www.mcn.net/~jimloy/billion.html for that information.)

- ***int*** Integer (whole number) data from –2^31 (–2,147,483,648) through 2^31 – 1 (2,147,483,647). The storage size for this data type is half that of bigint, 4 bytes.
- ***smallint*** Integer data from –2^15 (–32,768) through 2^15 – 1 (32,767). Storage size is 2 bytes.
- ***tinyint*** Integer data from 0 through 255. This is the smallest of integer data types, weighing in at 1 byte.

Bit:

- ***bit*** Integer data with either a 1 or 0 value. SQL Server 2000 stores bit data types in an interesting way. If there are 8 or fewer bit columns in a table, it uses a combined total of 1 byte for all 8 columns. If there are between 9 and 16 columns, 2 bytes are used, and so on.

Decimal and Numeric:

- ***decimal*** Fixed precision and scale numeric data from –10^38 + 1 through 10^38 – 1. Decimal precision indicates how many total digits stored, both to the left of the decimal and to the right. The decimal itself does not count as a digit. Scale determines how many digits to the right of the decimal are stored. So a decimal with a precision of 10 and scale of 5 might look like 99999.99999. The maximum precision is 38. Storage size depends on the precision. It is at least 5 bytes, and at most 17 bytes.
- ***numeric*** Functionally equivalent to decimal.

Money and Smallmoney:

- ***money*** Monetary data values from –2^63 (–922,337,203,685,477.5808) through 2^63 – 1 (+922,337,203,685,477.5807), with accuracy to a ten-thousandth of a monetary unit. Storage size is 8 bytes.
- ***smallmoney*** Monetary data values from –214,748.3648 through +214,748.3647, with accuracy to a ten-thousandth of a monetary unit. Storage size is 4 bytes.

Approximate Numerics:

- ***float*** Floating precision number data from –1.79E + 308 through 1.79E + 308. Floating point numbers are considered approximate values, because they can never be fully represented accurately. Storage size depends on precision, ranging from 4 to 8 bytes.
- ***real*** Floating precision number data from –3.40E + 38 through 3.40E + 38. Storage size ranges between 4 and 8 bytes.

Datetime and Smalldatetime:

- ***datetime*** Date and time data from January 1, 1753, through December 31, 9999, with an accuracy of three-hundredths of a second, or 3.33 milliseconds. Microsoft SQL Server stores values with the datetime data type internally as two 4-byte integers. The first 4 bytes store the number of days before or after the base date, January 1, 1900. The base date is the system reference date. Values for datetime earlier than January 1, 1753, are not permitted. The other 4 bytes store the time of day represented as the number of milliseconds after midnight.
- ***smalldatetime*** Date and time data from January 1, 1900, through June 6, 2079, with an accuracy of one minute. The smalldatetime data type stores dates and times of day with less precision than datetime. SQL Server stores smalldatetime values as two 2-byte integers. The first 2 bytes store the number of days after January 1, 1900. The other 2 bytes store the number of minutes since midnight. Dates range from January 1, 1900, through June 6, 2079, with accuracy to the minute.

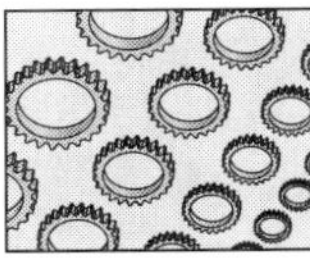

NOTE

I actually wish there were a date data type in between datetime *and* smalldatetime*. I rarely need to worry about dates as high as December 31, 9999, as allowed with datetime, but I do like the accuracy down to a second the data type provides.*

Character Strings:

- ***char*** Fixed-length, nonUnicode character data with a maximum length of 8,000 characters. Storage size depends on the size of the column. Because *char* is fixed in size, use it when you expect your data to be consistent in size from row to row.
- ***varchar*** Variable-length, nonUnicode data with a maximum of 8,000 characters. Storage size depends on the size of the data in the column. Use *varchar* when data is expected to vary considerably in size from row to row.

- ***text*** Variable-length, nonUnicode data with a maximum length of 2^31 – 1 (2,147,483,647) characters. Storage size depends on the amount of text.

Unicode Character Strings:

- ***nchar*** Fixed-length Unicode data with a maximum length of 4,000 characters. Storage size is twice the size of the same size *char*. Typically you'd use *nchar* in applications where supporting multiple languages was an issue.
- ***nvarchar*** Variable-length Unicode data with a maximum length of 4,000 characters. Storage size is twice the size of *varchar*.

Binary Strings:

- ***binary*** Fixed-length binary data with a maximum length of 8,000 bytes. Storage size varies depending on length of the column.
- ***varbinary*** Variable-length binary data with a maximum length of 8,000 bytes. Storage size varies depending on the length of the data in the column.
- ***image*** Variable-length binary data with a maximum length of 2^31 – 1 (2,147,483,647) bytes. Storage size depends on the size of the image. The actual binary data of an image is stored. This data type is really just a much larger version of *varbinary*.

Other Data Types:

- ***cursor*** A reference to a cursor. The *cursor* data type is only used when referring to a cursor in a stored procedure or other code. You can assign the cursor data type to a column when creating a table.
- ***sql_variant*** A data type that stores values of various SQL Server-supported data types, except text, ntext, timestamp, and sql_variant. Basically, you can use sql_variant to allow different data types to be applied to one column. To keep your life simple, I'd recommend not messing with this. It's a neat feature, but in most cases, you'd never want to use it.
- ***timestamp*** A database-wide unique number that gets updated every time a row gets updated. This is a tricky. Microsoft's idea of *timestamp* is a unique automatically generated piece of binary data that was updated each time a row was added or updated. The rest of the SQL world considered the *timestamp* data type to be the same as Microsoft's *datetime* data type. This could have

obvious compatibility problems, so Microsoft is giving *timestamp* back to the SQL world, and replacing it with *rowversion*. SQL Server 2000 can use *rowversion*, but will still treat *timestamp* the same as Microsoft has always treated it. In future releases SQL Server will treat the *timestamp* data type just like everyone else, and continue use of the *rowversion* datatype.

- ***uniqueidentifier*** A globally unique identifier (GUID). A GUID looks like this: – 6F9619FF-8B86-D011-B42D-00C04FC964FF and is supposedly 100 percent unique. No two GUIDs should be the same worldwide.

Designing Your Tables

You can determine which tables you need directly from the project requirements. If we study our list of final requirements from Chapter 4, it shouldn't be difficult to determine the content of our main tables. Once we determine this, we can easily figure out what other tables might be needed to complete the picture.

Let's take a look at our project requirements to refresh our memory:

- Skateboard configurator
- Category drill-down
- Keyword search
- Customer login
- Fast checkout
- Shopping cart
- Content
- Syndicated content
- Help system
- Marketing
- Beginner packages
- Backend
- Order processing

For now, let's not worry about all the details of each table, let's just begin making a list of the tables we think we need. We can worry about the columns a bit later. Take each feature of the application, and think about what tables are required. Let's start with the **skateboard configurator** feature.

We know the following right off the bat based on the configurator's features:

- If a customer is to select components, we'll need a table to draw the components from. Thus, we need a *Product* table.
- We also need to track the selected components some how, so we need a table that shows which products a customer has selected for their skateboard; let's call it *board_config* for now. If we think of a more appropriate name we'll rename it.
- It may be premature to think about, but it doesn't hurt. If we're to have customers use the configurator, we need a *Customers* table. If the customer is logged in, we can track their ID in the *board_config* table. If the customer is not logged in, we have to think of a way to track them in the *board_config* table.

Even though our focus was on figuring out what tables we'd need for the configurator, we came up with a couple more that can also be used in other mini-applications on the site. If we follow this method of walking through the features one by one, we'll end up covering most of the tables that we need.

Rather than waste a lot of paper walking through every step, let's just look at a list of tables we need in Table 5-1, along with a brief description of each.

We'll come up with more tables as we go along, but this is plenty to start with. Again, the best way to understand what databases you'll need is to look at each required feature, and think about what kind of tables will be needed to support the

Table	Description
Product	Stores base product information for the site.
product_var	Stores color and size variations of each product.
Customers	Stores customer information.
board_config	Stores skateboard configurator tracking.
Categories	Stores the site categories.
Orders	Contains the base order information for a customer.
order_details	Contains the items and quantities in an order.
Scart	Stores customers' shopping cart items. Data is purged when user orders, or if the user hasn't touched the cart for a certain length of time.
Articles	Stores imported content in the form of written articles.
Reviews	Stores reviews on products in our database.
help_system	Stores help articles.
help_tips	Stores tips.
Specials	Stores discount product packages.

Table 5-1 *The Tables for the skate.shop Application*

feature. It's OK to think about columns and data types, but don't let that slow you down. The important part right now is knowing what tables to use.

Data Modeling Tools and Methods

Now that we know what tables we want to use, we should begin sketching out the relationships between each table.

The cheapest, most efficient, and most flexible tool you can use to model your data is a pencil and a piece of paper. Big surprise, right? I've already made a big deal about using pencil and paper, but it's true. The cheapest data modeling tool that I can come up with is Visio at around $100 or so, and it can't even do as good a job as you can with pencil and paper. Not only that, but initially you need a lot of flexibility. You don't want to spend a few hours on a nice pretty Visio document, and then realize that you need to redo the entire thing because someone thought of a new table.

There are good data modeling programs, but the good ones usually cost a load, with prices starting in the $2,000 range, per seat. This might be a wise investment for some, but for others, is either out of reach, unreasonable, or just not worth it.

Pencil and paper offer excellent flexibility. If you mess up, you use the built in undo feature, the eraser. If you *really* mess up, you delete the file (wad up the paper and throw it at the cat). Once you've decided that you can plan the relationships no further, *then* you create a Visio document. If you don't have or want to use Visio, you can create a diagram of the site using SQL Diagrams, which you'll end up doing anyway, with or without a Visio doc.

It doesn't hurt to be thinking about columns and data types while modeling your data, but again, don't let it stop you from laying out the relationships on paper.

Tables, Columns, and Data Types

Now is the time to think of what columns you'll need in your tables, and what type of data those columns will contain. Let's look at the columns and data types for the *Product* table:

Column	Data Type
product_id	int identity
title	varchar(200)
details	varchar(1000)
img	varchar(200)
dateadded	smalldatetime
product_status_id	tinyint
brand_id	int
category_id	int

I hope that it's obvious that this table relates to four other tables. The column count might also seem a bit slim, but remember, there's also a product_details table. That's where we'll store sizes and colors for each product, inventory amounts, as well as prices.

You might be thinking, "Shouldn't the prices column be in the Product table? Otherwise you're breaking 3NF rules." Well, that's true, but this is one of those times when I need to bend the rules. It's possible that for every size and color variation of a product, I'll have the same price repeated for each product. This actually breaks the rules of 1NF, but there's the possibility that a product variation might have a different price. For example, some skateboarding shoe manufacturers make shoes in all sizes—from adult sizes to toddler sizes. Even though it's the same model of shoe, the toddler size shoe may be priced quite differently than the adult size shoe. It may not happen often, but I have to be prepared if it does, and it's a trade-off I'm willing to make.

It might be possible to create another table that helped handle prices better, but I'm not willing to add the extra complexity. The rules of database modeling are not set in stone; it's OK to bend them to your needs. Just don't bend so far they break.

Another interesting part of the table is the status_id field. I set its data type to *tinyint*, which means I can only have a number up to 255 in that column. It seems like it might be a bad idea, but the *product_status* table is linked exclusively to the *Products* table, and no other. The *product_status* table contains information about whether the product is discontinued, drop shippable, or other important flags. It's nearly impossible that I'll have over 255 available statuses, so *tinyint* is a good space saving choice.

Let's look at the *product_var* table since it closely relates to the *Product* table.

Column	Data Type
variation_id	int identity
product_id	int
size_id	int
color_id	int
price	decimal
product_status_id	tinyint

There's really only one piece of data here that's truly unique—the price. Every other field besides the primary key relates to another table.

I won't go into detail on every table; you should be able to determine what columns you'll need and what data types to use. You can look at Figure 5-3 as a reference to see if you're on track.

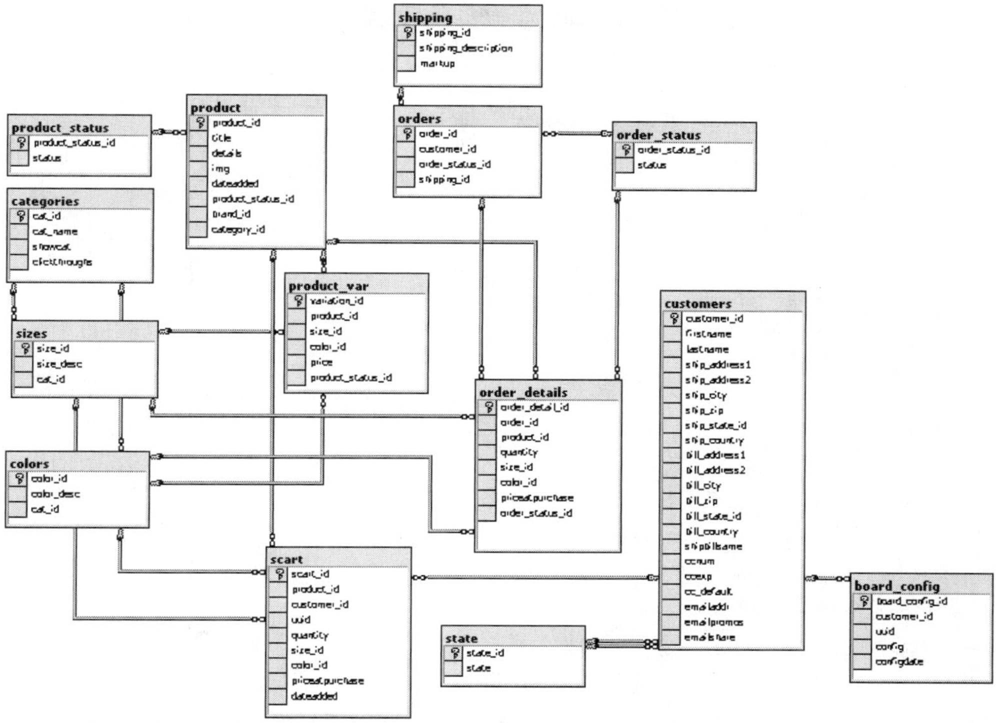

Figure 5-3 *A diagram of the skate.shop main tables. It looks a bit crazy on the surface, but if you study the relationships, it's very organized.*

Building Our Database

Building the database is one of my favorite steps in creating my application. I get to be organized to the point of near insanity, and no one has a problem with it.

In this section, I walk you through building a few tables in the Enterprise Manager, as well as using T-SQL to generate every table with the mere press of a button.

Creating a Table with the Enterprise Manager

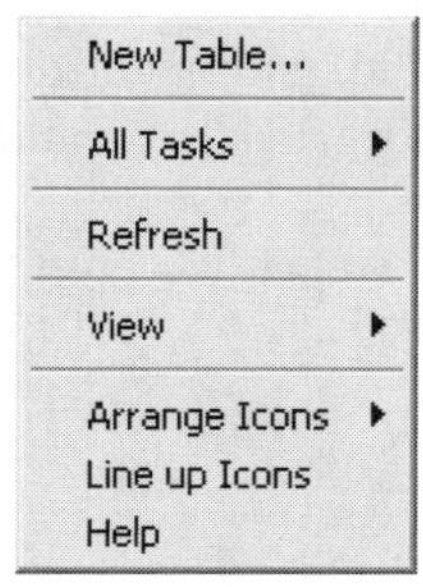

To create a table in the Enterprise Manager, right-click on the tables pane. The menu shown on the left will appear.

Click New Table. The table creation dialog box appears, allowing you to add columns. The top half of the dialog is where you enter table names, data types, and assign keys. The bottom half of the dialog is where you set the size, scale, precision, and whether or not a field is an identity field or not.

Figure 5-4 shows the details of a table in the process of being created.

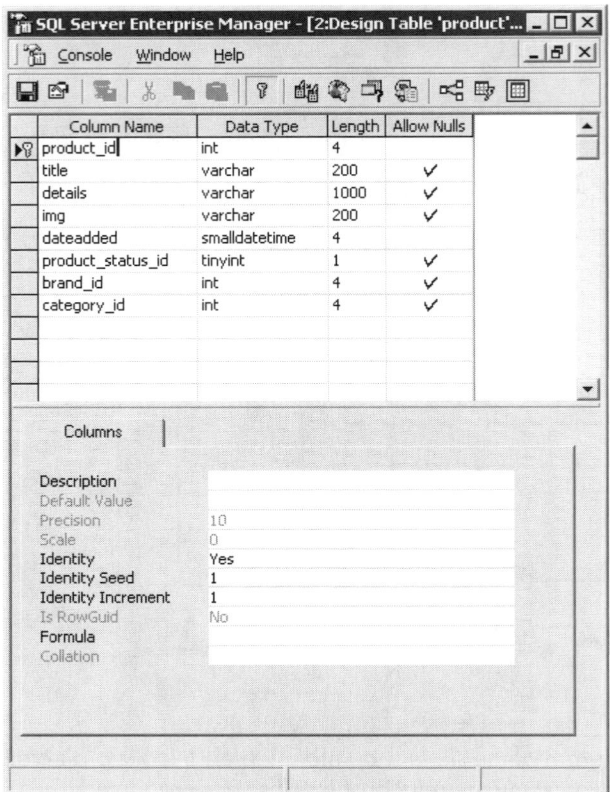

Figure 5-4 *The table design dialog.*

Once you've created your tables, you should use SQL Diagrams to create relationships between the tables.

Creating a Table with T-SQL

Personally, I think building tables in the Enterprise Manager is a slow process. Creating your tables using T-SQL code is much faster and a little more flexible. Although it looks more complicated, it requires the same technical mindset that it takes to create the same tables in the Enterprise Manager.

We're going to use the CREATE TABLE command to build our tables. We could execute the following code in SQL Query Analyzer:

```
CREATE TABLE product_status
(
```

```
    product_status_id tinyint IDENTITY(1,1) PRIMARY KEY,
    status varchar(30)
)
```

It's pretty easy to understand—the first line starts the process for creating the *product_status* table. Within the parenthesis, we define our columns. The first column is the product_status_id column, which is an identity field, as well as our primary key. So we make a declaration after we assign the *tinyint* data type of INDENTITY(1,1), which means the field should be an identity field, starting with the number 1, and incrementing one step for each row. The next declaration indicates that we want the column to be a primary key.

The second column pretty much explains itself. It's a varchar column called status, with a possible length of 30 characters. You might assume that because we can create a primary key, we should be able to also create a foreign key. Well, you're correct in that assumption. Here's a sample:

```
CREATE TABLE product
(
    product_id int IDENTITY(1,1) PRIMARY KEY,
    title varchar(200),
    details varchar(1000),
    img varchar(200),
    dateadded smalldatetime not null DEFAULT getdate(),
    product_status_id tinyint REFERENCES
product_status(product_status_id),
    brand_id int,
    category_id int
)
```

I use a REFERENCES declaration on the product_status_id column to create a relationship between the *product_status* table and the *Product* table. This will create a one-to-many relationship between *product_status* and the *Product* tables.

To create every table in one shot, execute the following code in SQL Query Analyzer:

```
use skateshop
CREATE TABLE product_status
(
    product_status_id tinyint IDENTITY(1,1) PRIMARY KEY,
    status varchar(30)
)

CREATE TABLE categories
(
```

```
   cat_id int IDENTITY(1,1) PRIMARY KEY,
   cat_name varchar(30),
   showcat bit,
   clickthroughs int
)

CREATE TABLE product
(
   product_id int IDENTITY(1,1) PRIMARY KEY,
   title varchar(200),
   details varchar(1000),
   img varchar(200),
   dateadded smalldatetime not null DEFAULT getdate(),
   product_status_id tinyint REFERENCES
product_status(product_status_id),
   brand_id int,
   category_id int
)

CREATE TABLE sizes
(
   size_id int IDENTITY(1,1) PRIMARY KEY,
   size_desc varchar(30),
   cat_id int REFERENCES categories(cat_id)
)

CREATE TABLE colors
(
   color_id int IDENTITY(1,1) PRIMARY KEY,
   color_desc varchar(30),
   cat_id int REFERENCES categories(cat_id)
)

CREATE TABLE product_var
(
   variation_id int IDENTITY(1,1) PRIMARY KEY,
   product_id int REFERENCES product(product_id),
   size_id int REFERENCES sizes(size_id),
   color_id int REFERENCES colors(color_id),
   price decimal(7,2),
   product_status_id tinyint
)

CREATE TABLE state
```

```
(
   state_id tinyint IDENTITY(1,1) PRIMARY KEY,
   state varchar(2)
)

CREATE TABLE customers
(
   customer_id int IDENTITY(1,1) PRIMARY KEY,
   firstname varchar(70),
   lastname varchar(70),
   ship_address1 varchar(100),
   ship_address2 varchar(100),
   ship_city varchar(100),
   ship_zip varchar(10),
   ship_state_id tinyint REFERENCES state(state_id),
   ship_country varchar(100),
   bill_address1 varchar(100),
   bill_address2 varchar(100),
   bill_city varchar(100),
   bill_zip varchar(10),
   bill_state_id tinyint REFERENCES state(state_id),
   bill_country varchar(100),
   shipbillsame bit,
   ccnum varchar(20),
   ccexp varchar(10),
   cc_default bit,
   emailaddr varchar(30),
   emailpromos bit default 1,
   emailshare bit default 0
)

CREATE TABLE shipping
(
   shipping_id int IDENTITY(1,1) PRIMARY KEY,
   shipping_description varchar(30),
   markup tinyint, -- percentage increase
)

CREATE TABLE order_status
(
   order_status_id tinyint IDENTITY(1,1) PRIMARY KEY,
   status varchar(30)
)
CREATE TABLE orders
```

```
(
   order_id int IDENTITY(1,1) PRIMARY KEY,
   customer_id int,
   order_status_id tinyint REFERENCES order_status(order_status_id),
   shipping_id int REFERENCES shipping(shipping_id)
)

CREATE TABLE order_details
(
   order_detail_id int IDENTITY(1,1) PRIMARY KEY,
   order_id int REFERENCES orders(order_id),
   product_id int REFERENCES product(product_id),
   quantity int,
   size_id int REFERENCES sizes(size_id),
   color_id int REFERENCES colors(color_id),
   priceatpurchase decimal(7,2),
   order_status_id tinyint REFERENCES order_status(order_status_id)
)

CREATE TABLE board_config
(
   board_config_id int IDENTITY(1,1) PRIMARY KEY,
   customer_id int REFERENCES customers(customer_id),
   uuid varchar(35), -- generated by ColdFusion if a customer isn't
logged in.
   config varchar(300),
   -- comma delimited list of id's/breaks 1NF rules, but needed for
simplicity.
   configdate datetime default getdate()
)

CREATE TABLE scart
(
   scart_id int IDENTITY(1,1) PRIMARY KEY,
   product_id int REFERENCES product(product_id),
   customer_id int REFERENCES customers(customer_id),
   uuid varchar(35), -- generated by ColdFusion if a customer isn't
logged in.
   quantity int,
   size_id int REFERENCES sizes(size_id),
   color_id int REFERENCES colors(color_id),
   priceatpurchase decimal(7,2),
   dateadded datetime default getdate()
)
```

Wrapping Up

We've seen examples of how to design our tables, and then build them using Enterprise Manager or T-SQL. We now have a database that is ready to use. We might need to make a few changes as we go along, but for the most part, we have a firm foundation to work with.

Now is where the real fun begins. We've done all our prep work, we've built the database, and we're ready to begin coding a site in ColdFusion.

CHAPTER

6

Building the skate.shop Front End

IN THIS CHAPTER:

Discussing the Skate.shop Code Standard

Building the Interface

Building the Mini-Applications for the Interface

In this chapter, we take a detailed look at the skate.shop application, where we build the front end of the site—those parts that are immediately visible to the customer. We also look at each module, or part of the application, and give detailed explanations for the various techniques that are introduced. Keep in mind that ColdFusion is very flexible in how it's coded, meaning, there isn't simply one way of writing code in ColdFusion. The skate.shop application could be coded in any number of ways—the way it's shown here is simply one of those ways.

Discussing the Skate.shop Code Standard

In the design phase of our skate.shop application, we developed a code standard for the developer to follow. For more information on this discussion, refer to Chapter 4. The code standard sets forth some guidelines as to how the application is to be built. Let's take a moment to quickly refresh the concept of our code standard:

- A shell page for each main part of the site points to, or includes, a main switch (content.cfm).
- Content.cfm acts as the main dispatcher, so each module executes through this page.
- A query switch is included to execute queries before the corresponding mini-application requires them.
- Each main part of the site interface, or mini-application, has its own directory-called pages underneath the modules directory, or modules/pages for short, and contains its own set of templates.

We may actually add or elaborate specifications to the code standard as we develop, but we shouldn't take away from the base standard. For example, we might want to suggest that modules set a minimum amount of **Caller** scope variables, and that all attributes should have default values (using <CFPARAM>). This suggestion simply elaborates on the idea of maintaining mini-applications.

As we look at the code for the skate.shop application, I make suggestions for what should be considered standard practices in our application. I also suggest best practices, although the application may not follow best practices. Remember, every situation is different and calls upon different techniques, some of which might not be best practices. The application also intentionally uses different approaches to similar problems, so that we can see different solutions to a problem.

Why We Use <CFMODULE>

Following our code standard, we're going to make wide use of the <CFMODULE> tag, which actually works almost identically to the way a custom tag works. Like a custom tag, <CFMODULE> has its own scope—only <CFMODULE> can access variables set within the code, unless the variable is set to a scope that's available to the calling template, or beyond.

The <CFMODULE> tag differs slightly from custom tags, in that you can supply a relative path to the module. Custom tags must reside in custom tag directories set up in the ColdFusion Server Administrator, or reside in the same directory as the calling template. <CFMODULE> allows you to store reusable blocks of code in directories of your choice, without you needing to worry about server settings. It's flexible though—you can if you want refer to the cfmodule by name, which is basically identical to calling the code as a custom tag.

Let's assume that the module sits in the modules/general directory off our main root application directory, and the name of the module is page_title.cfm. Here are several ways to call that module from a file in the root application directory, using both <CFMODULE> and custom tags.

First, we'll call the file using a relative path. This method requires no server administration:

```
<cfmodule template="modules/general/page_title.cfm">
```

It's obviously a simple tag. The first attribute is the relative path to the code. If the code required attributes, we could add the attributes and values to the tag.

Next, here's a method that requires a mapped directory, named foo, to be set up in the administrator, pointing to our root modules directory:

```
<cfmodule template="/foo/general/page_title.cfm">
```

Same concept there—the only difference is the reference to the mapped directory. This method comes in handy when you're nesting modules—using relative paths can get tricky.

If the code resides in a registered custom tag path, or sits in the custom tags directory, we can use either of the following methods:

```
<cfmodule name="page_title">
```

or

```
<cf_page_title>
```

Registered custom tag paths can be created in the ColdFusion Administrator under the Custom Tag Paths menu item. The *name* attribute is the name of the template, without the .cfm extension. The second method is the custom tag method, and works the same as the first shown method.

Personally, I prefer using relative paths. I don't have to worry about messing with the server, and I don't mind working out the paths in nested modules. And, if I move the code to a different server, I don't need to worry about it producing errors, because no mapped folder exists (or the custom tag doesn't exist).

Because <CFMODULE> maintains its own scope, it's also oblivious to the "outside world," or the caller template, without parameters being properly scoped. The following scopes are readily available to <CFMODULE>:

- Attributes
- Server
- Application
- Session
- Client
- CGI
- Request

Any variables set using the above scopes are available to the calling template, as well as the **Caller** scope. The **Caller** scope allows you to set an unscoped parameter within the module that is available to the calling template.

By making wide use of <CFMODULE>, we'll have a high degree of control over the parameters set within our code. It also encourages reusability. If a block of code needs to have its own set of variables and logic, it's likely that you will be able to use that block of code somewhere else.

Main Pages Detail

The main pages of the site are very simple, and aren't even really vital to the operation of the application. They're used as wrappers to the content.cfm file, and set the request.page parameter used to drive the switch in content.cfm.

Here's an example of the details.cfm file:

```
<cfparam name="request.page" default="details">
<cfinclude template="content.cfm">
```

It's plain to see why the file isn't vital to the operation of the application—the *request.page* variable could originate from a *URL* parameter or *form* parameter. But for aesthetic and readability reasons, we use the main pages. There are other benefits also, as we've covered earlier.

For each possible *request.page* value, we want a main page created. It becomes more evident how the main pages work when we look at the main switch in the content.cfm file.

Building the Interface

The interface for the skate.shop application is going to be kept very simple. On every page, we'll see the following:

- Category drill-down
- Site logo
- Site information
- Shopping cart (except during checkout process)

The shopping cart is probably the only interface feature that differs from the overall norm of interface design. Generally in online stores, shopping carts are accessible from a "shopping cart" link, and are rarely visible throughout the shopping process. I can only speculate why most sites operate this way—I think having the cart visible at all times is very useful. Not having the shopping cart on the page might make it easier to cache entire pages. The only truly dynamic document on a site with "separate" shopping carts is the shopping cart itself, which with less feature-rich programming languages, makes the most sense.

That's not a big enough argument for me, however, to disable the viewing of the shopping cart at all times. There is a lot we can do using ColdFusion's features, such as query caching and scooping, which can cache the majority of the page for performance benefits, while allowing us to keep the shopping cart active.

For skate.shop, we will use an interface that I've developed that is simple and straightforward. It's certainly not the only way to accomplish the task, although I think it does a very good job. I don't yet claim to be an interface expert, so don't let my way of doing things stop you from going with what you feel works.

The main advice I can give on interface design is to keep things as simple as possible, both from a usability aspect and a coding aspect. Fancy, flashy interfaces usually are more difficult to create, and are usually more difficult to use. Whatever kind of interface you use, the best way to test it is to literally watch people use it. Stand over someone's shoulder while they use your site. If you feel like you have to coach them on how to use the interface, chances are the interface is confusing. If the person using it can find and do what they need to on the site, chances are the interface does its job.

Here's an example of the layout of our site, with all content removed. The left column contains navigation, the middle contains content, and the right column contains the shopping cart. This layout never changes on the site; it remains consistent from the Home page to the last checkout page.

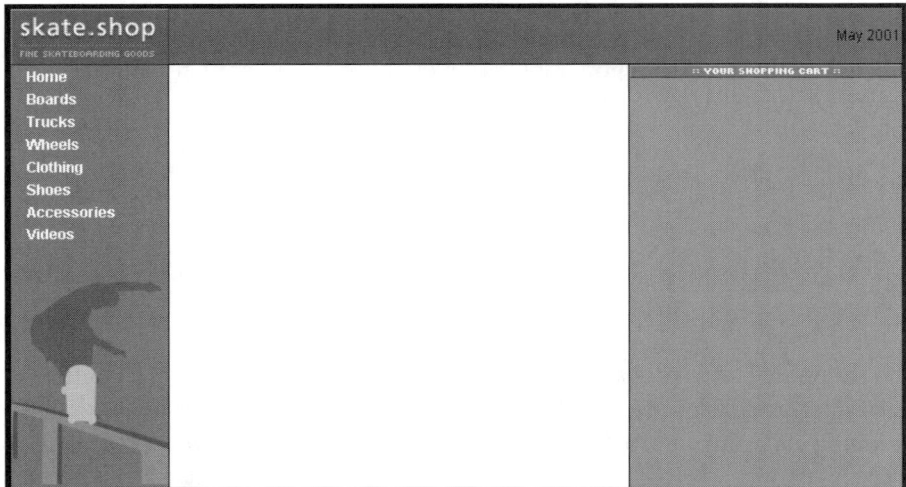

The only time the shopping cart isn't shown is during the checkout phase. We disable the editing of the shopping cart during the checkout phase because we want to separate the concept of "product choosing" from "product purchasing." While the user can get halfway through the checkout process, change his or her mind, and add a new product to the order without a problem, we still want to keep the user in the right frame of mind for the task at hand, and really, the application has two distinct tasks—picking products and purchasing those products.

During the checkout phase, we show a checkout progress mini-application where the shopping cart usually resides. We're making the space useful for the context of the content on the screen.

I've also designed the site to be *fixed width*, meaning that instead of stretching to the width of the browser, the site remains at a constant 720 pixels wide, regardless of the user's resolution or browser width. It's not required that you do this, but I like it because it makes my job as a designer easier. I don't have to worry about my design looking different on different browsers. Designing it to have a fixed width has its advantages as well as disadvantages—you can design what works best for your situation, or you can get yourself into trouble with different resolutions that perhaps don't display your fixed-width site well.

In the following sections, we'll look at each file in detail. I'll be stopping at certain points to discuss the reasoning behind the code, and pointing out best practices, and anything else that seems helpful. I'll be going in the order that the files are executed in the application, and when we hit the main switch in content.cfm, I'll take them in the order that they appear.

Looking at the Skate.shop Application.cfm File

Application.cfm is a special file in ColdFusion; for every ColdFusion file that executes, so does the application.cfm file. ColdFusion searches up the directory tree for the first application.cfm file that it finds. If you have the application.cfm file in the root directory, and there is no application.cfm file in root\modules, then for every ColdFusion file executed directly from the root\modules directory, application.cfm executes before any other code.

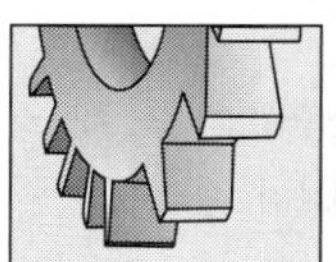

TIP

You can also execute code at the end of each request by creating a file called onrequestend.cfm. You must have an application.cfm file contained within the same directory as the onrequestend.cfm file for the file to execute; otherwise the code won't run (and won't even give you an error).

This has great benefits; it's easy to execute code globally without having to worry about including the code on every template. Here's the first part of our application.cfm file:

```
<cfapplication
  name="skateshop"
  clientmanagement="Yes"
  sessionmanagement="Yes"
  setclientcookies="Yes"
  sessiontimeout="#CreateTime(0,45,0)#"
  applicationtimeout="#CreateTime(2,0,0)#"
  clientstorage="skateshop_client"
>
```

Using the <CFAPPLICATION> tag sets up the **Application** scope for the skate.shop application. The first attribute defines the name of our application. It's actually an optional attribute if you're only going to be using the **Client** scope, but our application uses the **Session**, **Client**, and **Application** scopes. The second attribute, *clientmanagement*, indicates that we want to be able to use variables in the **Client** scope. Setting *sessionmanagement* to yes indicates that we want to be able to use session management. Our application will timeout session variables for a particular client after 45 minutes of inactivity. Application variables can be timed out using the *applicationtimeout* attribute, which is set to two hours.

Client Variable Storage

The *clientstorage* attribute of the <CFAPPLICATION> tag allows you to store client information in your own datasource. By default, ColdFusion stores client information in the registry, which isn't the best thing to do. Depending on the setup of your operating system, you might have a file size cap on the registry, which causes some interesting problems for ColdFusion when it tries to store client information. Additionally, it's simply a good idea to separate the client information from the registry—it's not what the registry is built for. Databases are built for rapid insert and changing of data—the registry is not.

To create a datasource to use for client storage, simply create a new database in SQL Server called skateshop_client. Don't worry about creating any tables for it yet; they'll be built automatically in the ColdFusion Administrator.

Once the database has been created, add the datasource just like any other in the ColdFusion Administrator, and called it skateshop_client.

Client Variable Storage *(continued)*

In the Administrator, click the Client Variables link.

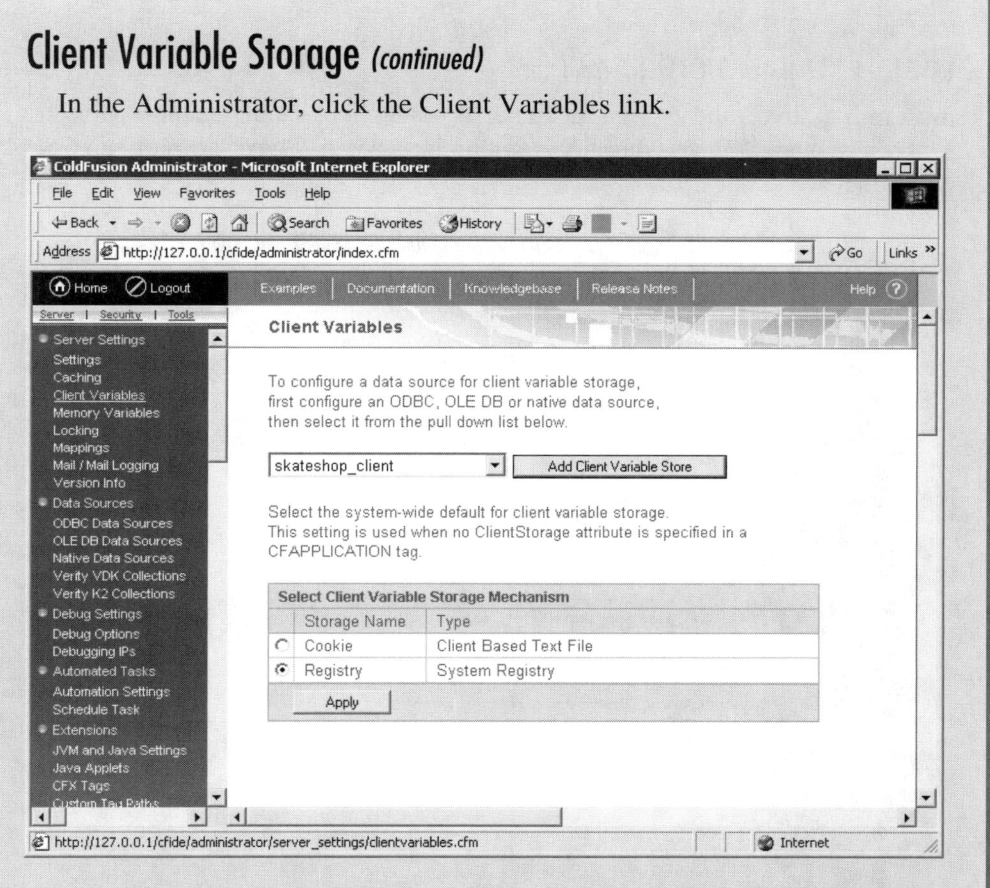

Select the datasource you've just created, then click Add Client Variable Storage. Because this datasource hasn't been set up to be used as client variable storage, the

Client Variable Storage *(continued)*

most important setting on this page is the Create client databases tables option. Make sure that at the very least, this option is selected. Click Submit to apply the changes.

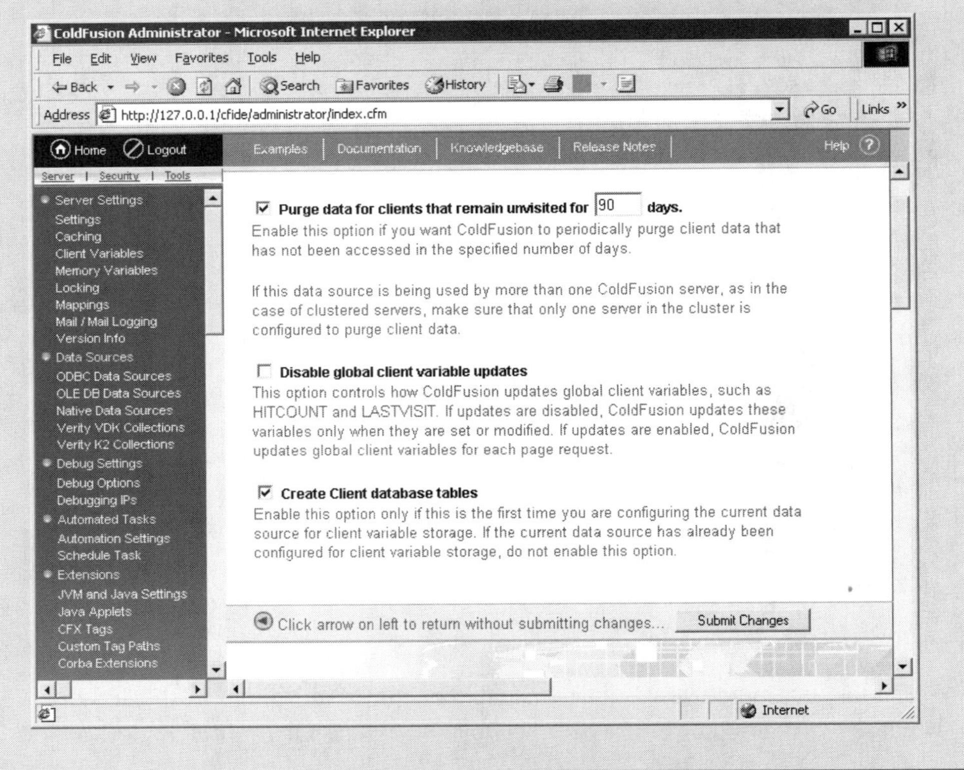

Client Variable Storage *(continued)*

It's also possible to set a default, systemwide Client Variable Storage Mechanism in the Clients Variables window. By default, the system uses the system registry, but we could make a datasource just like we did for skate.shop, and use it systemwide. When the <CFAPPLICATION> tag doesn't specify a *clientstorage* attribute and value, the default system will be used.

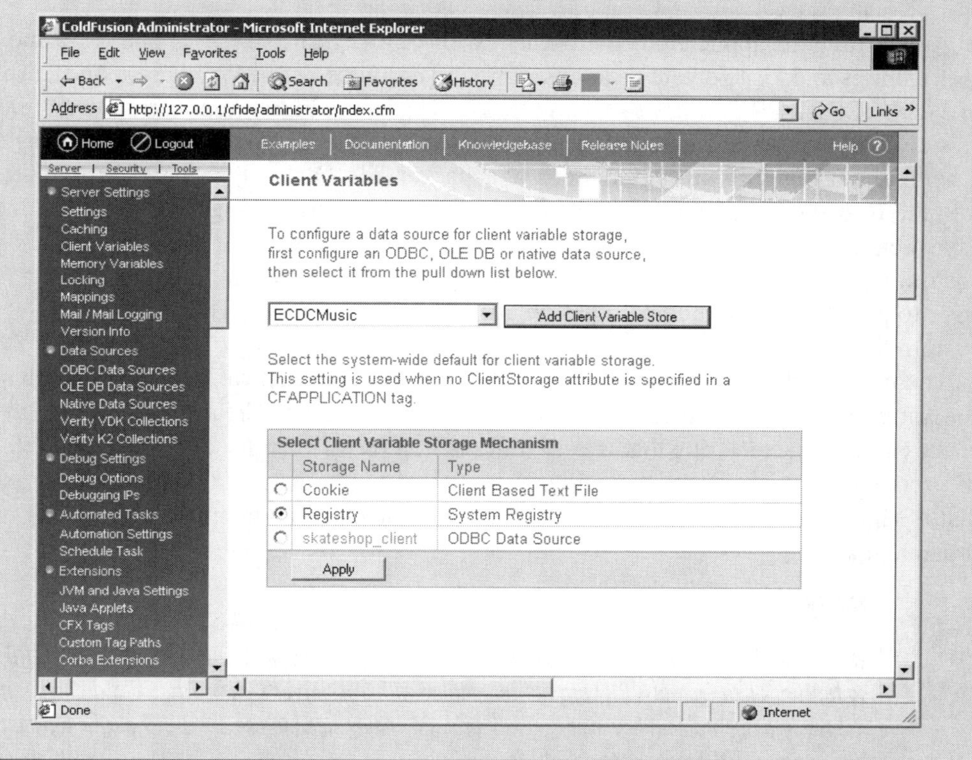


```
<cfset request.dsn = "skateshop">

<!--- take care of giving the customer a UUID --->
<cflock scope="session" timeout="10" type="exclusive">
```

```
<cfif IsDefined("session.uuid") is false>
   <!--- if they don't have a UUID, set one --->
   <cfset session.uuid = CreateUUID()>
<cfelse>
   <cfif session.uuid eq 0>
      <cfset session.uuid = CreateUUID()>
   </cfif>
</cfif>
</cflock>
```

After setting the application environment with <CFAPPLICATION>, one of the most useful things to do is create a variable for our datasource name. We'll use request.dsn in every <CFQUERY> tag or <CFSTOREDPROC> tag in our application when the tags as for a datasource because if the datasource name ever changes, we simply change it here, rather than dig through dozens of separate ColdFusion templates. We've set it to the **Request** scope so that it can easily be used by custom tags and modules that have their own scope. The **Request** scope is available to the entire application, including custom tags and modules, which will make our lives a little easier since we won't have to pass the datasource name as an attribute to every <CFMODULE> tag or custom tag.

The next block of code assigns a unique ID to each user that we'll use to distinguish shopping cart items and other session-specific information. The CreateUUID() function creates a 35 character string that is very difficult to reproduce, in fact, nearly impossible. It's very similar to the *uniqueidentifier* data type of SQL Server 2000, and is so unique that it's highly unlikely that it could even be reproduced on another completely separate machine.

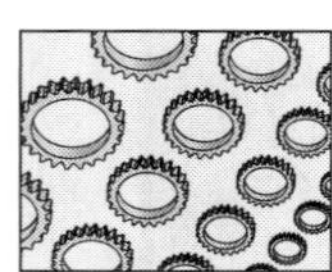

NOTE

The uniqueidentifier *data type in SQL Server 2000, is* not *the same format as ColdFusion's UUID, so functions like CreateUUID() are not compatible with SQL Server's* uniqueidentifier *datatype. It's not really a big problem however—you'll probably never need to use any UUID-pecific functions on a piece of SQL Server data.*

If the client connecting to our application hasn't already started a session, we'll create the session variables for them. But, before we do that, we need to put a lock around the block of code to avoid thread deadlocking. Because our application shares the memory space of the **Session** scope with the rest of the application, it's possible that multiple threads could corrupt each others data. Using the <CFLOCK> tag guarantees that the thread will execute exclusively. Exclusive thread execution is granted on a first-come, first-served basis. It's wise to use <CFLOCK> only when necessary, as it can slow down an application if used excessively. For example, don't use <CFLOCK> on an entire template—any data set to shared space in between the tags would have to wait its turn to be set, and that could get very slow.

<CFLOCK> should be used when writing to a session, application, or server variable, and it should also be used around CFX tags. Some CFX tags do not intrinsically support multithreading, so you need ColdFusion to handle the locking. You don't need to use <CFLOCK> when setting cookies, or client variables, because this data isn't stored in memory. Client variables are either stored in the registry or in a database, and cookies are stored on the user's machine.

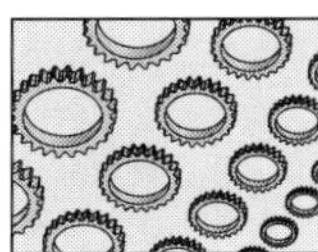

NOTE

You can write custom tags using the ColdFusion Application Programming Interface in C++ or Java. CFX, or ColdFusion Extensions, are registered in the ColdFusion administrator and are different than CFML custom tags because they are compiled DLLs. They can usually perform repetitive tasks more quickly than ColdFusion, or provide functionality not available in CFML.

We set our sessions in application.cfm because we can never be sure of where the user will enter our site. A search engine could index a *details* page, and that could be the user's main point of entry, so we want to be diligent in making sure they establish a session no matter where they arrive at in our site.

It's possible to use different scopes to establish the customer in our application. We could use a cookie, but we've already sent them two cookies when we executed the <CFAPPLICATION> tag—it sends the CFTOKEN and CFID cookies, which establish the identity of the client. We could use the **Client** scope without any problems, except for one—security. If the user closes the browser, and someone else logs onto the site using the same computer, the skate.shop application would think that the first user was still in an active session. When we can do things security-wise, it doesn't hurt to be cautious.

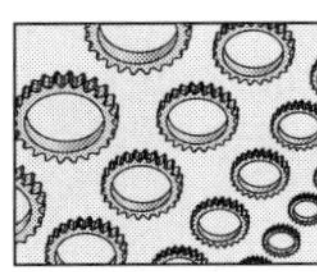

NOTE

It might be worth knowing that when the ColdFusion server sends the CFTOKEN and CFID cookies to the client browser, it creates the cookie names in uppercase. When referring to the cookie in your CFML code, it doesn't matter whether you use upper- or lowercase, because variable names in CFML are case insensitive. If you're developing in an environment like Linux, where filenames are case sensitive, knowing that the CFID and CFTOKEN cookies are all uppercase might come In handy. I can't say how exactly, but it's always good to know how the ColdFusion server does things so you can be prepared to do what you need to do.

If we used the **Application** scope, or even the **Server** scope, that would obviously cause problems. Assigning a UUID to the **Application** scope would essentially force the application to treat every user as one user because the application UUID would never get reset. It would always exist as long as people were hitting the site, and would never time out. Setting the UUID to the **Server** scope would make the UUID server-wide (so ANY application on the ColdFusion server would see the UUID as one unchanging value).

It might seem silly to think of putting the UUID in any other scope besides **Session** or **Client**, so why even talk about doing it differently? Well, it's a good stopping point for a discussion of scoping, and the differences between each scope. Let's talk about a few scopes in detail.

Server Scope

The **Server** scope allows you to set variables that are available to the entire server, regardless of the application framework. Server variables are structures, and can be manipulated just like any other structure. Server variables will remain persistent until the server is restarted, at which point they will not exist until you create them again.

Application Scope

The **Application** scope allows you to set variables specific to the application itself. Before you can use the scope, the <CFAPPLICATION> tag must have already executed with a name assigned to the application. Any value set to the **Application** scope is available to the entire application. The **Application** scope is good for making information available globally to the entire application.

You can also have the application variables timeout, either by setting the default timeout value in your ColdFusion administrator or by setting the timeout value in the <CFAPPLICATION> tag.

Client Scope

The **Client** scope stores persistent data that is specific to a browser. For example, you might want to personalize a site to a particular user by creating a variable that stores the user's favorite animal:

```
<cfset client.favorite_animal = "pig">
```

That value of *client.favorite_animal* would remain persistent for that particular user, and you could use it to personalize the site by showing a picture of a pig for instance.

A couple of neat objects are associated with the **Client** scope. The following code is an example of one of those objects in use:

```
<cfoutput>
  #client.HitCount#
</cfoutput>
```

This would return how many hits have been tracked for this particular client. Here are the available objects for the **Client** scope:

- CFID
- CFToken
- URLToken
- HitCount
- TimeCreated
- LastVisit

You can access these objects, but you cannot set them. ColdFusion automatically stores the data for each client.

Session Scope

Session variables are used to track a set of requests from a given client. Because of the stateless nature of the Web, tracking a session helps determine the identity of a single person from one request to the next.

When we refer to a session, it usually means all the connections that a single client would make to the server while using our application. Because the session is specific to each individual user, each user has a separate **Session** scope.

The session starts when the first connection of a client occurs, and ends when the user doesn't access the site within your specified timeout period. You can set a default timeout for the session in the ColdFusion Administrator, or in your <CFAPPLICATION> tag. When the user's session is timed out, ColdFusion clears out all variables associated with that user's session.

One of the most important variables we set in our application is the *session.uuid* variable. This variable contains a unique code that's assigned to a specific session. Because the value remains specific for the session, this allows us to show the user a shopping cart with items they've added during this session.

Looking at the Skate.shop Content.cfm File

Content.cfm is the heart of our application—it acts as a dispatcher for all of the *request.page* parameters. It also includes all of the main queries, user defined functions, and other widely used blocks of code in our application.

I name the file content.cfm perhaps inappropriately—I started calling the file content.cfm because this is where most of my content was showing up (as opposed to application.cfm, or other files I was including in my applications). The name isn't really important; as you develop the application, this will quickly become the most important part of the site, and probably the most widely used file in the application. You could name the file jellybeans.cfm, and you'd still know exactly what it did, just because of the usage. I would suggest naming it something descriptive—you don't want a new developer to be too confused. I used the example to illustrate the point that you will become quickly familiar with the file.

Let's look at the content.cfm file:

```
<!--- include any custom functions --->
<cfinclude template="functions/general.cfm">
<!--- include queries --->
<cfinclude template="queries/global.cfm">
<cfinclude template="queries/main_switch.cfm">

<!--- call the general page modules --->
<cfmodule template="modules/general/page_title.cfm">
<cfmodule template="modules/spiderweb/meta_gen.cfm">
<cfmodule template="modules/display/style.cfm">
<cfmodule template="modules/general/html_wrapper.cfm">

<cfflush interval="10">

  <!--- include the site HTML --->
  <cfmodule template="modules/display/master.cfm">
    <!--- main switch for the pages --->
    <cfswitch expression="#request.page#">
      <cfcase value="home">
        <cfmodule template="modules/pages/home/home.cfm">
      </cfcase>
      <cfcase value="results">
        <cfmodule template="modules/pages/results/results.cfm">
      </cfcase>
      <cfcase value="details">
        <cfmodule template="modules/pages/details/details.cfm">
```

```
      </cfcase>
      <cfcase value="checkout">
        <cfmodule template="modules/pages/checkout/checkout.cfm">
      </cfcase>
      <cfcase value="help">
        <cfmodule template="modules/pages/help/help.cfm">
      </cfcase>
    </cfswitch>
  </cfmodule>
</cfmodule>
```

Content.cfm also includes a whole lot of other files. We'll look at each file in detail, but first let's look at the structure of content.cfm. The first couple of lines include general user defined functions, global queries, and a main query switch. The next block contains modules that execute on every page. The major block contains our main switch, wrapped with some HTML formatting modules.

One of the interesting parts of the content.cfm file is the <CFFLUSH> tag.

<CFFLUSH>

<CFFLUSH> is a new tag to ColdFusion. <CFFLUSH> flushes the current buffer to the browser, so anything that ColdFusion has already processed gets sent to the user. This can improved the perceived performance of the application, as the user will start seeing results before ColdFusion has finished the entire CFML template. Traditionally, ColdFusion processed the entire template before returning the results to the user.

<CFFLUSH> modifies the HTML headers of the document that get sent back to the browser, which means that it's incompatible with other ColdFusion tags that modify the HTML headers. <CFLOCATION>, for example, modifies the headers; therefore, if <CFLOCATION> were run after CFFLUSH, an error would occur.

functions/general.cfm

This file is where we create any globally available user defined functions (UDFs). The following shows what the functions/general.cfm file looks like. (Note that to accomodate the need to wrap lines of text in this book, we've used the ¬ character to indicate the continuation of a line. The ¬ character is not part of the code; the code line should be entered as one complete line.)

```
<!--- general functions --->

<cfscript>
/*
```

```
once a custom function is created, in order to allow custom tags
and cfmodule's to use it "copy" the function to the Request scope
*/

function LongDate(date)
{
  DateFormat(date, 'mmmm yyyy');
}
request.LongDate = LongDate;

function CurrentLocation()
{
 udfCurrentLocation = ListGetAt(cgi.script_name,¬
    ListLen(cgi.script_name, '/'), '/');
 udfCurrentLocation = udfCurrentLocation & "?";

 if (IsDefined("url.cat"))
       udfCurrentLocation = udfCurrentLocation & "cat=#url.cat#" & "&";
if (IsDefined("url.id"))
      udfCurrentLocation = udfCurrentLocation & "id=#url.id#" & "&";
if (IsDefined("url.searchcrit"))

      udfCurrentLocation = udfCurrentLocation &¬
         "searchcrit=#url.searchcrit#" & "&";

return udfCurrentLocation;

}

request.CurrentLocation = CurrentLocation;
</cfscript>
```

ColdFusion 5.0 allows us to create our own functions, which you can use just like the native ColdFusion functions. The functions/general.cfm file creates the custom functions that we use in our skate.shop application, as well as copying the functions to the **Request** scope.

If we didn't copy the functions to the **Request** scope, we would have to pass the functions to our custom tags and modules as attribute/value pairs. This could get tedious, as our application is almost entirely made up of <CFMODULE> tags.

It seems like it would make more sense to create the function in the **Request** scope to begin with, without having to copy it later on, but that's simply not possible in ColdFusion 5.0.

The UDFs are pretty self-explanatory, and act as simple examples of what UDFs can be used for. These examples certainly don't show off the true potential of UDFs. You can write much more complex code than what I've shown.

You can call a UDF anywhere in the template (even before the function has been created) by simply treating the UDF like a regular function. It's best to create the function before using it for performance reasons. You will experience a slow down if you create the function after using the function in your template.

queries/global.cfm

This file contains queries that need to be available to every page:

```
<!---
These are queries that need to be present on every page, or globally available.
In order for queries to be passed to custom tags, the query has to be set to
the Request scope.
--->

<cfquery
  name="request.qryCatDrill"
  datasource="#request.dsn#"
  cachedwithin="#CreateTimeSpan('1,0,0')#"
>
exec dspCatDrill
</cfquery>
```

The first query is used to generate the category drill-down menu. We want this to execute right away, because we may add features that use the category information later on that would require that the query execute here.

Later on, there's a file called queries/main_switch.cfm that contains a switch with nearly all of the main-level queries in our application. The only reason why the category drill down query is in this file is because we want it to execute on every page, regardless of any other criteria.

We could get away with not having this file and putting the code into the queries/main_switch.cfm file, but because these kinds of queries execute always, it makes organizational sense to put them here.

queries/main_switch.cfm

This file organizes our queries for each of our mini-applications in a switch. It allows us to execute a query ahead of time in case we need the query to be available to the entire application. If we executed a query halfway down the page, we'd be in trouble if we needed the data from the query in a previous part of the template.

```
<!---
The main query should contain an entry for each page that requires a query.
Standalone CFMODULEs need not be represented here, just included pages.
--->
<cfinclude template="qryScart.cfm">
<cfswitch expression="#request.page#">
  <cfcase value="home">
    <cfinclude template="qryHome.cfm">
  </cfcase>
  <cfcase value="results">
    <cfinclude template="qryResults.cfm">
  </cfcase>
  <cfcase value="details">
    <cfinclude template="qryDetails.cfm">
  </cfcase>
</cfswitch>
```

modules/general/page_title.cfm

This module controls our page titles. We want each page title to be as relevant as possible to the content of the page. In order to do this, we have to know what content is on the page. For now, the page title module is able to place the product name in the title:

```
<!--- page title module --->

<cfset request.page_title.results = "www.skate.shop">
<cfif IsDefined("request.qryDetails")>
  <cfset request.page_title.results =
     request.page_title.results & " - " & request.qryDetails.title>
</cfif>
```

We set a variable called *request.page_title.results*. We'll use this variable later on in our modules/general/html_wrapper.cfm file. If the product details query has executed, the product title will be added to the rest of the title.

modules/spiderweb/meta_gen.cfm

The idea of this module is to dynamically create metatags that might help visiting spiders determine the content of the site. It works very similarly to the modules/general/page_title.cfm module in that it uses the request.qryDetails query to build a list of keywords. It's not a perfect science, but it's a quick and easy way to make an improvement over the alternative, which is to have no dynamically created relevant keywords.

```
<!--- meta tag generator module --->
<cfset request.meta_gen.description = "www.skate.shop sells skateboarding gear">
<cfset request.meta_gen.keywords = "Skateboards, skateboarding,
     wheels, videos, tricks, skateboarders, bearings, street skate">

<cfif IsDefined("request.qryDetails")>
  <!--- we need to generate a clean comma
     delimited list of all the words in the product --->
  <cfscript>
  // combine all the database fields into one string
  strAllWords = request.qryDetails.title & " " &
     request.qryDetails.details & " " & request.qryDetails.brand_name;
  // strip all HTML
  strAllWords = REReplace(strAllWords, "<[^>]*>", "", "All");
  // strip all punctuation
  strAllWords = REReplace(strAllWords, "[[:punct:]]", "", "All");
  // strip carraige returns and line feeds
  strAllWords = Replace(strAllWords, chr(10), "", "ALL");
  strAllWords = Replace(strAllWords, chr(13), "", "ALL");
  // replace all spaces with commas
  strAllWords = Replace(strAllWords, " ", ",", "ALL");
  // mix all the ingredients and bake at 350 for 30 minutes
  request.meta_gen.keywords = request.meta_gen.keywords & "," & strAllWords;
  </cfscript>
</cfif>
```

The first two lines set up the default states of the metatags. Within the "IsDefined" block, we generate a list of keywords taken from the request.qryDetails query.

We could get much more elaborate than this. If you've ever dabbled with trying to balance the right number of keywords in a meta tag for the best placement in a search engine, you know there's an entire science to it, and you probably also know that our little tag is probably a little underpowered to do a perfect job at it. But it is better than having nothing at all, and that's what's important right now.

When we have more time, or even in the next version of the software, we can come back to this tag and make considerable strides forward, without having to change the structure of the code base. We can simply modify the modules/ spiderweb/ meta_gen.cfm module, making sure that our variables remain the same, and anything we change should be seamless.

modules/display/style.cfm

This module is more or less a placeholder for future growth. Right now, it's very simple:

```
<cfset request.style.results = '<link rel="STYLESHEET"
     type="text/css" href="basic.css">'>
```

In the future, we could decide to display different style sheets based on detected browser versions, or instead of linking to a style sheet, we could define style blocks with <STYLE> tags.

modules/general/html_wrapper.cfm

This module has a open tag and a close tag. It wraps the html and body tags around our entire template to ensure proper HTML form:

```
<cfif thistag.executionmode is "start">
  <!DOCTYPE HTML PUBLIC "-//W3C//DTD HTML 4.0 Transitional//EN">
  <html>
  <head>
    <cfoutput>
    <title>#request.page_title.results#</title>
    <META name="description"
content="#request.meta_gen.description#">
    <META name="keywords" content="#request.meta_gen.keywords#">
    #request.style.results#
    </cfoutput>
  </head>

  <body bgcolor="Black">
</cfif>

<cfif thistag.executionmode is "end">
  </body>
  </html>
</cfif>
```

The most interesting thing about this module is that it has an opening and closing tag. The thistag.executionmode object is what makes this possible. It's pretty easy to see how this works—anything between the first two <CFIF> statement tags is the start of the module. Anything between the second <CFIF> tags is the end of the module. If the expression in the <CFIF> tag is true, the code between the opening and closing tags will execute.

We also output the results of page_title.cfm module and the meta_gen.cfm module.

modules/display/master.cfm

This module controls the HTML guts of our site. This is where we put all of the HTML tables and link images, and position our navigational elements. We also include the category drill-down module, the shopping cart module, and the checkout progress module:

```
<cfif thistag.executionmode is "start">
<!--- logo bar --->
  <table width="720" cellpadding="0" cellspacing="0" border="0">
    <tr>
      <td width="128"><a href="index.cfm"><img
      src="images/general/logo.gif" width="128" height="47"
      alt="www.skate.shop" border="0"></a></td>
      <td width="592">
        <table width="592" cellpadding="0" cellspacing="0" border="0">
          <tr>
            <td colspan="3" bgcolor="#41545C"><img
            src="images/general/clear.gif" width="592" height="1" border="0"></td>
          </tr>
          <tr>
            <td bgcolor="#41545C"><img src="images/general/clear.gif"
            width="1" height="44" border="0"></td>
            <td width="590" bgcolor="#41545C"
align="right"><cfoutput>#request.LongDate(Now())#</cfoutput></td>
            <td bgcolor="#41545C"><img src="images/general/clear.gif"
            width="1" height="44" border="0"></td>
          </tr>
          <tr>
            <td colspan="3" bgcolor="#41545C"><img
            src="images/general/clear.gif" width="592" height="1" border="0"></td>
          </tr>
        </table>
      </td>
    </tr>
  </table>
  <table width="720" cellpadding="0" cellspacing="0" border="0">
    <tr>
      <td bgcolor="#526773" width="127" valign="top">
      <cfmodule template="/modules/nav/cat_drill.cfm">
      <img src="images/general/boarder.gif" width=127
      height=172 border="0">
      </td>
      <td bgcolor="black" width="1"><img src="images/general/clear.gif"
      width=1 height=16 border="0"></td>
      <td width="100%" valign="top" bgcolor="White" align="center">
</cfif>

<cfif thistag.executionmode is "end">
      </td>
```

```
        <td bgcolor="black" width="1"><img src="images/general/clear.gif"
        width=1 height=16 border="0"></td>
        <td width="220" bgcolor="Gray" valign="top">
          <cfswitch expression="#request.page#">
            <cfcase value="checkout">
              <cfmodule
              template="../../modules/pages/checkout/steps.cfm">
            </cfcase>
            <cfdefaultcase>
              <cfmodule template="../../modules/pages/cart/cart.cfm">
            </cfdefaultcase>
          </cfswitch>
        </td>
      </tr>
    </table>
</cfif>
```

This is mostly HTML formatting, but there are some essential application parts to this module. The first half of the module formats the HTML all the way up to the start of the main content window, where we end up displaying all of the content of our site. Remember, we have three main sections: the drill down, the content area, and the shopping cart area. Notice that there is a "hanging" <TD> at the end of the first half of the module. This is because we wrap this module around the main content switch in content.cfm, and the closing half of the module will finish up with a </TD>.

The closing half of the module also contains the shopping cart/checkout progress switch. There's only one way the checkout progress module will show, and that's if the value of the *request.page* variable is "checkout." Otherwise, it will always show the default case: the shopping cart.

The modules leading up to this point take care of nearly all of the site format details. Now it's time to get into the real workings of the application—the mini-applications.

The Main Switch

The last part of content.cfm contains the main switch for our site. Based on the *request.page* variable, which is set in our main pages, one of the cases is executed. Each item in this main switch represent one of the major sections of our application, or as I've been calling them, the mini-applications. The next section, "Building the Mini-Applications for the Interface," will look at each mini-application in detail.

Error Trapping

We've wrapped the entire content.cfm file with <CFTRY> tags. These tags allow us to try the code first, and if any errors occur, to hand off the error handling to the <CFCATCH> tags nested within the <CFTRY> tags.

The idea we had for our site was that there should be minimal possibility for an ominous ColdFusion error, regardless of the condition of the application. If for whatever reason the application gags, the code within <CFCATCH> still executes. Our <CFCATCH> tag uses the catch type of "any," which means that if anything at all bad happens, the code with the tag will execute. In our case, we're including a basically static error page that tells the user, in general terms, that there has been an error.

The <CFCATCH> tag can get more specific. Let's say we wanted to display a specific error if we were having troubles connecting to the database. We could use something like this:

```
<cftry>

<cfquery name="foo" datasource="wrongDatasourceName">
SQL statement here
</cfquery>

  <cfcatch type="database">
  There's been a database error!
  </cfcatch>
</cftry>
```

Because we used a wrong datasource name, the error message within the CFCATCH tags would be displayed.

Building the Mini-Applications for the Interface

Each mini-application is almost a standalone program, relying as little as possible on the rest of the application. In some cases, no information is needed from the rest of the program, but in most other cases, queries are needed. Each mini-application makes up the entire application, with content.cfm acting as the coordinator. In this chapter we've been interchanging the terms *mini-application* and *module* when referring to pieces of the application that perform distinct tasks, and we will continue to do so.

One of the ideas behind the mini-application is that several different files, or steps, might be needed for its functionality. This is especially evident in the checkout process, where the user progresses step by step to finalize their order. Each step in the checkout process has its own file, with a coordinator or dispatcher set aside just for that mini-application. In the case of the checkout process, the checkout.cfm file is a large switch that acts as the coordinator for each step, just like the content.cfm file does for the main application.

In this section, I get a little more detailed about the code being used for each mini-application, and I discuss my rationale for choosing to do something a certain way. Keep in mind that ColdFusion is flexible—there is no one way to do something. I'd love for you to install the skate.shop application and play around with it, but I'd also encourage you to try and figure out better ways of performing the same task.

With that in mind, I've decided to do certain things a little differently in the mini-applications, to give a feel for what can be done. I'll point out the best practices, and other performance related issues as I go along. If I've shown a code example that affects the performance of the site negatively, I'll make sure to point it out, and offer alternatives.

Category Drill-Down Module

The category drill-down is the primary means by which customers can navigate through our site. I'm not exactly sure where the term *drill-down* came from, but what it describes is the act of a user clicking through a list of links, getting deeper into a category. A good illustration of this is when you're clicking on categories on Yahoo or Google, getting deeper and deeper into the site until you find what you're looking for.

Our category drill-down is far simpler. There is only one level of categories. When you click on a category, you see products immediately, rather than more subcategories. We still use the term, however, because it seems to be a kind of Internet standard—the act of finding something by clicking on links has earned the term *drill-down*.

Based on the lack of complexity of the category drill-down mini-application, it's probably a bit confusing that I would even consider it a mini-application. The reason for considering it a mini-application is that it performs a vital function on the site. It will probably be the primary method that people will use to find products on our site. Additionally, it meets the criteria of a mini-application. It requires very few, if any, pieces of information from the main application, and it can theoretically be pulled out of the main application without harming the main application, while still functioning on its own. The fact that it's simple doesn't stop it from being a powerful part of the site.

We call the module in the modules/display/master.cfm file. The module requires the request.CatDrill query, which is executed in the global queries file called from content.cfm.

The code for the category drill down exists in two places:

- Queries/global.cfm, which creates the request.qryCatDrill object by running the stored procedure dspCatDrill

- Modules/nav/cat_drill.cfm., which displays the results of the request.qryCatDrill object

queries/global.cfm

```
<cfquery name="request.qryCatDrill"
  datasource="#request.dsn#"
  cachedwithin=" #CreateTimeSpan(1,0,0,0)#">
exec dspCatDrill
</cfquery>
```

We execute this query in the global.cfm file because we want to possibly use the query data for future functionality. Keeping it in the global file maintains our organization because the category drill-down exists on every page; the query should also run on every page.

However, there's a performance flaw to running the query on every page. Our categories are probably not going to change often, if ever, so we're going to cache the query using the *cachedwithin* attribute. Using the CreateTimeSpan function, we set the query to cache for one day. This way, we dramatically reduce the amount of times that ColdFusion has to go to the database server to retrieve information. It also speeds up the application, because rather than waiting for results to come back from the database server, it gets the results from local memory.

We're executing a stored procedure within the <CFQUERY> tag, which is a perfectly legitimate way of executing a stored procedure. One of the more common questions asked at my local ColdFusion User Group meetings is "How do you execute a stored procedure in ColdFusion?" Stored procedures can be called with standard SQL, and <CFQUERY> supports standard SQL.

We'll look at some stored procedures that return multiple result sets later on, which you won't be able to use <CFQUERY> to execute.

dspCatDrill Stored Procedure

```
CREATE PROCEDURE dspCatDrill AS

SELECT cat_id, cat_name, showcat
FROM categories
WHERE showcat = 1
GO
```

You can create this stored procedure in the Enterprise Manager, or even easier, the SQL Query Analyzer.

The SELECT statement is easy to figure out. We're doing a simple SELECT for every category row where the showcat column is equal to one. Records with a showcat value of zero are considered hidden categories according to our spec.

TIP

*Avoid using the SELECT * FROM table. Using the wildcard symbol (*) requires that the database server determine what tables are available before returning any records. This is an extra bit of overhead that isn't necessary, and can be avoided. Even when selecting all columns from a table with very few columns to begin with, using the wildcard is a bad practice. Also, if the DBA decided to add several more columns to the table later on, you'd be pulling back extra columns that aren't needed, unnecessarily adding more overhead to the query. Always be specific when selecting your columns. When developing, it's not such a bad rule to break, but before the application is being used by hundreds of people at a time, you should make sure you're selecting specific columns.*

modules/nav/cat_drill.cfm

```
<table width="127" border="0" cellspacing="0" cellpadding="2">
  <tr>
    <td rowspan="9"><img src="images/general/clear.gif"
    width=3 height=1 border="0"></td>
    <td><b><a href="index.cfm" class="nav">Home</a></b></td>
  </tr>
  <cfoutput query="request.qryCatDrill">
    <tr>
      <td><b><a href="results.cfm?cat=#cat_id#"
       class="nav">#cat_name#</a></b></td>
    </tr>
  </cfoutput>
  <tr>
    <td colspan="2"><img src="assets/img/clear.gif"
      width=1 height=25 border="0"></td>
  </tr>
</table>
```

Displaying the data is also simple. We simply want a new HTML table row for each record in request.qryCatDrill.

Notice the href. We're pointing to results.cfm, adding a URL variable named *cat* with the value of cat_id. Results.cfm expects one of two values—either a *url.cat* variable or a *form.searchcrit* variable (which we'll talk about next).

Keyword Search Module

The keyword search mini-application uses the integrated Verity search engine. ColdFusion 5.0 adds new Verity functionality by including an OEM version of the Verity K2 server. The skate.shop application doesn't need the full functionality of the K2 server, so we're going to stick with the traditional Verity integretation. However, we will discuss the K2 server in Part III of this book.

Verity was designed to index static documents, but it can also be used to create indexes based on query results. In our keyword search mini-application, we'll build a very simple administrator to help build and maintain Verity collections, and we'll hand search criteria to <CFRSEARCH> to return product_ID values to our request.qryResults query.

Creating Verity Collections

Before we can search a Verity collection, we need to create one. We can use the ColdFusion Server administrator to create a collection, but it's a lot easier to use the <CFCOLLECTION> tag in our administrator.

Let's take a look at the administrator. For now it's very simple—it's just one

file that has a switch for the possible actions. We can easily integrate this simple administrator into the site administrator that we build in Chapter 7.

admin/verity/index.cfm

```
<a href="index.cfm?action=create">Create Collection </a><br>
<a href="index.cfm?action=refresh">Refresh Collection</a><br>
<a href="index.cfm?action=optimize">Optimize Collection </a><br>
<a href="index.cfm?action=delete">Delete Collection </a><br>
<a href="index.cfm?action=repair">Repair Collection </a><br>

<cfif IsDefined("url.action")>
  <cfswitch expression="#url.action#">
    <cfcase value="create">
      <cfquery name="qryForIndexing" datasource="#request.dsn#">
      SELECT details, brand_name, title
      FROM results_view
      </cfquery>

      <cfcollection action="CREATE"
              collection="skate_shop_coll"
              path="d:\inetpub\wwwroot\skate.shop\admin\verity">
```

```
        <cfindex action="REFRESH"
           collection="skate_shop_coll"
           key="product_id"
           type="CUSTOM"
           title="title"
           query="qryForIndexing"
           body="details,brand_name,title">

        <cfindex action="UPDATE"
           collection="skate_shop_coll"
           key="product_id"
           type="CUSTOM"
           title="title"
           query="qryForIndexing"
           body="details,brand_name,title">

       <cfoutput>#qryForIndexing.recordcount#</cfoutput>
        records indexed.

      </cfcase>
      <cfcase value="refresh">
        <cfquery name="qryForIndexing" datasource="#request.dsn#">
        SELECT product_id, details, brand_name, title
        FROM results_view
        </cfquery>

        <cfindex action="REFRESH"
           collection="skate_shop_coll"
           key="product_id"
           type="CUSTOM"
           title="title"
           query="qryForIndexing"
           body="details,brand_name,title">
      </cfcase>
      <cfcase value="optimize">
        <cfcollection action="OPTIMIZE" collection="skate_shop_coll">
      </cfcase>
      <cfcase value="delete">
        <cfcollection action="DELETE" collection="skate_shop_coll">
      </cfcase>
      <cfcase value="repair">
        <cfcollection action="REPAIR" collection="skate_shop_coll">
      </cfcase>
    </cfswitch>
  </cfif>
```

The first <CFCASE> tag handles the creation and population of the collection. The first thing we do is to execute a query that contains every possible item we want our users to be able to search on. We should only include the columns that we want to match keywords on. If our product descriptions were very wordy, and had tons of information, it might be a better idea to leave the product descriptions out of the collection, as they might produce far too many, seemingly irrelevant results. But because there's really not much data in our product descriptions, we're not worried about that.

The From clause in qryForIndexing refers to a view in our database called results_view. Views are like temporary tables in SQL Server. Views offer a performance increase in complex queries, because they cache the execution plan for a query, reducing the amount of time it takes to return records.

We feed the results of the view to the <CFCOLLECTION> tag, which creates a collection based on the results of qryForIndexing. When this <CFCOLLECTION> tag executes, it automatically creates the necessary directories and files (admin/verity/) that we specified in the tag.

The other actions are used to update the index, delete it, optimize it, or repair it. It's possible to do all of these kinds of maintenance tasks through the administrator, but it just makes more sense to handle them here.

Building a Verity Query

Getting Verity to produce some results is relatively easy. Simply pass some criteria to a <CFSEARCH> tag. The results that the <CFSEARCH> tag produce aren't exactly pretty, and they are not suitable to use with our results.cfm module. Therefore, we're going to pass the results of the Verity search to a query that will generate the proper results for results.cfm.

Because we only want one results file, regardless of how the user gets there, we need to do a little bit of thinking in queries/queryResults.cfm. The first thing we try to determine is what kind of search are we doing—a keyword search or a category drill-down? If the *url.cat* parameter exists, then we're doing a drill-down search. If *form.search* exists, then it's a keyword search.

Skip down to the second <CFIF>, where we're looking for the *form.searchcrit* variable. This is where we build our Verity query.

```
<cfset request.resultsError = 0>

<cfif IsDefined("url.cat")>
  <cfquery name="request.qryResults" datasource="#request.dsn#">
  SELECT brand_name, brand_id, cat_id, cat_name, title, img,
  product_status_id, showcat, price, product_id
  FROM results_view
  WHERE cat_id = #url.cat#
```

```
  </cfquery>

  <cfif request.qryResults.recordcount eq 0>
    <cfset request.resultsError = 1>
  </cfif>
</cfif>

<cfif IsDefined("form.searchcrit")>
  <!--- this is where all the verity action takes place --->
  <cfsearch collection="skate_shop_coll" name="verityResults"
criteria="#form.searchcrit#">

  <cfif verityResults.recordcount neq 0>
    <cfquery name="request.qryResults" datasource="#request.dsn#">
    SELECT brand_name, brand_id, cat_id, cat_name, title, img,
    product_status_id, showcat, price, product_id
    FROM results_view
    WHERE product_id IN (#ValueList(verityResults.key)#)
    </cfquery>
  <cfelse>
    <!--- set a flag that the results.cfm will
     check for to see if there are any results --->
    <cfset request.resultsError = 1>
  </cfif>
</cfif>
```

The first thing we do is pass the search criteria to the <CFSEARCH> tag. We specify the collection we want to search, and pass the search criteria. When <CFSEARCH> executes, it creates a query object, which we've named verityResults.

If <CFSEARCH> comes up with anything, we pass verityResults.key to the SQL statement. Forgive me for being redundant, but there are two key concepts here. When we created the skate_shop_coll collection, in the <CFCOLLECTION> tag we set what value we wanted to set as the key. We used the Product_ID from the query we used to populate the collection. We could have used almost anything unique, but we used the Product_ID so that we could easily pass the list of key values to a traditional SQL query.

The Where product_id IN (#ValueList(verityResults.key)#) part of the query selects every record within the generated comma-delimited list of Product_IDs.

In both queries, if no results are retrieved, we set *request.resultsError* to be equal to one. If results.cfm sees that the value of this variable is one, it displays a "no products found" error message.

modules/pages/search/searchbox.cfm

The search criteria has to originate from somewhere. Here's the code for the search box. It doesn't need much explanation, but for the sake of being consistent in showing all the code, here it is:

```
<table width="100%" cellpadding="0" cellspacing="0"
   border="0" bgcolor="#3E4E56">
  <form action="results.cfm" method="get">
  <tr>
    <td rowspan="4"><img src="images/general/clear.gif"
     width="5" height="1"  border="0"></td>
    <td class="searchbox"><b>Search:</b></td>
  </tr>
  <tr>
    <td><input type="text" name="searchcrit" size="15"></td>
  </tr>
  <tr>
    <td><img src="images/general/clear.gif"
    width="1" height="3"  border="0"></td>
  </tr>
  <tr>
    <td><input type="image" src="images/general/search_action.gif"
      width="75" height="15"></td>
  </tr>
  <tr>
    <td colspan="2"><img src="images/general/search_box_cap.gif"
    width="127" height="7" border="0"></td>
  </tr>
  </form>
</table>
```

I broke an HTML rule in this code. The <FORM> tags should be outside of the <TABLE> tags, but whenever I do that, I get undesirable spacing above and below the form, both in Netscape and in Internet Explorer. I simply can't allow something like that to screw up my design, so I just break the rules. The funny thing is that it looks and works fine in Netscape and in Internet Explorer.

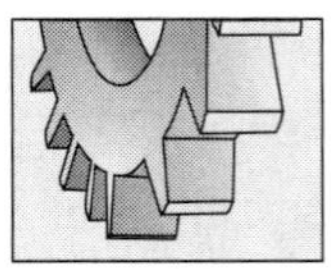

TIP

Our modules are deep within a directory structure, like modules/pages/search/searchbox.cfm. It's a good idea to remember that the paths to images should be entered as if the page was executing from the root directory, because in reality, it is executing from the root directory. If you use ColdFusion studio, and you rely on what it thinks the paths of the images are, you'll likely end up with broken images, because the path will be something like "../../images/general/clear.gif" when it should be "images/general/clear.gif".

Product Results Module

One of our goals for the application was that we'd reuse code as much as possible. The product results module is a perfect example of reuse. It only requires one thing—a query with the columns it's looking for, results or no results.

Technically, there is very little to this mini-application, but it still plays an important role in our main application. Combined with the qryResults.cfm module, the results module displays the list of available products for purchase. There's no need to belabor the point that it plays one of the most important roles in our application.

When displaying products, consistency is everything. We should confuse our customers as little as possible, and one of the ways to do that is by remaining consistent in how we display products. We might be able to remain consistent in the way we display products by using separate modules for category drill-down results and keyword search results, but if the modules became more complex, it could get tedious to keep the files consistent, and we would run the risk of the files becoming out of synch in how they display products.

Using one results file makes the most sense for maintaining consistency, and it makes it easier for the developer in the long run. Changing something once is unarguably easier than changing the same thing twice.

With all of that said, I should point out the possible pitfalls of using one file. The query that is used to display results must be identical in its structure. The columns need to be the same, and the grouping needs to remain consistent. It reduces our flexibility in the way we display products by using one file—it means that the results need to be identical. Ideally, this shouldn't ever really be a concern, but if even the slightest thing needs to be different for one search method versus another, we need two separate files (or we need to dynamically display the results differently based on the search method).

modules/pages/results/results.cfm

```
<cfif request.resultsError eq 0>
  <cfoutput query="request.qryResults" group="cat_id">
    <p>
    <table width="362" cellpadding="0" cellspacing="0" border="0">
      <tr>
        <td colspan="3"><b><img src="images/general/downarrow.gif"
        width="10" height="8"  border="0"> #Cat_Name#</b></td>
      </tr>
    <cfoutput group="Brand_ID">
      <tr>
        <td colspan="3" bgcolor="##C0C0C0"><b>#Brand_Name#</b></td>
      </tr>
      <cfoutput group="Product_ID">
        <tr>
          <td width="30"><a href="details.cfm?id=#product_id#"><img
            src="images/product/thumbnail/#img#"
            border="0" alt="#title#"></a></td>
          <td width="292"><a
          href="details.cfm?id=#product_id#">#title#</a></td>
          <td width="40">#DollarFormat(price)#</td>
        </tr>
      </cfoutput>
    </cfoutput>
    </table>
  </cfoutput>
<cfelse>
nothing found, show no products error.
</cfif>
```

The first thing we do is determine whether we have products to display. If we don't, we show the "sorry no products" error. If we do, we get right into outputting the query. There are three levels of grouping, with the idea that products should be organized by category, then by brand, then by product. Grouping by product isn't really necessary, but can act as a reminder of the organizational structure.

The grouping has a big effect on the HTML code that is generated. Each category of products sits within its own table, and each brand gets a table data cell that spans the entire table, while each product gets a row, with table data cells for the thumbnail image, the title, and the price.

Product Details Module

The product details module uses two files: queries/qryDetails.cfm and modules/pages/details/details.cfm. The first file is the query file. It executes ahead of time so that we can use the results of the query for the metatag generator and the page title generator. Let's look at the code for queries/qryDetails.cfm.

queries/qryDetails.cfm

```
<cfquery name="request.qryDetails" datasource="#request.dsn#"
cachedwithin="#CreateTimeSpan(0,2,0,0)#">
SELECT *
FROM details_view
WHERE Product_ID = #url.id#
</cfquery>
```

The first noticeable thing about this query is that I'm doing exactly what I said you shouldn't do earlier. I'm using SELECT * when I said that it wasn't a good thing to do. But I'm using SELECT * with a view, and performance-wise, there is no difference in using a wildcard to select all columns and explicitly naming each column to select.

A good way of evaluating query performance is by using the SQL Query Analyzer. This program not only lets you execute SQL statements and view results, but it also analyzes queries. Some people are curious why SQL Query Analyzer is called what it is, because it seems more a SQL client than anything else. SQL Query Analyzer has a feature that allows you to view the estimated query execution plan. This tool can provide valuable feedback about how the query is running, and where it's encountering bottlenecks.

To access the SQL Query Analyzer, you can either open it by going to Start Menu | Programs | Microsoft SQL Server | Query Analyzer, or you can open it from within Enterprise Manager by clicking Tools | SQL Query Analyzer.

To view the estimated execution plan, shown in Figure 6-1, you can either click the button directly to the right of the database drop-down menu on the upper toolbar, or press CTRL-L.

I still might face problems with the view changing—but I run that risk with views anyhow. If the view changes, regardless of whether or not I use a wildcard or specific column-naming convention, someone could change the view and I'd be up a creek. The benefits of views outweigh that risk, though. As with stored procedures, their executing plans are cached, but I get the added flexibility of "pretending" that the view is a table (which I don't get to do with stored procedures).

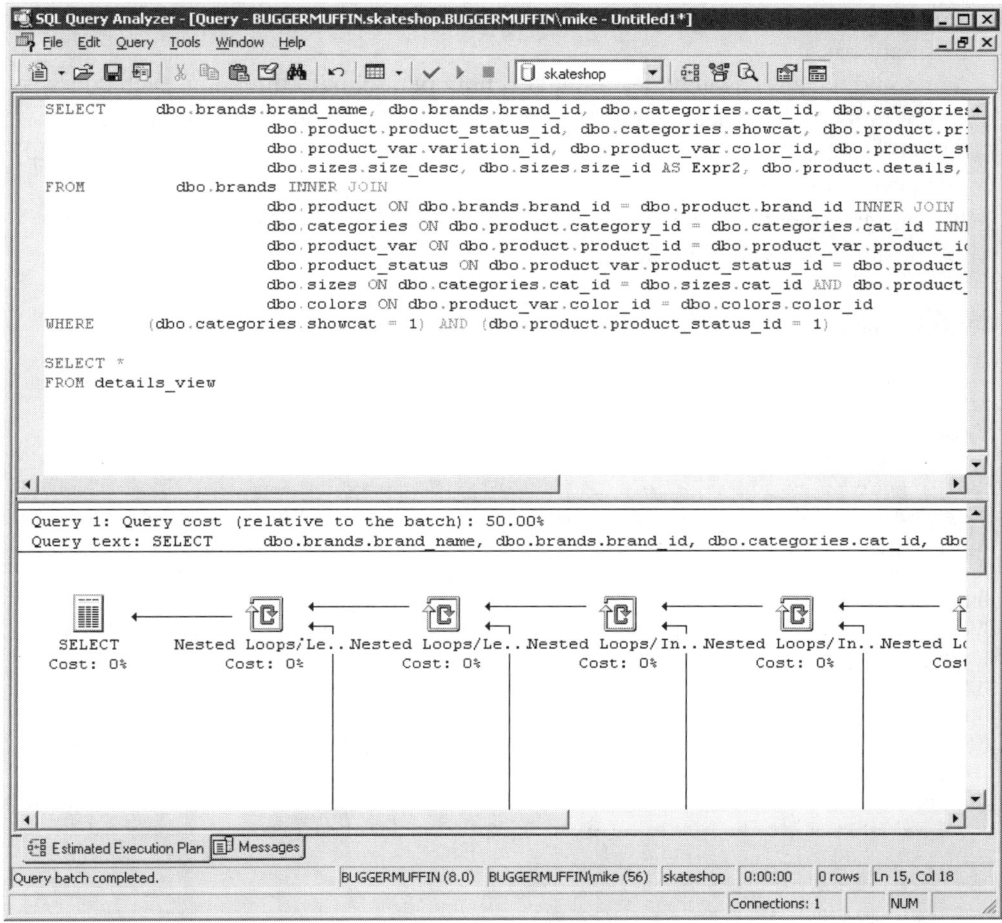

Figure 6-1 *Accessing the SQL Query Analyzer*

This query is cached—product details don't change often. The only data that we can readily say might change is the pricing information and stock status. Setting the query to be cached within two hours allows us to change prices without a huge lag. If the product you're selling is of a very volatile nature, then it might make sense to do away with caching altogether, or to consider a redesign of the query. It's relatively simple to split the details query from the prices query, but doing so would increase the number of times it would take to connect to the database. Balancing the performance needs with the business needs can sometimes be tricky, but both sides should be open for compromise. You may need to reduce performance to accommodate your business structure, or you may need to rethink your business structure to accommodate performance issues.

We could have set a sitewide, default caching period, but I think that each query is different in its caching needs. A site developer should be well aware of what queries need to be cached for what amount of time, and of course, these requirements should be well documented.

This query selects all the columns we use for the display of the product. Here's what the actual view looks like.

details_view

```
CREATE VIEW dbo.details_view
AS
SELECT
dbo.brands.brand_name, dbo.brands.brand_id, dbo.categories.cat_id,
dbo.categories.cat_name, dbo.product.title, dbo.product.img,
dbo.product.product_status_id, dbo.categories.showcat, dbo.product.price,
dbo.product.product_id, dbo.product_var.size_id, dbo.product_var.variation_id,
dbo.product_var.color_id, dbo.product_status.status, dbo.colors.color_desc,
dbo.colors.color_id AS Expr1, dbo.sizes.size_desc, dbo.sizes.size_id AS Expr2,
dbo.product.details, dbo.product_status.product_status_id AS prodvar_status_id
FROM dbo.brands
INNER JOIN dbo.product ON dbo.brands.brand_id = dbo.product.brand_id
INNER JOIN dbo.categories ON dbo.product.category_id = dbo.categories.cat_id
INNER JOIN dbo.product_var ON dbo.product.product_id =
dbo.product_var.product_id
INNER JOIN dbo.product_status ON
dbo.product_var.product_status_id = dbo.product_status.product_status_id
LEFT OUTER JOIN dbo.sizes ON
dbo.categories.cat_id = dbo.sizes.cat_id
AND dbo.product_var.size_id = dbo.sizes.size_id
LEFT OUTER JOIN dbo.colors ON dbo.product_var.color_id = dbo.colors.color_id
WHERE (dbo.categories.showcat = 1) AND (dbo.product.product_status_id = 1)
```

It's probably easy to see why views can help simplify things. This relatively complex query is much easier to work with than a view, and the performance benefits are worthwhile. Now that we've seen the view and know of all the available columns, let's look at the display.

modules/pages/details/details.cfm

The goal of the details page is to show the product image and description as efficiently as possible, and to allow customers to add any one of the product variations to their shopping carts.

```
<cfoutput query="request.qryDetails" group="cat_id">
  <p>
  <table width="362" cellpadding="0" cellspacing="0" border="0">
    <tr>
      <td colspan="2"><b><img
        src="images/general/downarrow.gif"
        width="10" height="8"
        border="0"> #Cat_Name#</b></td>
    </tr>
  <cfoutput group="Brand_ID">
    <tr>
      <td colspan="2" bgcolor="##C0C0C0"><b>#Brand_Name#</b></td>
    </tr>
    <cfoutput group="Product_ID">
      <tr>
        <td width="200" valign="top"><img
        src="images/product/medium/#img#"
        border="0" alt="#title#"></td>
        <td width="162" valign="top">
        <b>#title#</b><br>#details#
        </td>
      </tr>
      <tr>
        <td colspan="2">
          <table width="100%"
           cellpadding="2"
           cellspacing="0" border="0">
            <tr bgcolor="##C0C0C0">
              <td><b>Size</b></td>
              <td><b>Color</b></td>
              <td><b>Stock Status</b></td>
              <td><b>Price</b></td>
              <td><b>Add</b></td>
            </tr>
            <cfoutput group="variation_id">
            <cfif currentrow/2 eq int(currentrow/2)>
            <tr bgcolor="##EAEAEA">
            <cfelse>
            <tr>
            </cfif>
              <td>#size_desc#</td>
              <td>#color_desc#</td>
              <td>#status#</td>
```

```
                <td>#DollarFormat(price)#</td>
                <cfif prodvar_status_id eq 4>
                <td><img src="images/general/addcart_un.gif"
                width="87" height="15"  border="0"></td>
                <cfelse>
                <td>
<a href="details.cfm?cart=add&id=#Product_ID#&var_id=#variation_id#">
<img src="images/general/addcart.gif"
  width="87" height="15" alt="Add to Cart" border="0"></a></td>
                </cfif>
              </tr>
              </cfoutput>
            </table>
          </td>
       </tr>
     </cfoutput>
  </table>
  </cfoutput>
</cfoutput>
```

This code is your basic query output, using grouping to keep the data organized. Some of the more interesting parts of the code occur in the product variation display (the fourth nested <CFOUTPUT> tag). For readability purposes, I want each row to alternate in color, so I do a simple little trick:

```
<cfif currentrow/2 eq int(currentrow/2)>
show one color
<cfelse>
show another color
</cfif>
```

If I divide the current row by two, and it is equal in value to the integer value of the current row divided by two, then I must have an even number. Only even numbers divide perfectly in half, without any leftover decimal places, so wherever that condition is true, I'll show one color, and for everything else, I'll show another color.

When product variations are not in stock, we don't want to hide them—we still want customers to know that we carry the product, but that it's just not currently available. So we simply disable the shopping cart button.

The "Add to shopping cart" link simply passes *product_id* and *product_variation_id* to the details.cfm page. The most important URL attribute it passes is the *url.cart* tag, which in this case has the value of *add*.

The *url.cart* attribute indicates that the shopping cart should be ready to perform some type of action, and the value tells the shopping cart what that action is.

Shopping Cart Module

The shopping cart is probably the most complex mini-application in our main application; if not, it's a close second to the customer checkout system. There are several ways to track shopping cart information. For this application, I chose to track the information in a database. It's possible to store the information in a session variable, or a cookie, but I have much more flexibility and control over the shopping cart when it's in a database. There are performance issues when using a database—storing shopping cart entries in the **Session** scope is a lot faster than storing the entries in a table, but again, I gain flexibility and control using a database table.

Regardless of how we store the data, the concept of the cart is pretty much the same. Let's look at the following list of shopping carts requirements:

- Allow customers to add items to the cart.
- Allow customers to delete items from the cart.
- Allow customers to change quantities.
- Display the products in an orderly fashion.
- Allow customers to determine shipping cost and tax.

With these requirements in mind, let's look at the code.

queries/qryScart.cfm

This file is included on every page (it's in queries/main_switch.cfm, which executes on every page). If *url.cart* is present, then it will kick off some type of shopping cart action. The qryScart.cfm file is long, and I'll be showing one piece of it at a time, and talking about it in between. I'll be showing every line of it, though, so don't worry about missing anything.

Let's look at the first part of the code, where we perform the initial query of the shopping cart.

```
<cfquery name="request.qryScart" datasource="#request.dsn#">
SELECT *
FROM scart_view
WHERE uuid = '#session.uuid#'
</cfquery>
```

We're selecting all the products in the shopping cart where the uuid column is equal to *session.uuid*. Remember, *session.uuid* is initialized in application.cfm. We're using a view for this, so let's take a look at the view.

TIP

On operating systems where file case sensitivity is an issue, remember to make sure the first letter in Application.cfm is in uppercase. If your file is all lowercase, ColdFusion will not execute it, because It looks for Application.cfm. It's a good habit to consider this even when developing on a Windows machine, in case you port the code to a Linux server.

scart_view

```
CREATE VIEW dbo.scart_view
AS
SELECT dbo.scart.uuid, dbo.scart.quantity, dbo.scart.variation_id,
dbo.sizes.size_desc, dbo.colors.color_desc, dbo.product.title,
dbo.product.price, dbo.product.product_id, dbo.categories.cat_name,
dbo.categories.cat_id, dbo.product.weight
FROM dbo.scart
INNER JOIN dbo.product_var ON
dbo.scart.variation_id = dbo.product_var.variation_id
INNER JOIN dbo.product ON
dbo.product_var.product_id = dbo.product.product_id
INNER JOIN dbo.categories ON
dbo.product.category_id = dbo.categories.cat_id
LEFT OUTER JOIN dbo.sizes ON
dbo.product_var.size_id = dbo.sizes.size_id
LEFT OUTER JOIN dbo.colors ON
dbo.product_var.color_id = dbo.colors.color_id
```

Now, let's look at the new Query of Queries feature in ColdFusion 5.0, and actually use it to avoid having to connect to the database again.

```
<cfif IsDefined("url.var_id")>
  <!--- QofQ of qryScart for this row --->
  <cfquery name="QofQ_qryScart" dbtype="Query">
  SELECT quantity
  FROM request.qryScart
  WHERE variation_id = #url.var_id#
  </cfquery>
</cfif>
```

If *url.var_id* is present, then we know we need some data for a specific product variation in this customers shopping cart. We're actually simply narrowing down data from the request.qryScart query that we performed earlier. Rather than making a new database connection with a more specific query, we simply run a query on the previous query. We only have to submit the *url.var_id* variable as part of the WHERE clause, because the first query has already narrowed down the records to the session.uuid we're currently dealing with.

Querying the previous query kills two birds with one stone for us. First, we get a functional query that provides the data for the output of the shopping cart. Second, we get to eliminate a database connection by narrowing down on that previous query. Querying a query in ColdFusion is a pretty powerful feature, and can be used to increase performance.

Why do we need to focus on a particular product variation? Where is the query QofQ_qryScart used? To answer that question, let's look at the next few lines:

```
<cfif IsDefined("url.cart")>
  <cfswitch expression="#url.cart#">
    <cfcase value="add">
      <!-- products now get added to the cart, or qty is updated --->
      <cfif QofQ_qryScart.recordcount eq 0>
        <!--- if the product isn't in the customer's cart, add it --->
        <cfstoredproc procedure="AddScart" datasource="#request.dsn#">
          <cfprocparam type="In"
           cfsqltype="CF_SQL_VARCHAR" value="#session.uuid#"
           dbvarname="@uuid" maxlength="35" null="No">
          <cfprocparam type="In"
           cfsqltype="CF_SQL_INTEGER"
           value="#url.var_id#"
           dbvarname="@var_id" null="No">
          <!--- this brings back a refreshed cart --->
          <cfprocresult name="request.qryScart" resultset="1">
        </cfstoredproc>
      <cfelse>
        <!--- if the product is already there,
        bump it's quantity up by one --->
        <cfstoredproc procedure="UpdateScart"
         datasource="#request.dsn#">
          <cfprocparam type="In" cfsqltype="CF_SQL_VARCHAR"
           value="#session.uuid#" dbvarname="@uuid" maxlength="35" null="No">
          <cfprocparam type="In" cfsqltype="CF_SQL_INTEGER"
          value="#url.var_id#" dbvarname="@var_id" null="No">
          <!--- this brings back a refreshed cart --->
          <cfprocresult name="request.qryScart" resultset="1">
```

```
        </cfstoredproc>
      </cfif>
    </cfcase>
```

The first line checks for the existence of *url.cart*. This parameter is required for the cart to do anything at all. The following <CFSWITCH> tag uses *url.cart* to decide which case to execute.

Let's look at the <cfcase value="add"> section. This code deals simply with adding a product to the shopping cart.

Right away within the case we ask if the QofQ_qryScart has any records. If QofQ_qryScart found anything, then the product is already in the shopping cart, so instead of creating a duplicate record for it, let's simply bump the quantity up by one.

Let's look at how we do that—there's a new type of tag here that we haven't used in the application yet, the <CFSTOREDPROC> tag. This tag allows us to execute a stored procedure, but more importantly, it allows us to receive multiple result sets back. Basically, we can perform multiple queries in one stored procedure, and come back with multiple queries. This can provide performance increases, because it reduces the amount of connections that need to be made to the database server. Let's look at the first stored procedure that adds the product to the cart if it doesn't already exist.

AddScart Store Procedure

```
CREATE PROCEDURE AddScart
(
@uuid varchar(35)= NULL,
@var_id int = NULL
)
AS
INSERT INTO scart
(uuid, quantity, variation_id)
VALUES
(@uuid, 1, @var_id)

SELECT *
FROM scart_view
WHERE uuid = @uuid
GO
```

The first half of the stored procedure adds the product. Nested within the <CFSTOREDPROC> tag are <CFPROCPARAM> tags that we use to pass parameters to the stored procedure. We pass the *@uuid* parameter and the *@var_id* parameter so that we add the right product variation to the current UUID.

The second query looks exactly like the request.qryScart query—it is exactly the same, and it's used for the same purpose. Because the request.qryScart query has already executed by the time we add a product to the cart, and because by adding a product to the cart we've changed the data, we need to refresh the request.qryScart query.

Using a <CFPROCRESULT> tag, we indicate that the first result set should be called request.qryScart, which effectively overwrites the first request.qryScart. The result set is considered the first result set even though it's the second query in the stored procedure, because the Insert query doesn't produce a result set.

If the product variation already exists in the shopping cart, we simply increment the quantity by one.

UpdateScart Stored Procedure

```
CREATE PROCEDURE UpdateScart
(
@uuid varchar(35)= NULL,
@var_id int = NULL
)
AS

UPDATE scart
SET quantity = quantity + 1
WHERE uuid = @uuid AND variation_id = @var_id

SELECT *
FROM scart_view
WHERE uuid = @uuid
GO
```

We return the second query just like we did in the first query.

Let's look at the next case, the removal of a product:

```
<cfcase value="rm">
  <!--- remove the product --->
  <cfstoredproc procedure="RmScart" datasource="#request.dsn#">
    <cfprocparam type="In" cfsqltype="CF_SQL_VARCHAR"
    value="#session.uuid#" dbvarname="@uuid" maxlength="35" null="No">
    <cfprocparam type="In" cfsqltype="CF_SQL_INTEGER"
    value="#url.var_id#" dbvarname="@var_id" null="No">
    <!--- this brings back a refreshed cart --->
    <cfprocresult name="request.qryScart" resultset="1">
  </cfstoredproc>
</cfcase>
```

Based on *session.uuid* and *url.var_id*, we simply remove the item from the cart using the RmScart stored procedure.

RmScart Stored Procedure

```
CREATE PROCEDURE RmScart
(
@uuid varchar(35)= NULL,
@var_id int = NULL
)
AS

DELETE
FROM scart
WHERE uuid = @uuid AND variation_id = @var_id

SELECT *
FROM scart_view
WHERE uuid = @uuid
GO
```

We remove the product, and refresh the cart just like we did with the previous queries. This case also only executes when the *url.cart* value is rm. There will be a link on a product in the shopping cart that allows the customer to remove a product that supplies this value.

Now, on to the next case—reducing the quantity of an item in the shopping cart:

```
<cfcase value="sub">
      <cfif QofQ_qryScart.quantity lte 1>
        <!-- if the quantity for this product_var is less
        than or equal to 1, then we want to delete it --->
        <!--- remove the product --->
        <cfstoredproc procedure="RmScart" datasource="#request.dsn#">
          <cfprocparam type="In" cfsqltype="CF_SQL_VARCHAR"
          value="#session.uuid#" dbvarname="@uuid" maxlength="35" null="No">
          <cfprocparam type="In" cfsqltype="CF_SQL_INTEGER"
          value="#url.var_id#" dbvarname="@var_id" null="No">
          <!--- this brings back a refreshed cart --->
          <cfprocresult name="request.qryScart" resultset="1">
        </cfstoredproc>
      <cfelse>
        <!---subtract a value from customers cart --->
        <cfstoredproc procedure="SubScart" datasource="#request.dsn#">
          <cfprocparam type="In" cfsqltype="CF_SQL_VARCHAR"
```

```
          value="#session.uuid#"
          dbvarname="@uuid" maxlength="35" null="No">
          <cfprocparam type="In" cfsqltype="CF_SQL_INTEGER"
           value="#url.var_id#" dbvarname="@var_id" null="No">

<!--- this brings back a refreshed cart --->
          <cfprocresult name="request.qryScart" resultset="1">
        </cfstoredproc>
      </cfif>
    </cfcase>
```

It's possible to execute one of two stored procedures here. If the customer subtracts an item from their cart when they only have one item, it would make sense to remove the item from the cart completely. (It would be silly to track an item with zero quantity.) To do this, we use our QofQ_qryScart query of a query to determine the quantity for this item. If it's less then or equal to one, we remove it, using the RmScart stored procedure we looked at a second ago. If the product has a quantity greater than one, then we use the SubScart stored procedure.

SubScart Stored Procedure

The SubScart stored procedure updates the quantity of the shopping cart where the *UUID* column is equal to the supplied *@uuid* variable, and the *variation_id* is equal to the supplied *@var_id*.

```
CREATE PROCEDURE SubScart
(
@uuid varchar(35)= NULL,
@var_id int = NULL
)
AS

UPDATE scart
SET quantity = quantity - 1
WHERE uuid = @uuid AND variation_id = @var_id

SELECT *
FROM scart_view
WHERE uuid = @uuid
GO
```

This is almost getting redundant, but the preceding code shows how simple this kind of mini-application is if you make it simple. I've seen some very complex code for shopping carts, and I've seen some very simple code for shopping carts, and I'm sure you agree—simpler is better.

The last case in the switch helps out with the shipping calculations, and it might seem a bit out of place now, but you'll probably understand it once you've seen the entire picture.

```
<cfcase value="resetship">
  <cfset session.zipcode = 0>
  <cfset session.shipMethod = 0>
</cfcase>
```

Once a customer has entered a ZIP code and state to determine shipping and tax, they have the option of changing the ZIP code and tax. Because when a user enters their ZIP code and shipping method, we can't delete the *session.zipcode* and *session.shipMethod* variables created. If they want to change them, we need to set the to zero. Later on, if the *session.zipcode* and *session.shipMethod* variables are zero, we'll allow the customer to enter new information.

Here are a couple of more shipping-related pieces of code, as well as the remainder of the qryScart.cfm module. The bulk of shipping-related code is actually located in the last few lines, as a custom tag created by a third party.

```
<cfif IsDefined("form.zipcode")>
  <cfset session.zipcode = form.zipcode>
  <cfset session.shipMethod = form.shipMethod>
  <cfset session.state = form.state>
</cfif>

<cfif IsDefined("session.zipcode")>
  <cfif session.zipcode neq 0>
    <!--- determine total weight of items --->
    <cfquery name="QofQ_qryWeight" dbtype="Query">
    SELECT sum(weight*quantity) as total_weight
    FROM request.qryScart
    </cfquery>

    <cfif IsDefined("QofQ_qryWeight")>
      <!--- Perform Shipping Table Lookups --->
      <cfmodule template="../modules/shipping_calc/FedexMonger.cfm"
      weight="#QofQ_qryWeight.total_weight#"
      servicetype="#session.shipMethod#" zip="#session.zipcode#">
    </cfif>
  </cfif>
</cfif>
```

The first <CFIF> statement sets the shipping session variables. The form elements that the code refers to originate from the shopping cart module that we'll be looking at soon. If *session.zipcode* exists, we run a query of a query on request.qryScart to determine the total weight of this customers shopping cart. The shipping calculator, CF_FedExMonger, requires the weight, ZIP code, and shipping method to calculate the weight.

CF_FedEMonger is a third-party custom tag written by Matt Robertson. I won't go into all the details about the calculator and how it works. You could probably use almost any calculator—I found this one on Allaire's developer exchange site (http://devex.allaire.com/developer/gallery/index.cfm).

That's the entire qryScart.cfm file, and that's where most of the action takes place. The other half of the shopping cart is the display half.

modules/pages/cart/cart.cfm

The cart.cfm file is mostly just an output of the request.qryScart query. There are few bits of logic thrown in that I'll explain as well. This one is a long one, so I'll break it into pieces as well.

```
<table width="220" cellpadding="0" cellspacing="0" border="0">
  <tr>
    <td><img src="images/general/cart_title.gif" width="220"
    height="11" alt="shopping cart" border="0"></td>
  </tr>
</table>
```

This is the title of our shopping cart:

```
<table width="220" cellpadding="1" cellspacing="0" border="0">
<cfset cart.subTotal = 0>
<cfoutput query="request.qryScart" group="cat_id">
  <tr>
    <td colspan="5" bgcolor="White"> <b>#Cat_Name#</b></td>
  </tr>
  <cfoutput group="Product_ID">
    <tr>
      <td colspan="5" bgcolor="##82A8D1"> 
      <a href="details.cfm?id=#product_id#" class="carttitle">#title#</a>
      </td>
    </tr>
    <tr bgcolor="##233B55">
      <td align="center"><img
      src="images/general/cart_del.gif" width="16" height="9"
      alt="delete" border="0"></td>
```

```
        <td align="center"><img src="images/general/cart_size.gif"
        width="40" height="9" alt="size" border="0"></td>
        <td align="center"><img src="images/general/cart_color.gif"
        width="37" height="9" alt="color" border="0"></td>
        <td align="center"><img src="images/general/cart_qty.gif"
        width="49" height="9" alt="quantity" border="0"></td>
        <td align="center"><img src="images/general/cart_price.gif"
         width="50" height="9" alt="price" border="0"></td>
    </tr>
```

The first thing notable is the <cfset cart.subtotal = 0> section. We'll be tracking the shopping cart totals in this file as we go along, so we want to initialize this variable to zero before we start.

There are three levels of grouping in the output of the shopping cart. Up until now, we've included Category, Brand, Product, Product Variation, but for the shopping cart we drop the brand. We're limited on space, and we assume that at this point the customer is somewhat familiar with the products they've added to the cart. While we still think organizing the products by category is important, the brand isn't required, so we won't show it here.

The last <TR> contains the table column headers for the product variation output:

```
<cfoutput>
    <tr>
      <td align="center"><a href="#request.CurrentLocation()#?
#cgi.query_string#&cart=rm&var_id=#variation_id#"><img
src="images/general/cart_x.gif" width="18" height="15" alt="delete item"
border="0"></a></td>
      <td class="carttxt" align="center">#size_desc#</td>
      <td class="carttxt" align="center">#color_desc#</td>
      <td align="center">
        <table width="100%" cellpadding="0"
         cellspacing="0" border="0">
          <tr>
                <td><a href="#request.CurrentLocation()#cart=sub
&var_id=#variation_id#"><img src="images/general/cart_sub.gif"
width="18" height="15" alt="Subtract" border="0"
hspace="2"></a></td>
                 <td class="cartqty">#quantity#</td>
                 <td><a href="#request.CurrentLocation()#cart=add
&var_id=#variation_id#"><img src="images/general/cart_add.gif"
width="18" height="15" alt="Add" border="0" hspace="2"></a></td>
          </tr>
        </table>
```

```
      </td>
      <cfset cart.extPrice = (price*quantity)>
      <td class="cartprice"
align="right">#DollarFormat(cart.extPrice)#</td>
    </tr>
    <cfset cart.subTotal = cart.subTotal + cart.extPrice>
    </cfoutput>
  </cfoutput>
</cfoutput>
</table>
```

This is the last block of code before we begin adding up the subtotals, shipping costs, and taxes. The first <A> tag is the Remove Item link. One of the challenges of a shopping cart that shows up on every page is that you need to be able to modify the data of the cart from any location on the site, and be able to return to that page when the modification has been made. We could make it simpler by pointing the user to a page that said "Cart Updated," but that could effectively get the user lost within the site.

We use the user defined function CurrentLocation() to generate the URL that the user was last at before modifying the shopping cart. Because the shopping cart queries can run on any page just by supplying the *url.cart* variable, we simply make the Remove Item link point to the page the user was just on, along with the *url.cart=rm* variable. We do the same for the quantity buttons, the only difference being the *url.cart* value.

We use ColdFusion to display the price multiplied by the quantity of the item. We set this value to a variable called *cart.extPrice*, which we then immediately display. We use the DollarFormat() function to format the number as a price since we're adding two decimal values. We add the *cart.extPrice* to *cart.subtotal* (which started at zero). We'll hold onto this value and add it to the grand total once the user has entered in ZIP code and state information.

The last part of the file shows grand totals, and tackles the ZIP code and state form:

```
<cfif cart.subtotal gt 0>
<p>
<table width="100%" cellpadding="1" cellspacing="0" border="0">
  <tr bgcolor="#2C65A0">
    <td class="cartprice">Subtotal:</td>
    <td class="cartprice"
align="right"><cfoutput>#DollarFormat(cart.subTotal)#</cfoutput></td>
  </tr>
</table>
```

We output the *cart.subTotal* variable here once the subtotal is greater than zero, which means that the cart won't show anything unless there is something in the shopping cart.

```
<cfif IsDefined("request.shipcharge") is false>
  <p>
  <cfform action="#request.CurrentLocation()#?#cgi.query_string#"
  method="post">
    <table width="100%" cellpadding="1" cellspacing="0" border="0">
      <tr bgcolor="#0067CE">
        <td class="cartprice">Get an instant total!</td>
      </tr>
      <tr>
        <td class="cartprice">1. Select a shipping method:</td>
      </tr>
      <tr>
        <td>
        <cfif IsDefined("application.qryShipMethod") is false>
          <cfquery name="application.qryShipMethod"
           datasource="#request.dsn#">
          SELECT description, codename
          FROM shipping
          ORDER BY sortorder
          </cfquery>
        </cfif>
        <cfselect name="shipMethod" query="application.qryShipMethod"
value="codename" display="description"></cfselect>
        </td>
      </tr>
      <tr>
        <td class="cartprice">2. Enter a 9 digit zip</td>
      </tr>
      <tr>
        <td><cfinput type="Text" name="zipcode"
        message="A zip code is required to determine
        shipping costs." validate="zipcode"
        required="Yes" size="7" maxlength="7"></td>
      </tr>
```

The request.shipcharge query is initialized in the <CF_FEDEXMONGER> tag, and is the outcome of calculated shipping cost. If it doesn't exist, we want to allow the user to select a shipping method, and then enter a ZIP code. We're using <CFFORM>

so that we can easily make certain fields required without having to do a lot of extra coding. <CFFORM> automatically generates JavaScript code that will generate a pop-up window if the field is left blank, or entered incorrectly.

```
        <tr>
          <td class="cartprice">3. Enter your state</td>
        </tr>
        <tr>
          <td><cfinput type="Text" name="state"
          message="A state is required to determine tax rate."
          required="Yes" size="2" maxlength="2">
          <input type="submit" name="submit" value="Calculate"></td>
        </tr>
      </table>
    </cfform>
```

It might seem redundant to ask the user to enter their state once we know their ZIP code, and you're correct, it is redundant. We're asking this question because we had to make a bit of a sacrifice—we could probably develop a system that would tell us what ZIP code went to which state, but in this case, the performance hit wouldn't justify what we'd get in return. We really only care if they're in the same state that the skate.shop is located in, which for the purposes of this example is California. Our application will be faster if we simply let the user do a little bit of the work. Of course, we run the risk of frustrating users as well, who know very well that we could program something to do the thinking for them. It's a judgment call.

If determining the state based on the ZIP code became a requirement, we could design the system as efficiently as possible, and cache the queries that contained the data to reduce the number of database-related overhead issues.

```
<cfelse>
    <cfif session.state IS 'ca'>
      <cfset cart.tax = (cart.subtotal * 0.0825)>
      <table width="100%" cellpadding="1"
      cellspacing="0" border="0">
        <tr bgcolor="#2C65A0">
          <td class="cartprice">CA Sales Tax:</td>
          <td class="cartprice"
align="right"><cfoutput>#DollarFormat(cart.tax)#</cfoutput></td>
        </tr>
      </table>
    </cfif>
  <table width="100%" cellpadding="1" cellspacing="0" border="0">
    <tr bgcolor="#2C65A0">
```

```
      <td class="cartprice"><cfoutput>Fedex #session.shipMethod#</cfoutput>
<a href="<cfoutput>#request.CurrentLocation()#?#cgi.query_string#
&cart=resetship</cfoutput>">Change</a></td>
      <td class="cartprice" align="right">
      <cfoutput>#DollarFormat(request.shipcharge)#</cfoutput></td>
    </tr>
  </table>
  <table width="100%" cellpadding="0" cellspacing="0" border="0">
    <tr>
      <td bgcolor="#0070DF"><img src="images/general/clear.gif"
      width="1" height="1" border="0"></td>
    </tr>
  </table>
```

If the *request.shipcharge* variable does exist, and the state entered is California, we'll proceed to total the entire cart. The customer can change their shipping options by clicking the Change link, which sends the *url.cart* parameter with a value of "resetship", which resets the shipping information to zero.

```
<cfparam name="cart.tax" default="0">
  <cfset cart.grandtotal = cart.subtotal +
  cart.tax + request.shipcharge>
  <table width="100%" cellpadding="1" cellspacing="0" border="0">
    <tr bgcolor="#2C65A0">
      <td class="cartprice">Total:</td>
      <td class="cartprice"
      align="right"><cfoutput>#DollarFormat(cart.grandtotal)#</cfoutput></td>
    </tr>
  </table>
  </cfif>
  <table width="100%" cellpadding="0" cellspacing="0" border="0">
    <tr>
      <td><a href="checkout.cfm"><img src="images/general/cart_checkout.gif"
      width="220" height="17" alt="Checkout" border="0"></a></td>
    </tr>
  </table>
</cfif>
```

The remainder of the code totals the shopping cart, and shows the checkout button.

Customer Checkout Module

The customer checkout system allows returning customers to resubmit information we've already stored, and it allows new customers to sign up for our service. To keep things simple, there are very few differences between the code required for current customers and previous customers.

Each part of the checkout process is broken down into steps, both logically and within our code. The site progresses the user through the process, and presents the user with the appropriate form.

During the entire checkout process, and progress indicator displays what step the customer is working on within the entire process. This indicator is important, as it gives the customer some sense of how long they'll need to sit there before they're finished. I've never met anyone who enjoys filling out forms on web sites, so letting them know when they'll be finished is very helpful.

Each step in our site is broken down into a separate file. I'll go over each file individually. I'm going to break from tradition on Step 8 however, and only show the most important parts. It's over 200 lines, and a great deal of it is simply HTML formatting. If you want to get a detailed look at it you can find it on the CD-ROM.

pages/checkout/step1.cfm

We ask the user to login at this step. For current users, the login and password form elements are present. New users can click on the new users link.

```
<cfform action="checkout.cfm?step=2" method="POST"
enablecab="no" enctype="application/x-www-form-urlencoded">
  <cfmodule template="../../display/formwrapper.cfm"
   formtitle="1. Current Customers Login">
    <table width="100%" cellpadding="1" cellspacing="0" border="0">
      <tr>
        <td><b>Login:</b></td>
        <td rowspan="4" valign="top"><b>New customers:</b><br><a
        href="checkout.cfm?step=2&new=1">Click here</a>
        to create an account.</td>
      </tr>
      <tr>
        <td><cfinput type="Text" name="login"
        message="You must enter a login name."
        required="Yes" size="15" maxlength="100"></td>
      </tr>
      <tr>
        <td><b>Password:</b></td>
      </tr>
      <tr>
        <td><cfinput type="Password" name="password"
        size="15" maxlength="15"
        message="You must enter a password" required="Yes"></td>
      </tr>
      <tr>
```

```
        <td align="right" colspan="2"><input type="submit"
        name="submit" value="Next >>"></td>
      </tr>
    </table>
  </cfmodule>
</cfform>
```

Each steps uses a display module called formwrapper.cfm. This tag surrounds our form with a black border, and with a title bar. It's an example of how we can quickly reproduce common HTML themes using custom tags.

We're using <CFFORM> again to take care of data validation. In this step, both the login and password fields are required, and the user will get a message if either one is missing.

page/checkout/step2.cfm

```
<cfif IsDefined("url.new") is false>
  <cfmodule template="login.cfm" login="#form.login#"
  password="#form.password#">
  <cfif IsDefined("login.returncode")>
    <cfif login.returncode eq 1>
      <cfset session.customer_id =
       request.qryCustomer_ID.customer_id>
      <cflocation url="checkout.cfm?step=4">
    </cfif>
  </cfif>

<cfelse>
  <cfform action="checkout.cfm?step=3" method="POST" enablecab="no"
enctype="application/x-www-form-urlencoded">
    <cfmodule template="../../display/formwrapper.cfm"
    formtitle="2. Create Account">
      <table width="100%" cellpadding="1" cellspacing="0" border="0">
        <tr>
          <td><b>Choose a Login:</b></td>
        </tr>
        <tr>
          <td><cfinput type="Text" name="login"
          message="You must enter a login name."
          required="Yes" size="15" maxlength="100"></td>
        </tr>
        <tr>
          <td><b>Choose a Password (5-15 characters):</b></td>
        </tr>
```

```
        <tr>
          <td><cfinput type="Password" name="password1"
          size="15" maxlength="15"
          message="You must enter a password" required="Yes"></td>
        </tr>
        <tr>
          <td><b>Confirm Password:</b></td>
        </tr>
        <tr>
          <td><cfinput type="Password" name="password2" size="15"
          maxlength="15"
          message="You must confirm your password" required="Yes"></td>
        </tr>
        <tr>
          <td align="right" colspan="2"><input type="submit"
          name="submit" value="Next >>"></td>
        </tr>
      </table>
    </cfmodule>
  </cfform>
</cfif>
```

This first thing we do in this step is error check the login if the login is a current user, using the login.cfm module. We'll look at the login.cfm module as soon as I cover the rest of this step. New users are asked to enter a login name, and enter and reconfirm a password.

modules/checkout/login.cfm

When a current customer logs in, we need to check to make sure the login and password are correct:

```
<cfif IsDefined("attributes.login")>
  <cfstoredproc procedure="LoginCheckout" datasource="#request.dsn#">
    <cfprocparam type="In" cfsqltype="CF_SQL_VARCHAR"
     value="#attributes.login#" dbvarname="@login"
     maxlength="100" null="No">
    <cfprocparam type="In" cfsqltype="CF_SQL_VARCHAR"
     value="#attributes.password#"
     dbvarname="@password" maxlength="15" null="No">
    <cfprocparam type="Out" cfsqltype="CF_SQL_TINYINT"
     variable="request.login_status"
     dbvarname="@login_status" null="No">

  <!--- this brings back a customer id --->
    <cfprocresult name="request.qryCustomer_ID" resultset="1">
```

```
</cfstoredproc>

  <cfif request.login_status eq 1>
    <cfset caller.login.returncode = 1>
  </cfif>
  <cfif request.login_status eq 0>
    <cfmodule template="../../display/formwrapper.cfm"
     formtitle="Login Error">
      <table width="100%" cellpadding="1" cellspacing="0" border="0">
        <tr>
          <td>
          I can't find you in the database. Try the following:
            <ul>
              <li>Check the spelling of your login
              <li><a href="checkout.cfm?step=2&new=1">Create a new user</a>
            </ul>
          </td>
        </tr>
      </table>
    </cfmodule>
    <cfset caller.login.returncode = 0>
  </cfif>
  <cfif request.login_status eq 2>
    <cfmodule template="../../display/formwrapper.cfm"
      formtitle="Login Error">
      <table width="100%" cellpadding="1" cellspacing="0" border="0">
        <tr>
          <td>
          Password incorrect:
            <ul>
              <li>Please go back and check your password
            </ul>
          </td>
        </tr>
      </table>
    </cfmodule>
    <cfset caller.login.returncode = 0>
  </cfif>
</cfif>
```

The first thing the login.cfm module does is check to see if the login exists. If the login doesn't exist, it suggests that the user should check the spelling of their login, or click the new user link.

In the first <CFSTOREDPROC> tag, we're using a <CFPROCPARAM> with a type attribute of "Out". Within our stored procedure, we can pass a parameter to the "outside world" by using <cfprocparam type="Out" variable="request.login_status">.

This is different than returning a result set, as it's just passing a single variable. The *request.login_status* variable will let us know whether we should ask the user to check the spelling of their login or to reenter their password. A status of zero means the login doesn't exist. A status of two means the password is incorrect. A status of one indicates that user login exists, and the password is correct. The login.cfm module sets *caller.returncode* to one if the login is successful, and to zero if unsuccessful.

The LoginCheckout stored procedure is a good example of the kind of logic that can be embedded into a stored procedure.

LoginCheckout Stored Procedure

```
CREATE PROCEDURE LoginCheckout
(
@login varchar(100),
@password varchar(15),
@login_status tinyint OUTPUT
)
/*
@login_status must contain the OUTPUT
declaration in order to use <cfprocparam type="out">
*/

AS
set @login_status = 0

select customer_id
from customers
where login = @login and password = @password
if @@rowcount = 0
 begin
 -- customer doesn't exist or password is bad
 select login from customers where login = @login
  if @@rowcount = 0
   begin
    -- customer doesn't exist
    set @login_status = 0
   end
  else
   begin
    -- customer exists - password wrong
    set @login_status = 2
   end
```

```
 end
else
 begin
  set @login_status = 1
 end
GO
```

You'll probably notice a lot of begin-end statements. They're used to group multiple SQL statements into logical blocks, and to help control program flow. Begin-end statements aren't required in all cases, but when in doubt, it doesn't hurt to use them.

In this statement, *@@rowcount* returns the number of rows affected in the most recent query run. In this case, it is used as part of the first check to see if there is a problem with the user name or password. The next if statements evaluate the login and password separately.

If the login name exists, and the password is correct, a customer_id is assigned to *session.customer_id*, and the customer skips Step 3.

modules/pages/checkout/step3.cfm

Step 3 performs the required error checking for the new user creation, and adds the user if everything checks out:

```
<cfif IsDefined("form.submit")>
  <cfquery name="checkFirst" datasource="#request.dsn#">
  SELECT login FROM customers WHERE login = '#form.login#'
  </cfquery>

  <cfif checkFirst.recordcount gt 0>
    <cfmodule template="../../display/formwrapper.cfm"
     formtitle="Login Error">
      <table width="100%" cellpadding="1" cellspacing="0" border="0">
        <tr>
          <td>That login already exists.</td>
        </tr>
      </table>
    </cfmodule>
  <cfelse>
    <cfif form.password1 neq form.password2>
      <cfmodule template="../../display/formwrapper.cfm"
      formtitle="Password Error">
      <table width="100%" cellpadding="1" cellspacing="0" border="0">
        <tr>
```

```
        <td>Your passwords don't match.</td>
      </tr>
    </table>
  </cfmodule>
  <cfelse>
    <!--- we can FINALLY add the user --->
    <cfstoredproc procedure="AddCustomerLogin"
     datasource="#request.dsn#">
      <cfprocparam type="In" cfsqltype="CF_SQL_VARCHAR"
      value="#form.login#" dbvarname="@login" maxlength="100" null="No">
      <cfprocparam type="In" cfsqltype="CF_SQL_VARCHAR"
       value="#form.password1#" dbvarname="@password" maxlength="15" null="No">
      <!--- this brings back a customer id --->
      <cfprocresult name="request.qryCustomer_ID" resultset="1">
    </cfstoredproc>
    <cfset session.customer_id = request.qryCustomer_ID.customer_id>
    <cflocation url="checkout.cfm?step=4">
  </cfif>
 </cfif>
</cfif>
```

When we finally add the user, you can see that the last <CFPROCRESULT> ends up supplying the data for the *session.customer_id* variable. Notice that we didn't use a <cfprocparam type="out">. It is possible to not use <CFPROCPARAM> to create an "out" variable, but in this case, it's not a good practice. If our intention is to output a single value, rather than a result set, it's better to use <cfprocparam type="out"> than it is to generate that same value with an result set.

modules/pages/checkout/step4.cfm

Step 4 allows the user to enter his/her billing information. There's an important distinction that needs to be made between billing information and shipping information. They are not always one and the same. Often customers want a product shipped to their office because they're not going to be home during the day, or they want to ship it to someone as a gift.

If a user ends up at this step and doesn't have a *session.customer_id* assigned, they are asked to login. In fact, this happens on every step from this point forward, where a *session.customer_id* value is required at every step.

Step 4 gathers the information and validates it, and Step 5 stores it. I won't show all the code for Step 4; it's not really all that exciting. But I will show the check for the *session.customer_ID* variable, and how we handle the error.

```
<cfif IsDefined("session.customer_id")>
  Billing info form.
<cfelse>
  <cfmodule template="../../display/formwrapper.cfm" formtitle="Sorry...">
    <table width="100%" cellpadding="0" cellspacing="0" border="0">
      <tr>
        <td>You cannot access this step until you've logged in, or
        created a customer account.</td>
      </tr>
    </table>
  </cfmodule>
  <cfmodule template="step1.cfm">
</cfif>
```

modules/pages/checkout/step5.cfm

Step 5 stores the information gathered in Step 4, and asks the customer if the Billing Address and Shipping Address are identical. We want to save the customer the effort of entering their address twice if the billing and shipping address are the same.

```
<cfif IsDefined("session.customer_id")>
<cfif IsDefined("form.submit")>
  <cfquery name="UpdateInfo" datasource="#request.dsn#">
  UPDATE customers
  SET
  firstname = '#form.firstname#',
  lastname = '#form.lastname#',
  bill_address1 = '#form.bill_address1#',
  <cfif bill_address2 is not ''>
  bill_address2 = '#form.bill_address2#',
  </cfif>
  emailaddr = '#form.emailaddr#',
  phone = '#form.phone#',
  ccnum = '#form.ccnum#',
  ccexp = '#form.ccexp#',
  bill_city = '#form.bill_city#',
  bill_state_id = #form.bill_state_id#,
  bill_zip = '#form.bill_zip#',
  bill_country = '#form.bill_country#'
  WHERE customer_id = #session.customer_id#
  </cfquery>
</cfif>

<cfform action="checkout.cfm?step=6" method="POST" enablecab="No"
enctype="application/x-www-form-urlencoded">
  <cfmodule template="../../display/formwrapper.cfm"
```

```
     formtitle="5. Shipping & Billing Same?">
    <table width="100%" cellpadding="0" cellspacing="0" border="0">
      <tr>
        <td>Is the <b>shipping address</b> identical
          to the <b>billing address</b> you just entered?</td>
      </tr>
      <tr>
        <td><cfinput type="Radio" name="shipbillsame"
        value="1" checked="Yes">Yes<cfinput type="Radio"
        name="shipbillsame" value="0">No</td>
      </tr>
      <tr>
        <td><input type="submit" name="submit" value="Next >>"></td>
      </tr>
    </table>
  </cfmodule>
</cfform>
<cfelse>
  <cfmodule template="../../display/formwrapper.cfm"
   formtitle="Sorry...">
    <table width="100%" cellpadding="0" cellspacing="0" border="0">
      <tr>
        <td>You cannot access this step until you've logged in,
        or created a customer account.</td>
      </tr>
    </table>
  </cfmodule>
  <cfmodule template="step1.cfm">
</cfif>
```

modules/pages/checkout/step6.cfm

If the customer's billing address and shipping address are identical, we instantly push them up to Step 7. But if their billing address is different from their shipping address, we need to present them with a form to enter that information. I'll show the first part of step6.cfm where we send the user to Step 7 if needed. The rest of the file is just a form asking for input.

```
<cfif IsDefined("form.shipbillsame")>
  <cfquery name="UpdateInfo" datasource="#request.dsn#">
  UPDATE customers
  SET
  shipbillsame = #form.shipbillsame#,
  ship_zip = bill_zip
  WHERE customer_id = #session.customer_id#
```

```
  </cfquery>
</cfif>

  <cfquery name="customerInfo" datasource="#request.dsn#">
  SELECT *
  FROM customers
  WHERE customer_id = #session.customer_id#
  </cfquery>

<cfif IsDefined("form.shipbillsame")>
    <cfif form.shipbillsame is 1>
       <cflocation url="checkout.cfm?step=7">
    </cfif>
<cfelse>
  Shipping information form.
</cfif>
```

Once Step 6 is filled out, Step 7 stores the data.

modules/pages/checkout/step7.cfm

Step 7 stores the shipping information if it needs to, and presents the user with a shipping option. The form uses the application.qryShipMethod query if it's available, and if not, executes the query.

```
<cfif IsDefined("session.customer_id")>
<cfif IsDefined("form.submit")>
  <cfquery name="UpdateInfo" datasource="#request.dsn#">
  UPDATE customers
  SET
  ship_address1 = '#form.ship_address1#',
  <cfif ship_address2 is not ''>
  ship_address2 = '#form.ship_address2#',
  </cfif>
  ship_city = '#form.ship_city#',
  ship_state_id = #form.ship_state_id#,
  ship_zip = '#form.ship_zip#',
  ship_country = '#form.ship_country#'
  WHERE customer_id = #session.customer_id#
  </cfquery>
</cfif>

<cfform action="checkout.cfm?step=8" method="POST" enablecab="No"
enctype="application/x-www-form-urlencoded">
  <cfmodule template="../../display/formwrapper.cfm"
   formtitle="7. Choose a Shipping Method">
```

```
    <table width="100%" cellpadding="0" cellspacing="0" border="0">
      <tr>
        <td><b>Select a Shipping Type</b>*</td>
      </tr>
      <tr>
        <td>
        <cfif IsDefined("application.qryShipMethod") is false>
          <cfquery name="application.qryShipMethod"
           datasource="#request.dsn#">
          SELECT description, codename
          FROM shipping
          ORDER BY sortorder
          </cfquery>
        </cfif>
        <cfselect name="shipMethod" query="application.qryShipMethod"
         value="codename" display="description"></cfselect>
        </td>
      </tr>
      <tr>
        <td><input type="submit" name="submit" value="Next >>"></td>
      </tr>
    </table>
  </cfmodule>
</cfform>
<cfelse>
  <cfmodule template="../../display/formwrapper.cfm"
   formtitle="Sorry...">
    <table width="100%" cellpadding="0" cellspacing="0" border="0">
      <tr>
        <td>You cannot access this step until you've logged in, or
         created a customer account.</td>
      </tr>
    </table>
  </cfmodule>
  <cfmodule template="step1.cfm">
</cfif>
```

Creating the application.qryShipMethod query allows for a performance increase. The query only needs to be run once, and then it's available to the entire application within the application variable timeout period.

modules/checkout/pages/step8.cfm

Step 8 is where the entire order is shown to the user, ready for final approval. A record is created in the *Orders* table, and all of the shopping cart contents for this customer are transferred over to the *Order_Details* table.

Let's look at the first major block of code:

```
<!--- 1. gather shipping cost --->
<cfif IsDefined("form.shipMethod")>
  <cfquery name="customerInfo" datasource="#request.dsn#">
  SELECT ship_zip
  FROM customers
  WHERE customer_id = #session.customer_id#
  </cfquery>
  <cfquery name="shipMethodID" datasource="#request.dsn#">
  SELECT shipping_id
  FROM shipping
  WHERE codename = '#form.shipMethod#'
  </cfquery>
  <cfquery name="orderDetails" datasource="#request.dsn#">
  SELECT sum(quantity * weight) as total_weight
  FROM scart_view
  WHERE uuid = '#session.uuid#'
  </cfquery>
 <!--- time to determine final shipping cost --->
  <cfmodule template="../../shipping_calc/FedexMonger.cfm"
weight="#orderDetails.total_weight#" servicetype="#form.shipMethod#"
zip="#customerInfo.ship_zip#">
  <cfset request.shipcharge = DecimalFormat(request.shipcharge)>
```

This first block of code stores the shipping information, and calculates the final shipping cost using the CF_FedExMonger.

```
<!--- 2. build order --->
<cfstoredproc procedure="BuildOrder" datasource="#request.dsn#">
  <cfprocparam type="In" cfsqltype="CF_SQL_VARCHAR"
    value="#session.uuid#" dbvarname="@uuid" maxlength="115" null="No">
  <cfprocparam type="In" cfsqltype="CF_SQL_INTEGER"
    value="#session.customer_id#" dbvarname="@customer_id" null="No">
  <cfprocparam type="In" cfsqltype="CF_SQL_INTEGER"
    value="#shipMethodID.shipping_id#" dbvarname="@shipping_id" null="No">
  <cfprocparam type="In" cfsqltype="CF_SQL_DECIMAL"
    dbvarname="@shipping_id" value="#request.shipcharge#"
    maxlength="12" scale="2" null="No">
</cfstoredproc>
</cfif>
```

The second block kicks off the BuildOrder stored procedure, which creates the records for the order, and in turn, executes the BuildOrderDetails store procedure. Let's look at both of those. The code following the building of the order simply displays the entire order back to the user, and then updates the final price of the order.

BuildOrder Stored Procedure

```
CREATE PROCEDURE BuildOrder
(
@uuid varchar(35),
@customer_id int,
@shipping_id int,
@shipcost decimal(7,2)
)
AS

declare @order_status_id int, @order_id int

set @order_status_id = 1

-- build order record if it doesn't exist

select customer_id, uuid
from orders
where customer_id = @customer_id and uuid = @uuid
if @@rowcount = 0
 begin
 -- no order for this customer's session - build one
 insert into orders
 (customer_id, uuid, shipping_id, shipcost, order_status_id)
 values
 (@customer_id, @uuid, @shipping_id, @shipcost, @order_status_id)
 end
else
 begin
/*
order exists (maybe user changed shipping)
update shipping info just in case

*/
 update orders
 set
 shipcost = @shipcost,
 shipping_id = @shipping_id
 where customer_id = @customer_id AND uuid = @uuid
 end

set @order_id =
```

```
(select order_id
from orders
where customer_id = @customer_id AND uuid = @uuid)

exec BuildOrderDetails @uuid = @uuid, @order_id = @order_id
GO
```

BuildOrderDetails Stored Procedure

```
CREATE PROCEDURE BuildOrderDetails
(
@uuid varchar(35), @order_id int
)
AS

declare @order_status_id int
set @order_status_id = 1
-- if this query is repeated for this session, rebuild

delete from order_details
where order_id = @order_id

 insert order_details
 (order_id, variation_id, quantity, order_status_id)
 select @order_id, variation_id, quantity, @order_status_id
 from scart
 where uuid = @uuid
GO
```

Even at this point, the customer has the ability to go back into the site and add or subtract products from their shopping cart. If this stored procedure is run again, we want to discard any of the old order_details records, and copy the shopping cart over again.

For a small site like this, it's easier to just dump all the old records than it is to try to compare the differences between the shopping cart and the order details. On a larger, heavier-trafficked site, it might be a good idea to first determine if the records are indeed different before going through the steps of rebuilding, although both cases require the same amount of database calls. If we can avoid an Insert or an Update, we'll be saving ourselves some CPU power, which speeds up over database performance.

Keep in mind that this is all under the assumption that comparing the records takes less CPU than simply dropping the records and re-inserting them.

modules/pages/checkout/step9.cfm

Step 9 finalizes the order, clears out the shopping cart, and supplies the customer with order confirmation information.

```
<cfif IsDefined("session.customer_id")>
<cfif IsDefined("form.submit")>
  <!--- order is confirmed, process --->
  <cfquery name="completeOrder" datasource="#request.dsn#">
  UPDATE Orders
  SET Order_Status_ID = 2
  WHERE Order_ID = #form.Order_ID#
  </cfquery>

  <cfquery name="purgeCart" datasource="#request.dsn#">
  DELETE
  FROM
  scart
  WHERE uuid = '#session.uuid#'
  </cfquery>

  <cfset session.uuid = 0>
</cfif>

<cfmodule template="../../display/formwrapper.cfm"
   formtitle="9. Order Complete">
   <table width="100%" cellpadding="3" cellspacing="0" border="0">
    <tr>
      <td><b>Order Complete</b></td>
    </tr>
    <tr>
      <td>A confirmation email has been sent to your email address.</td>
    </tr>
    <tr>
      <td>For future reference,
      refer to <cfoutput><b>#form.Order_ID#</b></cfoutput> as the order
      number for this purchase.</td>
    </tr>
    <tr>
      <td>Your credit card will not be billed until
      your order has been shipped.</td>
    </tr>
    <tr>
      <td>Don't hesitate to email
      <a href="mailto:service@skate.shop">customer service</a> or
      call 888-888-8888 with any questions.</td>
    </tr>
```

```
  </table>
</cfmodule>
<cfelse>
  <cfmodule template="../../display/formwrapper.cfm"
   formtitle="Sorry...">
  <table width="100%" cellpadding="0" cellspacing="0" border="0">
      <tr>
        <td>You cannot access this step until you've
        logged in, or created a customer account.</td>
      </tr>
    </table>
  </cfmodule>
  <cfmodule template="step1.cfm">
</cfif>
```

modules/pages/checkout/steps.cfm

There's one last block of code for the site, and that's the Checkout Progress indicator. This file uses the *url.step* variable to determine which step to place an indicator next to. I'll show a simplified two-step version; the concept is exactly the same for 9 steps or 20 steps.

```
<table width="220" cellpadding="0" cellspacing="0" border="0">
       <tr>
             <td><img src="images/general/checkout_title.gif"
             width="220" height="11" alt="Checkout Steps" border="0"></td>
       </tr>
</table>

<cfscript>
stepIndicator1 = 0;
stepIndicator2 = 0;

switch(url.step)
{
    case "1":
    {
        stepIndicator1 = 1;
        break;
    }
    case "2":
    {
        stepIndicator2 = 1;
        break;
    }
} //end switch
```

```
indicatorOn = "<td width='20' align='right'>
<img src='images/general/doublerightarrows.gif' width='13'
height='10' alt='Current Step' border='0'></td>";

indicatorOff = "<td width='20' align='right'><img
src='images/general/clear.gif'
width='13' height='10' alt='Current Step' border='0'></td>";
</cfscript>

<table width="220" cellpadding="1" cellspacing="0"
border="0" bgcolor="#495B70">
  <tr>
    <cfif stepIndicator1 eq 1>
      <cfoutput>#indicatorOn#</cfoutput>
    <cfelse>
      <cfoutput>#indicatorOff#</cfoutput>
    </cfif>
    <td width="200"><div class="checkoutStatusWhite">1.</div> 
    <div class="checkoutStatusBlue">Login</div></td>
  </tr>
  <tr>
    <cfif stepIndicator2 eq 2>
      <cfoutput>#indicatorOn#</cfoutput>
    <cfelse>
      <cfoutput>#indicatorOff#</cfoutput>
    </cfif>
    <td width="200"><div class="checkoutStatusWhite">2.</div> 
    <div class="checkoutStatusBlue">Create Account</div></td>
  </tr>
</table>
```

Wrapping Up

In this very long chapter, we've stepped through the entire customer side of the skate.shop application. We've explored different methods for taking advantage of SQL Server to increase the performance of the application, and examined how to use ColdFusion to reduce the amount of workload on the SQL Server. We've used some of ColdFusion 5.0's new features, including <CFFLUSH>, Query of Queries, and UDFs.

Our next chapter details the entire administration backend, where we'll take advantage of other ColdFusion 5.0 features, including <CFGRAPH>.

CHAPTER

7

Building the skate.shop Administrator Tool

IN THIS CHAPTER:

Administrator Overview

Order Processing

Reporting

An e-commerce site doesn't do us any good if we don't have a way to process the orders and perform the day-to-day tasks of running the site. In this chapter, we build the Administrator tool for our site. We follow the same format as Chapter 6, where we review each file in the application, and talk about what it does and how it works.

Since the Administrator deals with business practices that depend on how the organization runs behind the site, we'll keep it simple and general, and allow for the flexibility of adding in functionality later on. The functionality of the Administrator should provide a substantial base to get started with.

There are alternatives to using a web-based Administrator. For instance, it's possible to create an Administrator using Microsoft Access as a client to SQL Server, or by writing a program using C++ or Visual Basic. Yet, using ColdFusion allows for a lot of flexibility, as well as rapid development.

Administrator Overview

The primary function of the Administrator tool is to process orders. We could successfully run the business of the site without any other feature, but without being able to process orders, we could never fulfill the orders and subsequently never collect a check. We've all heard plenty about dot com businesses not making money, but without order processing, we'd be taking this to the extreme.

In addition to order processing, we'll create sections that allow us to view reports, as well as a maintenance section that allows us to schedule tasks and maintain Verity collections.

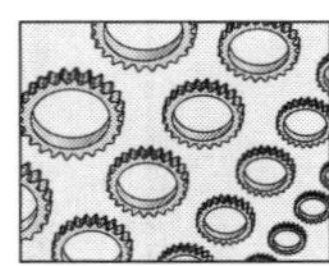

NOTE

In Chapter 6, we built a simple interface for maintaining the Verity search engine. This interface will be migrated into the site Administrator under the maintenance section of the Administrator.

The structure of the Administrator is somewhat similar to the overall application, except that we'll be using a frameset, in addition to the content.cfm. Because the Administrator is a smaller, simpler application, our directory structures storing the files are far less complicated as well. Let's look at the directory structure:

Directory	Description
skate.shop/admin	The root directory for the Administrator.
skate.shop/admin/maint	Stores all maintenance related files, including the scheduler, and the Verity interface.

Directory	Description
skate.shop/admin/maint/ skate_shop_coll	Stores the Verity collection. It's automatically created when creating a Verity index.
skate.shop/admin/maint/ scripts	Stores scripts that run under the scheduler.
skate.shop/admin/modules	Contains modules or custom tags used throughout the site Administrator. The concept behind this directory is simpler than the storefront. Because we only have a few major sections to the Administrator, there's no need to nest the major sections deeper than needed. However, one could argue that being consistent with the storefront would outweigh the inconvenience of nesting directories too deep.
skate.shop/admin/orders	Contains the order processing files.
Skate.shop/admin/reporting	Contains the reporting files.

Let's see how our skate.shop application is put together, first by looking at the HTML frameset, then the navigation elements and other graphic details, and finally, content.cfm.

skate.shop/admin/application.cfm

This file, and the concept behind it, should be familiar. The file is nearly identical to the file used on the front end. If you remember the concept of how application.cfm works (for more information, see Chapter 6), you'd know that if we didn't have an application.cfm in the skate.shop/ admin directory, that the application.cfm file in skate.shop would execute for any file in the admin directories. So, why have an application.cfm here at all? Well, because it's not entirely identical, and we don't want any of the extra stuff that our first file has.

We've set the session lengths to be four hours, which is more time then we set aside for the storefront's application.cfm. Because our employees are likely to keep the browser open all day, we want to maintain their sessions for a reasonable length of time.

```
<cfapplication name="skateshop_admin"
               sessionmanagement="Yes"
               setclientcookies="Yes"
               sessiontimeout="#CreateTimeSpan(0,4,0,0)#"
               applicationtimeout="#CreateTimeSpan(1,0,0,0)#">
<cfset request.dsn = "skateshop">
```

In our current site Administrator, the **Session** scope isn't used that often—the only spot it is used is in the order processing section, where the salesperson enters their intials. If their session is active, it remembers the initials the salesperson entered during that session. But we may decide later on to add more functionality to the site that requires session management, so we'll put it in now so we don't have to try and wedge it in later.

skate.shop/admin/index.cfm

This file sets up our frameset. I am no supporter of frames, I think they're a pain to work with, cause too much unneeded page loads, and don't always look good on every browser. When I committed to using frames for the Administrator, I could almost feel the collective shivers of those who feel the same way I do about frames—well, not literally, but I needed to add that for dramatic effect—frames are evil by nature for the havoc they wreak with browsers and the user experience as a whole.

So why use something we should be opposed to?

We have a captive audience, or at least the theoretical skate.shop business has a captive audience of sales people. Our imaginary network admin guy, who we'll call Tony, after one of the best network admin guys I've worked with, will inflict a great deal of pain on any sales person who decides to use a browser that doesn't work with our frameset.

Because our browsing environment is very controlled, the problems that plague frames are drastically reduced, making the benefits outweigh the disadvantages. The frameset also makes the application structure a little easier to deal with. We don't have to include graphical elements on every page, or include the navigation menu on every page. Because we'll never look at the traffic on our administration site, extra page hits are not a concern, and because the framesets never get reloaded, it doesn't increase the number of files that have to execute. My rule of thumb: for public sites, frames should be avoided at all costs. For private or intranet sites where you can expect all browsers to be of a certain platform, and where logging is either ignored or disabled, frames are OK.

```
<cfmodule template="modules/head.cfm">
<!-- frames -->
<frameset rows="47,*" framespacing="0" frameborder="0">
      <frame src="logo_bar.cfm"
             name="logo_bar"
             frameborder="0"
             scrolling="No"
             noresize
             marginwidth="10"
```

```
            marginheight="10"
            framespacing="0">
      <frameset  cols="128,*">
            <frame src="nav.cfm"
                   name="nav"
                   frameborder="0"
                   scrolling="Auto"
                   marginwidth="10"
                   marginheight="10">
            <frame src="content.cfm"
                   name="content"
                   frameborder="0"
                   scrolling="Auto"
                   marginwidth="10"
                   marginheight="10">
      </frameset>
</frameset>
</html>
```

skate.shop/admin/modules/head.cfm

Before the preceding frameset loads, we execute a module called head.cfm. We did something like this in the storefront—the theme here is the same, and again, on a simpler level. The concept is that we don't want to have to write all the head information on every template we make, so we'll do it once, and reference to it every time we need it.

```
<!DOCTYPE HTML PUBLIC "-//W3C//DTD HTML 4.0 Transitional//EN">

<html>
<head>
    <title>Skateshop Admin</title>
    <link rel="STYLESHEET" type="text/css" href="../basic.css">
</head>
```

We're using the same style sheet that we used for the storefront. There's no need to create a new style sheet when we've already done all the work. Notice that we're also not doing anything fancy with the title, or adding any metatags, or anything special at all. We don't need any of that since this is a private part of our site that the general public will never have access to.

skate.shop/admin/logo_bar.cfm

We maintain the site branding on the site Administrator by including the logo in a logo bar. The logo bar is basically uninteresting except for the fact that we wrap the html_wrapper.cfm file around the table. Let's take a look at it, because it is different than the html_wrapper.cfm used on the storefront.

```
<cfmodule template="modules/head.cfm">
<cfmodule template="modules/html_wrapper.cfm" bgcolor="##42555A">
<table width="100%" cellpadding="0" cellspacing="0" border="0">
    <tr>
        <td><a href="index.cfm"><img
        src="../images/general/logo.gif" width="128"
        height="47" alt="www.skate.shop" border="0"></a></td>
    </tr>
</table>
</cfmodule>
```

skate.shop/admin/modules/html_wrapper.cfm

We use this module to simply wrap the HTML body and closing /html tags. We also have the ability to pass the *bgcolor* attribute to this module, controlling the background color of the page. The storefront html_wrapper.cfm file contains a lot more HTML formatting, but we don't need that here.

```
<cfif thistag.executionmode is "start">
<cfparam name="attributes.bgcolor" default="white">
   <cfoutput>
   <body bgcolor="#attributes.bgcolor#" leftmargin="0" topmargin="0">
  </cfoutput>
</cfif>
<cfif thistag.executionmode is "end">
    </body>
    </html>
</cfif>
```

skate.shop/admin/nav.cfm

This file sets up the navigation links to each area of the administration site. The first thing to notice is that the URLs point to content.cfm, with a familiar page parameter. Another part to look at that often gets overlooked is the *target* attribute in the anchor tag. It loads the URL in the "content" frame, which we named in our frameset. If we neglected to add this attribute, the content.cfm file would load in the same frame as our navigation frame, and that wouldn't be good.

```
<cfmodule template="modules/head.cfm">
<cfmodule template="modules/html_wrapper.cfm" bgcolor="##526573">
<table width="127" border="0" cellspacing="0" cellpadding="2">
```

```
    <tr>
        <td><img src="../images/general/singlerightarrow.gif" width="7"
 height="11" border="0"></td>
        <td class="nav"><b>Orders</b></td>
    </tr>
    <tr>
        <td><img src="../images/general/clear.gif" width="7" height="11"
 border="0"></td>
        <td><b><a
        href="content.cfm?page=orders_new"
        class="nav" target="content">New Orders</a></b></td>
    </tr>
    <tr>
        <td><img src="../images/general/clear.gif" width="7" height="11"
border="0"></td>
        <td><b><a
        href="content.cfm?page=orders_current"
        class="nav" target="content">Current Orders</a></b></td>
    </tr>
    <tr>
        <td><img src="../images/general/clear.gif" width="7" height="11"
border="0"></td>
        <td><b><a
        href="content.cfm?page=orders_shipped"
        class="nav" target="content">Shipped Orders</a></b></td>
    </tr>
</table>
<p>
<table width="127" border="0" cellspacing="0" cellpadding="2">
    <tr>
        <td><img src="../images/general/singlerightarrow.gif" width="7"
height="11" border="0"></td>
        <td class="nav"><b>Reporting</b></td>
    </tr>
    <tr>
        <td><img src="../images/general/clear.gif" width="7" height="11"
border="0"></td>
        <td><b><a href="content.cfm?page=Reporting_GeneralSales" class="nav"
target="content">Product Sales</a></b></td>
    </tr>
    <tr>
        <td><img src="../images/general/clear.gif" width="7" height="11"
border="0"></td>
        <td><b><a href="content.cfm?page=Reporting_SiteMetrics" class="nav"
target="content">Site Metrics</a></b></td>
    </tr>
</table>
```

```
<p>
<table width="127" border="0" cellspacing="0" cellpadding="2">
    <tr>
        <td><img src="../images/general/singlerightarrow.gif" width="7"
height="11" border="0"></td>
        <td class="nav"><b>Maintenance</b></td>
    </tr>
    <tr>
        <td><img src="../images/general/clear.gif" width="7" height="11"
border="0"></td>
        <td><b><a
        href="content.cfm?page=maint_verity"
        class="nav" target="content">Verity Admin</a></b></td>
    </tr>
    <tr>
        <td><img src="../images/general/clear.gif" width="7" height="11"
border="0"></td>
        <td><b><a
        href="content.cfm?page=maint_schedule"
        class="nav" target="content">Scheduled Tasks</a></b></td>
    </tr>
</table>
</cfmodule>
```

skate.shop/admin/content.cfm

I know that by saying that this file is similar to its storefront counterpart, I'm risking sound redundant, but it's simply a fact of the matter. This file is just a switch that reacts to the value of url.page. Something we didn't use in the storefront version of the content.cfm file is the <CFDEFAULTCASE> tag. If the value of *url.page* isn't represented by any of the cfcase tags, then the code within the <CFDEFAULTCASE> tag executes. <CFDEFAULTCASE> doesn't make the application failsafe—if *url.page* doesn't exist, you will get an error.

```
<cfmodule template="modules/head.cfm">
<cfmodule template="modules/html_wrapper.cfm" bgcolor="white">
<table width="100%" cellpadding="0" cellspacing="0" border="0">
  <tr>
    <td align="center">
    <img src="../images/general/clear.gif" width="1" height="20"
     border="0">
      <cfparam name="url.page" default="orders">
      <cfswitch expression="#url.page#">
        <!--- orders --->
        <cfcase value="orders_new">
```

```
          <cfmodule template="orders/orders_new.cfm">
        </cfcase>
        <cfcase value="orders_process">
          <cfmodule template="orders/orders_process.cfm">
        </cfcase>
        <cfcase value="orders_current">
          <cfmodule template="orders/orders_current.cfm">
        </cfcase>
        <cfcase value="orders_shipped">
          <cfmodule template="orders/orders_shipped.cfm">
        </cfcase>
        <!--- reporting --->
        <cfcase value="Reporting_GeneralSales">
          <cfmodule template="reporting/Reporting_GeneralSales.cfm">
        </cfcase>
        <cfcase value="Reporting_SiteMetrics">
          <cfmodule template="reporting/Reporting_SiteMetrics.cfm">
        </cfcase>
        <!--- maintenance --->
        <cfcase value="maint_verity">
          <cfmodule template="maint/maint_verity.cfm">
        </cfcase>
        <cfcase value="maint_schedule">
          <cfmodule template="maint/maint_schedule.cfm">
        </cfcase>
        <cfdefaultcase>
          <cfmodule template="orders/orders_new.cfm">
        </cfdefaultcase>
      </cfswitch>
    </td>
  </tr>
</table>
</cfmodule>
```

Order Processing

The order processing module is designed around business practices. The idea is that several sales people are able to access the order processing information, view new orders, and take responsibility for the orders. This is obviously a very simple way to process orders. If this were a larger-scale operation, we might want to automate everything, including credit card processing and shipping and fulfillment, but we want to keep things simple to help keep us on the subject of ColdFusion. There are literally hundreds of ways to process an order, and it all depends on the business practice, or what the business needs are.

In the case of a skateboard shop, we want to keep things simple. The companies we do business with are often not capable of handling automated tasks, and still rely on doing things in more traditional ways. Because of this, we've decided that reducing the amount of automation better fits in with our business partners. Different business models might require that we do things entirely automated, either to be competitive, or because our business partners require it.

The skate.shop order processing is incredibly simple. There is one column in the *Order_details* table (which we created in Chapter 6) called order_status_id that controls the status of the order, which is what our order processing system is most concerned with. This column is a foreign key for the *Order_status* table. In our system, we only need to know what the order_status_id values mean. Here's the *Order_status* table, which contains the definitions of the order_status_id values. Understanding what these values mean will help you to understand how the system works.

order_status_id	Status definition
1	Customer is still building the order—shipping information has been chosen.
2	Customer has submitted the order—order is ready for processing and is considered a new order.
3	Salesperson has taken responsibility for the order, and the order is waiting to be shipped. This status doesn't change until the credit card has been authorized, and the order has been officially shipped.
4	Order has been shipped, and is kept for archival purposes.

skate.shop/admin/orders/orders_new.cfm

The NewOrders query selects all records in the SQL view AdminOrdersView with an order_status_id of two, which we know means that the customer has submitted the order and it's now ready for processing. The *AdminOrdersView* table selects all order related tables. We don't build any criteria into the view because we want to do the same kind of thing, without having to build a new view, for the other order states.

A user-defined function is introduced if there are orders to view. This function will help us determine the relative age of the function. It's important that we know how old the orders are, so we know which ones to process first. We could simply sort the orders by their date, but I want the actual age of each order to be evident to a salesperson. In our business model, order-processing speed is a key factor in customer satisfaction, so anything the application can do to help that process makes a difference.

```
<cfquery name="NewOrders" datasource="#request.dsn#">
SELECT *
FROM AdminOrdersView
WHERE Order_Status_ID = 2
</cfquery>

<cfif NewOrders.recordcount gt 0>

<cfscript>
function OrderAge(date1, date2)
{
   d1 = ParseDateTime(date1);
   d2 = ParseDateTime(date2);
   tmp = DateDiff("n", d1, d2);

   if (tmp GT 0)
   {
      num = tmp;
      myvar = num & IIF(num is 1, DE(" minute"), DE(" minutes"));
   }

   if (tmp GT 60)
   {
      num = Int(tmp/60);
      myvar = num & IIF(num is 1, DE(" hour"), DE(" hours"));
   }

   if (tmp GT 1440)
   {
      num = Int(tmp/1440);
      myvar = num & IIF(num is 1, DE(" day"), DE(" days"));
      if (num GT 4)
      {
         baddie = 1;
      }
   }

   if (tmp GT 10080)
   {
      num = Int(tmp/10080);
      myvar = num & IIF(num is 1, DE(" week"), DE(" weeks"));
      baddie = 1;
   }
```

```
   if (IsDefined("baddie"))
   {
      myvar = "<font color=""red""><b>" & myvar & "!</b></font>";
   }
   return myvar;
}
request.OrderAge = OrderAge;
</cfscript>

  <cfmodule template="../modules/tablewrapper.cfm"
   title="New Orders">
  <table width="100%" cellpadding="0" cellspacing="1" border="0">
    <tr>
      <td bgcolor="#2C65A0"><b>Order ID</b></td>
      <td bgcolor="#2C65A0"><b>Date/Time</b></td>
      <td bgcolor="#2C65A0"><b>Order Age</b></td>
      <td bgcolor="#2C65A0" colspan="2"><b>Name</b></td>
    </tr>
    <cfoutput query="NewOrders" group="Order_ID">
      <tr>
        <td><a
href="content.cfm?page=orders_process&id=#order_id#">#Order_ID#</a></td>
        <td>#DateFormat(orderdate, 'mm/dd/yy')#
        #TimeFormat(orderdate, 'h:mm tt')# PST</td>
        <td>#request.OrderAge(orderdate, now())#</td>
        <td>#FirstName# #LastName#</td>
        <td><a href="content.cfm?page=orders_process&id=#order_id#"><img
src="../images/general/order_process.gif" width="18" height="15" alt="Process
Order" border="0"></a></td>
      </tr>
    </cfoutput>
  </table>
  </cfmodule>
<cfelse>
  <cfmodule template="../modules/tablewrapper.cfm"
   title="No Orders" width="35%">
  <table width="100%" cellpadding="2" cellspacing="0" border="0">
    <tr>
      <td>There are no new orders to process.</td>
    </tr>
  </table>
  </cfmodule>
</cfif>
```

I mentioned that the function should show the relative age of the order. This means that if the order is 15 minutes old, the age should be displayed as "15 minutes," and if the order is 6 days old, the order should display "6 days." This may sound easy, but there's a bit more to it than you'd think. It would be much simpler if we decided that we want to show everything in minutes, whether it was "15 minutes" or "900 minutes," but because we want to break things down in the simplest form, it gets more complicated.

There are two other considerations to be made as well that complicate the logic. If an order is over say, 5 hours old, the display for the age should be "5 hours!" in bold red letters. This goes back to our goal of fast order processing—if something is over 5 hours old, it needs to stick out like a red-hot fire poker in your eye. Also, we need to keep the data relatively simple—we don't want to say "5 hours, 10 minutes, 4 seconds"; we want to round to the nearest whole.

Let's take a closer look at the OrderAge function, piece by piece:

```
<cfscript>
function OrderAge(date1, date2)
{
   d1 = ParseDateTime(date1);
   d2 = ParseDateTime(date2);
   tmp = DateDiff("n", d1, d2);
```

Using the *function* keyword, we create a function called OrderAge that requires two dates. We use the ParseDateTime() function to clean up the date in a way that will always be the same for the function. This speeds things up a bit when parsing the dates, and eliminates any unexpected surprises. The ParseDateTime() function takes any date string, like "January 1, 2000" or "1/1/00" and format it like this: "{ts '2000-01-01 00:00:00'}".

We then use the DateDiff() function to determine how many more minutes d2 is over d1. The "n" in DateDiff("n", d1, d2) means that we want to compare minutes.

```
if (tmp GT 0)
   {
      num = tmp;
      myvar = num & IIF(num is 1, DE(" minute"), DE(" minutes"));
   }
```

This is the first of a few questions we ask of the value returned by the DateDiff() function. The first thing we try to determine is whether the difference between the two dates is greater than 0. If it is, we use the IIF() function to ask if the value is 1. If it's 1, then we want to drop the "s" off the end of minutes so we look like we know how to speak proper English. If the value is not 1, then we keep the "s" on the end of minutes.

Because we decided earlier that the function needs to return the simplest form of the age of the order, we need to ask some more questions to determine whether the number of minutes is equal to an hour, a day, or weeks. The following three conditions ask those questions, and set the *myvar* variable to show the right measurement:

```
if (tmp GT 60)
{
   num = Int(tmp/60);
   myvar = num & IIF(num is 1, DE(" hour"), DE(" hours"));

   if (num GT 4)
   {
      baddie = 1;
   }
}

if (tmp GT 1440)
{
   num = Int(tmp/1440);
   myvar = num & IIF(num is 1, DE(" day"), DE(" days"));
   baddie = 1;
}

if (tmp GT 10080)
{
   num = Int(tmp/10080);
   myvar = num & IIF(num is 1, DE(" week"), DE(" weeks"));
   baddie = 1;
}
```

The if statements do just about the same thing as the first one, except this time when we get into the days statement, we also want to set a flag for anything over four hours old. The variable we use to store this flag is called *baddie*, and we'll use it later in the function to help make our order age stand out. If the number of minutes exceeds 1,440, then the age of the order is over a day old, and it automatically gets flagged as a baddie, because it's obviously over four hours old.

```
  if (IsDefined("baddie"))
   {
      myvar = "<font color=""red""><b>" & myvar & "!</b></font>";
   }
   return myvar;
}
request.OrderAge = OrderAge;
</cfscript>
```

If the *baddie* flag was created, then we know we need to format the returned age in a way that catches the employee's attention. Bold, red, and with an exclamation point should do the trick for now. We'll avoid making the age blink; employee retention is also a goal of ours, and blinking text on web pages has the adverse effect of driving people completely insane.

We return the value of *myvar*, and place the OrderAge function of the **Request** scope, just in case we use it later in a custom tag or module. When we call the function in our new orders table, we'll use the following code:

```
#request.OrderAge(orderdate, now())#
```

The value of *orderdate* comes from our query, and the now() function is used to supply the current date and time.

We display general information about the order, with the order number and an image linked to content.cfm?orders_process&id=#order_id#, along with the customer's first and last name, the age of the order, and the time it was submitted. Notice that we don't show the total dollar amount of the order—this isn't showing based on some of the business needs. In our business model, salespeople don't have any incentive to take one order over another. Their job description requires that they process the oldest order first, regardless of any other motivation. If our salespeople were paid based on commission, or by the number of orders processed, our design might be entirely different. Again, that's a business model-driven decision. As developers writing business applications, we need to flexible with what we create.

skate.shop/admin/modules/tablewrapper.cfm

We wrap the output of the NewOrders query with tablewrapper.cfm. The tablewrapper.cfm file sits in skate.shop/admin/modules, and is used to add some HTML formatting to the table. This allows us to have a consistent look and feel for the tables in our Administrator, while only having to worry about it once.

```
<cfparam name="attributes.title" default="{need a title}">
<cfparam name="attributes.width" default="90%">
<cfif thistag.executionmode is "start">
  <table width="<cfoutput>#attributes.width#</cfoutput>" border="0"
cellspacing="1" cellpadding="0" bgcolor="Black">
    <tr>
      <td>
        <table width="100%" cellpadding="0" cellspacing="0"
         border="0" bgcolor="White">
          <tr>
            <td bgcolor="#657E8F"
class="nav"><b><cfoutput>#attributes.title#</cfoutput></b></td>
          </tr>
          <tr>
            <td>
</cfif>
<cfif thistag.executionmode is "end">
            </td>
          </tr>
        </table>
      </td>
    </tr>
  </table>
</cfif>
```

skate.shop/admin/orders/orders_process.cfm

Now, let's look at the order processing file. We'll break the file down into two parts. The first part is the order processing part, and the second is the detailed display of the order.

The first query builds the list of order_status_id values and their descriptions. This is used in a drop-down list. The sales person selects one of the possible states of the order. Incidentally, the orders_process.cfm file doesn't "care" what page the sales person came from. In every order status page, whether it is orders_new.cfm, orders_current.cfm, or orders_shipped.cfm, the link to orders_process.cfm is the same. The page simply allows for the changing of the status of the order.

We use the same SQL view for pulling the order details that we did for displaying new orders, except this time we're looking for a particular order_id.

```
<cfquery name="OrderStatus" datasource="#request.dsn#">
SELECT *
FROM AdminOrderStatusView
</cfquery>
```

```
<cfif IsDefined("form.update")>
  <cfset session.salesrep = form.salesrep>
  <cfquery name="UpdateOrderStatus" datasource="#request.dsn#">
  UPDATE Orders
  SET Order_Status_ID = #form.Order_Status_ID#,
  Sales_Rep = '#form.salesrep#'
  WHERE Order_ID = #url.id#
  </cfquery>
</cfif>

<cfif IsDefined("session.salesrep")>
  <cfset request.salesrep = session.salesrep>
<cfelse>
  <cfset request.salesrep = "">
</cfif>

<cfquery name="OrderDetails" datasource="#request.dsn#">
SELECT *
FROM AdminOrdersView
WHERE Order_ID = #url.id#
</cfquery>

<cfform action="content.cfm?page=orders_process&id=#url.id#"
method="POST" enablecab="no">
<cfmodule template="../modules/tablewrapper.cfm"
title="Assign a Sales Rep" width="200">
<table width="100%" cellpadding="2" cellspacing="0" border="0">
  <tr>
    <td><b>1. Enter Your Rep Code</b></td>
  </tr>
  <tr>
    <td><cfinput type="Text" name="salesrep"
       value="#request.salesrep#" required="No" size="5"
       maxlength="10"></td>
  </tr>
  <tr>
    <td><b>2. Update Order Status</b></td>
  </tr>
  <tr>
    <td><cfselect name="Order_Status_ID"
    query="OrderStatus" value="Order_Status_ID"
    display="status"
    selected="#OrderDetails.Order_Status_ID#"></cfselect></td>
```

```
  </tr>
  <tr>
    <td><input type="submit" name="update" value="Update"></td>
  </tr>
</table>
</cfmodule>
</cfform>
```

Once the OrderDetails query has been executed, we display a form that lets the sales person assign their initials, or salesperson code, to the order. This assignment can change at any time, and it's not even required. Yet again, the business model drives the design of this part of the application. Salespeople, in this business model, are asked to take responsibility for an order. Once their name is assigned to it, they follow it through, and make sure it gets to the customer without any problems. But we need to keep it flexible too, if Joe W. assigns his name to the task, but gets overloaded, Steven N. can take over without any difficulty.

Once the order status has been changed, and it has been recorded using the UpdateOrderStatus query, the salesperson's initials are stored in *session.SalesRep* in the same step. A few lines later, after the UpdateOrderStatus block, we look for the existence of *session.SalesRep*. If it exists, we pass its value to *request.SalesRep*; if it doesn't, we pass a blank value to *request.SalesRep*.

We use *request.SalesRep* in the processing form to help reduce the number of times a sales rep needs to add their initials. We could build a salesperson table, complete with login names, passwords, and security roles, but we really don't need it here, yet. If, as a business, we decide later that we need this increased complexity, then the application is flexible enough, and simple enough, to allow that kind of change.

Let's look at the second part of the file, the order details part:

```
<p>
<cfmodule template="../modules/tablewrapper.cfm"
title="Order Details">
<cfoutput query="OrderDetails" group="Order_ID">
  <table width="100%" cellpadding="2" cellspacing="0" border="0">
      <tr>
        <td>
          <table width="100%" cellpadding="2"
          cellspacing="0" border="0">
            <tr>
              <td><b>Customer Information</b></td>
            </tr>
            <tr>
              <td>#firstname# #lastname# &lt;#emailaddr#&gt;</td>
```

```
        </tr>
        <tr>
          <td>#phone#</td>
        </tr>
      </table>
    </td>
  </tr>
  <tr>
    <td>
      <table width="100%" cellpadding="2"
       cellspacing="0" border="0">
        <tr>
          <td><b>Credit Card Information</b></td>
        </tr>
        <tr>
          <td>#ccnum#</td>
        </tr>
        <tr>
          <td>Expires #ccexp#</td>
        </tr>
      </table>
    </td>
  </tr>
  <tr>
    <td width="50%" valign="top">
      <table width="100%" cellpadding="2"
       cellspacing="0" border="0">
        <tr>
          <td><b>Billing Address</b></td>
        </tr>
        <tr>
          <td>#bill_address1#
          <cfif bill_address2 is not ''>
          <br>#bill_address2#</cfif></td>
        </tr>
        <tr>
          <td>#bill_city#</td>
        </tr>
        <tr>
          <td>#bill_state# #bill_zip#</td>
        </tr>
      </table>
    </td>
    <td width="50%" valign="top">
      <table width="100%" cellpadding="2"
       cellspacing="0" border="0">
        <tr>
```

```
              <td><b>Shipping Address</b></td>
            </tr>
            <cfif shipbillsame eq 1>
              <tr>
                <td>#bill_address1#
                <cfif bill_address2 is not ''>
                <br>#bill_address2#</cfif></td>
              </tr>
              <tr>
                <td>#bill_city#</td>
              </tr>
              <tr>
                <td>#bill_state# #bill_zip#</td>
              </tr>
            <cfelse>
              <tr>
                <td>#ship_address1#
                <cfif ship_address2 is not ''>
                <br>#ship_address2#</cfif></td>
              </tr>
              <tr>
                <td>#ship_city#</td>
              </tr>
              <tr>
                <td>#ship_state# #ship_zip#</td>
              </tr>
            </cfif>
          </table>
        </td>
      </tr>
    </table>
    <table width="100%" cellpadding="0" cellspacing="0" border="0">
      <tr>
        <td colspan="7"><b>Order Information</b></td>
      </tr>
      <tr bgcolor="##233B55">
        <td align="center"><img src="../images/general/checkout_part.gif"
width="20" height="11" alt="Part Number" border="0"></td>
        <td align="center"><img src="../images/general/checkout_desc.gif"
width="48" height="11" alt="Description" border="0"></td>
        <td align="center"><img src="../images/general/checkout_size.gif"
width="16" height="11" alt="Size" border="0"></td>
        <td align="center"><img src="../images/general/checkout_color.gif"
width="23" height="11" alt="Color" border="0"></td>
        <td align="center"><img src="../images/general/checkout_qty.gif"
width="39" height="11" alt="Quantity" border="0"></td>
        <td align="center"><img src="../images/general/checkout_price.gif"
```

```
width="20" height="11" alt="Price" border="0"></td>
      </tr>
      <cfset rowtick = 0>
      <cfset checkout.subtotal = 0>
      <cfoutput group="variation_id">
      <cfif rowtick/2 eq int(rowtick/2)>
      <tr>
      <cfelse>
      <tr bgcolor="##F0F8FF">
      </cfif>
        <td class="carttxt" align="center">#variation_id#</td>
        <td class="carttxt">#title#</td>
        <td class="carttxt">#size_desc#</td>
        <td class="carttxt">#color_desc#</td>
        <td class="carttxt" align="center">#quantity#</td>
        <td class="carttxt"
           align="right">#dollarformat(quantity*price)#</td>
      </tr>
      <cfset rowtick = rowtick + 1>
      <cfset checkout.subtotal = checkout.subtotal + (quantity*price)>
      </cfoutput>
    </table>
    <table width="100%" cellpadding="0" cellspacing="0" border="0">
      <tr>
        <td align="right">
          <table cellpadding="0" cellspacing="0" border="0">
            <tr>
              <td bgcolor="Black" colspan="2"><img
              src="../images/general/clear.gif"
              width="1" height="1"  border="0"></td>
            </tr>
            <tr>
              <td class="carttxt"><b>Subtotal</b></td>
              <td class="carttxt"
align="right">#dollarformat(checkout.subtotal)#</td>
            </tr>
            <cfset checkout.tax = 0>
            <cfif bill_state eq 'CA'>
            <cfset checkout.tax = (checkout.subtotal * 0.0825)>
            <tr>
              <td
              class="carttxt"><b>CA Sales Tax (8.25%)</b> </td>
              <td class="carttxt"
              align="right">#dollarformat(checkout.tax)#</td>
            </tr>
            </cfif>
            <tr>
```

```
              <td class="carttxt">#description# </td>
              <td class="carttxt"
              align="right">#dollarformat(shipcost)#</td>
            </tr>
            <tr>
              <td bgcolor="Black" colspan="2"><img
              src="../images/general/clear.gif"
              width="1" height="3"  border="0"></td>
            </tr>
            <cfset checkout.grand_total = checkout.subtotal +
            checkout.tax + shipcost>
            <tr>
              <td bgcolor="##A6D2FF"
              class="carttxt"><b>Grand Total</b> </td>
              <td bgcolor="##A6D2FF" class="carttxt"
              align="right">#dollarformat(checkout.grand_total)#</td>
            </tr>
          </table>
        </td>
      </tr>
    </table>
  </cfoutput>
</cfmodule>
```

This code is nearly identical to the code found in the checkout part of the site; in fact, the only differences are the paths to the images. This is a perfect example of when it's a good idea to make a module out of something. The slight difference between the two blocks of code can easily be overcome with an attribute called *imagepath*, or something similar, in which we pass the path to the images.

I didn't do that for a couple of reasons—I wanted to be able to show an example of when it's a good idea to use a module or custom tag. Also, I wanted to easily show what the rest of the orders_process.cfm file would output, without having to add any complexity. In a real life situation, I would have made this a cfmodule.

skate.shop/admin/orders/orders_current.cfm and orders_shipped.cfm

These two files are identical to the orders_new.cfm file that we covered in a preceding section except for one detail—the *order_status_id* value. In orders_current.cfm, we're looking for orders with an *order_status_id* of 3, and in orders_shipped.cfm, we're looking for orders with an *order_status_id* of 4.

These two files are also prime candidates for modularization, but in this case, I left them separate. It's possible that different functionality may quickly be added depending on the needs of the business.

For instance, it might be determined that orders in the orders_shipped.cfm file should show dollar amounts, totaling the number of orders sold, just as an "at-a-glance" piece of information. Or we may decide to add a phone number column to the orders_current.cfm file, or an interface to FedEx tracking systems.

Given that these two files are likely to be very different as time goes on, it didn't seem like a good idea to use modularization, only to throw that modularization away very soon. We don't need to look at the code, simply because we've seen it before in the orders_new.cfm file.

Reporting

Even a humble little skateboard shop needs to know about what's going on with their site, and ColdFusion 5.0 makes it especially easy to view gathered data. ColdFusion 5.0 comes with a new tag called <CFGRAPH> that lets you create graphical representations of data. The <CFGRAPH> tag itself is a nice addition, but what's even nicer is that it uses Macromedia Generator—a very powerful tool that allows developers to create dynamic Flash files. We'll look at the integration of ColdFusion and Flash in later chapters, but for now, it's perfectly alright to get excited about the inclusion of Generator. In this section, we get a taste of what Generator is capable of with the <CFGRAPH> tag.

Deciding what kind of data to track depends on how you run your business. This data is often referred to as *key metrics*, or *site metrics*. Metrics are the key pieces of data that tell you the performance of your site, or your business. For instance, knowing how many of the people who visit your site actually purchase something is a key metric—it helps you know what kind of return you're getting on your marketing and advertising dollars.

We could spend a huge amount of time discussing what kinds of things are key metrics and what kinds of things aren't—it's really something that becomes most evident as you're running your business. What we will go over though is how to use cfgraph to graphically display data that we've collected. Let's check out the first file in our reporting section, reporting_generalsales.cfm.

skate.shop/admin/reporting/reporting_generalsales.cfm

This file consists of two parts—the pie graph part and the details part. We'll look at the pie graph part. The second part is pretty self-explanatory—simply build a page based on the GeneralSales query, with a product_id as criteria.

```
<cfquery name="GeneralSales" datasource="#request.dsn#">
SELECT *
FROM Reporting_GeneralSales
</cfquery>

<cfgraph type="pie"
  query="GeneralSales"
  valueColumn="Quantity"
  itemColumn="title"
  showValueLabel="rollover"
  title="Products Sold"
  URL="content.cfm?page=reporting_generalsales&details="
  URLColumn="Product_ID"
  >
</cfgraph>
```

The GeneralSales query selects a view, which goes as follows:

```
SELECT
dbo.product.product_id,
SUM(dbo.order_details.quantity) AS Quantity,
dbo.product.title
FROM dbo.product
INNER JOIN dbo.product_var
ON dbo.product.product_id = dbo.product_var.product_id
INNER JOIN dbo.order_details
ON dbo.product_var.variation_id = dbo.order_details.variation_id
INNER JOIN dbo.orders
ON dbo.order_details.order_id = dbo.orders.order_id
WHERE (dbo.orders.order_status_id IN (3, 4))
GROUP BY dbo.product.product_id, dbo.product.title
```

This query counts every sold product, indicated by the order_status_id value of three or four. Our pie graph only really needs the calculated Quantity column, the product title, and the product_id column (which are the only things we've indicated in the Select statement). All the joins ensure that we're getting accurate product sales breakdowns in one shot.

<CFGRAPH> is a pretty simple tag—supply it with the right attributes and values, and it will generate a graph in the format you've indicated. Let's break down the attributes and values of the cfgraph example above.

Attribute	Value	Description
Type	Pie	Indicates that we want to generate a pie graph, as opposed to a line or bar graph.
Query	GeneralSales	Shows the name of our query, with the data we want to display.
valueColumn	Quantity	Determines the sizes of the pie slices.
itemColumn	Title	Shows the name of the product.
showValueLabel	Rollover	Indicates that we want the actual value of the pie slice to show up when the mouse rolls over the slice.
Title	Product Sales	Shows the title of our graph.
URL	content.cfm?page= reporting_generalsales&details=	Makes the pie slices clickable, and this is the URL of the slice.
URLColumn	product_id	Product_id will be added to the end of the URL value above, giving each slice a unique URL.

By default, <CFGRAPH> generates a graph in Flash format. If we added the attribute and value *fileformat="gif"*, it would generate a graph in GIF format. Graphs can be generated in Flash, GIF, and JPG formats.

skate.shop/admin/reporting/reporting_sitemetrics.cfm

This is the second example file. The first query gathers the data we'll need for the graph. We haven't yet talked about the clickthroughs column in the *Categories* table. We've added this query to the skate.shop/queries/qryResults.cfm to track the number of times someone clicks on a category:

```
<cfquery name="CategoryCounts" datasource="#request.dsn#">
SELECT cat_name, clickthroughs
FROM Categories
WHERE showcat = 1
```

```
</cfquery>

<!--- determine highest quantity value to use
for the scale of the graph --->
<cfquery name="QofQ_ScaleTo" dbType="query" maxrows="1">
SELECT clickthroughs
FROM CategoryCounts
ORDER BY clickthroughs DESC
</cfquery>

<cfset GraphScale = QofQ_ScaleTo.clickthroughs + 2>
<cfgraph type = "horizontalbar"
  query = "CategoryCounts"
  valueColumn = "clickthroughs"
  itemColumn = "cat_name"
  title = "Category Popularity"
  scaleTo = "#GraphScale#"
  fileFormat = "flash"
  depth = 4
  borderWidth="0"
  >
</cfgraph>
```

This query executes right before the request.qryResults query. This is a very simple way of tracking clickthroughs—if it ever became really important, we'd want to build a stored procedure that tracked category clickthroughs broken down by date. In fact, we'd want an entirely separate table set aside just to track clickthroughs by date, so that we could see seasonal trends, and so on.

```
<cfquery name="qryTrackCatImpression" datasource="#request.dsn#">
  UPDATE Categories
  SET clickthroughs = clickthroughs + 1
  WHERE cat_id = #url.cat#
</cfquery>
```

The second query in reporting_sitemetrics.cfm is a query of a query that figures out the greatest clickthrough count on any one of the categories. This value determines the scale of the chart. If we didn't determine this value, we'd have to supply an arbitrary value in the *scale* attribute of cfgraph.

A few lines down we add two to the overall scale for aesthetic purposes only in the *GraphScale* variable. Let's look at the attributes and values like we did previously.

Attribute	Value	Description
Type	Horizontalbar	Indicates that we want a horizontal bar graph, where the bars start on the left and extend to the right.
Query	CategoryCounts	The query name.
ValueColumn	Clickthroughs	Determines the width of our bars.
ItemColumn	cat_name	The label of the bar.
Title	Category Popularity	The title of the graph.
ScaleTo	#GraphScale#	The padded value generated for the query of queries.
FileFormat	Flash	Indicates that we'd like to generate the graph using Flash.
Depth	4	Gives each of the bars a 3D look. The higher the number, the more 3D the bar.
BorderWidth	0	Indicates that we don't want to show any borders on this graph.

Wrapping Up

In this chapter, we've built a very simple Administrator for our skate.shop application. The architecture of the Administrator allows for future expansion without too much difficulty, and does an effective job of handling the most important task—order processing.

You might have noticed that we didn't talk about the maintenance section of the site—that's what we'll be talking about in Chapter 8. We'll be building our own interface to the ColdFusion schedule, which will include some messing around with the registry—don't worry; we'll play it safe. We'll be launching the site (or at least theoretically), and we'll talk about how to monitor the ColdFusion server for performance, as well as the SQL Server.

CHAPTER

8

Launching and Maintaining the Site

IN THIS CHAPTER:

Building a Maintenance Scheduler

Staging and Launching skate.shop

Monitoring Performance

Tweaking Performance

Listening to the Customer

We've spent a lot of time designing and building our application. But before we launch the site, we need to make sure that we're ready to do business—that our web site is bug free, that our customers can tell us what they think of the site, and that our "house-cleaning" tasks are running on a regular basis.

In this chapter, we build a maintenance scheduler, and then stage, test, and launch the skate.shop site. We talk about ways to monitor site performance, and ways to increase that performance. Finally, we add a customer feedback system that allows customers to quickly and easily send feedback to the site, routed to the correct department.

Building a Maintenance Scheduler

One of the important parts of our skate.shop administration site is the maintenance scheduler. We'll cover the actual maintenance tasks later on in this chapter, but before we can launch the site, we need to have the scheduler framework in place.

Overview

The scheduler uses <CFSCHEDULE> and <CFREGISTRY> tags to access the ColdFusion task scheduler. We could use the ColdFusion task scheduler, but it's a good exercise to see examples of how to read and modify the registry, and it provides a useful tool for our site. Our scheduler allows us to view and modify skate.shop related tasks, filtering out any other task scheduled on the server.

Building the Scheduler

The scheduler consists of four files and one directory. In this section we look at each file, and break each down into digestible bits.

skate.shop\admin\maint\maint_schedule.cfm

This file displays the scheduled tasks, and allows us to add and delete tasks:

```
<cfset stringEntryPrefix = "skate.shop">

<cfset
  key_location =
  "HKEY_LOCAL_MACHINE\Software\Allaire\ColdFusion\CurrentVersion\Schedule">

<cfif IsDefined("url.action")>
  <cfif url.action is "del">
```

```
      <cfregistry action="DELETE" branch="#key_location#\#url.task#">
    </cfif>
</cfif>

 <!--- scan the registry for current skate.shop tasks --->
 <cfregistry action="GETALL"
           branch="#key_location#"
           name="AllScheduledTasks"
           type="Key">
```

This first block of code consists of three parts. The first part sets up values we'll use later on. The format of stringEntryPrefix is a big deal—the only tasks that our customer scheduler will show are tasks that start with "skate.shop." This is so we don't have other tasks scheduled on this server that don't have anything to do with our application.

The second <CFSET> stores the full path of the branch where we'll be adding keys. The registry is basically a hierachal database, and this branch is where ColdFusion stores its scheduled tasks.

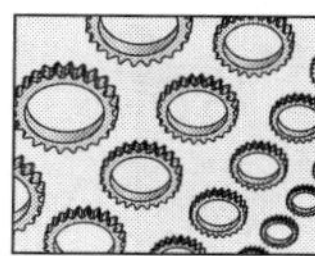

NOTE

We probably could have built our own scheduler, forgoing ColdFusion's registry method and using a combination of batch files or other methods. Using the registry works pretty well, however, and it gives us an opportunity to access some rarely used features of ColdFusion. I should warn you, before we go any further, that if you're careless with your registry, you can really mess things up. I would exercise extreme caution when deleting, or even updating keys—double check and make sure that your code is going to do what you think it will, and when in doubt, check again.

Setting the branch in the *key_location* variable helps keep us safer—if we only set the value once, then it's easier to maintain where we're editing and deleting in the registry. But, disastrous results can be just as easy if the value of *key_location* is something else that shouldn't be messed with.

Now that I'm done freaking you out about what you can do your registry, let's talk about the third block of code from above. If the url parameter *action* exists, we then look to see if the value of *action* is "del" (for delete). If the value is "del," we use <CFREGISTRY> to completely remove a branch from the registry, or in our case, a task. ColdFusion stores each task as a branch in the path, or tree, of the registry. Each branch, or task, has it's own set of values. The code we've just described deletes the branch indicated, and all of its values, without complaint. You don't have to delete its child values before killing the parent, so keep that in mind. If you were to delete the top level in the registry, every level below it would also be deleted, which would make getting kicked in the neck sound like a very desirable alternative. While I've been kicked in many places, I can't say for sure that I've been kicked in the neck, but I'm sure it's very painful—the pain of deleting your registry is far worse—which I've done for kicks, pun intended, just to see what would happen. I should move on; I already promised that my talk of registry doom was over, so let's reverse the attitude—playing with the registry is *fun!*

The fourth block of code generates a query object of all the task names, or more specifically, it looks at each branch below the *key_location* variable, and stores the name of each branch in a query called AllScheduledTasks. We'll use this query to output a list of tasks on the server. Now, for the next digestible bit:

```
<!--- first chunk --->
<cfmodule
   template="../modules/tablewrapper.cfm"
   title="Scheduled Tasks">

 <table width="100%" cellpadding="2" cellspacing="1" border="0">
  <tr>
    <td bgcolor="#2C65A0"><b>Task Name</b></td>
    <td bgcolor="#2C65A0"><b>Script</b></td>
    <td bgcolor="#2C65A0"><b>Duration</b></td>
    <td bgcolor="#2C65A0"><b>Interval</b></td>
    <td bgcolor="#2C65A0"><b>Controls</b></td>
   </tr>

   <!--- second chunk --->
   <cfloop query="AllScheduledTasks">
   <tr>
     <cfset stringTaskName = entry>
     <cfif Left(entry, len(stringEntryPrefix)) eq stringEntryPrefix>
      <cfregistry action="GETALL"
            branch="#key_location#\#entry#"
            name="TaskKeyValues"
            type="Any">

     <!--- third chunk --->
     <cfquery name="QofQ_URL" dbtype="Query">
     SELECT value
     FROM TaskKeyValues
     WHERE entry = 'URL'
     </cfquery>
     <cfquery name="QofQ_Duration" dbtype="Query">
     SELECT value
     FROM TaskKeyValues
     WHERE entry = 'Duration'
     </cfquery>
     <cfquery name="QofQ_Interval" dbtype="Query">
     SELECT value
```

```
      FROM TaskKeyValues
      WHERE entry = 'Interval'
      </cfquery>

      <!--- fourth chunk --->
      <cfoutput>
       <td><a
href="content.cfm?page=maint_scheduleedit&action=edit&task=#stringTaskName#">
#stringTaskName#</a></td>
       <td>#QofQ_URL.value#</td>
       <td>#QofQ_Duration.value#</td>
       <td>#QofQ_Interval.value#</td>
       <td>[<a
            href="content.cfm?page=maint_scheduleedit&task=#stringTaskName#">
             Edit</a>]
[<a href="content.cfm?page=maint_schedule&action=del&task=#stringTaskName#">
 Delete</a>]</td>
     </cfoutput>
     </cfif>
  </tr>
   </cfloop>
 </table>
 </cfmodule>
```

This first chunk of code is probably all too familiar now, so I won't spend any time on that other than to mention that it sets up the table for our outputted list of tasks.

The second chunk of code begins a loop using the query we generated with the <CFREGISTRY> tag that we talked about earlier in this section. For each item in that query, we'll do another <CFREGISTRY> call, this time, using the value of the task to show all the keys, or attributes, in that branch.

The third chunk gets interesting—remember that the <CFREGISTRY> tag generates a query, but we only want a couple of pieces of data from this query for each key in the branch. For each key in the branch, we'll use a query of a query to get three different values, the URL, the duration, and the interval.

The fourth and final part of this half of the maint_schedule.cfm file is the actual output of each key, using the values from each of the query of queries. Each task is linked to maint_scheduleedit.cfm.

The last piece of the file is a form that allows us to add a new task to the task scheduler:

```
<cfmodule
            template="../modules/tablewrapper.cfm"
                  title="Add New Task"
                  width="300">
 <cfform action="content.cfm?page=maint_scheduleedit"
```

```
        method="POST"
        enablecab="No">
 <table width="100%" cellpadding="2" cellspacing="1" border="0">
   <tr>
     <td bgcolor="#2C65A0" colspan=2><b>Task Name</b></td>
   </tr>
  <tr>
    <td><cfinput type="Text"
       name="task"
       value="skate.shop."
       message="A task name is required."
       required="Yes"
       size="15"
       maxlength="50"></td>
    <td><input type="submit" name="submit" value="Add Task"></td>
  </tr>
</table>
</cfform>
</cfmodule>
```

This block of code links back to the first block of code in our file, which we talked about at the beginning of this section.

skate.shop\admin\maint\maint_scheduleedit.cfm

This file is the actual interface to the task, and it allows us to modify the settings for the particular task. This file handles all the reading of the registry, and the actual updating of the registry, and does a few other interesting things that we'll see as well.

The first block of code handles the form action for adding a new task, which comes from the maint_schedule.cfm file, and sets the *key_location* string.

```
<cfset
      key_location =

"HKEY_LOCAL_MACHINE\Software\Allaire\ColdFusion\CurrentVersion\Schedule">

<cfif IsDefined("form.task")>
      <cfregistry action="SET"
            branch="#key_location#"
            entry="#form.task#"
            type="Key">
      <cfset url.task = form.task>
      <!--- create entries --->
      <cfregistry action="SET"
```

```
       branch="#key_location#\#url.task#"
       entry="Operation"
       type="String"
       value="HTTPRequest">
<cfregistry action="SET"
       branch="#key_location#\#url.task#"
       entry="URL"
       type="String"
       value="http://">
<cfregistry action="SET"
       branch="#key_location#\#url.task#"
       entry="File"
       type="String">
<cfregistry action="SET"
       branch="#key_location#\#url.task#"
       entry="Path"
       type="String">
<cfregistry action="SET"
       branch="#key_location#\#url.task#"
       entry="StartDate"
       type="String"
       value="#DateFormat(Now(), 'mm/dd/yy')#">
<cfregistry action="SET"
       branch="#key_location#\#url.task#"
       entry="StartTime"
       type="String">
<cfregistry action="SET"
       branch="#key_location#\#url.task#"
       entry="EndDate"
       type="String">
<cfregistry action="SET"
       branch="#key_location#\#url.task#"
       entry="EndTime"
       type="String">
<cfregistry action="SET"
       branch="#key_location#\#url.task#"
       entry="Interval"
       type="String"
       value="DAILY">
<cfregistry action="SET"
       branch="#key_location#\#url.task#"
       entry="ProxyServer"
       type="String">
<cfregistry action="SET"
       branch="#key_location#\#url.task#"
       entry="Publish"
       type="String">
```

```
        <cfregistry action="SET"
              branch="#key_location#\#url.task#"
              entry="RequestTimeout"
              type="String">
        <cfregistry action="SET"
              branch="#key_location#\#url.task#"
              entry="Password"
              type="String">
        <cfregistry action="SET"
              branch="#key_location#\#url.task#"
              entry="Username"
              type="String">
        <cfregistry action="SET"
              branch="#key_location#\#url.task#"
              entry="ResolveURL"
              type="String">
        <cfregistry action="SET"
              branch="#key_location#\#url.task#"
              entry="HttpPort"
              type="String"
              value="80">
        <cfregistry action="SET"
              branch="#key_location#\#url.task#"
              entry="HttpProxyPort"
              type="String"
              value="23">
</cfif>
```

Unfortunately, there's no sure-fire way to create the task. Each key for the task needs to be set beforehand. It might be possible to query an already existing task, but we can never be sure that a task will exist, so it's better to just create it.

```
<cfif IsDefined("form.fieldnames")>
      <cfif form.fieldnames does not contain "task">
            <cfloop list="#form.fieldnames#" index="field">
                  <cfregistry action="SET"
            branch="#key_location#\#url.task#"
            entry="#field#"
            type="String"
            value="#Evaluate('form.#field#')#">
            </cfloop>
      </cfif>
</cfif>
```

While it took a bit of effort to create the task, updating the task is much easier, thanks to the *form.fieldnames* parameter. Whenever a form is submitted, the form field names are placed in a comma-delimited list called *form.fieldnames*. This simple little list can reduce the amount of code we have to write by leaps and bounds for this particular task.

Rather than explicitly naming each key to set with the <CFREGISTRY> tag, we simply loop over the *form.fieldnames* list, and evaluate each item in the list. The *list* attribute in the loop tells the <CFLOOP> tag which list to use, and the *index* attribute is the name of the variable that will receive the value of the item in the list.

With each iteration of the loop, we use <CFREGISTRY> to update the value of the entry. This only works if each of our form elements is named exactly the same as the registry key entry. If it's named anything else, a new key entry will be created, and while it doesn't exactly hurt anything in this case, we want to avoid cluttering up our registry.

In the entry attribute of the <CFREGISTRY> tag, we use the *field* parameter, which should be a name of a key value. We then use the evaluate function to determine what the actual value of the form field is. The evaluate function in this example gives us the actual name of the form field, which is contained in the field index. If we haven't evaluated the field index, we get the value contained within the form field, rather than its name.

One of the things you'll notice in the form that actually kicks off this block of code is that the submit button isn't named. If we named the button, the value would show up in the *form.fieldnames* parameter, which would in turn create a key value pair in our registry. The fact that this value isn't passed might differ among different browsers and platforms, so keep in mind that it should be tested before it is put into production.

```
<cfregistry action="GETALL"
            branch="#key_location#\#url.task#"
            name="TaskKeyValues"
            type="Any">
<cfmodule
          template="../modules/tablewrapper.cfm" title="#url.task# Task Editor"
          width="400">
<cfform action="content.cfm?page=maint_scheduleedit&task=#url.task#"
        method="POST"
        enablecab="Yes">
<table width="400" cellpadding="2" cellspacing="0" border="0">
      <cfoutput query="TaskKeyValues">
      <tr>
            <td><a href="javascript:void(0)"
onmouseover="displayPopup('content.cfm?page=maint_scheduletermpopup&lookup=#entry#
','popup',300,150,(version4 ? event : null))"
onmouseout="closePopup()">#entry#</a></td>
            <td><cfinput type="Text"
```

```
        name="#entry#"
        value="#value#"
        required="No"
        size="25"></td>
       </tr>
       </cfoutput>
       <tr>
             <td colspan="2"><input type="submit" value="Update"></td>
       </tr>
</table>
</cfform>
</cfmodule>
```

The second half of the file displays the form and values for our task. The most interesting part of the form is the link we have for each entry name. One of the things that make the ColdFusion scheduler very useful is the fact that each setting is described in detail. We want to have that same kind of functionality as well, but we don't want it cluttering up the interface, so we'll use JavaScript to pop up a window with a description, or definition, of each entry.

skate.shop\admin\maint\maint_scheduletermpopup.cfm

To keep the interface to the task editor uncluttered, we provide an information link for each task attribute that will call a pop-up window, with the description of the attribute. This is a useful concept, and could easily be used in other parts of the site. It is probably one of the tricks that people want to know how to do the most.

Before our pop-up window can work, we need to add some JavaScript to our skate.shop/admin/modules/head.cfm:

```
<script language="JavaScript1.2">
// Quick way to test for Nav4 and IE4
version4 = false
if(navigator.appVersion.charAt(0) == "4") version4 = true

function displayPopup(url,name,height,width,evnt) {
 var properties = "toolbar=0,location=0,height="+height
 properties = properties+",width="+width
 if(evnt != null) {
  if(navigator.appName == "Microsoft Internet Explorer") {
  properties = properties+",left="+(evnt.screenX + 10)
   properties = properties+",top="+(evnt.screenY + 10)
  }else { // Navigator coordinates must be adjusted for scrolling
   properties = properties+",left="+(evnt.screenX - pageXOffset + 10)
   properties = properties+",top="+(evnt.screenY - pageYOffset + 10)
  }
 }
```

```
 popupHandle = open(url,name,properties)
}
function closePopup() {
 // mouseOut was introduced with JavaScript 1.1, so Navigator 2 users will
 // have to manually close the window
 if(popupHandle != null && !popupHandle.closed) popupHandle.close()
}
</script>
```

We also need to include maint_scheduletermpopup.cfm in our content.cfm file, so we add the following case to the main switch in content.cfm:

```
<cfcase value="maint_scheduletermpopup">
  <cfmodule template="maint/maint_scheduletermpopup.cfm">
</cfcase>
```

The skate.shop\admin\maint\maint_scheduleedit.cfm file contains the anchor tags that call the displayPopup function when a user mouses over the link. I actually didn't like the idea of having a new browser window pop up when I simply mouse over something, but now that I've been using it, I enjoy the functionality. The window pops up right where I need it, and it disappears when I'm done. I don't have to worry about the window getting lost, and I don't have to close it—it's automatic, which I like. For those who can't stand the window popping up, simply change the *onMouseOver* attribute in the anchor tag to *onClick*. Get rid of the *onMouseOut* attribute, and you're all set.

Here's the code for maint_scheduletermpopup.cfm, which is called by the pop-up window:

```
<cfmodule template="/modules/general/terms.cfm" lookup="#url.lookup#">
<cfmodule template="../modules/tablewrapper.cfm" title="#url.lookup#">
<cfoutput>#definition#</cfoutput>
</cfmodule>
```

It's an obviously simple template that includes the terms.cfm file, which we'll look at in the next section, and wraps a table around the definition variable, which is created in the terms.cfm file.

skate.shop\modules\general\terms.cfm

This file is actually designed to act as a standalone <CFMODULE>, which is why it sits in the main site's modules directory. The idea is that this file can be used for different parts of the site later on to define terms. For example, we could use it to help users understand what certain skateboarding terms mean. The interface to this module will always remain the same—feed it a term, and it spits out a definition.

In the future, we could create a terms table that stored all terms and definitions, but for now because we're only using the terms in the Administrator. We'll avoid making a database call and build a query on the fly of terms and definitions. Because there are about 17 terms in our file, each with lengthy, page-filling definitions, I'll just show an example of how we set two terms and definitions. The full code can be found on the CD.

If our terms were changing regularly, or we had more than 10 or 20 terms and definitions, it would make much more sense to use a table within a database. Some might suggest that doing it this way at any size is silly, and they would be reasonably within their right to say so. Doing it this way, however, shows a good example of how to build your own query on the fly, the knowledge of which could easily come in handy later on.

```
<cfscript>
 qryDefinitions = QueryNew("term,definition");

 QueryAddRow(qryDefinitions);
 QuerySetCell(qryDefinitions, "term", "Operation");
 QuerySetCell(qryDefinitions, "definition", "The definition");

 QueryAddRow(qryDefinitions);
 QuerySetCell(qryDefinitions, "term", "URL");
 QuerySetCell(qryDefinitions, "definition", "The definiton");
</cfscript>

 <cfquery name="QoQ_qryDefinitions" dbtype="query">
 SELECT definition
 FROM qryDefinitions
 WHERE term = '#attributes.lookup#'
 </cfquery>

 <cfset caller.definition = QoQ_qryDefinitions.definition>
```

The first line in the <CFSCRIPT> block creates a new query object with the column names "term" and "definition." Creating a query using the QueryNew function is pretty helpful in a situation like this. Rather than create an array or structure, or combinations of the two, we can create an actual query object that we use just like any other query.

We have to create each row in the query before we populate the query using the QueryAddRow function. It might look odd to see QueryAddRow(qryDefinitions); sitting all by itself, as opposed to something like tmp = QueryAddRow(qryDefinitons);. Both do the same thing, and both are valid. I just enjoy not having to worry about a *tmp* variable floating around without a purpose.

After we create the row, we populate it using the QuerySetCell function. QuerySetCell will by default set its data to the last row in the query, which, because of they way we've coded this query, will always be the row we added right before using QuerySetCell.

Once the query is generated, we use <CFQUERY> to pull the definition of the term we're looking for and set it to caller.definiton.

Hopefully, one of the things you noticed about this tag is that it's a bit overkill—building a query, then querying the query just for a single definition. A simpler way, and perhaps even faster way, might be to use a switch, like so:

```
<cfscript>
switch(term)
{
	case "Operation":
	{
		def="The definiton";
		break;
	}
	case "URL":
	{
		def="The definition";
		break;
	}
}
caller.definiton = def;
</cfscript>
```

Both examples show that it's possible to end up with equal results with some very different methods. In the second example, we show how to use a switch within <CFSCRIPT>. If you're familiar C/C++, you're probably very familiar with the switch used in <CFSCRIPT>. Unfortunately, <CFSCRIPT> only has similarities—don't try pasting a bunch of C/C++ code in and expect it to work.

skate.shop\admin\maint\scripts

This directory holds the files associated with each of the tasks we've set up. At this point in our application, there are only a couple of scripts that need to run on a regular basis, but they serve as good examples of the kinds of things that can be scheduled. Let's look at this script, and then schedule it with our newly created scheduler:

```
<cfparam name="intDays" default="-5">

<cfquery name="qryPurgeScart" datasource="#request.dsn#">
DELETE
```

```
FROM scart
WHERE dateadded < '#DateFormat(DateAdd('d', intDays, Now()), 'mm/dd/yy')#'
</cfquery>
```

This script deletes all shopping cart entries older than five days. We don't want our shopping cart table bogged down with abandoned shopping carts. It's probably safe to assume that after five days of not checking out, the customer will probably never check out, so we should clean the records up.

We'll save this file as skate.shop\admin\maint\scripts\purge_scart.cfm. Using <CFPARAM> to set the default amount of days to go back allows us to change that amount by calling the purge_scart.cfm template through a URL with a URL parameter, like this:

```
http://www.skate.shop/admin/maint/scripts/purge_scart.cfm?intDays=2
```

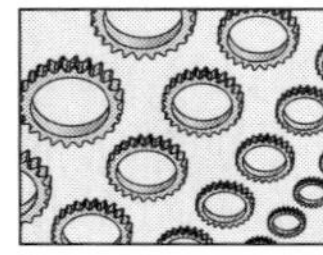

NOTE

It's highly recommended that you do something to block access from unauthorized people to your Administrator web directory. IIS 5.0 can allow you leave the doors wide open, or it can be set up to only allow a particular IP address to have access. Whatever you do, make sure it's secure. If someone gains access to the purge_scart.cfm template, they might be able to aggravate your customers a bit.

Let's add the script to our server's scheduled events, using our scheduler:

1. Open your skate.shop Administrator (probably located at http://127.0.0.1/skate.shop/admin).
2. Click Scheduled Tasks.
3. In the Add New Task box, type **skate.shop.purge_scart**. The skate.shop prefix separates the skate.shop scheduled tasks from other scheduled tasks on our server.
4. Click Add Task.
5. Leave the operation field with the value of HTTPRequest.
6. Enter the following URL in the URL field: http://yourdomain/admin/scripts/purge_scart.cfm. Notice that I used *yourdomain* as a placeholder—use what you know will work (127.0.0.1 will also work).
7. Leave the File field blank—you could use this field to save the output of the above template to a file.
8. Leave the Path field blank—it's used in conjunction with the File field.
9. Enter the day you want the task to start in the StartDate field. You must enter a start date, or your task will never start. Funny how that works.

10. Enter a start time in the StartTime field. This is also a required field.
11. The EndDate and EndTime fields are optional. If we leave these fields blank, the task will repeat based on your StartDate and StartTime and the value of the Interval field. If the Interval field is DAILY, then the task will repeat every day at the time you've specified in the StartTime field. Leave EndDate and EndTime blank.
12. Make sure Interval contains DAILY. (The value is not case sensitive.)
13. All of the other fields can be left blank, or with their default values.
14. Click Update, and the task will be updated. When you added the task name in the first step, the task was created, so at this point you're simply updating its blank or defaulted values with your own. To return to the scheduled tasks menu, click Scheduled Tasks.

This task will now run on a regular basis. If we wanted to purge records more frequently than every five days, we could simply add the *intDays=n* URL parameter to the end of our HTTPRequest value.

Staging and Launching skate.shop

The whole purpose of designing our application and writing a big pile of code is to have a successful launch. In order to have a successful launch, there is a certain type of attitude we need to have.

Our application is a piece of software, just like ColdFusion and Microsoft Office are pieces of software. Yes, there are some significant differences, but when it comes to launching or releasing a piece of software, the same considerations need to be made.

When a professional software company creates a piece of software, they perform rigorous testing on it. The developers test for memory leaks, glitches, critical bugs, and possible conflicts with other software, among many other exhaustive tests. Once the developers are finished with it, a quality assurance teams picks over it, making sure that the developers didn't miss anything.

I know I may be committing near blasphemy by suggesting that a developer might miss something, and believe me, my allegiances belong to the development team—but the truth is, as developers, we're often too busy to have to worry about "little" bugs. We shouldn't be making them in the first place, but we have bigger fish to fry—if there's a quality assurance team (even if it's your kid brother), then by all means, use the quality assurance team.

Once quality assurance has submitted formalized bug reports to the development team, and the development team has squashed any final bugs, it's time to really test the software.

Staging the Site

Prior to launching the site, and after the development team has buttoned up any loose ends, we begin the staging phase. The staging phase might also be known as an alpha phase—the software hasn't yet been released to the public, but it is undergoing internal testing.

The staging phase is the phase where you get as many people as you know personally to try and break your application. Depending on your environment, it could be the entire development team, usability experts, and if you're brave, the marketing and sales team. (But give your development and usability experts plenty of time before inviting the sales and marketing force.)

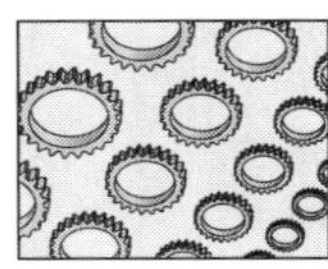

NOTE

It may sound as if I loathe sales and marketing teams, and the truth is, part of me does, even though I know that a good sales and marketing team is absolutely vital to an e-commerce business. What I dislike about most sales and marketing teams is that they usually ignore the design process where their input is essential, and when staging comes along, suddenly new functionality must be implemented or a business partner is going to jump off a bridge and never talk to us again. Marketing teams need to be well aware of when it's time to talk about functionality, and when it's time to test the functionality.

Information about how the site could be made better, or the discovery of bugs should be reported back to the person in charge of the design team so that any crucial changes can be made. I can be very idealistic and say that this process should execute smoothly without and snags, but we all know how businesses run—not everyone in an organization does everything exactly according to plan. But at this phase, imperfection in communications is not that big of a problem. All crucial bugs should have been worked out by now, and the staging process is simply a final test to make sure it's ready to go.

Sometimes it helps to create a list of all the possible interactions between the user and the site, a sort of script, and have as many people available follow the script. If all goes well with several people, chances are it will go well with a lot more people. During the staging process, those responsible for the application should be making sure that everything that is supposed to be happening on the back end of the site is indeed happening, and all is running well.

Launching the Site

Finally, the moment we've been building up to after weeks of development—the launch. This is a crucial stage, if we rush the launch process, we could do some serious damage to our reputation as an e-commerce site. One of the top complaints made by consumers looking to shop online is that site performance is poor. Launching our site only to have it crash and burn is the last thing we want to do. In order to have a successful launch, we need a formalized launch plan.

A launch plan is something the entire organization should be aware of and prepared to execute in unison. If you're a 100-person company, every department in the organization needs to be aware of how the launch will occur. If you're the only person in your organization, let your significant others know that there is a high potential that your energies within the next 24 hours are going to be spent babysitting your several week old application as it takes its first steps. I may be sounding a bit over dramatic, but in all seriousness, if your site goes live taking customer's orders, and crashes as they're putting in their credit card numbers, you've lost a customer for good, and will likely lose more as that customer relates their experience to others.

Why, after all of our testing and staging, do we still need to be hypersensitive to the needs of our site? The performance of your site is a matter of life or death for your business. If you cannot keep the site up and bug-free, you will not succeed as an e-commerce business, plain and simple.

Now, with all the doom and gloom taken into account, let's talk about how to have a successful launch. First of all, success is somewhat in the eye of the beholder, so let's separate business milestones of success from the technical end of things. First, the technical milestones you should be trying to achieve with the launch:

- **Crash free** The server should be available to service customers as near 100 percent as possible from launch day forward.
- **Bug free** Bugs should be worked out of the system by now, and if they do surface, they must be squashed immediately without pulling apart the entire application.
- **Backup plan** If catastrophe does occur, a backup plan should be available. A backup plan could be as elaborate as replacing the server farm with a new server farm, or as simple as putting up a page on the web server that states what the problem is, and that the site will return in a certain number of minutes or hours.

Now, I mentioned that success is in the eye of the beholder, but not technically. Technically, regardless of anything else, if the site fails in any one of the above milestones, the entire thing is a failure. Business-oriented success milestones (that was a mouthful) depend on the attitudes and requirements of those running the business. Here are my success markers on the business end of things for http://www.skate.shop:

- Customers need to know about the launch—a small budget PR campaign of handing out http://www.skate.shop stickers and flyers with the launch date should generate some local buzz, which can be followed up with similar events later on. A press release will be given to skateboarding- and consumer-related news wires. If I get *any* customers on or near my launch day, I'll be happy.

- If the PR campaign does *too* good a job, I need to have a plan in place. Do I turn away customers because my sales people can't handle the orders fast enough? Do I hire more people? Do I hire a company to help fulfill the orders? The site will be a success if I can process the orders in a manner that provides a high degree of customer satisfaction.

These business success markers are modest, and that's because this operation is modest. It is not yet setting out to dominate the market, so it's not having a huge launch. Even though the launch goals as a business are modest, on the technical end of things the goals will always be the same—the site has to perform under any circumstance.

Let's go over an example launch plan for http://www.skate.shop. The order of simplicity or complexity in which we deliver the launch plan can vary—I'm choosing to write a white paper with launch details that will be handed out to the staff of my company. If I were a much bigger organization, I'd probably print up some formal documents, bound if needed, and distribute to the departments who needed to know about the launch, followed by manager meetings discussing the material, and a company wide memo with a summary of the launch. An example of a launch plan follows:

The skate.shop Launch Plan

The moment we've all been working towards is soon to be. This document outlines how we plan to launch the site, and details some possible emergency plans as well. It's suggested that each part be studied carefully, and that dates and times be noted. We need everyone to be aware and attentive during the launch, and aware of each other department's roles and responsibilities as well. If we all know the plan, the launch will go smoothly and we'll be able to continue doing excellent work.

Date and Time

- Go live officially on, Monday, September 10, 2001 at 8:00 A.M., PST.

Pre-launch Events

- Lock the internal staging site two weeks prior to the launch. All bug reports should be submitted at this time.
- Provide a press preview site a week prior to the launch—this site will be the actual live site. It's encouraged that the tech team iron out any hardware or network issues before the press preview. Sales and marketing should be aware that the press needs to know the launch date, and that the site they are seeing is a preview. It's possible that during the press preview week we may get actual customers; fulfillment needs to be aware that real orders may appear and to consider every order as a customer (in other words, do not assume it's development testing).
- The tech team should iron out any final network and hardware-related issues, and verify that the site is ready by the end of the press preview week, and that it remains up until launch time the following Monday morning. No changes in the setup should occur during this time; if a change in the setup is required, it should be an emergency.

Launch Day

- Send press releases to several different news wires around 8:00 A.M., EST, which means orders could start appearing before the actual launch time. The tech team should be watching the site closely starting at 7:30 A.M., EST.
- Ensure that order fulfillment is working without any glitches. If the workload exceeds the abilities of the fulfillment team, we'll invite fulfillment team members to work overtime, and we'll split the money we would have used to hire a third party fulfillment team among the overtime volunteers. If the workload is too high even for the overtime volunteers, we'll hire ACME Fulfillment to handle the overflow. ACME Fulfillment is aware of our launch date, and has the means and ability to handle any of our overflow for a price. The management team felt that our money would be better spent on our in house fulfillment team, rather than a third party. Please let your manager know if you'll be available to volunteer for overtime at least a week before launch date, and to discuss any further details.

- Run the customer service team according to the company's customer service guidelines. If the workload becomes to high, ACME Customer Service is on standby. Unfortunately, because of the nature of customer service calls, overtime doesn't really apply. Customer services calls and inquiries must be answered immediately, and that requires more bodies.
- Guide all other teams to support the tech team, the order fulfillment team, and the customer service team as much as possible. These teams and their associated task and responsibilities have top priority during the two to three weeks following the launch.

Post Launch Events

- The tech team should monitor application performance, hardware performance, and network performance closely. Any changes to the system configuration must first be tested on the test server, and then applied to a single live server. Once the change has been made and monitored during normal traffic load, the change can be made to all servers. If a critical adjustment needs to be made that may result in server failure (such as, site errors or no server response) then a page must be displayed that informs customers that a critical change is being made, and that the site will be available as soon in an estimated amount of time. It's suggested that you pad your time estimates–it's better be back up before the user expects it, rather than after. A template "critical change" page can be found on the file server under tech\docs\criticalchange.html.
- Display any serious hardware outages on the "critical change" document to customers. A spare web server should be ready to put behind the incoming network stream to handle this.
- Set up a third-party hosting server, in case the network stream is severed completely, with the "critical change" error message—DNS can be forwarded to it with relative ease.
- Provide a detailed emergency plan, including phones numbers and who specifically is responsible for certain types of emergencies. Look at the tech\docs\emergencyplan.doc on the file server for more information.

So there's the launch plan for the sample company skate.shop. Your plan will certainly be different depending on your business. And yes, I know that most businesses don't have the luxury of being able to hire third parties to come in and handle what they can't, but everything else in the launch plan is very realistic. And being able to hire third parties to handle your overflow isn't unrealistic—it happens all the time, but being able to afford them might be difficult.

The plan itself is designed so that anyone in any part of the company can read it and know what is going to happen. Obviously, the sales and marketing team don't need to know how to set up an emergency server, but they do need to know that in an emergency, the technical team will be busy setting up an emergency server. The entire organizations duties and responsibilities are laid out so that everyone knows what is happening.

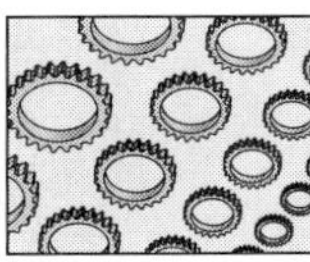

NOTE

I make mention of putting up a "critical change" error message that shows generally what the problem is, and when the site will be back up. Personally, I think it's a good idea to let your customers know what's going on when they can't get to your site. Primarily, it satisfies their curiosity. Imagine going to your local hardware store on a regular, nonholiday Saturday, during normal business hours, only to find the place completely boarded up with a sign that said, "Come back later." When is later? What the heck happened? On the Web, regular business hours are 24 hours a day, 7 days a week. If both of your two servers literally catch on fire, what does it hurt to display a message that says "Our servers literally caught on fire–we're replacing them. We should be back online in about two hours." Letting your customers know what's going on increases the chances that your customers will come back when you are up. Don't let the "I'm a big fat corporation who can get away with treating the customers like sawdust" attitude infect you; be personal with the customer, communicate with the customer, and maintain a relationship with the customer. I'll step off my soapbox now.

Monitoring Performance

In this section, we talk about how to monitor ColdFusion using the Windows NT System Monitor, and how to find bottlenecks in SQL queries using SQL Trace.

Using NT System Monitor

The NT System Monitor is a great tool for understanding system performance. System Monitor provides real-time feedback showing hardware usage metrics and service usage statistics. In addition to providing real-time feedback, it can also archive performance over a time span. Archived reports can be displayed using System Monitor in either of its two modes, bar graph, or the default line graph mode. In Windows 2000, the System Monitor tool can save graphed data as HTML, making it easy to place on a web site for remote viewing or printing.

Overview

NT System Monitor lets you tracks three different types of data, as follows:

- **Performance Objects** Performance objects are collections of counters that are associated with a hardware resource or a service.
- **Performance Counters** Performance counters are data items associated with a particular performance object. For example, ColdFusion Server has a subset of performance counters that let us track running requests, queued requests, and so on. These performance counters relay their respective values back to the NT System Monitor.
- **Object Instances** Object instances separate duplicate resources into their own identifiable object, or instance. If we have two CPUs in our machine, each will have its own object instance. Separating objects by instances lets us see how often we use the second CPU.

System Monitor allows you track data from different sources. You can track your local performance metrics, or you can track a computer on the network, and as we mentioned earlier, it can view archived performance reports.

System Monitor allows you to set sampling parameters. You can set System Monitor to automatically report statistics at user-defined intervals, like every ten seconds, or you can use manual mode, which requires you to click a button to view a snapshot of the current statistics.

A new feature to this version of System Monitor is Alerts. Alerts allow you to monitor the performance of certain actions when a performance counter meets specified criteria. Alerts can run a program, send a message, or start a new archive of performance statistics if the criteria are met. This has a lot of potential, for example, if you suspected a certain program of causing huge CPU usage spikes, you could configure an alert to start logging the performance of the suspicious program. Without this feature, you might have to sit and watch the box until something happened, or sift through a lot of recorded performance logs.

Tracking ColdFusion Performance

Before we can use System Monitor to track the performance of ColdFusion, we need to make sure that performance monitoring is enabled under the Debugging Options page in the ColdFusion Administrator (as shown in Figure 8-1).

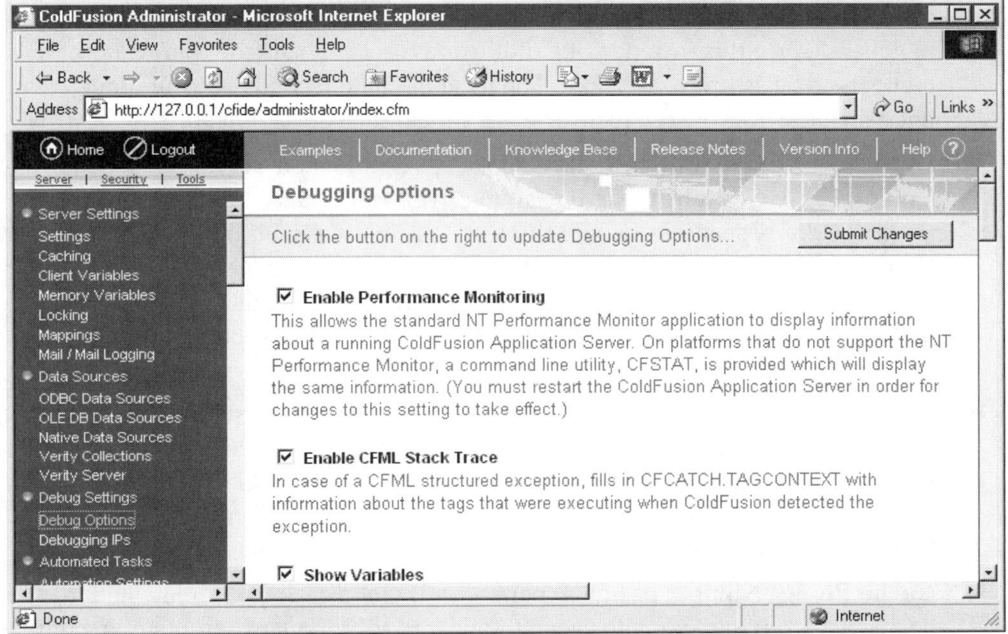

Figure 8-1 *Enabling performance monitoring in the ColdFusion administrator*

Once you've enabled performance monitoring, apply the changes. You'll have to start and stop ColdFusion in order for these changes to take effect.

ColdFusion allows us to track the following performance counters:

- **Average DB Time** Running average of the amount of time, in milliseconds, an individual database operation, launched by ColdFusion, took to complete. This is a good indicator of the health of your database since this instance of ColdFusion was started. Lower numbers are of course better. This doesn't include the amount of time it took to run the actual ColdFusion template, just the database connections.
- **Average Queue Time** Running average of the amount of time, in milliseconds, requests spent waiting in the ColdFusion input queue before ColdFusion began to process that request. Ideally this should be zero, but typically it never is. We'll go over queued requests in a moment and I'll explain further.
- **Average Request Time** Running average of the total amount of time, in milliseconds, it took ColdFusion to process a request. In addition to general page processing time, this value includes both queue time and database

processing time. This is a good indicator of the health of your application in general since this instance of ColdFusion has been started. You want these numbers to be as low as possible. The ideal number depends on your application, but over time you'll get a feel for what's ideal for your application .

- **Bytes In** Number of bytes received by the ColdFusion Server per second. You probably won't be using this counter very often. I've never needed to use it. The only scenario I could think of to use it in would be to see if the ColdFusion Server was acting funny—if the bytes in didn't match what you expected, perhaps something might be wrong, but then again, it would still be hard to determine. I'd guess it's more for informational purposes than it is diagnostics.
- **Bytes Out** Number of bytes returned by the ColdFusion Server per second. Again, this goes under the category for me as Bytes In. It's a conversation piece to use while at lunch with your other geek friends. "Guess how many bytes the ColdFusion Server spit out? 39,403,023 bytes. That's 2 more bytes than the weight of a Chewbacca's head in milligrams!" Imagine the envy.
- **Cache Pops** Number of times (per second) that a cached template had to be ejected from the template cache to make room for a new template. A high number here might be an indication that you should increase the size of your template cache.
- **DB Hits** Number of database operations performed per second by the ColdFusion Server. You might refer to this statistic when trying to optimize the performance of the application. If you can get away with using fewer database hits, your performance will increase.
- **Page Hits** Number of web pages processed per second by the ColdFusion Server.
- **Queued Request** Number of requests currently waiting to be processed by the ColdFusion Server. A waiting request means the user is getting an hourglass—they're waiting their turn to process the page. Queued requests aren't the end of the world, but they should be avoided if at all possible. If you're getting a lot of queued requests, chances are your server doesn't have the right amount of CPU power. Consider increasing the CPU strength, or adding more CPUs, or both. The next possible solution is to add another server to the web server cluster, which is more expensive.
- **Running Requests** Number of requests currently being actively processed by the ColdFusion Server. This is an important metric to watch—if it runs over the amount you have set in the Administrator, the requests will turn into queued requests.

- **Timed-out Requests** Total number of requests that timed out waiting to be processed by the ColdFusion Server. These requests never got to run. That's very bad. This number should be absolutely zero. If this number is more than zero, either you didn't pay attention to the queued requests, or you did pay attention, but took no action against getting queued requests. Timed-out requests are queued requests that keeled over and died. The user on the other end probably also keeled over and died from waiting for so long. There is a catch to this statistic though—if in the ColdFusion administrator you set the "Timeout Requests after *n* seconds" value to say, one second, you'll get a lot of timed out requests. A reasonable time for a request to run is 15 seconds. Anything after that is far to long, and should be timed out.

Typically, the best way to monitor the immediate health of your ColdFusion server is to track the performance of the running requests and queued requests. The other counters will give you a good idea of the overall performance of your application, but queued and running requests tell you exactly how well the ColdFusion server is performing.

Let's add these counters to our System Monitor.

1. To open the System Monitor, click Start | Settings | Control Panel | Administrative Tools, then click the Performance icon. You can also find the System Monitor by clicking Start | Programs | Administrative Tools, and then double-clicking the Performance icon.

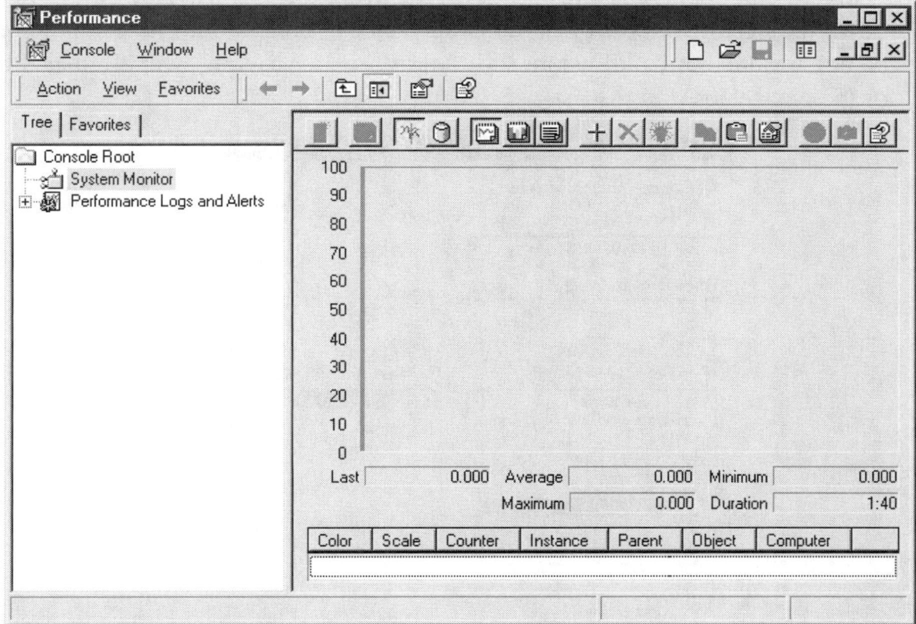

2. Click the System Monitor node in the left-hand column. To add a counter to the graph, click the button that looks like a plus sign, or right-click in the right-hand pane on the graph, and then click Add Counters.

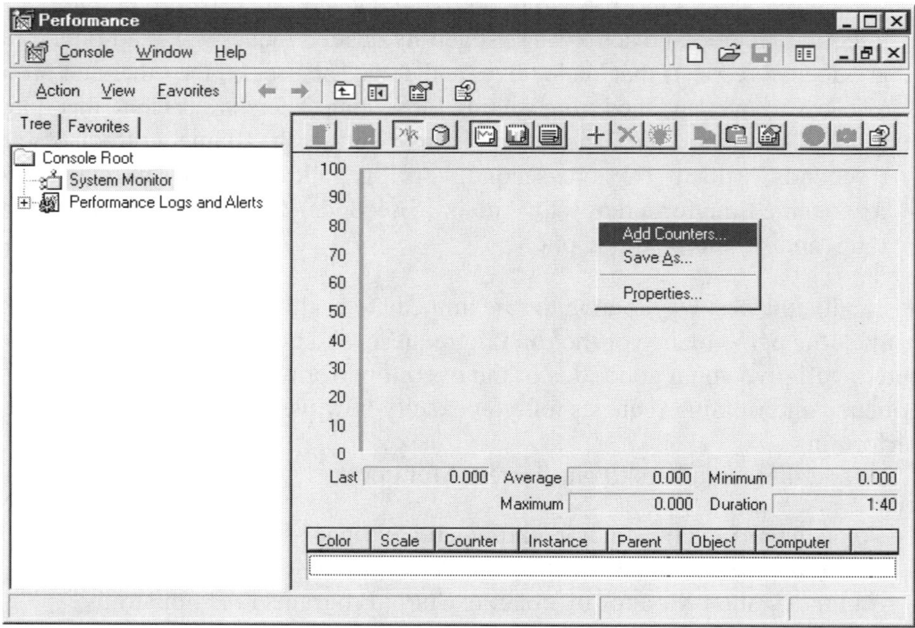

3. A dialog box opens that shows you all the available performance objects. Pull down the Performance Object menu and select ColdFusion. There should only be one instance of ColdFusion, so it doesn't matter if you select all instances, or the one selected in the list.

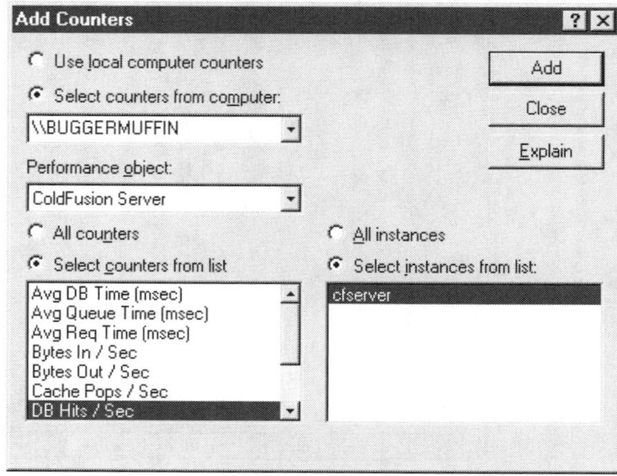

Below the Performance Object drop-down list is a list of the performance counters available to ColdFusion. Select Running Requests and click Add. The window will stay open to make it easy to add another counter. Select Queued Requests and click Add. Then click close.

The counters have now been added to the graph, and the graph should be tracking in real time, updating every second. If you're on a development server, you probably won't see any activity at all—probably just a red line passing from left to right. Even if there were some activity on this box, we'd probably see pretty much the same thing, because the scale of the graph is a lot greater than it should be.

By default, the scale, or height of the graph, is set to 100. The highest our running requests will ever get is the same as the value we set in the ColdFusion administrator under Server Settings | Settings | Maximum Running Requests. We want the scale of our graph to be about 10 more than what we set for the Maximum Running Requests. If the queued requests goes 5 to 10 points over the running requests, ColdFusion is probably in trouble, and needs to be restarted.

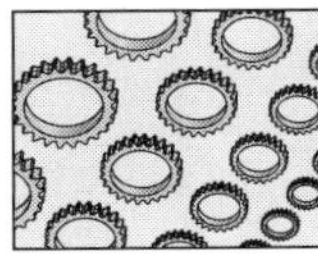

NOTE

ColdFusion can restart itself if requests start to become unresponsive. The default number of unresponsive requests is set in the ColdFusion Administrator under the Server Settings | Settings tab.

To change the scale of the graph, right-click the graph, and select Properties. Click the Graph tab, and change the Vertical Scale to 15 (10 more than our default Maximum Running Requests), as shown in Figure 8-2. Click OK.

Now, it's much easier to see fluctuations in the graph. But if you're on a development server with little or no activity, the graph will be flat lined. Open up a browser and play around in the sample application. Then, switch back to the System Monitor and you'll probably see some activity. If you're the only person on this server, you might find it difficult to get any activity at all, but you might see some spikes. On a normal live server, the running requests should be bouncing up and down and the queued requests should be flat. In fact, you won't get any queued requests until you see the running requests flat line at the Maximum Running Requests level.

It's a good idea to save this performance profile to use later. It's best to look at the other counters in a separate window because the scale is likely to different. To save the profile, do the following:

1. Click Console.
2. Click Save As.
3. Use a filename you'll remember, like cf_monitor.msc, and save it somewhere where you'll be able to find it. I keep mine on the desktop.

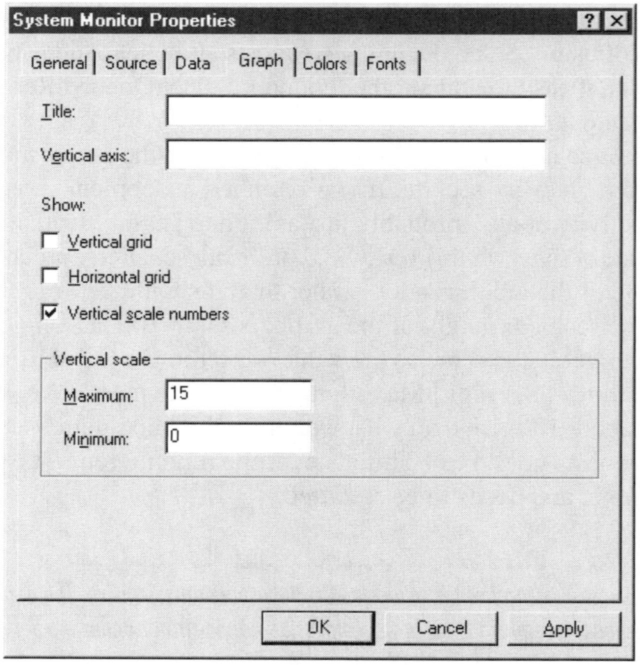

Figure 8-2 *Editing the graph properties*

Using SQL Profiler

SQL Profiler is a complicated and powerful tool, as are most things SQL Server-related, so we won't be able to become SQL Profiler gurus by the end of this section. We will at least be able to get a good idea of where to start, and most importantly, we'll understand enough to be able to use it to pinpoint bottlenecks in our application.

SQL Profiler is an external SQL Server tool, and the easiest way to get to it if you already have SQL Enterprise manager open is to click Tools, then SQL Profiler. If you don't have Enterprise Manager open, click Start | Programs | Microsoft SQL Server | Profiler, as shown in the following menu.

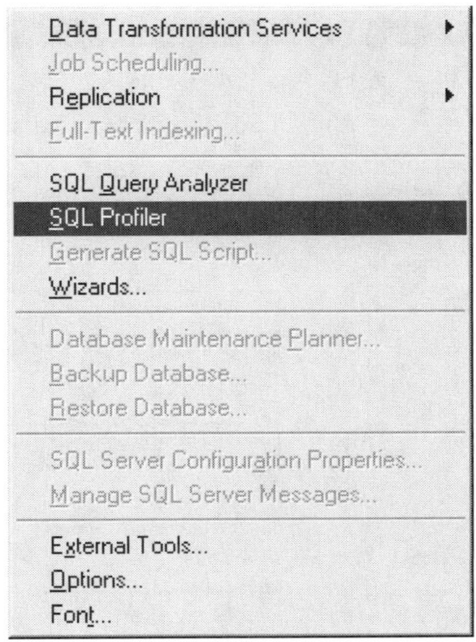

SQL Profiler allows you to capture the executions of your SQL Server to a file or to a SQL Server table, which you can analyze later to find slow running executions. SQL Profiler allows you to track every event, or only events you are interested. For example, if you wanted to track only Select queries, you could set the Profiler to only track Select queries.

To start a new SQL Profiler session, open the SQL Profiler, and click File | New | Trace, or press CTRL-N. A dialog box pops up asking you to connect to a server. Connect to your server, and click OK. The Trace Properties window will open upon connecting, as shown in Figure 8-3.

Give this trace a name (anything goes really; I chose skateshop), and use the default trace template. You can choose to save the results of the trace to a file or a table. A file will make it possible to easily analyze the data on another SQL server without having to copy tables over. Depending on your setup, a table might provide better performance—it's up to you. In this example, we'll use the File option. Save the file anywhere that makes sense to you. The Profiler allows us to limit the size of the file, which is a good thing. A very busy server could easily make a very large file, so we want to have some control over this.

We won't be filtering or changing any other settings, so go ahead and click Run. The second you click the Run button, the server will start tracking executions. On a busy server, you see a flash of activity—on a less frequented server, the activity may

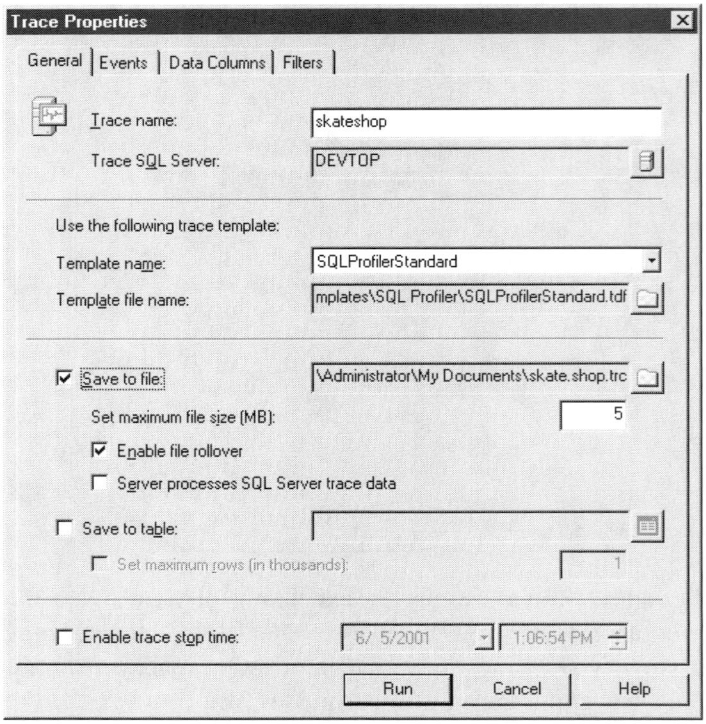

Figure 8-3 *The trace properties window allows you to set trace options.*

not be as high. If you're the sole developer on a development server, you might not see *any* activity. Open up the skate.shop application and just start shopping, doing what a normal user might do. You should start seeing some activity. The longer you track the activity, the better your results will be.

After a long trace, you can then feed the results to the Index Tuning Wizard, which determines if the indexes on your queries are set up for the best possible performance. It uses your SQL Trace to make this determination.

In the SQL Profiler, click Tools | Index Tuning Wizard to start the Wizard.

1. The first screen tells you what's going to happen. Click Next.

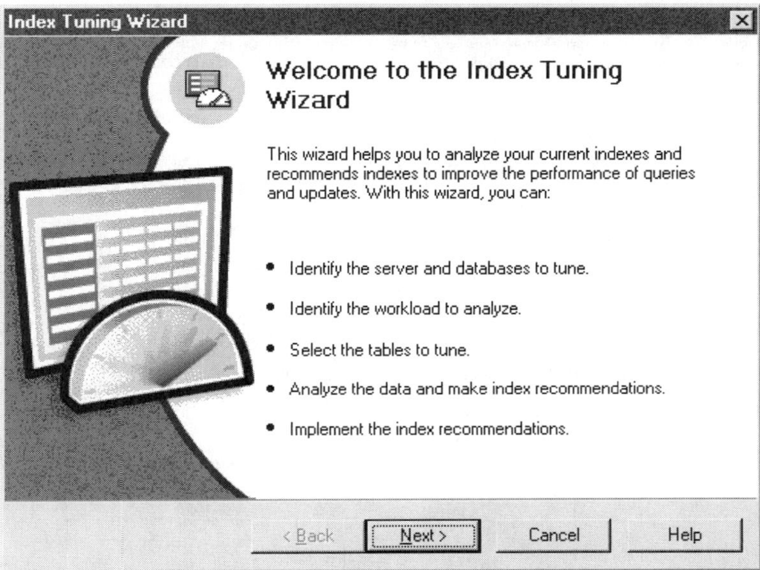

2. This screen asks for you to select the database to tune. Select skateshop. Be sure to keep all existing indexes unselected. Make sure "Add indexed views" is selected, and select the Thorough tuning mode. Click Next.

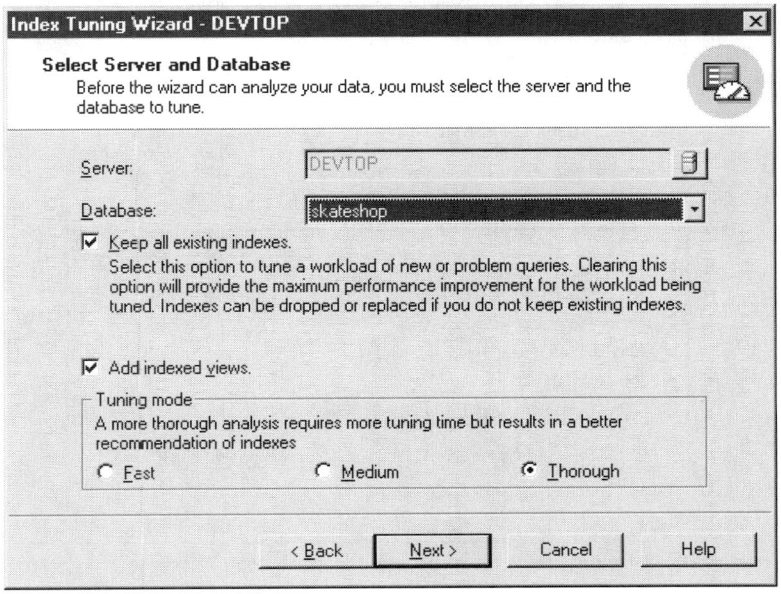

3. Click "My workload file," enter the name of the file you just created in the SQL Profiler, and then click Next.

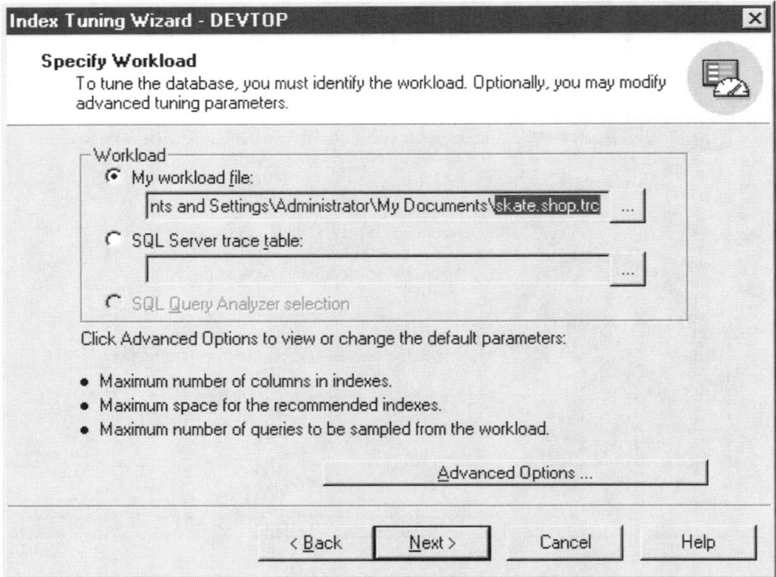

4. Click Select all tables, and then click Next.

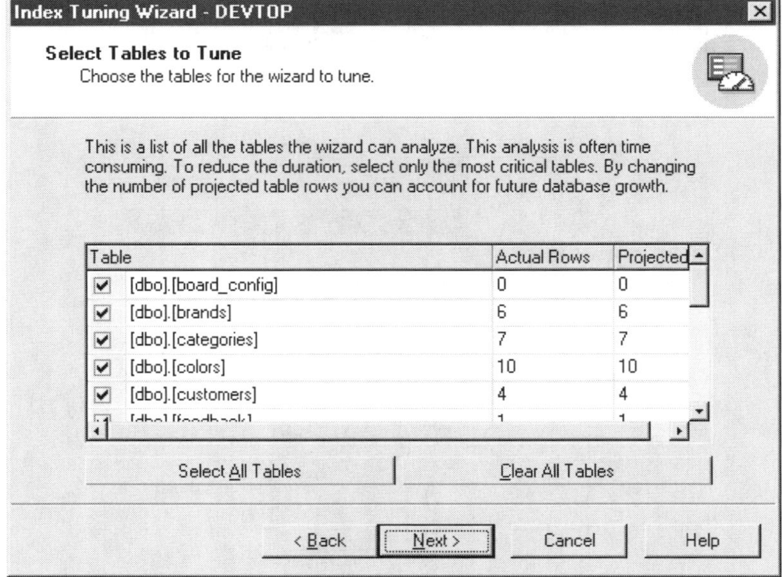

5. The Index Tuning Wizard analyzes your SQL Profiler file, and then determines whether the tables need to be indexed.

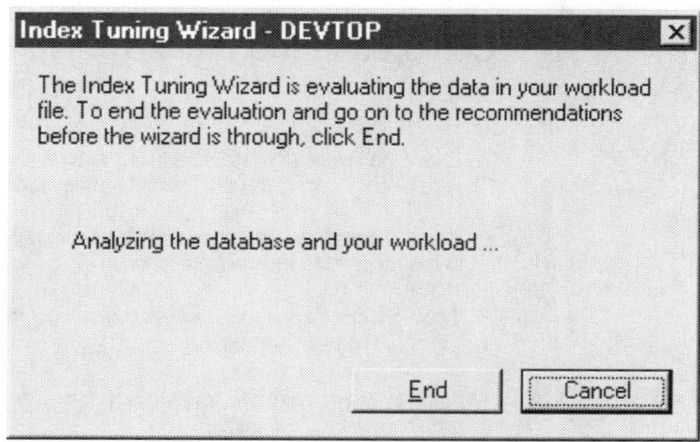

6. Once it's finished, it will show a list of recommendations. Chances are, for the skateshop database, the Wizard won't make any suggestions because during the creation of the database we did a good job making the indexes. Click Next to apply any of the suggested changes.

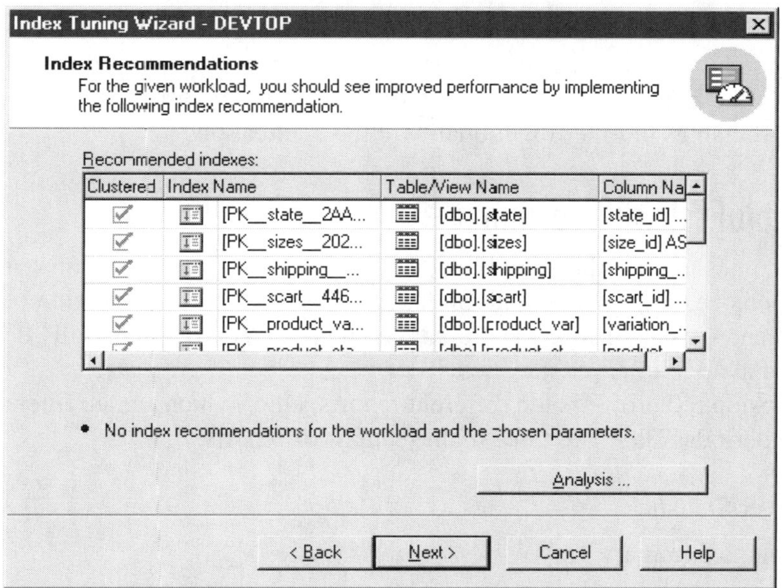

7. Click Finish.

It's a good idea to run a SQL Profile for a few hours during your peak time, and then to run the Index Tuning Wizard on the results. It's an especially good idea to do it if you add tables or other functionality to the application.

Using ColdFusion Reporting

When it comes to reporting, ColdFusion 5.0 provides a significant improvement over any previous version. The amount of data available and the presentation of the data are excellent—a statistics junkie's dream come true. You could literally drown in the amount of available server statistics.

ColdFusion 5.0 provides ten different reports, all of which can be filtered by date and time periods. There are three main sections of reports:

- Server Statistics
- Settings Summary
- Settings Changelog

The last two deal strictly with changes made to the server. The first category of reports is the one we should be most interested in. Including the Server Statistics Summary, there are eight reports we can choose from, all of which break down the statistics on an hourly basis:

- **Server Statistics Summary** Summary of all the more specific reports, covering everything from the number of .CFM requests made per second to the average ColdFusion thread count.
- **Requests** Shows request related statistics, including requests per second, and average CPU load per request.
- **Database Operations** Shows database-related statistics, including databases requests per second and the highest number of database requests.
- **Cache Pops** Show the cache pops per second and the highest cache pops per second, broken down by hour.
- **Queued Requests** Shows averages, broken down by hour, of queued requests.
- **Requests In Progress** Shows averages, broken down by hour, of running requests.
- **Timed Out Requests** Shows averages, broken down by hour, of timed-out requests.
- **Throughput** Shows how many bytes went in and out through ColdFusion, broken down by hour.

While the reporting is great, and covers pretty much everything you could think to cover, it would be great if the reports were easier to print, or if you could have the reports e-mailed to you on a scheduled basis. Hopefully, in the next release, the functionality will be expanded here.

The available metrics for the ColdFusion reports might seem awfully familiar to the performance counters in the System Monitor—they're exactly the same. In fact, the performance counters available to the System Monitor are also available to ColdFusion templates.

Using the GetMetricData function, you can build a structure that contains the performance counters and their values. For example:

```
<cfset pmData = GetMetricData( "PERF_MONITOR" ) >

<cfoutput>
  Current PerfMonitor data is: <P>
```

```
  InstanceName:  #pmData.InstanceName# <P>
  PageHits:     #pmData.PageHits# <P>
  ReqQueued:      #pmData.ReqQueued# <P>
  DBHits:          #pmData.DBHits# <P>
  ReqRunning:      #pmData.ReqRunning# <P>
  ReqTimedOut:    #pmData.ReqTimedOut# <P>
  BytesIn:          #pmData.BytesIn# <P>
  BytesOut:          #pmData.BytesOut# <P>
  AvgQueueTime:  #pmData.AvgQueueTime# <P>
  AvgReqTime:      #pmData.AvgReqTime# <P>
  AvgDBTime:          #pmData.AvgDBTime# <P>
  CachePops:         #pmData.CachePops# <P>
</cfoutput>
```

This block of code would output the current metric values. If you were feeling brave, you could create a tag that would execute on every page in your application, and store this data over time, making your own reporting application. It sounds like a simple task, but remember that by doing this you'd be adding overhead to the application, and you'd be repeating work because ColdFusion would already be capturing this data. But you could do it if you wanted to.

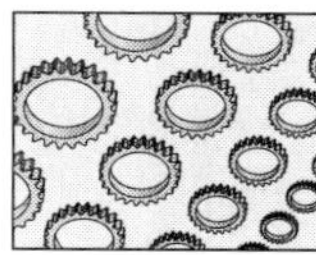

NOTE

I've thought of some interesting things to do with the data that the GetMetricData() function can provide that I've never actually put into practice. For example, it might be useful to only allow a user to execute a known long-running request if the current running requests were below a certain number. I've never put these kinds of ideas into practice because I feel that as a developer, it's my job to make the application work without waiting for "ideal" CPU conditions. If a ColdFusion request might bring a server to its knees, I should probably rethink how to execute that request, rather than simply telling a user to wait their turn. I could see where in an Intranet, or in an environment where the ColdFusion server is used to kick off data crunching tasks or other similar processor intensive tasks, it might be practical to use the GetMetricData() function in this manner, but then again, perhaps ColdFusion isn't the best program to run major data-crunching tasks.

Managing the Error Log Files

One of the most important post launch activities to perform is the daily study of the ColdFusion error logs. ColdFusion tracks every error reported to a user, and with ColdFusion 5.0, it provides a very sharp interface to the log files. In previous versions, the log files were simply stored, and if you wanted to look at them, you'd have to open them up in a text viewer. Now, in addition to nice formatting, ColdFusion provides some tools to manage the log files as well.

The application.log file contains all application related errors. If you were to look at this log file on a development box that would have a high degree or possibility of errors, you'd see a lot of entries in this log file. On a production box, any error you see here is something that needs to be fixed right away, as at least one user saw the error.

The ColdFusion Administrator has some impressive filtering tools for the logs that allow you to only show specific types of errors, or to show errors during a certain time span. Getting rid of errors speeds up your server, and increases customer confidence. With ColdFusion 5.0 and its very functional logging features, there really is no excuse for recurring errors.

Tweaking Performance

Now that we've covered how to monitor the performance and how to get rid of errors, it's time to milk the system for all we can by widening bottlenecks discovered in our monitoring, and by putting a little icing on the cake by caching queries effectively.

The Index Tuning Wizard took care of our indexing problems (or told us that we had no problems). We don't need to worry about that, but we can still increase the performance of our queries. There are two query-specific practices we can adopt to increase performance: make sure the queries themselves are running efficiently and cache the queries.

Optimizing Queries

When a query executes, an execution plan is generated. An execution plan is a roadmap that SQL creates to get to the data requested. In order to return the data, it has to figure out the fastest way to get there.

It would make sense that one way to increase performance would be to store that roadmap somewhere handy, rather than generate it on the fly. It's a common misperception that in SQL Server, only stored procedures cache their execution plans. After SQL Server 6.5, any SQL statement, whether it's in a View, a Stored Procedure, or a regular SQL statement, gets a cached execution plan.

ColdFusion advocates used to literally hammer the idea into developers that they should use stored procedures or nothing at all, and that if they didn't use stored procedures, their application was going to be as slow as a snail. It's simply not the case. There are only a few reasons I can see that make using a stored procedure a must—for security reasons and to generate multiple result sets with one database call.

It's OK to use a <CFQUERY> tag with a plain old SQL statement—as long as it's secure. This isn't really an optimization technique, it's a security technique, but it's worth stating just the same. If someone deletes all the data in your database, your application won't run very optimally, now will it?

Look at this query:

```
<cfquery name="foo" datasource="#request.dsn#">
SELECT columnA
FROM table
WHERE columnA = "#url.foo#"
</cfquery>
```

This query seems perfectly safe right? Well, not really. If I were a bad person, I could, with relative ease, do some bad things. What if I, as a user, changed my URL to this page to look like this:

```
http://www.skate.shop/index.cfm?foo=1%20drop%20database%20master
```

The foo query would run just fine, and immediately after it ran the entire master database would be deleted, crippling your SQL Server. You can execute multiple SQL statements in one <CFQUERY> tag, and the "drop database master" statement counts as a query. (The "%20" is the URL encoded value of a space). By the way, don't run that query, it'll hurt really bad if you do.

So how do we avoid having bad people do this? Well, if the query looked like this, that "bad" URL would cause an error:

```
<cfquery name="foo" datasource="#request.dsn#">
exec fooSP @columnA="#url.foo#"
</cfquery>
```

The stored procedure would be designed to only accept the *@columnA* parameter, and because the *@columnA* parameter would be declared as an integer, the extra SQL statement would cause an error.

The same protection could be built into the query without having to create a stored procedure using the <CFQUERYPARAM> tag. Here's an example:

```
<cfquery name="foo" datasource="#request.dsn#">
SELECT columnA
FROM table
WHERE columnA = <cfqueryparam value="#url.foo#" cfsqltype="cf_sql_integer"> </cfquery>
```

If #url.foot# weren't an integer, an invalid datatype error would occur.

I just got through ranting that errors are such a bad thing in the previous section—yes they are very bad, but when they stop someone from messing around with the URL and deleting our database, they're a good thing. I'll talk about error trapping for stuff like this in Chapter 14.

Query optimization can be a bit tricky, and if you're not a SQL expert, the best way to optimize a query is to experiment with different ways of writing the query. For example, the following two queries do the exact same thing, but one of them will run faster:

```
Query 1
SELECT *
FROM table

Query 2
SELECT column_A, column_B, column_C
FROM table
```

This is a very simple example—obviously the second query will run faster. The first query has to figure out what columns exist in the table before returning the data, whereas the second query takes care of what columns exist right from the start.

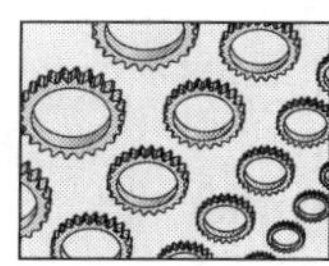

NOTE

The first time a query runs, it generates an execution plan that works as a roadmap to the data. The second time the exact same query is run, the execution plan doesn't need to be created, making the first query run a bit longer. When experimenting with queries, run the query a few times to ensure that an execution plan has been created. Don't use the first run of a query as the "benchmark" for your experimentation.

The SQL Query Analyzer tool allows you to view the execution plan of query. While a full explanation of exactly how to determine which query runs faster based on the results of the Execution Plan view would be quite lengthy, a good rule of thumb is that Execution Plans with fewer nodes, or for lack of a better definition, fewer icons, are faster.

Caching for Performance

In ColdFusion, you can cache a query. When you cache the query, the results of the query are stored in memory, and rather than making a database call, the query is supplied directly from ColdFusion, which can produce significant speed increases.

Traditional Query Caching

The <CFQUERY> tag has the ability to cache a query using the *cachedwithin* or *cachedafter* attribute.

Cachedwithin allows you to cache a query with the same name and SQL statement within a timespan. For instance, if you wanted a query to be cached for the next six hours, you'd use the following syntax:

```
<cfquery
  name="qryAnimals"
  datasource="#request.dsn#"
  cachedwithin="#CreateTimeSpan(0,6,0,0)#">
```

The CreateTimeSpan function generates a value that represents the timespan from this point forward. The actual value that's created for the example looks like 0.25. Six hours is exactly one twentyfifth of a day. If we use CreateTimeSpan(1,0,0,0) the value would be one. If we use CreateTimeSpan(0,0,0,1), which is one second, the value would be 1.15740740741E–005. You get the idea.

With the *cachedwithin* attribute in the <CFQUERY> tag, that query will now reside in memory until it times out or gets pushed out. In the ColdFusion Administrator under the Server Settings | Caching page, there is an option to set how many possible cached queries can be held in memory. The default value is 100. If there are 100 queries in memory and a new one is added, the oldest of the bunch gets dropped from memory.

The *cachedafter* attribute achieves the same results in a slightly different manner. Instead of caching from this point forward, it caches queries specific to the date. For example, if we used cachedafter="4/20/2005" the query would be cached after the date of April 20, 2005.

In both cases, caching queries can provide some nice results. But you also need to be selective—memory on the server isn't unlimited. You should cache queries where the result sets rarely differ from one query execution to the next.

It wouldn't be a good idea in the skate.shop application to cache shopping cart queries. First of all, you'd get a ton of queries being added to memory because dynamic queries based on the customer unique ID would be generated, and second of all, if you cached the query that selects the items in the shopping cart, the shopping cart will look the same within the cached time period, even if someone were to add something to the shopping cart.

A good query to cache in our sample application would be the qryResults query that generates results from a category drill down. New products are added once a day on a regular basis on our site, and the query doesn't need fresh data at every request. Caching the query speeds up the site, and doesn't cause any problems or inconveniences for the user or the business.

Using the Application Scope

There is another way to cache queries might provide a little more flexibility. In our application, we've use the <CFAPPLICATION> tag that allows us to use the

Application scope. We can set variables like *application.backgroundcolor* and other persistent variables. These variables stick around until they time out. The timeout for this scope is set in the <CFAPPLICATION> tag. Here's the skate.shop <CFAPPLICATION> tag:

```
<cfapplication name="skateshop"
               clientmanagement="Yes"
               sessionmanagement="Yes"
               setclientcookies="Yes"
               sessiontimeout="#CreateTimeSpan(0,0,45,0)#"
               applicationtimeout="#CreateTimeSpan(1,0,0,0)#">
```

The last attribute, *applicationtimeout*, says that variables in the **Application** scope should remain persistent for a day. If we were to create a query in the **Application** scope, its results would also remain persistent. Here's an example:

```
<cfquery name="application.qryAnimals" datasource="#request.dsn#">
```

This query and its data will now reside in the **Application** scope. It differs from using the *cachedwithin* attribute of the <CFQUERY> tag because if we were to run this query again, it would execute again. The data in *application.qryAnimals* would refresh as well.

In order to make this useful for caching purposes, we need to add a little more logic to it.

```
<cfif IsDefined("application.qryAnimals") is false>
   <cfquery name="application.qryAnimals" datasource="#request.dsn#">
   ...
   </cfquery>
</cfif>
```

Before running the query, we check to see if it already exists in the **Application** scope. If it doesn't, we create it. If it does, we do nothing. Having this kind of control can also allow us to refresh the query regardless of the **Application** scope timeout.

Let's illustrate a possible business scenario. Our queries are cached using the traditional *cachedwithin* attribute. All queries will be cached within one day of their creation. The company has a partnership with a certain manufacturer, and this manufacturer wants us to begin selling their product on a certain date. A day before the date, the company realizes that the date is actually today, and that if we don't start selling the product we'll cause some serious friction between the company and manufacturer. Because of our caching, new products added into the system won't show up until the next following business day. How do we add this manufacturer's products and have them start showing up immediately? Well, we can rename the query, we can change the SQL statement slightly, or we can restart the server to purge the memory. All of these solutions are pretty poor, and illustrate the lack of control you have when using *cachedwithin.*

Here's what you could do with the **Application** scope. Let's say that the business rule would be that all queries should be cached, but new products should show up the moment they are added. Here's a very simple example of how we could exercise control over the cached query:

```
<cfif IsDefined("application.qryAnimals") is false or
IsDefined("url.purgeQuery")>
   <cfquery name="application.qryAnimals" datasource="#request.dsn#">
   ...
   </cfquery>
</cfif>
```

If we were to pass the *url.purgeQuery* parameter to the request, the query would be run again, and the results would be refreshed. The example is quite simple, and while you might not be comfortable allowing just anyone to purge your cached queries from the URL, it goes to show that you can do it with simply one little bit of code.

Listening to the Customer

Customers provide our company with its sole stream of revenue, so we had better treat the customers right. In this section, we add a feedback system to the site that allows customers to complain, compliment, ask questions, and write us haikus if they feel like it. We also build a back end to the feedback system. The section may seem a bit out of place in this chapter, but I consider feedback a part of maintenance, so it fits if you look at it from that perspective.

Building a Feedback System

The feedback system should allow customers to quickly and easily send us a comment. There should be no required fields, if all they feel like doing is filling out the comments form with a single letter, by all means, they should be able to do that. If they feel like filling out the comments form, adding their name, their e-mail address, their phone number, and the category the comment is related to, then they should be able to do that too.

Customers will be able to access the feedback system from any page on the site. The feedback system needs to remember what page the user came from so that when they are finished, they can be provided with a link back to where they were. The following pieces of information can be provided by the user:

- First and last name
- E-mail address
- Phone number
- The comment itself

We will also gather the following information by our own means:

- The customer's browser type, version, and operating system
- The customer's IP address
- The date and time of the comment
- The page the customer was on when they clicked the feedback link
- The customer's UUID
- The customer's customer ID if they are logged in

The information gathered both from the user and the site assists the customer if they are having problems with their order, or technical problems with the site.

Let's break down each file in the feedback system, both on the front end and the back end.

skate.shop\modules\nav\cat_drill.cfm

This file needs to have a feedback link added to it. The code we'll be adding is in bold.

```
<cfset rowspan = request.qryCatDrill.RecordCount + 2>
<table width="127" border="0" cellspacing="0" cellpadding="2">
  <tr>
    <td rowspan="<cfoutput>#rowspan#</cfoutput>"><img
 src="images/general/clear.gif" width=3 height=1 border="0"></td>
    <td><a href="index.cfm" class="nav"><b>Home</b></a></td>
  </tr>
  <cfoutput query="request.qryCatDrill">
  <tr>
    <td><a href="results.cfm?cat=#cat_id#" class="nav"><b>#cat_name#</b></a></td>
  </tr>
  </cfoutput>
  <cfoutput>
```

```
<tr>
<td><a href="feedback.cfm" class="nav"><b>Feedback</b></a></td>
</tr>
</cfoutput>
  <tr>
    <td colspan="2"><img src="assets/img/clear.gif" width=1 height=25
 border="0"></td>
  </tr>
</table>
```

skate.shop\feedback.cfm

This file is the shell file for the feedback page:

```
<cfparam name="request.page" default="feedback">
<cfinclude template="content.cfm">
```

skate.shop\content.cfm

I've decided not to show the entire content.cfm file, as you should already be pretty familiar with it at this point. I'll show the code we need for the feedback system in bold, and a few lines above and below the code.

```
    <cfcase value="help">
        <cfmodule template="modules/pages/help/help.cfm">
      </cfcase>
      <cfcase value="feedback">
<cfmodule template="modules/pages/feedback/feedback.cfm">
</cfcase>
    </cfswitch>
  </cfmodule>
</cfmodule>
```

skate.shop\modules\pages\feedback\feedback.cfm

This is where all the action takes place on the customer's end. We need to create the feedback directory under skate.shop\modules\pages before creating the following file:

```
<img src="images/general/clear.gif" width="1" height="10" border="0"><br>

<cfif IsDefined("form.feedback_submit")>
<cfquery name="qrySendFeedback" datasource="#request.dsn#">
INSERT INTO Feedback
(
<cfif form.name is not ''>name,</cfif>
```

```
<cfif form.email is not ''>email,</cfif>
<cfif form.phone is not ''>phone,</cfif>
<cfif form.comment is not ''>comment,</cfif>
browser,
userip,
<cfif IsDefined("session.customer_id")>
customer_id,
</cfif>
uuid
)
VALUES
(
<cfif form.name is not ''>'#form.name#',</cfif>
<cfif form.email is not ''>'#form.email#',</cfif>
<cfif form.phone is not ''>'#form.phone#',</cfif>
<cfif form.comment is not ''>'#form.comment#',</cfif>
'#cgi.http_user_agent#',
'#cgi.remote_addr#',
<cfif IsDefined("session.customer_id")>
#session.customer_id#,
</cfif>
'#session.uuid#'
)
</cfquery>

<cfmodule template="../../display/formwrapper.cfm" formtitle="Feedback"
width="80%">
<table width="100%" cellpadding="1" cellspacing="0" border="0">
  <tr>
    <td>
    <p><b>Thank you.</b><br>
    We will contact you either by email or by phone within the next business day.
    If you have immediate needs, please call customer
    service at <b>800-555-5555</b>
    </td>
  </tr>
</table>
</cfmodule>

<cfelse>
<form action="feedback.cfm" method="post">
<cfmodule template="../../display/formwrapper.cfm" formtitle="Feedback"
width="80%">
<table width="100%" cellpadding="1" cellspacing="0" border="0">
  <tr>
    <td>
    <p>Customer service is our <b>top priority</b>.
```

```
    If you have a question, have a problem, or would like to make a
    comment about anything, feel free.
    <p>All information will be kept confidential, your email address
    won't be added to a list - it will just be used to provide a prompt
    reply.
    <p><b>All fields are optional</b>, although the more information
    you can give, the better we'll be able to assist you.
    </td>
  </tr>
  <tr>
    <td><b>First & Last Name:</b></td>
  </tr>
  <tr>
    <td><input type="text" name="name" size="25"></td>
  </tr>
  <tr>
    <td><b>Email:</b></td>
  </tr>
  <tr>
    <td><input type="text" name="email" size="25"></td>
  </tr>
  <tr>
    <td><b>Phone Number:</b></td>
  </tr>
  <tr>
    <td><input type="text" name="phone" size="25"></td>
  </tr>
  <tr>
    <td><b>Your Question/Comment:</b></td>
  </tr>
  <tr>
    <td><textarea cols="30" rows="12" name="comment"></textarea></td>
  </tr>
  <tr>
    <td><input type="submit" name="feedback_submit" value="Submit Feedback"></td>
  </tr>
</table>
</cfmodule>
</form>
</cfif>
```

Because all of the fields are optional, in the insert query near the top of the file, we must check to see if the values are empty or not. It's not a very graceful way of doing things, but it gets the job done while remaining flexible. Now, on to the Administrator's side.

skate.shop\admin\nav.cfm

Once again, I won't show the entire file. This time, I'll show the HTML table that we'll be adding a row to, with the added code in bold:

```
<table width="127" border="0" cellspacing="0" cellpadding="2">
    <tr>
        <td><img src="../images/general/singlerightarrow.gif"
        width="7" height="11" border="0"></td>
        <td class="nav"><b>Maintenance</b></td>
    </tr>
    <tr>
        <td><img src="../images/general/clear.gif" width="7"
        height="11" border="0"></td>
        <td><b><a href="content.cfm?page=maint_verity"
        class="nav" target="content">Verity Admin</a></b></td>
    </tr>
    <tr>
        <td><img src="../images/general/clear.gif" width="7"
        height="11" border="0"></td>
        <td><b><a href="content.cfm?page=maint_schedule"
        class="nav" target="content">Scheduled Tasks</a></b></td>
    </tr>
      <tr>
<td><img src="../images/general/clear.gif" width="7"
height="11" border="0"></td>
<td><b><a href="content.cfm?page=maint_feedback"
class="nav" target="content">Feedback</a></b></td>
</tr>
</table>
```

skate.shop\admin\content.cfm

Same drill here—the new code is in bold, and I've only included a few lines before and after the new code to help give you an idea of where it goes in the file:

```
  <cfcase value="maint_scheduletermpopup">
    <cfmodule template="maint/maint_scheduletermpopup.cfm">
  </cfcase>
  <cfcase value="maint_feedback">
<cfmodule template="maint/maint_feedback.cfm">
</cfcase>
  <cfdefaultcase>
```

```
    <cfmodule template="orders/orders_new.cfm">
  </cfdefaultcase>
</cfswitch>
```

skate.shop\admin\maint\maint_feedback.cfm

This file is a very basic output of the feedback, ordered by date, and with a very simple delete function. If we need to increase the functionality of this, we can do so later. Before we can do anything for the feedback system, we need to create the table. The following code creates the table in the skateshop database:

```
USE skateshop
CREATE TABLE feedback (
  feedback_id int IDENTITY (1, 1) NOT NULL PRIMARY KEY CLUSTERED,
  name varchar (100) NULL ,
  email varchar (100) NULL ,
  phone varchar (100) NULL ,
  comment varchar (700) NULL ,
  browser varchar (100) NULL ,
  userip varchar (50) NULL ,
  customer_id int NULL ,
  uuid varchar (35) NULL ,
  feedbackdate datetime NULL DEFAULT getdate()
)
GO
```

Here's what the actual maint_feedback.cfm file looks like:

```
<cfif IsDefined("url.delete")>
<cfquery name="deleteFeedback" datasource="#request.dsn#">
DELETE
FROM feedback
WHERE feedback_id = #url.delete#
</cfquery>
</cfif>

<cfquery name="feedback" datasource="#request.dsn#">
SELECT feedback_id,name, email, phone, comment,
browser, userip, customer_id, uuid, feedbackdate
FROM feedback
ORDER BY feedbackdate
</cfquery>

<cfmodule template="../modules/tablewrapper.cfm" title="Feedback">
<table width="100%" cellpadding="0" cellspacing="1" border="0'>
```

```
  <tr>
    <td bgcolor="#2C65A0" colspan="2"><b>Date</b></td>
    <td bgcolor="#2C65A0"><b>Name</b></td>
    <td bgcolor="#2C65A0"><b>Email</b></td>
    <td bgcolor="#2C65A0"><b>Phone</b></td>
    <td bgcolor="#2C65A0"><b>User IP</b></td>
    <td bgcolor="#2C65A0"><b>Customer ID</b></td>
    <td bgcolor="#2C65A0"><b>UUID</b></td>
    <td bgcolor="#2C65A0"><b>Comment</b></td>
  </tr>
  <cfoutput query="feedback" group="feedbackdate">
  <tr>
    <td><a
href="content.cfm?page=maint_feedback&delete=#feedback_id#">
    <img src="../images/general/cart_del.gif" width="16" height="9"
    alt="Delete" border="0"></a></td>
    <td>#DateFormat(feedbackdate, 'mm/dd/yy')#</td>
    <td>#name#</td>
    <td>#email#</td>
    <td>#phone#</td>
    <td>#userip#</td>
    <td>#customer_id#</td>
    <td>#uuid#</td>
    <td>#comment#</td>
  </tr>
  </cfoutput>
</table>
</cfmodule>
```

Wrapping Up

In this chapter, we've launched the site, talked about how to monitor site performance, and explored how to use SQL tools to help increase performance. This chapter concludes the second part of our book. Part III will cover advanced topics, some of which we may have used in the creation of the skate.shop application.

PART

Advanced Topics

OBJECTIVES

- Look at ways to extend ColdFusion
- Learn about WDDX and related technologies
- Find out about the new *connectString* attribute
- Perform transaction rollbacks and commits
- Learn about ColdFusion's different debugging options
- Learn about error-handling tags available to ColdFusion developers
- Learn why and how to use custom tags
- Learn how to write and use regular expressions
- Learn about SMTP and POP e-mail
- Create a simple FTP client
- Use <CFHTTP> to pull web sites back for processing

CHAPTER

9

Scripting with <CFSCRIPT>

IN THIS CHAPTER:

When <CFSCRIPT> was introduced with the 4.0 release of ColdFusion, the idea was to allow for a robust yet easy to use scripting language that worked as a subset of ColdFusion. In this chapter, we cover just about everything there is to know about the <CFSCRIPT> subset. Learning how to script with <CFSCRIPT> is not difficult. In fact, I had a personal debate over where to put this chapter in the book. While it's not entirely an advanced concept, it ended up as the first chapter in this part of the book because it seems that ColdFusion programmers, in general, still struggle with the technology. The <CFSCRIPT> documentation provided by Allaire for previous versions has been sparse, to say the least, so it makes sense that it's not used as much as it could be by the ColdFusion community.

<CFSCRIPT> plays an even bigger role in ColdFusion 5.0. In order to make full use of the new User Defined Functions feature, <CFSCRIPT> is a requirement.

<CFSCRIPT> is a scripting language within ColdFusion. You can set variables, do conditional processing, and even write output to the screen (or more appropriately, the HTML file that is returned to the browser). Any variables that are available to the ColdFusion template are available to the code with <CFSCRIPT>, as well as ColdFusion functions.

Here's what a <CFSCRIPT> block looks like. We talk about the syntax later in the "<CFSCRIPT> Conventions" section:

```
<cfscript>
lstAnimals = "Crab, Turkey, Rabbit, Donkey";
szFavoriteAnimal = ListGetAt(lstAnimals, 1);
</cfscript>
```

Let's learn more about <CFSCRIPT> by first understanding its advantages and disadvantages. Then, we'll get into more details about the language itself.

Advantages of <CFSCRIPT>

One of the ideas behind creating <CFSCRIPT> was that it needed to be easy to use right from the beginning. So rather than introduce an entirely new language, the designers of <CFSCRIPT> decided to use the already available set of features and general functionality of ColdFusion. This means that the learning curve of <CFSCRIPT> is extremely low—if you know CFML, then you'll have very few problems learning <CFSCRIPT>.

There is also no need to use tags. In fact, you can't use tags at all, which we'll cover in the following "Disadvantages of <CFSCRIPT>" section. Here's a comparison of code snippets; both produce identical results. One snippet uses traditional CFML, and the other uses <CFSCRIPT>:

```
<cfset request.szProName = "Bob Burnquist">
```

Now, the same snippet, but using <CFSCRIPT> instead:

```
<cfscript>
request.szProName = "Bob Burnquist";
</cfscript>
```

Aside from some differences in syntax, the code looks nearly the same.

Another one of the benefits of using <CFSCRIPT> is that, at times, it makes code more readable. Readability of code may not seem like much, but when you're looking at someone else's code, or even looking or your own code for the first time in a while, the benefits of readability become quickly obvious. Code that is easier to read reduces frustration, and increases productivity.

Let's compare the differences in readability with an example of traditional CFML first:

```
<!--- Create the Structure --->
<cfset strProName = StructNew()>
<cfset tmp = StructInsert(strProName, "FirstName", "Tony")>
<cfset tmp = StructInsert(strProName, "LastName", "Hawk")>
<cfset tmp = StructInsert(strProName, "Age", "35")>
<cfset tmp = StructInsert(strProName, "YearsPro", "21")>
<cfset tmp = StructInsert(strProName, "Stance", "Goofy")>
<cfset tmp = StructInsert(strProName, "YearsRiding", "25")>
<cfset tmp = StructInsert(strProName, "SignatureTrick", "The 900")>
<cfset tmp = StructInsert(strProName, "NickName", "Birdman")>
<cfset tmp = StructInsert(strProName, "Weight", "170")>
<cfset tmp = StructInsert(strProName, "Height", "6' 2""")>
```

Now, using <CFSCRIPT>:

```
<cfscript>
// Create the Structure
strProName = StructNew();
StructInsert(strProName, "FirstName", "Tony");
```

```
StructInsert(strProName, "LastName", "Hawk");
StructInsert(strProName, "Age", "35");
StructInsert(strProName, "YearsPro", "21");
StructInsert(strProName, "Stance", "Goofy");
StructInsert(strProName, "YearsRiding", "25");
StructInsert(strProName, "SignatureTrick", "The 900");
StructInsert(strProName, "NickName", "Birdman");
StructInsert(strProName, "Weight", "170");
StructInsert(strProName, "Height", "6' 2""");
</cfscript>
```

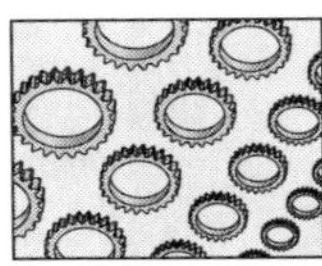

NOTE

I really don't know that much about the skateboarding legend Tony Hawk—most of the stuff I made up for the sake of the example. Notice that on his height measurement I have to escape the double quote in 6' 2" with another double quote. This is so ColdFusion doesn't assume that the first double quote mark is the end of the literal value.

It might be my own preference, but I think it's safe to assume that most developers would agree that the <CFSCRIPT> snippet is a lot cleaner and seems simpler. There were obviously fewer keystrokes, and it's simply easier to read. Magnify this little block of code to a full-size application, and the idea of simplicity becomes very enticing.

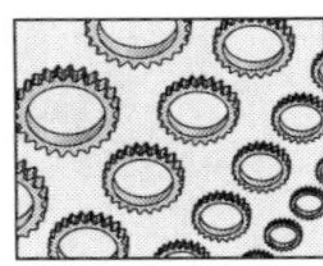

NOTE

Does it seem like something is missing from this code snippet? In the CFML example I use a tmp *variable. But, in the <CFSCRIPT> snippet, I make no reference to a* tmp *variable. In ColdFusion 4.5 and later, temporary variables for functions like StructInsert aren't required, not even in the CFML <CFSET> statement. But they've never been required in <CFSCRIPT>.*

<CFSCRIPT> was also designed to look and behave similarly to other languages to help make the transition to using it easier. <CFSCRIPT> looks and works a lot like JavaScript, and there are also similarities to C and C++. These similarities can also work as disadvantages however, but we'll cover those in the following section.

Disadvantages of <CFSCRIPT>

One of the complaints I've heard about <CFSCRIPT> is that it looks *too much* like other languages. Having a block of JavaScript next to a block of <CFSCRIPT> can make readability a bit more difficult. Here's an example:

```
<cfscript>
function LongDate(date)
{
  DateFormat(date, 'mmmm yyyy');
}
</cfscript>

<script>
function checktime()
{
  var thisday=new Date();
  var hour=thisday.getHours();
  if ((hour < 12) && (hour >=6))
    {alert ("Good Morning!");}
  if ((hour >= 12) && (hour < 18))
    {alert ("Good Afternoon!");}
  if ((hour >=18) && (hour < 22))
    {alert ("Good Evening!");}
  if ((hour >=22) || (hour < 4))
    {alert ("Time for bed!");}
  if ((hour >= 4) && (hour < 6))
    {alert ("You're up early!");}
}
</script>
```

Between the two blocks of code, there aren't too many differences, which can be confusing for beginners, or for those who are quickly trying to track down a bug. Though it doesn't take much to figure out whether it's ColdFusion or JavaScript, it's an extra step, and one that can make the code similarities a disadvantage.

Another possible disadvantage of <CFSCRIPT> is that it disallows all use of tags. While you can use every function available to regular CFML, you cannot use any tags within a <CFSCRIPT> block. I say that this is a possible disadvantage because really when you think about it, if we could do everything in <CFSCRIPT>, then we might lose a lot of the simplicity of tags. There's no doubt that if every CFML tag had a <CFSCRIPT> equivalent, then the equivalent would likely take more effort than its tag counterpart to invoke. <CFSCRIPT> is designed for simplicity, and it improves upon parts of CFML that were more complicated than they should be. Together, the CFML and <CFSCRIPT> tags take advantage of the strengths and weaknesses of both.

<CFSCRIPT> Conventions

If you're familiar with JavaScript, then understanding the syntax of <CFSCRIPT> shouldn't be a problem. Let's go over the list of syntax rules required for <CFSCRIPT>.

- All expressions must end with a semicolon (;):

```
// Correct
szParkLocation = "Laguna Hills";
// Incorrect
szParkLocation = "Laguna Hills"
```

- Expressions are case insensitive, meaning that the following two variables are considered the same:

```
Animal = "cow";
aNIMAL = "cow";
```

- Literal string values must be surrounded by double or single quotes:

```
// Correct
szParkState = "CA";
// Incorrect
szParkState = CA;
```

As we've seen in the previous code examples, single-line comments are preceded by double slash symbols:

```
// This is a single line comment, you should write lots of these.
```

Sometimes a single-line comment is not enough, so a comment block is needed. A comment block is entered like this:

```
/* This block of comments starts off as shown, using a forward slash,
then and asterisk. This allows the developer to have a more extended
block of comments than a single line comment. It's closed by using
an asterisk, then another forward slash, like this. */
```

Of course, comments aren't executed, so the ColdFusion parser will ignore anything within a comment.

These are the basics of <CFSCRIPT> syntax. We'll go over more programming conventions when we introduce conditional processing a little later in the "Using Conditional Statements" section.

Setting Variables

Setting variables in <CFSCRIPT> is a piece of cake. Everything that you know about <CFSET> applies here, with the normal <CFSCRIPT> rules applied. Here's an example:

```
ThisVariable = 25;
```

The following expressions are valid for a lot programming languages, although you might assume that it would cause ColdFusion to return an error:

```
1;
1 * 1;
"dog";
```

ColdFusion doesn't really do anything with the preceding expressions. The second expression in the snippet performs a calculation, but the result of the calculation isn't set to anything. The result of an expression can only be set to something if the *set to* operator is used, more commonly known as the equals sign (=).

The previous bit of information by itself doesn't really mean much. How many of us are going to write a program with a completely meaningless expression? Probably not too many, but I brought it up to help explain another piece of the <CFSCRIPT> phenomena—expressions without variables.

Earlier in the "Advantages of <CFSCRIPT>" section, I showed an example of an expression that used no variables. Let's take a look at it again:

```
<cfscript>
// Create the Structure
strProName = StructNew();
StructInsert(strProName, "FirstName", "Tony");
StructInsert(strProName, "LastName", "Hawk");
StructInsert(strProName, "Age", "35");
StructInsert(strProName, "YearsPro", "21");
StructInsert(strProName, "Stance", "Goofy");
StructInsert(strProName, "YearsRiding", "25");
StructInsert(strProName, "SignatureTrick", "The 900");
StructInsert(strProName, "NickName", "Birdman");
StructInsert(strProName, "Weight", "170");
StructInsert(strProName, "Height", "6' 2""");
</cfscript>
```

The reason no variable is set with the StructInsert function is because the value of the variable would normally be of no use to us. The StructInsert function modifies an already existing value, in this case, the strProName structure.

If you're curious about what would happen if we did set the StructInsert() function to a value, try executing the following code:

```
<cfscript>
// Create the Structure
strProName = StructNew();
tmp = StructInsert(strProName, "FirstName", "Tony");
</cfscript>
<cfoutput>#tmp#</cfoutput>
```

The value of tmp will be "YES" when you output it, although it's really a Boolean value, which means it's the same as saying Yes, True, or 1. It's obvious in the examples of <CFSCRIPT> that I've shown so far that you can create structures in <CFSCRIPT>. You can also create arrays:

```
<cfscript>
// Create the Array
arryPros = ArrayNew(2);
arryPros[1][1] = "Tony";
arryPros[1][2] = "Hawk";
arryPros[2][1] = "Rodney";
arryPros[2][2] = "Mullen";
arryPros[3][1] = "Mark";
arryPros[3][2] = "Gonzales";
arryPros[4][1] = "Chet";
arryPros[4][2] = "Thomas";
arryPros[5][1] = "Daewon";
arryPros[5][2] = "Song";
</cfscript>
```

Again, there's no need for a temporary variable, and all of the normal <CFSCRIPT> rules apply.

I said earlier that using CFML tags wasn't possible within a <CFSCRIPT> block. This includes tags like <CFQUERY>, which are used to query a database and return a query object, but I didn't say that creating a query wasn't possible. Remember that all functions are allowed in <CFSCRIPT>, which means that Query functions such as QueryNew are perfectly valid. Here's how you'd create a query object in <CFSCRIPT>:

```
<cfscript>
// Create the Query
qryPros = QueryNew("FirstName, LastName");
QueryAddRow(qryPros, 1);
QuerySetCell(qryPros, "FirstName", "Tony");
QuerySetCell(qryPros, "LastName", "Hawk");
QueryAddRow(qryPros, 1);
QuerySetCell(qryPros, "FirstName", "Rodney");
QuerySetCell(qryPros, "LastName", "Mullen");
QueryAddRow(qryPros, 1);
QuerySetCell(qryPros, "FirstName", "Mark");
QuerySetCell(qryPros, "LastName", "Gonzales");
QueryAddRow(qryPros, 1);
QuerySetCell(qryPros, "FirstName", "Chet");
QuerySetCell(qryPros, "LastName", "Thomas");
QueryAddRow(qryPros, 1);
QuerySetCell(qryPros, "FirstName", "Daewon");
QuerySetCell(qryPros, "LastName", "Song");
</cfscript>
```

The QueryAddRow function adds another row to the qryPros object, and then the QuerySetCell function adds our values to that row. This query object can be used just like a query generated with <CFQUERY>. While we still can't pull data straight from a database in <CFSCRIPT>, we can make a query object that can be used with the Query of Queries feature, and anything else you'd normally be able to do with a query.

Using WriteOutput()

WriteOutput() only works inside <CFSCRIPT>. It cannot be used outside of the <CFSCRIPT> blocks. The function allows you to output a string to the generated HTML of an executed ColdFusion template. For example, the following code programmatically outputs our list of professional skateboarders:

```
<cfscript>
ct = 1; //the loop count
while (ct lte qryPros.RecordCount)
{
    WriteOutput(qryPros.FirstName[ct] & " " & qryPros.LastName[ct] & "<br>");
    ct = ct + 1;
}
</cfscript>
```

The WriteOutput function spits out whatever it finds between the parentheses. In this case, we're doing a little more than just outputting a simple value; we're actually outputting the query we built earlier. We'll come back to this example when we talk about looping in <CFSCRIPT>, and I'll explain in detail everything that is going on to output the query.

Using Conditional Statements

<CFSCRIPT> allows you to use the if/else and switch conditional statements. These statements are similar in syntax to JavaScript conditional statements, and they are also similar in behavior to their CFML counterparts.

IF/ELSE

The if statement is followed by an expression that evaluates to either true or false. Here's an example of a simple if statement:

```
<cfscript>
if (DayofWeekAsString(DayOfWeek(Now())) eq "Tuesday")
    WriteOutput("Taco Tuesday!");
</cfscript>
```

Notice that the expression DayofWeekAsString(DayOfWeek(Now()) eq "Tuesday" is contained with parentheses. If you're not used to the syntax, forgetting to add the parentheses can happen with embarrassing frequency.

The if statement also executes the first statement that follows, in this case, if the day is Tuesday. Consider the following snippet:

```
<cfscript>
if (DayofWeekAsString(DayOfWeek(Now())) eq "Tuesday")
    WriteOutput("Taco Tuesday!");
    WriteOutput("I'll have a burrito!");
</cfscript>
```

The statement that outputs "I'll have a burrito!" will always execute, regardless of whether it's Tuesday or not. In order to execute multiple statements based on a condition, we need to surround the statements with a set of parentheses, like this:

```
<cfscript>
if (DayofWeekAsString(DayOfWeek(Now())) eq "Tuesday")
```

```
{
    WriteOutput("Taco Tuesday!");
    WriteOutput("I'll have a burrito!");
}
</cfscript>
```

Both “Taco Tuesday!” and “I’ll have a burrito!” will execute if the day is Tuesday.

If we want to execute statements when the condition doesn’t meet our first set of criteria, we use the else statement:

```
<cfscript>
if (DayofWeekAsString(DayOfWeek(Now())) eq "Tuesday")
{
    WriteOutput("Taco Tuesday!");
    WriteOutput("I'll have a burrito!");
}
else
{
    WriteOutput("Give me some cheese enchiladas.");
}
</cfscript>
```

We actually don’t need to use the parentheses around the “Give me some cheese enchiladas.” statement. That said, it doesn’t hurt, and it’s a good idea to remain consistent with the rest of the code.

So, how do we write an else if statement?

```
<cfscript>
if (DayofWeekAsString(DayOfWeek(Now())) eq "Tuesday")
{
    WriteOutput("Taco Tuesday!");
    WriteOutput("I'll have a burrito!");
}
else if (DayofWeekAsString(DayOfWeek(Now())) eq "Monday")
{
   WriteOutput("How old are those donuts?");
}
else
{
    WriteOutput("Give me some cheese enchiladas.");
}
</cfscript>
```

The else if statement works just like the if statement, requiring an expression that evaluates to true or false, surrounded by parentheses.

The same performance rules apply for conditional statements in <CFSCRIPT>, as they do traditional in CFML—too many ifs and else ifs can slow things down, and switches should be considered in their place.

SWITCH/CASE

The rules of switch in <CFSCRIPT> are nearly the same as in <CFSWITCH>, but there are some minor differences. Let's look at an example:

```
<cfscript>
switch (DayofWeekAsString(DayOfWeek(Now())))
{
    case "Tuesday":
      {
          WriteOutput("Taco Tuesday!");
          WriteOutput("I'll have a burrito!");
          break;
      }
      case "Sunday":
      {
          WriteOutput("How old are those donuts?");
          break;
      }
}
</cfscript>
```

The switch statement needs an expression that ends up evaluating to one of the case values. Each case is contained within the switch statement's curly brackets. Each case statement requires the *break* expression. If none of the case values match the switch expression, a default set of instructions can be executed by adding the following code shown in bold:

```
<cfscript>
switch (DayofWeekAsString(DayOfWeek(Now())))
{
    case "Tuesday":
      {
          WriteOutput("Taco Tuesday!");
          WriteOutput("I'll have a burrito!");
          break;
```

```
        }
        case "Sunday":
        {
            WriteOutput("How old are those donuts?");
            break;
        }
        default:
        {
                WriteOutput("Give me some cheese enchiladas.");
        }
}
</cfscript>
```

Notice that for the default case, the break statement is not allowed. You only need the break statement when defining cases that match your condition.

Using Loops

There are four possible types of loops that can be executed in <CFSCRIPT>: while loops, for loops, do-while loops, and for-in loops. In this section, we talk about everything except the for-in loop, and show examples of how to use each type of loop. The for-in loop isn't actually a loop, and only fucntions as one when trying to determine whether a structure key exists. We'll skip it for right now.

While Loops

A while loop continues to loop while a certain condition is true. For example:

```
<cfscript>
ct = 1;
while (ct lte 10)
{
    WriteOutput(ct & "<br>");
    ct = ct +1;
}
</cfscript>
```

The WriteOutput statement executes ten times, because the condition indicates that we want to loop while the variable *ct* is less than or equal to 10. After each

WriteOuput, we increment the value of *ct* by one. Eventually *ct* is equal to 10, which stops the loop. If we didn't increment *ct,* the loop would theoretically loop infinitely.

For Loops

The for loop works a little more efficiently in the example we used for the while loop:

```
<cfscript>
for (ct=1; ct lte 10; ct = ct +1)
{
    WriteOutput(ct & "<br>");
}
</cfscript>
```

The for loop iterates while the condition remains true, just like the while loop, yet its condition is set up a little bit differently. The value is initialized in the first part of the condition, and the actual condition is set next while the incrementing follows.

Do-While Loops

The do-while loop works just like the while loop except for one difference. The while loop tests the condition before executing the code within the loop. The do-while loop executes the code within the loop, and *then* tests the condition. Here's an example:

```
<cfscript>
ct=1;
do
{
    WriteOutput(ct & "<br>");
    ct = ct +1;
}
while (ct lte 10);
</cfscript >
```

User Defined Functions

One of the more interesting features of ColdFusion 5.0 is the ability to create user defined functions in <CFSCRIPT>. User defined functions can be used just like built-in ColdFusion functions, and can only be created within a <CFSCRIPT> block. They can then be called anywhere from within the same template.

User defined functions make it easier to do repetitive tasks, such as formatting a date string or calculating the tax of a price. Already there are a few sites that are collecting and creating user defined functions that you can use in your code. The creators of http://www.cflib.org have a bunch of very handy user defined functions that they've organized in libraries. As ColdFusion 5.0 becomes more popular, there are sure to be more sites with similar types of offerings.

Creating User Defined Functions

The creation of user defined functions is pretty intuitive, especially if you've used JavaScript. Here's our LongDate() example:

```
<cfscript>
function LongDate(date)
{
  DateFormat(date, 'mmmm yyyy');
}
</cfscript>
```

This first part of creating the function is done by using the *function* keyword. Following the *function* keyword is the name you'll be calling the function. If you intend to pass arguments to the function, then you can do so by supplying a comma-separated list of argument names within the parentheses. In our example, we only pass a date argument. The name of the argument doesn't have to be anything special; it will only be used within the scope of the function.

We can perform any number of instructions within the function separated by curly brackets. The example above formats a date string to look like "January 2001."

User defined functions cannot be passed to a custom tag unless they're placed in a scope that is visible to a custom tag. Here's an example of how you'd put a function in the **Request** scope:

```
function LongDate(date)
{
  DateFormat(date, 'mmmm yyyy');
}
request.LongDate = LongDate;
```

We basically copy LongDate to the **Request** scope. This may not be a very clean way of doing it, but it does work without any adverse side effects.

Using User Defined Functions

In our own sample application, we use the user defined function LongDate() to format a date in a specific format. Using this function enables us to bypass having to format the date using DateFormat() every time we want the date to look like "January 2001".

```
<cfoutput>#request.LongDate(Now())#</cfoutput>
```

Another one of the user defined functions we use is the CurrentLocation() function. This function takes no arguments, and returns a value called udfCurrentLocation.

```
<cfscript>
function CurrentLocation()
{
    udfCurrentLocation = ListGetAt(cgi.script_name, ListLen(cgi.script_name, '/'),
'/');
    udfCurrentLocation = udfCurrentLocation & "?";
 if (IsDefined("url.cat"))
    udfCurrentLocation = udfCurrentLocation & "cat=#url.cat#" & "&";
if (IsDefined("url.id"))
    udfCurrentLocation = udfCurrentLocation & "id=#url.id#" & "&";
if (IsDefined("url.searchcrit"))
    udfCurrentLocation = udfCurrentLocation & "searchcrit=#url.searchcrit#" & "&";
return udfCurrentLocation;
}
request.CurrentLocation = CurrentLocation;
</cfscript>
```

This function helps to format the URLs in our shopping cart so that when a user deletes an item or increases a quantity, the original URL they were on before taking the action is retained.

Wrapping Up

As you can see, <CFSCRIPT> is a great tool for keeping your code simple, and is capable of performing many useful tasks. Because you're unable to make use of the powerful ColdFusion tags, <CFSCRIPT> doesn't entirely replace CFML. <CFSCRIPT> is primarily used for looping, switches, and if/else statements, and quite often can do these things faster than CFML.

I like using <CFSCRIPT> because it's simply easier to code. It may sound a bit trivial, but using <CFSCRIPT> requires fewer keystrokes. Think about writing a very large <CFSWITCH> statement in CFML. For each case, I need to open the case with <CFCASE>, and then close it with </CFCASE>. If I can avoid just the few extra characters in those two tags, I can code more quickly. <CFSCRIPT> also helps me avoid having to use my SHIFT key for each < and > that I need to code—again, it may sound trivial, but it makes a big difference in a large block of code.

And finally, <CFSCRIPT> code is easier to read, even with its similarities to JavaScript. It helps delineate the code from HTML, and because of its similarity in structure to other languages like JavaScript, <CFSCRIPT> helps new developers understand the logic behind the template more quickly.

CHAPTER

10

Advanced Technologies

IN THIS CHAPTER:

Locking

ColdFusion Extensions

WDDX

Using Advanced Security

I like to think of this chapter as a deli—you can choose macaroni salad, or you can be daring and go for the mysterious day-glow, jello stuff with raisons and shreds of carrot. This chapter doesn't have everything, but it has a couple of topics to choose from.

Some of the topics in this chapter simply weren't complicated enough or interesting enough to warrant an entire chapter, so they've each been given their own section. Publishers aren't fond of short chapters, so I outsmarted them and snuck these topics into one chapter. This keeps the topics short, sweet, and most importantly, in the book.

Locking

Locking is an easily misunderstood subject for many ColdFusion developers. This section should give developers a good understanding of when and how to use locking, and what kind of benefits can be achieved by using good locking practices.

Locking properly should really be considered a requirement of any good application that makes use of any *shared data scopes*. Shared data scopes are scopes that reside in system memory. Shared data scope variables remain persistent on the server, even if a user closes their browser. The following scopes are considered shared data scopes:

- **Server** scope
- **Application** scope
- **Session** scope

ColdFusion 4.5 and later take a lot of the hassles out of locking by providing settings in the ColdFusion Administrator that automate shared scope variable locking. For now, let's pretend that no automatic locking is taking place so that we can better understand locking practices. Understanding good locking practices will help you better understand how to use the ColdFusion automatic locking feature. It will also help if you host your application somewhere where the Administrator has disabled any of the automatic locking features. Once we've talked about locking sufficiently, we'll briefly talk about how the ColdFusion Administrator handles automatic locking.

The reasons for locking aren't brutally obvious at first. We might not be using any locking on an application that makes heavy use of shared data scopes, and everything might work flawlessly. However, that same application might begin exhibiting some strange behavior if the traffic levels start to increase to a level where locking is necessary.

Earlier we read that shared data scope variables are persistent variables. They don't reside in a cookie on the user's machine, nor do they reside in a database anywhere. They reside in memory on the server. The memory used by unlocked shared variables runs the risk of becoming corrupt if multiple requests access the variable at the same time. To eliminate the possibility of multiple requests accessing the same variable at the same time, we use the <CFLOCK> tag.

The <CFLOCK> tag locks variables as they are being accessed. The tag itself is only needed in the following situations:

- When writing to a shared scope variable.
- When reading a shared scope variable.
- When checking for the existence of a shared scope variable.
- When executing CFX tags (we cover this later in this section).

There are two modes in which <CFLOCK> works, both of which can be specified using the *type* attribute. Let's describe each mode, and what it specifically performs:

- **Exclusive Locks** Exclusive locks allow a single request to access the variable one at a time. This completely prevents any data corruption because it's impossible for another process to do anything to the variable. No other code from any other request will execute while the code between an exclusively locked set of <CFLOCK> tags is executing. Locks are given on a first come first serve basis. Exclusive locks can have obvious repercussions if the code within the <CFLOCK> tags takes a while to execute. We'll discuss best practices shortly. Using <CFLOCK TYPE="Exclusive"> will grant an exclusive lock. This mode is the default mode, so specifying <CFLOCK> without any attributes will also grant an exclusive lock.
- **Read-only Locks** Read-only locks are less restrictive in that they allow other requests to read the variable without halting all other requests. Read-only locks prevent the data being read from changing mid-read. If an exclusive lock is being performed on a shared data variable, a read-only lock will pause until the shared data variable is updated, then perform the read. Read-only locks are ignored until an exclusive locks occurs, so there's no performance hit when using them. Using <CFLOCK TYPE="ReadOnly"> will allow a read-only lock.

Now, with all that said about <CFLOCK>, let's throw a monkey wrench into your understanding. <CFLOCK> doesn't actually lock shared data variables. It locks blocks of code. If variables are written within the block of code, then they too are locked along with the code. The <CFLOCK> tag by default doesn't discriminate about what kind of variables to lock, nor does it assume that two different blocks of code that write or read the same variable are indeed writing or reading the same variable.

This is where the *name* and *scope* attributes come into play. Consider two different blocks of code; both write to the same variable within the **Server** scope. The two blocks of code are actually different (the differences aren't important right now, just that they *are* different). In fact, the blocks of code could be identical, but it's easier to grasp if you consider two truly different blocks of code because ColdFusion by default sees the blocks as two different and completely unassociated blocks of code, even if they are the same. Specifying the *name* attribute allows you to assure that the two blocks of code don't run at the exact same time. If they are both given the same name, ColdFusion knows not to run the two blocks simultaneously. Here's a syntax example of the *name* attribute in use:

```
<cflock type="exclusive" name="lockSiteConstants">
   <cfset application.constRootURL = "http://www.stompzine.com/">
</cflock>
```

Only blocks of code with the same name will be locked, which is a good reason to use the *name* attribute when locking. This increases performance, but there is also a risk to using named locks. Because <CFLOCK> with the name attribute will only lock blocks of code with the exact same name; if you accidentally use a different name to lock a block of code that accesses shared data variables, then you're not doing any locking at all.

Using the *scope* attribute is somewhat similar, except that it locks an entire scope rather than just a block of code. The scope attribute takes the following values:

- **Server** All code sections with this attribute on the server share a single lock.
- **Application** All code sections with this attribute in the same application share a single lock.
- **Session** All code sections with this attribute that run in the same session and application share a single lock.

Locked blocks of code can be assigned timeout values so that a problematic lock doesn't hold up your entire server. If you add the *timeout* attribute to a <CFLOCK>

tag, the lock will end regardless of whether or not the operation is finished, if the timeout value in seconds has been exceeded.

Another attribute can be added to the <CFLOCK> tag that allows you to debug timed-out locks. Adding the *thowOnTimeOut* attribute with the value of "yes" will cause the <CFLOCK> tag to throw an error. The <CFCATCH>/<CFTRY> tags can be used to gracefully handle the error. With the attribute set to "no," or even left out of the tag entirely, a timed-out lock will make no "noise," and the code will continue to process.

<CFLOCK> should be used for a few other things besides the **Server**, **Application**, and **Session** scopes to assure consistent data. When using <CFHTTP>, <CFFILE>, or any other process that reads or writes a file from a disk, the <CFLOCK> tag should also be used. A text file on the server that can be written to by multiple processes can run into the same problems that shared data variables can.

It's also a good practice to lock CFX tags. CFX tags are extensions to ColdFusion that are written in C++ or Java, and are called as tags. For example, <CFX_PING> is a CFX tag that performs a ping operation, written in C++. Locking CFX tags using the name attribute in the <CFLOCK> tag is considered a good practice because it's quite possible that the CFX tag hasn't been written to handle multiple threads simultaneously. What I usually do when calling CFX tags is simply name the lock the same as the CFX tag. For example:

```
<cflock name="cfx_ping" timeout="2">
   <cfx_ping address="www.stinkmachine.com">
</cflock>
```

Whenever I execute the CFX tag, as long as I remain consistent with the naming, I can be assured that if the tag is executed simultaneously then it will be locked properly.

Now that we understand how locking works, let's consider the settings available in the ColdFusion Administrator under the Server | Locking page. The following table describes these settings, and the role of each setting.

Setting	Description
Single-Threaded Sessions	When this setting is enabled, no locking is required on variables in the **Session** scope. ColdFusion will automatically lock variables within the same **Session** scope.

Setting	Description
Variable Scope Lock Settings	Each variable scope can be set to automatically lock in three different ways: • **No Automatic checking or locking** If this is selected, then ColdFusion keeps its hands out of things, and requires that the developer handle all locking requirements. • **Full Checking** If selected, ColdFusion tries to ensure that all shared data variables are properly locked. If not properly locked, ColdFusion will throw an error. ColdFusion doesn't do any of the locking for you, it simply checks to see if something is locked. Named locks shouldn't be used when this setting is enabled because ColdFusion doesn't consider it a full lock (named locks will only lock if the same named lock is already running). • **Automatic Read Locking** If selected, ColdFusion automatically performs read-only locks on shared data variables, but will throw an error if a write to a shared data variable is not locked.

In summary, even with the aid of the ColdFusion Administrator automatic settings, locking should be part of any application that makes use of any type of shared data variable. Here are some tips to keep in mind when writing your locks:

- Do not use an excessive number of exclusive locks, and when you do lock, make sure the least amount of code is locked.
- If you need to create shared data variables using complex routines that could possibly take some time to perform, rather than lock the code that creates the routines, create the variables as local, unshared variables first, then lock the block of code that copies the local variables to the shared data variables.
- Be sure to use consistent names when using named locks, otherwise your locks will not execute.
- Always lock CFX tags, just to play it safe.

ColdFusion Extensions

ColdFusion by itself is reasonably powerful and can perform quite a few advanced tasks, but sometimes it simply makes sense to use different technologies that might perform tasks in a quicker, or more efficient way. Using the CFX tag technology, and the

<CFOBJECT> tag, ColdFusion can make use of functionality from leading languages and technologies such as C++, Server-side Java, COM objects, and Java classes.

CFX Tags

CFX tags are C/C++/Java tags written specifically for ColdFusion using the ColdFusion Custom Tag API. CFX tags are registered in the ColdFusion Administrator under the Server | CFX Tags page. Both C/C++ and Java tags can be registered here.

CFX tags are called using familiar CFML tag naming. The following example calls an imaginary tag that takes a few attributes. The tag itself creates a structure with some values that we immediately output:

```
<cfx_dissect fruit="Orange">

<cfoutput>
#strDissect.Skin#<br>
#strDissect.Pulp#<br>
#strDissect.Seeds#<br>
#strDissect.Core#<br>
</cfoutput>
```

The point of the example is that CFX tags can be developed to be very integrated into ColdFusion. This type of extension to ColdFusion, other than CFML Custom Tags, is easily the most seamless method of introducing functionality from different languages into ColdFusion.

COM Objects

Component Object Model (COM) is a technology developed by the Digital Equipment Corporation and Microsoft Corporation that allows developers to create functional blocks of code, or objects, that can be reused with relative ease in other programs. COM objects can do very simple tasks, or they can perform quite complex tasks. COM objects are also very versatile because they can run on multiple development environments. For example, just as ColdFusion developers can integrate COM objects into their applications, so can ASP programmers, or even C++ programmers.

COM objects are compatible with ColdFusion when using the <CFOBJECT>, but only in a Windows environment. While Microsoft has ported COM to other platforms, ColdFusion only supports COM and Distributed Component Object Model (DCOM) objects on Windows platforms.

Before a COM object can be used, it needs to be registered on the system it will be executing on. Registration for each COM object can differ, but typically, running the regsvr32 program from the command will register the object.

```
regsvr32 comobject.dll
```

To unregister the object, the following command would work:

```
regsvr32 /u comobject.dll
```

To call a COM object, we must use the <CFOBJECT> tag. The following example calls an imaginary COM object. We discuss the use of the attributes and naming right after the example:

```
<cfobject
   type="COM"
   action="create"
   name="objectname"
   class="class.name">
```

Each COM object is typically called with syntax similar to the object above. Usually an understanding of the COM object you're calling is required once it's called, as COM objects can differ extensively in the tasks that they perform.

The following is an example of Lewis Sellers' TCP Client COM object. It's a very useful COM object, and can be found at http://www.intrafoundation.com. In the example, we use the COM object to perform a **whois** command on the Macromedia domain. The **whois** command will look up the domain name record for http://www.macromedia.com, and return information about who owns the domain, and where it's registered.

```
<cfobject
   action="create"
   name="obj"
   class="Intrafoundation.TCPClient"
>

<cfset c=obj.Open("whois.networksolutions.com","whois")>
<cfset obj.timeout=3.0>
<cfset obj.SendRN("macromedia.com")>
<cfset page=obj.Recv()>
<cfoutput>#HTMLCodeFormat(page)#</cfoutput>
<cfset obj.Close()>
```

Server-side Java

Java classes, as well as Enterprise Java Beans (EJB), can be called using the <CFOBJECT> tag. EJB is a server-side component based architecture based on the Sun Java 2 Enterprise Edition platform (J2EE). EJBs can provide the same kind of functionality that CFX tags or COM objects can. Whether or not there is an advantage to using Java is up to the developer.

Calling a Java object is very similar to calling a COM object. The following example assumes that the foo.class file is in the C:\Cfusion\Java\Classes directory, or in the directory specified under the Server | JVM and Java Settings page in the ColdFusion Administrator. It also assumes that a Java Virtual Machine is running. Default installations of ColdFusion should already have a Java Virtual Machine running.

```
<cfobject
   type="Java"
   action="create"
   name="objectname"
   class="foo">
```

CORBA

CORBA stands for *Common Object Request Broker Architecture*. The technology was developed in 1992 by the Object Management Group, a consortium that included IBM, Apple, and Sun Microsystems. The object of the consortium was to develop a standardized object model that worked independently on different platforms and environments.

Before we get into calling a CORBA object, I should mention that it's probably safe to say that the vast majority of ColdFusion developers will never need to know a single thing about how to call a CORBA object. Developing CORBA objects is a difficult and expensive process, and CORBA support in ColdFusion is mainly added so that companies that have already invested a great deal in CORBA can continue to maximize their investment with ColdFusion.

The <CFOBJECT> tag is used to call a CORBA object. The following example calls an imaginary CORBA object:

```
<cfobject
   type="CORBA"
   action="connect"
   name="objectname"
   class="c:\\corbaobject.ior2"
   context="IOR">
```

In this example, the context attribute along with the class attribute indicates that we're bypassing a naming service for CORBA objects, and making a direct connection to the file for a CORBA object.

If you're still interested in CORBA, the CORBA web site has more information (http://www.corba.org), as well as the Object Management Group's web site (http://www.omg.org). There is also a Usenet newsgroup dedicated to CORBA at comp.object.corba.

WDDX

Web Distributed Data Exchange (WDDX) is a technology introduced by Jeremy Allaire, the creator of ColdFusion, that allows for complex data exchange between different types of web-based applications.

The benefits of using WDDX are that a ColdFusion server can pass standardized data to a Microsoft ASP server, or a PHP-based application, or any other server that supports WDDX. While ColdFusion was developed by the makers of ColdFusion, it was designed to work as flawlessly as possible with other languages to promote the transfer of complicated data structures between different types of systems. To learn more about the roots of WDDX, look at http://www.openwddx.org.

Data Syndication and Distributed Computing

One of the most obvious benefits of the Internet is that tons of computers are essentially on the same network, with the ability to communicate with each other through a small army of different protocols and services. Unfortunately, however, distributed computing on the Internet is difficult due to security issues. Firewalls and other security measures do a lot to block the ability to perform true distributed computing tasks. Rather than being always connected, computers on the Internet today have many obstacles in between them that discourage true, distributed computing.

Think of what it takes to connect several hundred computers together to perform a particular task in today's Web environment. It's very difficult to do, because the HTTP protocol is designed to be fairly "unintelligent" and disconnected. When a web browser connects to a web server, the request from the web browser is very brief. It asks to download a particular resource, and asks little else beyond that. The browser takes over from there, rendering the HTML, or displaying the image. As soon as the request is completed, the connection is cut, and the web server considers the next request from the client an entirely new connection. This kind of environment is also not very good for distributed computing, where data exchange needs to be a little more intelligent, and structured.

WDDX tries to overcome these barriers by allowing developers of different platforms to exchange data seamlessly between the different platforms. ColdFusion programmers can develop all of the functionality that they require to be performed on the server side, and then hand off WDDX packets to a different server running PHP. The PHP server can than perform tasks based on the WDDX packets, without ever being concerned about how the data was produced.

WDDX itself doesn't replace any protocol. It works with the HTTP protocol to pass data from one server to another, which helps overcome some of the obstacles to traditional distributed computing. Most security measures on the Internet, like firewalls, readily accept HTTP packets because for the most part, they're completely benign.

WDDX can be used to create sophisticated data syndication applications. Imagine an ASP-driven, weather-related web site that you could connect to with your ColdFusion server to get the raw data for the day's weather forecast. The data could be formatted exactly the way you wanted to format it, with little or no parsing. In ColdFusion, the data could be placed right into ColdFusion-friendly structures that could be used to create your own forecast page.

While WDDX doesn't solve every problem associated with distributed computing, it does create a functional way to pass structured data to and from disparate web server applications, which makes things like data syndication more robust and easier to execute.

WDDX and XML

WDDX is a subset of *Extensible Markup Language* (XML). XML was created to allow developers to create their own markup languages, or data schemas, much like HTML. In HTML, the browser renders the document based on the type of tags within the HTML document. Table rows are represented as <TR> tags, and cells within the table are represented as <TD> tags. The browser is programmed to understand a certain specification of HTML, and while HTML isn't XML, it helps describe the association between XML and WDDX.

The browser knows that, based on the official HTML specification, certain tags are to be rendered in certain ways. XML by itself doesn't do anything to describe the data within its tags—this is what a schema is for. The schema describes what data within XML tags are supposed to contain. WDDX acts as a schema. It describes what kinds of values are contained within the data, and allows different web servers to interpret what the values are.

<CFWDDX>

The <CFWDDX> tag is used to *serialize*, or format, data into WDDX packets. The WDDX packets themselves are merely text strings, but with the XML based WDDX markup language applied. We'll see some examples of the language shortly. <CFWDDX> is also used to *deserialize* WDDX packets, or take WDDX packets and return them to a ColdFusion-friendly form.

Let's look at an example of <CFWDDX> that pushes data to another server. Afterwards we'll look at a template that receives WDDX packets.

```
<cfsetting showdebugoutput="No">
<cfquery name="qryRockStars" datasource="#request.dsn#">
SELECT rockstar_id, rockstar_name, rockstar_talent
FROM Rockstars
</cfquery>
<cfwddx action="cfml2wddx" input="#qryRockStars#"
output="wddxRockStars">

Resulting WDDX packet is:
<xmp><cfoutput>#wddxRockStars#</cfoutput></xmp>
```

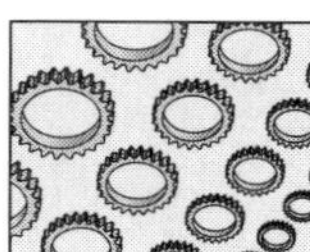

NOTE

Notice the <CFSETTING> tag in the example code. Without this code, ColdFusion might throw a funny error that says: XML parsing error: junk after document element. *The <CFSETTING> tag in the example reduces whitespace that might produce the error. Erik Goodlad, the technical editor for this book, discovered this error, and is amused because it uses the nontechnical term "junk." In the receiving template it's a good idea to use the Trim() function to reduce any added whitespace as well. We'll look at that example shortly.*

The output of the above block of code would look something like the following, except all on a single string. It has been broken up here to look pretty in the book:

```
<wddxPacket version='1.0'>
<header></header>
<data>
   <recordset rowCount='4'
    fieldNames='ROCKSTAR_ID,ROCKSTAR_NAME, SPECIAL_TALENT'>
   <field name='ROCKSTAR_ID'>
      <number>34920</number>
      <number>34922</number>
```

```
      <number>34930</number>
      <number>34945</number>
   </field>
   <field name='ROCKSTAR_NAME'>
      <string>Neil Diamond</string>
      <string>Elvis Presley</string>
      <string>Yanni</string>
      <string>Michael Jackson</string>
   </field>
   <field name='SPECIAL_TALENT'>
      <string>Confusion Ray</string>
      <string>Lethal Hip Gyration</string>
      <string>Aural Torture Method</string>
      <string>Shape Shifting Action</string>
   </field>
   </recordset>
   </data>
</wddxPacket>
```

If we were to receive this packet from another source, we'd use <CFWDDX> to deserialize it, or turn it back into useable data within ColdFusion:

```
<cfhttp url="http://server.com/feeds/rockstars/pushfeed.cfm" method="GET"/>
<cfwddx action="WDDX2CFML" input="#Trim(cfhttp.filecontent)#"
output="qryRockStars">

<cfoutput query="qryRockStars">
   #rockstar_id# #rockstar_name# #rockstar_talent#<br>
</cfoutput>
```

<CFWDDX> parses the WDDX packet automatically, and creates a query object with the resulting data, which can be used just like any other query object.

Using Advanced Security

ColdFusion 5.0 provides robust security features that can be integrated into ColdFusion applications. With ColdFusion security features, login functionality can be created that allows a user to log in and be given permissions based on the user group they belong to, or other specific permissions that pertain to that particular user.

In this section, we talk about the tags used to authenticate users, and some of the functions as well. Towards the end of the section, we include sample code that puts all of the security pieces together into a miniature application.

Before any advanced security features can be used, an administrator must set up the proper security contexts in the ColdFusion Administrator. Earlier, in Chapter 3, we talked about some of the features under the Security section of the ColdFusion Administrator. We pick up here where that chapter left off. It's assumed that advanced security is enabled in the Administrator, and that you're at least somewhat familiar with the Administrator.

Setting Up the Advanced Security Environment

In this section, we set up a sample security context, some users, resources and policies, and user groups. We do all of this from the ColdFusion Administrator, and there will be plenty of screen shots to use as reference points. If you're already familiar with the concept of security contexts, then it doesn't hurt to skip this section.

Security Contexts

Before we do anything else, we need to create a security context. A security context is sort of like a box that stores security policies. These security policies end up applying to users and resources.

Creating a security context isn't required as the first step; it's possible to create users first, and then apply them towards a security context, but it's easier to explain the concept if we start off by creating the "box" to hold things in.

To create a security context, follow these steps:

1. Click the Security Contexts button on the Security | Security Configuration page in the ColdFusion Administrator.
2. Click on the Security Contexts box toward the top of the page.

3. Enter a name into the box, and then click Add Security Context, as shown here:

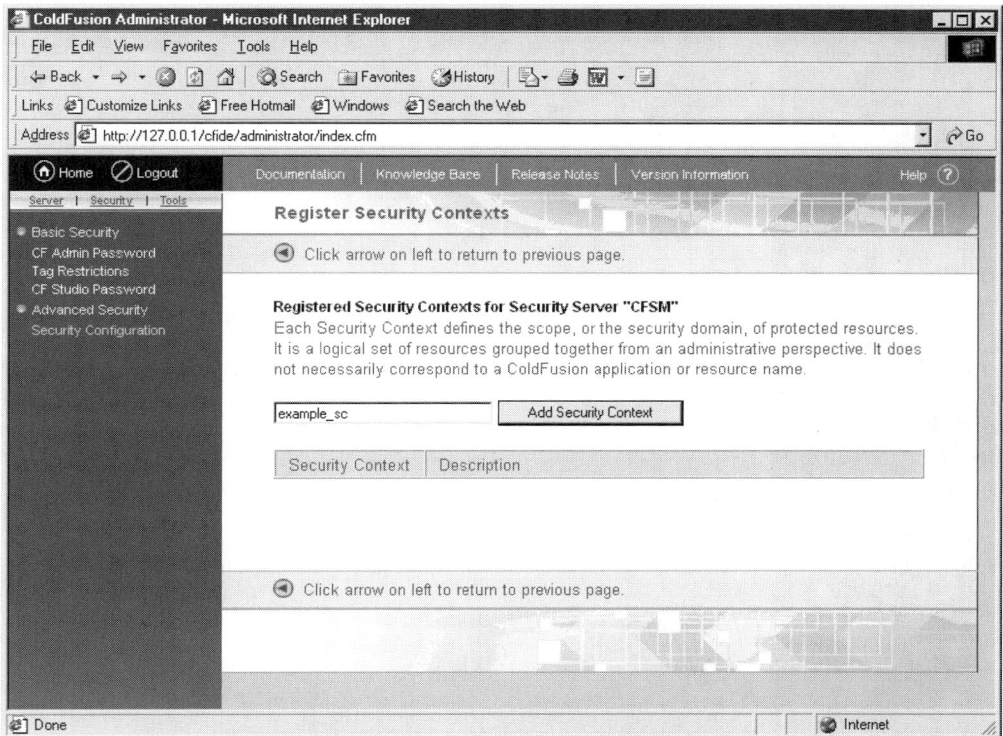

4. Add a description to your security context. While it might seem like a minor detail at this point, it's a good idea to add a description, because it's possible

that other administrators might not know what your security context is for. It's also helpful when you have to manage many security contexts.

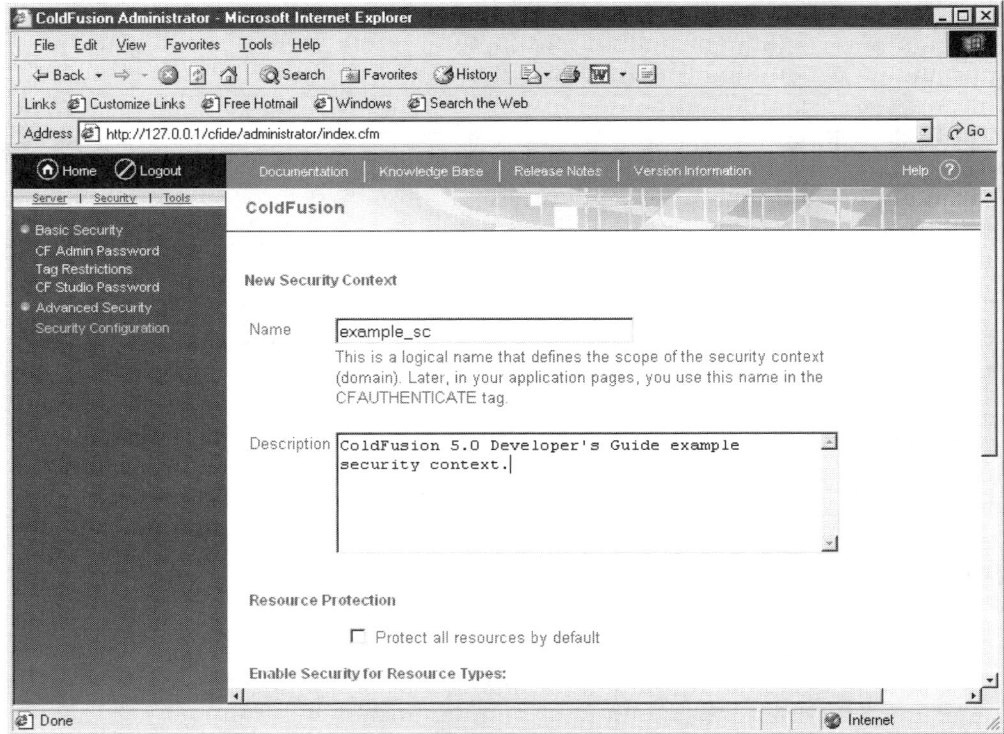

5. Below the description box, when you scroll down the screen, you will see several options to choose (as shown next). For the sake of the example, we select each option as shown. This allows us to create rules for every possible

rule type. We then create rules shortly. If we were to not select some of the items, it would simply mean that we wouldn't be able to create a rule for that item, which isn't really a bad thing or a good thing. It just means we wouldn't have control—some applications might call for that.

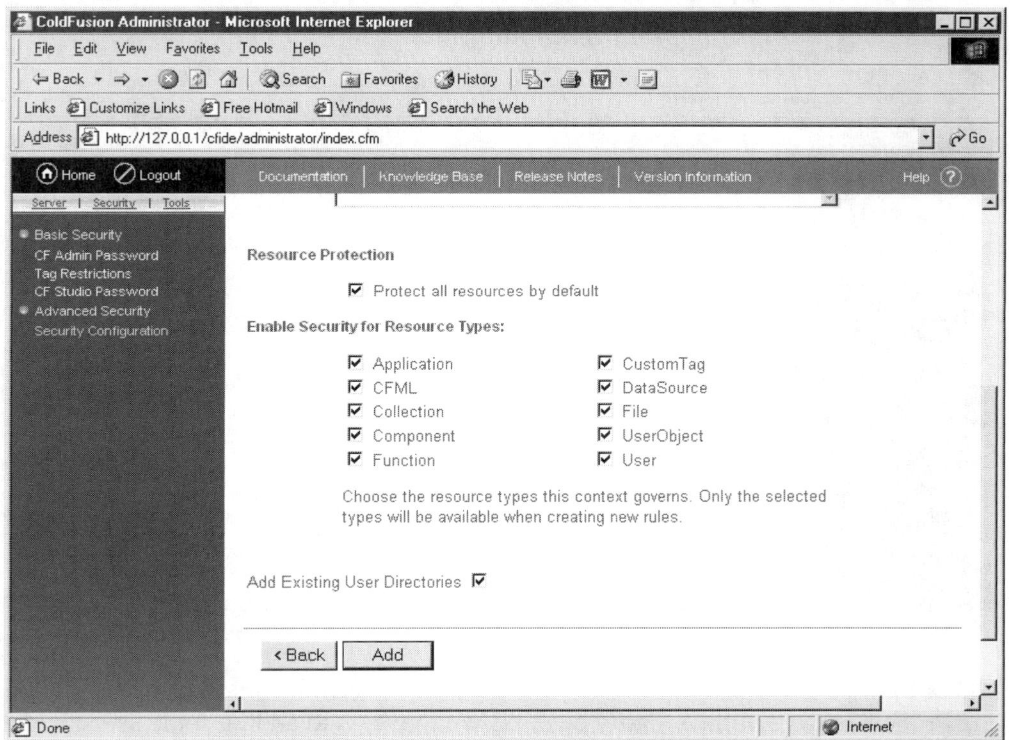

6. Click the Add button, and the page reloads, except now the security context is active, and a new choice of buttons appears at the bottom of the page, as shown here:

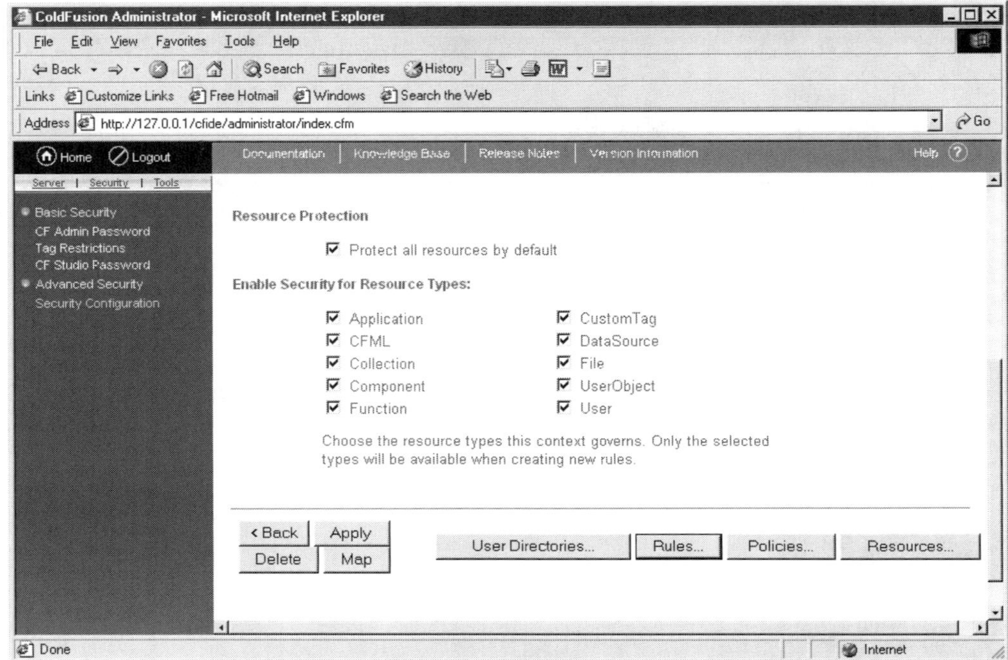

For right now, don't worry about the buttons. Just remember that they're located on the Properties page of the security context. We move on to adding some users, which will bring us back to the main menu of the Security | Security Configuration page.

Users Directories

Now that we've created a security context, it's time to add some user groups to it. From the Security | Security Configuration page, click the User Directories button.

Enter a name for the user directory you'll be creating in the box (see Figure 10-1), and then click the Connect Directory button. The screen shown in Figure 10-2 will appear.

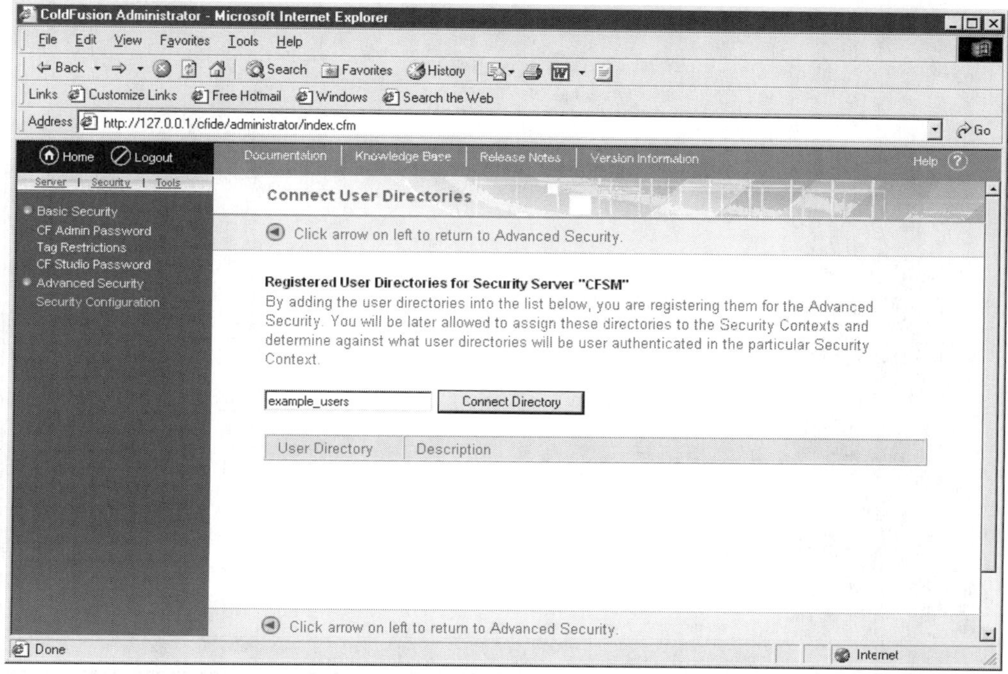

Figure 10-1 *Registering a new user directory within a security context*

In our example, we're using the upsized ODBC database that we created in Chapter 3. This requires that we select ODBC as the Namespace, and the Location should be the name of the SQL Server our security database is on. Supply the appropriate user name and password, and click the Add button at the bottom of the page. The LDAP and ODBC settings shouldn't need to be changed from the default values.

Resources and Policies

Make your way back to the main security menu under Security | Security Configuration, and click Security Contexts. Click the security context we created earlier, then click

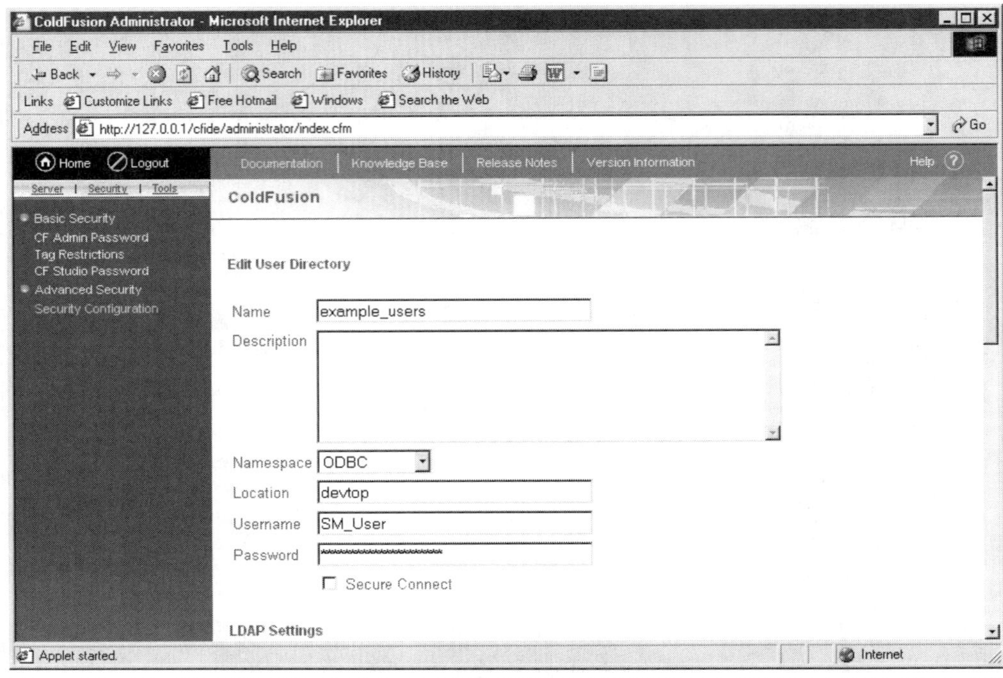

Figure 10-2 *Editing the User Directory specifics*

the User Directories button. This menu allows you to add the user group you just created to this security context (see Figure 10-3).

Move the user group, or groups, that you want to fall under this security context to the left-hand pane (it's likely to already be selected). Now make your way back to the Security | Security Configuration page again. Click the Resources button. This loads a Java application that displays all of the items that were indicated as configurable in the Security Context creation process (see Figure 10-4). Make sure your browser can properly display a Java application, as this is the only way you can modify the resources through the Administrator. The Java applet itself may take a considerable amount of time to load for the first time.

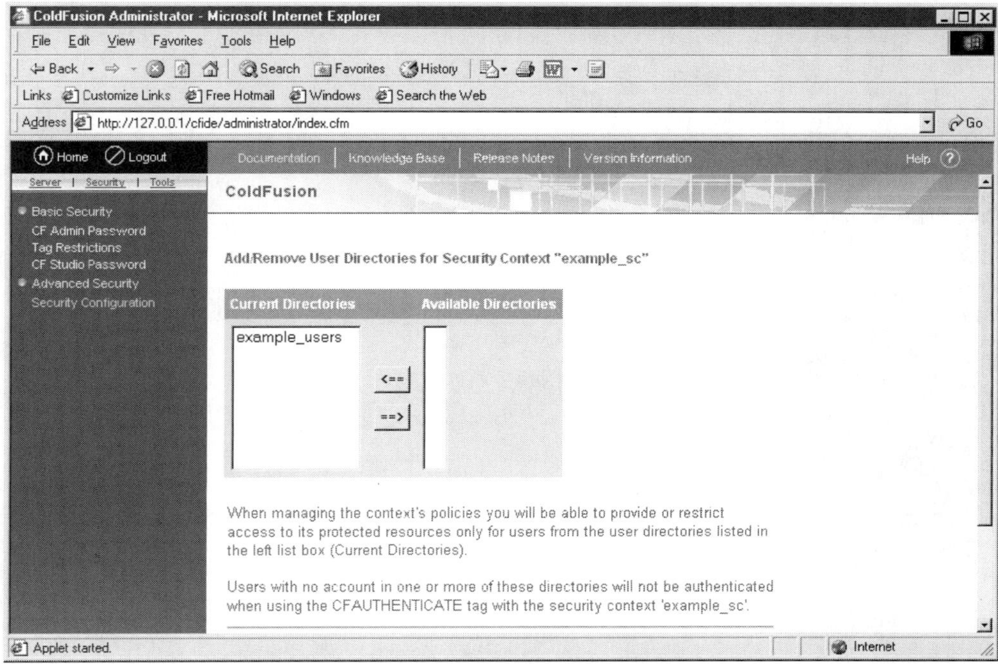

Figure 10-3 *Adding a User Directory to a Security Context*

The first thing we'll do is add a user to our recently created user group. To do this, click the USER node, and then click the Add Resource button. A window pops up that asks for a user name:

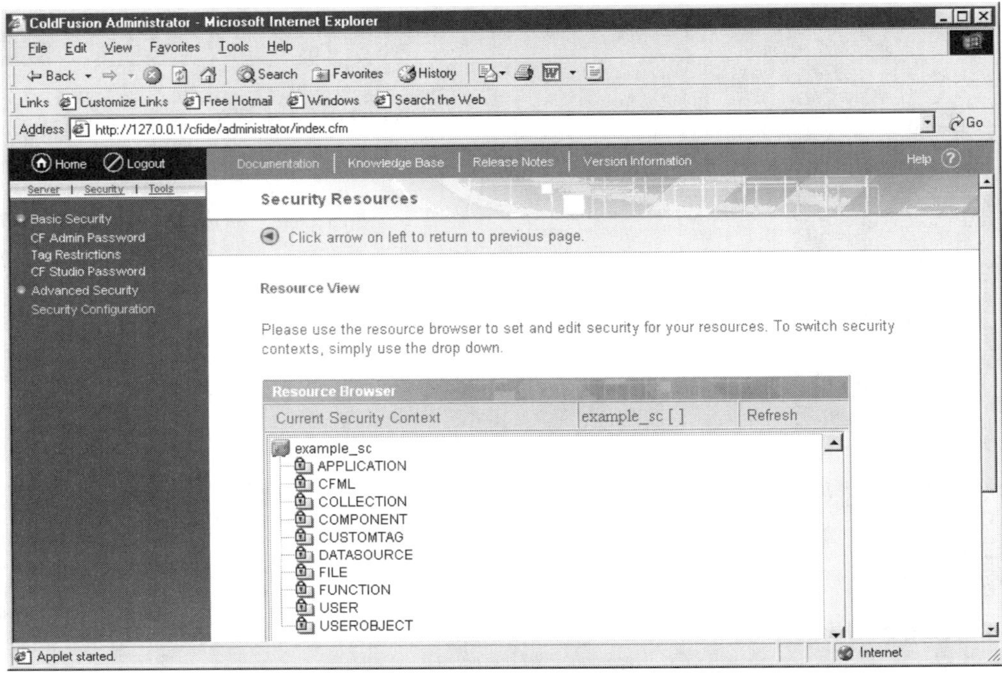

Figure 10-4 *Security Resources page*

Enter a user name and press OK. This creates the user underneath the USER node. Each resource type has a pop-up window just like the one that you just used, each with different settings for each resource. Click the CFML resource type, and then click Add Resource.

This time, the window is specific to what CFML tags you'd like to protect. Select a tag, and then click OK. The <CFEXECUTE> tag is now added underneath the CFML node. This process can be performed on each of the resource types.

The idea behind the resource browser is that it can be used to protect resources on a machine. By default, all access is granted, and permissions to certain resources need to be taken away.

Policies

Underneath Security | Security Configuration, click the Security Contexts button, and then click the security context you're interested in creating a policy for (hopefully the one you've been testing with up until this point). Click the Policies button, and then enter a policy name and press Add. Enter a description for the policy, and then press Add again (see Figure 10-5).

Once the policy is created, you'll be returned to a list of policies — click the policy you just created. Click the Rules button to add any existing rules (rules are

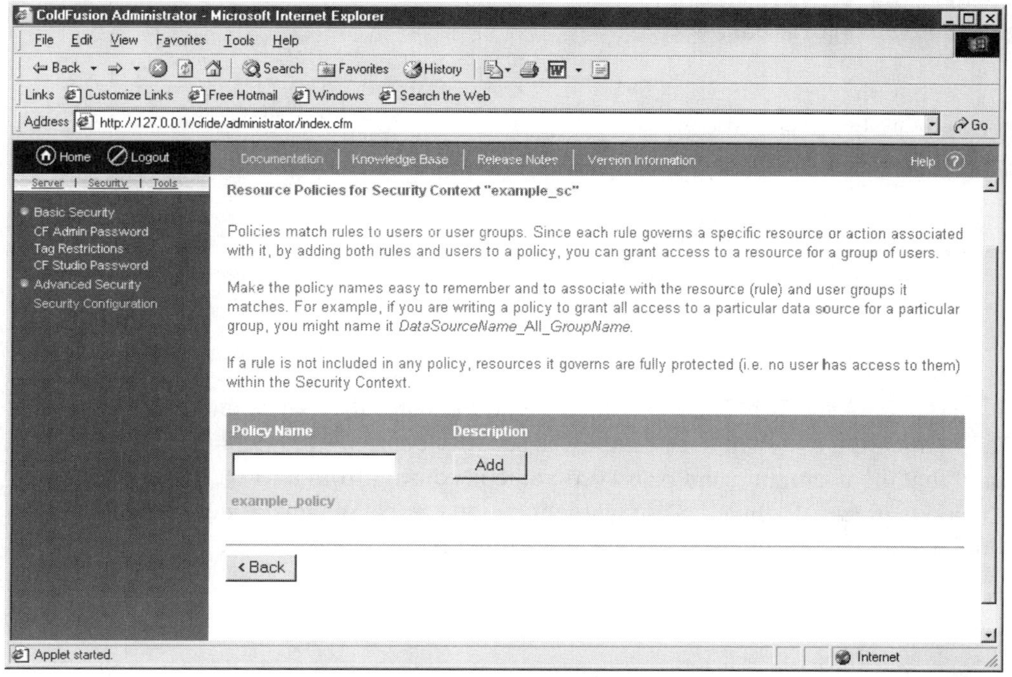

Figure 10-5 *Adding a new Security Policy.*

associated with Security Contexts and can be created from the Security Context properties page).

<CFAUTHENTICATE>

The <CFAUTHENTICATE> tag authenticates a user. Ideally, this tag should be executed before any other ColdFusion tags execute if you're working in a secure application. Typically, developers place the tag in the Application.cfm file because the Application.cfm file is sure to execute for each ColdFusion request. The following code example shows the <CFAUTHENTICATE> tag in use in an Application.cfm file:

```
<cfif NOT IsAuthenticated()>
  <cftry>

  <cfauthenticate
throwonfailure="Yes"
securitycontext="example_sc"
username="#form.user#"
password="#form.password#">

   <cfcatch type="security">
    <b>Authentication error:<b>
    <p>
    <cfoutput>
    <p>#CFCATCH.message#
    </cfoutput>
   </cfcatch>
  </cftry>
</cfif>
```

The <CFAUTHENTICATE> tag in bold indicates that we're interested in authenticating a user in the example_sc security context (this field is required), and that the user name and password value is coming from a form. The rest of the code gracefully handles any authentication errors. We talk about <CFTRY> in Chapter 14, and the IsAuthenticated() function in the next section.

The following attributes are available to the <CFAUTHENTICATE> tag:

Attribute	Description
securitycontext	Required. This should be the name of an established security context in the ColdFusion Administrator
username	Required. This is the name of the user to authenticate.
password	Required. The user's password.
setcookie	Optional. This can be either "yes" or "no." By default, the option is "yes." When enabled, an encrypted cookie is sent to the user that includes user name, security context, browser IP, and the browser type.
throwonfailure	Optional. This can be either "yes" or "no." Default is "yes." When enabled, this attribute indicates that if an error occurs, the tag should throw a security error, which can be used by <CFTRY>/<CFCATCH>.

Security Functions

There are four functions related to ColdFusion's advanced security features. Let's look at all of them.

IsAuthenticated()

This function returns a value of TRUE if the user is authenticated using the <CFAUTHENTICATE> tag. If you supply an optional argument containing the name of a security context, it will return TRUE if the user is authenticated for that particular security context.

IsAuthorized()

This function returns the value of TRUE if the user is authorized to perform a task on a specific resource. The function can take up to three arguments: *resourcetype*, *resourcename*, and *action*. *Resourcetype* indicates the type of resource you'll be checking, out of the following list:

- Application
- CFML
- File

- DataSource
- Component
- Collection
- CustomTag
- UserObject

Resourcename indicates the name of the resource being checked. In the case of a custom tag, *resourcetype* would be CustomTag, and *resourcename* could be CF_HelloWorld.

The action attribute shouldn't be used with the Component and CustomTag resource types. For the remaining resource types, the *action* attribute is required. The *action* attribute takes different values depending on the resource type. The following table indicates what action values go with each resource type:

Resource Type	Possible Action Values
Application	ALL, USECLIENTVARIABLES
File	READ, WRITE
Datasource	ALL, CONNECT, SELECT, INSERT, UPDATE, SP
Collection	DELETE, OPTIMIZE, PURGE, SEARCH, UPDATE

The CFML and UserObject resource types were deliberately excluded from the table because they require a little more discussion. The action value for the CFML resource type can be any valid action for the particular CFML resource.

The possible values available for the UserObject resource are defined in the ColdFusion Administrator in the Security | Security Configuration | Resource View page.

AuthenticatedContext()

Outputting this function returns the current security context that the application runs under. For example:

```
Secure context is: <cfoutput>#AuthenticatedContext()#</cfoutput>
```

AuthenticatedUser()

Using this function returns the name of the current authenticated user. Here is an example:

```
Current user: <cfoutput>#AuthenticatedUser()#</cfoutput>
```

<CFIMPERSONATE>

<CFIMPERSONATE> allows you to assume the identity of a user, which includes assuming all of the user's permissions. The tag is typically used to help test a document, to make sure the permissions for a particular user are working correctly without having to worry about any other authentication-related tags or functions. For instance, using <CFIMPERSONATE> eliminates the need to use <CFAUTHENTICATE>, or to check to see if a user is logged in using the IsAuthenticated() function. Take a look at the tag in action:

```
<cfimpersonate securitycontext="example_sc"
   username="Michael"
   password="AJ79YEGhd3"
   type="CF">
...
</cfimpersonate>
```

While most of the attributes speak for themselves, the *type* attribute is interesting. This attribute with the value of "CF" means that permissions on resources within ColdFusion's control will be assumed. The other possible value, "OS," will assume the permissions of an operating system user. The OS method is faster because ColdFusion isn't doing the work of authenticating at that point, but the OS type also doesn't have the ability to control access to a CFML tag. If all you're protecting in your security context is OS related items like directories, then using the OS type is probably the best way to test. If you're protecting access to CFML tags and other ColdFusion-specific resources in your security context, it's best to use the CF type.

Advanced Security Example

In this section, we look at some example code that one might use to implement advanced security. Rather than show an entire application, we focus on the relevant parts to advanced security. We show portions of two files, the application.cfm file that contains the authentication code, and a template that checks to see if a user is authorized to perform a DELETE query.

The example can be used to model your own type of advanced security framework, and shows off a few of the functions used for authorization that we talked about earlier in this chapter. User security is typically handled in this format; the application.cfm file contains the authentication code, because it will always execute before the called template. If authentication is successful, the called template is then executed because the user has passed the security checkpoint.

Application.cfm

This example checks to see if the user is authenticated, and if they are, allows the user to proceed. If they're not authenticated, it displays a login form, and aborts any other processing. The URL that the user originally requested is retained, and is used as the form action. This is done to prevent from losing where the user originally was. It's a usability thing; we don't want to completely confuse the user by sending them to an arbitrary URL of our choosing once they've logged in. We want the login to come up if needed, and get out of the way with as little confusion as possible when they've logged in.

The security related parts of the application.cfm file are shown here. The comments provide insight into what the code is actually doing:

```
<cfif NOT IsAuthenticated()>
   <!--- The user hasn't been authenticated, set flag --->
   <cfset intShowLoginFlag = 0>

   <cfif IsDefined("form.szUserName") AND IsDefined("form.szPassword")>
      <!--- User submitted login info. Give it a go --->
      <cftry>
         <cfauthenticate setcookie="Yes"
               throwonfailure="Yes"
               securitycontext="skateshopadmin_sc"
               username="#form.szUserName#"
               password="#form.szPassword#">

         <cfcatch type="security">
            <!--- Authentication didn't work, show error --->
            <cf_error errortype="sec.login.bad">
            <cfset intShowLoginFlag = 1>
         </cfcatch>
      </cftry>

   <cfelse>
      <!--- User didn't submit login information, give chance to re-enter --->
      <cfset intShowLoginFlag = 1>
   </cfif>

      <!--- Show the login form --->
      <cfif intShowLoginFlag eq 1>
         <!--- construct the url of the
              calling page (prevents user from losing their place) --->
         <cfset szURL = cgi.script_name>

         <cfif cgi.query_string neq "">
```

```
            <!--- if there are parameters, squeeze the required ? in --->
            <cfset szURL = szURL & "?" & cgi.query_string>
         </cfif>

         <form action="<cfoutput>#szURL#</cfoutput>" method="post">
            <table>
               <tr>
                  <td>Username:</td>
                  <td><input type="text"
                      name="szUserName" size="12" maxlength="20"></td>
               </tr>
               <tr>
                  <td>Password:</td>
                  <td><input type="password"
                  name="szPassword" size="12" maxlength="20"></td>
               </tr>
            </table>
            <input type="submit" value="Login">
         </form>
      <!--- halt any further processing (not graceful, but works) --->
      <cfabort>
   </cfif>
</cfif>
```

Called Template Example

Let's assume that the user has passed the authentication test. Now we want to make sure they have the correct permissions to execute the DELETE query. Our security policies contain the rules that would allow or disallow a user to perform a DELETE query, but we need to programmatically determine if those rules apply to our current user.

The following example is a very small portion of a called template that controls access to an INSERT query:

```
<cfif IsAuthorized("DataSource", request.dsn, "delete")>
      <cfquery name="qryDeleteProduct" datasource="#request.dsn#">
      DELETE
      FROM Products
      WHERE Product_ID = #url.id#
      </cfquery>
<cfelse>
      <!--- display error indicating that this user
             doesn't have delete permissions --->
     <cf_error type="sec.perm.delete">
</cfif>
```

Wrapping Up

Locking, CFX tags, WDDX, and advanced security are all important things, although relatively easy to understand when it comes to how they work within ColdFusion. If I were to pick a personal favorite of the topics in this chapter, it would be the locking topic. It's rarely used properly, but hopefully, as more developers start to learn of its importance, good locking practice will become more pervasive.

CHAPTER

11

Stored Procedures and Advanced Database Connectivity

IN THIS CHAPTER:

Stored Procedures

Advanced Database Connectivity

In this chapter, we start by talking about how to write advanced SQL Server stored procedures. Knowing how to write stored procedures that reduce the load of ColdFusion can contribute big performance gains. Developers often use ColdFusion to do work that SQL Server can do much faster, with far fewer CPU and memory requirements. SQL Server stored procedures have the ability to perform loops, use conditional statements, create and access variables, and use an entire set of functions.

We also talk about the new ColdFusion 5.0 advanced database connectivity features that give you much more flexibility when connecting to a datasource than the standard DSN attribute of the <CFQUERY> tag. Using some of the new attributes available to <CFQUERY>, you can avoid the need to create datasources in the ColdFusion Administrator by supplying the required information in the <CFQUERY> tag. We talk more about that later in this chapter, but first, let's talk about stored procedures.

Stored Procedures

We've already seen some examples of stored procedures earlier, in Part II. But, to make sure we cover everything, let's go over exactly what a stored procedure is.

A stored procedure is a SQL statement stored on the database server that can be executed by simply calling its name. The stored procedure itself, once created, becomes a named entity on the SQL server, which can be used in T-SQL. It's not like a SQL View that acts like a temporary table; it's more like a program that can be executed when needed. A stored procedure can consist of either a single T-SQL statement, or a group of T-SQL statements with conditional logic.

Stored procedures are compiled at run time, meaning that once executed, each subsequent execution will run off compiled code. This compilation is sometimes referred to as procedure caching. In Part II, we talked about how SQL Server stores the execution plan for both T-SQL statements and stored procedures. This compilation is the same that we discussed earlier. In SQL Server 7.0 and later, both stored procedures and queries are compiled or cached upon execution, and subsequent executions run off precompiled, or cached code.

Stored procedures help organize your application by storing often used code in a central location. Imagine an application with hundreds of queries spread across hundreds of CFML templates. The administrative task of keeping track of every query embedded in the CFML code becomes daunting when faced with a large application. Stored procedures provide a single point of control over the queries in your application. If a table name changes in the database, rather than digging through piles of CFML, you simply look at each stored procedure, which is a much easier task.

Stored Procedures in ColdFusion

ColdFusion has extensive stored procedure support using the <CFQUERY> and <CFSTOREDPROC> tags. One of the more commonly asked questions at ColdFusion User Group meetings, and on the CF-TALK list is, "What's the trick to using stored procedures with ColdFusion?" Well, there really is no trick—it's a fairly easy concept to understand, as you'll see here.

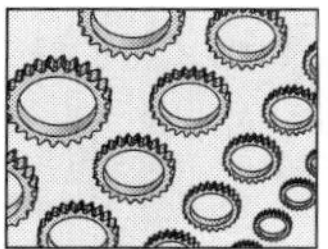

NOTE

The ColdFusion community is a very strong one. There are organized User Group meetings, and the CF-TALK list is easily the most popular ColdFusion related e-mail list.

<CFSTOREDPROC> is more robust than <CFQUERY>, and offers a few more advantages over <CFQUERY> when executing stored procedures. <CFQUERY> only allows open database connectivity (ODBC)-compliant code to be executed. This means that database servers that do not use ODBC-compliant code to execute stored procedures cannot make use of <CFQUERY>, and must use <CFSTOREDPROC> to execute the procedure. <CFSTOREDPROC> can also return output variables, retrieve multiple record sets, and also return status codes that aren't available in <CFQUERY>.

For the example code, we create a stored procedure that, in the beginning, is very simple, in order to establish the foundation for creating stored procedures. Later in this chapter, the examples get more complex as we introduce new types of abilities. The stored procedures themselves are introduced simply as examples—for the most part, they don't have a very useful real-world application. You might be able to use them for something effectively, but the intention here is to focus on the syntax, capabilities, and execution of stored procedures. If you find that the stored procedures fill a need, then by all means use them.

In the very beginning we use both <CFQUERY> and <CFSTOREDPROC> to execute the stored procedures, but as the examples get more complicated, we'll be sticking to <CFSTOREDPROC>.

<CFQUERY>

<CFQUERY> allows you to execute stored procedures using the following form:

```
<cfquery name="qryScriptLog" datasource="#request.dsn#">
exec ScriptLogger @ScriptName = '#cgi.script_name#'
</cfquery>
```

To execute a stored procedure using <CFQUERY>, simply use the EXEC statement, followed by the name of the stored procedure. The EXEC statement is actually shorthand for the EXECUTE statement. Both do the exact same thing, and using EXEC is considered perfectly good form.

The stored procedure in this example requires a parameter called *@ScriptName*. Both parameters and variables in T-SQL are called by placing the @ symbol before the variable name. Let's look at the code for the first stored procedure. The idea behind this stored procedure is to keep track of how many times a certain ColdFusion template has been executed on the server. The stored procedure assumes that the *ScriptLog* table exists. Here's the code to create that table:

```
CREATE TABLE ScriptLog
(
   ScriptName varchar (100) NULL,
   DateTimeStamp datetime NULL
)
```

And now, the stored procedure:

```
CREATE PROCEDURE ScriptLogger
(
@ScriptName varchar(100)
)
AS
INSERT INTO ScriptLog
(ScriptName, DateTimeStamp)
VALUES
(@ScriptName, GetDate())
```

The first line indicates that we want to create the stored procedure named ScriptLogger. Immediately following in parentheses, we must declare what variables we'll be using in the SQL statement. If you need to declare more than one variable, make sure to separate the variable name and data type definitions with commas. The queries that we use, or any other logic, should be placed after the AS statement. In this example, we insert the value of *@ScriptName*, and we use the GetDate() function to insert the most current date.

We talk more about this particular example in a second; but first, let's see how to use the <CFSTOREDPROC> tag to execute the stored procedure.

<CFSTOREDPROC>

<CFSTOREDPROC> gives you more control over the execution of your stored procedure than <CFQUERY> does. For example, you cannot retrieve multiple result sets using <CFQUERY>; you must use <CFSTOREDPROC>.

Let's use <CFSTOREDPROC> to execute our example stored procedure:

```
<cfstoredproc procedure="ScriptLogger" datasource="#request.dsn#">
<cfprocparam type="In"
             cfsqltype="CF_SQL_VARCHAR"
             dbvarname="@ScriptName"
             value="#cgi.script_name#">
</cfstoredproc>
```

In the <CFSTOREDPROC> tag, we name the stored procedure we want to execute. We also make sure not to forget the datasource. Because we are passing a parameter to the stored procedure, we need to use the <CFPROCPARAM> tag nested within <CFSTOREDPROC>.

<CFPROCPARAM> is used to pass parameters between the stored procedure and our application. We can send parameters to the stored procedure, or we can receive parameters from the stored procedure into our application. Let's look at an example of a simple stored procedure that creates an output variable, and use <CFSTOREDPROC> to pass that variable to the CFML template. We look at the stored procedure first:

```
CREATE PROCEDURE ReturnSomething
(
@ReturnThis int OUTPUT
)
AS
SET @ReturnThis = 12345
GO
```

This procedure doesn't do anything except set the value of *@ReturnThis* to 12345. When we declare *@ReturnThis*, the OUTPUT statement at the end is what tells the stored procedure that we're expecting to use the value outside of the stored procedure. To pull the value of *@ReturnThis* into a ColdFusion variable, we need to use the <CFPROCPARAM> tag:

```
<cfstoredproc procedure="ReturnSomething" datasource="#request.dsn#">
             <cfprocparam type="Out"
             cfsqltype="CF_SQL_INTEGER"
             variable="Returned"
```

```
            dbvarname="@ReturnThis">
</cfstoredproc>

<cfoutput>#Returned#</cfoutput>
```

The type attribute of <CFPROCPARAM> indicates that we're looking for an "Out" variable. By default, the type is "In", but we're going the opposite direction here. The variable attribute creates the variable we'll be placing in the value of the SQL variable listed in the *dbvarname* attribute.

You can create as many output variables as you like in a stored procedure, as long as you have a matching <CFPROCPARAM> tag. If you neglect to use the <CFPROCPARAM> tag for an output variable defined in a stored procedure, you get an error.

Conditional Expressions and Statements

If we were to include the <CFQUERY> query tag shown earlier on every page in our skate.shop application, then the *ScriptLog* table would quickly begin growing with each request. Whether or not it's wrong or right, for the sake of argument, we don't want a ton of records piling up.

Rather than inserting a new record for each request, let's change things a bit so that we start counting the number of times the script is hit on the fly. When we do this, the DateTimeStamp field of the table *ScriptLog* becomes a bit useless because we're going to aggregate the counts of the script names on the fly—the concept behind the data being stored is different, as we're now simply counting the scripts executed rather than keeping a historical record.

We're going to drop the DateTimeStamp field from the table entirely. We're also going to add a column called HitCount. To do this, you can run the following code in Query Analyzer:

```
ALTER TABLE ScriptLog
DROP COLUMN DateTimeStamp
ALTER TABLE ScriptLog
ADD HitCount int DEFAULT 0
```

Now that we've removed the DateTimeStamp column and added a HitCount column, it's time to modify the ScriptLogger stored procedure to reflect the new changes. In order to perform this new task of counting the executed scripts, we need to introduce some conditional logic into the stored procedure.

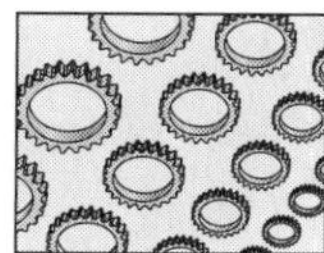

NOTE

Almost all of the programming elements discussed in this chapter, such as IF, CASE, etc., can be used in a regular query, and are not exclusive to stored procedures. It makes sense to talk about the syntax and form of these elements while talking about stored procedures because stored procedures are usually used to handle sets of tasks. When performing a number of tasks in a single procedure, you'll inevitably need to use most of what you see in this chapter.

IF

In order to count the scripts executed on our server, the stored procedure has to ask some questions first. If the value of the supplied variable, *@ScriptName*, doesn't exist in our *ScriptLog* table, then we need to add it before we can start counting it. Let's look at the code:

```
ALTER PROCEDURE ScriptLogger
(
@ScriptName varchar(100)
)
AS
IF (
   SELECT count(*)
   FROM ScriptLog
   WHERE ScriptName = @ScriptName
   ) = 0
BEGIN
INSERT INTO ScriptLog
(ScriptName, HitCount)
VALUES
(@ScriptName, 0)
END

UPDATE ScriptLog
SET HitCount = HitCount + 1
WHERE ScriptName = @ScriptName
GO
```

The IF statement checks to see if there are any records with the value of *@ScriptName*. If the value is zero, then we insert the value of *@ScriptName*, with a HitCount value of zero. The value of *HitCount* is initially set to zero because we want to keep our code simple—the subsequent update statement that simply increments the value of *HitCount* where the ScriptName equals the value of *@ScriptName* would need to be much more complicated if we inserted the record any other way.

CASE

The CASE statement in T-SQL evaluates a list of conditions and returns one of multiple possible result expressions. There are two forms of the CASE statement—a simple form and a "searchable" form. Here's an example of the CASE statement using the simple form:

```
SELECT animal,
   ProperName =
   CASE animal
    WHEN 'chicken' THEN 'Blue Beaked Kentucky Rooster'
    WHEN 'frog' THEN 'Red Spotted Albino Guatemalan Bullfrog'
    WHEN 'cow' THEN 'South American Pygmy Steer'
    WHEN 'goat' THEN 'North Canadian Weiner Goat'
    ELSE 'Not yet titled'
    END
FROM Animals
```

In this statement, we check for the existence of a specific animal, for instance, chicken, and replace that instance with a proper name. The value 'chicken' becomes 'Blue Beaked Kentucky Rooster', and so on. It's not changing the data in the database; it's simply changing the results. This statement returns a column called ProperName, and for every WHEN statement that is true, returns the THEN result. If none of the WHEN statements are true, the ELSE statement is returned. The results returned when running this query would look like this:

```
animal  ProperName
------- --------------------------------------
frog    Red Spotted Albino Guatemalan Bullfrog
chicken Blue Beaked Kentucky Rooster
goat    North Canadian Weiner Goat
cow     South American Pygmy Steer
fish    Not yet titled

(5 row(s) affected)
```

Because we didn't set up a case for 'fish', the ProperName column we created is filled with the value of the ELSE statement, 'Not yet titled'.

Replacing animals' types with imaginary proper names probably won't come in handy very often, so now that we know the format a little better, let's look at something that might come in more useful. Using the CASE statement, we can avoid performing a join to a table with generally static values, like a stock status table. Let's pretend that we have a table with a structure similar to the following:

```
Status_ID Status_Description
1         In Stock
2         Backordered
3         1-2 Weeks
```

Now, let's look at an example of a products table:

```
Product_ID Product_Name Status_ID
20123      Fork         1
20329      Ice Pick     1
23043      Swiss Cheese 2
21203      Rice         1
21234      Corvette     3
```

If we wanted to output the stock status of each product, we'd need to create a query that joined the two tables so that we could show the Status_Description column to the user. Here's what we'd have to do:

```
SELECT Product_Name, Status_Description
FROM Product
INNER JOIN Status
ON Product.Status_ID = Status.Status_ID
```

Joining the tables might not be that hard to perform in a query, but JOIN statements slow down queries. Because the values of our *Status* table will rarely change, it's probably safe to use a CASE statement instead, which eliminates the need for the JOIN statement, let alone the table. Here's how we could produce the same results using a CASE statement, which would also speed up our query:

```
SELECT Product_Name,
CASE status_id
   WHEN 1 THEN 'In Stock'
   WHEN 2 THEN 'Backordered'
   WHEN 3 THEN '1-2 Weeks'
   END
FROM Product
```

This query is much faster than using a JOIN statement, and reduces the need for an extra table. This, of course, isn't practical if either the values need to change, or if the number of WHEN statements become unruly. The more WHEN statements within the CASE, the slower the query gets. It's hard to say when it would be better to use a JOIN versus a CASE, but in this example, the CASE wins. The best way to know which one will provide better results is to test both. Try it out and see which one is faster, and use the faster one.

The second form of CASE is called a Searched CASE. This form is more powerful than the simple evaluation we used for our previous CASE examples. Here's an example of the Searched CASE form:

```
SELECT 'Price Range' =
   CASE
      WHEN price < 20 THEN '20 and Under'
      WHEN price BETWEEN 20 AND 40 THEN '20-40'
      WHEN price > 40 THEN '40 and Above'
   END
FROM Product
```

With the Searched CASE form, the WHEN conditions can be ranges. In this example, it's clear that you're not limited to simple less than or greater than expressions. You can use pretty much any kind of expression you might be able to use in a WHERE statement.

Looping

Yes, you can loop in T-SQL. This comes as a surprise to a lot of ColdFusion developers who are so used to using ColdFusion to do everything, and using SQL to spit out data. As we've seen so far, SQL can do a quite a bit in the ways of conditional statements and processing, so the fact that you can loop shouldn't be a surprise.

To use a loop in T-SQL, we use the WHILE statement. The WHILE statement sets a condition for the repeated execution of a SQL statement or statement block. The statements are executed repeatedly as long as the specified condition is true. The loop can be controlled from within the loop using BREAK and CONTINUE. We'll talk about these controls in a second, but first let's set up an example of a loop.

For this example, assume that we have a product table with a price column. Someone in the organization has decided that all the products in the store will have their prices doubled until the average price is greater than $15 dollars. Here's what the code would look like:

```
WHILE (SELECT AVG(price) FROM product) < $15
BEGIN
   UPDATE product
      SET price = price * 2
   SELECT MAX(price) FROM product
   IF (SELECT MAX(price) FROM product) > $40
      BREAK
   ELSE
      CONTINUE
END
```

This example doubles every price until the highest price is greater than $40, in which case it stops looping. If every price in our table were $1.00, the loop would iterate only four times and then finish, because the average price would exceed $15 dollars after four iterations. If every price were $1.00, the final price after doubling four times would be $16, which, of course, is more than $15. With every price at $1.00, the price never exceeds $40, because the average price is exceeded before any of the prices hit $40.

Let's pretend that all of the prices are $1.00, except for one, which is $10. The loop would only iterate three times, because the $10 price would exceed the limit of $40 set within the IF statement, which would execute the BREAK statement, stopping the loop.

This example is an interesting one to play with, so to make it easy to test, you can use the following code. It uses a temporary table, which we'll talk about later in this chapter. You can modify the following testing code to suit your needs; each commented block can be executed one after another, or you can execute the entire block at once.

```
-- ONLY RUN IF THE TABLE EXISTS
DROP TABLE ##temp_prices
-- REFRESH THE TEMP TABLE
CREATE TABLE ##temp_prices
(
price money
)

-- TOSS SOME VALUES INTO THE TABLE
INSERT INTO ##temp_prices (price) VALUES (1.00)
INSERT INTO ##temp_prices (price) VALUES (1.00)
INSERT INTO ##temp_prices (price) VALUES (1.00)
```

```
INSERT INTO ##temp_prices (price) VALUES (10.00)
INSERT INTO ##temp_prices (price) VALUES (1.00)
INSERT INTO ##temp_prices (price) VALUES (1.00)

-- RUN THE LOOP
DECLARE @loop_iteration int
SET @loop_iteration = 1

WHILE (SELECT AVG(price) FROM ##temp_prices) < $15
BEGIN
   PRINT(@loop_iteration)
   SET @loop_iteration = @loop_iteration + 1
   UPDATE ##temp_prices
      SET price = price * 2
   SELECT MAX(price) FROM ##temp_prices
   IF (SELECT MAX(price) FROM ##temp_prices) > $40
      BREAK
   ELSE
      CONTINUE
END
PRINT 'Too high'

-- SEE WHAT IT DID
SELECT *
FROM ##temp_prices
```

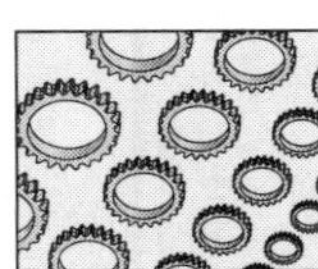

NOTE

The code example shown here will throw an error if you've never executed it before because of the DROP TABLE statement in the first line. To avoid this, simply comment out the first line of code when executing the statement for the first time. It is possible to determine programmatically whether the table already exists, but that goes a bit beyond the scope of the subject at hand.

There's an obvious flaw in this example: if the price exceeds $40.00, the loop will quit, leaving all of the other prices well below our $15.00 average. If we *really* wanted to perform such a blanket procedure on our prices without the process being thwarted by a single high price, we could, but it would change the process entirely. We could flag the high price, and remove the BREAK, letting the WHILE condition take care of stopping the loop when the average price hit $15.00 or more.

The WHILE statement is like a simplified version of <CFLOOP>. If we wanted to step through a record set like we can with <CFLOOP QUERY="whatever">, then we need to use a different feature of SQL Server: cursors.

Cursors

Operations in T-SQL normally act on a complete set of rows. When you perform an UPDATE statement, you're updating all the rows that meet a certain criteria. When you execute a SELECT statement, you receive records that meet a certain criteria, just like the UPDATE and DELETE statements. We call the results of these statements a result set, or record set. Both terms are interchangeable, and no harm is done in doing so.

Cursors, if set up to do so, allow the developer to perform operations on each record, one record at a time. If this sounds processor intensive to you, then you've hit the nail right on the head. It's very processor intensive.

Cursors require lots of system resources because of their nature—stepping through a record set in SQL can have the following adverse affects:

- Cursor use can lead to deadlocking and concurrency issues. Even when making provisions to avoid these deadlocks by using cursor options such as READ_ONLY and OPTIMISTIC, problems can still occur.
- Cursors use the tempdb database for temporary storage of cursor data. If cursors are in wide use on your server, tempdb can reach undesirables sizes.
- It's very easy to tie up a lot of resources with improper cursor programming practices. For instance, developers often forget to deallocate the resources provided to a cursor, which requires an extra step. (We'll show an example a bit later.)

Hopefully by now I've discouraged you from ever using cursors. Some developers claim there are tasks that absolutely must use cursors, but I don't feel that way. I have personally never seen the need to use a cursor—if I need to step through a set of records, I hand it off to ColdFusion. Using <CFLOOP QUERY="queryname"> can provide any functionality I'd need when using a cursor, and more. But even before I get to that point, I usually try to step back and rethink my application a bit. Chances are I can redesign the process to the point where stepping through each record isn't needed.

While I know that I've bad-mouthed cursors quite a lot, I still think it's important to know what they are and how to write them. Some developers still swear by cursors, and knowing how cursors work can help you think of alternatives, and give you some well grounded ammunition to use in your next "cursors vs. alternative methods" battle.

Here's an example of a cursor that uses data from a temporary table, for testing purposes only. It just wouldn't be a good idea to do this on a production box—this simply makes it easier for you to test the cursor examples we'll be going over, without having to make any "permanent" tables. (Permanent isn't exactly the right word considering how easy it is to remove a table in SQL, but I think you get the idea.)

```
-- CREATE LOCAL TEMP TABLE
CREATE TABLE #temp_animals
(
animal_name varchar(20),
animal_type varchar(20),
animal_profession varchar(20)
)

-- INSERT VALUES
INSERT INTO #temp_animals
(animal_name, animal_type, animal_profession)
VALUES
('Horchata', 'Chimpanzee', 'Actor')

INSERT INTO #temp_animals
(animal_name, animal_type, animal_profession)
VALUES
('Mr. Ed', 'Horse', 'Actor')

INSERT INTO #temp_animals
(animal_name, animal_type, animal_profession)
VALUES
('Dog', 'Dog', 'Pet')

INSERT INTO #temp_animals
(animal_name, animal_type, animal_profession)
VALUES
('Mr. Belvedere', 'Cat', 'Pet')

-- DECLARE VARIABLES FOR CURSOR
DECLARE @animal_name varchar(20),
@animal_type varchar(20),
@animal_profession varchar(20)

-- CREATE CURSOR
DECLARE animals_cursor CURSOR
   FOR SELECT * FROM #temp_animals
OPEN animals_cursor
FETCH NEXT FROM animals_cursor
INTO @animal_name, @animal_type, @animal_profession
```

```
WHILE @@FETCH_STATUS = 0
BEGIN
   PRINT ' '
   PRINT 'Animal: ' + @animal_name
   PRINT 'Type: ' + @animal_type
   PRINT 'Profession: ' + @animal_profession

   -- Get the next animal.
   FETCH NEXT FROM animals_cursor
   INTO @animal_name, @animal_type, @animal_profession
END
CLOSE animals_cursor
DEALLOCATE animals_cursor
GO
DROP TABLE #temp_animals
```

The first half of this block of code creates and inserts data into the *#temp_animals* table. We talk about temp tables in the next section in more detail. I find that using animals as examples completely absolves me from any type of political backlash, although it just occurred to me that I won't be able to put the "Never tested on animals" sticker on the box. (That was a shameless joke, and you can blame the editors if it happens again, because I can't make any promises that I *won't* do something like that again.) After inserting the data, we declare some variables that we'll use in the cursor.

For each column we'll be using in the cursor, we'll need a variable declared. In this example, we use each column in the *#temp_animals* table, so we need a variable for each column. Giving the variables the same name as the column helps to avoid confusion. There's no conflict in SQL because *@animal_name* is a variable, whereas the column animal_name is an entity. SQL knows the difference between the two.

The life of the cursor officially starts when we issue the following command:

```
DECLARE animals_cursor CURSOR
   FOR SELECT * FROM #temp_animals
```

CURSOR is actually a special kind of data type in SQL Server, which makes it possible to create a cursor with a command as simple as the one above. We could do all sorts of things in between the time we create the cursor and the time we actually start to use it. To use the cursor, we have to open it using the OPEN command, like so:

```
OPEN animals_cursor
```

Once the cursor is open, we can begin using it by populating our local variables with the values of the first record in the cursor:

```
FETCH NEXT FROM animals_cursor
INTO @animal_name, @animal_type, @animal_profession
```

You'll see the command again a bit later, in the code at the end of a WHILE loop. Before I explain this first command, let's look at the rest of the code. Doing so will help you understand why we repeat the command.

```
WHILE @@FETCH_STATUS = 0
BEGIN
...
   FETCH NEXT FROM animals_cursor
   INTO @animal_name, @animal_type, @animal_profession
END
```

For now, ignore any code right after BEGIN. *@@FETCH_STATUS* is a global system variable, and can contain one of a few possible values:

- 0 (FETCH statement was successful.)
- –1 (FETCH statement failed.)
- –2 (The fetched row was missing.)

The WHILE loops over each record while *@@FETCH_STATUS* is 0. The second FETCH command fetches the next record at the end of each iteration, and if there is a row to fetch, *@@FETCH_STATUS* remains 0. If there is no row, *@@FETCH_STATUS* will not equal 0, which will stop the loop.

The first FETCH statement outside of the loop establishes the first record, and also sets the *@@FETCH_STATUS* variable to equal 0, which kicks off the loop.

Within the loop, we perform some type of operation on each row. In the supplied example, we simply print the name of the animals and their professions, using the following code:

```
PRINT ' '
PRINT 'Animal: ' + @animal_name
PRINT 'Type: ' + @animal_type
PRINT 'Profession: ' + @animal_profession
```

The results of the above would look something like this:

```
Animal: Horchata
Type: Chimpanzee
Profession: Actor

Animal: Mr. Ed
Type: Horse
Profession: Actor

Animal: Dog
Type: Dog
Profession: Pet

Animal: Mr. Belvedere
Type: Cat
Profession: Pet
```

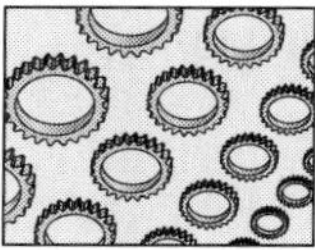

NOTE

When I was a kid, there was a guy in my neighborhood who ended up becoming a professional skateboarder, and is now a pretty well-known actor. He had a dog named Dog. I remember playing with his kid brother, and this dog came out and someone ran out saying "Dog, get back in the house right now!" and I thought that maybe they weren't very bright. I ended up finding out that Dog was indeed the dog's name, and I have always thought that was funny. I've never felt confident enough with my dry humor to be able to name my fish Fish, but maybe someday. Mr. Belvedere is the name of a cat I had, which was named after the TV show of the same name.

Printing the stuff is a very elementary task; you could just as easily INSERT the data in the cursor into another table, like so:

```
INSERT INTO another_table
(name, date_entered)
VALUES
(@animal_name, getdate())
```

You can pretty much perform any valid SQL statement for each record. This is just another reason why I don't like cursors—it's very easy to get carried away. From the looks of the code, it seems like no big deal to insert something for each record, but imagine doing it for 500,000 records, or worse yet, 10,000,000 records. That could bring a server to its knees, not to mention cause all sorts of deadlocking issues. The cursor would take forever to run, and would lock the table used to populate the cursor. My wife thinks this phrase is funny, but in this context there's nothing funny about it—cursors give you a lot of rope to hang yourself with.

The most important thing to do if a cursor is used is to close and deallocate the cursor, using the following code:

```
CLOSE animals_cursor
DEALLOCATE animals_cursor
```

A lot of developers forget to deallocate the cursor, which means that the cursor is still using resources. Remember how we had to declare the cursor, and then open it? We now have to do the same thing, in reverse order; otherwise the cursor will just sit there, hogging up our precious system resources.

Here are some tips for using cursors if you absolutely must use them (which you should never need to do):

- Do everything you can to avoid using them.
- Try putting the tempdb database on its own physical drive. Speeding up the tempdb database can increase performance, because the cursor will use the tempdb database to store temporary tables.
- Always CLOSE and DEALLOCATE a cursor.
- Try to FETCH as small a result set as possible. Don't SELECT the entire table of 200,000 records when you only need ten.
- Find a very good SQL book, and learn all you can about cursors. I've only given a general overview of cursors; there are more performance gains available for those willing to dive into the many ways of setting them up.

Temporary Tables

There are two types of temporary tables, and we've seen both of them in the examples in this chapter: global temporary tables that are available to the entire set of sessions on the server, and local temporary tables that are available to the current session only. Creating a local or global temporary table takes the exact same code, except the table names are referenced in a slightly different way. Here's how to create a local temporary table:

```
CREATE TABLE #temp_animals
(
animal_name varchar(20),
animal_type varchar(20),
animal_profession varchar(20)
)
```

And here's how to create a global temporary table:

```
CREATE TABLE ##temp_animals
(
animal_name varchar(20),
animal_type varchar(20),
animal_profession varchar(20)
)
```

There is only one difference between the two blocks of code—the name of the table. Global temporary tables use two # signs, and local temporary tables use a single # sign. When referring to the table later on, you call the table by its name, either *#temp_animals,* or *##temp_animals* if it's global.

SQL Server transparently places a unique sequence of numbers at the beginning of your temporary table name. It does this because several people could execute a stored procedure that creates multiple renditions of the same temporary table, and SQL Server needs to know which one to actually use for which person. It stores the names of the temporary tables in the *sysobjects* table in the tempdb database. Because SQL needs some room to insert this unique suffix, temporary table names cannot exceed 116 characters. This sentence is less than 116 characters. In fact, it's only 41 characters, including spaces. That should give you an idea of how big you can actually make the names.

You can still drop a temporary table just like any other table by using the following command:

```
DROP TABLE #temp_animals
```

Of course, it's not a good idea to do that to your regular tables, but it's a perfectly OK way of getting rid of a temporary table. Temporary tables will also drop by themselves. Local tables will drop in the following ways:

- If the temporary table is in a stored procedure, the table drops when the stored procedure completes execution. Nested stored procedures still have access to the table, as it's dropped at the end of the execution of the main stored procedure. The calling process does not have access to the temporary table.
- Local temporary tables drop when the session ends. In ColdFusion, the session usually ends shortly after the request is made to the SQL Server, and SQL Server returns the requested data.

Global temporary tables are dropped when the session that created the tables ends, and all other sessions using the table have finished.

Temporary tables within stored procedures or triggers are entirely different entities than tables created in regular SQL Statements. They are basically scoped—within stored procedures and triggers, they are scoped to stored procedures, nested procedures, and triggers.

You cannot assign a FOREIGN KEY to a temporary table, although you can assign other constraints just like a regular table.

Multiple Result Sets

Using <CFSTOREDPROC>, it's possible to execute a stored procedure that produces multiple result sets that can be used within your ColdFusion code as separate query objects. Consider this example for a moment:

```
CREATE PROCEDURE multiples
AS
SELECT *
FROM table1
SELECT *
FROM table2
```

This stored procedure would return multiple result sets. To access those result sets in ColdFusion, we'd need the following code:

```
<cfstoredproc procedure="multiples" datasource="#request.dsn#">
   <cfprocresult name="qryTable1" resultset="1">
   <cfprocresult name="qryTable2" resultset="2">
</cfstoredproc>
```

Each <CFPROCRESULT> tag nested within the <CFSTOREDPROC> tags will return each result set. The result set number corresponds with the order in which the query was executed within the stored procedure.

We can then use the name of each result set and treat it as if it were like any other query. We can output it using <CFOUTPUT> and we can use it within a query of queries, or anywhere else a query object is valid. This has obvious benefits, the first being that only one transaction was made for two sets of records. If we were to use <CFQUERY>, two transactions would occur, as well as two separate connections.

It is entirely possible to run a single stored procedure that produces every result needed for a page request. In our skate.shop example, we use <CFSTOREDPROC> with multiple result sets several times this way, although we don't go so far as to execute a single stored procedure.

Advanced Database Connectivity

ColdFusion 5.0 includes an entire set of new database connection options, with an attribute available to <CFQUERY> and <CFSTOREDPROC> called *connectString*. With the *connectString* attribute, developers can connect to databases in ways never possible in any previous version of ColdFusion. One of the most interesting things that *connectString* allows is to connect to a database without ever creating a datasource.

The connectString attribute can also help you do the following:

- Pass additional parameters to a preexisting ODBC datasource. Some database platforms allow you to pass more information than the ColdFusion Administrator passes. For instance, you can pass the application name and workstation ID to a Sybase database.
- Bypass ColdFusion Administrator settings. For example, if you have set up a connection in the ColdFusion Administrator to use a particular login and password to the database, you can supply a different user name and password with *connectString* to override the ColdFusion settings.
- Access databases on the database server without ever creating a datasource in the Administrator. This can be helpful for applications with several ColdFusion servers; rather than defining a datasource for each ColdFusion server, you can use the *connectString* variable to make the connection, thus eliminating the need to add the datasource on each server.

The *connectString* attribute is available to following tags:

- <CFQUERY>
- <CFSTOREDPROC>
- <CFUPDATE>
- <CFINSERT>
- <CFGRIDUPDATE>

The *connectString* attribute itself requires a list of arguments and values. Here's an example:

```
<cfquery
   name="qryGetShorty"
```

```
    datasource="#request.dsn#"
    connectString="UID=oscar;PWD=dde0d3csr3;">
...
```

The rest of the code is cut short to put emphasis on the *connectString* attribute. In this example, we're still using a datasource set up in the ColdFusion Administrator. We're simply supplying the user name and password, which overrides anything we have set in the Administrator.

The value of the connectString attribute should be a set of arguments and values separated by semicolons. You can't just make up arguments; each database server has its own unique set of arguments. SQL Server 2000 accepts the following arguments:

- **DRIVER** The database driver to use; in the case of SQL Server 2000 it would contain {SQL SERVER}.
- **SERVER** The name of the server, or IP. Can be a qualified network name, like BUGGERMUFFIN, or an IP.
- **UID** The user name for the database.
- **PWD** The password for the database.
- **DATABASE** The name of the database to connect to.

To connect to a datasource without setting up the datasource in the Administrator, use the following form:

```
<cfquery
   name="qryGetShorty"
   dbtype="dynamic"
   datasource="_ _dynamic_ _"
   connectString="DRIVER={SQL SERVER};SERVER=SQL0126;UID=cf;PWD=;DATABASE=movies">
```

Once again, I've cut off everything after the first half of the <CFQUERY>. In order to make a completely dynamic connection to a datasource, we need to indicate that the *dbtype* is "*dynamic*" and the *datasource* is "_ _*dynamic*_ _." There are two underscores before and after the word dynamic. If you don't supply these underscores, your query will return an error. The *connectString* attribute supplies all of the necessary arguments to the server.

If we wanted every query in our application to be dynamic, it would be a good idea to create a variable in application.cfm. We would call it *request.CS*, or something of that nature, to place the connection string value; that way we wouldn't have to enter a lengthy string into the connectString attribute for every query. For example:

```
<cfset request.CS = "DRIVER={SQL SERVER};SERVER=SQL0126;UID=cf;PWD=;DATABASE=movies">

<cfquery
   name="qryGetShorty"
   dbtype="dynamic"
   datasource="__dynamic__"
   connectstring="#request.CS#">
```

Wrapping Up

We've taken a closer look at some of the capabilities of stored procedures, and looked at some of the new ColdFusion database connectivity features. I'd encourage you to learn as much as you can about writing stored procedures and using more advanced language in the procedures. But always remember—sometimes SQL can do things better and faster than ColdFusion, and vice versa. Even if you're satisfied with the performance of a block of code run on one platform, try to see how it runs on another platform. You'll learn very quickly where the strengths and weaknesses of each platform lie.

CHAPTER

12

<CFTRANSACTION>

IN THIS CHAPTER:

Database Transactions

How SQL Server 2000 Handles Transactions

Locking

The <CFTRANSACTION> Tag

Controlling Transactions

One of the most commonly misunderstood tags in ColdFusion is the <CFTRANSACTION> tag. The ColdFusion documentation states that <CFTRANSACTION> groups multiple queries into a single unit. This definition is pretty weak, considering all of the things that the tag can do besides simply grouping queries into a single transaction.

In order to fully understand how <CFTRANSACTION> works, we need to know about database transactions. Therefore, before talking about <CFTRANSACTION> in detail, we'll learn about database transactions, transaction locking, commits and rollbacks, and isolation levels. All of these topics will greatly aid in the understanding of the tag, and will help you to write better applications.

Database Transactions

Relational databases, like SQL Server 2000, are designed to be used by many people at the same time reading and writing data from multiple databases, or even a single database, simultaneously. If we did not have database transactions, the requests to change, access, or add data to a database would become a near impossible feat, as the data would undoubtedly become corrupt. Transactions prevent data from being written by two people at the same time. Without transactions, two users could attempt to edit the same data, which would possibly become corrupt. Transactions make it possible for the database to support thousands of requests to change data.

To understand transactions, it's good to think of a real world example. One of the easiest examples to understand is that of a bank transaction. Most of us have at least some experience with making deposits and transferring money from one account to another, or even from bank to bank. Each action involves a transaction of some sort. I'm not a banker myself, so I wouldn't be able to describe exactly what happens in a bank transaction, but if we think in laymen's terms of how bank transactions work, it will serve as a good example of how to describe database transactions.

I use a bank that allows me to transfer money from one account to another. I also have a credit card with that bank, and I can transfer money from any one of my accounts to my credit card, which would effectively be the same as making a payment to the card. Let's say I want to transfer $125 into my credit card from my checking account to make a payment. When I make the request to transfer these funds, the transaction probably performs the following tasks in order:

- It checks to see if $125 is available in the checking account.
- It checks to see that there are no restrictions on transferring to the credit card.

- If all conditions are met, it transfers funds from the checking account into the credit card.
- It logs the transactions for statements, auditing, and whatever else banks are interested in tracking.

Nothing is done in this transaction until everything checks out, which means that the money must be available, and the credit card account must have no restrictions that would impede the ability to make the transfer. The money doesn't leave the checking account until the second to last step in the transaction, where the transaction is committed.

Let's show another example. In this case, let's think about a much more lengthy process involving money. If you've been involved in the purchasing of a home, or even if you haven't, you probably know that there is nothing simple about the process. Once you find the home you want, you kick off a serious transaction, both in the amount of money at stake, and in the number of actions that take place within that transaction. Here's a basic run down of what happens when you are settled on buying a particular home, and the current owners of the home have accepted your offer. I'm not an expert on home buying, so the steps may differ from home purchase to home purchase, but I think you'll get the idea. Each one of the steps here usually has a lot of subtasks within it, but we don't need to worry about those. Assume that each step is relatively complicated, perhaps more than it should be.

- Get approved for a loan.
- Enter the escrow period.
- Order home inspections.
- Undergo a detailed credit history examination.
- Agree to any covenants, conditions, and restrictions.
- Agree to any Homeowners Association rules.
- Notarize all important documents.
- Transfer money from the loan company to the previous owner.
- Close of escrow period.
- Get keys from previous owner.

I've oversimplified the process. I'm sure there's a lot more to purchasing a home (I've done it once myself, and it was a blur of paperwork), but the idea behind the transaction is more important. The escrow period acts as a sort of transaction, and the transaction isn't final, or committed, until the escrow period closes, and the keys are handed over to the new owner.

With those two examples in mind, let's get our minds back to relational databases. Imagine that you have a set of SQL statements that each depend on each other. Rather than getting too deep into the details for now, let's assume that there are four separate SQL statements, and the fourth SQL statement depends on the previous three statements to succeed before it will run. Now, to make things a little more complicated, let's assume that the second statement inserts some data, and the third statement updates some data. Database transactions allow you to commit those four statements in a single step, rather than four distinct steps, and additionally, database transactions allow you to not execute the transaction if any one of its subtasks fail.

This kind of functionality is what makes it possible to execute complicated tasks with possibly thousands of transactions per second, without widespread data corruption. But, as is usually the case with databases, there is a cost to this kind of functionality. Transaction support means that resources must be set aside temporarily to support the results of the transaction until the transaction completes. Also, depending on how the transaction is executed, records involved in a transaction can be locked exclusively until the transaction is complete, which means that other clients are prevented from accessing the records until unlocked. We'll talk more about how to effectively write transactions in the next section.

How SQL Server 2000 Handles Transactions

Because we've put so much focus on SQL Server 2000 in this book, I thought it would be a good idea to get a further understanding of how transactions work specifically on SQL Server 2000. A lot of the descriptions and explanations might equally apply to previous versions of SQL Server, or even perhaps other relational databases that support transactions.

We won't be talking about it much more than beyond this paragraph, but it's worth pointing out that the version of MySQL that we talked about in Part I of this book does not support transactions, although the latest version apparently does. The developers of MySQL felt that individual, or *atomic operations* (a term we will discuss shortly), were more stable than transactional operations. They've recently updated their software to support transactions based on the publics' request for the feature, but they still feel transactional operations aren't the best way of doing things. I mention this merely to make the point that there are alternative theories behind data concurrency, not as a criticism of MySQL. I probably also make the point that Microsoft isn't your only option, since MySQL now supports both paradigms of operations.

ACID

ACID is not a warm and fuzzy sounding acronym when it comes to databases. Visions of databases being eaten away by a liquid with corrosive abilities promote bad feelings to say the least, but the term itself really is a good thing. The acronym ACID is used when describing how a transaction should be designed. ACID stands for the following four properties, each of which must be present in order to consider a block of statements a true transaction. Consider them rules to live by when designing transactions:

- Atomicity (a term we heard in the previous section)
- Consistency
- Isolation
- Durability

Atomicity

The term *atomic operations* was brought up earlier when talking about MySQL transaction support. Unfortunately, MySQL has a different definition of the term *atomic* as it relates to transactions. When MySQL uses the term atomic operation, it means a single SQL statement, or database operation, not a sequence of SQL statements.

In SQL Server 2000, *atomicity* means that a transaction must be an atomic unit of work. If every step in the transaction succeeds, then the entire transaction is committed. If any one part of the transaction fails, the entire transaction fails.

Consistency

Consistency suggests that all data modified by a transaction should remain in a consistent state. The transaction should follow any rules set by the design of the database. For example, a transaction shouldn't bypass the primary key rule of a table, and insert its own generated value. The transaction should allow the database to set its own value for a primary key column. Basically, transactions should do things above and beyond what a normal single SQL statement would do. I realize that is a rather vague definition, but unfortunately there's no real blanket statement that can be made, except that data should remain consistent. In my own terms, your transaction shouldn't alter the database structure, or primary key structures, or indexes, or anything "internal".

The reason for consistency will become more evident when we talk about rollbacks. Rollbacks allow a previous transaction to work as a sort of undo button, returning the database to an original statement. Imagine a transaction that renames every table in the database to the table's names in Pig Latin. These new tables are used by developers—who write billions of lines of code that depend on the accuracy of these table names. Someone decides, after having some kind of epiphany, to rollback the transaction that gave birth to the Pig Latin tables. Think for a moment of the chaos that would ensue, as developers begin to hunt down the person who rendered their billions of lines of code useless. Billions of lines of code based on Pig Latin–named tables that are then reverted to normally named tables is the reason why the rule for consistency exists.

Isolation

Transactions should use the state of data in the database that existed when the transaction started. Modifications made by transactions running concurrently must be isolated from modifications made by any other concurrent transactions. This means that if Transaction A starts, it uses a set of data that existed when it started, and if Transaction B starts while Transaction A is still running, Transaction B also sees the same set. If Transaction B started after Transaction A has already completely, Transaction B will see a data set that has been modified by Transaction A. Neither Transaction A nor B sees data in an intermediate state — they only see data when the transaction has been committed.

Durability

A transaction is designed to provide permanent results. If the server crashes miserably halfway through a transaction, the transaction is never committed; therefore, no permanent changes are made to the database. Once the transaction has been committed, the changes are permanent.

Locking

Before I explain locking as it relates to SQL Server 2000, I should point out that I'm not referring to ColdFusion locking using the <CFLOCK> tag. <CFLOCK> performs a different kind of function — it maintains data consistency for variables on the ColdFusion server. Database transaction locking is a similar, but, at the same time, much different animal.

SQL Server 2000 uses locking to ensure transactional integrity and database consistency. Locking prevents users from reading data being changed by other users, and prevents multiple users from changing the same data at the same time. If locking isn't used, data within the database could become corrupt. Locking is pretty much automatic in SQL Server. When you run an update statement, the table is temporarily locked as the update occurs.

To help explain locking, let's step back a bit and think about our fund transfer example. Remember that we wanted to transfer $125.00 from my checking account to my credit card. In order for this to happen without money flying all over the place, the banking system needs to do some locking as the transaction occurs. At the start of the transaction, the banking system locks the checking account so that no other transactions try to change the balance. Imagine the problems that could occur if the account wasn't locked, and during the transfer of $125.00, the account was emptied somehow during the transaction. The money the bank was transferring wouldn't really be there at all, and might end up being credited to my credit card account. While it might be nice, it would be wrong. The lock is vital in making sure that the money, or data, is updated correctly. That kind of lock would be considered an exclusive lock, which would disallow any kind of activity on the account while the transaction was in progress.

In this case, it might be safe to only use a shared lock, which might allow me to check the balance of my account as the transaction was executing. It might show I still had $125.00 in my account, but if I were to try and move that money anywhere, it would disallow me to do so until the transaction that was moving $125.00 to my credit card was complete. I know bank processes are more sophisticated than this, but you get the idea.

We'll talk more about exclusive and shared locks in a moment, but before we do, I'd like to point out that ColdFusion doesn't have any control over how the database performs its locks. That kind of thing is usually handled on the fly by the database itself. SQL Server locks resources automatically at a level appropriate to the task. SQL Server uses the following types of locks for their respective tasks:

Lock Type	Description
Shared	Used for operations that do not change or update data (read-only operations), such as SELECT statements.
Update	Used on resources that can be updated. Prevents a common form of deadlock that occurs when multiple sessions are reading, locking, and potentially updating resources later.

Lock Type	Description
Exclusive	Used for data-modification operations, such as INSERT, UPDATE, or DELETE. Ensures that multiple updates cannot be made to the same resource at the same time.

As you can see, SQL Server has a pretty set plan for how it will lock individual SQL statements automatically. You can override these plans, but for now we're not concerned with overriding the plans. There isn't much of a need to lock a single UPDATE statement; if you feel there is a need, either because you're getting deadlocking errors, or for other, similar issues, then your application could probably do well with a performance overhaul. Something is wrong in the application when you need to override SQL's automatic locking modes.

Deadlocking errors are a pretty big concern for most developers, as they do occur. We should take a look at what causes deadlocks, and how to reduce them.

Avoiding Deadlocks

Before we even start talking about how to avoid deadlocks, let's make one thing clear—you cannot avoid deadlocks entirely. There is always a possibility that deadlocks will occur in a transactional database. The number of deadlocks can be drastically reduced using a few good techniques and design principles, but always keep in mind that they will never be fully eradicated.

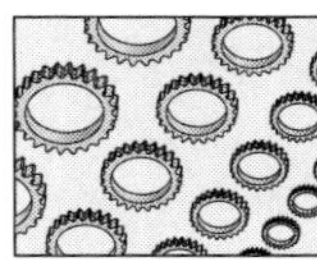

NOTE

Deadlocks are often confused with normal locking. They're somewhat similar in how they work, and locking in general is the root cause of deadlocking, but they're not the same thing. Normal locks wait for a resource to be released, and will keep waiting until the resource is released. There is no timeout on a normal, SQL-initiated lock. Deadlocks, as we'll learn in this section, are locks that fall into cyclical dependency. We'll understand over the course of the section how a deadlock occurs, but put in simple terms, for deadlocks to occur, it requires at least two locks to lock each other out of a resource.

Deadlocks are always a possibility because of the way SQL Server locks transactions. As we talked about in previous sections, if SQL Server didn't lock tables during updates and inserts, there would be a possibility of data corruption.

Deadlocks occur when there is a cyclical dependency between two or more transactions, or threads, for a set of resources. A transaction may acquire one or more resources (for example, locks). If the resource being acquired is currently owned by another transaction, the first transaction may have to wait for the owning, or original transaction to release the target resource. The waiting transaction is said to have a dependency on the owning transaction for that particular resource. This is where the term cyclical dependency comes from—each transaction goes back and forth waiting for the resource to be free, each locking the other out. If this kind of thing went unchecked, the server might start to hog resources for these deadlocks, so SQL Server detects them immediately and kills both transactions.

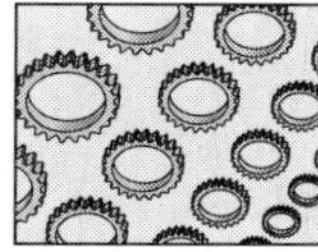

NOTE

When a deadlock occurs, SQL Server chooses to kill one of the transactions involved in the deadlock. It does a rollback on the victim, and notifies the victim of the deadlock, and continues the other transaction involved in the deadlock. SQL Server usually chooses the transaction that is the least expensive, CPU-wise, to rollback.

Minimizing Deadlocks

There are a lot of benefits to reducing deadlocks in your application, despite the most obvious one, which is the reduction of errors displayed to your users. Also, more system resources will be available because fewer rollbacks will occur from failed transactions. Users of your site who encounter deadlock errors will get a very nasty error that looks something like this:

```
Your transaction (process ID #52) was deadlocked on thread
 resources with another process and has been chosen as the
deadlock victim. Rerun your transaction.
```

To minimize deadlocks, follow these simple rules:

- Within transactions, always access database entities like tables in the same order. We'll see why in a bit.
- Avoid user interaction within a transaction. This rule isn't that relevant to ColdFusion developers, but to developers who use things like cursors on a client machine, where user interaction is the norm, this can be a problem. If the transaction has to wait for a user to do something, the resources in the transaction are like waiting for that user. Users are notorious for doing things like going to lunch, going into a meeting, or going home for the night while in the middle of things like transactions.
- Keep transactions short, and in one batch. If you have several very short transactions that could be lumped into a single transaction, it might be a good idea to do so, although you have to be careful. Sometimes several smaller

transactions can reduce the possibilities of deadlocks better than a larger single transaction. There's no real set rule of thumb for this, but the closest we can come is to keep transactions as short as possible.

- Use a low isolation level. We haven't talked about isolation levels in detail yet, but we do in the section called "Isolation Levels."

Access Entities in the Same Order If all concurrent transactions access objects in the same order, deadlocks are less likely to occur. For example, if two concurrent transactions obtain a lock on the *Products* table, and then on the *Product_Var* table, one transaction is blocked on the *Products* table until the other transaction is completed. After the first transaction commits or rolls back, the second continues. A deadlock does not occur.

If we were to run two concurrent transactions that access the *Products* and *Product_Var* tables in opposite orders, we'd be guaranteed a deadlock. For this example, Transaction A is designed to update the *Products* table, and then the *Product_Var* table. Transaction B does the same thing, but in exact opposite order. It updates the *Product_Var* table first, and then the *Products* table. If both transactions are started at the same time, Transaction A gets a lock on *Products*, while Transaction B gets a lock on *Product_Var*, because Transaction A has to wait for the lock on the *Product_Var* table to expire in order to continue processing. Transaction B has the same problem, but in reverse order. Because Transaction A is waiting for the lock to expire on the *Product_Var* table, it cannot expire the lock on the *Products* table. Transaction B cannot let go of its lock on the *Product_Var* until the *Products* table is unlocked. This creates a deadlock, because neither transaction can move forward.

Avoid User Interaction in Transactions Like we said earlier, this rule doesn't really apply to the ColdFusion stateless environment. Because there is never a point during a ColdFusion request that waits for user input, we may never run into this problem.

Keep Transactions Short A deadlock typically occurs when several long-running transactions execute concurrently in the same database. The longer the transaction, the longer the exclusive or update locks are held, blocking other activity and leading to possible deadlock situations. Keeping transactions in one batch minimizes network roundtrips during a transaction, reducing possible delays in completing the transaction and releasing locks.

Use a Low Isolation Level We'll be talking about isolation levels in the following section, with a higher degree of detail, so don't get worried if the description of this rule seems a bit short. Isolation levels basically determine what kind of lock a transaction should initiate, some locks are "stronger" than others. The lower the isolation level, the less strict the lock is. If Transaction A has a lower isolation level than Transaction B, Transaction A will bow down to Transaction B, and let Transaction B have control, which would avoid a deadlock.

Detecting Deadlocks

It's nearly impossible to detect deadlocks on a production server unless you have a lot of people testing the development server. Deadlocks occur on busy servers because there's a higher frequency of transactions being run that could possibly clash. Development servers typically don't have these problems, because there's simply less traffic.

The best way I've found to detect deadlock errors is to keep track of the ColdFusion error logs. In the ColdFusion administrator, click the link called Tools in the upper left-hand corner of the administrator. Click Log Files, then application.log, and look for occurrences of deadlocks. If you don't find any, wait until your traffic gets higher. I know of very few high traffic sites that don't get deadlock errors. They're just something most developers experience at least sooner or later.

Isolation Levels

There's no way to control locking from ColdFusion, except through isolation levels. Isolation levels are supported in the <CFTRANSACTION> tag, which we cover in the next section. Isolation levels are not a ColdFusion thing; they're part of SQL Server, and were created to work as a sort of plan for executing transactions. Isolation levels can help performance issues with transactions, because they tell the database server which transaction has precedence over another.

Isolation levels are important when they relate to performance. It allows a developer to increase or decrease the degree to which a transaction should lock itself. For example, some transactions might need to be completely isolated from the rest of the server — no other concurrent transaction should mess with the first transaction; all other transactions have to wait their turn after the first one. This type of isolation level provides the best chances for the transaction to execute completely undisturbed, but it would also make every other transaction that accessed the same objects wait their turn, which slows things down. On the other side of the spectrum, think of a transaction that is very low priority—any other transaction should always be able to access the objects this transaction is accessing. This would offer the lowest level of isolation, but the highest degree of performance, because no other transaction would have to wait its turn.

There are four isolation levels available: READ UNCOMMITTED, READ COMMITTED, REPEATABLE READ, and SERIALIZABLE. I list each of these in capital letters because they are originally SQL statements that would be included in a transaction, and good SQL programming form usually keeps SQL statements in capital letters for readability issues. Not being one to stray from protocol, I'll keep referring to the isolation levels in capital letters.

Just listing some names of isolation levels probably doesn't help you understand what they are and how they work, but we'll begin to understand that as we describe each isolation level. We'll really start to see the isolation levels in action when we talk about the <CFTRANSACTION> tag in the next main section.

READ UNCOMMITTED

This level of isolation is the best performing of the four isolation levels, it's also a risky isolation level to use if doing important updates or inserts, because there is a possibility of what's called a *dirty read*. A dirty read occurs when a record is selected that may still be in the process of being updated, and could very well change after the transaction affecting the row commits. A simple real world example of this would be if the marketing team at your company sent out a press release to several public relations agencies, stating to the agencies that the release might possibly change. The public relations agencies decide to release the press release to news wires, knowing the release might change. This would be a dirty read in real world terms. It's risky because your marketing team might change a statement after the public relations agency has already digested the data and done something with it.

Transactions with a READ UNCOMMITTED isolation level allow other transactions to read data that has been updated within the transaction. There could be four UPDATE statements in a transaction, and other transactions could see the data affected by the first of the four UPDATE statements before the entire transaction even got to the fourth UPDATE statement. That reminds me of another example that helps describe some of the risk.

I remember when I was in school as a child and the teacher passed out a test. There were few lines of instructions, and about fifteen questions on the test. The first line of instructions read "Read each question of the test before answering a single question," followed by other similar questions. The first few questions were arithmetic questions, but by around the fifth question, kids in the classroom began acting strangely. The fifth question asked the student to "Stand up, and pat your head three times," and the sixth question asked the student to "Raise your hands in the air and count backwards, out loud from 10 to 1." The questions continued to get more absurd, until the last question, which read, "Skip every question but the last question. When you get to this question, you've finished the test."

All of these kids, including myself, were performing dirty reads on the questions, acting on the questions before completing the entire transaction, which was reading the test. Had we paid attention to the isolation level, which would have been the instruction to read each question before doing anything, we would have known that all of the questions were bogus, and that only the last question counted.

READ COMMITTED

This level of isolation is the default level of isolation assigned by SQL Server. READ COMMITTED means that shared locks are held while the data is being read to avoid dirty reads, but the data can be changed before the end of the transaction. So a transaction could update a table, and then SELECT the newly updated information within the same transaction. Other transactions would have to wait until the transaction doing the updating is complete before seeing new data.

If we think of the marketing team's press release example again with a few changes we can describe this in a sort of real world example. Let's say that the marketing team has created a new press release, but rather than send it off to the public relations agency, they send it internally within the company for review. The creation of the press release is like the update statement, and review is like the subsequent SELECT statement on the data. The public relations agency doesn't see the press release until the company is ready for its release, which is like the completion of the transaction. The public relations agency is like a separate transaction.

REPEATABLE READ

A REPEATABLE READ isolation level locks all data used in the queries within a transaction, preventing other users from updating the data, but new *phantom rows* can be inserted into the data set by another user, and are included in later reads in the current transaction. Phantom rows are rows inserted or deleted within a transaction that has not yet completed. Any transaction that reads these new rows cannot commit any changes because of these phantom rows. Phantom rows can occur from transactions that allow dirty reads, or transactions with an isolation level of READ UNCOMMITTED.

We now return back to the press release example. The marketing team has sent the press release to several people within the company, and those people have decided to make their own changes to the press release. They get sent back to the marketing director, whose job it is to send the approved version to the public relations agency, but he can't because he suddenly has six different versions of his press release. These changes can be thought of as phantom rows. With an isolation level of REPEATEABLE READ, the changes can be read within the company (a transaction), but not yet by the public relations agency (a different transaction) because the marketing director needs to figure out which changes to keep.

SERIALIZABLE

This level of isolation is the most restrictive, because it locks everything within the transaction. Other transactions can't do a single thing until this kind of transaction has committed or been rolled back. Because it's the most restrictive, it's also the slowest method. All other transactions that access the same objects must wait until this transaction is finished. This kind of isolation is basically the same as an exclusive lock on the data being accessed by the transaction.

The real world example for this is simple — the marketing director will not release a press release to the PR agency until the release is final and complete. During the processing of making the press release final and complete, the marketing director doesn't do any other task but finish the press release. He cannot be bothered to go to lunch, make statements on new products, or do anything else until his task is finished.

The <CFTRANSACTION> Tag

Everything we've been leading up to in this chapter describes the things that <CFTRANSACTION> has control over. Queries enclosed in <CFTRANSACTION> tags are treated as a single transaction, with a default isolation level of SERIALIZABLE.

Let's recall the credit card payment example; this time, however, we'll see what it looks like using ColdFusion. Because we don't know all of the details about how bank transactions works, we'll just pretend that it's a lot simpler than it actually is. Consider the examples one step above pseudocode, in that the code looks like normal ColdFusion code, but the actual queries might normally be much more complex.

Here's a general run down of what we'll be doing in this transaction:

- Checking for the availability of funds in the checking account.
- Checking to see if we're allowed to transfer funds into the credit card account.
- If everything checks out, pulling funds from the bank account, and crediting the funds to the credit card account.

In this block of <CFSCRIPT> code, we create a variable called *transStatus*, and set it to 0. If the funds exist, the value of *transStatus* is incremented by one. If the credit card is allowing payments to be made, *transStatus* is again incremented by one. This is how we tell the transfer queries that "everything checks out." If the value of transStatus is 2, then we've met our conditions.

```
<cftransaction>
   <!--- check for fund availability --->
   <cfquery name="qryFundCheck" datasource="#request.dsn#">
   SELECT Balance
   FROM Checking_Account
   WHERE AccountID = 100000203
   </cfquery>

   <!--- check to see if credit card can be credited --->
   <cfquery name="qryCCStatus" datasource="#request.dsn#">
   SELECT CCStatus
   FROM Account_Details
   WHERE AccountID = 100000203
   </cfquery>

   <cfscript>
   transStatus = 0;
   if (qryFundCheck.Balance GTE 125)
      IncrementValue(transStatus);
   if (qryCCStatus.CCStatus eq 1)
      IncrementValue(transStatus);
   </cfscript>

   <cfif transStatus eq 2>
      <!--- pull $125 out of the account --->
      <cfquery name="qryPullFunds" datasource="#request.dsn#">
      UPDATE Checking_Account
      SET Balance = Balance - 125
      WHERE AccountID = 100000203
      </cfquery>

      <!--- credit the credit card --->
      <cfquery name="qryCreditCard" datasource="#request.dsn#">
      UPDATE CreditCard_Account
      SET Balance = Balance + 125
      WHERE AccountID = 100000203
```

```
        </cfquery>
    </cfif>
</cftransaction>
```

Because we're using ColdFusion to run the queries that actually change the account conditionally, it might seem that the <CFTRANSACTION> tags aren't required, or at least that they're not required around the entire block of code. You might think that we could make do with <CFTRANSACTION> tags around the queries that do the changing of the bank balances.

Having the SELECT statements outside of the <CFTRANSACTION> block would cause a problem. If the page were called twice in a row, the SELECT statements would both run, and the <CFSCRIPT> block would set the value of *transStatus* to 2. The first request would start a transaction transferring the funds, and the second request would wait for the first. When the first request finished, the second request would start, making it possible for the account to reflect a negative balance. Keeping the SELECT statements within the block is important so that the UPDATE statements from the first request will end before the SELECT statements from the second request begin. Additionally, if the query that checks for the funds is interrupted, or fails for whatever reason, we want the entire transaction to fail. We want to treat the block of code as an atomic unit—it's an all or nothing proposition, no single piece should execute if the rest of the code doesn't also execute.

Controlling Transactions

So far we've said a lot about committing transactions and performing rollbacks, but we've seen no examples of how to actual use <CFTRANSACTION> to perform these kinds of actions. In this section, we detail each of the possible values of the *action* attribute of <CFTRANSACTION>. We also talk about how to suggest your own isolation levels when running a transaction.

The *action* attribute of the <CFTRANSACTION> tag has three possible values:

- begin
- commit
- rollback

We won't talk about the begin value, because it's the default action that <CFTRANSACTION> performs. There's really not much to say about it, except that it simply starts the transaction. There is no benefit in specifying the action as *begin*, other than perhaps for readability.

Commit

In ColdFusion, when we wrap a set of queries with the <CFTRANSACTION> tag, the closing tag is what actually commits the transaction by default. There might be times, however, when it is appropriate to force a commit. A commit action releases any of the resources and locks gathered by the transaction, and makes any changes to the data performed by queries within the transaction. Sometimes it might make sense to commit earlier within a transaction, to free up resources.

To see a commit in action, let's modify the example we've been using about transferring money from my checking account to my credit card. This time, we transfer $125 to my credit card, and $125 to my savings account as well. The code will be modified a bit to run a little more gracefully. It's still very simple in terms of banking. This time, the savings account and credit card account are distinguished using account numbers:

```
<cftransaction>
   <cfscript>
   // set bank account id's for each account
   customerID = 100000203;
   checking = 233832;
   lstAccount = "233491,246231";
   xferAmount = 125;
   </cfscript>

   <!--- loop through each account, and make the transfer --->
   <cfloop list="#lstAccounts#" item="account">
      <!--- check for fund availability --->
      <cfquery name="qryFundCheck" datasource="#request.dsn#">
      SELECT Balance
      FROM Account
      WHERE AccountID = #checking# AND CustomerID = #customerID#
      </cfquery>

      <cfscript>
      transStatus = 0;
      if (qryFundCheck.Balance GTE xferAmount)
         IncrementValue(transStatus);
      </cfscript>
```

```
        <cfif transStatus eq 1>
            <!--- pull $125 out of the checking account --->
            <cfquery name="qryPullFunds" datasource="#request.dsn#">
            UPDATE Account
            SET Balance = Balance - #xferAmount#
            WHERE AccountID = #checking# AND CustomerID = #customerID#
            </cfquery>

            <!--- credit the proper account --->
            <cfquery name="qryCreditCard" datasource="#request.dsn#">
            UPDATE CreditCard_Account
            SET Balance = Balance + #xferAmount#
            WHERE AccountID = #account# AND CustomerID = #customerID#
            </cfquery>
            <cftransaction action="commit" />
        </cfif>
    </cfloop>
</cftransaction>
```

This time around we automatically assume that the account we're going to be transferring into allows transfers, so the *transStatus* variable only needs to equal 1, which indicates that the right amount of funds are available. In this code, we're looping over a list of accounts, then basing our queries on the account number and customer ID.

Notice the code in bold — this is the code that commits the transaction. When we commit the transaction, the tables that we've locked are now free for the next iteration of the loop. It might seem like there's a typo, with a forward slash at the end of the tag. The <CFTRANSACTION> tag requires a closing tag. Adding the forward slash at the end of the tag is the equivalent of supplying a matching closing tag to the <CFTRANSACTION> tag. If you're familiar with XML syntax, this probably isn't that new to you, but I know that if you haven't seen it before in ColdFusion, it can be a bit confusing.

Rollback

The rollback action allows us to force the transaction to fail. Let's look at the example we showed previously, with some additional logic. Instead of listing each of the queries that do the transfer, for simplicity we'll include an imaginary template that performs all of the transferring. The template returns a status code with a value of 1 or 0. If the return code is 1, the fund transfer was successful; if the status code is 0, then the fund transfer failed. The template checks for fund availability, and does everything we need it to do:

```
<cftransaction>
   <cfscript>
   // set bank account id's for each account
   customerID = 100000203;
   lstAccounts = "233831, 246231";
   xferAmount = 125;
   </cfscript>

   <!--- loop through each account, and make the transfer --->
   <cfloop list="#lstAccounts#" item="account">
      <cfinclude template="fundxfer.cfm">
      <cfif FundXfer.ReturnCode eq 1>
         <cftransaction action="commit" />
      <cfelse>
         <cftransaction action="rollback" />
      </cfif>
   </cfloop>
</cftransaction>
```

In this example, if the fund transfer fails, then we roll back the queries that were involved, throwing out any changes they would have made. If the transfer is successful, then we commit the transaction as we did in the previous example.

Suggesting Isolation Levels

<CFTRANSACTION> allows for an optional attribute called *isolation*. The following four values are accepted:

- read_uncommitted
- read_committed
- repeatable_read
- serializable

The values coincide with the isolation levels we discussed earlier in the chapter. By default, serializable is the value that <CFTRANSACTION> uses, but you need to remember that this might not always be the best isolation level to use. The best isolation level to use depends on a lot of factors, but a good rule of thumb is to use the isolation level that provides the highest degree of performance, and the lowest degree of deadlocks or data corruption. Serializable provides the lowest degree of deadlock or data corruption because it completely isolates itself; everything within a serializable transaction is completely locked, and cannot be touched by any outside transaction. This is the "safest" isolation level, but offers the worst performance (because everything has to wait its turn).

Wrapping Up

We've learned in this chapter that transactions in ColdFusion can be a valuable safeguard against data corruption. We've also learned how to avoid deadlocks, how to use the <CFTRANSACTION> tag, and how to perform transactions within the tag.

CHAPTER 13

Debugging

IN THIS CHAPTER:

Debugging ColdFusion Applications

In this chapter, we discuss the debugging options available to your application. Quickly fixing bugs is one of the best things you can do for your application, and knowing how to quickly understand error messages and debugging information will help you develop the best application possible. ColdFusion allows for a number of different debug options that can be turned on from the ColdFusion Administrator. We'll be discussing each one of these options in detail, as well as providing examples of their use where we can.

Debugging ColdFusion Applications

Debugging, in very simple, plain English terms, is the act of chasing down a bug and squashing it. In developer terms, a "bug" is actually called an *exception*. An exception is what happens when ColdFusion is parsing a template, and finds a problem with it. The term *exception* is a bit more fitting in that regard, because ColdFusion may or may not know if there is a genuine error, it just knows something is wrong, and it has been thrown off course.

In this chapter, when I say either exception or error, I mean the same thing. In my opinion, if ColdFusion cannot parse a page for any reason at all, whether it is a syntax problem or a database connection that can't be made, that's an error. When something breaks in the application, I don't argue whether exception is the right word to use or not, I simply know that users are seeing an error, and I need to fix it. Exceptions and errors are the same in my book.

It might seem silly to make a big deal about these words that basically mean the same thing, but they are different in different contexts. We'll be looking at both errors and exceptions in the same context, so they are the same for the purposes of this chapter.

One of the things we won't be talking about in this section is ColdFusion Studio debugging. Believe it or not, not everyone uses ColdFusion Studio to write ColdFusion code. So far I haven't mentioned ColdFusion Studio in this book, and I don't really plan to beyond this mention of it. ColdFusion Studio offers debugging tools that aid developers in testing code within the ColdFusion Studio editor. Personally, I find that setting up the debugging environment in ColdFusion Studio is far more difficult and time-consuming than just seeing the error in a browser and tracking it down with my favorite editor (which happens to be ColdFusion Studio, but that's another subject).

We talk about how to use debugging information to fix errors in Chapter 14, which covers error handling. For now, let's talk about what information is available to the developer when writing a ColdFusion application.

Debugging Options in the ColdFusion Administrator

Debugging information is made available to a developer through the ColdFusion Administrator. Before we talk about the available information, let's talk about how to enable debugging information to different developers.

When debugging information is turned on, the Administrator has the ability to show the information to every user that hits a page, or just to particular IP addresses. The debugging information is displayed at the bottom of an executed page. To control who sees the debugging information, go to your ColdFusion Administrator, and click the Debugging IP option in the left column.

The IPs that appears in your IP list may be blank, or different. On my server, I've decided that when browsing my ColdFusion applications locally, I want to see debugging information. The debugging information will not appear to any other machine except my server. If there are no IPs in the list, then debugging information is displayed to every user. Unless it's an in-house, development server, I wouldn't recommend showing off the debugging information to everyone. Debugging information exposes a lot of information about an application and the server that the application runs on. It would be very easy for a hacker, or even a simply mischievous individual, to do bad things to your site.

To add an IP address to the list, enter the IP address in the input box and click the Add button. The Add Current button adds the IP address that you're currently using. If you're accessing the ColdFusion Administrator from the server, the IP address is 127.0.0.1. If it's a different machine other than the server, than it uses the machine IP address.

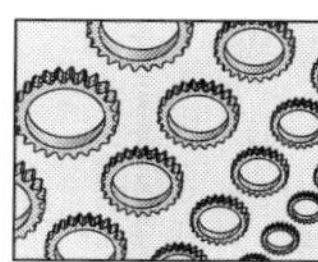

NOTE

It might seem a little exaggerated when I say that I really enjoy that in ColdFusion 5.0, you don't have to apply the IP address list changes. In ColdFusion 4.5, the debugging information and IP address list were on the same page, and you'd happily enter in ten IP addresses, thinking that they were being stored somewhere; if you left the page without applying the changes, the IP addresses you entered would be lost. Perhaps I'm low in the IQ department and this has only happened to me, but in my opinion, not having to apply the changes when adding an IP is a really nice thing.

To remove the IP address from the list, select the IP address, and then click Remove. Remember though, if you remove all the IP addresses, debugging information will be visible to all users.

TIP

It's not a bad idea to always leave the 127.0.0.1 IP address in the list. This prevents the debugging information from showing up to all users, and rarely will you want the debugging information turned off when you're browsing your site from the server. You shouldn't be using up vital resources on the server by browsing in the first place, so it makes perfect sense to do this, unless of course you want all your debugging information available to every user.

As much as I like the new IP address list interface in ColdFusion 5.0, I still wish that I could temporarily disable an IP address. As a developer, I sometimes want to see the site exactly as a user does. The debugging information can interfere with the way the site displays, or expose errors in different ways than might occur to a regular users, so I will often remove my IP address from the list. After testing, I add my IP address once again. It's just a pain to have to do it this way.

I suppose one could write a custom tag that could generate debugging information, and that would have its own, database-driven interface with features that make up for the lack of features available in the default installation of ColdFusion, but it would just be so much easier if it were built into the ColdFusion Administrator from the beginning. However, the fact that you *could* if you wanted to build this functionality points out one of ColdFusion's strengths—ColdFusion is a versatile program.

Let's talk about each of the possible debugging information pieces. Each of these options can be enabled in the ColdFusion Administrator, under the Debug Options link on the lefthand side of the ColdFusion Administrator. I find it helpful when describing each option to show an example of the kind of information the option provides. I'll be including these examples in the descriptions of the options, but screenshots simply won't do the trick, so for readability, they'll be displayed as code examples.

Enable Performance Monitoring

Enabling this option does two things. First, it begins reporting ColdFusion metric data to the Windows 2000 Performance Monitor, and second, it makes metric data available to the GetMetricData() function. We talk about that function in the "GetMetricData()" section.

On platforms other than Windows 2000 or Windows NT, the metric information can be obtained through a command line utility included with ColdFusion called CFSTAT. Actually, the CFSTAT utility is included with all ColdFusion 5.0 versions, and Windows 2000 and Windows NT users can use it, although the performance monitor is much more useful. The utility is located in CFUSION\BIN, and is named cfstat. On Windows machines, it's named cfstat.exe.

This option provides information via CFSTAT, the Performance Monitor, or through the GetMetricData() function. When using CFSTAT, the results might look like this:

```
Pg/Sec  DB/Sec  CP/Sec  Reqs Reqs
Now Hi  Now Hi  Now Hi  Q'ed Run'g
2   9   3   7   0   0   0    1
```

There are actually several more columns of data, but I left them off for formatting reasons. We don't yet need to see each column of data; we talk about that more when we discuss the GetMetricData() function.

You can see from this example that the CFSTAT tool does what it should, but that the information isn't exactly presented in the best of ways. Unfortunately, there's not much that can be done about it. The utility was designed to make up for the fact that other operating systems don't have an NT Performance Monitor.

The NT Performance Monitor provides an excellent overview of the server's metric data. We'll look at an example of the GetMetricData() function in the next section.

Enable CFML Stack Trace

The stack trace exposes an array of structures in the CFCATCH collection. We haven't yet talked about the CFCATCH collection because it's part of the <CFCATCH> tag, which we'll read about in the second half of this chapter. The <CFCATCH> tag allows a developer to catch errors, and the CFCATCH collection that is exposed aids in determining what to do with an error.

The stack trace allows a developer to determine the exact line number of code that an error occurs on, programmatically (meaning that the developer must program a routine of code that exposes the values of the CFCATCH collection). We'll see detailed examples of the CFCATCH collection in action in the second half of this chapter.

The CFML stack trace, when enabled, is processor intensive, and it's recommended that it be turned off if you don't plan to use the CFCATCH collection. Keep in mind that by turning it off, you do not disable to the use of the <CFCATCH> tag, you just lose the ability to access the CFCATCH collection.

Because we look at the <CFCATCH> tag in detail later in the chapter, we'll forego examples for now.

Show Variables

By enabling show variables, the following scopes of variables will be visible with their values at the bottom of each ColdFusion template processed by the ColdFusion server, if they are present within the template:

- CGI
- Form
- URL
- Cookie Variables

The following example of a CFML template shows each of the following variables being set, except for the CGI scope. ColdFusion does not let you create a variable in the **CGI** scope:

```
<cfset form.var1 = 1>
<cfset url.var2 = 2>
<cfset cookie.var3= 3>
```

It is perfectly acceptable to create variables in the **Form** or **URL** scope, as shown in the preceding example. As a matter of preference, I don't like seeing a *form* variable set within the template; I think *form* variables should be created and set when a user submits a form, but I understand that sometimes it just makes sense to do it.

At the bottom of each ColdFusion template processed by the ColdFusion server, the following information will be shown for the preceding example:

```
Parameters
Form Fields:

VAR1=1

URL Parameters:

VAR2=2

CGI Variables:
```

The results are cut off before showing all of the CGI variables. There are about forty CGI variables that are always present, and we've already covered their names and values in previous chapters.

Cookie variables do not have a specific section within the debugging information, but you can determine what cookie variables exist by looking at the *CGI.HTTP_COOKIE* variable. The *CGI.HTTP_COOKIE* variable is a list of sorts, containing the cookie name followed by a value, with each set followed by a semicolon. The following code loops over the *CGI.HTTP_COOKIE* value, and displays each cookie name, followed by its value, in an easy-to-read format. The code itself is a good base for code that works with each cookie and value, one at a time:

```
<cfloop list="#CGI.HTTP_COOKIE#" index="szCookie" delimiters="; ">
   <cfset szCookieName = ListGetAt(szCookie, 1, "=")>
   <cfset szCookieValue = ListGetAt(szCookie, 2, "=")>
   <cfoutput>#szCookieName# = #URLDecode(szCookieValue)#<br></cfoutput>
</cfloop>
```

The *delimiters* attribute of the <CFLOOP> tag is what separates each cookie name and value pair from the list. The delimiter value separates each item in the list, which is set to the *szCookie* variable. The *szCookie* variable is treated like a list within the loop, and because we know the first item in the list will always be the cookie name, we set that value to *szCookieName*. The second item in the list will always be the value, so we set that value to *szCookieValue*. The delimiter for the *szCookie* variable is the equals sign, which separates the cookie name from the value. We then output both variables.

This little block of code can come in handy when trying to understand what cookies are being sent to your browser, and with a little bit of modification, can help you start fresh by removing the cookies from your browser. The modifications are in bold:

```
<cfloop list="#CGI.HTTP_COOKIE#" index="szCookie" delimiters="; ">
   <cfset szCookieName = ListGetAt(szCookie, 1, "=")>
   <cfset szCookieValue = ListGetAt(szCookie, 2, "=")>
   <cfoutput>#szCookieName# =
   #URLDecode(szCookieValue)# killed<br></cfoutput>
   <cfcookie name="#szCookieName#" expires="NOW">
</cfloop>
```

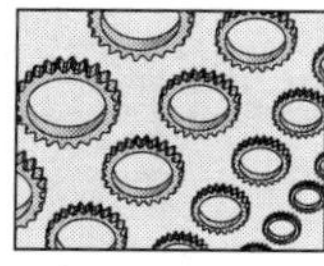

NOTE

It may appear, after running the cookie killer example, that the cookies are not being deleted because their names still appear in the CGI.HTTP_COOKIE *variable. They are indeed being removed. The variables with* CGI *scope are determined before the display of the template, which means by appearances, the cookies still seem to exist. Because the cookie killer example also outputs the names of the cookies it has killed, if you refresh the page, you'll notice that no cookies are displayed, or killed, because they were killed in the previous execution of the script.*

Show Total Processing Time

This option quite simply enables the display of how long it takes, in milliseconds, to actually execute the ColdFusion template. The amount of time taken is calculated based on the total execution of all included templates and queries. Here's some example output:

```
Execution Time

240 milliseconds
```

Show Detailed Processing Time Breakdown

Let's assume that 240 milliseconds is far too much time for a template to execute. How do we pin down which part of the code is taking the longest? There are programmatic ways in ColdFusion to determine this, but what if we want the easy way? This option is the easy way; it displays each included template along with its individual execution time. Here's an example, combined with the above example:

```
Execution Time

240 milliseconds
0 ms C:\INETPUB\WWWROOT\SKATE.SHOP\APPLICATION.CFM
10 ms C:\INETPUB\WWWROOT\SKATE.SHOP\CONTENT.CFM
0 ms C:\INETPUB\WWWROOT\SKATE.SHOP\FUNCTIONS\GENERAL.CFM
10 ms C:\INETPUB\WWWROOT\SKATE.SHOP\INDEX.CFM
10 ms C:\INETPUB\WWWROOT\SKATE.SHOP\MODULES\DISPLAY\MASTER.CFM
0 ms C:\INETPUB\WWWROOT\SKATE.SHOP\MODULES\DISPLAY\STYLE.CFM
0 ms C:\INETPUB\WWWROOT\SKATE.SHOP\MODULES\GENERAL\HTML_WRAPPER.CFM
0 ms C:\INETPUB\WWWROOT\SKATE.SHOP\MODULES\GENERAL\PAGE_TITLE.CFM
0 ms C:\INETPUB\WWWROOT\SKATE.SHOP\MODULES\NAV\CAT_DRILL.CFM
0 ms C:\INETPUB\WWWROOT\SKATE.SHOP\MODULES\PAGES\CART\CART.CFM
0 ms C:\INETPUB\WWWROOT\SKATE.SHOP\MODULES\PAGES\HOME\HOME.CFM
0 ms C:\INETPUB\WWWROOT\SKATE.SHOP\MODULES\PAGES\SEARCH\SEARCHBOX.CFM
0 ms C:\INETPUB\WWWROOT\SKATE.SHOP\MODULES\SPIDERWEB\META_GEN.CFM
0 ms C:\INETPUB\WWWROOT\SKATE.SHOP\ONREQUESTEND.CFM
0 ms C:\INETPUB\WWWROOT\SKATE.SHOP\QUERIES\GLOBAL.CFM
0 ms C:\INETPUB\WWWROOT\SKATE.SHOP\QUERIES\MAIN_SWITCH.CFM
0 ms C:\INETPUB\WWWROOT\SKATE.SHOP\QUERIES\QRYHOME.CFM
210 ms C:\INETPUB\WWWROOT\SKATE.SHOP\QUERIES\QRYSCART.CFM
0 ms STARTUP, PARSING, & SHUTDOWN
```

As you can see, we now have much more data to work with, and the slowpoke in this bunch is the qryscart.cfm file. This option provides very valuable information that can save developers a lot of time. Imagine how long it might take to step through each included template called by this request, trying to figure out which one was slowing things down. It would be a difficult task.

This option also exposes another valuable piece of information. The above list of files and execution times also exposes the included files that executed in this request. We could probably find this information out by looking through our code, and determining which switches executed which code, but that too would take time—this option makes it much easier to find out that information.

Show SQL and Datasource Name

This option allows you to display database information if a database error occurs. Disabled, the information is vague, not giving specifics about what exactly has gone wrong. Here's what a database error might look like if the option were disabled:

```
Error Diagnostic Information
ODBC Error Code = S0022 (Column not found)

[Microsoft][ODBC SQL Server Driver][SQL Server]Invalid column name 'xuuid'.

The error occurred while processing an element with a general identifier
of (CFQUERY), occupying document position (1:1) to (1:60) in the
template file C:\INETPUB\WWWROOT\SKATE.SHOP\QUERIES\QRYSCART.CFM.
```

The error is hopefully obvious; I simply tossed an x into a query where I shouldn't have. The error doesn't expose the SQL or the datasource name. Now, look at the same error with the option enabled:

```
Error Diagnostic Information
ODBC Error Code = S0022 (Column not found)

[Microsoft][ODBC SQL Server Driver][SQL Server]Invalid column name 'xuuid'.

SQL = "SELECT * FROM scart_view
WHERE xuuid = '1E4EF081-3948-4670-B459057980101339'"

Data Source = "SKATESHOP"

The error occurred while processing an element with a general identifier
of (CFQUERY), occupying document position (1:1) to (1:60) in the
template file C:\INETPUB\WWWROOT\SKATE.SHOP\QUERIES\QRYSCART.CFM.
```

The differences are highlighted in bold. When the option is enabled, the entire SQL query is exposed, including the datasource. This information is very nice to have when a complex dynamic query is being built in the template. The SQL displayed is what the database server ended up with, and that generated query can be very helpful in determining what is wrong in your application.

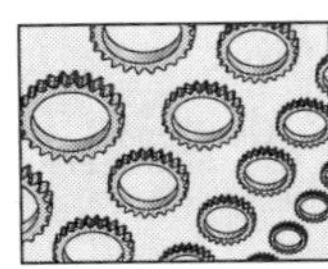

NOTE

If your IP address is on the debugging information IP list, then you'll see all query information regardless of whether or not the Show SQL and Datasource Name option is selected. I find this kind of weird; why would you want to expose the SQL code to users who are not on the IP list? Seems to me the tables need to be shifted; if the option is selected, then users on the IP list should see it. If it's not selected, users on the IP list should not see the extra information. Users who are not on the IP list should always see a vague SQL error message, regardless of the status of the option in the Administrator—or least that's what I think.

Show Query Information

A bit earlier we talked about tracking down which parts of your template were taking up the most time to execute. By enabling the Show Detailed Processing Time Breakdown option, we were able to expose the execution time of each included template. In the section previous to that, we talked about how the total execution time of a template was figured out by the time it took to execute the CFML and the queries on the page.

The Show Query Information option allows you to expose the execution time of a query, how many records it pulled back, and whether or not the query was cached. It also allows you to expose the exact SQL statement executed for a particular query, which as we read earlier, can be very helpful in troubleshooting a query that produces an error.

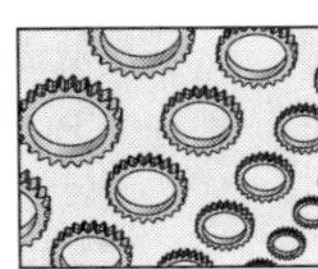

NOTE

The Show Query Information exposes the exact SQL statement executed for each query, but it does not show the information for an erroneous query. The erroring query will be displayed in the error message. However, sometimes queries don't produce an error to the point of crippling the application. Sometimes a query might work perfectly fine, but it might do so in a way that the developer hadn't intended. By exposing the query information, each query can be examined to determine whether or not they're executing as intended.

Here's an example of the exposed query information for the query that is taking the most time in the qryscart.cfm file. In previous sections, we determined that qryscart.cfm was executing slower than we'd like, so now we're tracking down which query is slowest in that file.

```
request.qryScart (Records=1, Time=160ms)
SQL =
SELECT *
FROM scart_view
WHERE uuid = '1E4EF081-3948-4670-B459057980101339'
```

There are two ways to figure out which query was running the slowest within qryscart.cfm. The first way is the more scientific approach; open up the qryscart.cfm file, determine the names of the queries, and look for the slowest one within the list of executed queries exposed by the Show Query Information debugging option. The second approach is called a wild guess; based on the execution time of the qryscart.cfm and the names of the queries, it's possible to figure out which query is the slow one in the qryscart.cfm file.

A nice improvement on this debugging option might be to have the option of exposing the exact template that a query was executed in. This would make tracking down slow queries even easier. Once again, it is possible to programmatically make this information available, but the effort required is probably more than the benefits gained.

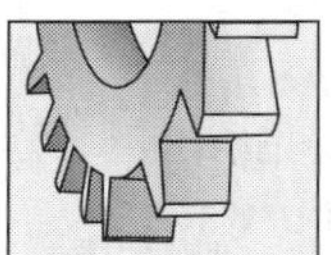

TIP

Adding the attribute debug to the <CFQUERY> tag forces query debugging information to show, regardless of the settings in the ColdFusion Administrator.

Display Template Path in Error Messages

This option, when enabled, exposes the exact location of the template where an error is occurring. This also goes for included templates that use <CFINCLUDE>, <CFMODULE>, or are included as custom tags. This is a great improvement over older versions, which didn't expose what template an error was occurring in. Here's an example:

```
Error Diagnostic Information
Context validation error in tag CFIF

The tag is not correctly positioned relative to other tags in the
template: tag CFIF must have some content. This means that there
must be at least one tag, some text, or even just white space
characters between the <CFIF> and </CFIF> markers.

This problem may be due to a CFML comment that has no end comment mark.

The error occurred while processing an element with a general identifier
```

```
of (CFIF), occupying document position (14:8) to (14:13).

The specific sequence of files included or processed is:
C:\INETPUB\WWWROOT\SKATE.SHOP\INDEX.CFM
  C:\INETPUB\WWWROOT\SKATE.SHOP\CONTENT.CFM      CFInclude
    C:\INETPUB\WWWROOT\SKATE.SHOP\QUERIES\MAIN_SWITCH.CFM      CFInclude
      C:\INETPUB\WWWROOT\SKATE.SHOP\QUERIES\QRYSCART.CFM      CFInclude

The error occurred while processing an element with a general identifier
of (CFINCLUDE), occupying document position (6:1) to (6:35) in the template
file C:\INETPUB\WWWROOT\SKATE.SHOP\QUERIES\MAIN_SWITCH.CFM.
```

In addition to the specific error message, this option makes tracking down an error much easier.

GetMetricData() Function

There's relatively little official documentation on the GetMetricData() function when there really should be more. It's a valuable function that exposes system performance metrics, and can aid developers in building system aware tools. In this section, we talk about what the GetMetricData() function does, both on Windows NT machines and other operating systems, and we talk about the data returned from the function.

The last part of the section will be a discussion about a custom tag that demonstrates some very basic functionality using the data derived from the GetMetricData() function. This tag detects system load by using the GetMetricData() function, and diverts requests to a different server.

Using GetMetricData() on Windows NT or 2000

The GetMetricData() function takes one of four possible arguments, each producing different types of system performance information. We look at each argument, and the syntax for each, next.

PERF_MONITOR If the Enable Performance Monitoring option is enabled in the Debugging Options, using GetMetricData("PERF_MONITOR") creates a structure with the following keys:

Key	Value
avgDBTime	The average amount of time it takes to make and receive requests to and from the database
avgQueueTime	The average length of time queued ColdFusion requests must wait before being completed

Key	Value
avgReqTime	The average length of time it takes to complete ColdFusion requests
bytesIn	The number of bytes received by the ColdFusion server since it was started
bytesOut	The number of bytes sent out by the ColdFusion server since it was started
cachePops	The number of times the cache has been filled to capacity, kicking out the oldest cached page to make room for a newly cached page
dbHits	The number of times the database has been hit since the ColdFusion server started
InstanceName	The name of the instance of ColdFusion you're running
pageHits	The number of overall ColdFusion page requests since the server was started
reqRunning	The current active running requests
reqQueued	The current active queued requests
reqTimedOut	The number of timed-out requests since the ColdFusion server was started

Creating the structure with GetMetricData() is very simple. In the following code example, we create the structure, as well as output its contents:

```
<cfset strPMData = GetMetricData("PERF_MONITOR")>

<cfoutput>
  Current PerfMonitor data is:<br>
  InstanceName: #strPMData.InstanceName#<br>
  PageHits: #strPMData.PageHits#<br>
  ReqQueued: #strPMData.ReqQueued#<br>
  DBHits: #strPMData.DBHits#<br>
  ReqRunning: #strPMData.ReqRunning#<br>
  ReqTimedOut: #strPMData.ReqTimedOut#<br>
  BytesIn: #strPMData.BytesIn#<br>
  BytesOut: #strPMData.BytesOut#<br>
  AvgQueueTime: #strPMData.AvgQueueTime#<br>
  AvgReqTime: #strPMData.AvgReqTime#<br>
  AvgDBTime: #strPMData.AvgDBTime#<br>
  CachePops: #strPMData.CachePops#<br>
</cfoutput>
```

This data can be used in any number of ways. We create a tag later on that uses some of this data, but before we do that, let's look at the other possible arguments.

SIMPLE_LOAD Versions previous to ColdFusion 5.0 didn't support this argument. Supplying this argument to the GetMetricData() function produces, surprisingly, a simple value that represents the load of the site. It's not perfectly clear from testing and ColdFusion documentation, but it's assumed that the integer the argument produces is actually the same as the number of queued requests on the server. Healthy servers generally have no queued requests, so if the value you get is 0, your server is in good shape.

Here's the syntax of the GetMetricData() function with the SIMPLE_LOAD argument:

```
<cfset intSimpleLoad = GetMetricData("SIMPLE_LOAD")>
```

The idea behind this argument was to simplify things. Those who requested the feature were typically using the PERF_MONITOR argument in older versions, but only using the *ReqQueued* key within the entire structure. Avoiding the creation of a structure avoids taking up more resources than needed, and makes the developer's job a little bit easier.

PREV_REQ_TIME Supplying this argument exposes the time, in milliseconds, the last request took to complete. Personally, I'm not sure how useful this is, other than to satisfy curiosity. I'm comforted in knowing that it's there, in case I do decide to use it someday. Here's the syntax:

```
<cfset intPrev_Req_Time = GetMetricData("PREV_REQ_TIME")>
```

AVG_REQ_TIME This argument exposes the average request time. This is a bit different from the PERF_MONITOR structure key *AvgReqTime*, because its data gathering is separate from the Performance Monitor. The value of the registry key located at HKEY_LOCAL_MACHINE\SOFTWARE\Allaire\ColdFusion\CurrentVersion\Server\ReqAvgWindowSec is the number of seconds to look back on in order to calculate the average. For example, the default value is 120, which means that the server stores the time it takes to complete a request for all requests that were executed within the past 120 seconds. If you were to drop the number to 20, it would only look back 20 seconds. If you were drop it completely to 0, there would be no tracking, so the average would be very inaccurate. Here's the syntax:

```
<cfset intAvg_Req_Time = GetMetricData("AVG_REQ_TIME")>
```

<CF_DivertLoad>

In this section, we dissect a small application that displays debugging information gathered by a scheduled ColdFusion template. The application uses several new ColdFusion 5.0 features that we'll point out in the text, and is a good example of how to take advantage of the GetMetricData() function that we've been talking about.

The application consists of two ColdFusion templates, and a database with a single template. Both ColdFusion templates can be placed within a unique directory on your web server. Before we look at the templates, let's create the table we'll be using in the database, using the following script:

```
CREATE TABLE perf_history (
   entry_id int IDENTITY (1, 1) NOT NULL ,
   InstanceName varchar (50) NULL ,
   ReqQueued int NULL ,
   ReqRunning int NULL ,
   ReqExecTime int NULL ,
   Entry_Date datetime DEFAULT GetDate() NOT NULL
)
GO
```

It's perfectly all right to create this table on an existing database; I placed mine in its own database. We use the *connectString* attribute of the <CFQUERY> tag later to connect to this table, so you don't need to be too picky about where to put it—just place it where you think you should.

In fact, when discussing this application, our focus is more on the code itself than the structure of the application. The application itself isn't anything all that special, but the code within it helps us talk about the GetMetricData() function, and shows off some new ColdFusion 5.0 features at the same time. Personally, I think that some of the reporting features in the ColdFusion 5.0 Administrator provide much better data, but they lack one feature—graphing. If this application inspires someone to create a more significant performance tracking and graphing application, that would be great!

Now, back to the application. Let's look at the file that we should schedule. This file is called perf_track.cfm, although it can be named whatever you like. Perf_track.cfm gathers data using the GetMetricData() function, and shows an example of the *connectString* attribute in action. In order to get consistent data for the graphs, it's probably best to schedule the file to run at regular intervals. I tested the application using hourly data, as well as including the file within a few of my applications, located at http://www.michaelbuffington.com. When the data was collected randomly it still worked, but it just didn't seem to report the data that well. Here's the code:

```
<cfset strPMData = GetMetricData("PERF_MONITOR")>

<cfquery
name="qryTrack"
dbtype="dynamic"
datasource="_ _dynamic_ _"
connectstring="
DRIVER={SQL SERVER};
SERVER=(local);
UID=perf;
PWD=d0woe23;
DATABASE=perf_tracker">
INSERT INTO perf_history
(InstanceName,
ReqQueued,
ReqRunning,
ReqExecTime)
VALUES
('#strPMData.InstanceName#',
#strPMData.ReqQueued#,
#strPMData.ReqRunning#,
#GetMetricData("PREV_REQ_TIME")#)
</cfquery>
```

The first line of code uses the GetMetricData() function with the PERF_MONITOR argument. This argument generates a structure, which we assign to *strPMData*. We use some of the keys in this structure when we insert the performance data into the database.

The next block of code is the query that inserts the data. The code might look confusing; each attribute/value has been separated onto its own line for readability. The first attribute name is familiar, but the next one might seem odd. The *dbtype* attribute used with dynamic value indicates that we're going to be making a dynamic connection. The next attribute, *datasource*, requires the value of _ _dynamic_ _. That includes two underscores, the word dynamic, and two more underscores. When making a dynamic connection, the *dbtype* and *datasource* connections must be formatted like this.

We've talked about the *connectString* attribute in previous chapters, but we haven't yet used it in an application example. The arguments/values of the *connectString* attribute are separated for readability as well. The first argument, *driver*, indicates the driver we'll be using. The next argument, *server*, is the SQL server we'd like to connect to. If connecting to a local *server*, as I've shown here, then surround the word *local* with parentheses. If connecting to another server, replace *(local)* with a server name or IP address.

The next two arguments are the UID and PWD arguments. These are the login and password values. Notice that I've used an account called "perf." This SQL login is very limited in what it can do. The only thing it can do is insert data into a table within a database, and select data. It can't delete anything and it can't insert data into other databases—it's locked down. The reason for this is of course for security reasons, but it's also because there's always a possibility that this code might get into the wrong hands no matter how secure I make my system. I probably don't even need to mention this, but Internet Information Server (IIS) continues to have security issues pop up. With a secure login, it would be difficult for a malicious user to do much of anything to our databases.

Following the login and password arguments, indicate what database we'd like to connect to. As I said earlier, I set up a specific database for this application, called perf_tracker.

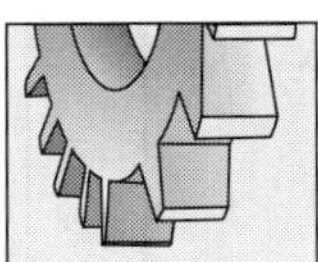

TIP

You can connect to any datasource with the connectString *attribute. Here's an example of a* connectString *that connects to a Microsoft Access database:*

Driver={Microsoft Access Driver (.mdb)};Dbq=perf.mdb;DefaultDir=C:\inetpub\wwwroot\perf_tracker\db;Uid=Admin;Pwd=;*

The SQL query inserts three of the *strPMData* key value pairs into the database, then, for the ReqExecTime column, uses the GetMetric() function to insert the value of time it took to execute the last template. The four columns tracked were picked because they're basically live. The application is intended to take snapshots of live site metrics and store them, which we'll be able to graph at a later date.

Let's look at the graphing application saved to a file as perf_track_grapher.cfm. The idea behind this file is that it acts as both the form that will be used to filter the graph, and as the file that displays the graph. In addition to the application, we point out the use of some new ColdFusion 5.0 features.

The application itself is contained within one file, but for the purposes of talking about the code, I'll break it into pieces. It's not a particularly large file, but it's difficult to plop the entire thing down and then discuss it with any sort of clarity. I'll show the code first, then talk about it:

```
<!DOCTYPE HTML PUBLIC "-//W3C//DTD HTML 4.0 Transitional//EN">

<html>
<head>
   <title>Performance Tracker</title>
   <style type="text/css">
   BODY, TD
   {
      font: 11px Arial, Helvetica, sans-serif;
   }

   .error
   {
      color:navy;
   }

   .forms
   {
      font: 11px Arial, Helvetica, sans-serif;
      border-style:0;
      border:1px black solid;
      color: black;
      padding:2px 2px 2px 2px;
   }
   </style>
</head>
```

No rocket science going on here—we're just setting up the HTML document, and defining the styles we use later on. I'm very much into style sheets, and would encourage anyone who's not into style sheets to spend some time figuring them out. (Note that in the following code, the ¬ symbol indicates a line that had to be broken in this book because of space restrictions, but it should be entered as one continuous line.)

```
<!--- SETUP DEFAULT VARIABLES --->
<cfscript>
// setup default error messages
```

```
arryMessages = ArrayNew(1);
arryMessages[1] = "";
arryMessages[2] = "";
arryMessages[3] = "";
arryMessages[4] = "";
intErrors = 0;
cs = "DRIVER={SQL SERVER};SERVER=(local);¬
UID=perf;PWD=perf;DATABASE=perf_tracker";
</cfscript>
```

These are some of the variables we'll be using in the application. It might seem foolish to create an array, and then make static assignments immediately afterwards. Well, it gets a little more foolish than that later on. Only one of the cells in the array are used in the application, but the idea behind creating the array in the first place was to have a possible error message for each form element. It turns out that there is only one possible way to screw things up. Rather than convert everything, I left the array in the name of expansion. Someday this application might need the array, and it doesn't really hurt to have it now. The messages are blank right now for a reason, which we'll come back to later.

The *intErrors* variable is used in conjunction with some form validation. If any of the form values have a problem or conflict somehow, this value will increase in value. The graph will only be created if there are no errors in the form.

The *cs* variable is our connect string. All queries in this application have dynamic datasources, and it would be tedious to mess around with each query. It also enhances in the readability of the code.

```
<!--- FORM VALIDATION --->
<cfif IsDefined("form.szColumn")>
   <!--- make sure that the start date is earlier than the end date --->
   <cfif DateCompare(form.szStartDate, form.szEndDate) eq 1>
      <cfset intErrors = intErrors + 1>
      <cfset arryMessages[2] =
        "<b>Error:</b> Start date is greater than end date.">
   </cfif>
</cfif>
<!--- END OF FORM VALIDATION --->
```

This is the mighty form validation. Before we get into it, let's talk a little bit about what the application is allowed to do. Among other things, the user should be able to select a start date and an end date for the time period in which he or she would like to see data. If the user were to select a start date that was greater than the end date, it would present a problem, so we need to let the user know if it happens.

The first thing we do is check for the existence of the form.szColumn name variable. If it is defined, then we know the form was submitted, and it's time to begin our validation. The nested <CFIF> statement compares the two dates. If the start date is greater then the end date, the DateCompare() function returns the number 1. If DateCompare() returns the number 1, we increase the *intErrors* variable by one, and then reset the second cell in arryMessages to contain the new, more visible error message. Remember that the first time we set this cell, the error message was completely blank. Now we've filled it with something. You'll see later in the code that we output the arryMessages cells regardless of what's in them. This saves us from having to do a lot of <CFIF> code for each error message. The cell is only modified if there is a message. This system of error reporting works pretty well, even on large forms, where using the array really comes into play.

Later in the code, we'll check the value of *intErrors*, and if it's 0, we build a graph, but if it's 1 or more, then no graph will be built.

```
<cfquery name="qryPossibleDates"
dbtype="dynamic" datasource="__dynamic__" connectString="#cs#">
SELECT CONVERT(varchar(10), Entry_Date, 101) as SmallEntryDate
FROM Perf_History
GROUP BY CONVERT(varchar(10), Entry_Date, 101)
ORDER BY CONVERT(varchar(10), Entry_Date, 101)
</cfquery>
```

This is a small block of code, but there's a lot to talk about. In the form, we use drop menus for the start date and end date, and this query helps generate those dates. Let's step back for a second and remember the structure of our *Perf_History* table. If you remember the code we used to create the table, you'll recall that the Entry_Date column has a default value of getdate(). GetDate() is a SQL function that produces the exact time. You'll also recall that the Entry_Date column is a datetime field, which is accurate down to the second. This was done also for expansion reasons. Those hours, minutes, and seconds after the date might be important someday.

But in this application, we only want to see things by date. We want to ignore time values and only focus on dates. We take care of this by using the SQL function called Convert(). This function takes three arguments. The first argument is the datatype that you'd like the column to be converted to. The second argument is the column that you'd like to convert, and the last column is called the style column. This has nothing to do with pimps, disco, or Charlie's Angels sunglasses. The argument indicates how we'd like to format the Entry_Date column. When it comes to converting date/time values, the convert function can take the optional style argument and apply a preset style to the column. In our case, we want the date to look like 7/20/2001. SQL has a style for this, it's called 101. If you're curious about why 101 magically converts our date into the proper format, don't feel too bad; so am I. I can't find a good reason why 101 has the effect that it does, I just know it works. If you want see more preset styles, check out your SQL Server Books Online documentation.

We also only want to output one record for each possible date, so we group the Entry_Date column. We need to maintain the conversion every time we reference the column because we're grouping on that column. There is no WHERE clause because we want all of the possible dates in the *Perf_History* table. We use this query for both the start date and end date drop-downs.

```
<body bgcolor="#BBBDC4">
<div style="font: 16px;"><b>Performance Tracker</b></div>
<table cellpadding="0" cellspacing="0" border="0">
   <tr>
      <td>
         <form action="perf_track_grapher.cfm" method="post">
            <p>
            <b>Select a Column:</b><br>
            <select name="szColumn" class="forms">
                  <option value="ReqQueued"
                  <cfif IsDefined("form.szColumn")>
                    <cfif form.szColumn eq "ReqQueued">selected</cfif>
                    </cfif>>Queued Requests</option>
                  <option value="ReqRunning"
                  <cfif IsDefined("form.szColumn")>
                    <cfif form.szColumn eq "ReqRunning">selected</cfif>
                    </cfif>>Running Requests</option>
                  <option value="ReqExecTime"
                   <cfif IsDefined("form.szColumn")>
                   <cfif form.szColumn eq "ReqExecTime">selected</cfif>
                   </cfif>>Execution Times</option>
            </select>
            <cfoutput><div class="error">#arryMessages[1]#</div></cfoutput>

          <p>
            <b>Select a Start Date</b><br>
            <select name="szStartDate" class="forms">
               <cfloop query="qryPossibleDates">
                  <option value="<cfoutput>#SmallEntryDate#</cfoutput>" <cfif
IsDefined("form.szStartDate")><cfif form.szStartDate eq SmallEntryDate>
selected</cfif></cfif>><cfoutput>#SmallEntryDate#</cfoutput></option>
               </cfloop>
            </select>
            <cfoutput><div class="error">#arryMessages[2]#</div></cfoutput>
```

```
            <p>
            <b>Select an End Date</b><br>
            <select name="szEndDate" class="forms">
               <cfloop query="qryPossibleDates">
                  <option value="<cfoutput>#SmallEntryDate#</cfoutput>"
                  <cfif IsDefined("form.szEndDate")>
                    <cfif form.szEndDate eq SmallEntryDate>selected</cfif>
                    </cfif>>
                 <cfoutput>#SmallEntryDate#</cfoutput>
                 </option>
              </cfloop>
            </select>

            <p>
            <b>Select a Calculation Type</b><br>
            <select name="szAggregate" class="forms">
               <option value="sum"
               <cfif IsDefined("form.szAggregate")>
               <cfif form.szAggregate eq "sum">
                selected</cfif>
               </cfif>>sum</option>
               <option value="avg"
               <cfif IsDefined("form.szAggregate")>
               <cfif form.szAggregate eq "avg">
                selected</cfif>
               </cfif>>avg</option>
               <option value="max"
               <cfif IsDefined("form.szAggregate")>
               <cfif form.szAggregate eq "max">
                selected</cfif>
               </cfif>>max</option>
               <option value="min"
               <cfif IsDefined("form.szAggregate")>
               <cfif form.szAggregate eq "min">
                selected</cfif>>
               </cfif>min</option>
            </select>

            <p>
            <input type="submit" value="Generate Graph">
         </form>
      </td>
```

We'll cut it off there. The form allows a user to select the column of data they'd like to see, the start date, the end date, and a type of calculation to perform on the data before graphing it. It might seem a little overcomplicated to have that much code for four form elements, but the code increases usability. When a user submits the form, the values they've picked are retained. This is possible by checking to see if the form has been submitted, and if it has, by checking to see if the particular form value is equal to the *select* option. It might seem tedious, but it will make your application much easier to use application.

```
      <!--- DISPLAY GRAPH --->
      <cfif IsDefined("form.szColumn")>
         <td>
            <cfif intErrors eq 0>
               <cfquery name="qryBuildGraph" dbtype="dynamic"
                 datasource="__dynamic__" connectstring="#cs#">
               SELECT #form.szAggregate#(#form.szColumn#) as sumColumn,
               CONVERT(varchar(10), Entry_Date, 101) as SmallEntryDate
               FROM Perf_History
               WHERE CONVERT(varchar(10), Entry_Date, 101)
                   >= '#form.szStartDate#'
               AND CONVERT(varchar(10), Entry_Date, 101) <= '#form.szEndDate#'
               GROUP BY CONVERT(varchar(10), Entry_Date, 101)
               ORDER BY CONVERT(varchar(10), Entry_Date, 101)
               </cfquery>

               <cfgraph type="BAR"
               query="qryBuildGraph"
               valuecolumn="sumColumn"
               itemcolumn="SmallEntryDate"
               showvaluelabel="Yes"
               valuelabelfont="Arial"
               valuelocation="OVERBAR"
               title="#form.szAggregate# History"
               barspacing="2"
               backgroundcolor="##BBBDC4"/>
            </cfif>
         </td>
      </cfif>
   </tr>
</table>
</body>
</html>
```

If the form has been submitted, and the error count is still 0, we execute the query that will be used to populate the graph. We use the values from the *form.szColumn* variable and the *form.szAggregate* variable to choose what column we want from the database, and what aggregate function we'd like to perform on it. The *form.szColumn* variable will be one of the four possible columns in the database, and because we're using the GROUP BY clause on the Entry_Date column, we have to aggregate the values for the selected column as well.

We then use <CFGRAPH>, which is new to ColdFusion 5.0, to generate a graph based on the data. The default format of the graph is Flash, and default size of the graph is 320×240 pixels, which is adequate for this application. The <CFGRAPH> tag requires a closing </CFGRAPH> tag, but in this example we use the / symbol at the end of the <CFGRAPH> tag to close it. For tags that require closing tags, using the / symbol at the end of the tag is the equivalent of supply the closing tag.

We finish off the HTML document, and that's the end of the application. The most important thing to take away from the example is that there are practical uses for the GetMetricData() tag. Combined with something like <CFGRAPH>, the tag can provide you with value information about your server.

GetTickCount() Function

It's possible to single out a particular block of code in your application and determine how much time it takes for that particular block of code to execute using the GetTickCount() function. The GetTickCount() function returns the current value of the execution time of a page. The following code is an example of the GetTickCount() function that is used to determine the length of time it takes to execute a loop:

```
<cfscript>
intStartTick = GetTickCount();

i = 1;

while (i lte 10000)
   {
      i = i + 1;
   }

intEndTick = GetTickCount();
intExecTime = intEndTick - intStartTick;

WriteOutput(intExecTime);
</cfscript>
```

The first line of code sets the *intStartTick* value. This value will be the value of the millisecond counter at that point in time, so if there was a ton of code that executed previous to this variable assignment, the tick count could be significant.

We'll loop some code ten thousand times just for kicks to give us something to measure. After the loop is complete, we measure the tick counter once more, and place its value into the *intEndTick* variable. To figure out the elapsed time for our loop, we subtract the end tick count with the start tick count, then output the value.

Wrapping Up

In this chapter, we've talked about the many debugging possibilities built into ColdFusion. We've also discussed a few functions that can help you to write your own debugging information. Using the information exposed by these debugging options increases the speed of your applications, and tells you a lot more about what your servers can handle, and the affect certain ways of programming your application can have on the overall responsiveness of your site.

Debugging alone will not help you have a smooth running site, however. In Chapter 14 we talk about how to programmatically handle errors, bypassing the standard, user-unfriendly ColdFusion server errors.

CHAPTER

14

Error Handling

IN THIS CHAPTER:

If you found a tarnished, old oil lamp while trekking through the vast Sahara desert, and gave it a rub, releasing a wish-granting genie, I'd hope one of your requests would be: "Oh, Genie of the lamp, please grant me the ability to write superb error handling code in ColdFusion." When it comes to coding in ColdFusion, if you could only do one thing truly well, it should be writing good error handling code, because good error handling code can mask all your bad code. Think of it: if every error you inadvertently wrote into your application was handled by another part of your application, you'd be set.

Good error handling code is like good health insurance. Some of us may need to see a doctor on a regular basis, while some of us haven't been to the doctor for several years, even though we still pay the insurance premiums. Writing good error handling code is like paying the insurance premium. You may not need the error handling, or you might *really* need it, in which case, you'll be very glad you have it.

But good error handling code goes beyond saving yourself from a lot of ugly errors on your site. It can also increase the performance of your site. For example, imagine that you have a custom tag that is called from the majority of your application's template. Now, let's get crazy and suggest that the custom tag you wrote is prone to errors (we all know that ColdFusion programmers produce the fewest errors, but just stick with me here). If that tag were to error for even just half of your users, your server would come to a crawl. Every time ColdFusion has to report an error on its own, it does a couple of things.

First, it stores the error message and some other bits of information to its log files. Second, it figures out what line the error message is on, and in what template. Third, it has to determine whether or not to show more information to some users than it does to others because of ColdFusion Administrator debugging options. That kind of processing doesn't come out of thin air, it's snatched up from the same resource pool that non-erroring pages use.

You can write error handling code that bypasses all of this, or does all of this, or uses a mix of the two. The most important part is that you can do it. You can also program a lot more into your error handling. Imagine an error that figures itself out, or e-mails a database administrator when there's a database error. I've even thought of having the site send a text message to my cell phone with a very brief error message. The possibilities are only limited by your effort, imagination, and technology.

With all the error handling evangelism out of the way, let's expose one more truth about error handling—ColdFusion developers don't use it enough. It's one of those types of technologies that don't jump right out at you requiring your attention. <CFQUERY> jumps right out at you; it's hard to get data from a database without a query. It's not always obvious where ColdFusion error handling tags fit in.

In this chapter, we try to make ColdFusion error handling capabilities easy to understand, and give good, valid reasons to use them. Writing good error handling takes a little more time in the beginning, but saves a lot of headaches in the end, not to mention the fact that it probably makes impressions of stability and quality to your site visitors.

Using <CFERROR>

<CFERROR> allows developers to display a particular error-handling template when an error occurs. There are four different types of errors that <CFERROR> checks for: EXCEPTION, REQUEST, VALIDATION, and MONITOR. We'll look at each of these types in the following sections. <CFERROR> is probably the easiest type of custom error handling you can perform, especially on already existing applications. Only one <CFERROR> tag needs to exist per request, so it's easy to retrofit an old application by placing the tag in the Application.cfm file.

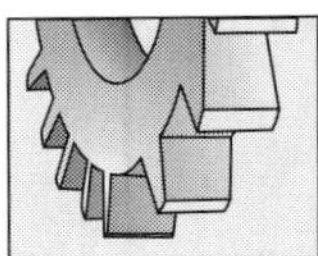

TIP

You shouldn't use the cfencode utility to encrypt error handler files. You might run into problems, according to Macromedia.

The <CFERROR> tag requires two attributes: *type* and *template*. We'll discuss the four possible types in a second, but first let's continue talking about the <CFERROR> attributes. The template attribute should be an absolute path to the file name. If the error handler file is in the same directory as the file that executed the <CFERROR>, then the following syntax would be used:

```
<cferror type="request" template="errorhandler.cfm">
```

There are two other possible attributes as well. The *mailto* attribute can contain the e-mail address of an administrator. Supplying this e-mail address won't send off an e-mail to someone whenever an error occurs, it simply passes the value to your error handler as *error.mailto*. We'll explain the error scope shortly. The *exception* attribute is required if the error type is exception or monitor. It contains the type of exception to handle. For example, the following tag would handle files that are included in the template using <CFINCLUDE>, but that in reality don't exist:

```
<cferror type="EXCEPTION" exception="MissingInclude"
template="errorhandler.cfm">
<cfinclude template="does_not_exist.cfm">
```

When an error type of request, exception, or monitor occurs, <CFERROR> creates the **Error** scope, and passes a certain set of parameters within that scope to the error handling page. The following table lists the variables available to the error handler, as well as their descriptions:

Variable	Description
Error.diagnostics	A detailed description of the error. It's something we're also already accustomed to, as it's the same form as a regular ColdFusion error.
Error.mailto	If the *mailto* attribute is specified in the <CFERROR> tag, then the value of that attribute is placed in *error.mailto*.
Error.datetime	This is a timestamp of the error.
Error.browser	The browser type that encountered the error. It contains the same data as *cgi.remote_addr*.
Error.generatedcontent	This is the failed request's generated content. This is important, because your program flow is being passed to the error handler template. It's good to know what did get generated on the erroring page.
Error.remoteaddress	This is the IP address of the user making the request.
Error.httpreferer	This is the URL to the page the user was at before encountering the error. If the user typed in a direct URL to the error, then this will be blank. If a user clicked on a link that brought him or her to the error, then this variable will contain that URL.
Error.template	This is the exact path and name of the ColdFusion template that produced the error.
Error.querystring	The URL query string of the user's request. Basically, the URL parameters attached to the end of the ColdFusion template.

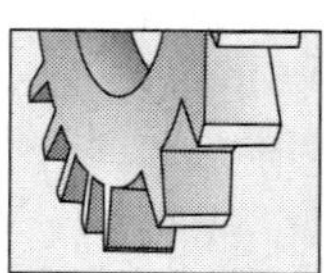

TIP

If you're using the exception or monitor error type, you can replace the scope name of error with cferror.

As mentioned earlier, it's easy to place the <CFERROR> tag within the Application.cfm file, which will make that <CFERROR> tag available for every page. There are no restrictions on where you can place the <CFERROR> tag, but you should always place the <CFERROR> tag before the error. If you place the <CFERROR> tag at the end of a request, it will not do any good for errors that occur before the <CFERROR> tag is executed.

Only one <CFERROR> tag is needed for each error type (except for the validation error type, which we'll detail soon). Also, you can have multiple <CFERROR> tags, but you only really need one for each error type. The first error encountered is the first error that will get passed to the error handler. There is no type precedence or anything like that. The following example will error on the <CFSET> tag before it errors on MissingInclude, even though the order of the <CFERROR> tags are opposite:

```
<cferror type="EXCEPTION" exception="MissingInclude"
template="handler_mi.cfm">
<cferror type="EXCEPTION" exception="Expression"
template="handler_exp.cfm">

<cfset hello = hello>
<cfinclude template="does_not_exist.cfm">
```

Each error type is designed to work differently in different situations. Let's check out each error type, and talk a bit further about what they're good for, and how they work.

TYPE=REQUEST

The REQUEST error type indicates that any error that occurs within the request should be handled by the indicated error handler. The entire error scope is passed to the error as we talked about in the previous section. This type is probably the easiest to implement, because it will handle any exception, or error. It will not, however, catch improperly formatted code (like an extra # sign or the lack of a required one). Let's look at an example of the two files that use the <CFERROR> tag with the request type. The first file is the calling file, with the error, and the second file is the actual error handler.

```
<cferror type="REQUEST" template="errorhandler.cfm">

<cfscript>
lstExample = "one,two,three";
szfour = ListGetAt(lstExample,4);
</cfscript>
```

The first line of code assigns the errorhandler.cfm file to any error within the request. Keep in mind that context errors cannot be handled by <CFERROR>. A context error is something like forgetting to close a <CFIF> tag, or any other tag that requires a closing tag. In our example, the ListGetAt() function will have a problem, because there is no fourth item in the list we set up.

Now, let's look at our errorhandler.cfm file. The errorhandler.cfm file handles things a bit differently from the ColdFusion standard error. In this example, it's very much simplified, because we're going to continue to add to it during this chapter as we introduce new technologies. Consider this a fully stripped down version of the error handler.

```
Woops, an error has occurred, don't you dare do
that again or we'll send nanobots to steal your face or a
dingo to steal your baby, whichever scares you more.<br>
```

Okay, so that is an insanely stripped down version of an error handler. This error handler does absolutely nothing except tell the user that something happened. Nothing is logged, no administrator is told that anything has happened, and we've even scared the user into thinking they'll be accosted by microscopic robots, or they'll lose their first-born to wild Australian koninis.

This is an extreme example of some good things about the request type, as well as one of the bad parts. One good thing is that it caught the error without the developer having to be too specific. A bad thing is that you cannot do the following:

```
<cf_errorformatting>
Woops, an error has occurred, don't you dare do
that again or we'll send nanobots to steal your face or a
dingo to steal your baby, whichever scares you more.<br>
</cf_errorformatting>
```

In this example, we've surrounded the error with some formatting tags. Just pretend they make the error nice and pretty. The request type error does not support a full range of CFML code. You cannot include files, or execute custom tags or use <CFMODULE>. The reason for this is a good one—because the request error catches everything, you could end up in a nasty loop if a custom tag on the page also had an error. ColdFusion ignores all tags, including any CFML code or comments.

Another interesting thing about this error type is that you can only use the **Error** scope variables like *error.browser*, *error.diagnostics*, and so on. In addition, you do not need to surround them with <CFOUTPUT> tags; they're output automatically. ColdFusion will ignore any other variables set or called in the error handler. The only variables that ColdFusion "sees" are the *error.whatever* variables.

Obviously, this is a bit limiting, because it will probably be difficult without being able to use much CFML to keep your site's look and feel while displaying the error, and about the most you can do is output the results of the error to the user.

TYPE=EXCEPTION

The EXCEPTION error type gives us a lot more options than the REQUEST error type, but requires a little more effort to implement. But, with the EXCEPTION error type, the error handler file is able to support the entire CFML code base, which means that the site's look and feel can be maintained, and actual actions can be taken based on the error.

When using the EXCEPTION type, you must include the *exception* attribute in <CFERROR>. The *exception* attribute can have one of the following values, which I'll also describe as they're introduced:

Exception Type	Description
application	This is a custom exception type that we'll cover when we talk about the <CFTHROW> tag.
database	Any type of database related error. This wouldn't include something like forgetting the datasource attribute of a <CFQUERY> tag though; that's a different kind of error.
expression	This type of error occurs when an expression evaluation has a problem. For example, if we tried to add the number 2 to the string *foo*.
lock	This occurs when a lock-related error occurs.
missinginclude	This handles missing included files, such as <CFMODULE> references, but not missing custom tag references.
object	This occurs when code using <CFOBJECT> fails.
security	This type of error is caught when using tags like <CFAUTHENTICATE>, or other security related tags.
custom	This could be a custom named exception type that you assign with a <CFTHROW> tag. We'll talk about the <CFTHROW> later, in the section "Using <CFTHROW>."
any	This is the "all of the above" choice, and covers any type of error.

Let's update our files to use the EXCEPTION error type. The first file that creates the error will use the expression exception type, and the error handler will be more specific to that exception type.

```
<cferror type="EXCEPTION" exception="expression"
template="errors\expression.cfm">
<cfset var1 = 2>
<cfset var2 = "foo">
```

```
<cfif var1 + var2 eq 0>
This is here just to look pretty.
</cfif>
```

This code will return an error when trying to add the two variables together. The errorhandler.cfm itself has been changed to a more specific file within an errors directory called expression.cfm. This error handles all expression exceptions. It's not a requirement to do it this way; it's simply an example. There are many possibilities of how to set up error handling, and this is just one of them. Here's the new code for the errors/expression.cfm file.

```
<cf_errorbox title="Expression Error">
There's been an expression error:<br>
<p>
<cfoutput>
#error.diagnostics#
</cfoutput>
</cf_errorbox>
```

The expression.cfm file uses a custom tag that provides the formatting for the error. Here's what the code looks like for that tag:

```
<cfparam name="attributes.title" default="{no title}">

<cfif thistag.executionmode IS "start">
   <table width="300" cellpadding="0"
   cellspacing="0" border="1">
      <tr>
         <td>
            <table width="100%" cellpadding="2"
            cellspacing="0" border="0">
               <tr>
                  <td bgcolor="#9EC900">
                  <b><cfoutput>#attributes.title#</cfoutput></b>
                  </td>
               </tr>
               <tr>
                  <td>
</cfif>
```

```
<cfif thistag.executionmode IS "end">
                  </td>
               </tr>
            </table>
         </td>
      </tr>
   </table>
</cfif>
```

This places a fancy HTML table around our error message. The idea behind the tag is that it can be expanded to also include site elements, or whatever else is needed that isn't exactly specific to an expression error. Just like the expression.cfm file uses the custom tag for formatting, so can other specific error message files.

Right now the specific expression.cfm file doesn't really do much as far as expressions go, but it could. In fact, let's think of the same example above, but instead of an expression error, it's a database error. The following database.cfm file could handle the error specifically for a database error:

```
<cf_errorbox title="Database Error">
The following actions have been taken:<br>
<ul>
   <cf_massmedia employee="DBA" messagecount="100">
   <li>We've paged, e-mailed, IM'd the DBA with the error</li>
   <cfif SleepingHours("DBA") is true>
      <cf_electrocution employee="DBA" level="maximum">
      <li>The electrocution wake device has been initiated on the DBA</li>
   <cfelse>
      <li>DBA is in the office, and has been
        hog tied in front of the SQL server.</li>
   </cfif>
</ul>
<p>
<cfoutput>
#error.diagnostics#
</cfoutput>
</cf_errorbox>
```

This error handler makes quick work of alerting the database administrator that something is wrong. There are obviously some imaginary custom tags, and an imaginary user defined function or two. Please don't electrocute your database administrator; that would be cruel.

The last part you should know about the EXCEPTION error type is that you can use all of the **Error** scope variables listed in the previous section.

TYPE=VALIDATION

This type of error handling is used when validating form elements, and is sometimes referred to as server-side validation. In the following example, the form.cfm error handler would execute to take care of any errors related to the form input.

```
<cferror type="validation" template="errors/form.cfm">
```

The way the <CFERROR> tag knows there's an error depends on how you set up your form. Look at the following form (we'll talk about the bold part following the example):

```
<form action="formaction.cfm" method="post">
<input type="text" name="intNumeric"><br>
<input type="hidden" name="intNumeric_integer">
<input type="submit" name="submit" value="Submit">
</form>
```

This form assumes two things: first, that there is a formaction.cfm file, and second, that the <CFERROR> tag we showed earlier exists in application.cfm. Putting the <CFERROR> tag in the application.cfm file isn't a requirement, but makes it easier to do blanket form error validation (which <CFERROR> is good at).

Notice the line in bold. The first question that should come to mind when looking at the above code is "How does ColdFusion know there's an error?" The way it knows is by the hidden field that is matched with the text input field. The name of the text input field isn't that important, but the *_integer* part is. This indicates that the intNumeric form field should contain integer-type data. Adding a hidden form element, with the desired datatype added to the form element name of the field we want to validate, is what triggers ColdFusion to watch the field for an error.

If we were to submit the above form with a string instead of an integer, <CFERROR> would produce the following error:

```
Form Entries Incomplete or Invalid

One or more problems exist with the data you have entered.

Data entered in the Intnumeric field must be a number (you entered 'test').

Use the Back button on your web browser to
return to the previous page and correct the listed problems.
```

We've seen how to trigger an error if the form element doesn't contain integer data, so why don't we look at the other types of triggers we can put into effect. The following table lists the values and a description for each:

Value	Description
date	Validates a US date in the form of *dd/mm/yyyy*.
eurodate	Validates European formed dates (*dd/mm/yyyy*).
time	Validates time values in the form of *hh:mm:ss*.
float	Validates floating-type values, although it will accept integer values as well.
integer	Validates integer-type data, although just like float, it accepts floating values as well.
required	This will make the form element a required element.

For lack of a better term, I'll continue to call the hidden fields that trigger form validation errors *validation triggers*. As far I know, there doesn't seem to be an official ColdFusion term for them, which isn't really that big a deal because quite honestly, you'll probably find that using <CFERROR> for form validation isn't really that valuable.

Let's look at an example that makes a field required, and that limits the data to be entered to integer-type data:

```
<form action="formaction.cfm" method="post">
<input type="text" name="intNumeric"><br>
<input type="hidden" name="intNumeric_required">
<input type="hidden" name="intNumeric_integer">
<input type="submit" name="submit" value="Submit">
</form>
```

If the field is left blank, an error will be displayed indicating that the field cannot be left blank because it is a required field. If the user goes back and adds a string, the error will indicate that a number is required. So what happens when multiple fields require validation? Let's look at another example:

```
<form action="formaction.cfm" method="post">
<input type="text" name="intNumeric"><br>
<input type="hidden" name="intNumeric_required">
<input type="hidden" name="intNumeric_integer">
<input type="text" name="szDate"><br>
<input type="hidden" name="szDate_required">
<input type="hidden" name="szDate_date">
<input type="submit" name="submit" value="Submit">
</form>
```

If all of the above fields were left blank, the error message would indicate that both fields were required. The error handler validates the entire form, not just one field at a time.

TYPE=MONITOR

The <CFERROR> MONITOR error type is used in conjunction with <CFTRY>/<CFCATCH> combinations. We haven't yet talked about <CFTRY> and <CFCATCH> in great length, so we'll give a very brief description of how <CFTRY> and <CFCATCH> work, in order to better explain this error handling method.

<CFRY> combined with <CFCATCH> will completely bypass ColdFusion error handling, including writing the error to the application.log file. When using <CFTRY> and <CFCATCH> to handle errors, it is sometimes difficult to record the errors. When an error occurs using this combo, the <CFERROR> tag first handles the error, then passes the program flow back to the <CFTRY>/<CFCATCH> block, where the error first occurred. <CFTRY> and <CFCATCH> will then do their thing with the error. The important part to understand is that the template indicated in the <CFERROR> tag will never be seen by a user because it's instantly passed back to the calling template.

Here's an example of a template with an intentional error within the <CFTRY> and <CFCATCH> tags. We talk about <CFTRY> and <CFCATCH> in the next section, so don't worry too much about them yet; the idea here is to understand how the error handler template behaves.

```
<cferror type="MONITOR" template="errors/monitor.cfm">

<cftry>
   <cfset var1 = 2>
   <cfset var2 = "foo">

   <cfif var1 + var2 eq 0>
   This is here to look pretty.
   </cfif>

   <cfcatch>
   This is where the above error is really handled.<br>
   </cfcatch>
</cftry>

<cfif IsDefined("server.monitor_count")>
   <cfoutput>#server.monitor_count#</cfoutput>
</cfif>
```

The first line indicates that the file errors/monitor.cfm should execute when there is an error within the <CFTRY> tags. The staged error is the same one we've been using often in the chapter, surrounded by <CFTRY> tags. The <CFCATCH> block is where the actual error is handled. The errors/monitor.cfm is responsible for modifying the *server.monitor_count* variable. Let's take a look at that file:

```
<cfparam name="server.monitor_count" default="0">

<cfset server.monitor_count = server.monitor_count + 1>
```

If you run the erroring example code we just talked about, the above code will execute whenever there is an error. This is a very rudimentary example of the monitor error type at work. It does a good job at showing what the method can do, but ideally you'd probably want a better errors/monitor.cfm file that would do a lot more, like e-mail the error to someone.

The same **Error** scope variables exist for the MONITOR error type; in fact, you can basically consider the MONITOR error-handling type the same as the EXCEPTION handling type. This means that you can use any ColdFusion code within in the indicated error handling template, like <CFMAIL> or any other code to assist you in tracking the error.

Using <CFTRY> and <CFCATCH>

Using <CFTRY> and <CFCATCH> together is truly the most versatile way of catching and taking care of errors. Previous to this, we've been talking about <CFERROR>, and while <CFERROR> is good at catching errors, it's nowhere near as flexible as <CFTRY> and <CFCATCH>. In this section, we talk about how to use <CFTRY> and <CFCATCH> to trap errors, and we'll examine several examples illustrating how the tags are used within the context of an application.

Used with one or more <CFCATCH> tags, the <CFTRY> allows developers to catch and process errors. When <CFTRY> and <CFCATCH> were first introduced to ColdFusion, I had a difficult time understanding the purpose of each tag. In retrospect, the tags are about as perfectly named as possible, but at the time, I came up with a kind of rule to help remember how the tags worked, and the rule still comes to mind when I'm explaining <CFTRY> and <CFCATCH>.

I use the word *rule* for lack of a better term; it's more like a story. The rule is that wrapping a block of code with <CFTRY> is akin to giving Evel Knieval a Plan B button. If the daredevil is trying to jump six-dozen full-size buses on his famous motorcycle, and as he's flying through the air over the ramp realizes that he's going to land, he has the option of pressing his Plan B button, which is <CFCATCH> in the story.

The Plan B button suspends him in midair and stops time and gravity as his Evel Knieval team scrambles to take a few dozen vehicles out and to move the landing ramp closer. Once they're done, Evel lands the jump with no broken bones or egos, and everyone is happy. The Plan B button, or I should say <CFCATCH>, gives Evel, or the code, a chance to fix an error as the program is processing (or as the daredevil is dare devilling). The only problem is that in real life, Evel Knieval never had a Plan B button, and ended up breaking a lot of bones. That's why I'd recommend sticking to ColdFusion as your profession, because you always have the option of using <CFTRY> and <CFCATCH> to avoid bone-breaking events.

Let's look at an example custom tag I use on my personal web site. The application itself uses <CFHTTP> to connect to another web server on my network that displays the current MP3 playing over my office speakers. There is a plug-in for the WinAmp MP3 Player that serves the data for me, but for right now that part isn't important. I then display the data on my personal web site. The reason for the application is really kind of pointless. I'd seen it done on a friend's site a while ago, and thought I'd try it out.

Because I can never be absolutely sure that the WinAmp server will be available, I need to use <CFTRY> and <CFCATCH> to make sure that no error is displayed when the server is unavailable. There are a lot of other parts to this application that might be of interest, and that I'll explain briefly after showing the code itself:

```
<cftry>
   <cfhttp url="http://192.168.1.101" method="GET" port="8989"
resolveurl="false"/>
   <cfscript>
   string = REReplace(cfhttp.filecontent, "<[^>]*>", "|", "All");

   title = ListGetAt(string, 7, '|');
   Replace(title,' - ', '-');

   position = ListGetAt(string, 9, '|');
   quality = ListGetAt(string, 11, '|');
   status = Trim(ListGetAt(string, 13, '|'));
   band = Trim(ListGetAt(title, 1,'-'));
   tmp = title;
   song = Trim(ListDeleteAt(tmp, 1, '-'));
   </cfscript>

   <cfquery name="findBand" datasource="new_stomp" maxrows="1">
   SELECT Band_Title, Band_OfficialSite
   FROM Bands
   WHERE Band_Title = '#band#' AND Band_OfficialSite <> ''
```

```
   </cfquery>

   <cfif findBand.RecordCount gt 0>
      <cfset band_link = "<a href='" & findBand.Band_OfficialSite & "'
target='_blank'>">
      <cfset linkup = 1>
   </cfif>

      <table width="98" cellpadding="0" cellspacing="0" border="0">
         <tr>
            <td><cf_titlegen title="CURRENT MP3"></td>
         </tr>
         <tr>
            <td bgcolor="Black"><img src="images/space.gif" width="1"
height="1" border="0"></td>
         </tr>
         <tr>
            <td><cfif
IsDefined("linkup")><cfoutput>#band_link#</cfoutput><cf_mp3gen
string="#UCase(band)#" color="0000FF"></a><cfelse><cf_mp3gen
string="#UCase(band)#"></cfif></td>
         </tr>
          <tr>
            <td><cf_mp3gen string="#UCase(song)#"></td>
         </tr>
         <tr>
            <td><cf_mp3gen string="#UCase(position)#" color="FF0000"></td>
         </tr>
         <cfif status is 'paused'>
         <tr>
            <td><cf_mp3gen string="#UCase(status)#" color="FF0000"></td>
         </tr>
         </cfif>
         <cfif IsDefined("linkup")>
         <tr>
            <td><cf_titlegen title="INFO BY"></td>
         </tr>
         <tr>
            <td><a href="http://www.stompzine.com"><img
src="http://www.stompzine.com/assets/images/stomp.gif" width="44" height="11"
alt="www.stompzine.com" border="0"></a></td>
         </tr>
         </cfif>
      </table>
      <br>
   <cfcatch type="Expression">
      <cfmail to=errors@stompzine.com
        from="michaelbuffington.com error"
        subject="mp3 player is messed!"
```

```
      type="HTML">
    Your MP3 player is messing up. You better fix this soon
    because if you don't, you'll get a ton of e-mails that
    look exactly like this.
    <p>
    <b>Error Type:</b> #cfcatch.type#
    <p>
    <b>Message:</b>
    #cfcatch.message#
    <p>
    <b>Full Error:</b>
    #cfcatch.detail#
    </cfmail>
  </cfcatch>
</cftry>
```

The most important tags in this custom tag are highlighted in bold. If an expression-related error occurs, the block of <CFCATCH> code indicated in bold will send an e-mail indicating the error. Now, this isn't exactly the best use of the <CFCATCH> tag, because all we're doing is sending an e-mail off. This can be done using <CFERROR> alone. But on my site, displaying the currently playing MP3 isn't a top priority, so it I don't try to fix the problem. I could, if I wanted to, write a block of code that displays a message to the user that the MP3 server was having a problem, but the design of the site works well, so I'll just not do anything.

Notice that the <CFCATCH> has the attribute *type*. The example shows that I want to catch errors with a type of expression. There are nine exception types, and they are the same as the ones discussed in the section on <CFERROR> using the exception error handler. To be consistent, here's the list once again:

- Application
- Database
- Expression
- Lock
- MissingInclude
- Object
- Template
- Security
- Custom type
- Any

Just like <CFERROR>, the custom exception type is a type used in conjunction with <CFTHROW>, which we'll talk about soon.

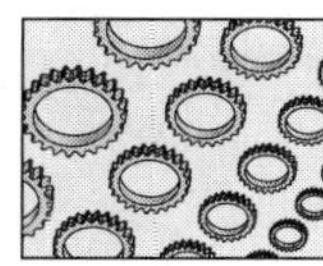

NOTE

If <CFTRY> and <CFERROR> were to arm wrestle, <CFTRY> would, with fierce concentration and brute force, pin <CFERROR> and win. Actually, the "battle" is far less exciting—if <CFERROR> and <CFTRY> are used on the same page, the <CFTRY> tags override any <CFERROR> tag. There is no indication from the ColdFusion server that this happens; it just does, so it's something you should be aware of, especially if you have your money on <CFERROR>. If you want <CFERROR> to execute along with <CFTRY>, you must use the MONITOR type handler.

Several of these exception types create variables available to the block of <CFCATCH> code. The following table lists the exception type, along with the variables created:

Exception Type	Variable Name	Description
Database	NativeErrorCode	The error code associated with the particular error when using native drivers or OLE DB drivers.
Database	SQLState	The error code associated with the database when using ODBC drivers.
Expression	ErrNumber	An internal expression code number.
Lock	LockName	The name of the lock that errored. If there is no lock name in the <CFLOCK> tag, the name *Anonymous* is used instead.
MissingInclude	MissingFileName	The name of the file that couldn't be included.
Custom	ErrorCode	The values you set when using custom error types (which we talk about soon).
Custom	ExtendedInfo	Extended information for custom error types that you set.

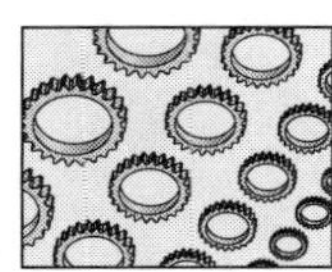

NOTE

Regardless of the driver type you use for a database connection, both the NativeErrorCode *and* SQLState *variables will contain data. Depending on whether you use ODBC or native/OLE drivers, the value will be relevant. If you use ODBC, then* SQLState *is the relevant variable. If you use native or OLE drives, then* NativeErrorCode *is the relevant variable.*

In our example custom tag you might have noticed that there is a query being made. This query check the http://www.stompzine.com database to see if there is a biography for the artist of the current MP3, and if there is, it will link to that band's web site.

As the code is presented, if that query were to error somehow, the user would see a nasty database error.

By nesting a <CFTRY> and <CFCATCH> block, we can reduce the chances that the entire custom tag will fail. For example, the following block of code changes the code surrounding the query in the example custom tag:

```
<cftry>
   <cfquery name="findBand" datasource="new_stomp" maxrows="1">
   SELECT Band_Title, Band_OfficialSite
   FROM Bands
   WHERE Band_Title = '#band#' AND Band_OfficialSite <> ''
   </cfquery>

   <cfcatch type="Database">
<cfset findBand.RecordCount = 0>
</cfcatch>
</cftry>
```

If there is a SQL error, or if the datasource has a problem connecting, there will be an error that we catch with <CFCATCH>. We then set the record count to 0 for the findBand query. We could also very easily put some type of code within the <CFCATCH> block that notifies the site administrator that something is wrong. The remaining code in the site assumes the query has executed, but comes back with zero records. The connection to the database server could be completely severed, and the site would remain functional.

Using <CFTHROW>

<CFTHROW> allows you to create a custom exception type, just like a MissingInclude, Database, or one of the other of the possible exception types available to <CFCATCH>. Here's an example of <CFTHROW> in action:

```
<cftry>
   <cfif NOT IsDefined("url.category")>
       <cfthrow type="missingURLParam"
message="Missing a URL Parameter">
   </cfif>
   ...
   <cfcatch type="missingURLParam">
   <!--- error handling code here --->
   </cfcatch>
</cftry>
```

In this example, if the URL parameter category doesn't exist, we throw an error with the custom type name of *missingURLParam*. We can use this error type later on in the <CFCATCH> tag, and do something about the error. If we used the <CFCATCH> type of Any, the custom type would be caught. When <CFCATCH> says any, it really does mean any type of exception.

If we didn't name the <CFTHROW> exception type, it would automatically fall under the Application type. The Application exception is designed solely to catch unnamed <CFTHROW> tags.

The preceding example includes two attributes. There actually five total attributes for the <CFTHROW> tag, all of them optional. Here is a list of the attributes and their descriptions:

Attribute	Description
type	The name of the custom exception.
message	An error message that describes the actual error.
detail	Detailed information about the error. Again, you define this.
errorcode	An error code that you've selected.
extendedinfo	Any type of extended information that you'd like to add.

With all of these custom attributes, it seems like the designers of ColdFusion should have just let you pass a structure to the tag that could be used later on. Having set attributes forces consistent code though, so it's not that big a deal.

Using <CFRETHROW>

The <CFRETHROW> tag is designed to throw the error one more time if the first error handler cannot fix the problem. For instance, if the <CFCATCH> block is unable to resolve the error, the <CFRETHROW> tag will throw the error to the calling template.

It makes the most sense to use this tag within a custom tag. For example, imagine a custom tag that has its own error handling, but you want the calling template to take care of the error handling. The following example shows what the custom tag might look like:

```
<cftry>
   <cfset this_will = error>
   <cfcatch type="expression">
      <cfrethrow>
   </cfcatch>
</cftry>
```

The error here will get thrown to the calling template, which looks like this:

```
<cftry>
   <cf_example_tag_from_above>
   <cfcatch type="expression">
      Error handling code for custom tag here.
   </cfcatch>
</cftry>
```

Sitewide Error Handler

The ColdFusion Administrator allows you to assign a sitewide error handler, underneath the Server Setting page. If you've assigned an error handler here, it's the equivalent of including the <CFERROR TYPE="Exception"> tag on every single page on the ColdFusion server. This allows you to catch every error with your own custom error handler, rather than the standard ColdFusion error handling.

All of the rules that apply to <CFERROR TYPE="Exception"> also apply to this sitewide error handler, which means you can write CFML code, include custom tags, and so on to your heart's content. All of the *error.scope* variables are also available to the sitewide error handler.

If you do end up using <CFERROR> within the Application.cfm file of a site that has a sitewide error handler, the <CFERROR> tag will override the sitewide error handler.

Missing Template Handler

If you've tried executing a ColdFusion template on your server that doesn't exist, you get a ColdFusion-generated 404 error message. Your web server might have the option of providing custom 404 error messages, but these won't apply to ColdFusion templates on a standard web server setup. ColdFusion allows you to set a missing template handler in the ColdFusion Administrator, under the Server Settings page.

The missing template handler can be standard CFML code. Unfortunately, there are no special variables exposed when a missing template is encountered. However, if you'd like to somehow track which missing template was called, the *cgi.cf_template_path* variable is available, and can tell you what file was being called.

Wrapping Up

In this chapter, we've discussed ColdFusion error-handling possibilities. Hopefully, using tags like <CFTRY> and <CFCATCH> will become a strong part of your application writing. The amount of time saved by writing code to take care of possible errors is beneficial by itself, but the fact that you're reducing the number of errors seen by a user is far more beneficial, even if the result isn't measurable. Errors reduce user confidence, and unfortunately, users might assume that if your site is unreliable, then your company must be unreliable as well. Proper error handling simply makes things better for your users, your application, and your company.

CHAPTER

15

Custom Tags

IN THIS CHAPTER:

Simple Custom Tags

Advanced Custom Tags and Functionality

Using <CFASSOCIATE>

Using <CFMODULE>

One of the goals of anyone who writes code, regardless of the language or platform, should be reusability. Blocks of code should be designed in ways that allow the functionality to be used in multiple places, without having to rewrite the code again. With reusability comes efficiency, and efficiency in code comes with a lot of benefits like lower overhead, fewer bugs, more organization, and fewer headaches, just to name a few.

In this chapter, we talk entirely about custom tags. Custom tags allow ColdFusion developers to make modular blocks of code that can be made available to the entire ColdFusion server, or just a particular application. They help promote code reuse, as well as provide several other hidden benefits as well, which we'll talk about as we go along.

We start by talking about simple custom tags. Most of us have probably at least dabbled with custom tags, but you may still find the first section useful even if you've been using custom tags for a while. Once we cover the basics, we get into advanced custom tags. Keep in mind that while a distinction is being made between simple and advanced custom tags, in reality there is no real defining line between simple and advanced. There is no official ColdFusion term for advanced custom tags. For this chapter, advanced custom tags take advantage of tag pairs, tag nesting, child and parent tags, and other more complicated techniques.

In both the simple custom tag sections and advanced custom tag sections, we introduce an example custom tag. Both can be used in the real world with little or no modification—hence the reusability of custom tags. But before we break down the tags, we'll cover all the techniques in the sections leading up to the examples.

Simple Custom Tags

ColdFusion as a language derives a lot of its simplicity from the fact that it uses tags that perform certain tasks. As a developer, you don't need to know all of the algorithms that a tag like <CFQUERY> performs when invoking the tag. As developer, you're able to maintain your focus on the task at hand, rather than get into the nitty-gritty of how to do whatever is required to create a recordset for instance. The idea of custom tags comes directly from the ColdFusion tag-based language, allowing you to perform tasks by using tags. This allows you to write the code once (or use code that someone else has written), and move on to figuring what you need to do to complete functionality within a ColdFusion template.

There isn't anything special about the technology behind custom tags. Custom tags themselves are regular ColdFusion templates that follow a few rules, which we discuss in "How to Create Custom Tags." The tags themselves should run as self-contained programs for portability and reusability reasons. You want to be able to copy the file of a custom tag to another completely different server and application, and expect it to work in the same way. If you design custom tags without this kind of an approach the purpose of custom tags are somewhat defeated, although the flexibility of custom tags would also allow you to create a custom tag that depended entirely on its server/ application environment.

How to Create Custom Tags

As we read earlier, tags are simply ColdFusion templates with a few rules applied to them. Any valid CFML is valid within a custom tag, and there no restrictions as to the template size or anything like that. Just as in a regular ColdFusion template, HTML, JavaScript, and so on, are acceptable. You're free to do what you want with custom tags.

Custom tags can be as simple as a single <CFSET> tag, or as complicated as an entire application consisting of tag pairs and nested tags. Let's look at a very simple custom tag:

```
<cfparam name="attributes.firstvalue" default="1">
<cfparam name="attributes.secondvalue" default="1">

<cfset caller.result = attributes.firstvalue + attributes.secondvalue>
```

Yes, this is an almost insultingly simple custom tag that merely adds two values together. The point is that custom tags use standard CFML, and can be as simple and tiny as the above example. There are some new variables and scopes introduced in the custom tag, but they're easy to understand. We talk about the attributes and caller scopes in some of the following sections.

There are a few places that you can store custom tags. The first place is the ColdFusion custom tag directory, which for standard Windows installations is located in the C:\CFUSION\CustomTags directory. Custom tags saved to this directory, or any subdirectory beneath this directory, will be available to any application on your ColdFusion server. For example, even though the CustomTags directory is in an entirely different location from your application, you'd still be able to call it and use it in your application. If you share the server with someone else, they too would be able to access your custom tags, which brings up the point that if you're on a shared environment, it's a good idea to write tags that can't be used against you. Shared environments and custom tags bring up a whole other subject to talk about; for now we avoid getting sidetracked and move on. We address shared environments later on. We also talk about how to actually call a custom tag in the "Calling Custom Tags" section.

Custom tags can also be stored within the same directories as your application, but there are some rules to keep in mind. When a custom tag is called, ColdFusion first looks for that custom tag in the directory of the calling template, then in the ColdFusion CustomTags directory. Custom tags stored in your application's directories cannot be accessed by other applications, which might provide some security benefits. For example, an application in c:\wwwroot\inetpub\skate.shop would not be able to use a custom tag in c:\wwwroot\inetpub\stompzine.

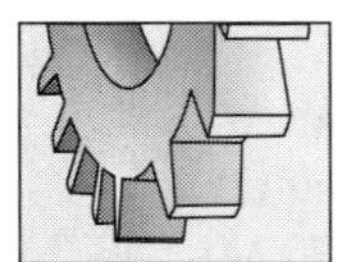

TIP

You can tell ColdFusion where to look for your custom tags by appending the path to the HKEY_LOCAL_MACHINE\SOFTWARE\ALLAIRE\COLDFUSION\CURRENTVERSION\CUSTOMTAGS key. Always keep in mind that messing around in the registry can produce undesirable results if you're not careful; modifying this key, however, won't give you any trouble.

Calling Custom Tags

To call a custom tag, you would use the following syntax:

```
<cf_stupidcalc firstvalue="123" secondvalue="342">
```

This code would call the file stupidcalc.cfm. Custom tag filenames can be whatever you like, and the way to call them is by adding CF_ to the beginning of the filename, and leaving off the .CFM file extension. ColdFusion then looks for the file in the calling template's directory, then the ColdFusion CustomTags directory.

It should be noted that calling a custom tag is much different than using the <CFINCLUDE> tag. The <CFINCLUDE> simply pulls whatever logic exists in the specified template into the calling template. The application acts as if the included template was the same as having the included template's logic within the logic of the calling page. Custom tags are individual programs, complete with their own variable space that cannot be automatically accessed by the calling template. They require a few more resources than a <CFINCLUDE> would, because they need to be loaded into memory when they are first executed. The amount of resources the tag requires is pretty minimal, and without a doubt the amount of time saved maintaining and building the application will make up for the possible extra resources required.

There are no real set rules for custom tag syntax, but it's good to follow a certain form. First and foremost, each custom tag should contain a comment block that describes the purpose of the tag, the author, some contact info, and a creation date. It's a good idea to do this even if you know no one else will ever see the code. *You* might see it a year later, and without a comment block, you might have a hard time figuring out what the tag does without digging into the code.

For extra credit, it's good to list which attributes are expected to be passed from the calling template, with a brief description of what they're used for. This will help you understand further what each tag does, and will also help you understand what its requirements are. Let's look at an example of the comment block that will end up describing the simple custom tag for this chapter:

```
<!---
NAME:
<cf_linkmonster>

DESCRIPTION:
This tag takes a string, and based on a query of keywords, links
the keywords to the URL of choice.

ATTRIBUTES:
attributes.string      - (required) String that should be scanned for
                          keywords to link.
request.qryKeywords    - (required) Query containing keywords and IDs.
                          See notes for format.
attributes.href        - (required) URL to link to. See notes for
                          format and examples.
attributes.output      - (required) Name of the variable to place modified string.

NOTES:
The request.qryKeywords query should contain the following columns:
   ID, WORD
The ID column is used within the attributes.href string to make a
dynamic link.
For each record in the query, the attributes.string variable is
scanned for the a string that matches the WORD column.

The attributes.href string should formatted like the following examples
   http://www.domain.com/file.cfm?id=[id]
   index.cfm?var1=foo&id=[id]
The [id] value will be replaced with the ID column from the
request.qryKeywords query for each matched keyword.

The more records in the request.qryKeywords tag, the slower this
tag will perform. For each record in request.qryKeywords the tag
must scan the attributes.string variable for that particular keyword.
```

```
EXAMPLES:
<cfscript>
qryKeywords = QueryNew("id, word");

QueryAddRow(qryKeywords);
QuerySetCell(qryKeywords, "id", "1");
QuerySetCell(qryKeywords, "word", "blue");

QueryAddRow(qryKeywords);
QuerySetCell(qryKeywords, "id", "2");
QuerySetCell(qryKeywords, "word", "green");

QueryAddRow(qryKeywords);
QuerySetCell(qryKeywords, "id", "3");
QuerySetCell(qryKeywords, "word", "red");

request.qryKeywords = qryKeywords;
string = "The colors blue, red, and green should be linked in this string";
</cfscript>

<cf_linkmonster
   string="#string#"
   href="test.cfm?id=[id]"
   output="linked">

AUTHOR:
Michael Buffington (mike@stompzine.com)
VERSION: 1.0 - 7/25/2001
VERSION: 1.1 - 8/05/2001 - MB: Added <CFEXIT> error handling.
--->
```

The comment block itself is clear and concise. There are probably more details we could add, but there is such thing as too much of a good thing. Comment blocks should be clear, to the point, and readable too. The whole point of having comments is so that someone will read them, and programmers have lazy eyes. They don't want to be bothered with confusing or overly wordy comments.

We've gotten a peek at the custom tag we'll be going into later, but for now, let's continue with the basics. Once the comment block is in place, the first thing to do is to assign default values to the custom tag attributes, or define some error handling if a required attribute is missing.

Let's look at another example that assigns default values, as well as checking for required attributes. This example is just a general example, and isn't the <CF_LINKMONSTER> tag we snuck in earlier. We talk about that tag in detail later in "Using <CF_LINKMONSTER>." Before looking into the tag, we look at how the tag is called. Assume that the following two blocks of code are in separate files, the first block in the calling template, and the second block, the custom tag itself.

```
<cf_calendar month="July" highlight="#Now()#">
```

Now, the example code from the custom tag:

```
<cfparam name="attributes.highlight" default="1">
<cfparam name="attributes.background" default="white">
<cfparam name="attributes.highlightcolor" default="red">
<cfparam name="attributes.displaystyle" default="classic">

<cfif NOT IsDefined("attributes.month")>
   <cfset caller.error = "The month attribute is required">
   <cfexit>
</cfif>
```

Let's stop there. Assume that the tag creates some type of calendar. Notice that we've only passed two attributes to the custom tag, but there are five possible attributes. The first four are optional. If they aren't included in the calling template, then the <CFPARAM> tags will default them to a default value. The *month* attribute, however, is required. If it is not present, then we set an error message that can be accessed by the calling template, then we use the <CFEXIT> tag to stop processing the custom tag and return to processing the calling template.

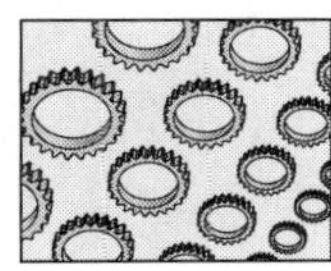

NOTE

If you used <CFEXIT> on a regular CFML template, not a custom tag, it would do the same thing <CFABORT> does, which is completely stop the ColdFusion template from processing. <CFABORT> within a custom tag is still <CFABORT>, and stops the request at the exact moment it's used.

Accessing Attribute Values

You've probably noticed that in some of the examples of custom tags we've been looking at, we refer to variables as something like *attributes.name* or *caller.name*. These two types of variable are important to understand. Custom tags have their own memory space, meaning they cannot see variables that exist on the calling template, nor can the calling template see what variables exist within the custom tag.

When you pass an attribute to a custom tag, as shown in the following example, the attribute's name and value are placed in the **Attributes** scope.

```
<cf_calendar month="Decemember">
```

To help me understand how the **Attributes** scope and **Caller** scope work, I thought of another real-world metaphor. Custom tags are like amusement park rides, and the people getting on the ride are custom tag attributes. The second they step off the loading platform and onto the ride, they are passed into the **Attributes** scope. While on the ride, no one else can mess with them from the outside world.

They are happy people, completed enthralled and distracted from anything else beyond the ride, except for perhaps their stomachs. The fact is, some people get sick on amusement park rides, and some weaker-bellied folks need to purge their stomachs while riding. The contents of their stomachs, when launched from the fast moving ride, are now part of the **Caller** scope. The outside world is now privileged to have something come from within the ride into their world (the same world the amusement park riders were once in).

The outside world in the metaphor is the calling template, the loading dock is the invocation of the custom tag, and the riders are the attributes and values. The flying stomach contents of the queasy rider is a variable within the **Caller** scope that an employee (some logic in the calling template, or perhaps even a different custom tag called within the calling template) will have to deal with.

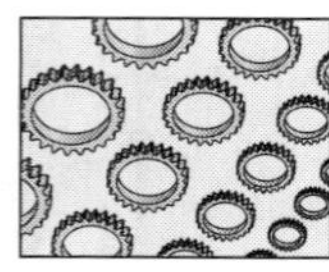

NOTE

You'll be happy to know that within the entire book, that metaphor contains the highest degree of bodily function talk. You'll also be glad to know that I got rid of my initial metaphor of a seagull and an activity they perform that is commonly referred to as target practice.

Variables passed from the calling template must always be referred to as *attributes.variablename*. If you neglect to use the **Attributes** scope name, ColdFusion assumes you're referring to a different variable contained within your custom tag.

Passing Structures as Attributes

Imagine having a custom tag that required a lot of attributes, so many that it began to get a little bit crazy each time you called the tag. For example, check out this custom tag invocation:

```
<cf_tablemaker
  bgcolor="brown"
  width="300"
  padding="2"
  border="0"
  column1="Name"
  column2="Job Description"
  column3="Extension"
  >
```

First of all, the idea of having attributes like *column1* and *column2* is probably a bad idea. This means that within the custom tag, we have to accept and prepare for the possibility that a dynamic number of columns might be assigned, which would be tedious. There are better ways of doing this, which we'll show in a second. Also, notice that there are attributes here that appear as they are there just for formatting. These too could be handled differently. But for the formatting attributes, we'll be doing it differently purely for readability reasons. It's perfectly acceptable to do it as shown. We'll modify how column names are handled for functionality reasons.

Let's look at changing the formatting attributes first. Custom tags allow you to pass an attribute collection by using the following syntax:

```
<cf_tablemaker attributecollection="#strTableFormat#">
```

The *attributecollection* attribute takes the key-value pairs of a structure and passes them to the custom tag. However, the custom tag has no idea that the key-value pairs came in the form of a structure, or as a regular attribute. Let's look at the following code to help explain it. The first block is the calling template, and the second block is the custom tag:

```
<cfscript>
strTableFormat = StructNew();
StructInsert(strTableFormat, "bgcolor", "red");
StructInsert(strTableFormat, "width", "300");
StructInsert(strTableFormat, "padding", "2");
StructInsert(strTableFormat, "spacing", "2");
StructInsert(strTableFormat, "border", "0");
</cfscript>

<cf_tablemaker attributecollection="#strTableFormat#">
```

Within the custom tag, we'd refer to the key-value pairs contained within the structure as if they were the same as any other attribute. For example, the block of code below is pulled out of the fictitious <CF_TABLEMAKER> tag where the attributes in the structure are actually used:

```
<table width="<cfoutput>#attributes.width#</cfoutput>"
   border="<cfoutput>#attributes.border#</cfoutput>"
   cellspacing="<cfoutput>#attributes.spacing#</cfoutput>"
   cellpadding="<cfoutput>#attributes.padding#</cfoutput>"
   bgcolor="<cfoutput>#attributes.bgcolor#</cfoutput>">
```

We'll cut it off there; the important part to notice is that the structure name is lost, and the key names are now within the **Attributes** scope.

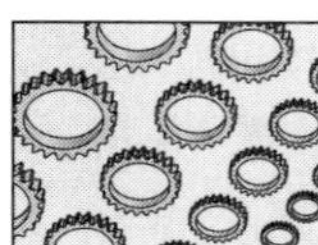

NOTE

There's an actual performance benefit from having as little extraneous text between <CFOUTPUT> tags as possible. In the example, the <CFOUTPUT> tags handle the bare minimum, which in this case are the attributes available to the custom tag. This practice applies to CFML in general, not just to custom tags. However, sometimes being this meticulous with your <CFOUTPUT> tags makes the code harder to read. Personally, I prefer readability and code cleanliness more than I do perfect code. That readability and code cleanliness might make it easier for other developers within my organization to work with my code, which might save more time and money than almost immeasurable performance increases.

Now, how do we handle multiple structures? I suggested earlier that the column attributes for this tag was a bad idea, and that it could be handled differently. Basically what we have are two structures that need to be combined into one: the formatting structure, which was done purely for readability reasons that we saw earlier, and the columns structure, which we look at shortly. Only one structure can be passed to a custom tag at a time. That might seem like a problem, but really it's not. When the structure is passed to the custom tag, all of the key-value pairs are hacked to bits anyhow, placed into the **Attributes** scope, so maintaining two separate structures is out of the question from the very start.

So what we have to do is combine the two structures before passing them to the custom tag. Once in the custom tag, the keys are treated as attributes. Let's look at the calling template that combines the structures into one unit, then passes the structure to the tag.

```
<cfscript>
// Create Structures
strTableFormat = StructNew();
StructInsert(strTableFormat, "bgcolor", "red");
```

```
StructInsert(strTableFormat, "width", "300");
StructInsert(strTableFormat, "padding", "2");
StructInsert(strTableFormat, "border", "0");

strColumns = StructNew();
StructInsert(strColumns, "column1", "Name");
StructInsert(strColumns, "column2", "Job Description");
StructInsert(strColumns, "column3", "Extension");

// Move strTableName into strCombined
strCombined = StructNew();
strCombined = strTableFormat;

// Create New Entries for the columns
i = 1;
while (i lte StructCount(strColumns))
{
   StructInsert(strCombined, "column" & i, Evaluate("strColumns.column" & i));
   i = i + 1;
}
</cfscript>

<cf_tablemaker attributecollection="#strCombined#">
```

Adding the strColumns structure to the strTableFormat structure might seem like it's a bit complicated, but the reason it's done the way is to allow a dynamic number of key-value pairs. As long as we maintain the format of the existing strColumns structure, the loop within the <CFSCRIPT> block will insert the columns to the strCombined columns.

It's possible that there are other ways of doing this, but this method combines the two quickly, without much need for a lot of dynamic variable evaluations. Ideally, the most functional method of combining the two structures wouldn't rely on the keys in the structures to have a particular naming format.

Once passed into the custom tag using the *attributecollection* attribute, the key-value pairs are reassigned as variables in the **Attributes** scope. Each key within the structure we pass into the custom tag would be referred to like so (this example outputs the key-value pairs within the tag):

```
<cfoutput>
#attributes.bgcolor#<br>
#attributes.width#<br>
#attributes.padding#<br>
#attributes.border#<br>
#attributes.column1#<br>
#attributes.column2#<br>
```

```
#attributes.column3#<br>
</cfoutput>
```

Notice that the structure name is completely stripped. The custom tag will error if it sees any other scope other than the **Attributes** scope for these particular variables. The structure no longer exists within the tag, just variables within the **Attributes** scope.

The Caller Scope

Because custom tags maintain their memory space, there needs to be some way to pass a variable from the custom tag to the calling template. The **Caller** scope is what enables us to do this. Variables set to the **Caller** scope are available to the calling template. If invoking the following custom tag, the *caller.foo* variable would be available to the calling template once the tag was finished executing:

```
<cfparam name="attributes.color" default="red">
<cfparam name="attributes.mode" default="display">

Assume there's some useful code happening here.

<cfset caller.foo = "This value is passed to the calling template">
```

The **Caller** scope is the vehicle that allows you to pass a variable outside of the template. It also allows you to modify values in already existing variables within the calling template. For instance, there would be no conflict in our above example if the variable *foo* already existed within the calling template.

You can also set variables of other scope types within a custom tag using the **Caller** scope. For instance, all of the following <CFSET> statements would work:

```
<cfset caller.request.dsn = "newdsn">
<cfset caller.application.count = caller.application.count + 1>
<cfset caller.server.servertime = Now()>
```

However, with these scopes, setting the variable to the **Caller** scope isn't required because custom tags have access to those scopes automatically. In fact, custom tags can "see" the following scopes:

- Request
- Session
- Application
- Client

- Cookie
- CGI
- URL
- FORM

The fact that custom tags can see these scopes makes things a lot easier. For example, in the previous "Passing Structures as Attributes" section, we talked about passing a structure of attributes to a custom tag. If you were to scope the structure to the **Request** scope, the structure would be automatically visible to the custom tag, requiring no tricks to passing the data to the custom tag. For example, the following block of code creates a structure within the **Request** scope. This structure will be automatically available to a custom tag invoked in the same block of code:

```
<cfscript>
// Create Structures
request.strTableFormat = StructNew();
StructInsert(request.strTableFormat, "bgcolor", "red");
StructInsert(request.strTableFormat, "width", "300");
StructInsert(request.strTableFormat, "padding", "2");
StructInsert(request.strTableFormat, "border", "0");
</cfscript>

<cf_tablemaker>
```

And now, let's look at the pretend <CF_TABLEMAKER> tag to see how to access the values of the structure. We'll just output them to give an idea of how they are referenced:

```
<cfoutput>
#request.strTableFormat.bgcolor#<br>
#request.strTableFormat.width#<br>
#request.strTableFormat.padding#<br>
#request.strTableFormat.border#<br>
</cfoutput>
```

Notice that we reference the key in the structure just as we would anywhere else, except that this structure is maintained within the **Request** scope. If we neglected to include the **Request** scope reference, we'd generate an error. Because the **Request** scope is visible to a custom tag, variables within its scope are called the same way they would be on the calling template.

Using <CF_LINKMONSTER>

Now that we're experts on the basics of custom tags, let's look at a useful custom tag from start to finish. The idea for the tag came up when I was developing http://www.stompzine.com. Within http://www.stompzine.com are articles and reviews on music, movies, bands, and games, and one of the business rules behind the site is that there should always be a healthy amount of linking within the site articles to other sources of information about a particular topic within the site.

With that business rule in mind, there are two possible ways of accomplishing this goal; format links within the article by hand, or try to automate the process. The tag automates the process by taking in the body of the article, scanning for keywords, and changing those keywords into links, pointing to appropriate information. The tag itself relies on the developer to point its links in the right direction, but other than that it's completely automatic.

Originally, this tag was designed to link band names to band biographies, but it quickly became apparent that it could be designed to be an all-purpose linking utility. The tag is used extensively throughout http://www.stompzine.com, and drastically reduces the amount of work required to actually format the links by hand.

There seems to be only one major drawback—the tag has the potential of hogging resources. We'll talk about this possibility as we outline the tag.

The tag itself isn't that large or complex, but it's important to understand how to make it work within the context of your application. We look at the entire tag, from start to finish, and afterwards I'll pull out particular sections of the tag to talk about. Once the code for the tag itself is covered, we look at a calling template that serves as example of how to call the tag.

```
<!---
NAME:
<cf_linkmonster>

DESCRIPTION:
This tag takes a string, and based on a query of keywords, links
the keywords to the URL of choice.

ATTRIBUTES:
attributes.string      - (required) String that should be scanned for
                          keywords to link.
request.qryKeywords    - (required) Query containing keywords and IDs.
                          See notes for format.
attributes.href        - (required) URL to link to. See notes for
                          format and examples.
attributes.output      - (required) Name of the variable to place
                          modified string.
```

```
NOTES:
The request.qryKeywords query should contain the following columns:
   ID, WORD
The ID column is used within the attributes.href string to make a
dynamic link.
For each record in the query, the attributes.string variable is
scanned for a string that matches the WORD column.

The attributes.href string should formatted like the following examples:
   http://www.domain.com/file.cfm?id=[id]
   index.cfm?var1=foo&id=[id]
The [id] value will be replaced with the ID column from the
request.qryKeywords query for each matched keyword.

The more records in the request.qryKeywords tag, the slower this
tag performs. For each record in request.qryKeywords, the tag
must scan the attributes.string variable for that particular keyword.

EXAMPLES:
<cfscript>
qryKeywords = QueryNew("id, word");

QueryAddRow(qryKeywords);
QuerySetCell(qryKeywords, "id", "1");
QuerySetCell(qryKeywords, "word", "blue");

QueryAddRow(qryKeywords);
QuerySetCell(qryKeywords, "id", "2");
QuerySetCell(qryKeywords, "word", "green");

QueryAddRow(qryKeywords);
QuerySetCell(qryKeywords, "id", "3");
QuerySetCell(qryKeywords, "word", "red");

request.qryKeywords = qryKeywords;
string = "The colors blue, red, and green should be linked in this string";
</cfscript>

<cf_linkmonster
   string="#string#"
   href="test.cfm?id=[id]"
   output="linked">

AUTHOR:
Michael Buffington (mike@stompzine.com)
VERSION: 1.0 - 7/25/2001
VERSION: 1.1 - 8/05/2001 - MB: Added <CFEXIT> error handling.
--->
```

```
<cfif NOT IsDefined("attributes.string")>
   <!--- don't do anything, exit --->
   <cfexit>
</cfif>

<cfif NOT IsDefined("request.qryKeywords")>
   <!--- can't link without words, exit --->
   <cfexit>
</cfif>

<cfif NOT IsDefined("attributes.href")>
   <!--- need someplace to link to, exit --->
   <cfexit>
</cfif>

<cfif NOT IsDefined("attributes.output")>
   <!--- need someplace to send the string, exit --->
   <cfexit>
</cfif>

<cfscript>
// copy variables
string = attributes.string;
href = attributes.href;
qryKeywords = request.qryKeywords;

// loop counter
i = 1;

// loop over each keyword
while (i lte qryKeywords.recordcount)
   {
      dynHref = Replace(href, "[id]", qryKeywords.id[i]);
      link = "<a href=" & dynHref & ">" & qryKeywords.word[i] & "</a>";
      string = replacenocase(string, qryKeywords.word[i], link, "ALL");
      // increment count
      i = i +1;
   }

// send it back to the calling template
"caller.#attributes.output#" = string;
</cfscript>
```

As you can see, this tag is more comments than it is code, which isn't a bad thing. This tag could potentially be used by hundreds of developers, and the comments are a vital guide for those developers.

The first bit of functionality in the tag itself checks for the existence of required attributes. Every attribute in this tag is required. If the attribute isn't defined, then the processing of the custom tag is simply skipped. The request.qryKeywords query is also required, and if it doesn't exist, then processing of the tag is skipped. The <CFEXIT> tag kills the processing of this current tag and returns to the calling template, and resumes the processing.

Within the <CFSCRIPT> block is where the entire bulk of the processing of this custom tag occurs. Let's look at the first few lines within that block:

```
<cfscript>
// copy variables
string = attributes.string;
href = attributes.href;
qryKeywords = request.qryKeywords;

// loop counter
i = 1;
```

To make the code a little more readable, and to reduce the amount we'll have to type later when we copy the attributes and the request.qryKeywords query into new variables. Remember, the custom tag maintains its own memory space, so there's no worry that these variables will conflict with variables outside of the custom tag. We also set up a loop counter. It's important that the value of the counter be set to 1, rather than 0, because we're going to be looping over a recordset, and recordsets always start out at 1.

Let's look at the next block of code in detail:

```
1. // loop over each keyword
2. while (i lte qryKeywords.recordcount)
3.    {
4.       dynHref = Replace(href, "[id]", qryKeywords.id[i]);
5.       link = "<a href=" & dynHref & ">" & qryKeywords.word[i] & "</a>";
6.       string = replacenocase(string, qryKeywords.word[i], link, "ALL");
7.       // increment count
8.       i = i +1;
9.    }
```

Admittedly, this code isn't very easy to follow, so we'll review each line. I've numbered the lines in the particular block for ease of reference. If you were to copy this block exactly as it's printed, you'd probably get an error due to the line numbers. In addition, the line numbers represent this block only, which is why the first line here starts with the number 1, not the actual line number, as it would if we were looking at the entire body of code.

Line 2 starts the While loop that loops over the set of records in the qryKeywords query. The counter is what controls the iterations, so if the counter is less than or equal to the total number of records in the qryKeywords query, it will continue to loop. At the end of each iteration, we increment the value of the counter (at Line 8).

Line 4 creates a new variable called *dynHref*, which is short for *dynamic href*. This is where we replace the *[id]* string within the *attributes.href* variable with the ID column of the qryKeywords column. This might be confusing because we haven't yet talked about the format of the qryKeywords query, or about the *[id]* string. Let's step out of the context of the custom tag for a second and cover the requirements of the query and string.

The qryKeywords query requires two columns. The first column is the ID column, and the second is the WORD column. Because we want to be able to generate a list of keywords from our current database, and then link to information about those keywords within our site, the custom tag assumes that for every keyword, there will also be an ID column.

For example, on http://www.stompzine.com there is a *Bands* table. Let's assume that we want to link every possible band name within a string, and link it back to a page with information about the band. Here's the query that would generate the list:

```
SELECT Band_ID as ID, Band_Title as WORD
FROM Bands
```

This query selects all the bands from the *Bands* table and renames the columns to ID and WORD. Now, let's think about the *attributes.href* string. On http://www.stompzine.com, this string would look something like *music/ bands.cfm?id=[id]*. The expression on Line 4 in the example code will replace the *[id]* string with the ID column value from our query for whatever particular record the loop is on. The tag assumes that we'll be linking to a URL that we can pass an ID value to. Let's look at the code again:

```
1. // loop over each keyword
2. while (i lte qryKeywords.recordcount)
3.    {
4.       dynHref = Replace(href, "[id]", qryKeywords.id[i]);
5.       link = "<a href=" & dynHref & ">" & qryKeywords.word[i] & "</a>";
6.       string = replacenocase(string, qryKeywords.word[i], link, "ALL");
7.       // increment count
8.       i = i +1;
9.    }
```

Now that we have a better understanding of the *href* variable and its use of the *[id]* string, let's examine the rest of Line 4. The replace function replaces the *[id]* string within the href string with the ID column in the qryKeywords query. The counter variable *i* serves double duty by indicating what row we're referencing within the variable *qryKeywords.id[i]*.

On Line 5, we take the *dynHref* variable we just created, and surround it with the HTML anchor tag along with the word from the qryKeywords query, again referenced using array style referencing. We append the closing HTML anchor tag to the end of the string.

On Line 6, we go ahead and replace each keyword within the string with our newly generated *link* variable. The replacenocase() function matches any keyword within the *string* variable regardless of its case, which is important. Within http://www.stompzine.com, authors might refer to band without the proper case. For example, if the keyword we were looking to replace was "Foo Fighters," the following variations on the band names within the string variable would be missed if we didn't use the replacenocase() function:

- foo Fighters
- Foo fighters
- foo fighters
- FOO fighters
- and so on.

Another added benefit of using the ReplaceNoCase() function at this step is that we replace the keyword within the string variable with the actual database representation of that keyword. So if in the stompzine *Bands* table "Foo Fighters" was the correct representation of the band name, versions with improper cases would be replaced. It adds an extra level of site consistency with very little effort. Within the ReplaceNoCase() function on Line 6 we also make sure that we replace every keyword by using the "ALL" scope. Without the scope of "ALL," only the first instance of the keyword would get linked.

Line 8 increments the counter variable, and the process starts over again. Let's look at the remainder of the code:

```
// send it back to the calling template
"caller.#attributes.output#" = string;
</cfscript>
```

The last line within the <CFSCRIPT> block creates a variable within the **Caller** scope with the name of the *attributes.output* variable.

Let's look at an example template that invokes the <CF_LINKMONSTER> tag, as well as builds the required queries and string before hand:

```
<cfscript>
qryKeywords = QueryNew("id, word");

QueryAddRow(qryKeywords);
QuerySetCell(qryKeywords, "id", "1");
QuerySetCell(qryKeywords, "word", "blue");

QueryAddRow(qryKeywords);
QuerySetCell(qryKeywords, "id", "2");
QuerySetCell(qryKeywords, "word", "green");

QueryAddRow(qryKeywords);
QuerySetCell(qryKeywords, "id", "3");
QuerySetCell(qryKeywords, "word", "red");

request.qryKeywords = qryKeywords;

string = "The colors blue, red, red and green should be linked in this string";
</cfscript>

<cf_linkmonster
   string="#string#"
   href="test.cfm?id=[id]"
   output="linked">

<cfoutput>#linked#</cfoutput>
```

Advanced Custom Tags and Functionality

In addition to some of the more basic capabilities of custom tags, there are also some more advanced ways of writing and invoking custom tags. In this section, we discuss and show examples of what I consider more advanced aspects of custom tags. We also introduce a custom tag that makes use of each of the more advanced subjects that we discuss in this section, which includes nesting, tag pairs, and child/parent tags.

While I'm referring to the functionality as advanced, you'll probably see that the subject matter is pretty intuitive, especially if you're very familiar with custom tags to begin with. Suggesting that the tags are advanced simply means that by using some of these techniques your tags will be more capable of performing more complex functions.

In each subsection, we show examples that may or may not be all the useful in the real world. This is done for the sake of simplicity, and because we want to focus on the technique itself. We show a real world example in the final subsection and discuss the code just like we did in the "Simple Custom Tags" section earlier in this chapter. The main idea is to introduce the concepts, and then show the real thing when we're ready for it.

Tag Pairs

With custom tags you have the ability to create custom tag pairs. Most of us are probably very accustomed to using tag pairs, especially when programming in ColdFusion. Some examples of tag pairs include <CFQUERY>…</CFQUERY>, <CFLOOP>…</CFLOOP>, and <CFIF>…</CFIF>. Custom tags allow you to create the same kind of functionality, as shown in the following example:

```
<cf_customtag>
...
</cf_customtag>
```

In order to create a custom tag pair, we need to use the **ThisTag** scope of variables within the custom tag. When a custom tag is invoked, a set of variables is created in the **ThisTag** scope. The following variables are created when a tag is invoked:

- ThisTag.ExecutionMode
- ThisTag.HasEndTag
- ThisTag.GeneratedContent

We cover the later two variables shortly, but for now let's focus on *ThisTag.ExecutionMode*. When you execute a custom tag using tag pairs like the previous code example, the custom tag is executed twice. For example, pretend that the following is a custom tag:

```
<cfparam name="attributes.month"
default="#MonthAsString(DatePart('m',Now()))#">

<cfoutput>#attributes.month#</cfoutput>
```

If we were to invoke the above custom tag using the following form, the current month would be printed twice:

```
<cf_month>
</cf_month>
```

This is because the tag is executed twice. During the first half of the pair of tags, the tag prints the month, and in the second half of the pair, it also prints the month. The *ThisTag.ExecutionMode* variable contains which half of the tag is currently executing. Using this variable, you can design the tag to make full use of tag pairs. The following example shows the same month tag, but this time making use of tag pairs:

```
<cfparam name="attributes.month"
default="#MonthAsString(DatePart('m',Now()))#">

<cfif ThisTag.ExecutionMode eq "start">
   <cfoutput>#attributes.month#</cfoutput>
</cfif>

<cfif ThisTag.ExecutionMode eq "end">
   <cfset nextMonth =
   MonthAsString(DatePart('m',DateAdd('m', 1, attributes.month)))>
   <cfoutput>#nextMonth#</cfoutput>
</cfif>
```

The *ThisTag.ExecutionMode* variable can contain one of two values, *start* or *end*. When the first half of the tag pair executes, the mode is **Start**. During the second half, the mode is **End**. In the above example, the current month would be displayed, along with the next month. If we removed the second half of the tag pair, only the current month would be displayed, because the latter half of the tag pair wouldn't execute.

It's possible, using ThisTag.HasEndTag, to programmatically determine whether or not there is an ending tag pair. A custom tag might require that the latter half of the tag be invoked, or that the tag shouldn't be executed at all. The following example requires a closing tag to be present; otherwise it won't execute.

```
<cfparam name="attributes.firsthalf" default="This is the first half">
<cfparam name="attributes.lasthalf" default="of the sentence.">

<cfif ThisTag.HasEndTag eq 1>
   <cfif ThisTag.ExecutionMode eq "start">
      <cfoutput>#attributes.firsthalf#</cfoutput>
   </cfif>
```

```
  <cfif ThisTag.ExecutionMode eq "end">
    <cfoutput>#attributes.lasthalf#</cfoutput>
  </cfif>
</cfif>
```

The third variable in the **ThisTag** scope is the *ThisTag.GeneratedContent* variable. This variable contains, as its name indicates, any generated content that happens between the two tag pairs. The following example contains content between the two tag pairs. Any generated content between the tag pairs will be stored in the *ThisTag.GeneratedContent* variable.

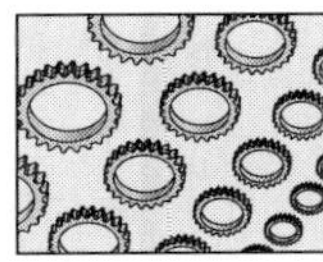

NOTE

When code is executing in Start mode, or more technically put, when ThisTag.ExecutionMode *is "start," the* ThisTag.GeneratedContent *variable is empty. Only when* ThisTag.ExecutionMode *is "end" does it have content. Also, if there is no end tag,* ThisTag.GeneratedContent *is still an empty parameter.*

```
<cf_sentence>
Hello, the time is <cfoutput>#TimeFormat(Now(), "hh:mmtt")#</cfoutput>
</cf_sentence>
```

Only generated content is captured, so the string would look something like "Hello, the time is 11:30 A.M.". The ability to store the generated content almost seems like a useless feature — what could you possibly use it for? A good example of the *ThisTag.GeneratedContent* variable in action is the <CF_HTMLHeadBlock> tag by Nate Weiss. Nate's original tag used <CFABORT> to end processing if a closing tag wasn't present, but I've changed it to use <CFEXIT> instead. I've also modified it slightly so that it simply ignores anything in between the tags, rather than error. I'll show the tag, and then explain how it works afterwards:

```
<cfsetting enablecfoutputonly="YES">
<!--- Make sure a closing tag exists in calling template --->
<cfif not thistag.hasendtag>
  <cfexit>
<cfelse>
  <!--- When the closing tag is encountered... --->
  <cfif thistag.executionmode is "End">
    <cfhtmlhead text="#ThisTag.GeneratedContent#">
  </cfif>
</cfif>
<cfsetting enablecfoutputonly="NO">
```

This custom tag enables you, using the <CFHTMLHEAD> tag, to write whatever lies between the <CF_HTMLHeadBlock> tags to the HTML head of the document. As an example, consider the following example from Nate's documentation on the tag:

```
<html>
<head></head>
<body bgcolor="White">
Creating the HTML Head block now...
<p><a href="javascript:ShowAlerts()">Click here to test function.</a>
</body>
</html>

<!--- All this will be inserted between the HEAD tags, above --->
<cf_htmlheadblock>
  <!--- Run a simple query --->
  <cfquery name="GetData" datasource="A2Z">
    SELECT * FROM Customers
  </cfquery>

  <!--- Put the query recordcount in the title of the page --->
<title><cfoutput>#GetData.RecordCount# Records Found</cfoutput></title>

  <!--- Send a javascript function to the HEAD area --->
  <script language="JavaScript">
    function ShowAlerts() {
    <CFOUTPUT QUERY="GetData">
      alert('Customer Number #CustomerID# is #FirstName# #LastName#');
    </CFOUTPUT>
    }
  </script>
</cf_htmlheadblock>
```

Anything generated within the <CF_HTMLHeadBlock> tags will be placed between the HTML <HEAD> tags of the template. This allows you to execute a pretty much unlimited amount of ColdFusion code anywhere on the template, and have it sent to the head of the HTML document.

Nesting Custom Tags

In addition to tag pairs, ColdFusion allows the developer to nest custom tags. Here's an example of some nested custom tags:

```
<cf_table>
  <cf_row value="Piranah">
  <cf_row value="Blue Ram">
  <cf_row value="Oscar">
</cf_table>
```

This imaginary set of tags might build a table with each row containing the names of South American based tropical fish. The creation of the rows could be handled by the nested <CF_ROW> custom tag.

It's also perfectly acceptable to use a custom tag within the custom tag template, although in both cases it's recommended that you avoid nesting too deep, for performance reasons. Too much nesting can lead to slower execution times because for each invocation of a tag, resources must be allocated to set up the memory space for the tag and its variables.

Custom Tag Functions

There are two functions designed exclusively for custom tags. These functions can help reduce custom tag-related errors, and then give you a way to make your custom tags more robust. We discuss the GetBaseTagList() and GetBaseTagData() functions in the following two sections.

GetBaseTagList()

The GetBaseTagList() function takes no arguments, and should be executed within a custom tag. The function generates a comma-delimited list of parent, or ancestor tags. In the previous South American Tropical Fish example, if we were to execute the GetBaseTagList() function within one of the <CF_ROW> tags, it would generate a list of every tag that executed before it, including normal CFML tags. For example, if in the <CF_ROW> tag the first thing we did was output the GetBaseTagList() function, we might see a list like so: "CFOUTPUT, CF_ROW, CF_TABLE." If we output the GetBaseTagList() function deeper within the <CF_ROW> custom tag, we might see something like: "CFIF, CFOUTPUT, CF_ROW, CF_TABLE." The first item in the list is the parent tag, climbing up the "family tree" in reverse order.

Using this tag, it's possible to determine if a parent tag has executed. Nested tags might require parent tags to execute before executing themselves, and parsing this list can help determine that. It's possible to use the ListFind() function to see if the parent tag is somewhere within the list, and if it is, then to proceed with the execution of the nested, or child, custom tag.

GetBaseTagData()

The GetBaseTagData() functions makes it possible to "see" what variables exist within the parent tag. For example, imagine that you had a custom tag nested within a set of parent tags, like the following:

```
<cf_HTMLHeadBlock showTitle="1">
   <cf_title>
</cf_HTMLHeadBlock>
```

Within the nested tag, it's possible to get a list of the data available to the <CF_HTMLHeadBlock> tag, which in this case, is the *showTitle* attribute. In this example, we may only want to execute the <cf_title> tag if the *showTitle* attribute is present within the parent tag. To determine this, we'd use the following block of code within our <CF_TITLE> tag. To keep things focused and simple, I'm only showing the pertinent lines of code:

```
<cfset parentData = GetBaseTagData("CF_HTMLHEADBLOCK")>

<cfif IsDefined("parentData.attributes.showTitle")>
   <cfif parentData.attributes.showTitle eq 1>
      <title>[title here]</title>
   </cfif>
</cfif>
```

In this example, the title is only generated if the attribute *showTitle* is present in the <CF_HTMLHEADBLOCK> tag, and furthermore, if the *showTitle* attribute is equal to 1. Remember that the <CF_HTMLHEADBLOCK> tag sends any generated content to the HTML <HEAD> tags, so the title would only show up in between the head tags if the *showTitle* attribute was present and set to 1.

The GetBaseTagData() function provides the means to allow a nested custom tag to pull information from the parent tag.

<CF_SIDEBAR> Tag

I wrote the <CF_SIDEBAR> for http://www.stompzine.com. The tag came about because there wasn't a consistent way of adding a sidebar to templates that displayed articles or album reviews. The <CF_SIDEBAR> is highly configurable, and can run in any application without the need of any external files. The tag itself is actually two tags: a parent called <CF_SIDEBAR> and a child called <CF_SIDEBARITEM>. The <CF_SIDEBARITEM> tag is nested within the <CF_SIDEBAR> tags. The <CF_SIDEBAR> tag builds an HTML table around the content items, which are handled by <CF_SIDEBARITEM>.

The tags make extensive use of the some of the things we've been talking about in the previous sections. There's a lot to talk about as we look at the tag, so I'll split it up into manageable chunks.

Let's look at the first, most important part of the <CF_SIDEBAR> custom tag: the comment block. It may be long, but this comment block does a great deal to help explain how the <CF_SIDEBAR> tag works.

```
<!---
NAME:
<cf_sidebar>

DESCRIPTION:
This tag, with the help of <cf_sidebaritem> creates a formatted sidebar looks
good next to news articles, product descriptions, etc.

ATTRIBUTES:
attributes.color_title_bg   - (optional) Color of the title background
attributes.color_title_tip  - (optional) Color of the title corner box
attributes.color_content_bg - (optional) Color of the sidebar background
attributes.color_outline    - (optional) Color of the sidebar outline
attributes.width_tip        - (optional) Width of the title corner box
attributes.width_table      - (optional) Width of the sidebar
attributes.sidebar_title    - (optional) Title of the sidebar
attributes.align_content    - (optional) Aligns sidebar content items
attributes.class_title      - (optional) CSS class for the sidebar title
attributes.class_tick       - (optional) CSS class for the content item
bullets
attributes.class_content    - (optional) CSS class for the content items
attributes.style_title      - (optional) CSS style for the sidebar title
attributes.style_tick       - (optional) CSS style for the content item
bullets
attributes.style_content    - (optional) CSS style for the content items

NOTES:
All attributes for both the <cf_sidebar> tag and
the <cf_sidebaritem> must be passed to the <cf_sidebar> tag.

The attributes scope is passed to all nested tags automatically.

Alternatively, this tag also accepts a structure with
keys that match the above attributes.
```

```
If passing a structure, it only needs to be done once
through the attributecollection attribute in the <cf_sidebar>
tag. ex: <cf_sidebar attributecollection="#strSideBarAttribs#">

Color values should be named values or hex values
(make sure to escape the # signs) ex: ##000000

If you pass any class_* attributes, the HTML will be
formatted automatically.

The same goes for style_* attributes.

EXAMPLES:

// define font classes/styles
StructInsert(strSidebar, "class_title", "title");
StructInsert(strSidebar, "class_tick", "tick");
StructInsert(strSidebar, "class_content", "content");

// define sidebar/sidebaritem colors
StructInsert(strSidebar, "color_title_bg", "##224466");
StructInsert(strSidebar, "color_title_tip", "##6699CC");
StructInsert(strSidebar, "color_content_bg", "##071727");
StructInsert(strSidebar, "color_outline", "##224466");
StructInsert(strSidebar, "width_tip", "5");
StructInsert(strSidebar, "width_table", "220");
StructInsert(strSidebar, "sidebar_title", "Sidebar");
StructInsert(strSidebar, "align_content", "left");
</cfscript>

<cf_sidebar attributecollection="#strSidebar#">
   <cf_sidebaritem content="This is a content item">
   <cf_sidebaritem notick
     content="<a href=""http://domain.com"">This is a link.</a>">
   <cf_sidebaritem content="This is another content item">
</cf_sidebar>

AUTHOR:
Michael Buffington (mike@stompzine.com)
VERSION: 1.0 - 8/09/2001
--->
```

In the Notes section of the comment block, I indicate that nested, or child tags of the main <CF_SIDEBAR> tag will inherit their attributes from the main tag. This doesn't automatically happen with custom tags; it's something that needs to be handled programmatically. This is done for a couple of reasons. The first reason is so that the child tags benefit from being able to read the **Attributes** scope of the parent tag. The second benefit is more of an organizational benefit: passing only a single set of attributes or a structure to the base tag is less work, and makes code more readable.

Because there are so many possible attributes, it also made more organizational sense to define the attributes in a structure prior to the custom tag invocation, and then pass that structure to the custom tag. Additionally, it made sense to, rather than pass the structure through the *attributecollection* attribute for each child tag, to inherit the attributes from the parent tag.

The <CF_SIDEBAR> tag is tightly integrated with its child <CF_SIDEBARITEM> tags. The <CF_SIDEBAR> tag will not execute if there are no child tags, and the child tags will not execute if there are no parent tags.

Let's look at the first block of code in the <CF_SIDEBAR> tag.

```
<cfif ThisTag.HasEndTag is 1>
  <cfif ThisTag.ExecutionMode is "start">
   <cfparam name="attributes.color_title_bg" default="##224466">
   <cfparam name="attributes.color_title_tip" default="##6699CC">
   <cfparam name="attributes.color_content_bg" default="##071727">
   <cfparam name="attributes.color_outline" default="##224466">
   <cfparam name="attributes.width_tip" default="5">
   <cfparam name="attributes.width_table" default="120">
   <cfparam name="attributes.sidebar_title" default="{specify title}">
   <cfparam name="attributes.align_content" default="left">

   <!--- define title style/class --->
   <cfif IsDefined("attributes.class_title")>
      <cfset css_title = "class=""" & attributes.class_title & """">
   <cfelseif IsDefined("attributes.style_title")>
      <cfset css_title = "style=""" & attributes.style_title & """">
   <cfelse>
      <cfset css_title = "">
   </cfif>
```

The first line of code has a matching <CFIF> at the very end of the custom tag. This tag will only execute if *ThisTag.TagHasEnd* equals 1, which means that there are indeed nested tags present.

We set up the default attributes. Nothing in this tag is required, so this list of default attributes is a complete list of possible attributes in the <CF_SIDEBAR> tag. Notice that after the <CFPARAM> tags we do some conditional processing of the *attributes.class_title* and *attributes.style_title* variables. These variables allow a developer to assign a Cascading Style Sheet (CSS) class or style to the title of the sidebar. Depending on the condition, the *css_title* variable will be set to contain something like class="class-name" or style="color:red;". The *css_style* variable is output later on in the <TD> tag that contains the sidebar's title. If none of the conditions are met (which would mean that the developer didn't specify a class or style), the *css_title* variable would be blank. This allows us to simply output the *css_title* variable without having to do any conditional processing within the HTML code later on.

Let's continue:

```
<cfoutput>
   <table
        width="#attributes.width_table#"
       bgcolor="#attributes.color_outline#"
       border="0" cellspacing="0" cellpadding="1">
         <tr>
            <td>
               <table
               width="#attributes.width_table#"
            border="0" cellspacing="0" cellpadding="1">
                  <tr>
                     <td width="#attributes.width_tip#"
                     bgcolor="#attributes.color_title_tip#">
                <div style="display:inline;
width:#attributes.width_tip#;"></div>
                </td>
                     <td

width="#int(attributes.width_table-attributes.width_tip)#"
                bgcolor="#attributes.color_title_bg#" #css_title#>
                 <b>#attributes.sidebar_title#</b>
                </td>
                  </tr>
                  <tr>
                     <td colspan="2"
                bgcolor="#attributes.color_content_bg#"
                align="#attributes.align_content#">
   </cfoutput>
</cfif>
```

This is the HTML code that makes up the first half of our sidebar table. All the attributes are applied to the appropriate parts of the HTML table, including the *css_title* variable we talked about earlier. The <DIV> tag in bold controls the width of what I'm calling a tip. It's really just a rectangle in the upper-left corner of the sidebar added for appearances only, but it is configurable through the tag attributes. Notice also that the *int(attributes.width_table – attributes.width_tip)* segment of code calculates the proper width of the title bar cell.

That takes care of the first half of the <CF_SIDEBAR> tag. Now, let's check out the last, entirely unexciting half:

```
   <cfif ThisTag.ExecutionMode is "end">
                        </td>
                     </tr>
                  </table>
               </td>
            </tr>
         </table>
   </cfif>
</cfif>
```

That's right, there's nothing here but HTML tags. The last half of the <CF_SIDEBAR> tag *is* important even though I'm making it sound unimportant. Without it, the HTML would be pretty screwed up, because the latter half closes all the <TD>, <TR>, and <TABLE> tags we used in the first half. The last <CFIF> closes the first <CFIF> that we talked about earlier that determines whether or not there are any nested child tags.

Now, let's look at the <CF_SIDEBARITEM> tag, starting with its comment block:

```
<!---
NAME:
<cf_sidebaritem>

DESCRIPTION:

This tag needs to be nested with its parent tag, <cf_sidebar>.
It does nothing by itself.

ATTRIBUTES:

attributes.content    - (optional) Any valid HTML
attributes.width_tick - (optional) Width of the bullet/tick <TD>
attributes.notick     - (optional) Indicates that no bullet should be shown.

NOTES:
This tag inherits attributes from the <cf_sidebar> tag;
essentially, the attributes scope of the <cf_sidebar> tag is
merged into the attributes scope of this tag.
```

```
EXAMPLES:
Look at the <cf_sidebar> tag for examples.

AUTHOR:
Michael Buffington (mike@stompzine.com)
VERSION: 1.0 - 8/09/2001
--->
```

The comment block is very similar to its parent tag's comment block, which goes to show that consistent comment blocks are a good thing. The developer using the tag knows the format, and knows where to look for his or her information.

While the <CF_SIDEBARITEM> tag inherits all of its attributes from the parent tag, it's still possible to set some individual attributes for the tag. The *attributes.width_tick* variable controls the width of the <TD> for the bullet, and the *attributes.notick* variable sets a flag that we'll use to hide the bullet if it's present, and the *attributes.content* variable contains the actual content we'd like to display. The *attributes.content* variable can contain pretty much any valid HTML tags, including <IMG> tags, <A> tags, or whatever else you'd want to use.

Let's look at the first block of code for the rest of the tag:

```
<cfparam name="attributes.content" default="{need content}">
<cfparam name="attributes.width_tick" default="5">

<!--- check to see if parent tags have executed --->
<cfif ListFind(GetBaseTagList(), "CF_SIDEBAR")>
```

First, we define the default variables for the tag, but then we do something that looks pretty interesting. The <CF_SIDEBARITEM> tag isn't supposed to execute without its parent tags. In order to find out if the parent tags have executed, we make use of the GetBaseTagList() function. As we discussed in earlier sections, the GetBaseTagList() function generates tags that execute before the current tag. If we use the ListFind() function to find "CF_SIDEBAR" in the list that GetBaseTagList() generates, we can determine whether or not the parent tag has executed. If the "CF_SIDEBAR" text is in the list, then the tag has executed, and we can move on. If it's not in the list, then the <CF_SIDEBARITEM> tag isn't nested, and shouldn't execute.

```
<!--- grab the base tag's attributes --->
<cfset strBaseTagAttributes = GetBaseTagData("cf_sidebar")>

<!--- replace this tag's attributes scope
      with the base tag's attributes scope --->
```

```
<cfloop collection="#strBaseTagAttributes.Attributes#" item="key">
<cfset StructInsert(attributes, "#key#",
"#Evaluate('strBaseTagAttributes.Attributes.#key#')#", 1)>
</cfloop>
```

This block of code uses the GetBaseTagData() function to copy the attributes from the <CF_SIDEBAR> tag to the <CF_SIDEBARITEM>. What follows is the merging of the base tag attributes into the <CF_SIDEBARITEM> tag's **Attributes** scope.

We loop over the base tag structure, and very every item in the structure, we append the key and its value to **Attributes** scope. The **Attributes** scope can be treated like a structure, but the structure that the GetBaseTagData() function creates is a little trickier. For whatever reason, the structure generated by the GetBaseTagData() function doesn't work with ColdFusion structure functions.

For instance, it would have been easier to use the StructAppend() function to simply append the strBaseTagAttributes structure to the attributes structure, but that doesn't work. The only sure fire way I've been able to treat the strBaseTagAttributes structure as a true structure is by using <CFLOOP> to loop over each key.

It's worth mentioning that the structure generated by GetBaseTagData() is actually an array of structures. Notice that when looping over the strBaseTagAttributes structure, we're actually looping over the strBaseTagAttributes.Attributes structure within the strBaseTagAttributes structure. It's a bit tricky to figure out, but it it might help if you think of it as a hierarchy. The strBaseTagAttributes structure is the parent; Attributes is a child (complete with its own keys and values).

Let's continue:

```
<!--- define tick style/class --->
<cfif IsDefined("attributes.class_tick")>
   <cfset css_tick = "class=""" & attributes.class_tick & """">
<cfelseif IsDefined("attributes.style_tick")>
   <cfset css_tick = "style=""" & attributes.style_tick & """">
<cfelse>
   <cfset css_tick = "">
</cfif>

<!--- define content style/class --->
<cfif IsDefined("attributes.class_content")>
   <cfset css_content = "class=""" & attributes.class_content & """">
<cfelseif IsDefined("attributes.style_content")>
   <cfset css_content = "style=""" & attributes.style_content & """">
<cfelse>
   <cfset css_content = "">
</cfif>
```

We perform a very similar set of instructions in the parent tag. In the <CF_SIDEBARITEM> tag, there two places that can contain style sheet classes or styles, so we have a conditional block for each one:

```
   <table
     width="<cfoutput>#attributes.width_table#</cfoutput>"
     cellpadding="2" cellspacing="0" border="0">
      <tr>
         <td valign="top"
           width="<cfoutput>#attributes.width_tick#</cfoutput>"
           <cfoutput>#css_tick#</cfoutput>>
            <cfif IsDefined("attributes.notick")> <cfelse>&#149;</cfif>
         </td>
         <td
          width="
          <cfoutput>
          #int(attributes.width_table-attributes.width_tick)#
          </cfoutput>"
          <cfoutput>#css_content#</cfoutput>>
          <cfoutput>#attributes.content#</cfoutput>
        </td>
      </tr>
   </table>
</cfif>
```

The rest of the code is simply HTML with our attribute values plugged in.

Let's look at an example of the <CF_SIDEBAR> tag from a calling template to get an idea of how they all work together:

```
<style type="text/css">
.title {
          font-family: Arial, Helvetica, Geneva;
          color:white;
          font-size: 11px;
          text-decoration: none
        }

.tick {
         font-family: Arial, Helvetica, Geneva;
         color:white;
         font-size: 11px;
         text-decoration: none
       }
```

```
.content {
            font-family: Arial, Helvetica, Geneva;
            color:white;
            font-size: 11px;
            text-decoration: none
          }
</style>

<cfscript>
strSidebar = StructNew();

// define font classes/styles
StructInsert(strSidebar, "class_title", "title");
StructInsert(strSidebar, "class_tick", "tick");
StructInsert(strSidebar, "class_content", "content");

// define sidebar/sidebaritem colors
StructInsert(strSidebar, "color_title_bg", "##224466");
StructInsert(strSidebar, "color_title_tip", "##6699CC");
StructInsert(strSidebar, "color_content_bg", "##071727");
StructInsert(strSidebar, "color_outline", "##224466");
StructInsert(strSidebar, "width_tip", "5");
StructInsert(strSidebar, "width_table", "220");
StructInsert(strSidebar, "sidebar_title", "Sidebar");
StructInsert(strSidebar, "align_content", "left");
</cfscript>

<cf_sidebar attributecollection="#strSidebar#">
      <cf_sidebaritem content="This is a sidebar item.">
      <cf_sidebaritem notick content="<a href=""##"">link</a>">
      <cf_sidebaritem content="So is this">
</cf_sidebar>
```

In the very beginning of the example, I set up some CSS style that I'll use later in the attributes for the tag. Normally these should be part of your CSS style that is included in the head, either as a file, or within the <STYLE> tags. Using CSS isn't a requirement.

Within the <CFSCRIPT> block I set up all of the colors, widths, and other settings for the tags. To help keep it organized, I segment my code with some comments to indicate what kinds of things I'm setting. It's not a requirement, but it helps other developers, or even myself if I happen to look at the code two months later.

Finally, I invoke the tags. I pass the structure that I use to store the attributes to the parent tag by using the *attributescollection* attribute. I can nest as many <CF_SIDEBARITEM> tags as I'd like. The capability of adding something other than plain text is shown in the second <CF_SIDEBARITEM> tag, where I use the *notick* attribute, and I pass an <A> tag to the custom tag. Removing the tick helps to visually tie the link to the previous content item. I could just as easily pass an <IMG> tag, or an entire <TABLE> structure, although things could get pretty ugly, literally, if I got carried away.

The <CF_SIDEBAR> tag is a good example of some of the things we talked about in the "Advanced Custom Tags and Functionality" section of this chapter. The tag itself, however, is fairly simple and straightforward in its design, and is by no means an indication of the limits of custom tags.

Using <CFASSOCIATE>

One of things that we didn't have an opportunity to discuss while talking about custom tags is the <CFASSOCIATE> tag. In the <CF_SIDEBAR> example, we talked about how to pull attributes from a parent tag into a child tag, but we didn't talk about how to do it the other way around, from a child to a parent.

The best way to describe the <CFASSOCIATE> tag is to show it in use. <CFASSOCIATE> by definition allows sub-tag data to be sent to its parent tag. By this definition, the <CFASSOCIATE> tag needs to be used in a subtag. Let's look at the subtag, discuss what it does, then look at the parent tag.

```
<cfif thistag.ExecutionMode IS "start">
<b>lilkim.cfm - start</b><br>
</cfif>

<cfif thistag.ExecutionMode IS "start">
   <cfassociate basetag="cf_bigpoppa">
   <cfif IsDefined("attributes.string")>
   <cfoutput>string = #attributes.string#</cfoutput><br>
   </cfif>
</cfif>

<cfif thistag.ExecutionMode IS "end">
<b>lilkim.cfm - end</b><br><br>
</cfif>
```

In this tag, which is named <CF_LILKIM>, the <CFASSOCIATE> tag is given the name of the parent tag, which is <CF_BIGPOPPA>. Now, let's look at <CF_BIGPOPPA>, the parent tag. We'll talk about what <CFASSOCIATE> is actually doing once we look at the parent tag.

```
<cfif thistag.ExecutionMode IS "start">
<b>bigpoppa.cfm - start</b><br>
</cfif>

<cfif thistag.ExecutionMode IS "end">
<b>bigpoppa.cfm - end</b><br>
</cfif>

<cfif thistag.ExecutionMode IS "end">
   <p>
   <!--- Protect against no sub-tags --->
   <cfparam Name="thisTag.assocAttribs" default="#arrayNew(1)#">

   <!--- Create structure --->
   <cfset subattribs = StructNew()>

   <!--- Loop through the array --->
   <cfloop index="i" from="1" to="#arrayLen(thisTag.assocAttribs)#">
      <!--- Loop through nested structures --->
      <cfloop item="x" collection="#thisTag.assocAttribs[i]#">
         <!--- Add nested structures to new structure --->
         <cfset tmp = StructInsert(subattribs,
         "child#i#.#x#", "#thisTag.assocAttribs[i][x]#")>
      </cfloop>
   </cfloop>

   <!--- Output new structure --->
   All values:<br>
   <cfloop item="x" collection="#subattribs#">
      <cfoutput>#x# = #subattribs[x]#<br></cfoutput>
   </cfloop>
   <br><br>
   <!--- Output single value from new structure --->
   Single value:<br>
   <cfoutput>#subattribs.child2.string#<br></cfoutput>
</cfif>
```

The <CF_BIGPOPPA> tag loops over an array called *thisTag.assocAttribs*. This array is created by the <CFASSOCIATE> tag that was executed in the <CF_LILKIM> sub-tag. Any attributes that we're passed to the <CF_LILKIM> tag are now present in the thisTag.assocAttribs array.

Let's look at the <CFASSOCIATE> tag from the <CF_LILKIM> tag again:

```
<cfassociate basetag="cf_bigpoppa">
```

Notice that we need to give the name "cf_bigpoppa" to the <CFASSOCIATE> tag. This is the name that ColdFusion assigns to <CF_BIGPOPPA> when executing a template that calls the <CF_BIGPOPPA> tag. The basetag attribute is required, so a tag name must be present. If you don't know the tag name, it's possible to use the GetBaseTagList() function to programmatically determine which tag executed last, therefore giving you the name of the parent tag.

Using <CFMODULE>

Custom tags are expected to be in certain directories — either in the caller templates directory, somewhere underneath the C:\CFUSION\CustomTags directory, or in a directory that you've placed in the registry. Sometimes this can cause problems. For instance, what if you had two tags with identical names, but with entirely different purposes? That might cause a naming conflict; the tag you were expecting to use might reside in the CustomTags directory, but the identically named tag might be in the caller template's directory, which would call the wrong tag.

The way around this conflict is to use the <CFMODULE> tag. The <CFMODULE> tag is simply another way to call custom tags, and by using it, all custom tag functionality remains, including tag pairs, nested tags, scopes, and so on.

There are two ways to call a custom tag using <CFMODULE>. Let's look at the first:

```
<!--- first method --->
<cfmodule name="tagname">
```

The first method allows you provide a specific name of the tag within the C:\CFUSION\CustomTags directories. The following list provides the rules in calling a custom tag by a specific name:

- The *name* attribute can only be used to call a custom tag using <CFMODULE> if the template for the custom tag resides beneath the C:\CFUSION\ CustomTags\ directory.
- The value in the *name* attribute of the<CFMODULE> tag is the name of the custom tag file without the extension. If the file name is calculate.cfm, then value of *name* would be "calculate."
- If the calculate.cfm file resides in the root C:\CFUSION\CustomTags\directory, the name would be "calculate." If the file resides in C:\CFUSION\ CustomTags\ myapp, the name would be "myapp.calculate." If the file is in C:\CFUSION\ CustomTags\myapp\math, the name would be "myapp.math.calculate." I think you get the idea. The name consists of the directories starting from the root custom tags directory separated by a period, down to the actual tag name. Let's look at some examples:

```
<cfmodule name="calculate">
<cfmodule name="myapp.calculate">
<cfmodule name="myapp.math.calculate">
```

You cannot call a tag using the *name* attribute within or relative to the calling templates directory; you can only call tags that are within the C:\CFUSION\ CustomTags directories, or directories beneath the root custom tags directory.

```
<!--- second method --->
<cfmodule template="../tags/tagname.cfm">
```

The second method, using the *template* attribute, is also very useful. The *template* attribute expects a relative path to the tag (meaning, relative to the calling template's location). By supplying a relative path to the tag, you're sure to execute the exact tag you want.

Another benefit to using <CFMODULE> becomes apparent when your site is hosted in a shared environment. Oftentimes, ISPs who host ColdFusion sites will not allow you to have access to the C:\CFUSION\CustomTags directory, for security reasons. (Imagine if everyone on the server could have access to everyone's custom tags; not safe.) The <CFMODULE> tag allows you to store and execute tags from within your application's directory structure.

Wrapping Up

In this chapter, we've talked about how to write and invoke simple custom tags. We've also examined how to write more advanced custom tags, using tag pairs, parent and child tags, and tag-specific functions, and to exchange data between parent and child tags.

One of the most important things about custom tags is that they change the way coding projects are done, both from a development perspective and a business perspective. From a development perspective, custom tags are centralized, more robust, and can be thought of as standalone programs. From a business perspective, standalone, robust, bug-free code can be sold as a product, or used as a way to show off the talent of the organization's programmers. Custom tags are good almost any way you look at them, and I encourage you to use them as much as possible.

CHAPTER

16

Pattern Matching with Regular Expressions

IN THIS CHAPTER:

Overview

The Rules

Character Classes

Multicharacter Regular Expressions

Anchoring

Backreferencing

Matched Subexpressions

Regular expressions in ColdFusion provide very powerful pattern-matching capabilities. In this chapter, we give a brief overview of how regular expressions work within ColdFusion, and we show some examples of how to use regular expressions in your code. By the end of this chapter, even the novice developer should be able to come up with basic, regular expressions, which should come in very handy.

Overview

A regular expression is a set of characters that a language like ColdFusion uses to find matches in a larger string. Regular expressions, on a basic level, allow a developer to use wildcards to find certain patterns. On a more advanced level, developers can use regular expressions to do very complicated things like strip HTML tags from a document, or replace repeating words with a single world.

While regular expressions are deeply rooted in the UNIX operating systems as a means of pattern matching, the idea of regular expressions came from Stephen Cole Kleene in the mid-1950s as a type of notation to manipulate "regular sets" that exist in regular algebra. Kleene was a mathematician who can be credited with several mathematical "inventions," and regular expressions are just one of a few big ones.

The fact that regular expressions have mathematical roots will probably help when learning how to use regular expressions. The notation of regular expressions isn't exactly easy to figure out at a glance. For example, the following is a regular expression that matches integer numbers (with or without a sign):

```
(\+|-)?[1-9][0-9]*
```

To someone who's never seen or heard of regular expressions, the above line of code seems like an alien language, but there is an order to the apparent chaos, which we'll talk about in "The Rules" section in this chapter.

In ColdFusion, regular expressions can be used to do complicated pattern matching. For example, most of us are probably familiar with the Replace() function. The following code does exactly what we want it to:

```
<cfset string = "Hello, replace this with cows">
<cfset string = Replace(string, "this", "cows")>
<cfoutput>#string#</cfoutput>
```

The result of the above would be "Hello, replace cows with cows", because we've indicated that the word "this" should be replaced with "cows". The function Replace() is good for doing what we've just shown, but what if the requirements were changed a bit, and we wanted to get rid of every word that repeated itself. The following example uses REReplace(), which stands for Regular Expression Replace. This function is similar to the Replace() function, but searches for a regular expression pattern as opposed to a particular substring:

```
<cfset string = "This word word is repeated repeated.">
<cfset string = REReplace(string, "([A-Za-z]+)[ ]+\1", "\1", "ALL")>
<cfoutput>#string#</cfoutput>
```

The result of the above would be "This word is repeated.", because the regular expression has been designed to look for any word that immediately repeats itself, and the REReplace function is replacing the second word with nothing. It's possible to get this kind of functionality by writing code that avoids using regular expressions, but it would be more complicated, and would easily be much slower than the regular expression.

The Rules

Let's start with the basics. Regular expressions can't just be created on a whim; they follow a certain set of rules. For the most part, these rules are true wherever regular expressions are used, whether it's on ColdFusion, Perl, PHP, or even SQL, but as a disclaimer, I'm required to state that sometimes the rules do not apply. Each language that supports regular expressions seems to support them in mildly different ways. Always consult with your languages documentation when it comes to regular expressions. Let's go over the rules for ColdFusion.

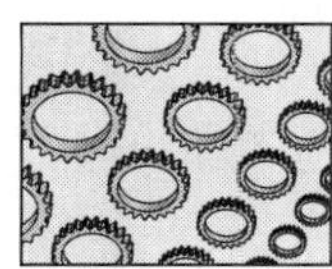

NOTE

ColdFusion regular expression support is very weak compared to that of Perl. Fortunately, Rick Osborne has created a CFX tag that can take a Perl formatted regular expression, and search a string within ColdFusion. The tag is located at http://www.rixsoft.com/ColdFusion/CFX/PCRegEx/cfx_pcregex.html, or on the Developers Exchange on the Allaire site.

Table 16-1 shows special characters used by a regular expression to do certain things. We talk about what these things are a bit later; right now it's important to establish what the special characters are so that you can avoid confusion in the future.

Character	Name
+	Plus sign
*	Asterisk
?	Question mark
.	Period
[	Left Square Bracket
^	Caret
$	Dollar Sign
(	Left Parenthesis
)	Right Parenthesis
{	Left Curly Bracket
|	Pipe Symbol
\	Backslash

Table 16-1 *Special Characters*

Any other character in a regular expression matches itself. For instance, if we were looking to find the first letter A in a string, we'd use the following regular expression (in bold):

```
<cfset intPosA = REFind("A" , "The letter A.")>
```

The bold text in the example above is indeed a regular expression—a very weak and pretty useless example of one to say the least. But, it is a valid regular expression. Any character in a regular expression that is not a special character matches itself.

To find one of the special characters in a string, the character needs to be escaped with the backslash character. For example, the following code looks for a question mark. The question mark, as we just learned, is a special character to regular expressions.

```
<cfset intPosQ = REFind("\?" , "Where's the question mark?")>
```

The backslash indicates that the question mark in the regular expression is not intended to be a special character; rather, it's just a literal question mark.

A period can be used as a character placeholder. The following example illustrates this rule best:

```
<cfset szNewWord =
  REReplace("Cot, Bog, Log, Cow, Chicken", "[CBL].[tg]", "*", "ALL")>
```

In the example, Cot, Bog, and Log would be replaced by the * symbol. The period matches any single character. If we output the szNewWord variable, we'll get the following string:

```
*, *, *, Cow, Chicken
```

Cow and Chicken are not replaced because of the bracketed characters in the string, which brings us to the next rule.

Brackets surrounding a character or characters indicate that we want the regular expression to search for one of those characters. In our previous example, the regular expression looked for any word that started with C, B, or L because of the [CBL] part of the regular expression. Notice also that the regular expression is uppercase — regular expressions are case sensitive (which is another rule).

Let's say that we wanted all uppercase letters to be replaced with a character. The following example would do just that:

```
<cfset szNewString = REReplace("This Is Gonna Get Munched", "[A-Z]", "x", "ALL")>
```

Every uppercase letter in this string will get replaced with the letter x, returning the string "xhis xs xonna xet xunched". The string really was munched. The rule: Brackets can surround a range of letters. The range is indicated by the hyphen. We could have narrowed the range by using A-G instead of A-Z, which would change the string to "This Is xonna xet Munched".

What if we wanted to exclude certain characters in our regular expression? Let's create a regular expression that replaces every character except the letter *G* with the letter *x*:

```
<cfset szNewString = REReplace("This Is Gonna Get Munched", "[^G]", "x", "ALL")>
```

This would turn the string into "xxxxxxxxGxxxxxGxxxxxxxxxx".

The caret is used within a range. The caret is only a special character if it's the first character in the range of letter. If it's not the first character, it's treated as a standard character (meaning the regular expression will try to match the literal caret character in the string).

If you intend to use a closing square bracket (]) in a regular expression, it must be the first character in the regular expression or in a character range. The regular expression will not look for the bracket if it's not the first character in the string, even if it's preceded with the backslash escape code. The following example shows how you'd find the literal closing square bracket character in a string:

```
<cfset szNewString =  REReplace("Here's the ] symbol", "[]]", "bracket")>
```

This would change the string to "Here's the bracket symbol".

Character Classes

Regular expressions support Portable Operating System Interface (POSIX) character classes. POSIX is an Institute of Electrical and Electronics Engineers (IEEE) standard designed to provide portability between different UNIX systems. Character classes can be used, as follows:

```
<cfset szNewString =  REReplace("Here's the ] symbol", "[[:punct:]]", "*", "ALL")>
```

The string would be changed to "Here*s the * symbol".

The character class is in bold. In this case, all punctuation marks will be replaced with an asterisk. Character classes are surrounded by square brackets, and sandwiched between two colons. Table 16-2 lists the available character classes in ColdFusion.

Class	Match
[:alpha:]	Matches any letter, upper or lowercase. Equivalent to using [A-Za-z].
[:upper:]	Matches any uppercase letter. Equivalent to using [A-Z].
[:lower:]	Matches any lowercase letter. Equivalent to using [a-z].
[:digit:]	Matches any numerical digit. Equivalent to using [0-9].
[:alnum:]	Matches any number or letter, upper- or lowercase. Equivalent to using [A-Za-z0-9].
[:xdigit:]	Matches any hexadecimal digit. Equivalent to using [0-9A-Fa-f].
[:space:]	Matches any tab, new line, vertical tab, form feed, carriage return, or space.
[:print:]	Matches any printable character, which includes all characters, and spaces, but not new lines, tabs, vertical tabs, form feeds, or carriage returns.
[:graph:]	Matches anything that is not white space, or basically anything but spaces, tabs, new lines, and any other "unseen" character.
[:punct:]	Matches any punctuation character. Includes ! ' # S % & ` ( ) * + , - . / : ; < = > ? @ [/] ^ _ { | } ~
[:cntrl:]	Matches any character that's not covered in any of the character classes. Good for cleaning garbage out of a string.

Table 16-2 *Character Classes*

Multicharacter Regular Expressions

Single-character regular expressions are useful, but they are nowhere near as handy as multicharacter regular expressions. Multicharacter regular expressions allow you to search for multiple string patterns with a single regular expression. For example, if we wanted to strip the HTML from a string, we'd use the following example:

```
<cfset szOldString = "
<table width=200 cellpadding=0 cellspacing=0 border=0>
   <tr>
      <td>Hello World</td>
   </tr>
</table>">

<cfset szNewString =  REReplace(szOldString, "<[^>]*>", "", "All")>
<cfoutput>#sznewstring#</cfoutput>
```

The regular expression, in bold, searches for every open less-than character (<) first, but leaves single greater-than characters (>) alone. The less-than character (<) must also have a matching greater-than bracket. These leave a string like the following alone:

```
Nothing > would happen < to this string.
```

The rules for multicharacter regular expressions are as follows:

- Use parentheses to group parts of regular expressions as subexpressions. This allows you to find a substring within a larger pattern.
- Use the plus sign to search for multiple instances of a single character or subexpression. For example: (is)+ matches multiple instances of the word "is".
- Use an asterisk (*) following a single character or subexpression to match zero or more instances of the regular expression. The HTML stripping example we showed earlier is a good example of this. The expression will match <> just as easily as <br>, because of the asterisk.
- Use a question mark (?) to match zero or one instance of the regular expression.
- Use the pipe symbol (|) as an OR symbol. For example, co(p|pper) matches cop or copper.

- To find a specific range of repeating patterns, use curly brackets preceding a subexpression in this form: {*m*,*n*}, where *m* is the start of the range, and *n* is the total number of repeating patterns you'd like to match. For example, (foo){1,3} would match foo, foofoo, foofoofoo, but not foofoofoofoo. Using {*m*,} by itself indicates that you'd like to match at least the amount of *m*. You cannot, however, use {,*n*} to match up to a certain amount; (use {0,*m*} instead.)

The ColdFusion 5.0 documents state that strings of more than 20,000 characters in length produce an error when using REFind() or REReplace. I'm not sure exactly what they're talking about because I've used regular expression functions on strings greater than 20,000 characters without a problem; in fact, strings as large as 250,000 characters can be used without a problem.

If for whatever reason your version of ColdFusion 5.0 errors on a string larger than 20,000 characters, the string can be broken up programmatically into smaller chunks, but there is a potential problem when doing so. Splitting a string might also split a pattern that would otherwise be matched if the string were whole.

This problem could be remedied by writing a "splitter" that would overlap the string chunks, allowing split patterns to be matched. But, as I said, despite what the ColdFusion 5.0 documents state, strings larger than 20,000 characters can be used.

Anchoring

ColdFusion allows you to anchor a regular expression to find a string that occurs either at the beginning of a string or the end of a string. The following rules apply:

- If a caret symbol (^) is encountered at the beginning of an expression or subexpression, the matched string must also begin at the beginning of the string being searched. For example:

```
<cfset szOldString = "Kermit the frog here.">

<cfset intPos = REFind("^Kermit", szOldString)>

<!--- This should return a value of 1 --->
<cfoutput>#intPos#</cfoutput>
```

- If a dollar sign ($) is used at the end of an expression or subexpression, the matched string must also be at the end of the string. For example:

```
<cfset szOldString = "Kermit the frog here. Big Bird is over there.">

<cfset intPos = REFind("here.$", szOldString)>

<!--- This should return a value of 42 --->
<cfoutput>#intPos#</cfoutput>
```

► If a caret is used at the beginning of an expression or subexpression, and a dollar sign is also used at the end of the expression or subexpression, the matched string must start at the beginning of the string, and end at the end of the string. For example:

```
<cfset szOldString = "Kermit">

<cfset intPos = REFind("^Kermit$", szOldString)>

<!--- This should return a value of 1 --->
<cfoutput>#intPos#</cfoutput>
```

If no anchoring is used, then the pattern can occur anywhere within the string. Without anchoring, the pattern isn't constrained, or "hooked," to any part of the searched string.

Backreferencing

Backreferencing is the ability to step back in the matched string to search for something else. This is especially useful when matching doubled words like "the the" and "is is".

To use backreference, precede the number of matches you'd like to step back with a slash. For example, to find doubled words, I'd use the following regular expression:

```
<cfset szI = REReplace("Doubled Doubled words.","([A-Za-z]+)[ ]+\1","\1","ALL")>
```

The backreference is in bold, and is the key to this regular expression. The expression itself matches all words that are followed by a space that occur more than once, with the backreference stepping back one step. The backreferencing in the replacement string replaces the doubled words with the matched string.

Matched Subexpressions

If we were doing some significant searching on a string, it might be important for us to know exactly where the regular expression found a match. Both the REFind() and REFindNoCase() functions accept a fourth attribute, *ReturnSubExpression*. When this attribute is set to True, the functions create an array containing two structures with the positions and lengths of the subexpressions found.

The returned structure has two arrays, *pos* and *len*. The *pos* array contains the position of the matched subexpressions. The *len* array has the length of each subexpression. The first element of each array points to the occurrence of the full pattern, and any index beyond the first index contains information about the matched subexpressions. Remember, subexpressions are surrounded in parentheses. If there are no matches in the regular expression, the *pos* and *len* arrays each contain a single element with a value of 0.

Wrapping Up

While the regular expression support in ColdFusion leaves a lot to be desired, it's still a useful method for messing around with strings. Some of the biggest time savers occur when you're stripping bad characters out of a string, or using regular expressions to find formatted data within strings. Regular expressions are difficult to grasp, and even to explain clearly, without experience. The old adage applies: practice makes perfect. Sometimes it takes some tweaking to get a regular expression to work correctly, but it usually saves development time if trying to reproduce the results in alternate ways.

CHAPTER

17

Internet Protocols

IN THIS CHAPTER:

E-mail and ColdFusion

File Transfer Protocol

Hypertext Transfer Protocol (HTTP)

ColdFusion allows a developer to interact with several different Internet protocols. The fact that it does is no big surprise, considering that for any web application language to be anywhere near competitive, it must provide comprehensive support for popular Internet standards. ColdFusion indeed does provide comprehensive support for several popular Internet standards, or protocols.

In this chapter, we discuss the following four Internet standards (actually, there are five, but two are grouped together as you'll see):

- SMTP and POP
- FTP
- HTTP
- LDAP

Each major section gives background on each protocol, and introduces what tags and methods are available in interacting with other computers on the Internet using the protocol.

In the several examples used in this chapter, all good programming practices are thrown right out the window, and downright dirty code is used. At this point in the book, it's assumed that you've done enough higher-level programming to not want to be bothered by extraneous code not related to the subject at hand. The code itself isn't necessarily bad, or harmful, it's simply stripped of any good programming practices like error trapping, checking for variables, and things like that. While I'm a firm believer in good programming practices, I want the examples in this chapter to be as streamlined as possible because there's a lot of ground to cover. Extra code at this point would simply be redundant and a waste of space. The code examples in this chapter are designed to be foundations to something bigger. But performance isn't compromised. If there is something that needs to said about how to code something for performance reasons, it will be covered.

E-mail and ColdFusion

E-mail is undoubtedly the most popular form of person-to-person communication on the Internet today—it always has been, and in one form or another, it always will be. E-mail as we know it today hasn't changed much since the days of its origin in the early 1970s. E-mail is originally a child of the ARPANET program, and e-mail-related protocols remain relatively unchanged since the early days of their existence.

The ColdFusion support of e-mail is adequate; e-mail can be sent using the <CFMAIL> tag, and ColdFusion can connect to a POP3 server and retrieve messages for processing (or to aid in making a web-based, e-mail client, which we'll do shortly).

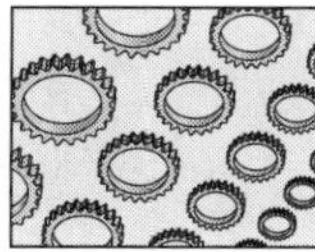

NOTE

Personally, I'm not a huge fan of using ColdFusion to do things like sending out thousands of e-mails to a customer base. I've had too many experiences where ColdFusion, for whatever reason, produced an error to the point where I had to restart the server while in the middle of sending out thousands of e-mails. I'm always paranoid that too many e-mails will be sent out, or that some won't be sent at all. ColdFusion has a sort of hands-off approach to the e-mail process, which produces a very uncomfortable feeling when you're trying to figure out why every third person e-mailed is getting a message three times. I'll explain the hands-off approach as I talk about sending e-mail with <CFMAIL>, but concisely, when it comes to very large mailings, I choose not to use ColdFusion.

In this section, we talk about ColdFusion e-mail-related technologies, and we build some very simple applications along the way that demonstrate how easy it is to use ColdFusion to perform e-mail-related tasks.

Sending E-mail

Sending e-mail is about the easiest e-mail-related task one can do in ColdFusion. The <CFMAIL> tag is used to relay a message from a ColdFusion application to a Simple Mail Transfer Protocol (SMTP) server. SMTP by definition is indeed a simple protocol. The protocol is designed for server-to-server communication—e-mail gets tossed around by servers that exchange very simple commands with each other in order to push e-mail around to the right destination.

In the case of <CFMAIL>, an existing SMTP server is required. ColdFusion cannot by itself send an e-mail; this is what the SMTP servers do. But, ColdFusion can hand a message to an SMTP server, which will examine the message and decide what to do with it based on the e-mail headers.

Because SMTP is considered a server-to-server protocol, other protocols are available that allow clients, or users, to download and read e-mail. We'll talk more shortly about sending e-mail.

The following conversation between two SMTP servers might give you some insight on how the protocol works. Each unnumbered line is a new command, and each numbered line is the response from the server. It's possible to Telnet into a server to experience this same experience in real time (although mail.stompzine.com doesn't exist, so don't try it):

```
HELO
250 stompzine.com Hello , pleased to meet you
VRFY mike@stompzine.com
250 Yeah, I know that one.  He (or she) is Michael Buffington <mike@stompzine.com>
MAIL From: <spammer@spam.com>
RCPT To: <mike@stompzine.com>
```

```
DATA I'm spamming you!
QUIT
250 <mike@stompzine.com>, Sender accepted
this is not a valid command
500 What? I don't understand that.
```

Now, whether or not anything happened from the conversation is another story. The language of servers for the most part is standardized, but there's always the possibility that you might ask a server to do something it's not willing to do. For instance, a lot of servers wouldn't have responded so politely if I'd asked them to verify an e-mail address with the VRFY command. Using this command is one way spammers obtain e-mail addresses; they hammer away at a server digging for information. Most servers these days are more strict in what commands they allow.

None of what we've talked about up until this point is required knowledge when it comes to <CFMAIL>. The <CFMAIL> tag, when sending an e-mail, might have a very similar conversation to the one we just had with the SMTP server, but it performs this conversation in the background. I mentioned earlier that <CFMAIL> is a hands-off approach and this is the proof of that statement. No understanding of SMTP server etiquette is required; just set the tag up and it'll do the talking for you.

This hands-off approach is fantastic if you care as much about SMTP conversations as you care about the "new offers for body part enlargement" e-mails you may get in your Hotmail inbox on a near-regular basis. But, for those who want to know the inner workings of how <CFMAIL> does its thing, then you're pretty much out of luck. If you want to have control over the conversation, you'd have to telnet into the SMTP server and do the talking yourself. Unfortunately, ColdFusion doesn't have built in Telnet support, so you're stuck with <CFMAIL>.

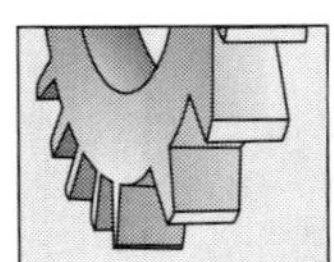

TIP

Lewis Sellers has created a set of COM objects called TCPClient, Second Edition. *These objects allow you to make connections with any TCP protocol, including Telnet. If you're the type who wants to control the conversation with an SMTP server, then you'll need this free software. More information can be found at http://www.intrafoundation.com/tcpclient.html.*

Sending Plain Text E-mails with <CFMAIL>

Now for some examples of <CFMAIL> doing its thing. The following example shows how one might send a plain text e-mail to a friend using ColdFusion:

```
<cfmail to="eg@stompzine.com"
  from="mike@stompzine.com"
  subject="Hey man.">
Erik,
```

```
I'm finally going to a Weezer concert.

- Mike
</cfmail>
```

At the most basic level, only three attributes are required, as shown. If there is no default SMTP server setup in the ColdFusion Administrator under the Server | Mail / Mail Logging page, the *server* attribute is required. It's a good idea to check out the mail setting page to make sure the settings are the way you'd like them to be set up.

Notice in the previous example that the body of the message is nested between the <CFMAIL> tags, and that it's formatted to be flush to the left-hand side of the ColdFusion template. ColdFusion sends everything between the <CFMAIL> tags, including things like Tabs used to make your code look pretty. There's not much you can do to get around this, other than making sure that plain text e-mails are flush left.

When this tag is executed as shown, ColdFusion will place the message in a mail spool. It will not immediately connect to the SMTP server and have a conversation in order to reduce the number of required connections. Think of this real world parallel: the spooler is like a manila folder file where letters are placed. Rather than drive down to the post office with each new letter created, the letters are placed in the folder that will be taken to the post office at a reasonable interval. In ColdFusion, the spool is processed at intervals that you can set within the ColdFusion Administrator. If, during the interval set in the Administrator, ten new e-mails are generated using ColdFusion, ColdFusion will hand off those ten new e-mails to the SMTP server. The default spool interval is 60 seconds, but it can be set as low as 15 seconds.

This spooling thing is a fact of life with ColdFusion, and cannot be avoided. There really is no need, though, to fight it, because it's there for a good reason. Spooling reduces the amount of load on the ColdFusion server, and also reduces the amount of server- to-server communication required. Also, when ColdFusion does end up making a connection to another e-mail server, it uses a request from the same requests that ColdFusion templates use. So if your server is set to process only three simultaneous requests, and the e-mail is being handed off to another server, only two requests are left over. Spooling also applies to any e-mail generated by <CFMAIL>, not just simple ones like the preceding example.

Sending HTML Formatted E-mails with <CFMAIL>

Let's look at a example, and then discuss it:

```
<cfmail to="eg@stompzine.com"
   from="mike@stompzine.com"
   subject="More about Weezer"
   type="HTML">
```

```
Erik,<br>
<a href="http://www.weezer.net">Weezer</a> might be what all
the kids are listening too, but it's still my favorite.
<p>
- Mike
</cfmail>
```

The only real difference between this example and the plain text e-mail example is the *type* attribute. The *type* attribute by default is "plain," but when set to "HTML," indicates that the body of the message is in HTML format. In the background it's really just modifying an e-mail header that indicates that the message is in HTML format. If the users' e-mail client doesn't care for HTML messages, it will show the HTML code as if it were plain text (exposing HTML tags and such).

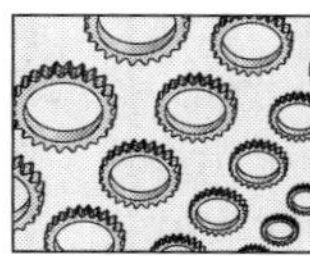

NOTE

I can't stand HTML e-mail. I have these pet peeves in life, and HTML-formatted e-mail is one of them. I don't think HTML has any place in e-mail, which has done just fine for years with simple, plain text messages. I don't like seeing images in my e-mail, and I don't mind seeing full URLs, even if they are ugly. E-mail was designed to be lightweight, and fast, and HTML support makes e-mail clients fatter, and makes the messages much larger than they need to be. I get spam messages sometimes that are more than 175K in total file size, when the same pointless "enhance your [insert body part]" message could have been reduced to about 2K if it were in plain text format. To help strengthen my opinions on HTML-formatted e-mail, it seems to me that nine out of ten spam e-mails I get are HTML-based. This opinion could branch off into all sorts of other topics, like quality content versus images, so I'll head it off right now by saying that I know I'm not alone in this opinion, and would suggest that when deciding between HTML e-mail and plain text that you consider my opinion on the subject.

Formatting-wise, the HTML between the <CFMAIL> tags is rendered by the user's e-mail client. Things like tabs for code formatting may or may not affect the users client; it all depends on how the client interprets the HTML. I will still make sure HTML-formatted e-mails are flush left, just to avoid any problems the client might have if it encounters extra tabs or white space. I really do hate the way it makes my code look, but that's just the way it is.

The <CFMAILPARAM> Tag

The <CFMAILPARAM> tag is used within <CFMAIL> tags to add extra headers, or to attach files to the e-mail message. The following example shows an extra header not handled in the base <CFMAIL> tag added to the message using the <CFMAILPARAM> tag:

```
<cfmail to="eg@stompzine.com"
  from="mike@stompzine.com"
  subject="Heard of Dashboard Confessional?">
Erik,

I've been listening to Dashboard Confessional a lot.  I think
it's pretty good, mostly acoustic guitar. It's a one man band
with the singer from some emo band.

- Mike
<cfmailparam name="Reply-To" value="mb10534@yahoo.com">
</cfmail>
```

The base <CFMAIL> tag handles most of the headers you'd be concerned with including, although the following brief list might also be helpful:

Header	Description
Reply-To	E-mail clients take this value and send replies to this address, rather than the address in the From header.
Envelope-To	This header takes precedence over the To e-mail header. E-mail lists use this header a lot to help e-mail list users filter their e-mail better. While the To header might contain gamers@ign.com, the Envelope-To header contains the actual users e-mail address. The user will be able to take all e-mail going to the gamers@ign.com e-mail address and filter the e-mail accordingly. This would be more difficult without the Envelope-To header.

You can also make up your e-mail headers, called *x-headers*. X-headers allow you to create headers that can be used by the recipient client. The only catch is that the recipient client needs to be able to do something with the headers for them to have any purpose. The following example shows an x-header using the <CFMAILPARAM> tag. Assume that it's nested within the <CFMAIL> tags.

```
<cfmailparam name="X-RapidMailer" value="1.0">
```

This header is completely made up, but the idea is that perhaps the client might react to this header in some way. Perhaps the client will display e-mails coming from the fictional RapidMailer 1.0 version of software differently than it would other e-mails.

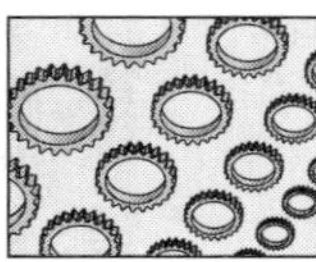

NOTE

It's interesting to note that when ColdFusion generates an e-mail, it includes a header called x-cf-version. The value of this version is 4.5.0, which doesn't seem right when you consider that ColdFusion 5.0 is responsible for creating the header. You can see this for yourself if you open one of the files in the C:\CFusion\Mail\Spool directory immediately after using the <CFMAIL> tag to send an email from ColdFusion in a text editor. Perhaps the "e-mail" portion of ColdFusion 5.0 is version 4.5.0, or perhaps it was missed by the Quality Control folks at Macromedia.

E-mail Attachments

The <CFMAILPARAM> tag is used to attach a file to an e-mail message within the CFMAIL> tags. The following example shows how it attaches a file to a message:

```
<cfmail to="eg@stompzine.com"
  from="mike@stompzine.com"
  subject="Saves the Day"
  type="HTML">
Erik,
<br>
I took about 80 pictures at the House of Blues when
<a href="http://www.savestheday.com">Saves the Day</a> played,
but only two or three turned out. I'll never use a film camera again.
<p>
- Mike
<cfmailparam file="c:\pictures\std\std_hob1.jpg">
</cfmail>
```

The file attribute of <CFMAILPARAM> indicates what file you'd like to include in the e-mail. A full path to the file is required. <CFMAIL> will look for a file on the ColdFusion server.

Data Driven E-mail

<CFMAIL> can be used with data from queries, or other objects or variable types within your application. The following example shows an e-mail with data from a query:

```
<cfquery name="qryNewBands" datasource="#request.dsn#">
SELECT band_name
FROM bands
WHERE band_new = 1
</cfquery>

<cfset newbands =  qryNewBands.RecordCount>
```

```
<cfmail
    to="eg@stompzine.com"
    from="mike@stompzine.com"
    subject="New Bands">
Greetings!

Stompzine.com has #newbands# new band<cfif newbands neq 1>s</cfif>:
<cfoutput query="qryNewBands">
#band_name#
</cfoutput>
</cfmail>
```

In this example, we can see that any properly formatted CFML code is valid within the <CFMAIL> tags. This provides great flexibility in how e-mails are generated. Possible uses for data-driven e-mails include order confirmations and other semi- unique and user-specific e-mails.

Notice that in the example the <CFMAIL> tag has a *query* attribute. This would allow us to avoid using the <CFOUTPUT> tag altogether within the <CFMAIL> tags, but because we're outputting a list of band names, we still use <CFOUTPUT> tags. <CFMAIL>, with the *query* attribute, will automatically group data. If the <CFOUTPUT> tags were removed, only a single band name would be listed. The nested <CFOUTPUT> tags loop over the entire record set indicated in the *query* attribute of the <CFMAIL> tag.

Example Mailers

When it comes to e-mail and ColdFusion, one very obvious strength is that ColdFusion can automate the process of sending out a lot of e-mail. Let's pretend that the company you work for is planning a Christmas party, and it's your responsibility to implement the technology that will e-mail several thousand employees information on the event.

We'll look at two examples, both of which share the same database structure. Both examples do things in a sort of similar fashion, but there are subtle differences between each. We'll talk about the advantages and disadvantages of both as we go along.

If you'd like to quickly make a test bed for these examples, run the following script within your SQL Server Query Analyzer to create the database tables and to insert some example e-mails to work with. Make sure to hook the database up to a data source so it can be used with ColdFusion.

```
CREATE DATABASE mailinglist

USE mailinglist
CREATE TABLE e-mail (
e-mail_id int IDENTITY(1,1),
```

```
e-mail_address varchar(100),
first_name varchar(100),
last_name varchar(100),
e-mail_sent int DEFAULT 0
)
GO

USE mailinglist
INSERT INTO e-mail
VALUES
('mike@stompzine.com', 'Michael', 'Buffington', 0)

INSERT INTO e-mail
VALUES
('eg@stompzine.com', 'Erik', 'Goodlad', 0)

INSERT INTO e-mail
VALUES
('wilford@quaker.com', 'Wilford', 'Brimley', 0)


INSERT INTO e-mail
VALUES
('bobdole@viagra.com', 'Bob', 'Dole', 0)
GO
```

Single-Request E-mailer

The single-request e-mailer gets its clever name from the fact that it performs the entire e-mailing operation in a single request. Let's look at the code, then we'll discuss its advantages and disadvantages.

```
<cfquery name="qryE-mailList" datasource="#request.dsn#">
SELECT DISTINCT e-mail_address, first_name, last_name
FROM E-mail
</cfquery>

<cfmail query="qryE-mailList"
to="#e-mail_address#"
from="mike@stompzine.com"
subject="You're my guinea pig.">
Greetings #first_name#!

I'm sending this to you because you're special.
- Mike
</cfmail>
```

An advantage to this method of mass e-mailing is that the code is very simple. A query is built, and the <CFMAIL> tag is looped, sending e-mail to each record within the query. A disadvantage is that there is no accounting going on. What I mean is that if the request gets interrupted halfway through the loop, there's no way of knowing who has already sent an e-mail, and who hasn't. It's embarrassing to send out multiples, so this method is kind of risky in that regard.

Multiple-Request E-mailer

Once again, this method is cleverly named the multiple-request e-mailer, because it makes a single request to send out a single e-mail. Let's look at the code:

```
<cfparam name="url.action" default="next">

<cfif url.action is "stop">
Finished!
<cfabort>
</cfif>

<cfif url.action is "next">
   <cftry>
      <!--- select first available e-mail address
         that hasn't been flagged as sent --->
      <cfquery name="qryE-mail" datasource="#request.dsn#">
      SELECT DISTINCT TOP 1 e-mail_id, e-mail_address,
      first_name, last_name
      FROM E-mail
      WHERE e-mail_sent = 0
      </cfquery>

      <!--- if a record exists, send e-mail --->
      <cfif qryE-mail.RecordCount GT 0>
         <cfmail query="qryE-mail"
           to="#e-mail_address#"
           from="mike@stompzine.com"
           subject="You're my guinea pig.">
Greetings #first_name#!

I'm sending this to you because you're special.

- Mike
</cfmail>

         <!--- update this record as sent --->
         <cfquery name="qryUpdateE-mail" datasource="#request.dsn#">
```

```
          UPDATE E-mail
          SET e-mail_sent = 1
          WHERE e-mail_id = #qryE-mail.e-mail_id#
          </cfquery>
       <cfelse>
          <cflocation url="cfmail_oneatatime.cfm?action=stop">
          <cfabort>
       </cfif>
       <cfcatch type="Any">
       <!--- error processing here in the future: for now move on --->
       </cfcatch>
    </cftry>
</cfif>

<cflocation url="cfmail_oneatatime.cfm?action=next">
```

In this example, each record in the table is handled by a single request. The first record that hasn't been flagged as sent is selected, e-mail is sent, and then the record is flagged as sent. The <CFLOCATION> tag at the end of the script starts it all over again by sending the *url.action* variable to the same script with the value of "next." If there are no more records to send e-mails to, the script relocates to the same script, except this time with a *url.action* variable of "stop," and aborts all further processing.

We could do nearly the same thing with a single request, using a stored procedure to select a record, then immediately update the record, but we can't be sure whether <CFMAIL> ever executes if we do it that way. With this method, the <CFTRY> tags will only allow code between the tags to execute if everything is error free between the tags, which ensures that all code is executed, or none at all. Once again, we could do this with a <CFLOOP> set of tags, <CFTRY> tags, with a select statement, <CFMAIL> tag, and update statement in between, but we'd still have a disadvantage.

If we decide to run the above example from a browser, a single request occurs, and immediately relocates the browser to a new request. If we did a <CFLOOP> block like in the first, single-request method, we'd run the risk of the browser timing out.

If the browser doesn't get a response back in a certain amount of time, it will time out. Having the browser time out doesn't kill the request. The request will continue to run on the ColdFusion server until it's finished, provided that the ColdFusion server doesn't decide to stop the request based on the time allotted for requests to run in the ColdFusion Administrator. The <CFLOCATION> tag might allow the request to send out e-mails faster than one might like. Instead of using <CFLOCATION>, the code could be modified to work with a <META> tag that refreshes the page after a certain number of seconds. This could help reduce the immediate load on a server.

Processing E-mail with <CFPOP>

We've learned a lot about how to send e-mail with <CFMAIL>, so how do we receive it? Well, technically, ColdFusion can't receive e-mail at all. It doesn't act as a mail server, which is good, because that would introduce a completely new activity to ColdFusion that could probably be done better by other pieces of standalone software.

ColdFusion can act as a client to a POP3 server. POP3 is the third version of the Post Office Protocol written in 1988 by Marshall Rose. POP3 simply allows for the retrieval of mail from a POP3 server by a POP3 client. POP3 doesn't allow you to send e-mail, only receive. It's sort of like the exact opposite of SMTP, which will generally only allow clients to send e-mail.

So, with that said, it makes more sense that ColdFusion can't receive e-mail; it can only retrieve messages from a POP3 server.

The <CFPOP> tag allows a developer to retrieve message headers, messages, and download attachments. Combined with <CFMAIL>, a ColdFusion-driven, fully functional e-mail client can be built, which is what we'll create in the next sections.

Building an E-mail Client

In this section, we build a very simple, and nearly crude e-mail client with ColdFusion. While it does allow a user to read and compose e-mail, it lacks most of the functionality that would make anyone want to use it on a regular basis. In fact, it doesn't even have a login screen—the POP3 user is hard-coded. The application is built to serve as an example of how to use the <CFPOP> tags more than it is to serve as a model for an e-mail client.

Each file of the application is broken down into its own section, and each is discussed individually within the sections.

Using Application.cfm

This file contains variable assignments that we'll use throughout the application. The POP3 login information is hard coded into this file, which is then used throughout the site. Obviously, this is for testing only—creating a production site with automatic login might not be the best thing to do.

```
<!--- set user specific info --->
<cfset request.pop_login = "info">
<cfset request.pop_password = "do30da368oe">

<!--- set application constants --->
```

```
<cfset request.pop_server = "192.168.1.100">
<cfset request.pop_port = "25">
<cfset request.dl_urlroot =
"http://127.0.0.1/pop/attch/#request.pop_login#/">
<cfset request.attachment_storage =
"E:\wwwroot\pop\attach\#request.pop_login#\">
```

Using Nav.cfm

This file will be included on most of the pages, and serves as very simple navigation:

```
<b>Navigation:</b>
[<a href="index.cfm">Inbox</a>]
[<a href="compose.cfm">Compose</a>]<br>
```

Receiving Headers (Index.cfm)

We break this file down into a few parts:

```
<cfinclude template="nav.cfm">
<cfinclude template="delete.cfm">
```

These first two lines include two files: nav.cfm and delete.cfm. We've already covered the nav.cfm file, and we'll cover what the delete.cfm file does shortly.

```
<cfpop action="GETHEADERONLY"
       name="qryHeaders"
       server="#request.pop_server#"
       username="#request.pop_login#"
       password="#request.pop_password#">
```

The <CFPOP> in this example uses the action GETHEADERONLY. Using this action will pull all the current headers for the logged in user from the server indicated, and place them in a query called *qryHeaders*.

```
<p>
<form action="index.cfm" method="post">
<input type="submit" name="delete" value="Delete Selected"><br>
<table>
   <tr>
      <td><b>Delete</b></td>
      <td><b>From</b></td>
      <td><b>Date</b></td>
```

```
      <td><b>Subject</b></td>
   </tr>
<cfloop query="qryHeaders">
   <tr>
      <td>
        <input type="checkbox" name="message_id"
value="#messagenumber#">
      </td>
      <td>
        <cfoutput><a
href="read.cfm?id=#messagenumber#">#from#</a></cfoutput>
      </td>
      <td><cfoutput>#date#</cfoutput></td>
      <td><cfoutput>#subject#</cfoutput></td>
   </tr>
</cfloop>
</table>
</form>
```

The remainder of the file displays the query generated by <CFPOP>. The following table lists the possible attributes for <CFPOP>, and what each attribute does:

Attribute	Description
server	Required. This is the host name or IP address of the POP3 server you'll be connecting to.
port	Optional. This is the port of the POP3 server. By default, the value is 110, which is the default POP3 port used by most servers.
username	Optional. This is the user name of the account you'd like to retrieve mail for. If it's left blank, the login is anonymous.
password	Required if the *username* attribute is used.
action	Required. This indicates what you'd like the <CFPOP> tag to actually do. The possible values are: GETALL GETHEADERONLY DELETE
name	Required when the action type is GETALL or GETHEADERONLY. This attribute is the name of the query object.

Attribute	Description
messagenumber	Required for the action type DELETE. This attribute can be a comma-delimited list of message numbers, or a single value. When used with the DELETE action, all messages referenced in the list will be deleted. When used with the GETALL or GETHEADERONLY actions, only the messages in the list will be received.
attachmentpath	Optional. When receiving messages with attachments using the GETALL action type, files will be saved to the ColdFusion server at the indicated path.
timeout	Optional. This attribute indicates the amount of time the connection to the POP3 server can remain active before timing out. The default amount is 60 seconds. Remember that the clock starts ticking the instant the connection to the server is made and will time out at the indicated value regardless of activity level.
maxrows	Optional. This indicates the maximum number of rows that should be pulled from the POP3 server.
generateuniquefilenames	Optional. This attribute takes a Boolean value, and indicates whether the downloaded attachment files should be renamed with unique names to avoid file-naming conflicts. The default value is FALSE.

<CFPOP> generates several variables after executing that can be used when outputting messages and headers. The following table describes each variable. Replace the query name *qryname* with the query name assigned within the <CFPOP> tag.

Variable	Description
qryname.date	The date of the message.
qryname.from	The value of the From header of the message.
qryname.messagenumber	A value assigned to the message by the POP3 server. It's supposed to be unique, but some mail servers will change a message's message number if it has been downloaded, which can obviously cause problems.
qryname.replyto	The value of the Reply-To header.
qryname.subject	The value of the Subject header.
qryname.cc	The value of the carbon copy (CC) header.
qryname.to	The value of the To header.

Variable	Description
qryname.body	The body of the message. Only available with the GETALL action type.
qryname.header	The entire list of headers and values. Available with the GETALL action type only.
qryname.attachments	A tab-delimited list of the filenames attached to an e-mail.
qryname.attachmentfiles	A tab-delimited list of the filenames as they appear on the ColdFusion server.

The format of the date that the POP3 server creates isn't recognized by ColdFusion as a valid date string, so the ParseDateTime() function should be used. The following example shows how one might use the function:

```
<cfoutput>#ParseDateTime(date,"POP")#</cfoutput>
```

Unfortunately, dates within e-mail messages are not always reliable, and will sometimes throw off the ParseDateTime() function. It's possible to use <CFTRY> to try parsing the date first, and if the ParseDateTime() function errors because of a malformed date, to avoid processing the date. There are plenty of ways that this can be handled; the best way depends on your application.

Getting the Message Body (Read.cfm)

This file will select a particular message based on the *url.id* value, and display the message, along with any attachments:

```
<cfinclude template="nav.cfm">

<cfpop action="GETALL"
       name="qryMessage"
       messagenumber="#url.id#"
       attachmentpath="#request.attachment_storage#"
       server="#request.pop_server#"
       username="#request.pop_login#"
       password="#request.pop_password#">

<p>
<cfoutput query="qryMessage">
<b>Date:</b> #date#<br>
<b>From:</b> #from#<br>
<b>Subject:</b> #subject#<br>
```

```
<b>To:</b> #to#<br>
<b>Body:</b><br>
<pre>#body#</pre>
<cfif attachments neq ''>
<b>Attachments:</b><br>
<cfloop list="#attachments#" index="file" delimiters="	">
<a href="#request.dl_urlroot##file#">#file#</a><br>
</cfloop>
</cfif>
</cfoutput>
```

This time, we use the GETALL action type with the <CFPOP> tag. This pulls back everything for the particular message we've selected, including the body of the message. We display the body of the message between <PRE> tags to preserve any tabs or white spaces within the e-mail body.

The *attachments* variable is a tab-delimited list of the files included with the message. Before looping through the list of attachments, we check to see if any attachments exist. If they do, we display the attachments, one after another.

Deleting Messages (Delete.cfm)

This file is actually included within the index.cfm file. If the form on the index.cfm file has been submitted, the code within this file will execute and delete the selected messages using the <CFPOP> tag, with the action type of DELETE.

```
<cfif IsDefined("form.delete")>
      <cfpop action="DELETE"
       messagenumber="#form.message_id#"
       server="#request.pop_server#"
       username="#request.pop_login#"
       password="#request.pop_password#">
</cfif>
```

Each form element on the index.cfm page is named message_id. If multiple check boxes are selected, form.message_id will contain a comma-delimited list of message numbers, which are then passed to the *messagenumber* attribute within the <CFPOP> tag. This allows for a clean, single-step deletion of the selected messages.

Composing and Sending Messages (Compose.cfm)

This actually doesn't have anything to do with <CFPOP>, because sending e-mail uses <CFMAIL>, but it's part of the overall application. The following file is basically just a form with a few input boxes for the To and From headers and the body of the message. Once the form has been submitted, <CFMAIL> sends the message to the message spool for further processing.

```
<cfinclude template="nav.cfm">

<cfif IsDefined("form.send")>
<cfmail to="#form.to#"
from="#form.from#"
subject="#form.subject#">
#form.body#
</cfmail>
Message sent to <cfoutput>#form.to#</cfoutput>.
<cfelse>
   <form action="compose.cfm" method="post">
      <b>From:</b><br><input type="text"
          name="from" size="25" maxlength="25"><br>
      <b>Subject:</b><br><input type="text"
          name="subject" size="45" maxlength="45"><br>
      <b>To:</b><br><input type="text"
          name="to" size="25" maxlength="25"><br>
      <b>Body:</b><br>
      <textarea cols="45" rows="8" name="body"></textarea><br>
      <input type="submit" name="Send" value="Send">
   </form>
</cfif>
```

File Transfer Protocol

Like SMTP, File Transfer Protocol (FTP) has been around since the early 1970s. FTP is designed specifically to transfer files between an FTP client and an FTP server. ColdFusion allows developers to write FTP functionality into their applications by using the <CFFTP> tag.

In this section, we talk about <CFFTP>, then we build a simple FTP client using ColdFusion that allows for browsing an FTP site, and for downloading and uploading files. We discuss each file used in the sample application, just as we did for the e-mail application.

Using <CFFTP>

<CFFTP> allows you to perform the following FTP-related actions:

- Establish connections to an FTP server
- Browse and change directories
- Download and upload files
- Delete files and remove directories
- Close a connection to an FTP server

Attributes

The <CFFTP> attributes are divided into two different tables here to help you make sense of their functions. The first table lists attributes that would be used when establishing a connection to an FTP server. The second table lists attributes that would be used when performing FTP tasks, once a connection has been established.

Here is a list of the attributes to use when establishing a connection to an FTP server:

Attribute	Description
action	Required. This attribute determines what FTP action should take place. The following actions are available: Open ChangeDir CreateDir ListDir GetFile PutFile Rename Remove GetCurrentDir GetCurrentURL ExistsDir ExistsFile Exists Close

Attribute	Description
username	Required when using the OPEN action type. This is the user name used to login to the FTP server.
password	Required when using the OPEN action type. This is, of course, the password used to login to the FTP server.
server	Required when using the OPEN action type. This is hostname or IP address of the FTP server that you're connecting to.
port	Optional. This is the port of the FTP server to connect to. The default value is 21.
timeout	Optional. This is the amount of time in seconds that the connection will take to timeout on an idle connection. The default value is 30 seconds.
connection	Optional. The *connection* attribute lets you perform connection caching. We'll talk about connection caching shortly.
proxyserver	Optional. If a proxy server is to be used, this attribute should contain its hostname or IP.
retrycount	Optional. This attribute indicates the number of retries of an action that <CFFTP> will perform in case of failure. The default value is 1.
stoponerror	Optional. This attribute can contain either "yes" or "no." When set to "yes" and an error occurs, <CFFTP> stops processing and displays an error. When set to "no" and an error occurs, <CFFTP> creates the following three variables: CFFTP.Succeeded CFFTP.ErrorCode CFFTP.ErrorText
passive	Optional. This attributes contains either a "yes" or "no" value. When set to "yes," the connection is set to passive mode. The default value is "no."

The *connection* attribute allows a developer to perform connection caching. The connection attribute is basically a connection name, and when that name is used again, the login information from the <CFFTP> with the action of OPEN is used. This makes it possible to only enter login information once, and helps simplify code. It also has performance benefits as well. Rather than make a new connection for each FTP action, when a connection name is used, the <CFFTP> tag simply picks up where the last <CFFTP> tag with the same connection left off.

The next table lists attributes that would be used when performing FTP tasks. The attributes can be combined with the previous set of attributes as well.

Attribute	Description
name	Required when the action type is ListDir. This is the name of the query object created as a result of the directory listing. We'll talk about what columns are contained within the query shortly.
transfermode	Option. This attribute can take three values: AutoDetect, ASCII, and Binary. The default value is AutoDetect.

Attribute	Description
asciiextensionlist	Optional. When a semicolon-delimited list of file extensions is supplied, files with extensions in the list are forced to download in ASCII mode when the *transfermode* attribute is set to AutoDetect.
failifexists	Optional. This attribute can contain either a "yes" or "no" value. If the action type is GetFile, and this attribute is set to "yes," then the <CFFTP> will fail if the user has a file with a conflicting name on their system. The tag will fail rather than try to overwrite the file. The default value is "yes."
directory	Required when the action type is ChangeDir, CreateDir, ListDir, or ExistsDir. This attribute indicates what directory the action type will be performed on.
localfile	Required when using the action type GetFile or PutFile. This attribute indicates the name of the file on the local system that will be used with either of these two action types.
remotefile	Required when using the action type GetFile, PutFile, or ExistsFile. This attribute indicates the name of the file on the remote system that will be used with any of these three action types.
item	Required when using the Exists or Remove action type. This attribute indicates the file or directory that will be used with either of these action types.
existing	Required when using the Rename action type. This attribute indicates the file or directory that will be changed when using the Rename action type.
new	Required when using the Rename action type. This attribute works with the *existing* attribute, and indicates the new name of the file or directory using the Rename action type.

Return Variables

When an FTP action is performed using the <CFFTP> tag, a variable called *CFFTP.ReturnValue* is created. The value of the variable is different depending on the action type performed. The following table lists the action types of the *CFFTP.ReturnValue* variable, and describes their values.

Action Type	Value
GetCurrentDir	Returns the name of the current directory.
GetCurrentURL	Returns the current URL.
ExistsDir	Returns a Boolean value. Yes means the directory exists, and No means it doesn't.
ExistsFile	Returns a Boolean value.
Exists	Returns a Boolean value.

When a directory listing is performed using the ListDir action type, a query is created that contains the filenames and other attributes within the directory. The following columns are available in the query indicated in the name attribute of the <CFFTP> tag:

Column	Description
name	The name of the file or directory.
path	The path of the file without the drive letter.
URL	A URL for the directory or file.
length	The size of the file or directory in bytes.
lastmodified	The date and time when the file was last modified. It's a good idea to use the ParseDateTime() function on this, because the date returned is unformatted.
attributes	A string value containing either "Normal" or "Directory." Files are called "Normal," and directories are called "Directory."
IsDirectory	A Boolean value indicating whether or not the item is a directory or a file.
mode	On UNIX machines, an octal value indicating the permissions of a file.

Building an FTP Client

The following application demonstrates the fundamentals of using <CFFTP>. The application takes a similar approach to the e-mail client we built in the previous section in that it's simple, get-to-the-point kind of code. Let's look at each file:

Using Application.cfm

This file contains all the login information, path information, and other important things for the FTP client:

```
<!--- set user specific info --->
<cfset request.ftp_login = "ftp_user">
<cfset request.ftp_password = "diq39do0">

<!--- create a connection --->
<cfset request.ftp_connection = "test">

<!--- set application constants --->
<cfset request.ftp_server = "192.168.1.100">
<cfset request.ftp_port = "21">

<cfset request.upload_temp = "C:\ftp\uploads">
```

```
<cfparam name="url.dir" default="">

<cfset url.dir = Trim(url.dir)>

<cfif Left(url.dir,1) IS "/">
   <cfset url.dir = RemoveChars(url.dir, 1, 1)>
</cfif>
```

Working with Navigation (Nav.cfm)

We use the same kind of simple navigation from the previous application, and simply include it on every page:

```
<b>Navigation:</b>
[<a href="index.cfm">Browse</a>]
[<a href="uploadfile.cfm
<cfif IsDefined("url.dir")><cfoutput>?dir=#url.dir#</cfoutput></cfif>
">Upload</a>]

[<a href="createdir.cfm
<cfif IsDefined("url.dir")><cfoutput>?dir=#url.dir#</cfoutput></cfif>
">Create Directory</a>]
<br>
```

In this example, we squeeze the value of *url.dir* into the query string of the link if the *url.dir* variable exists. This allows the navigation links to be specific for whatever directory we're in on the server, so when a user clicks on the upload file directory, the file will be uploaded to the current directory. The same goes for creating a directory.

Browsing Files (Index.cfm)

In this file, before getting a directory listing, we open the connection to the FTP server, using information that is set within the Application.cfm file.

```
<!--- open a connection --->
<cfftp action="OPEN"
       server="#request.ftp_server#"
       username="#request.ftp_login#"
       password="#request.ftp_password#"
       stoponerror="Yes"
       port="#request.ftp_port#"
       connection="#request.ftp_connection#"
       timeout="60">
```

```
<!--- create a list of files --->
<cfftp action="LISTDIR"
       stoponerror="Yes"
       name="qryFiles"
       directory="#url.dir#"
       connection="#request.ftp_connection#">

<cfinclude template="nav.cfm">
<cfinclude template="path.cfm">

<table>
   <tr>
      <td><b>Delete</b></td>
      <td><b>Name</b></td>
      <td><b>Size</b></td>
      <td><b>Last Modified</b></td>
      <td><b>Attributes</b></td>
   </tr>
   <cfloop query="qryFiles">
      <cfoutput>
      <tr>
         <cfif IsDirectory>
            <td><a
               href="deletedirectory.cfm?dir=#url.dir#/#name#">Del</a></td>
            <td><a href="index.cfm?dir=#path#">[#Name#]</a></td>
         <cfelse>
            <cfset download_url = Replace(url,
            "ftp://#request.ftp_server#",
"ftp://#request.ftp_login#:#request.ftp_password#@#request.ftp_server#"
 , "ALL")>

   <td><a href="#download_url#">#Name#</a></td>
         </cfif>
         <td>#Length#</td>
         <td>#LastModified#</td>
         <td>#Attributes#</td>
      </tr>
   </cfoutput>
</cfloop>
</table>
```

When outputting the list of files, we check to see if the object is a directory by using the IsDirectory column. Because the IsDirectory column is a Boolean value, saying <cfif IsDirectory> is the same as saying <cfif IsDirectory is TRUE>. Directories are surrounded by brackets in our listing, and are given different URLs. The delete link also points to a different ColdFusion template than a file would.

Downloading files is as simple as clicking the URL of the filename.

Uploading Files (Uploadfile.cfm)

First of all, uploading files is a bit tricky. <CFFTP> acts as a client between the ColdFusion server and the FTP server. This means that even though we can build an FTP client using ColdFusion, ColdFusion is still the client, not the user using the client through a browser. This means that two steps are required in order for a user using the ColdFusion-driven FTP client to upload a file from their local system. The file has to first be uploaded to the ColdFusion server using <CFFILE>, and then transferred to the FTP server using <CFFTP>.

```
<cfinclude template="nav.cfm">
<cfinclude template="path.cfm">

<cfif IsDefined("form.upload_file")>
<!--- send file to a temporary spot on the CF server --->
   <cffile action="UPLOAD"
        filefield="form.upload_file"
        destination="#request.upload_temp#"
        nameconflict="MAKEUNIQUE">

<!--- send the file from the CF server to the FTP server --->
   <cfftp action="PUTFILE"
       localfile="#request.upload_temp#\#file.serverfile#"
       remotefile="#url.dir#\#file.clientfile#"
      connection="#request.ftp_connection#">

   <cfoutput>#file.clientfile#</cfoutput> uploaded.

   <!--- now remove the file from the CF server --->
   <cffile action="DELETE"
        file="#request.upload_temp#\#file.serverfile#">

<cfelse>
   <form enctype="multipart/form-data"
   action="uploadfile.cfm?dir=<cfoutput>#url.dir#</cfoutput>"
   method="post">

   <b>Select a file:</b><br>
   <input type="file" name="upload_file" size="25"><br>
   <input type="submit" name="Upload" value="Upload">
```

```
   </form>
</cfif>
```

Creating Directories (Createdir.cfm)

Creating directories is a simple matter; the following code shows how it's done:

```
<cfinclude template="nav.cfm">
<cfinclude template="path.cfm">

<cfif IsDefined("form.dir")>
   <cfftp action="CREATEDIR"
          directory="#url.dir#/#form.dir#"
         connection="#request.ftp_connection#">

   <cfoutput>#form.dir#</cfoutput> created.
<cfelse>
   <form action="createdir.cfm?dir=<cfoutput>#url.dir#</cfoutput>"
     method="post">
   <b>Enter a valid directory name:</b><br>
   <input type="text" name="dir" size="25" maxlength="255"><br>
   <input type="submit" name="Create" value="Create">
   </form>
</cfif>
```

Removing Directories (Deletedir.cfm)

Deleting directories is also simple. In this example, we only allow empty directories to be removed:

```
<cfinclude template="nav.cfm">
<cfinclude template="path.cfm">

<cfftp action="LISTDIR"
       name="qryFiles"
       directory="#url.dir#"
      connection="#request.ftp_connection#">

<cfif qryFiles.RecordCount EQ 0>
   <cfftp action="REMOVE"
       item="#url.dir#/*.*"
      connection="#request.ftp_connection#">

   <cfftp action="REMOVE"
       item="#url.dir#"
```

```
      connection="#request.ftp_connection#">
      Directory removed.
<cfelse>
   Directory contains files or subdirectories, and wasn't deleted.
</cfif>
```

Hypertext Transfer Protocol (HTTP)

Of all the protocols used on the Internet today, HTTP wins in usage, hands down. HTTP is what allows the data on web sites to be passed from the web server to a web browser, and just like the other Internet protocols we've been talking about in this chapter, ColdFusion can perform HTTP specific tasks.

In this section, we examine the <CFHTTP> tag and other related tags, and show some examples of how to use the <CFHTTP> tag.

Using <CFHTTP>

The <CFHTTP> tag allows a developer to perform GET and POST operations. We'll talk about each of these operations soon, but first, let's look at the attributes available to <CFHTTP>.

Attributes

The following attributes are available to the <CFHTTP> tag:

Attribute	Description
url	Required. This is the URL of the HTTP resource you intend to connect to.
port	Optional. If the port is different than port 80, then you can supply a different port here.
method	Required. This is the operation you'd like to perform; either GET or POST.
username	Optional. If the web server requires a user name, this is where you'd indicate it.
password	Optional. This works in conjunction with the *username* attribute.
columns	Optional. This attribute takes a comma delimited list of column names. We'll look how to use this attribute later on.
path	Optional. This attribute is used when downloading a file using a GET operation. If a full path isn't specified, the contents of the URL are placed in the *cfhttp.filecontent* variable. We'll cover that variable in the next section.

Attribute	Description
file	Required if the path operation is used with the method of POST. This is the name of the file you'd like to save. For GET operations, the original filename in the URL is used as the default filename. Your own filename can be supplied.
delimiter	Required if using the *name* attribute. The default delimiter is a comma, but any character can be supplied here.
name	Optional. This is the name of the query that <CFHTTP> creates when generating a query from a GET or POST operation. We'll show an example of this soon.
textqualifier	Required when generating a query. This attribute is used to determine where columns begin and end within a file retrieved using a GET or POST operation.
resolveurl	Optional. This attribute takes a "yes" or "no" value. When set to "yes," ColdFusion attempts to make sure that any linked item within the *cfhttp.filecontent* variable will be resolved properly. For example, if we pulled back Yahoo's front page, and they normally set anchor tags to look like <a href="r/ar">, ColdFusion will attempt to change the anchor tag to <a href="http://www.yahoo.com/r/ar">. All links should work properly with this attribute turned on.
proxyserver	Optional. This should contain the hostname or IP address of a proxy server.
proxyport	Optional. This should contain the port of the proxy server indicated in the *proxyserver* attribute.
useragent	Optional. When used, this attribute will allow you to mimic a certain type of user again. For example, by default, ColdFusion shows up to web servers as "ColdFusion." By supplying the user agent of a popular browser, like "MSIE 5.5," the web server may assume that you're simply a regular user on a regular browser. Some site administrators block certain user agents because they fear automated tools or spiders, so this attribute can help bypass that kind of a block.
throwonerror	Optional. This attribute takes a Boolean value, and when enabled, allows you to throw an error code to accompanying <CFTRY><CFCATCH> tags. The error code and its message are placed in the *cfhttp.statuscode* variable. The default value for this attribute is FALSE.
timeout	Optional. This one is a bit tricky to explain, so we'll talk about it in a second.
redirect	Optional. This is a Boolean attribute. When enabled, it will continue the POST or GET operation even if a redirect is encountered. If *redirect* is disabled, and the *throwonerror* attribute is enabled, the location of the redirect is stored in the *cfhttp.responseheader[location]* variable. When disabled, the POST or GET operation is halted when it encounters a redirect.

The *timeout* attribute allows you to have the POST or GET operation halt after a certain amount of seconds. By default, ColdFusion will opt to timeout the operation based on a couple of different factors. It gets a bit tricky, so follow closely.

If the attribute is left out of the tag, by default, ColdFusion uses three different timers to determine the ultimate timeout value of the <CFHTTP> operation. If the user supplies the *url.requesttimeout* variable when calling the template that executes the <CFHTTP> operation, ColdFusion uses that value as the default timeout value. However, if the value of *url.requesttimeout* is greater than the default request timeout value set in the ColdFusion Administrator, the value in the ColdFusion Administrator will be used.

If the *timeout* attribute is present, ColdFusion determines which of the two values is smaller: the supplied timeout value, or the value stored in the ColdFusion Administrator. It will time out the <CFHTTP> operation based on the smaller of the two values.

If no timeout value is supplied in the URL, or the <CFHTTP> tag, or in the ColdFusion Administrator, then the <CFHTTP> operation will continue until it completes, or someone shuts off the power to the ColdFusion server. It will continue indefinitely until something else happens.

Return Variables

When the <CFHTTP> tag is used, the following variables are returned. Note that we're not including queries created by <CFHTTP>. We'll get to that in second.

Variable	Description
cfhttp.filecontent	Returns the contents of a GET or POST operation if the path/file attribute combo isn't used.
cfhttp.mimetype	Returns the MIME type of the file returned by a GET or POST operation.
cfhttp.responseheader	This is a structure containing the HTTP headers. Try using <cfdump var="#cfhttp.responseheader#"> to see the structure of this structure.
cfhttp.header	This is the raw data from the HTTP headers. Looking at this variable can help you determine what possible keys exists in the cfhttp.responseheader structure.
cfhttp.statuscode	Returns the error code and error message if the *thrownonerror* attribute is enabled in the <CFHTTP> tag.

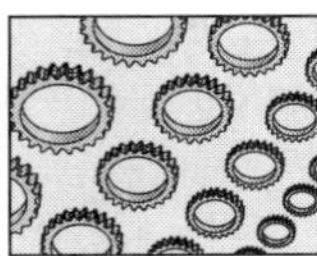

NOTE

MIME stands for Multipurpose Internet Mail Extensions. *That's right; while we are talking about HTTP and Web stuff, it really does say Mail Extensions. The creators of HTTP thought MIME would be perfect for HTTP, so they incorporated it into the design. MIME, in very simple terms, allows the web server to tell the client or browser what kind of file they're requesting. It is also what enables clients and browsers to download binary data-like audio files and images. For more information about MIME, check out http://www.faqs.org/rfcs/rfc2045.html.*

Getting Data

The following example shows a simple GET operation in action:

```
<cfhttp url="http://www.yahoo.com" method="GET"/>

<cfoutput>#cfhttp.filecontent#</cfoutput>
```

Notice the trailing / in the <CFHTTP> tag. This kind of notation is the same as writing the following:

```
<cfhttp url="http://www.yahoo.com" method="GET">
</cfhttp>

<cfoutput>#cfhttp.filecontent#</cfoutput>
```

The <CFHTTP> tag requires a closing tag, using the XML style notation reduces the amount of typing required, and gets rid of the silly hanging end tag.

Posting Data

This example shows how to use the POST method. Some sites have forms that use the POST method. The POST method allows a client to send data through a form, rather than the URL. Sometimes the data being sent is not just plain text that you might see in a URL; sometimes it's encrypted, or even in binary form. Also, if you think about how ColdFusion handles a form using the POST method as opposed to the GET method, you'll know there's a difference there as well. Form elements using the GET method are passed to the URL scope, while form elements using the POST method are passed to the FORM scope.

As for binary data, in the FTP client example we talked about earlier in the chapter, we used the POST method to pass a file from our local machine to the ColdFusion server. That would be impossible to do using the GET method.

Let's look at the following example:

```
<cfhttp url="http://www.bn.com/include/universal_qsearch.asp" method="post">
   <cfhttpparam type="FORMFIELD" name="product" value="1">
   <cfhttpparam type="FORMFIELD" name="query" value="Bahamas">
</cfhttp>

<cfoutput>#cfhttp.filecontent#</cfoutput>
```

In this example, we're connecting to the Barnes & Noble web site's search script. Never mind that they use ASP for a moment, and scan a bit further down until you see the <CFHTTPPARAM> tags nested within the <CFHTTP> tags.

Within the <CFHTTPPARAM> tags, we're passing two form fields, product and query. The script indicated in the URL attribute of the <CFHTTP> is expecting at least these two variables in order to generate a response. The product value of one indicates that I'm interested in searching the entire site, and the query value "Bahamas" indicates where I'd like to be as soon as I finish writing this book. With these values, the script on the Barnes & Noble web site will search for books about the Bahamas, the results of which will end up in my *cfhttp.filecontent* variable.

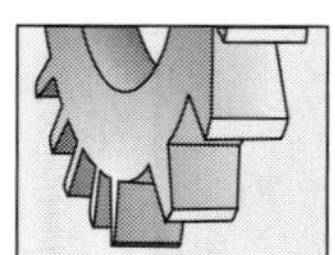

TIP

How did I know what variables to pass to the http://www.Barnes&Noble.com search script? I looked at the source of a page that had a search box on it. I noted where the form would be submitted to, which I used as my URL value, and I made note of the names of the fields within that form. This doesn't always work though—some sites are trickier to figure out, but more often than not, this method works.

The <CFHTTPPARAM> tag allows you to pass not only FORMFIELD data in a POST operation, it allows the following other types of data to be passed as well:

- URL
- COOKIE
- CGI
- FILE

The <CFHTTPPARAM> tag is only allowed to be used when doing a POST operation. (It's completely useless in a GET operation.) The tag takes the following attributes:

Attribute	Description
Name	Required. This is the name of the field you'll be passing to the URL in the <CFHTTP> tag.
Type	Required. This is the type of data you'll be passing to the URL. The following types are available: FORMFIELD URL COOKIE CGI FILE
Value	Required except when using the *file* attribute. This attribute should contain the value of the field indicated in the *name* attribute.
File	Required when using the *type* attribute with a FILE value. This attribute specifies the path of the file you're posting to the URL.

Parsing Results

So now that we have some information returned from the Barnes & Noble site, what can we do with it? If we wanted the returned data to remain exactly as it appeared on the Barnes & Noble site, then our job would be done, because that's exactly the data that ended up in the *cfhttp.filecontent* variable. But we're not content with that. We want to mess around with the data, extract the useful bits, and do something with them. The following custom tag uses some regular expressions to pull out all of the URLs on the page, and toss everything else out. The tag requires a string to be passed, which in this case is the *text* attribute of the <CF_GETLINKS> tag, and will optionally return a structure of links. The tag comments are specific as well:

```
<cfsetting enablecfoutputonly="yes">
<!---
   GetLinks 2.0 (10/23/98)

   THIS TAG REQUIRES CF 4.0

   This tag finds all anchor or frame tags in the passed text,
   and creates   a structure that you can use to look up a URL by name.

   Usage:

   <CF_GetLinks TEXT="#Body#" [OUTPUT="objLinks"]>

   Creates a structure with the following contents:
```

```
      link:  An array of all the URL's in the text.
      desc:  An array of all the descriptions in the text.
      index: A structure with the link description as the key, and the
             corresponding array position as the value.

   You can use the "index" structure to look up the array position of a
   particular URL.  For example, if you know the text contains a link
   titled "Next", You can look up "Next" in the index structure with
   StructFind(), and use the resulting number to get the corresponding
   URL from the link array.

   The name of the structure can be specified in the OUTPUT parameter.
   If no OUTPUT parameter is provided, it creates an array called
   "objLinks".

   NOTE: If you use this with CFHTTP, you may want to use the
   RESOLVEURL option.

   Let me (jmueller@creativeis.com) know if you find any anchor tags
   that are not detected by this function.

   Joel Mueller
   Creative Internet Solutions
--->

<cfparam name="BodyText" default="">

<cfif isdefined("Attributes.Text")>
   <cfset bodytext = attributes.text>
<cfelse>
   <cfabort showerror="<B>GetLinks Error:</b> You must
   specify the TEXT attribute.">
</cfif>

<cfscript>
   objLinks = StructNew();
   objIndex = StructNew();
   arrLink = ArrayNew(1);
   arrDesc = ArrayNew(1);
   Output = "objLinks";

   if (IsDefined("Attributes.Output")) {
      if (Len(Trim(Attributes.Output)) GT 0) {
         Output = Attributes.Output;
      }
   }

   nextMatch = 1;
   Counter = 1;
   do {
```

```
      // find opening anchor tag.
      objMatch = REFindNoCase("<(a|frame)[[:space:]]+[^>]*
        (HREF|SRC) ?= ?[""']?([^[:space:]""'>]+)(>|(([""']|[[:space:]])[^>]
        *>))", BodyText, nextMatch, true);
      nextMatch = objMatch.pos[1] + objMatch.len[1];
      if (ArrayLen(objMatch.pos) GTE 4) {
         thisURL = Mid(BodyText, objMatch.pos[4], objMatch.len[4]);
         thisTag = Mid(BodyText, objMatch.pos[2], objMatch.len[2]);
         if (CompareNoCase(thisTag, "A") EQ 0) {
            descEnd = FindNoCase("</a>", BodyText, nextMatch);
            thisDesc = Mid(BodyText, nextMatch, descEnd - nextMatch);
            nextMatch = descEnd + 4;
         } else {
            // get the frame name
            fullTag = Mid(BodyText, objMatch.pos[1], objMatch.len[1]);
            frameName = "";
            objFrame = REFindNoCase("NAME ?= ?[""']?([^[:space:]""'>]+)
                  (>|(([""']|[[:space:]])[^>]*>))", fullTag, 1, true);
            if (ArrayLen(objFrame.pos) GT 1) {
               frameName = Mid(fullTag, objFrame.pos[2],
                     objFrame.len[2]);
            }
            thisDesc = "FRAME: " & frameName;
         }

         StructInsert(objIndex, thisDesc, Counter, true);
         arrLink[Counter] = thisURL;
         arrDesc[Counter] = thisDesc;
         Counter = Counter + 1;
      }
   } while (nextMatch NEQ 0);

   StructInsert(objLinks, "index", objIndex);
   StructInsert(objLinks, "link", arrLink);
   StructInsert(objLinks, "desc", arrDesc);

   SetVariable("Caller." & Output, objLinks);
</cfscript>

<cfsetting enablecfoutputonly="no">
```

Creating Queries

Previously in this section, I promised we'd talk about how to create a query using the <CFHTTP> tags. The following example shows a query being generated using <CFHTTP>. We'll talk about what's going on immediately following the example:

```
<cfhttp url="http://127.0.0.1/http/getme.txt"
      method="GET"
```

```
        name="qryJasonLee"
        columns="id,title,price"
        delimiter=","
        textqualifier=""
>

<cfoutput query="qryJasonLee">
#id# #title# #price# <br>
</cfoutput>
```

The URL in this example points directly to a text file. The text file looks like this:

```
id,title,price
12,Chasing Amy,19.95
14,Almost Famous,19.95
23,Mallrats,19.95
25,Mumford,17.95
```

The text file is arranged into three columns: an ID column, a title column, and a price column. I made up these columns; there is really nothing special about them, or the data, except that they all star Jason Lee, an ex-pro skateboarder, and a guy who grew up down the street from me when we were kids.

The <CFHTTP> tag grabs this file, matches the columns in the file to the columns indicated in the *columns* attribute, and puts them into the "qryJasonLee" query object, which is then output.

Downloading Files

The <CFHTTP> file can be used to download files from a web server. The following example shows how to do it:

```
<cfhttp url="http://127.0.0.1/chapter17/http/getme.txt"
        method="GET"
        path="C:\incoming"
        file="getme.txt">
```

Wrapping Up

In this chapter we've seen that ColdFusion can interface with a lot of the most popular Internet protocols. Being able to access these protocols gives ColdFusion a great deal more flexibility than if it wasn't able to access them. Tools can be built that allow you to leverage to the simplicity and power of ColdFusion to perform complicated sequences of code, such as extracting URLs from a page or creating a fully functioning, web-based e-mail client. The possibilities are nearly endless—if it can be done by a human on the Internet, it's likely that ColdFusion code can be written to do it also.

CHAPTER

18

XML and SQL 2000

IN THIS CHAPTER:

Reading XML Data

Writing XML Data

The Extensible Markup Language (XML) has become a popular format for transferring structured data between different types of data repositories. XML documents describe what kind of data they contain and how the data should be formatted, making it possible to transfer data between different data repositories without losing important information about the data structure.

To discuss everything related to XML would go well beyond the scope and subject matter of this book, so we'll simply discuss the tools of the XML trade, and for brevity, forego extensive discussion about what XML is.

To get the most out of this chapter, the following is assumed of the reader:

- You know that XML documents can include Document Type Definition (DTD) files, External Data Representation (XDR) files, and XML files.
- You know that DTD files describe data within an XML document, and that XDR files describe, more or less, the structure of the data within an XML document.
- You know that XML documents are tag based, and that XML is a form of hypertext just like HTML.

In this chapter, we talk about how to read and write XML data structures in ColdFusion. ColdFusion doesn't have any true built-in XML functionality, but several developers have created custom tags and extensions that provide a great deal of XML functionality within ColdFusion.

We also talk about how to import XML data using the SQL Server Data Transformation Services (DTS), and how to create XML documents using the sp_makewebtask stored procedure. While SQL Server 2000 is touted as being very XML-centric, the truth is that it's not as easy as it seems. For instance, SQL Server 2000 doesn't have the ability to import XML data into tables within a database without the addition of some add-on components. We talk about how to install these components, and how to make effective use of XML with SQL Server.

Reading XML Data

There were a few ways to approach the discussion of XML in this chapter, and I felt it best to divide the chapter into two halves: reading XML data and writing XML data. These two actions in a typical development environment require distinct and separate types of tasks. So, in this first half, we talk about how to read XML data, first within the ColdFusion environment, and then within SQL Server 2000.

Using ColdFusion

ColdFusion has no native support for XML. I say that knowing full well that Web Distributed Data Exchange (WDDX) is a subset of XML. WDDX doesn't help in parsing or writing XML documents because it only deals with WDDX structures. ColdFusion doesn't have the ability right out of the box to read an XML document, and allow the developer to do something with the data structure.

Because of the need to have XML support within ColdFusion, and thanks to the ability to add functionality through custom tags and extensions, developers have created several very good packages to read XML. We now talk about several popular add-ons to ColdFusion that allow for both reading and writing XML in ColdFusion, and we'll show you some examples.

SOXML

Site Objects XML (SOXML) creates a lot of freely available add-ons to ColdFusion, and can be found at http://www.siteobjects.com. SOXML is probably one of the most popular sets of custom tags for processing XML documents within ColdFusion. SOXML uses the Document Object Model (DOM) to process XML documents.

Before we detail SOXML, let's have a very quick lesson on XML processing. We'll be very brief. This is the kind of discussion that can turn into several hundred pages of fascinating acronyms and technical jargon that could also double as potent general anesthesia. There are dozens of very good books on XML that do a much finer job at going deeper into XML related topics than this chapter will. We just need to cover the basics to get an idea for how SOXML and ColdFusion work together.

When it comes to XML, there are two types of processing: the DOM method and the Simple API for XML (SAX) method. SAX is an acronym of acronyms. SAX loads and processes only a few lines of XML at a time, which makes a SAX capable processor a good idea for XML documents over five megabytes. DOM processors load the entire XML document in a single shot, which makes for faster processing, but more importantly, allows for properties, methods, and collections. Using a DOM processor allows for more functionality for both reading and writing XML documents.

Within the DOM processor are two different types of technology that allow developers to make full use of XML documents within their applications: *Extensible Stylesheet Language Transformations* (XSLT) and *XPath*. XSLT allows for the transformation of an XML document into another form, like an HTML document or a comma-delimited document. XPath allows for searching or filtering of data within an XML document (much like T-SQL and database tables).

SOXML uses a DOM processor along with the processor's sub technologies to allow for the capability of parsing XML documents and handing off the data to ColdFusion query objects, as well as other capabilities.

Now that we know a bit more about SOXML, let's use it in ColdFusion. To download SOXML, go to http://www.siteobjects.com/ and click the products link. SOXML requires Microsoft XML (MSXML) 2.0 or later on the ColdFusion server. Most Windows 2000 Advanced server installations should already have MSXML 2.5 installed, and servers with SQL Server 2000 should have MSXML 2.6 installed. If you want the latest version or don't have MSXML installed, you can download it from MSDN. It would be great to give an exact URL, but it seems the Microsoft URL structure changes more often than technical books stay on the shelves. What seems to work though is to go to http://msdn.microsoft.com and search for MSXML, although I offer no guarantees of finding it. Most developers shouldn't need to look for it, because it will already be installed.

Installing SOXML To install SOXML on your ColdFusion server, download the SOXML installation files from the downloads area at http://www.siteobjects.com, then take the following steps:

- Unzip the soxml16.zip file into a temporary directory.
- Copy the soxml.cfm file into your custom tags directory.

To test the installation, copy the moreoverheadlines.xml file included within the ZIP file to a directory on your web server set aside for testing, and execute the following code:

```
<cf_soxml
   action="XML2CF"
   input="#GetDirectoryFromPath(CGI.Path_Translated)#\moreoverheadlines.xml"
   output="xmlTest"
   type="file">

<cfdump var="#xmlTest#">
```

The <CFDUMP> tag will display the contents of the query created using the <CF_SOXML> tag.

Creating a Query from an XML String Using the <CF_SOXML> tag is straightforward. The following example shows an XML file from a remote location being translated into a ColdFusion query object:

```
<cfhttp url="http://slashdot.org/slashdot.xml" method="GET"/>

<cf_soxml
   action="XML2CF"
   input="#cfhttp.filecontent#"
   output="structHeadlines">

<cfdump var="#structHeadlines#">
```

The example above pulls the latest headlines from http://www.slashdot.org and dumps the contents of the structure created with the <CFDUMP> tag. We look at a custom tag specifically geared towards grabbing the Slashdot headlines and formatting them later in this section.

<CF_SOXML> Attributes The following table shows the attributes available to the <CF_SOXML> tag:

Attribute	Description
Action	Required. This attribute can be one of the following values: • **CFX2XMLDOM** Allows a developer to take any ColdFusion data structure, and convert it to an XML DOM object. • **CF2XML** Allows a developer to transform any ColdFusion data structure into a standard XML string. • **XML2CF** Allows a developer to transform an XML string, or XML file into a ColdFusion structure. • **XML2DOM** Allows a developer to transform an XML string or XML file into an XML DOM object. • **XML2HTML** Turns any XML string or document into an HTML string.
Input	Required. When converting from ColdFusion to XML, this can be any value data type within ColdFusion. When reading XML, this can be any properly formatted string of XML, or the full path to an XML file.
Output	Required when reading XML data. This is the name of the structure that will be created upon executing the <CF_SOXML> tag.
Type	Required only when reading XML data from a file. When reading a file, the *type* attribute should use the "file" value.

Attribute	Description
rootname	Optional. Used when creating XML from ColdFusion, this attribute indicates the name of the root tag of the XML document to be created. The default value for this attribute is "ROOT."
encoding	Optional. Used when creating XML from ColdFusion, this attribute is used when creating documents with extended character sets. By default, the encoding attribute is not used.
standalone	Optional. This attribute takes a "yes" or "no" value, and is used when creating an XML document. When set to yes, the document is created with the <?xml version="1.0" standalone="yes"?> declaration which would force an XML parser to throw an error if an external reference to another resource were indicated in the XML document, like a reference to a DTD. By default, the *standalone* attribute is set to "no," which allows for external references, but doesn't necessarily mean that external references exist.
XSLinput	Optional. This attribute allows you to specify a URL, full path, or XML string to transform using the XSL method of transformation.
XSLType	Required if the *XSLinput* attribute references a file. The possible values are "file" or "variable." The default value is "variable."
r_type	Optional. This allows the developer to specify how the XSL transformation should be returned. The possible values are "text" or "object." The default value is "text."

<CF_SLASHDOT>

The <CF_SLASHDOT> tag was created by Timothy Larkin, and is an example of a different way of interpreting XML. In this case, the <CF_SLASHDOT> tag takes the current XML document containing the current Slashdot headlines, and parses them within the tag (bypassing any MSXML parser).

Let's take a look at the tag:

```
<!-----------------------------------------------------------------------
NAME:              CF_Slashdot
FILE:             Slashdot.cfm
VERSION:          0.2
CREATED:         08/20/2000
LAST MODIFIED:    08/20/2000
AUTHOR:      Timothy Larkin (tim@pmdb.org) icq=4976648
DESCRIPTION:The purpose of this tag is to parse the slashdot xml
            file containing the 10 latest headlines and store
            the information in an array of structures. It requires
            1 parameter, which is a url to the slashdot xml file.
```

```
            the one optional parameter is "number," which allows one
            to limit the number of headlines to retrieve, the default
            is10.
COPYRIGHT:  This tag is freeware and can thus be freely used, copied,
            modified, and distributed as long as this header is left
            intact.
DISCLAIMER: No warranties, either expressed or implied are granted
            with this software.  This program is provided "as is".
            The author, Amkor Electronics, and anyone else affiliated
            with the creation and use of this tag shall assume no
            liability for problems arising out of the use of this tag.
----------------------------------------------------------------------->

<cfif not isdefined("attributes.number")>
   <cfset attributes.number=10>
<cfelse>
   <cfif attributes.number gt 10><cfset number=10></cfif>
</cfif>

<cfif not isdefined("attributes.location")>
   ERROR: you must provide a url for the location of the slashdot xml file.
<cfelse>
   <cfhttp url = "#attributes.location#"></cfhttp>
   <cfset slashcode = cfhttp.filecontent>

<cfscript>
// create initial datastructures
caller.slashdot = ArrayNew(1);
position = 1;

for(i=1;i LTE attributes.number;i=i+1) {
caller.slashdot[i] = StructNew();

// pull out all information for 1 story
start = Find("<story>",slashcode, position)+ 7;
end = Find("</story>", slashcode, start);
storyinfo = Mid(slashcode, start, end - start);
position = end;

// parse story into the structure
start = Find("<title>", storyinfo, 1)+ 7;
end = Find("</title>", storyinfo, start);
StructInsert(caller.slashdot[i], "title", Mid(storyinfo, start, end - start));
```

```
start = Find("<url>", storyinfo, 1)+ 5;
end = Find("</url>", storyinfo, start);
StructInsert(caller.slashdot[i], "url", Mid(storyinfo, start, end - start));

start = Find("<time>", storyinfo, 1)+ 6;
end = Find("</time>", storyinfo, start);
StructInsert(caller.slashdot[i], "time", Mid(storyinfo, start, end - start));

start = Find("<author>", storyinfo, 1)+ 8;
end = Find("</author>", storyinfo, start);
StructInsert(caller.slashdot[i], "author", Mid(storyinfo, start, end - start));

start = Find("<department>", storyinfo, 1)+ 12;
end = Find("</department>", storyinfo, start);
StructInsert(caller.slashdot[i], "department",
          Mid(storyinfo, start, end - start));
start = Find("<topic>", storyinfo, 1)+ 7;
end = Find("</topic>", storyinfo, start);
StructInsert(caller.slashdot[i], "topic", Mid(storyinfo, start, end - start));

start = Find("<comments>", storyinfo, 1)+ 10;
end = Find("</comments>", storyinfo, start);
StructInsert(caller.slashdot[i], "comments",
Mid(storyinfo, start, end - start));

start = Find("<section>", storyinfo, 1)+ 9;
end = Find("</section>", storyinfo, start);
StructInsert(caller.slashdot[i], "section", Mid(storyinfo,
start, end - start));

start = Find("<image>", storyinfo, 1)+ 7;
end = Find("</image>", storyinfo, start);
StructInsert(caller.slashdot[i], "image", Mid(storyinfo, start, end - start));
}
</cfscript>
</cfif>
```

The following code takes the results of the <CF_SLASHDOT> custom tag and displays them in an HTML table:

```
<cf_slashdot number="10" location="http://slashdot.org/slashdot.xml">
<cfoutput>
   This is an example of how displaying links
```

```
   to the 5 most current headlines.
   <table>
      <cfloop index="i" from="1" to="5">
         <tr><td><a href="#slashdot[i].url#"
                target="_BLANK">#slashdot[i].title#</a></td></tr>
      </cfloop>
   </table>
   <br><br><br>
   This dumps all the information that was
   obtained from the xml file.
   <table>
      <cfloop index="i" from="1" to="10">
         <tr><td>title</td><td>#slashdot[i].title#</td></tr>
         <tr><td>url</td><td>#slashdot[i].url#</td></tr>
         <tr><td>author</td><td>#slashdot[i].author#</td></tr>

<tr><td>department</td><td>#slashdot[i].department#</td></tr>
         <tr><td>topic</td><td>#slashdot[i].topic#</td></tr>
         <tr><td>comments</td><td>#slashdot[i].comments#</td></tr>
         <tr><td>section</td><td>#slashdot[i].section#</td></tr>
         <tr><td>image</td><td>#slashdot[i].image#</td></tr>
         <tr><td> </td><td> </td></tr>
       </cfloop>
   </table>
</cfoutput>
```

Using SQL Server 2000

I'm a big fan of Distributed Transaction Services (DTS). DTS allows developers to link SQL Server related tasks together visually within the Enterprise Manager. The grouping of tasks is called a package, and a package can do many wonderful and complex things repeatedly. For example, let's create an imaginary set of tasks that need to be executed in a single larger step:

- Download Slashdot XML headlines.
- Store headlines in a headlines table.
- Store headlines in a comma delimited text file.
- Perform a full text search reindex on the headlines.
- E-mail the administrator that the set of tasks completed.

All six of these tasks could be executed in order within a DTS Package on a scheduled basis, except for one. You'd think that with all of the hype around SQL Server 2000 and how it can return query results in XML format and such that you'd also be able to easily import XML documents. Unfortunately, SQL Server 2000 cannot import XML documents in any way without the addition of some add-on components.

In this section, we detail how to download and install the required components, and then we create a DTS package that performs what we stated above, as well as give some insight on DTS packages.

Installing the SQL Server XML Tools

SQL Server needs some add-on components before it can import XML documents. To install these components, go to the following URL and download the SQL Server XML Tools package:

http://download.microsoft.com/download/SQLSVR2000/Install/Beta1/W98NT42KMe/EN-US/sqlxml.exe

Once the file is downloaded, execute the sqlxml.exe file and follow the prompts. There is no need for a restart because all the installing program does is register some new objects that will become immediately available to SQL Server.

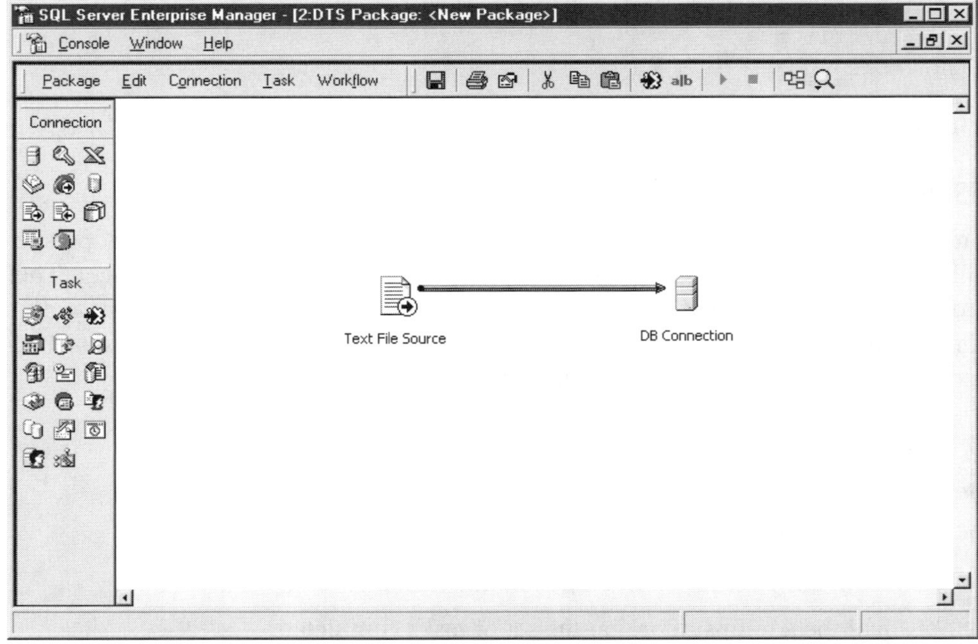

Figure 18-1 *A simple DTS package*

DTS Basics

DTS allows developers to use graphical tools to create sequentially executed tasks. DTS provides connection support, SQL tasks, data transformation tasks, and workflow assignments that allow the ability to create robust and complex sequences of tasks.

One of the best ways to think of how a DTS package works is to equate the sequence of tasks and workflow assignments with a sort of living and breathing flow chart. The sub tasks of a DTS can be set up visually just like a flow chart, and the flow chart type logic can be built into the workflow assignments. Figure 18-01 shows a very simple DTS package that imports data from a text file and inserts it into a template. The actual details of each step are not visible, because they're set within the properties for each task or object in the entire sequence.

DTS packages can range from being as simple as a single T-SQL query, to incredibly complex sequences of transformation tasks with thousands of database connections, complete with transactional support.

Creating a DTS Package To create a DTS package, do the following:

1. Select the Local Package node beneath the Data Transformation Services folder in the SQL Server Enterprise Manager:

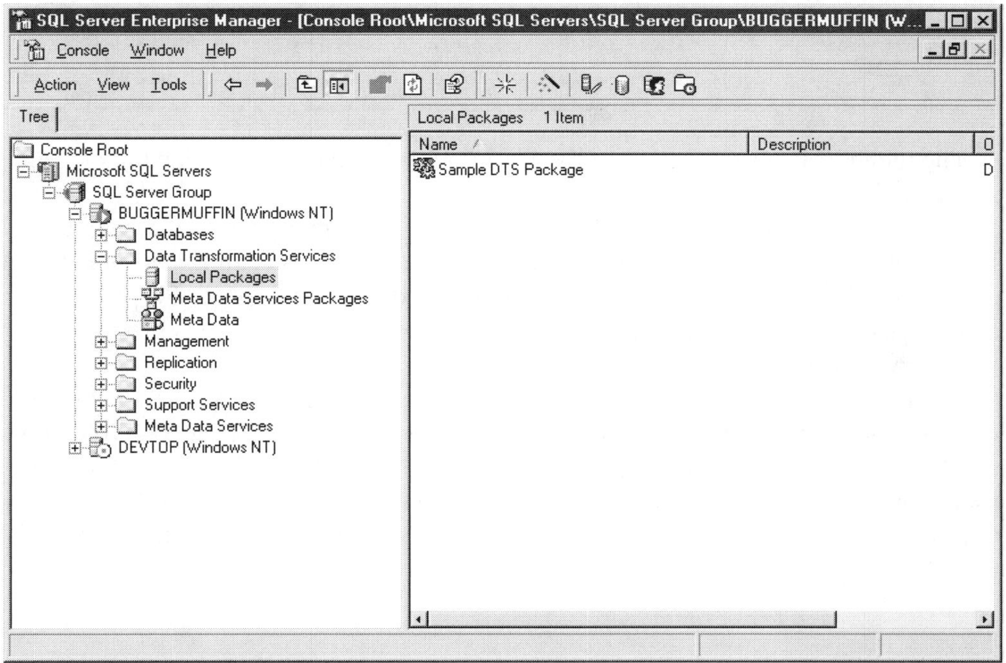

2. Right-click Local Packages and select New Package. The DTS Package designer loads, at which point you are ready to begin designing a new DTS package on a blank slate:

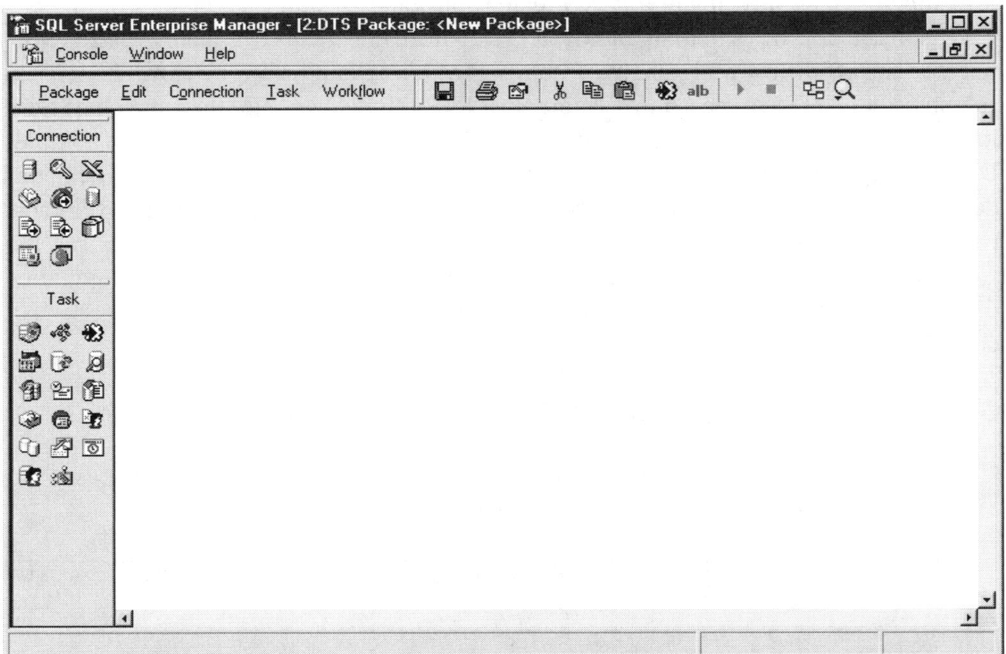

The menu of icons on the left of the DTS Package Designer is divided into sections: Connections and Tasks.

The Connections section contains icons of possible connections to data sources. For example, a text file source is considered a data source, as is an Excel spreadsheet connection. Connections are needed when pulling data from a source for processing, as well as to write data to a source. We see an example of connections in use when we begin importing XML.

The tasks section contains icons for the possible tasks that can be executed within the DTS package. We'll be using the ActiveX Script Task to pull our XML data into a SQL Server database table. Other tasks include the Send Mail Task, which can be used to notify e-mail recipients of a the progress of a DTS package, or the Data Driven Query Task, which can be used to insert T-SQL commands into the entire sequence of tasks.

One of the most important things about DTS packages is that while the tasks themselves might be simple, the effective uses of numerous tasks can perform some very heavy-duty tasks. It's a bit like in nature where relatively simple chemical reactions between molecules can produce behavior seen in animals and humans. At the most basic level, the interactions are simple, but as more systems work together, the interactions perform incredible tasks. DTS packages don't come anywhere near close to the complexity of animal and human behavior, but when it comes to pushing data around, it does a fine job.

To create a task within the DTS package, click the appropriate icon, and set the properties for the item. The DTS Designer places the icon for the task within the package pretty much randomly; it's up to you to decide where it goes visually.

Let's make a connection to a text file that we'll import into a database table. We're just making a dry run right now, so don't worry much about specifics—we'll never execute this package.

1. Click the Text File (Source) icon, and fill out the properties.

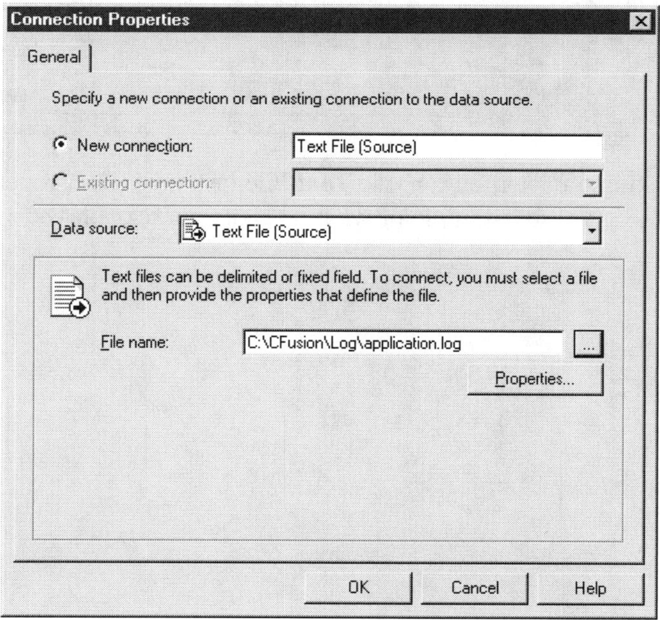

2. In this example, I've selected my application.log file for the ColdFusion server. This is merely an example; you can choose whatever you like. By clicking the Properties button, we have the ability to detail what kind of file we're dealing with.

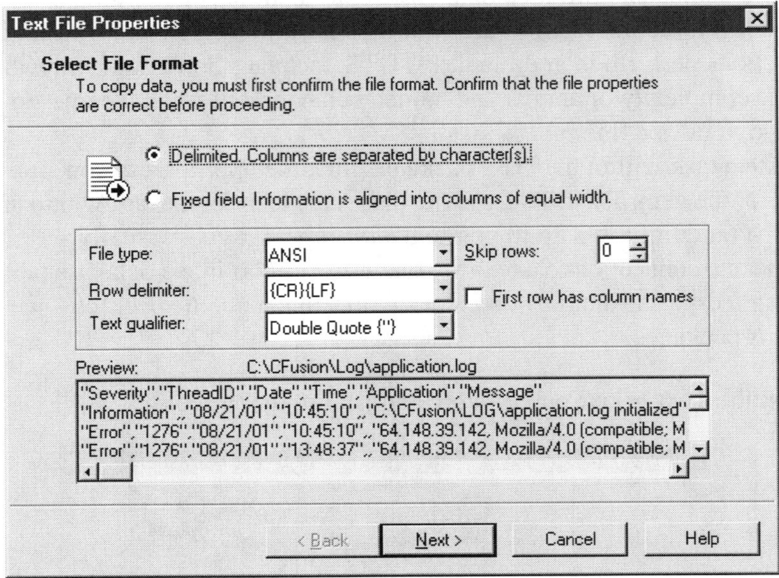

3. After clicking the Next button, the Text File task takes the properties we've defined and gives us a sample of what it thinks our text file's columns are.

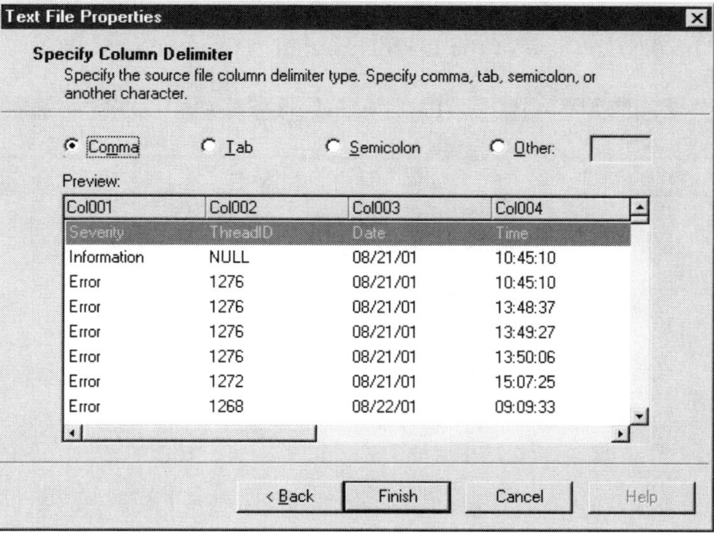

4. Click Finish when you're satisfied with the choices made in the Properties menus, and then click OK to close the Text File task properties. The DTS Designer will place the task in the Designer.
5. Now we add a database connection that we'll ultimately end up transferring data to. Click the Microsoft OLE DB Provider for SQL Server icon in the Connections section of the DTS Designer. The following dialog box should appear:

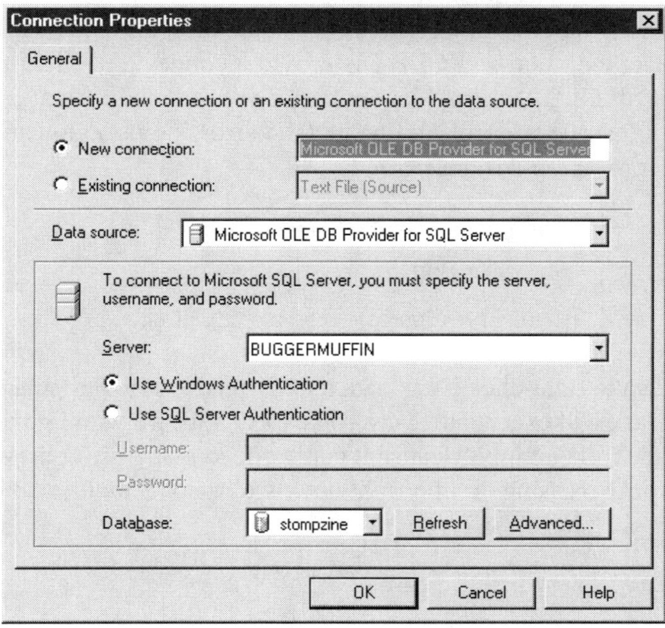

1. Fill out the properties, and then press OK. The connection will be placed within the design view of the DTS Designer, as shown next.

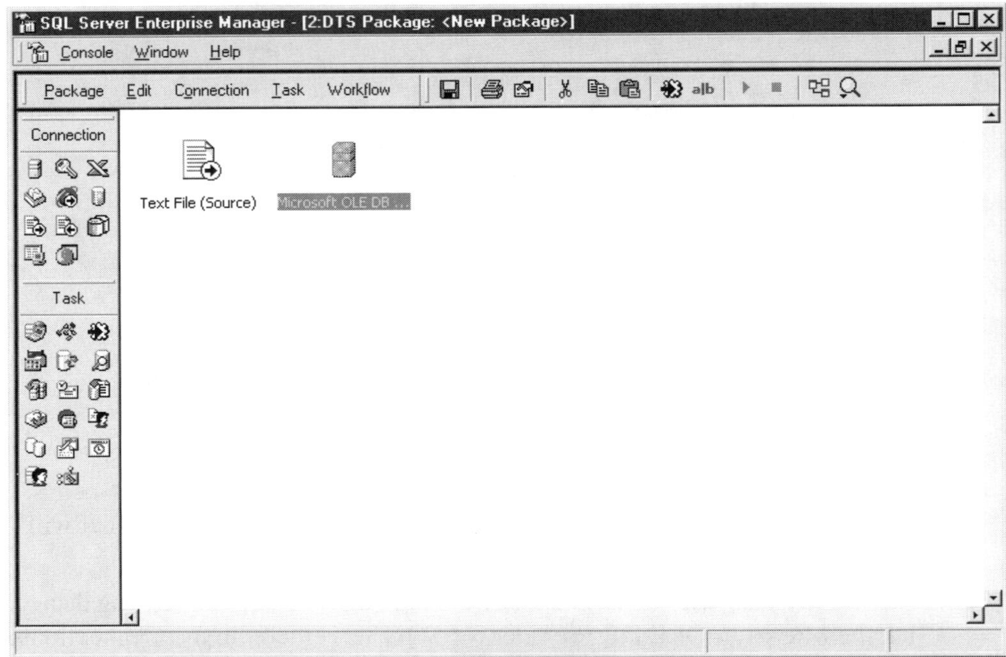

2. Now that both connections are available, it's time to make the connection between the two items. Select the Text Source task, and then use the Control key to select the Microsoft OLE DB Provider connection. Right-click on the Microsoft OLE DB Provider connection we created earlier, and select Transform Data Task. A black line with an arrow pointing towards the database connection will be created:

It's a good idea to right-click black data transformation arrow to make sure the data transformation task will execute the way you expect it to; we won't go into the details of how it should work, simply because it can work so many different ways, and also because we're only messing around right now; we're not actually making a useful package. We're just concerned about the mechanics of how to create package right now, not what will actually happen.

Saving & Loading DTS Packages To save the package we just created, click the floppy disk icon on the task bar of the DTS Designer, or click Package | Save. Go ahead and save the sample package, even though you know it's not functional. We're still going to talk about how to move packages from machine to machine.

To save a package as a file that can be transferred to another server, click on Package | Save As. To save the package as a DTS file, change the package location to Structured Storage File, and give the package a name. Pretty simple.

To load a package saved in the DTS format, right-click on the Data Transformation Services folder in the left pane of the SQL Server Enterprise Manager and select Open Package. The following dialog box will appear:

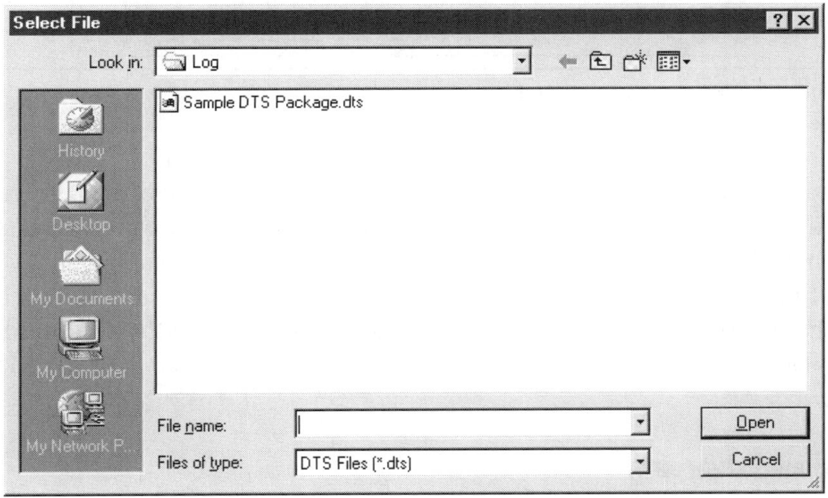

Select the DTS file, and click OK. The package will load in the DTS Package Designer.

Executing and Scheduling a DTS Package DTS Packages can be executed by pressing the Play button within the DTS Package Designer itself. You can also right-click the package within the Enterprise Manager, and select Execute Package.

To schedule a package, right-click the package in the Enterprise Manager and select Schedule Package. Modify the settings according to how you'd like the package to be scheduled (see Figure 18-2), and it will run according to your schedule. For more

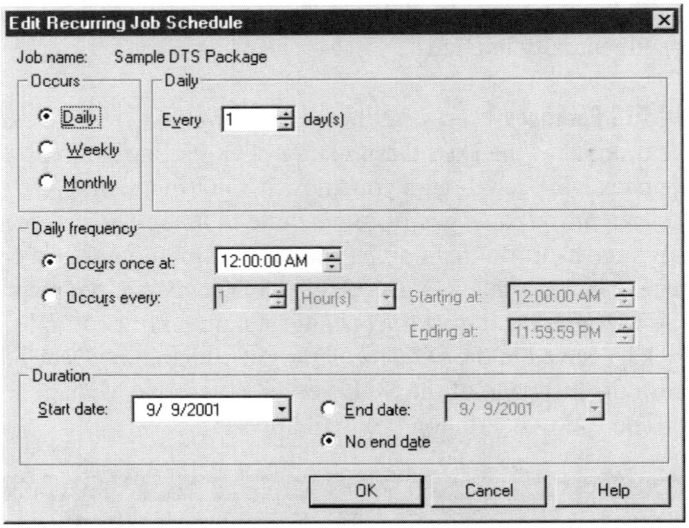

Figure 18-2 *Scheduling a package*

information about the finer points of building DTS packages, I'd recommend reading the online books provided with SQL Server 2000. Unfortunately, giving a complete rundown of DTS packages would go beyond the scope of this chapter, and we want to stick to the topic of XML. The best advice I can give on learning DTS packages is to do a lot of experimentation. The DTS package designer isn't the best interface in the world to deal with, but with some experience it will become very easy to understand and use.

XDR Schema Overview

Before we can load any XML into SQL server, we need to have a cursory understanding of XDR schemas. The XML Objects that come with the XML Tools package we installed earlier don't understand DTDs, which is a pain if you ask me. They do understand XDR schemas, which describe the data within a XML document a bit differently than a DTD would. Rather than simply describing what the data should be, the XDR file describes the relationships between the data and the SQL Server Database Table.

The following is the XDR file we'll be using in our examples. Its design is based on the slashdot.xml file available at http://www.slashdot.org/slashdot.xml.

```
<?xml version="1.0" ?>
<Schema
name="Untitled-schema"
xmlns="urn:schemas-microsoft-com:xml-data"
xmlns:dt="urn:schemas-microsoft-com:datatypes"
xmlns:sql="urn:schemas-microsoft-com:xml-sql" >

   <ElementType name="author" model="closed" content="textOnly"
      dt:type="string"/>
   <ElementType name="comments" model="closed" content="textOnly"
      dt:type="i2"/>
   <ElementType name="department" model="closed" content="textOnly"
      dt:type="string"/>
   <ElementType name="image" model="closed" content="textOnly"
      dt:type="string"/>
   <ElementType name="section" model="closed" content="textOnly"
      dt:type="string"/>
   <ElementType name="story" model="closed" content="eltOnly"
      order="seq" sql:relation="slash_headlines">
      <element type="title" minOccurs="1" maxOccurs="1" sql:field="title"/>
      <element type="url" minOccurs="1" maxOccurs="1" sql:field="url"/>
      <element type="time" minOccurs="1" maxOccurs="1"
           sql:field="time"/>
      <element type="author" minOccurs="1" maxOccurs="1"
           sql:field="author"/>
      <element type="department" minOccurs="1" maxOccurs="1"
           sql:field="department"/>
      <element type="topic" minOccurs="1" maxOccurs="1"
           sql:field="topic"/>
      <element type="comments" minOccurs="1" maxOccurs="1"
           sql:field="comments"/>
      <element type="section" minOccurs="1" maxOccurs="1"
           sql:field="section"/>
      <element type="image" minOccurs="1" maxOccurs="1"
           sql:field="image"/>
   </ElementType>

   <ElementType name="time" model="closed" content="textOnly"
      dt:type="string"/>
   <ElementType name="title" model="closed" content="textOnly"
      dt:type="string"/>
   <ElementType name="topic" model="closed" content="textOnly"
     dt:type="string"/>
   <ElementType name="url" model="closed" content="textOnly"
      dt:type="uri"/>
</Schema>
```

The XDR file was created using an XML editor called XML Spy, available at http://www.xmlspy.com, but it could have been made in any text editor. The benefit of using XML Spy is that it can generate XDR schemas based on the structure of an XML document.

The most important parts of the slashdot.xdr file are the *sql:relation* and *sql:field* attributes. These attributes link the element to a field in the database. So when the "department" element uses the *sql:field*="department" attribute, this tells the XML Bulk Load Object that items in the department element should end up in the department column. The sql:relation field in the root element defines the table to link to, in this case, slash_headlines.

Unfortunately, creating XDR schemas is another one of those topics that takes more than just chapter. I'd recommend studying the example XDR document closely, as well as the XML document, as well as read the Help files that are included with the XML Tools package we installed earlier.

Using the XML Bulk Load Objects

To load the slashdot.xml file into a database, we essentially only need a single ActiveX Script task within a DTS package. But we could, based on our needs, build further functionality into the package. In our example, we simply load the XML file into our database table, but we could, if needed, load the data into a type of holding tank, perform some data scrubbing tasks on the data to better fit our needs, append the data to a live table, and when the process was all complete, e-mail a success or failure e-mail to the owner of this project. To keep things simple, we'll just look at the details of the XML Bulk Load Object.

In a new DTS Package, click the ActiveX Script Task icon in the Tasks section of the icon bar on the left-hand side of the DTS Package Designer. In the code window that is presented, replace the default code with the following code:

```
Function Main()

set objBL = CreateObject("SQLXMLBulkLoad.SQLXMLBulkLoad")

objBL.ConnectionString =
"provider=SQLOLEDB.1;data source=server;database=slash;uid=user;pwd="

objBL.SchemaGen = True

objBL.ErrorLogFile = "c:\slash\slashdot.log"
objBL.Execute "c:\slash\slashdot.xdr", "c:\slash\slashdot.xml"
set objBL=Nothing


Main = DTSTaskExecResult_Success
End Function
```

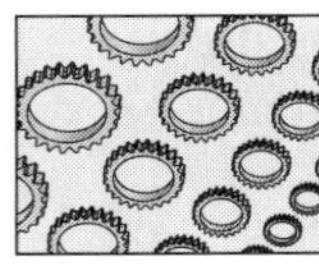

NOTE

The ActiveX script example shown here needs to be modified to point to your database server. The locations of files in the code also need to point to a specific location on your server. The code shown here wraps because of the formatting in the book. The line that starts with objBL.ConnectionString *needs to be contained on one line, otherwise an error will occur.*

This code loads the SQLXMLBulkLoad object, and is eventually executed. The connection string is important, because it defines what server we'll be connecting to, what database, and which user to use. The objBL.SchemaGen assignment forces the object to create the *Slash_headlines* table and columns based on the XDR schema. This completely replaces the table if the table already exists, so keep that in mind. With this option enabled, the bulk load object expects the tables defined in the XDR schema to already be present, so if you choose to disable automatic creation, make sure the tables and columns exist.

The objBL.ErrorLogFile assignment defines where we'd like to store any error logs. The next line executes the object, defining the XDR file and the XML file. The next line unloads the object.

When this script is executed within the DTS package, the XML file will be imported into the tables defined within the XDR. The bulk load object can quickly parse and import some pretty big XML files, so it's an efficient way to pull XML formatted data into SQL Server, despite the setup time.

I hope that with future releases of SQL Server, XML will be a much easier subject to tackle. It would be great if XML support was as strong as support for things like importing comma delimited text files, or importing from different database types. Downloading a separate package, setting up XDR Schemas, and writing ActiveX Scripts is not a fun or efficient way of importing XML data into SQL Server, but it is the best cheap option available currently.

Writing XML Data

Fortunately, pulling XML data out of SQL Server is a much easier subject, which we'll cover shortly, but first, we'll talk about the book's namesake, ColdFusion.

Using ColdFusion

Once again, ColdFusion has no built-in support for generating pure XML. I can generate WDDX packets, which are a subset of XML, but it cannot create an XML file from a query for instance. We'll use <CF_SOXML> to generate XML from within ColdFusion.

If you've skipped ahead to this section, it might be a good idea to read up on the attributes and background information for the <CF_SOXML> custom tag written earlier in the chapter. I'll assume in this section that we all know about how to use the tag, and I'll focus on supplying examples.

The following examples creates an XML string using the <CF_SOXML> tag:

```
<cfscript>
qryGoodStuff = QueryNew("deadlyanimal, killingtalent, hourstolive");

QueryAddRow(qryGoodStuff);
QuerySetCell(qryGoodStuff, "deadlyanimal", "King Cobra");
QuerySetCell(qryGoodStuff, "killingtalent", "venom spitting");
QuerySetCell(qryGoodStuff, "hourstolive", "a few");

QueryAddRow(qryGoodStuff);
QuerySetCell(qryGoodStuff, "deadlyanimal", "Grizzly Bear");
QuerySetCell(qryGoodStuff, "killingtalent", "skull crushing");
QuerySetCell(qryGoodStuff, "hourstolive", "depends on skull thickness");

QueryAddRow(qryGoodStuff);
QuerySetCell(qryGoodStuff, "deadlyanimal", "Upset Monkey");
QuerySetCell(qryGoodStuff, "killingtalent", "bacterial bite");
QuerySetCell(qryGoodStuff, "hourstolive", "many");

QueryAddRow(qryGoodStuff);
QuerySetCell(qryGoodStuff, "deadlyanimal", "Cow");
QuerySetCell(qryGoodStuff, "killingtalent", "falling on you");
QuerySetCell(qryGoodStuff, "hourstolive", "depends on size of cow");
</cfscript>

<cf_soxml
   action="CF2XML"
   input="#qryGoodStuff#"
   output="xmlSample">

<cffile action="WRITE"
   file="C:\chapter18\code\soxml_sample.xml"
   output="#xmlSample#"
   addnewline="Yes">
```

Using SQL Server 2000

Importing XML data in SQL Server 2000 proved to be an interesting process, but producing XML data from within SQL Server 2000 is a breeze. The following two sections show how to return XML data from a query, and how to save that data to an XML file.

Returning XML Data with the FOR XML Clause

SQL Server 2000 can generate XML from a standard T-SQL statement. The following T-SQL statement pulls the top five articles from the Slashdot headlines we imported earlier, and returns them in XML format:

```
SELECT *
FROM slash_headlines
FOR XML AUTO, ELEMENTS
```

The FOR XML clause directs SQL Server to return the data from the query in XML format. AUTO is a mode type, one of three. The possible modes are RAW, AUTO, and EXPLICIT. The T-SQL example shown above using the AUTO mode with the ELEMENTS argument directs SQL to produce results that look like the following:

```
<slash_headlines>
   <title>A Java-Based Handheld OS</title>
   <url>http://slashdot.org/article.pl?sid=00/08/18/0235252</url>
   <time>2000-08-20 12:33:20</time>
   <author>emmett</author>
   <department>one-lump-or-two</department>
   <topic>java</topic>
   <comments>34</comments>
   <section>articles</section>
   <image>topicjava.jpg</image>
</slash_headlines>
<slash_headlines>
   <title>Non Disclosure Agreements in Interviews?</title>
   <url>http://slashdot.org/article.pl?sid=00/08/18/1833229</url>
   <time>2000-08-20 11:27:47</time>
   <author>Cliff</author>
   <department>you-gotta-be-kidding-me</department>
   <topic>news</topic>
   <comments>93</comments>
   <section>askslashdot</section>
   <image>topicnews.gif</image>
</slash_headlines>
```

If we had used the following T-SQL statement, the XML would be returned in attribute mode:

```
SELECT TOP 5 *
FROM slash_headlines
FOR XML AUTO
```

The date from returned from the previous statement would look similar to the following:

```
<slash_headlines
   title="A Java-Based Handheld OS"
   url="http://slashdot.org/article.pl?sid=00/08/18/0235252"
   time="2000-08-20 12:33:20"
   author="emmett"
   department="one-lump-or-two"
   topic="java"
   comments="34"
   section="articles"
   image="topicjava.jpg"/>
<slash_headlines
   title="Non Disclosure Agreements in Interviews?"
   url="http://slashdot.org/article.pl?sid=00/08/18/1833229"
   time="2000-08-20 11:27:47"
   author="Cliff"
   department="you-gotta-be-kidding-me"
   topic="news"
   comments="93"
   section="askslashdot"
   image="topicnews.gif"/>
```

Creating XML Documents Using sp_makewebtask

The sp_makewebtask can be used to quickly write XML documents to a file. The stored procedure takes three arguments when creating an XML document. The first argument is the T-SQL statement itself, and the second argument is the location of a template file that needs to be created beforehand. Let's look at the template file first:

```
<root>
<%begindetail%>
<%insert_data_here%>
<%enddetail%>
</root>
```

This template should be saved as c:\slash\template.tpl according to our examples. The sp_makewebtask stored procedure will handle the rest. The file should look exactly as I've shown: the sp_makewebtask procedure will replace the <%...%> style tags with XML data. The following statement executes sp_makewebtask:

```
sp_makewebtask
@templatefile = 'c:\slash\template.tpl',
@query =
'SELECT TOP 5 *
FROM slash_headlines
FOR XML AUTO, ELEMENTS',
@outputfile = 'c:\slash\sp_slashdot.xml'
```

Wrapping Up

In this final chapter, we've seen how to read and write XML data in both SQL Server and ColdFusion. With more and more organizations using XML it will become a more important part of a developer's skill set. Hopefully, as time progresses, support for XML in both ColdFusion and SQL Server will become much more intuitive.

Index

D

E

F

G

H

I

J

K

L

N

O

P

Q

R

S

T

INTERNATIONAL CONTACT INFORMATION

AUSTRALIA
McGraw-Hill Book Company Australia Pty. Ltd.
TEL +61-2-9417-9899
FAX +61-2-9417-5687
http://www.mcgraw-hill.com.au
books-it_sydney@mcgraw-hill.com

CANADA
McGraw-Hill Ryerson Ltd.
TEL +905-430-5000
FAX +905-430-5020
http://www.mcgrawhill.ca

GREECE, MIDDLE EAST, NORTHERN AFRICA
McGraw-Hill Hellas
TEL +30-1-656-0990-3-4
FAX +30-1-654-5525

MEXICO (Also serving Latin America)
McGraw-Hill Interamericana Editores S.A. de C.V.
TEL +525-117-1583
FAX +525-117-1589
http://www.mcgraw-hill.com.mx
fernando_castellanos@mcgraw-hill.com

SINGAPORE (Serving Asia)
McGraw-Hill Book Company
TEL +65-863-1580
FAX +65-862-3354
http://www.mcgraw-hill.com.sg
mghasia@mcgraw-hill.com

SOUTH AFRICA
McGraw-Hill South Africa
TEL +27-11-622-7512
FAX +27-11-622-9045
robyn_swanepoel@mcgraw-hill.com

UNITED KINGDOM & EUROPE (Excluding Southern Europe)
McGraw-Hill Education Europe
TEL +44-1-628-502500
FAX +44-1-628-770224
http://www.mcgraw-hill.co.uk
computing_neurope@mcgraw-hill.com

ALL OTHER INQUIRIES Contact:
Osborne/McGraw-Hill
TEL +1-510-549-6600
FAX +1-510-883-7600
http://www.osborne.com
omg_international@mcgraw-hill.com